Analyzing the Impacts of Industry 4.0 in Modern Business Environments

Richard Brunet-Thornton
University of Economics, Czech Republic

Felipe Martinez
University of Economics, Czech Republic

A volume in the Advances in Business Information Systems and Analytics (ABISA) Book Series

IGI Global
DISSEMINATOR OF KNOWLEDGE

Published in the United States of America by
IGI Global
Business Science Reference (an imprint of IGI Global)
701 E. Chocolate Avenue
Hershey PA, USA 17033
Tel: 717-533-8845
Fax: 717-533-8661
E-mail: cust@igi-global.com
Web site: http://www.igi-global.com

Library of Congress Cataloging-in-Publication Data

Names: Martinez, Felipe, 1976- editor. | Brunet-Thornton, Richard, 1953- editor.
Title: Analyzing the impacts of industry 4.0 in modern business environments / Richard Brunet-Thornton and Felipe Martinez, editors.
Description: Hershey, PA : Business Science Reference, [2017] | Includes bibliographical references.
Identifiers: LCCN 2017017367| ISBN 9781522534686 (h/c) | ISBN 9781522534693 (eISBN)
Subjects: LCSH: Management. | Computer networks--Management. | Internet of things.
Classification: LCC HD30.37 .A52 2017 | DDC 658/.054678--dc23 LC record available at https://lccn.loc.gov/2017017367

This book is published in the IGI Global book series Advances in Business Information Systems and Analytics (ABISA) (ISSN: 2327-3275; eISSN: 2327-3283)

British Cataloguing in Publication Data
A Cataloguing in Publication record for this book is available from the British Library.

For electronic access to this publication, please contact: eresources@igi-global.com.

Advances in Business Information Systems and Analytics (ABISA) Book Series

Madjid Tavana
La Salle University, USA

ISSN:2327-3275
EISSN:2327-3283

Mission

The successful development and management of information systems and business analytics is crucial to the success of an organization. New technological developments and methods for data analysis have allowed organizations to not only improve their processes and allow for greater productivity, but have also provided businesses with a venue through which to cut costs, plan for the future, and maintain competitive advantage in the information age.

The **Advances in Business Information Systems and Analytics (ABISA) Book Series** aims to present diverse and timely research in the development, deployment, and management of business information systems and business analytics for continued organizational development and improved business value.

Coverage

- Business Decision Making
- Management Information Systems
- Geo-BIS
- Performance Metrics
- Data Strategy
- Statistics
- Business Process Management
- Business Intelligence
- Data Governance
- Forecasting

IGI Global is currently accepting manuscripts for publication within this series. To submit a proposal for a volume in this series, please contact our Acquisition Editors at Acquisitions@igi-global.com or visit: http://www.igi-global.com/publish/.

The Advances in Business Information Systems and Analytics (ABISA) Book Series (ISSN 2327-3275) is published by IGI Global, 701 E. Chocolate Avenue, Hershey, PA 17033-1240, USA, www.igi-global.com. This series is composed of titles available for purchase individually; each title is edited to be contextually exclusive from any other title within the series. For pricing and ordering information please visit http://www.igi-global.com/book-series/advances-business-information-systems-analytics/37155. Postmaster: Send all address changes to above address.

Titles in this Series

For a list of additional titles in this series, please visit: www.igi-global.com/book-series

Research, Practices, and Innovations in Global Risk and Contingency Management
Kenneth David Strang (State University of New York, USA & APPC Research, Australia) Maximiliano E. Korstanje (University of Palermo, Argentina) and Narasimha Vajjhala (American University of Nigeria, Nigeria)
Business Science Reference • copyright 2018 • 418pp • H/C (ISBN: 9781522547549) • US $245.00 (our price)

Modeling and Simulation Techniques for Improved Business Processes
Maryam Ebrahimi (Azad University, Iran)
Business Science Reference • copyright 2018 • 246pp • H/C (ISBN: 9781522532262) • US $185.00 (our price)

Value Sharing for Sustainable and Inclusive Development
Mario Risso (Niccolò Cusano University, Italy) and Silvia Testarmata (Niccolò Cusano University, Italy)
Business Science Reference • copyright 2018 • 398pp • H/C (ISBN: 9781522531470) • US $245.00 (our price)

Supporting Innovation Through National R&D Programs Emerging Research and Opportunities
Amiram Porath (Independent Researcher, Israel)
Business Science Reference • copyright 2018 • 158pp • H/C (ISBN: 9781522536529) • US $145.00 (our price)

Always-On Enterprise Information Systems for Modern Organizations
Nijaz Bajgoric (University of Sarajevo, Bosnia and Herzegovina)
Business Science Reference • copyright 2018 • 257pp • H/C (ISBN: 9781522537045) • US $215.00 (our price)

Knowledge Integration Strategies for Entrepreneurship and Sustainability
Neeta Baporikar (Namibia University of Science and Technology, Namibia & University of Pune, India)
Business Science Reference • copyright 2018 • 413pp • H/C (ISBN: 9781522551157) • US $265.00 (our price)

Business Architectures for Risk Assessment and Strategic Planning Emerging Research and Opportunities
James McKee (Wollongong University, Australia)
Business Science Reference • copyright 2018 • 118pp • H/C (ISBN: 9781522533924) • US $155.00 (our price)

Handbook of Research on Emergent Applications of Optimization Algorithms
Pandian Vasant (Universiti Teknologi Petronas, Malaysia) Sirma Zeynep Alparslan-Gok (Suleyman Demirel University, Turkey) and Gerhard-Wilhelm Weber (Middle East Technical University, Turkey)
Business Science Reference • copyright 2018 • 812pp • H/C (ISBN: 9781522529903) • US $445.00 (our price)

IGI Global
DISSEMINATOR OF KNOWLEDGE

701 East Chocolate Avenue, Hershey, PA 17033, USA
Tel: 717-533-8845 x100 • Fax: 717-533-8661
E-Mail: cust@igi-global.com • www.igi-global.com

List of Reviewers

Amitabh Anand, *SKEMA Business School, France*
Michelle Caron, *Southern New Hampshire University, USA*
Harish C. Chandan, *Argosy University, USA*
Eric Cohen, *State University of Campinas, Brazil*
Neha Gangwar, *Periyar Management and Computer College, India*
Abhishek Goel, *Indian Institute of Management, India*
Mohammad Ayub Khan, *Tecnologico de Monterrey, Campus Monterrey, Mexico*
Konstantinos Leftheriotis, *The American College of Greece, Greece*
Radek Liška, *University of Economics, Czech Republic*
Sergio Mazini, *Centro Universitário Toledo Araçatuba, Brazil*
Chandan Medatwal, *Poornima University, India*
Vikas Mehra, *Tata Motors, India*
Mahima Mishra, *Symbiosis Institute of Business Management, India*
Mateus Panizzon, *Universidade de Caxias do Sul, Brazil*
Gerardo del Cerro Santamaría, *Rutgers University, USA*
Marianela Sarabia, *Argentine University of Enterprise, Argentina*
Holli Semetko, *Emory University, USA*
Bruce Thomson, *MacEwan University, Canada*
Guilherme Tortorella, *Universidade Federal de Santa Catarina, Brazil*
Zsofia Toth, *Nottingham University Business School, UK*
Gabriel Vidor, *Universitário da Região dos Vinhedos, Brazil*

Table of Contents

Detailed Table of Contents

This chapter describes the development stage of China's optical fiber manufacturing industry, and then analyses the Yangtze Optical Fibre and Cable Joint Stock Limited Company (YOFC) development stage. According to YOFC case, the authors show that continuous learning and absorption, proprietary R&D and product innovation, good use of every opportunity and favorable development policy, talent reserve and intelligence support, active transformation by sizing up the situation, independent operation, and elimination of monopolization are the implications of transformation and upgrade of the optical fiber industry.

Malaysia intends to ride on the crest of the coming i.4.0 wave. According to the 2016 GE Global Innovation Barometer study, a significant number of Malaysian executives felt positive about embracing i4.0 vis-a-vis their global peers. On the surface, Malaysia appears ready for its own i4.0 revolution. According to the WEF's Networked Readiness Index on digital readiness, Malaysia was ranked 6th in terms of having the most tech-savvy government in the world. The automotive sector is ideally suited to kickstart the i4.0 revolution as it was traditionally regarded as the "industry of industries" – particularly due to its traditional role in spearheading wider, cross-sectoral industrialisation. However, Malaysia is not yet ready to embrace the 4th Industrial Revolution. This chapter discusses the obstacles, challenges, and opportunities facing i4.0 uptake in the Malaysian automotive industry. It ends by recommending a unique pathway for i4.0 adoption in the sector.

In this chapter, better understanding of Industry 4.0 is presented by investigating the role of different technologies and business partners on success of Industry 4.0. Enablers for smart factory are discussed in detail, and how to match these enablers with value chain partners of Industry 4.0 are identified as a

Balancing exploration and exploitation in entrepreneurial ventures enabled by Industry 4.0 has not been the focus of the existing literature. It is because the phenomenon is emerging and the focus has been to use practitioners' best practices in studying such phenomenon. In this chapter, the author combines the literature in balancing exploration and exploitation with the practitioners' best practices such as customer development model and lean startup. The author proposes that the existing models are good in principle but in order to really solve the problem in such an uncertain environment driven by big data, cloud computing, internet of things (IoT), and artificial intelligence, managers need to embed optimization algorithms in their decision making.

Knowledge tells us that increase in productivity decreases margins in a competitive market and increases margins in a growing market. Not much is known about Industry 4.0 and its position within the corporate strategy and its possible impact on corporate performance. This chapter discusses the position of Industry 4.0 within the corporate strategy and how it may impact corporate performance. The main points include that corporates have to reflect on their core resources, leadership, and knowledge portfolio to take advantage of the Industry 4.0 platform. The corporates engaging in cost and volume strategies and those engaging in fast new product development strategies may benefit greatly with Industry 4.0. The services of Industry 4.0 may be outsourced but with added risks. Finally, the increased productivity with Industry 4.0 under constraint market growth may lead to the potential risk of market failure and large-scale layoffs.

The promises of Industry 4.0 in the medical device industry needs to be built on sound cybersecurity infrastructures, polices, and practices. During 2011-2017, the authors interviewed many manufacturers of medical devices in China, Germany, Israel, Japan, Taiwan, and U.S. about their attitude towards cybersecurity. Many manufacturers are not committed to cybersecurity risk management because they pursue lower cost and shorter product life cycles; do not have sufficient knowledge of operating environments of hospitals; have defensive attitude toward vulnerability disclosure; and reap quick benefits from the low-trust level among stakeholders and unequal power between manufacturers and distributors. Only a few large U.S. manufacturers of medical devices have set up robust secure platforms and interoperable optimal standards which benefit the users. As cybersecurity is a shared responsibility, many small and medium-sized enterprises need to be empowered through the support of international organizations and local government policies.

Section 3
Frameworks

Systems engineering focuses on design, development, and implementation of complex systems. Not only does the Industry 4.0 concept consist of various technical components that need to be properly set and interconnected, but it is also tied to various managerial aspects. Thus, systems engineering approach can be used for its successful deployment. Overemphasis of technological aspects of Industry 4.0 represents the main starting point of this chapter. Then, collocation analysis, word clusters identification, selection and exemplification of selected domain in the business management realm, and frequency analysis are used in order to develop a holistic framework of Industry 4.0. This framework comprises six levels – physical, activity, outcome, content, triggers, and context. Moreover, the information and control level is integrated. The new holistic framework helps to consider Industry 4.0 from the complex systems engineering perspective – design and deployment of a complex system with required parameters and functionality.

The recent introduction of new disruptive technologies aimed at monitoring, controlling, optimizing, and automating production systems is shifting the manufacturing landscape towards a fourth industrial revolution. In this new industrial paradigm, manufacturing companies face complex challenges requiring the development of new organizational and technological capabilities. With this context in mind, this chapter is intended to provide a maturity assessment framework to understand the transformation process in manufacturing companies transitioning to Industry 4.0. The proposed framework is applied to 10 in-depth industrial case studies in Canada and Italy, two countries with increasing awareness of the Industry 4.0 revolution. A comparative case analysis revealed four different standards, or archetypes, for Industry 4.0 adoption, which are discussed and analyzed, highlighting a relationship between a company's manufacturing configuration and its path towards Industry 4.0 adoption.

Section 4
Knowledge Transfer and Education

Industry 4.0 is for most companies and especially for small and medium sized enterprises (SMEs) one of the major challenges after the wave of lean management. The aim of this chapter is to provide a methodological guidance for the practical use of the Industry 4.0 vision and principles in production system design in the specific context of SMEs. Based on the analysis of literature, a procedure model for the target-oriented introduction of Industry 4.0 principles in SMEs is proposed. A first practical evaluation of the approach is carried out based on two industrial case studies. The experiences made in the industrial cases show that Industry 4.0 is not limited to the application in large enterprises but is very suitable also for SME. This chapter contributes, with its case-study-based methodology, to the existing sparse knowledge on the introduction of Industry 4.0 in SME production systems.

A main challenge for academic writing for students at master thesis level is to find the right perspective from which to launch the argument of the thesis. In the context of international business (IB) studies, the eclectic theoretical paradigm of the field offers students myriad frameworks from which to frame their research questions. The purpose of this chapter is to illustrate how perspective in academic writing can be taught and learnt in a systematic manner. Taking the example of the teaching of culture theory in international business (IB) studies, this chapter illustrates how the deictic or "pointer" function of the pronoun system in language can be used to help perspective research position and research design.

Section 5
Process and Value

Industry is transforming from Industrie 3.0, automation, to Industrie 4.0, digitalization. Siemens intends to be a key player in Industrie 4.0, whose customer value proposition will shape manufacturing industries at customers. This chapter analyzes Siemens' customer value proposition for cyber-physical systems as manufacturing equipment and products in terms of this technology's impact on value. The goal is to identify concrete value drivers which cyber-physical systems technology in Industrie 4.0 brings. The

Foreword

Industry 4.0 or I4.0 – buzzword or reality; evolution or revolution? These are the issues at hand, questions that stimulate debate across all business sectors with models and scenarios that intrigue both management practitioners and academicians alike. The term itself, Industry 4.0, was coined at the 2011 Hannover Messe, an outcome of the German federal government's initiative to implement initiatives, recommendations, and guidelines to digitise manufacturing processes.

Similar with other contemporary issues, there exists a plethora of literature and documentation. However, at times, the individual is confronted with divergent and oppositional positions. Commercial brochures and flipbooks often attempt to sell products and services rather than the concept or reality of digital transformation. An overbearing emphasis is placed on potential increased profits and gains in productivity while overlooking the human impact. The nomenclature itself invites confusion in that it varies by country and oftentimes, by industry. I4.0 is equally known as, cyber-physical systems, the Internet of Things, cloud computing, Artificial Intelligence, cognitive computing, and digital transformation.

This book with its theme of *Analysing the Impacts of Industry 4.0 in Modern Business Environments* is a valuable addition to the extant body of knowledge. Written by both research scientists and industry specialists, it aims to clarify the nature of Industry 4.0 and its implications today as well as in the immediate future. Each chapter investigates a different aspect, some drawing from existing deployments whereas, others explore national considerations and implications. The content is not exhaustive, but it does provide an overview worthy of consultation and future exploration by the reader.

As governments develop their plans to enter a digitised world, the challenges, both positive and negative; difficult and interesting, for their citizens will become increasingly evident. This book is a thought-provoking initiative in that direction.

Stanislav Háša
University of Economics, Czech Republic

Stanislav Háša *is Head of the Department of Management at the Faculty of Business Administration of the University of Economics, Prague. Equally, he is a consultant and clinical psychologist with a practice in the Prague metropolitan area. Dr. Háša is a prime motivator to incorporate Industry 4.0 within the Department of Management curriculum to better prepare our students to transition to the workforce of the future.*

Preface

Organisations aspire to improve competitiveness and performance through digitalisation. This sentiment is shared with many companies that have demonstrated significant interest in I4.0 for several years. Digital transformation in any context requires not only a substantial change management plan but equally, the two essential components of Knowledge Management (KM): knowledge sharing and knowledge transfer. In a recent policy paper, Dittrich (2016) proposes that to implement a successful transition to a digital environment, the European Union "is bound to ...the mass upgrading of the digitals skills of European workers." To complete this formidable undertaking, knowledge is central.

In a recent report entitled, *Digital Transformation Monitor Czech Republic: Průmysl 4.0* (2007), the European Commission identifies that a threat to the Czech national strategy rests with the extant gap between industry needs and resources. Successful KM implementation in the Czech Republic is rare. One cause of this situation is that successful KM implementation at the organisational level depends on the condition and status of other levels where the attention to knowledge is significant. Bureš and Čech (2008) identify four knowledge levels: supranational, national, organisational, and management of knowledge. Each level describes the overall environment in which knowledge-related activities are performed. Each differs from the other in many aspects. An increase of the resolution of any one of the above permits further levels to be discovered. Exemplars of this refinement are economic sectors such as tourism, engineering, telecommunications, and education, or clusters that have different knowledge needs, utilisable tools, techniques, and procedures. They are frequently uncovered between the national and the organisational level demonstrating that the demarcation between levels is ambiguous.

SUPRANATIONAL LEVEL

This level is both the broadest and the most general. It operates by means of concepts of the Knowledge Economy (KE) and Knowledge Society (KS) wherein tangible knowledge does not play a role. Supranational corporations and institutions shape this level, for example the World Bank, the OECD, and the United Nations.

Within a Czech context this level is recognised particularly through the numerous strategic documents issued by the European Union (EU). The Lisbon Strategy published by the European Council emphasises the KE as a strategic and primary objective. The document states that the EU desires to become a world-leading economy that is competitive and knowledge-based. Although this strategy has been revised and objectives modified several times, it continues to influence EU members and their partners. In this vein, KE and knowledge- based competition are no longer theoretical concepts limited to academicians or manuscripts in scholarly journals (Drucker, 1993; Nonaka, 1995). Subsequently, the position of the Czech government reflects the EU initiative.

NATIONAL LEVEL

With globalisation, there exists a remarked increase in the flow of goods and services, and the migration of people, ideas, and wealth on an international basis. The advantages both tangible and intangible of this movement are numerous and significant. Companies of a national character must compete with international enterprises in their domestic market. In the Czech environment, former privately or state-owned corporations are now controlled by management boards located outside national borders. Companies must remain vital in the current highly competitive and trans-border environments. The lack of critical knowledge on an appropriate mix of personnel, technology, intellectual assets, and physical assets may lead to the demise of indigenous businesses and significantly influence organisational and national culture. The advent of the fourth industrial revolution that incorporates both guidelines and directives from the EU and the Czech government, augments the stress to remain competitive and profitable.

At the national level, KE and KS exhibit a Czech dimension that reflects the nation's historical, cultural, economic, legislative, and geopolitical specifics. KE and KS are associated with authentic conditions and the needs of the organisation in the country. Government support for KM is referenced in several ministerial publications that comprises the Strategy of the economic growth of the Czech Republic, and the Strategy of the Government of the Czech Republic in the EU framework to cite a few. Institutions outside the public domain also exercise a pertinent role. The Association for Information Society publication "Manifest of Knowledge Society" (SPIS, 2007) summarises the current situation and outlines the tasks to be undertaken to succeed in this new global context.

ORGANISATIONAL LEVEL

Genuine KM is practiced at this level. KM encompasses a knowledge-based and knowledge-orientated organisational management irrespective of the organisational mandate or nature. Therefore, KM can be introduced in business organisations, educational institutions or even, civil administration. Many Czech institutions including commercial interests realise that traditional assets are no longer the sole resources managed during the transition to KE and KS. In doing so, prominence to knowledge resources and knowledge processes is highlighted. Knowledge resources are of particular concern in this circumstance wherein labour force skills are compatible with or surpass industry requirements and experience.

Many problems exist at this level in the Czech Republic. The transition to KE and KS must be performed in parallel with other changes. Prior to its current economic successes, the Czech economy had been transitory and in flux given its historical past of sixty years of oppressive regimes. Cultural aspects, including social and individual barriers, contribute significantly (Bureš, 2003). KM is perceived in different ways that in turn create additional communication and cooperation problems. The perceptions are usually formed by substituting a KM system with off-the-shelf solutions of software-based applications. Although necessary in the overall scheme as implementation or deployment tools, KM in both theory and concentrates more on the human dimension. Lastly, there is a lack of KM implementation methodology available in and specific to the Czech Republic. Case studies of successful KM implementation tend to deal mostly with larger concerns outside the Czech borders (Ahmed, Lim & Loh, 2002). Many Czech companies are small or medium size enterprises. Subsequently, available models are not applicable to the Czech environment that contribute to the lack of successful KM implementation. For these reasons there exists a compelling need for further research and model- development to address the distinct Czech reality. Without the appropriate "Home-Made" tools, Czech organisations revert to services provided by consultancy companies that due to cost often render KM out of reach. In other instances, foreign-developed methodologies are sought. In both cases, the organisation is confronted with methods and procedures created in different settings that ignore the intercultural dimension. Moreover, they lack sufficient detail and guidelines and are seldom available in the Czech language.

MANAGEMENT OF KNOWLEDGE (MOK) LEVEL

Characterised by research in such fields as Artificial Intelligence and other I4.0 components, and knowledge-based systems, this level operates with tangible knowledge. MoK is an established technological discipline that embodies the lowest and the most basic level in which proper attention to knowledge is exercised. Methods, techniques, and principles of research work within fields such as pedagogy, psychology, sociology, and other cognitive sciences are also incorporated at this fundamental level. A relationship between managers and MoK exists. KM achieves its goals by utilising MoK outputs within the scope of its own activities. Managers are not usually cognisant of the principles on which the products of MoK are based. This is not an unusual situation and is comparable to other work activities in which the operations behind the result are tacit. However, MoK products or services require a degree of awareness and intent. Although many tools and applications are perceived as "easy-to-use" and quickly implemented, for example, wikis, discussion forums, videoconferencing, and document management systems, other applications that entail expert systems or multi-agent technologies require an awareness of knowledge acquisition, or knowledge storage.

RELATIONSHIP AMONG AND BETWEEN SINGLE LEVELS

The levels produce one coherent system that possesses its own considerable relationships. If MoK does not operate properly or efficiently, activities at higher levels will not be composite and complete, as MoK represents the basis for all knowledge related activities. Its subsequent products are applied at the organisational level. Regardless of the strong technological base at the MoK level, it neither supports a technological approach to KM, nor stresses its technological origin. It does draw the necessary attention to the notion that modern technologies catalyse change. Hence, the organisational level constitutes the basis of the KE both at the national and supranational level.

The higher the level, the lower is the significance of specific knowledge. While MoK operates with real knowledge and develops instruments and procedures, no matter how this knowledge is acquired, processed, distributed or exploited, at the organisational level it is not feasible to manage knowledge but rather to create the appropriate conditions for successful knowledge manipulation. Consequently, managers concentrate on the schematic and content (knowledge resources (Holsapple & Joshi, 2001). At the national and supranational levels, the objective of all activities remains the creation of an environment and framework wherein lower levels can operate successfully.

One compenent that forms a relationship between the national and the organisational level is culture. Heier and Borgman (2002) study the impact of national culture on the development, rollout, and usage of KM-based projects. Once identified and categorised the attributes of the research are validated against a conceptual framework substantiated by Hofstede's (2001) cultural dimensions. Although much criticism has been levied against Hofstede over the past decades, recent research not Hofstede based has equally justified this position (Brunet-Thornton & Bures, 2012). In a similar vein, Gulev (2005) seeks to develop two criteria to evaluate the cultural impacts on knowledge flows and knowledge sharing in four European countries. Although material prevalent to the Czech Republic is lacking, these two examples represent only a meagre sampling of the available and abundant current research. KM must be embedded into the context of a greater vision and by doing so, substantial relationships at any single level or among levels is not only preserved, but also emphasised.

KNOWLEDGE INTENSITY

Managers, Czechs are not an exception, require motivation for its deployment and experience the desired changes. Therefore, it is necessary to establish a concept of organisational knowledge intensity and to confirm the positive influence of a KM programme to this intensity.

It is understandable that the knowledge intensity of nations, industries, organisations, or departments is of crucial importance to the whole knowledge hierarchy. While measuring the benefits of KM implementation or of intellectual capital development in organisations is quite common today at the organisational level, overall organisational knowledge intensity quantification including both static and dynamic aspects of KM is rare. Autio, Sapienza and Almeida (2000) define knowledge intensity as the extent to which a firm depends on its knowledge as a source of competitive advantage. Davenport and Smith (2000) assert that knowledge intensive companies will allocate more resources to knowledge management. However, the criteria enabling the classification of organisations according to their knowledge intensity are not elaborated. Moreover, knowledge intensity may not be associated with KM programmes whatsoever. Every organisation possesses knowledge resources and realises knowledge processes, but few recognise such consciously.

In general, the concept of knowledge intensity is widely known. It consists of minimally four factors: involvedness of knowledge and understanding required to perform assignments; expertise necessary for the competent handling of work-related unpredictability; severity of consequences of potential work inaccuracy, and swiftness of action. However, there is not a generally accepted methodology that measures organisational knowledge intensity from the managerial perspective.

This view enables managers to view their organisations from a different standpoint. Firestone (1999) considers the organisational information and knowledge infrastructure to consist of two models. The first represents the organisational and human components and their continual interaction. The model is not determined by design, but emerges from the dynamics of the enterprise process and its activities. Thus, this model is natural. The second model is a conceptually distinct and integrated system that arises from the former. It includes computers, software, or electronic components. This model is artificial and developed by design. The resulting information-knowledge processing infrastructure is often a blend of the two. Since organisations are complex systems, humans are not able to fully design the infrastructure leaving one natural phenomenon to propagate an unexpected and emergent behaviour (Čech, 2005). Monitoring of the organisational knowledge intensity assists managers to evaluate how the models are interrelated, and developed.

RESEARCH PERSPECTIVE

From the research perspective, the entire knowledge hierarchy involves many scientific disciplines such as economics, international trade theory, management science, political science but also informatics, sociology, and psychology. One current problem is that these disciplines usually analyse at a single stratum without deep consideration or linkage to other levels. The more one escalates in the hierarchy, the more evident are the research problems related to economics or management; whereas, in the opposite direction research problems related to informatics or psychology are evident. This perspective must be considered when conducting research at the organisational level and organisational knowledge intensity respectively.

Therefore, the application of a systems approach and thinking is necessary to study organisational knowledge intensity in the context of the whole hierarchy. Moreover, a systems approach is applied when thinking about organisational knowledge intensity and using it as a practical indicator. However, most managers are not prepared as management education centres on a mechanism rather than a systems approach.

Increased knowledge and insight originate from interdisciplinary and multidisciplinary research. The proposal emphasises the multidisciplinary to explore organisational knowledge intensity. Knowledge economy development (Chen, 2005), knowledge intensive industries, cross-cultural management, knowledge management, modern managerial measurement systems (Kaplan, 1996), organisational culture, human resources, and knowledge technology applications (Mikulecký, Ponce & Hynek, 1997) are only some of the facets considered. Throughout the proposed study attention focuses on the possibilities of the further development of organisational knowledge intensity, the performance of organisations in knowledge management activities and on the general indicators of their performance.

PRACTICAL SIGNIFICANCE

Practical value is ensured through the methodology design enabling organisations to quantify their knowledge intensity and benchmark their performance from a knowledge perspective with others at an international level. The applied implication evolves from the composition of the research team. Moreover, the project benefits include not only the methodology but an amelioration to the existing body of knowledge. The theoretical results enhance managerial familiarity of the relationship between KM and organisational knowledge intensity. Organisational knowledge intensity is closely related to KM, wherein it can serve as a tool for the justification and substantiation of related initiatives. Therefore, the project output supports and facilitates managerial decision-making. KM-related decisions are strengthened by the managers' knowledge and awareness of processes, and resources. Equipped with this information, management takes efficient and more effective decisions as to resource allocation, financial budgeting, and in other day-to-day tasks. Incorporating cultural aspects within the total problem ensures an undisputable relationship between the proposed project and practice.

CONCLUSION

Knowledge oriented activities are viewed at several levels of the knowledge hierarchy. At the supranational level, objectives are interpreted as guidelines for national and organisational development. The Czech Republic is not an exception as Czech enterprise strive to improve their performance and competitiveness. Unfortunately, systematic KM is not envisioned as a viable option. Several reasons previously cited contribute to this condition. Previous efforts demonstrate that there is no "turnkey" solution available to meet the special circumstances of most companies in the Czech Republic.

To support further development on KM the proposed project focuses on the organisational knowledge intensity. Its ultimate result – a methodology for monitoring organisational knowledge intensity – provides managers with an appropriate tool for the justification of a KM programme and monitoring of its development. Once this tool is deployed, managers who lack system thinking ability should avoid the seemingly straightforward solutions that are obviously insufficient to implement KM.

ORGANISATION OF THE BOOK

The first segment of the book, "Country and Region Specific," discusses Industry 4.0 from a national or regional perspective. Chapters 1 and 2 provide the reader with in-depth analyses along with an appropriate case study on recent and future developments in China. Chapter 3 examines the challenges of the automotive industry in Malaysia, whereas, Chapter 4 delves into the opportunities possible for developing nations. "Management, Strategy, and Performance" investigates the Industry 4.0 impact on the way that business is conducted. Chapter 5 concentrates on management challenges in a digital age; whereas, Chapter 6 centres on logistics and risk management. The following Chapter, 7, delivers a detailed examination of logistics and supply chain. Chapter 8 discussed leveraging for sustainable performance. Corporate strategy forms the basis for Chapter 9. Lastly in this segment, Chapter 10 assesses issues relative to cybersecurity risk management in a specific industry. The third section, "Frameworks," comprises two chapters: 11 proposes an alternative holistic framework. Chapter 12 provides an assessment framework to gauge manufacturing maturity. Section 4, "Knowledge Transfer and Education," entails a five-step methodology to introduce Industry 4.0 (Chapter 13) and the challenges to teach cultural theory in the context of the digital era (Chapter 14). "Process and Value" presents the last segment of the book. Chapter 15 explores how corporate-specific to legacy devices transitioned to cyber-physical systems. Chapter 16 investigates synergies between process excellence and Industry 4.0.

Richard Brunet-Thornton
University of Economics, Czech Republic

REFERENCES

Ahmed, P., Lim, K. K., & Loh, A. (2002). *Learning Through Knowledge Management*. Oxford, UK: Butterworth- Heinemann.

Autio, E., Sapienza, H. J., & Almeida, J. G. (2000). Effects of age at entry, knowledge intensity, and imitability on international growth. *Academy of Management Journal*, *43*(5), 909–924. doi:10.2307/1556419

Brunet-Thornton, R., & Bureš, V. (2012). Cross-Cultural Management: Establishing a Czech Benchmark. E+M Economics and Management, 3(12), 46-62.

Bureš, V. (2003). Cultural Barriers in Knowledge Sharing. E+M Economics and Management, 6, 57-62.

Bureš, V. (2006). Knowledge Management and its Implementation. *WEBIST 2006: Proceedings of the Second International Conference on Web Information Systems and Technologies*, 115-118.

Bureš, V. (2009). Conceptual Perspective of Knowledge Management (in Czech). E+M Economics and Management, 12(2).

Bureš, V., & Čech, P. (2008). Knowledge Management: The Central European Experience. *Effective Executive*, *11*(6), 47–53.

Čech, P. (2005). *The Potential of Knowledge in Organizations* (Dissertation). Hradec Králové: University of Hradec Králové.

Chen, D. H. C., & Dahlman, C. J. (2005). *The Knowledge Economy, the KAM Methodology and World Bank Operations*. Washington, DC: World Bank. Available http://www.worldbank.org/

Davenport, T. H., & Smith, D. E. (2000). Managing Knowledge in Professional Service Firms. In *The Knowledge Management Yearbook 2000-2001*. Oxford, UK: Butterworth-Heinemann.

Dittrich, P. (2016). *Reskilling for the Fourth Industrial Revolution*. Formulating a European Strategy. Policy Paper 175. Available: http://www.institutdelors.eu/media/digitalskill-jdib-nov2016.pdf?pdf=ok

Drucker, P. F. (1993). *The post capitalist society*. Oxford, UK: Butterworth-Heinemann.

European Commission. (2017a). *Czech Republic: "Průmysl 4.0"*. Available: https://ec.europa.eu/growth/tools-databases/dem/monitor/sites/default/files/DTM_Prumysl%2040_CZ%20v1.pdf

European Commission. (2017b). *Digital Transformation Scoreboard 2017: Evidence of positive outcomes and current opportunities for EU businesses*. Available: http://s3platform.jrc.ec.europa.eu/-/digital-transformation-scoreboard-2017-evidence-of-positive-outcomes-and-current-opportunities-for-eu-businesses?inheritRedirect=true

Firestone, J. (1999). *The Artificial Knowledge Manager Standard: A "Strawman"*. Working Paper No. One, KM ANSI/ISO Standards Committee Meeting, Executive Information Systems, Inc. Available: http://www.dkms.com/papers/akmsstrawbak.pdf

Gulev, R. (2005, December). Economic Culture Impacts on Knowledge Flows and Knowledge Sharing within Selected EU Countries. *Journal of Knowledge Management Practice*, *6*.

Heier, H., & Borgman, H. P. (2002). *Knowledge Management Systems Spanning Cultures: The Case of Deutsche Bank's HRBASE*. Symposium conducted at the meeting of ECIS 2002, Gdansk, Poland.

Hofstede, G. (2001). *Culture's Consequences* (2nd ed.). London: Sage Publications.

Holsapple, C. W., & Joshi, K. D. (2001). Organizational Knowledge Resources. *Decision Support Systems*, *31*(1), 39–54. doi:10.1016/S0167-9236(00)00118-4

Kaplan, R. S., & Norton, D. P. (1996). *Balanced Scorecard: Translating Strategy into Action, Harvard*. Harvard Business School Press.

Mikulecký, P., Ponce, D., & Hynek, J. (1997) Knowledge-Based Projects in Industrial Applications. *Proceedings of 4th International Seminar on Mathematical Simulation in the Glass Melting, Horní Bečva*, 191- 201.

Nonaka, I., & Takeuchi, H. (1995). *The Knowledge Creating Company*. New York: Oxford University Press.

SPIS. (2007). *Manifest of Knowledge Society*. Prague: Association for Information Society. Available: http://www.spis.cz

Acknowledgment

The editorial team wishes to thank, in particular, the members of the Centre for Digital Transformation and the Cross-Cultural Management Centre of the University of Economics, Prague for their continued effort during this process.

The idea behind this book, to analyse the impacts of Industry 4.0 in modern business environments, prompted the team to sponsor, in collaboration with the MacEwan University School of Business (Canada), an international conference on Management in the Digital Era that was held in Prague during 27 – 28 October 2017. During the conference, many of the authors presented their findings to over 50 participants from 20 countries. To all attendees, our thanks and appreciation.

Due to the novel theme and discussion proposed by this book, one of the largest challenges of this project was to secure volunteer reviewers. The Editor wishes to thank the reviewers for their admirable work and dedication. A special thank you is extended to Eric Cohen, Egemen Hopali, Kostas Leftheriotis, Radek Liška, Sergio Mazini, Vikas Mehra, Mateus Panizzon, and Bruce Thomson. They each reviewed two or more manuscripts, and provided detailed notes to the author(s), as well as to have respected the deadlines – they have my sincere gratitude.

Above all, a sincere thank you to all the authors for their submissions and their contributions to the extant body of knowledge.

Richard Brunet-Thornton
University of Economics, Czech Republic
Prague, 22 November 2017

Section 1
Country and Region Specific

Chapter 1
Strategic Plan of "Made in China 2025" and Its Implementation

Ma Huimin
Huazhong University of Science and Technology, China

Xiang Wu
Huazhong University of Science and Technology, China

Li Yan
Hubei University of Economics, China

Han Huang
Huazhong University of Science and Technology, China

Han Wu
Rennes School of Business, France

Jie Xiong
Rennes School of Business, France

Jinlong Zhang
Huazhong University of Science and Technology, China

ABSTRACT

The US has introduced a package of policies and specialized plans to reinvigorate its manufacturing industry by revolving around "reindustrialization." It has put forward a national strategic plan for advanced manufacturing, aiming at strengthening advantages of its technology-intensive advanced manufacturing industry. Japan has a different focus. By releasing "New Robot Strategy," Japan attempts to accelerate development of cooperative robots and unmanned plants to revolutionize the robot industry, cope with aggravation of Japanese social and economic issues, and enhance international competitiveness of Japan's manufacturing industry. As to France, with "New Industrial France" promoted, layout optimization of the manufacturing industry is more important. Britain, however, is invigorating its manufacturing industry through the "High-Value Manufacturing" strategy, and the strategy has so far entered Phase II. China is no exception. This chapter explores "Made in China 2025."

DOI: 10.4018/978-1-5225-3468-6.ch001

INTRODUCTION

The US has introduced a package of policies and specialized plans to reinvigorate its manufacturing industry by revolving around "reindustrialization". Besides, it has put forward "A National Strategic Plan for Advanced Manufacturing", aiming at strengthening advantages of its technology-intensive advanced manufacturing industry. German is implementing "Industry 4.0" policy. Japan has a different focus. By releasing "New Robot Strategy", Japan attempts to accelerate development of cooperative robots and unmanned plants to revolutionize the robot industry, cope with aggravation of Japanese social and economic issues, and enhance international competitiveness of Japan's manufacturing industry. As to France with "New Industrial France" promoted, layout optimization of the manufacturing industry is more important. UK, however, is invigorating its manufacturing industry through the "high-value manufacturing" strategy, and the strategy has so far entered Phase II. South Korea, a neighboring country of China, has put forward the "advanced innovators' strategy" so as to promote mutual integration between the manufacturing industry and information technology, create new industries, and scale a new high for its manufacturing competitiveness. China is no exception; thus this article provides a comprehensive analysis of "Made in China 2025" strategic plan as well as its implementation. This article provides new insights to practitioners in manufacturing industries, with guidelines to benefit the decision making processes. Moreover, we also would like to enrich the academic literature by extending the focus of advanced manufacturing topics from advanced economics to emerging market perspective. Doing so also gives both practitioners and academia an open discussion on the newly formulated national policies of advanced manufacturing in a broader scope of countries.

1."MADE IN CHINA 2025"

1.1 Development and Status of China's Manufacturing Industry

From the start of the Industrial Revolution, the manufacturing industry has been an essential part of economy. China's manufacturing industry embarked on the path of development after China's adoption of the reform and opening-up policy in 1978. Its development generally includes three periods, namely period of recovery, period of emergence of private economy and foreign-invested manufacturing industry, and period of marching towards the international market (Wübbeke, Meissner, Zenglein, Ives, & Conrad, 2016).

The first period lasted from 1978 to the late 1980s. It was a period witnessing revival of China's manufacturing industry. Before this period, China had built a relatively complete manufacturing system according to the planned economy system of the former Soviet Union, which was mainly devoted to production of industrial products, thus resulting in lack of consumables. In the coming one decade after China's adoption of reform and opening-up policy, China's manufacturing industry gradually made a comeback, marked by entry of domestically-made electronic products and light industrial products into the market. Televisions, washing machines and refrigerators could almost be found in every Chinese household. There were more options for dressing of Chinese. Consumables especially foods gradually enriched. During this period, state-owned enterprises (SOEs) were without doubt a pioneering force of China's manufacturing industry. Some military industrial enterprises started producing products for civil use. However, short supply was still a striking characteristic of China's consumption market in this period.

The second period mainly referred to the whole 1990s. It was a period when the private enterprises and foreign-invested manufacturing industry emerged. Especially benefiting from appearance of private enterprises, establishment of special economic zones and stock markets, and launch of commercial housing, China's planned economy was transformed into market-oriented economy. Gradually, over-supply rather than short supply became a dominant characteristic of China's consumption market. The market-oriented economy along with the increasing degree of opening of the coastal areas contributed to flourishing of private economy and gained competitive advantage for it. During the period, a large number of management and technical personnel working in SOEs quit their jobs and started their own business. In addition, many SOEs, failing to get adapted to market changes because of weak awareness of competition, suffered serious losses in the market. The glory of time-honored brands held SOEs disappeared. Moreover, different kinds of industrial parks were set up in China. The huge potential of the Chinese market attracted many foreign-invested manufacturing enterprises to base themselves in China. Thanks to foreign-invested enterprises and joint ventures, advanced design and manufacturing techniques for industrial and consumption products were introduced from foreign countries. During this period, emergence of private economy and foreign investments fueled rapid development of the manufacturing industry in China's coastal areas. The gap between inland China and China's coastal areas started widening in terms of the manufacturing industry and even the regional economic power.

The third period lasts from the early 21st century to present. It is a period when China's manufacturing industry marches into the international market. In 2001, China entered the WTO. Foreign investments flooded into China, capitalizing on opening of the Chinese market to foreign competitors (Xia, 2017). Many of these foreign investments have been developed into today's tens of thousands of manufacturing enterprises either being joint ventures or being foreign-invested. Export-oriented manufacturing enterprises located in China's coastal areas give full play to their cost advantage to handle OEM orders from the developed countries. Gradually, China becomes the production outsourcing base of the international manufacturing industry. "Made in China" starts gaining popularity in the global market as a brand of Chinese products. The cost advantage of these coastal enterprises is derived from the gathering of surplus labor and industries. Apart from the cost advantage, China's infrastructure construction and Internet development have also contributed to thriving of the manufacturing industry. Acceleration of government input in infrastructure construction, notably railways, high-speed highways and communication facilities, has led to spreading of urbanization. On the other hand, infrastructure consumption and rising of the consumption level increase the demand for raw materials, industrial products, and consumables. Thanks to burgeoning of the shipping, tool machine, automobile, engineering machinery, electronics and communications, and steel industries, the whole manufacturing industrial chain has been updated. Development of IT represented by Internet is an important driving factor of the manufacturing industry. Information systems, such as ERP, PLM, CRM and SCM, are widely used among Chinese enterprises to facilitate e-commerce. During the period, China's industrial product and consumable market has been fully transformed from the seller-oriented market into the buyer-oriented market. Internationalization of the manufacturing market, on the one hand, enriches product categories. On the other hand, it intensifies market competition. Following entry of China into the WTO, China's manufacturing industry has also quickly integrated itself into the global economy. With skyrocketing of international trade volume, China is gaining more and more trade surplus. The local excellent manufacturing enterprises, such as Lenovo, Haier and Huawei, keep expanding their business on a global scale.

1.2 "Made in China 2025"

After decades of development, Chinese manufacturing industry needs a new strategic plan to cope with the current situation. Consequently, the State Council issued "Made in China 2025" on May 8, 2015 to transform China from a manufacturing giant into a world manufacturing power. The plan, endorsed by Premier Li Keqiang, is the country's first action plan focusing on promoting manufacturing.

1.2.1 Strategic Goals

"Made in China 2025" plan proposes a "three-step" strategy of transforming China into a leading manufacturing power by the year 2049 in line with the basic guideline of

innovation-driven, quality first, green development, structurally optimizes and human-oriented" and the basic principle of "market orientation, government guidance, focus on the present, look into the future, overall promotion, key breakthroughs, independent development, opening and cooperation (Liu, 2016; Li, 2017; Zhang, Peek, Pikas, & Lee, 2016).

The first step is to develop from a manufacturing giant into a manufacturing power by 2025. The second step is to reach the medium level of the world manufacturing powers by 2035. The third step is to further consolidate China's position as a manufacturing power and list China's comprehensive manufacturing strengthen into the world's top list by 2049.

1.2.2 Priorities

Revolving around the strategic goal of being a manufacturing power, "Made in China 2025" plan identifies nine tasks as priorities: 1) Improving manufacturing innovation; 2) Integrating information technology and industry; 3) Strengthening the industrial base; 4) Fostering Chinese brands; 5) Enforcing green manufacturing; 6) Promoting breakthroughs in 10 key sectors, including new information technology, numerical control tools and robotics, aerospace equipment, ocean engineering equipment and high-tech ships, railway equipment, energy-saving and new energy vehicles, power equipment, new materials, biological medicine and medical devices, and agricultural machinery; 7) Advancing restructuring of the manufacturing sector; 8) Promoting service-oriented manufacturing and manufacturing-related service industries; and 9) Internationalizing manufacturing.

"Made in China 2025" plan adopts intelligent manufacturing as the major area for it to make a breakthrough. To further promote intelligent manufacturing, China will set up intelligent plants and digitalized workshops as pilot projects in major fields; speed up applications of advanced manufacturing techniques and equipment, including human-machine intelligent interaction, industrial robots, intelligent logistics management and additive manufacturing, to the production process; promote simulation optimization, digital control, status information real-time monitoring and self-adaptive control of the manufacturing process. Besides, efforts will be made to fasten promotion and application of the product whole-life cycle management, customer relationship maintenance and supply chain management system; boost integration of key links, including group control and management, design and manufacturing, production-supply-marketing, business and finance; and realize intelligent control and management.

1.2.3 Guarantee Systems

"Made in China 2025" proposes achieving breakthroughs of key breakthroughs restricting development of China's manufacturing industry via government guidance, resource integration and five major projects, including construction of the National Manufacturing Industry, intelligent manufacturing, strengthening of the industrial basis, green manufacturing, and high-end equipment innovation. All these efforts made can also contribute to improvement of overall competitiveness of China's manufacturing industry. In order to realize the above objectives, "Made in China 2025" points out the necessity of deepening institutional reform, creating a market environment featuring fair play, improving financial support policies, reinforcing financial and tax policy support, building a multi-level talent training system, introducing more policies to support development of medium, small and micro-sized enterprises, further expanding opening of the manufacturing industry, and completing the organization and implementation mechanism. It is also emphasized that various central departments and local governments should realize significance of building a manufacturing superpower, strengthen their organization and leadership, improve their work mechanism, study and formulate specific implementation plans, detail policy measures, and guarantee implementation of various tasks. Under the background, local governments should launch policies to promote upgrade and transformation of the manufacturing industry in line with regional characteristics.

1.3 Advantages and Challenges of China's Manufacturing Industry

Over the past decades, China has shaped a firm domestic market with a complete range of sectors, and an independent and complete manufacturing system. Along with rapid development of China's economy, "Made in China" has been active in the global market, forging its own advantages (Tourk & Marsh, 2016). However, there is no doubt that China's manufacturing industry still has a long way to go.

1.3.1 Advantages

Up to 2017, the advantages of China's manufacturing industry can be summarized as follows:

1. China has a complete industrial system. There are 39 large-scale industries, 191 medium-scale industries, and 5252 small-scale industries in China. It is apt to say that China is the country with the most complete range of industrial classification in the world. The unparalleled industrial system including almost every sector enables China to compete in almost every field of industrial products, ranging from fashion and shoes to airplanes, from raw materials and minerals to machine tools. This provides an important source of competitiveness for China, and lays the foundation for China's industrial upgrade.
2. China is the world's largest consumption market. This guarantees transformation and upgrade of China's manufacturing industry. In 2015, China's retail sales accounted for nearly 20% of the global total, contributing nearly 37% to global industrial growth. As a contrast, Europe and North America together just contributed less than 5%. The sharp contrast indicated a strong vigor and growth potential of China's retail market. Benefiting from years of high-speed growth, China's online retail market scale increased to 3.8 trillion RMB, registering a year-on-year increase of 36.2% (Yang, Li, & Liu, 2015). Its percentage in the global online retail market and contribution rate were 35% and 46%, respectively. The impressive performance listed China on the top of the

global online retail market. An expanding consumption market usually indicates a growing demand, and the growing demand can create a favorable condition for transformation and upgrade of the manufacturing industry.

3. China has the world's largest industrial labor resources. A large population and abundance of labor resources—these are a part of China's basic national conditions. Since popularization of the nine-year compulsory education system in 2000, the educational level of Chinese has achieved a significant improvement. The sharp increase of the popularization rate of senior high education and the strengthening of occupational education have led to popularization of higher education. Since 2011, governments at all levels have fully implemented the *National Medium-and Long-term Educational Reform and Development Programme (2011~2020),* and remarkable achievements have been achieved especially in terms of giving priority to development of education, promotion of education equality, balanced development of compulsory education and preschool education reform. The balance between education supply and demand has fostered abundant industrial labor resources.
4. China has increased its input for basic R&D to boost update of its manufacturing industry. Competitiveness of the manufacturing industry is mainly reflected as innovation. China is a country pursuing innovation for a long time. In 2015, the national R&D input totaled at 1.4 trillion yuan, an increase of 38.1% over 2012. From 2012 to 2015, China's R&D input maintained an annual growth of 11.4%. If calculated by the exchange rate, China's R&D spending has well exceeded that of Germany and Japan to be the second largest R&D investor, just after the US. In the future, increasing R&D input of China will keep on promoting technological innovation and upgrade of the manufacturing industry.
5. China's regional development policies guarantee industrial completeness during the transformation process of the manufacturing industry. Industrial development policies vary in different parts of China. This lays the foundation for formulation of a nationwide industrial layout in China. Comparatively, development of China's manufacturing industry is the fastest in China's southeast coastal areas, followed by that of Central China, and West China is still retarding. Different industrial distributions and different development levels make it possible for industries to transfer between different regions. In this way, industrial completeness can be maintained even during the upgrade and transformation process of China's manufacturing industry.

1.3.2 Challenges

1. **A Low per Capita Increase:** Though development of China's manufacturing industry has been impressive, its total increase and per capital increase are still far behind that of the current manufacturing superpowers in the world, like the US an Germany. In other words, China's manufacturing industry is confined to the labor-intensive period with low technical content and added value. In 2008, Japan's per capita increase of the manufacturing increase was close to 9,000 USD, which was the highest in the world. However, the figure was just around 700 USD in China. From 1993 to 2008, the annual average increase of China's manufacturing increase was 26.6%, which was far overtaken by 47.2% of the US and 36.9% of Japan. This suggested that China's manufacturing industry still needed to increase its profitability, which was often reduced by the high percentage of material consumption, low degree of processing and low technical content.

2. **Weak Technological Innovation and Lack of Core Techniques:** That techniques and brands lack proprietary intellectual property rights is common to see in China's manufacturing industry (Siu & Contreras, 2016). About 60% of key techniques and core techniques come abroad. In 2012, the R&D input of China's top 500 manufacturing enterprises just accounted for around 1.87% of their operating income. In 2013, the R&D input of manufacturing enterprises above the designated scale accounted for just 0.85% of their operating income. Many Chinese manufacturing enterprises have not yet realized the importance of innovation, and their ability to digest the innovational techniques is wanting. These shortages have been hurdles of Chinese manufacturing enterprises to effectively absorb international innovation resources. Though human resource costs keep on increasing, top-notch technical personnel and technological innovation teams are still lacking. As China 's manufacturing industry keeps on improving its technological level, making technological import increasingly difficult, its late-mover advantage is losing. Most Chinese manufacturing enterprises are resource-intensive or labor-intensive. In international labor distribution, they are often at the bottom of the global industrial value chain. In the field of foreign trade, 80% of Chinese competitors with a competitive advantage are from the labor-intensive sector. The competitiveness index of China's manufacturing enterprises in the high-tech field represented by computer integration and manufacturing technology, material technology, aerospace technology and electronic technology is extremely low. For example, most electronic and communication devices exported from China to other countries include compute peripheral devices, electronic elements and audio devices for home use. All these are low-end products in the new-and high-tech industry. To sum up, China is still the "world's manufacturing plant", serving as a supplier of cheap, low-end products and parts for the rest of the world. It is full of challenges for China's manufacturing industry, being at the bottom of the value chain, to take the lead in the international manufacturing market. Worse still, the profit margin of China's manufacturing industry has been increasingly squeezed.
3. **Extensive Development Mode and Serious Environmental Pollution:** China is a major energy consumer in the world. Its energy supply structure is unreasonable (Hao, Qiao, Liu, & Zhao, 2017). The terminal energy consumption and total power generation of China rank No. 1 in the world. However, in terms of the energy generation mode, China's electricity is mainly generated by coals. The electricity generation mode is outdated and less environmentally-friendly. To support the rapid economic development, China has consumed large amounts of energies with a low energy utilization efficiency. For example, in 2011, China's GDP took up 10.48% of the world's total, but its energy consumption was around 18.33% of the global total. The GDP unit energy consumption of China was nearly 1.75 times higher than the world's average, 2.25 times higher than that of the US, 3.63 times higher than that of Germany and 4.18 times higher than that of Japan. There is a huge gap between China and the current manufacturing superpowers in terms of energy efficiency. In 2011, China's GDP unit carbon dioxide emission was 2.42 times higher than the world's average, 3.12 times higher than that of the US, 5.21 times higher than that of Germany and 5.39 times higher than that of Japan. All this proved an extensive development mode of China's economy. Though the energy consumption and the unit output pollutant emission of the manufacturing industry are declining on an annual basis, the rapid economic growth still leads to a sharp increase of pollutant emissions, seriously damaging the ecological environment (Binz, Gosens, Hansen, & Hansen, 2017).

At present, China's economic development has been ushered into a period of medium-rate growth. Resource and environmental constraint is strengthening; cost of production elements, such as labor resources, is increasing; and the investment and export increase rate is obviously slowing down. From the perspective of external environment, trade protectionism is prevailing in the international community and the trade environment is worsening. Meanwhile, foreign investments are withdrawing from the Chinese market to have their manufacturing bases located in Southeast Asia or other places with cheaper labor resources. After years of rapid development, China's manufacturing industry is embracing a hard time. The previously extensive development mode relying on input of resource elements and scale expansion could no longer bring sustainable benefits for China's manufacturing industry. It has become an imperative for China to adjust the structure of its manufacturing industry, upgrade and transform it, and increase its development level and efficacy. Under such a background, the Chinese government put forward "Made in China 2025" plan, at an attempt to achieve an all-around transformation and upgrade of its manufacturing industry, form new driving force for its economic development, and shape new advantages for it to compete in the international market.

2. ANALYSIS OF POLICIES FOR DEVELOPMENT OF THE MANUFACTURING INDUSTRY IN TYPICAL REGIONS OF CHINA

2.1 Regional Economic Layout of China

2.1.1 Overall Evaluation of China's Regional Manufacturing Industry

China has a vast territory. This leads to striking differences of the manufacturing industry in different regions. According to development characteristics of the manufacturing industry, this chapter divides 22 provinces, five autonomous areas, four municipalities directly under administration of the central government in China, excluding Hong Kong SAR, Macau SAR and Taiwan, into the east region, central region, western region, and northeast region. Most manufacturing enterprises concentrate in the east region. In the central region and the western region, the resource-intensive manufacturing industry concentrates. In the east region, communication devices, electric appliances and machinery devices form a major part of the manufacturing industry. In the northeast region, the traditional manufacturing industry dominates. It can be seen that regional distribution of China's manufacturing industry is not balanced. However, in recent years, under regulation of national policies, China's regional industrial economy has been increasingly coordinated (Li, Yang, & Liu, 2014).

1. **East Region:** The east region includes six provinces (Hebei, Jiangsu, Zhejiang, Guangdong, Fujian, Henan, etc.) and three municipalities (Beijing, Shanghai and Tianjin) directly under administration of the central government. For a long time, the east region, particularly, the Yangtze Delta Area and the Pearl River Delta Area, has been celebrated as the region with the most developed manufacturing industry in China.
    a. **The Yangtze River Delta Region:** The Yangtze River Delta Region mainly refers to two provinces (Jiangsu and Zhejiang) and one municipal (Shanghai) directly under administration of the central government. Here is the area with the largest manufacturing industrial scale in China. Revolving around Shanghai, the manufacturing industry in this region radiates along

major traffic axes, and has absolute advantage in terms of new-generation IT, marine engineering equipment, high-tech ships and new materials. After 2000, the Yangtze River Delta Region has been expanding obviously. The higher the degree of technological concentration is, the smaller the industrial expansion radius is. In the current Yangtze River Region, development of Jiangsu's manufacturing industry has been impressive; while Shanghai is shifting its focus from the manufacturing industry to the service industry, so the percentage of its manufacturing industry is declining.

b. **The Pearl River Delta Region:** The Pearl River Delta Region mainly covers nine cities of Guangdong Province, including Guangzhou, Shenzhen, Zhuhai, Dongguan, Foshan, Zhongshan, Huizhou, Jiangmen, and Zhaoqing. It is a major manufacturing base of China. Guangzhou is the central city of the Pearl River Delta Region. Though the Pearl River Delta Region exceeds the Yangtze River Delta Region in terms of economic aggregate, the former is still inferior to the latter in terms of the manufacturing industrial scale. Technological innovation is a highlight of the manufacturing industry in the Pearl River Delta Region. The new and high-tech industry is the largest contributor to Guangdong's manufacturing industry. At the same time, the low-tech industry is also taking up a high percentage in Guangdong's manufacturing industrial structure.

c. **Beijing-Tianjin-Hebei Region:** As the region name implies, the region includes one province, Hebei, and two cities, namely Beijing and Tianjin. The manufacturing industrial scale of the Beijing-Tianjin-Hebei Region is relatively small. Currently, the Beijing-Tianjin-Hebei Region is implementing the in-depth integration strategy, which combines growth of the manufacturing industry, technological research and talent advantage of Beijing and Tianjin to boost an overall promotion of Hebei's manufacturing industry. However, air pollution has hindered in-depth integration among Beijing, Tianjin and Hebei.

d. **Other Regions:** Shandong Province is a giant manufacturing province, because it is included in the top 5 of most segments of the manufacturing industry. The advantage of Shandong's manufacturing industry is mainly reflected in the sector of food manufacturing and textile. Fujian Province is advantageous in the field of new-generation IT, marine engineering devices, high-tech ships and new materials.

2. **Central Region:** The central region includes six provinces, namely Shanxi Province, Henan Province, Anhui Province, Jiangxi Province, Hunan Province and Hubei Province. Most of these provinces show a huge potential in many manufacturing sectors. For example, Henan Province has formed development advantages in the field of new-generation IT, power equipment, energy-saving and new energy vehicle, agriculture machines and new materials; Hubei, Hubei and Anhui have made remarkable achievements in the field of new-generation IT; Jiangxi has advantages in developing biomedicine and high-performance medical instruments, marine engineering devices, high-tech ships and new materials; and Shanxi is rising in the field of advanced rail transit devices and new materials.

3. **Western Region:** The west region includes 12 provinces, municipalities and autonomous areas, chiefly Shaanxi, Gansu, Ningxia, Qinghai, Xinjiang, Sichuan, Guizhou, Yunnan, Tibet, Inner Mongolia, Guangxi and Chongqing. Sichuan and Chongqing are two representative areas with an advanced manufacturing industry in the west region. Sichuan is a giant manufacturing province in the west region. More importantly, it is a major national equipment manufacturing base. Chongqing,

relying on the Yangtze River Economic Belt Strategy, has maintained a rapid development momentum (Hou, 2016).

4. **Northeast Region:** The northeast region includes three provinces, namely Heilongjiang, Jilin and Liaoning. It is known as the traditional industrial basis of China. The manufacturing industry is a pillar industry of this region. However, since 2013, the growth rate of the manufacturing industry in this region has been sharply declining. The manufacturing industry in the region mainly concentrates in the medium-and low-end sector with a low R&D input and lacking technological innovation. The manufacturing industry distribution in the northeast region has a close bearing on its development history. The competitive sectors of the region include high-end numerically controlled machine tools and robots, aerospace devices, marine engineering devices and high-tech shipping, advanced rail transit traffic devices, energy-saving and new energy vehicles, power equipment and agricultural machinery, etc.

2.1.2 Introduction of Manufacturing Superpowers in China

1. **Introduction of Manufacturing Superpowers in China:** Data analysis of China's industrial statistical yearbook shows that different sectors of China's manufacturing industry are low in concentration. Concentration of the top five provinces in every sector is around 50% (China State Statistics Bureau, 2017). Key sectors of "Made in China 2015" are found in the following provinces and municipalities with a high concentration, principally Jiangsu, Guangdong, Shanghai and Shandong (Hu & Sun, 2014). According to requirements of "Made in China 2025", the indexes are analyzed from four dimensions, namely innovation capability, quality effectiveness, integration between industrialization and informatization, and green development (see Table 1). Jiangsu and Guangdong are worthy of the top two in the list of China's manufacturing industry comprehensive strength, with their measuring indexes far exceeding those of others.

Table 1. China's manufacturing superpower evaluation index system

Dimensions	Indexes
Innovation ability	Percentage of the internal R&D spending in the total operating income of a manufacturing enterprise above the designated scale (%)
	Number of effective patterns and inventions in per 100 billion yuan of the operating income of a manufacturing enterprise above the designated scale (piece)
Quality effectiveness	Quality competition index of the manufacturing industry
	Increase of the added value of the manufacturing industry
	Increase rate of the overall labor productivity in the manufacturing industry (%)
Integration between industrialization and informatization	Broadband popularization rate (%)
	Digital R&D design tool popularization rate (%)
	Key process numerical control rate (%)
Green development	Decrease of energy consumption of unit industrial added value of an enterprise above the designated scale
	Decrease of carbon dioxide emission of unit industrial added value
	Decrease of water consumption of unit industrial added value
	Comprehensive utilization rate of industrial solid wastes (%)

Sources: Summarized by authors based on the national and provincial government reports.

After analyzing more than 600 cities, either large-scale or medium-scale or small-scale, in China according to the above evaluation indexes, it can be observed that Shenzhen and Guangzhou, both located in Guangdong Province; Suzhou, Wuxi and Nantong in Jiangsu Province; Ningbo in Zhejiang Province; and Qingdao in Shandong Province show outstanding performance.

2. **Analysis of Distribution of Ten Key Sectors of the Manufacturing Industry:** Based on the data from "China Manufacturing Big Data Platform", the distribution of ten key sectors listed in "Made in China 2025" is analyzed (see Table 2).

2.2 Government Action Schemes for Typical Regions

Since issuance of "Made in China 2025", there have been 29 provinces, autonomous areas and municipalities, including Jiangsu, Guangdong, Shandong, Fujian, Sichuan, Hubei and Beijing, gradually

Table 2. Provincial distribution chart of ten key sectors

Ten key Sectors	Distribution	Competitive Provinces and Cities
New information technology	The east region is the major competitive region, and the central region shows a strong development potential.	Beijing, Guangdong, Shanghai, Jiangsu, Zhejiang, etc.
Numerical control tools and robotics	Distribute in eastern central, west, and northeast region, and concentrate in areas with a maturely developed manufacturing industry.	Beijing, Shanghai, Jiangsu, Zhejiang, Shandong, Liaoning, Hubei, Hunan, Shaanxi, etc.
Aerospace equipment	With the Yangtze River Delta and Shaanxi in the central region at the core; the Pearl River Delta and northeast region on two wings; with Beijing, Tianjin and Sichuan as R&D support.	Aeronautic equipment: Shanghai, Tianjin, Shaanxi, etc.; Spaceflight equipment: Beijing, Shanghai, Shaanxi, etc.
Ocean engineering equipment and high-tech ships	Distribute mainly around ship and ocean engineering production bases and research institutes.	Guangdong, Shanghai, Jiangsu, Shandong, Tianjin, Fujian, Liaoning, Hubei, Anhui, Chongqing, Guangxi, etc.
Railway equipment	Mainly concentrate in the east region, northeast region and central region.	Jiangsu, Shandong, Hebei, Jilin, Liaoning, Hunan, etc.
Energy-saving and new energy vehicles	Consistent with the distribution of the traditional automobile industry, including the Yangtze River Delta cluster represented by Shanghai, the northeast industrial cluster represented by Changchun, central region cluster represented by Wuhan, Beijing-Tianjin-Circum-Bohai Sea Region cluster, Pearl River Delta area represented by Guangzhou, and southwest cluster represented by Chongqing.	Beijing, Guangdong, Shanghai, Zhejiang, Jilin, Hunan, Chongqing, etc.
Power equipment	Concentrate in the east region, and some provinces of the northeast region and west region show development advantages in the segments.	Shanghai, Jiangsu, Zhejiang, Tianjin, Liaoning, Henan, Shaanxi, Xinjiang, etc.
Agricultural machinery	Mainly concentrate in the eastern central region.	Jiangsu, Shandong, Heilongjiang, Henan, Hubei, Anhui, etc.
New materials	The Yangtze River Delta, Pearl River Delta, Beijing-Tianjin-Hebei-Shandong Region, central region, northeast region and west region.	Beijing, Guangdong, Shanghai, Jiangsu, Zhejiang, Shandong, Tianjin, Anhui, Jiangxi, etc.
Biological medicine and medical devices	The biological medicine industry revolves around the Yangtze River Delta and the Circum-Bohai Sea Region. The high-performance medical equipment industry concentrates in eastern coast areas, and Sichuan and Chongqing in the west region.	Biological medicine: Guangdong, Jiangsu, Henan, Sichuan, etc.; High-performance medical equipment: Guangdong, Shanghai, Jiangsu, Zhejiang, Shandong, Tianjin, Chongqing, Sichuan, etc.

Sources: Summarized by authors based on the national and provincial government reports.

issuing local implementation strategies and action schemes for "Made in China 2025". Besides, more than 30 cities, including Dongguan, Wuxi, Wuhan, Dalian, Harbin, Nanjing and Suzhou have introduced measures to more effectively implement "Made in China 2025". In terms of content, various places in China have formed a development strategy oriented towards high-end equipment manufacturing and industrial upgrade. On the whole, their strategies revolve around ten key sectors proposed by "Made in China 2025", but each of them gets different focuses.

In order to analyze "Made in China 2025" implemented on a local level, this chapter chooses Guangdong, Jiangsu and Hubei as well as representative cities of these provinces, namely Dongguan, Wuxi and Wuhan, for a contrastive analysis.

2.2.1 "Made in China 2025" Action Scheme in Guangdong, Jiangsu and Hubei

1. **"Made in China 2025" Action Scheme of Guangdong Province:** The Guangdong Provincial Government, Economic & Information Commission of Guangdong Province, Guangdong Provincial Development and Reform Commission, Guangdong Provincial Science & Technology Bureau and Guangdong Provincial Finance Bureau have issued a series of supporting documents based on practical situations of Guangdong and requirements of "Made in China 2025". The "Notice of the Guangdong Provincial People's Government on Issuing 'Guangdong Provincial Intelligent Manufacturing Development Plane (2015-2025)'" (No. 70 [2015]) released in 2015 was the first of its kind, closely followed by *Suggestions of the Guangdong Provincial People's Government on Implementing 'Made in China 2025'* (No. 89 [2015]). Later, around 20 documents related to task distribution, integration of the manufacturing industry and Internet, and so on have been launched. These documents show that

Guangdong is quick in responding to the national government's call for implementation of "Made in China 2025", and its action scheme is highly referential to the rest of provinces in China.

Major development sectors pinned down by the Guangdong Provincial People's Government include new information technology, advanced equipment manufacturing, new materials, and biological medicine. Under the four major sectors, there are 18 subsidiary categories. Four projects are clarified, including the

industrial infrastructure strengthening project, manufacturing internationalization project, green engineering project and manufacturing innovation engineering project.

Nine major tasks, including building a national intelligent manufacturing development demonstration area; promoting deep integration between informatization and industrialization; accelerating transformation, upgrade and structural adjustment of the manufacturing industry; implementation of the industrial infrastructure strengthening project; fully promoting green manufacturing; enhancing protection and utilization of quality, brand and intellectual property; boosting coordinated development of large-scale, medium-scale and small-scale enterprises; actively developing the service-oriented manufacturing industry and the production-oriented service industry; and raising the international development level of the manufacturing industry.

2. **"Made in China 2025" Action Scheme of Jiangsu Province:** Since 2015 after the CPC Jiangsu Provincial Committee and the Jiangsu Provincial People's Government issued "Notice on 'Made in China 2025 Jiangsu Action Scheme'" (No. 16 [2015]), the local government and various departments have subsequently introduced nine comprehensive documents. Meanwhile,

more documents haven issued in order to guide the development of dedicated industries, such as new energy vehicles, ships, chemical and metallurgical building materials, etc.

There are 15 key sectors involving in Jiangsu's action scheme for "Made in China 2025". Among them, eight are major sectors, including high-end equipment innovation; integration between military and civil manufacturing, manufacturing industry innovation center construction, intelligent manufacturing, industrial infrastructure foundation strengthening; quality and brand construction; manufacturing industry internationalization; and green manufacturing. The major tasks are clear, including eight categories, including strengthening of independent innovation and promotion of Jiangsu's core manufacturing competitiveness; acceleration of in-depth integration between industrialization and informatization and improvement of the corporate intelligent development level; continuous promotion of technical transformation and gathering of new driving force for industrial optimization and upgrade; strengthening of quality and brand construction and expansion of the international influence of products in Jiangsu Province; promotion of innovation of industrial models and speeding up of production-oriented service industry; increasing foreign exchange and cooperation to promote internationalization of the manufacturing industry; acceleration of the industrial structural adjustment and optimization of the productivity space layout; promotion of green production and manufacturing to support sustainable development of the manufacturing industry.

3. **"Made in China 2025" Action Scheme of Hubei Province:** The Hubei Provincial People's Government, Hubei Provincial Economic and Information Committee, Hubei Provincial Development and Reform Committee, Hubei Provincial Science and Technology Bureau and Hubei Provincial Finance Department have issued many documents concerning "Made in China 2025".

In order to coordinate different documents issued by different departments, the provincial government has specially set up the provincial manufacturing superpower construction leadership group.

In February 2017, the leadership group issued "Notice on '1+X Action Scheme or Implementation Plan of Hubei Province for 'Made in China 2025'" (No. 1 [2017]). Later, eight plans revolving around the Action Scheme have been subsequently launched, including "Hubei Provincial Intelligent Manufacturing Demonstration Project Implementation Plan", "Hubei Provincial Manufacturing Industry Innovation Center Construction Engineering Implementation Plan", Hubei Provincial Industrial Infrastructure Strengthening Implementation Plan", "Implementation Plan for Hubei's Development of the Service-oriented Manufacturing Industry", "Hubei Provincial New-Generation Technology and Industry Development Action Plan (2016-2020)", "Hubei Provincial Biological Medicine and High-end Medical Instrument Industrial Development Action Plan" (2016-2020), "Hubei Provincial New Materials Industry Development Implementation Plan" (2016-2020), and "Hubei Provincial Ocean Engineering Equipment and

High-Tech Ship Industry Development Action Plan" (2016-2020) (Li, 2016). The eight implementation plans cover multiple key development sectors of Hubei's manufacturing industry.

The key sectors in Hubei's "Made in China 2025" action plan includes ten categories and 42 items. To achieve development of the nine key sectors, nine projects have been launched, namely the intelligent manufacturing demonstration project, manufacturing entrepreneur development new center construction, industrial foundation strengthening project, enterprise fine management promotion project, intelligent technological transformation project, service-oriented manufacturing industry demonstration project, clean production demonstration project, manufacturing internalization project, and entrepreneur development project. Correspondingly, nine major tasks are pinpointed, including acceleration of intelligent manufacturing development and promotion of in-depth integration between informatization and industrialization; improvement of the manufacturing industry innovation system and promotion of the independent innovation ability; strengthening of "four fundamentals" development and improving the foundation of the manufacturing industry; improvement of the industrial standards and systems, and enhancement of quality and brand construction; boosting of the industrial structural adjustment and speeding up of the manufacturing industry transformation progress; development of the production-oriented service industry and promotion of service orientation of the manufacturing industry; promotion of green manufacturing and sustainable development capability; sticking to promoting development through increase of the opening degree to the outside world, and deepening of international industrial cooperation; acceleration of multi-layer talent development and full release of talent dividends.

2.2.2 "Made in China 2025" Action Scheme in Dongguan, Wuxi and Wuhan

1. **"Made in China 2025" Action Scheme of Dongguan**: Dongguan is the city of Guangdong responding the fastest to "Made in China 2025", from the issued time of city level policy and documents as responses to the central government policy change(s). Right after Guangdong Province issued the action plan for "Made in China 2025", Dongguan spearheaded to put forward "Made in Dongguan 2025", and issued "Suggestions on Implementing 'Made in Dongguan 2025'" (No. 1 [2015]). Later, more than 10 documents related to implementation measures and key development sectors have been introduced. Seen from the content of the documents, measures to implement "Made in Dongguan 2025" are relatively comprehensive.

The key sectors involving in Dongguan's action scheme fall into 23 categories. There are four major tasks, including strengthening the electronic information manufacturing industry; developing the intelligent manufacturing equipment and intelligent power distribution equipment; promoting the consumable manufacturing industry transformation; cultivating the emergence industry of strategic importance. There are six projects launched to realize development of the key sectors, including the innovation manufacturing project; quality manufacturing project; intelligent manufacturing project; green manufacturing project; service-oriented manufacturing project; cluster manufacturing project.

2. **"Made in China 2025" Action Scheme of Wuxi:** The Wuxi Municipal People's Government, Wuxi Municipal Economic and Information Committee and Wuxi Municipal Development and Reform Committee, Wuxi Municipal Science and Technology Bureau, and Wuxi Municipal Finance Bureau have nearly introduced ten documents and guidelines to ensure smooth progress of "Made in China

2015" in China. In particular, Wuxi has launched a guiding document specially for development of the local integrated circuit industry.

The key sectors involved in "Made in China 2025" action scheme of Wuxi falls into eight categories and 32 subsidiary categories. 16 major tasks have proposed, including promoting the intelligent workshop (plant) construction; accelerating intelligent manufacturing of key sectors; promoting Internet applications to industry; developing intelligent equipment and products; developing intelligent equipment and key parts; strengthening cooperation in the intelligent equipment industry; promoting the intelligent manufacturing coordination and innovation scheme; participating in the intelligent manufacturing standard formation; propelling intelligent manufacturing patent, brand and quality construction; developing software and information technology; developing the Internet-based manufacturing industry; cultivating intelligent manufacturing service suppliers; building the intelligent manufacturing service system; building a multilevel talent team; improving the talent development mechanism; and implementing the "Taihu Talents" plan. In response to the 16 major tasks, there are 11 projects, including the opening and cooperation project; service-oriented manufacturing project; talent support project; enterprise cultivation project; intensification and cluster project; green low-carbon project; intelligent manufacturing project; innovation-driven project; project leadership; and quality and brand project.

3. **"Made in China 2025" Action Scheme of Wuhan:** The Wuhan Provincial People's Government, Wuhan Provincial Economic and Information Committee and Wuhan Provincial Development and Reform Committee, Wuhan Provincial Science and Technology Bureau, and Wuhan Provincial Finance Bureau have nearly introduced ten guiding documents for implementation of "Made in China 2025". These documents cover a wide range of sectors and issues.

The key development sectors in "Made in China 2025" action scheme of Wuhan falls into four categories and 11 types. The major tasks fall into four categories and include 15 items. The four categories of tasks include promotion of the manufacturing industry independent innovation capability; acceleration of integration between the Internet and the advanced manufacturing industry; building of a new industrial development system; and acceleration of the traditional industrial transformation and upgrade. There are four major projects launched to realize the four tasks, including intelligent manufacturing project; green manufacturing project; green manufacturing project; service-oriented manufacturing project; and industrial foundation strengthening project.

2.3 Comparison of Government Implementation Policies in Typical Regions

2.3.1 Comparative Analysis of Government Implementation Policies in Guangdong, Jiangsu and Hubei

Comparison of key development sectors and supporting service systems of Guangdong, Jiangsu and Hubei are shown in Table 3.

The east region represented by Jiangsu and Guangdong is quick in responding to "Made in China 2025", proposing a new development mentality for local development. Benefiting from their favorable development basis of the manufacturing industry, their supporting service systems put forward are highly elaborate and feasible. The action scheme of Jiangsu resolves around major problems facing its manu-

Table 3. Key development sectors and supporting service systems of Guangdong, Jiangsu and Hubei

Provinces		Guangdong	Jiangsu	Hubei
Key development sectors	Similarities	Biological medicine and high-end medical equipment; new materials (high-performance compound materials); ocean engineering equipment and high-tech ships, aerospace equipment, railway equipment, energy-saving equipment and resource recycling, new energy vehicles, intelligent equipment (industrial robots and high-end numerically controlled machine tools); new information and technology (integrated circuit and specialized devices, cloud computing, big data and Internet of Things, network communication devices, operation systems and industries, software new energies); intelligent manufacturing (Internet Plus manufacturing, integration between industrialization and informatization, robots, industrial cloud platforms, industrial big data application, and industrial e-commerce).		
	Differences	New information and technology (new-type panel display); satellite application; intelligent manufacturing devices (sensors, automatic control systems, machine tools, and other major equipment, R&D and industrialization of intelligent devices, including intelligent production line, intelligent plant, servo and implementation components); new materials (materials with special functions, rare earth and nanometer materials); biological medicine and high-end medical equipment (southern medicine plants); new energies	Intelligent equipment (additive material manufacturing, such as 3D printing, and new-type intelligent textile machinery); engineering and agricultural machinery; new-type power equipment (large-sale efficient power generation devices and heavy-type gas turbines); new materials (new-type antiseptic coatings, green new materials using renewable resources, high-temperature superconducting materials, new-type electronic materials, high-performance, strong and light-weighted metal alloy materials, nanometer materials, etc.); new energies.	Beidou Navigation Satellite System: New information and technology (intelligent terminal and new panel display); intelligent manufacturing equipment (laser); biological medicine and high-end medical instruments (chemical pharmacy and Chinese patent medicines); new materials (high-performance metal materials, high-end chemical and industrial new materials, electronic information functional materials, new-type inorganic nonmetal materials, and leading new materials); specialized cars; energy-saving and environmentally-friendly devices (resource recycling).
Supporting service systems	Similarities	Promoting the institutional and system reform; changing the government functions (simplifying administration and delegating powers to lower levels); accelerating financial and tax support (for the first set of technical equipment); improving the financial support policies (introducing social capitals, financing leasing, property mortgage or pledge); fostering medium-and large-scale enterprises, development small-and micro-scale enterprises, and promoting coordinated development of enterprises of all sizes; creating a market environment featuring fair play; talent construction and intelligence support (entrepreneur development project and industry-research-university combination); playing a leading role; and promoting network security and information guarantee.		
	Differences	① Encouraging enterprises under administration of the central government and Guangdong provincial SOEs to set up "entrepreneurship and innovation" innovation funds, equity investment funds, and industrial investment funds; ② Providing land, housing and ocean use preferential policies; ③ Giving full play to the role of industrial associations; ④Promoting technology innovation cooperation of Guangdong with Hong Kong and Macau.	① Encouraging the government to purchase cloud computing and other specialized third-party services; Launching industrial integration cooperation demonstration sites; ③ Encouraging the financial institutions to make use of the "entrepreneurship and innovation" platform to provide one-stop systematic financial services, equity investment funds, and industrial investment funds; ④ Implementing the policy of maintaining the land use type and property type within five years of the transition period; ⑤ Giving full play to the role of industrial associations.	① Expanding all-around technology cooperation with the US, Germany, France, Britain and other developed countries; ② Strengthening exchange and communication of Wuhan city circle with the circum-Fanyang Lake city circle and the circum-Changsha-Zhuzhou-Xiangtan city circle; deepen cooperation and interaction of Wuhan with Changsha, Nanchang, and other central cities; ③ Assessing technology innovation, and launching "technology finance innovation project", "technology poverty relief project" and "carbon finance"; ④ Launching industrial integration demonstration sites, BOT model, industrial park investment and financing demonstration sites, financing and investment companies in industrial parks, loan and lease asset securitization demonstrates sites; attracting insurance funds into major development projects, and starting Internet equity fund-raising.

Sources: Summarized by authors based on the national and provincial government reports.

facturing industry and aims at strengthening its performance in the medium-and high-end manufacturing sector. Based on in-depth integration between new information and technology, and the advanced manufacturing industry, Jiangsu attempts to make a breakthrough in the field of intelligent manufacturing. Key industrial sectors and core technologies are its major focuses. In the future, it will march into the world market more vigorously. As a provincial manufacturing giant in China and a major global manufacturing base, Guangdong has deeply realized its shortages after years of development. A series of supporting policies introduced by it fully show its determination to transform from "manufacturing" to "intelligent manufacturing". Hubei Province is a critical province of the central region. In one year and a half after the provincial government issued 'Made in China 2025 Action Scheme of Hubei", concerted efforts have been made among more than 20 departments to form a "1+16" planning policy framework covering nine major tasks and ten key sectors. However, concerning the content of various policies, some measures are too complex; policies issued by different departments are sometimes inconsistent. Seen from their implementation effects, these policies still need to improve their feasibility. In fact, these problems are not facing Hubei Province, but are shared problems of areas with an underdeveloped manufacturing industry in the central region and west region of China.

All in all, provinces, cities and municipalities in different regions of China are still dominated by an enclosed, independent and "small but complete" development mentality. The homogenization of the regional industrial structure is becoming increasingly prominent, making structural complementation even an impossibility. Meanwhile, due to lack of regional balance and overall planning, some unnecessary repeated constructions have been found between different sectors and regions. This impairs the cost effectiveness and might easily trigger unjust competition.

2.3.2 Comparative Analysis of Implementation Policies in Dongguan, Wuxi and Wuhan

Comparison results of key development sectors and supporting service systems of Dongguan, Wuxi and Wuhan are shown in Table 4.

Dongguan has long been the manufacturing base of Guangdong Province. Its strategic significance to development of Guangdong's manufacturing industry is self-evident. This city includes "Made in Dongguan 2025" into the national strategy of "Made in China 2025", and clarifies the objective of "developing a model city of Made in China". Meanwhile, the strategic objective system of "Made in Dongguan 2025" is implemented through "six major projects". The series of measures adopted by Dongguan is in line with its industrial characteristics and almost covers every aspect of the manufacturing industrial development in Dongguan.

Comparatively, the action scheme of Wuxi to implement "Made in China 2025" is less systematic. Though many key development sectors and objectives are proposed, documents supporting overall development of the manufacturing industry and development of specific sectors are lacking. This is related to position of Wuxi in Jiangsu's manufacturing industry development plan. In Jiangsu, Suzhou is the manufacturing superpower. Thus, Wuxi becomes less important to Jiangsu in realizing its provincial manufacturing industry development. The policies issued are not closely integrated with industrial characteristics of Dongguan, and are highly homogenous to those for other parts of Jiangsu Province.

As a major industrial town of the central region, Wuhan, the provincial capital of Hubei, is contributing around one third to the industrial output of Hubei. In order to realize development of future industries, Wuhan has built a manufacturing innovation system. By 2020, the optoelectronics information indus-

Table 4. Comparison of key development sectors and supporting service systems of Dongguan, Wuxi and Wuhan

		Dongguan	Wuxi	Wuhan
Key development sectors	Similarities	Intelligent manufacturing equipment (numerically-controlled machine tool, industrial robots and 3D printing); new information and technology (integrated circuit, cloud computing, big data and Internet of Things, software and new display); new materials (metallic materials, compound materials, and special function materials); new energy vehicles; biological medicine sector (biological medicine and high-performance medical instruments).		
	Differences	Textile, clothing, shoes and hats; foods and drinks; toys, stationery and sporting goods (specialized electronic devices and intelligent production lines, modules and intelligent plastic molding equipment, and intelligent power distribution equipment); new information and technology (intelligent mobile phones, intelligent wearable devices, Internet of vehicles, intelligent home furnishing, fifth-generation mobile communications, new electronic devices, basic materials, Internet of Vehicles, etc.)	High-end equipment manufacturing; intelligent manufacturing devices (R&D and industrialization of intelligent sensing, intelligent test and installation, intelligent warehousing and logistics); power equipment; energy-saving and environmentally-friendly industry; new energies (photovoltaic and wind power); high-end textile and garment sector; production-oriented service sector; high-end ships and maritime work equipment.	New information and technology (intelligent terminal and optical communications); intelligent equipment manufacturing (laser); future industry (all optical network, quantum communication network, virtual reality technology, gene diagnosis and target treatment, stem cell, tissue and organ regeneration, artificial intelligence, human-computer manufacturing and equipment, key technology of driverless vehicles); applications of BeiDou Navigation Satellite System; high-tech ships and ocean engineering equipment; railway equipment.
Key supporting service systems	Similarities	Deepening the institutional reform, and optimizing industrial policies; strengthening financial policy support, and promoting integration between the financial industry and the manufacturing industry; enhancing the financial and tax policy support; increasing the degree of opening and international cooperation; optimizing the internal and external opening layout; improving the organizational leadership mechanism; doing a good job in talent introduction and development, and shoring up the talent team construction; improving the market monitoring system; reinforcing the land use guarantee; and improving the performance assessment mechanism.		
	Differences	Promoting the industrial spirit and manufacturing civilization; enhancing the fundamental guarantee for plan implementation (in terms of traffic, water electricity, communications, etc.); giving full play to the role of commercial associations; and promoting development of the Internet finance.	Giving full play to the role of industrial organizations; strengthening overall planning and top-level design; building a major problem negotiation mechanism; and reinforcing the organic connection between special plans.	Optimizing the industrial development environment (improving the connection mechanism between the upstream and downstream industries, and constructing the corporate credit system); adjusting and optimizing the spatial layout (increasing the scale and efficiency of four major sectors).

Sources: Summarized by authors based on the national and provincial government reports.

trial, new energy vehicle and intelligent vehicle national manufacturing and innovation centers will be set up. meanwhile, innovation intensity of Hubei's competitive industries, including biological health, intelligent manufacturing and high-end equipment, will be strengthened. Wuhan also clearly states its goal to build two to four national manufacturing and innovation centers by the year 2025.

On the whole, the supporting documents issued by various cities in the typical regions of China have a close bearing on the position of these cities in the manufacturing industry development of their respective province (China Academy of Information and Communications Technology, 2016). For example, major cities, including Dongguan and Wuhan, have their action scheme serve implementation of "Made in China 2025" in their respective province. Meanwhile, they integrate sectors with their own development characteristics in their action scheme. On the contrary, in terms of cities such as Wuxi which is less important to the province it is located in, the development planning is relatively generous, which cannot fully show their development characteristics.

2.3.3 "Made in China 2025" Regional Development Planning

Now, the Chinese government is organizing revision of "Guide to Provinces and Cities in Implementing 'Made in China 2025'" (hereinafter abbreviated as the "Guide"), and the revised version will hopefully be realized before the end of 2017. The Guide aims at combining key tasks of "Made in China 2025" with resource endowments and current industrial development in various places, avoiding repeated constructions, highlighting specialties of every region, giving full play to competitive industries in different places, and promoting transformation and upgrade of China's manufacturing industry and reasonable layout of the industrial structure. All these efforts will form a "new map" of "Made in China".

According to the Guide, provinces in the central region, such as Anhui, Henan and Shanxi, are required to explore development possibilities of their new energy, new materials, biological medicine, information and technology sectors, apart from further tapping development potential of their original competitive industries, including energy mining equipment, coal and chemical equipment, agricultural machinery and basic processing equipment. Besides, the Guide requires central provinces to further optimize the industrial structure of the manufacturing industry, increase the percentage of the technological industry in the whole manufacturing industry, and gradually eliminate the high-energy-consumption and high-pollution industries.

In terms of the west region and partial old industrial areas, the Guide is urging the focus to be put on cultivation of emerging competitive industries, while gradually weeding out backward production capacity. For example, Shaanxi, Sichuan and Chongqing are positioned to further develop their competitive industries, including information and technology, and aerospace. On the other hand, they are expected to seek development in emerging industries, including cloud computing, big data and Internet of Things.

The Guide also gives policy support to industrial upgrade of some old industrial bases in the northeast region and the northwest region. Places with the old industrial bases are required to seek their comparative advantages and support transformation and upgrade of the key sectors with comparative advantages. Meanwhile, the list of competitive industries for foreign investments is issued to attract more foreign investments, and guide the coastal industries to gradually shift to the inland. The northeast region and the southwest region are supported to take the lead to introduce key projects with favorable basic development conditions and which can hopefully make breakthroughs of "Made in China 2025". Meanwhile, a batch of competitive industrial bases with outstanding economies of scale and competitive industries highly competitive in various segments and with their own development characteristics will be developed.

Revision and implementation of the Guide is to guarantee continuous implementation of "Made in China 2025", and promote steady progress of industrial upgrade in different places. Meanwhile, the ten key development sectors raised by "Made in China" will get the priority of development. Additionally, emerging industries, such as robots, additive material manufacturing, industrial Internet and intelligent manufacturing, in recent years will be further cultivated.

After issuance of the Guide, various provinces, districts and municipalities can better implement "Made in China 2025" in the local level by giving full play to their comparative advantages and adopting the differentiated industrial development strategy; formulate more reasonable industrial transfer policies and promote coordinated development of the regional manufacturing industry; and fully improve the comprehensive development capability of China's manufacturing industry through overall planning.

CONCLUSION

Over the past several decades, China's manufacturing industry has experienced three stages of development, namely revival, emergence of private and foreign-invested manufacturing enterprises, and marching of products made in China to the international market. Now, China's manufacturing industry is facing with both development opportunities and challenges. On one hand, it has the most complete industrial system and the largest consumption market. The potential knowledge spillover of different sectors within the scope of national border will bring the manufacturing industries and other supporting sectors a valuable opportunity to enhance its competence. Due to its huge domestic market, the discrepancy between the rural regions and the east coast provinces can provide possibilities to the domestic leading sectors to restructure the manufacturing processes and distribution systems. These two factors will benefit both the regional government in the short run and the central government in the long term. On the other hand, its per capita growth rate is low; its innovation capability is lacking; and its environmental pollution is worsening. One of the common challenges Chinese manufacturing companies encountering is how to develop or build competitive advantages through innovation capabilities. In the development of Chinese manufacturing industry, a small group of leading domestic firms accumulated knowledge and built capabilities when expanding internationally. It is widely considered that the majority manufacturing companies do not have the similar competence. Therefore, China's manufacturing industry is calling for a new development strategy. "Made in China 2025" is a national strategy proposed for China's manufacturing industry. It attempts to develop China from a global manufacturing giant into a global manufacturing superpower.

China has a vast territory. In different regions, the economic development level is different, so it is with the development level of the manufacturing industry. Therefore, how to fully realize the strategic goals laid down by "Made in China 2025" should be considered carefully. This chapter attempts to provide references for transformation strategies, paths and policy support for different regions in implementing "Made in China 2025". For continental countries and other emerging countries such as India and Brazil, the experience of development and implementation of "Made in China 2025" strategy also offers a template model to refer. Particularly, the policy and policy modification of Chinese authority at national and regional level provides the other countries valuable lessons. However, due to the difference of economic characteristics of the manufacturing sectors from China to other nations, replication becomes difficult. This brings another possibility to these countries to cooperate in responding to the demands of advanced manufacturing. We would like to highlight the main findings of this article:

1. According to the national statistical yearbook, the industry in different regions of China is classified into different levels. Based on the indexes of the national statistical yearbook, a measurement model is built to measure the manufacturing industry of different regions in terms of informatization and intelligentization. Then, the manufacturing industry of different regions is classified into different levels according to the concept of informatization and intelligentization. In other words, the starting point of the regional manufacturing industry is clarified. Next, the author visits dozens of enterprises and plants to learn their demands, expectations and future action schemes.
2. The transformation and upgrade goals in different economic belts of China are examined through in-depth interview and observation in July to August, 2017. First, Guangdong Province, Jiangsu Province, Hubei Province and the surrounding regions are chosen for study. Then we chose representative industries and manufacturing companies to conduct interviews.
3. Based on industrial theories and interview materials, transformation and upgrade strategies and paths for different key sectors are outlined. Based on existing statistical data and in-depth interview, the foundation of key sectors, as well as their demands and expectations of transformation and upgrade, and characteristics of their manufacturing industry is investigated. According to the industry theories, different transformation and upgrade strategies and paths are put forward for different key sectors.
4. According to strategies and paths of different sectors, the role of the government played in the transformation and upgrade of China's and regional manufacturing industry is summarized. Furthermore, whether policies of the central government and the local government can effectively support upgrade of the manufacturing industry is examined. Hence, our description and analysis of "Made in China 2025" puts forward policy implications for the other countries.

ACKNOWLEDGMENT

This work is supported by The Major Project of National Social Science Foundation of China (16ZDA013) and The Project of National Natural Science Foundation of China (71772142).

REFERENCES

Binz, C., Gosens, J., Hansen, T., & Hansen, U. E. (2017). Toward Technology-Sensitive Catching-Up Policies: Insights from Renewable Energy in China. *World Development*, *96*, 418–437. doi:10.1016/j.worlddev.2017.03.027

China Academy of Information and Communications Technology. (2016). *China Industry Development Report 2016*. Beijing: Posts & Telecom Press.

China State Statistics Bureau. (2017). *China's Statistical Yearbook (2007–2016)*. Beijing: China Statistical Press. (in Chinese)

Hao, H., Qiao, Q., Liu, Z., & Zhao, F. (2017). Impact of recycling on energy consumption and greenhouse gas emissions from electric vehicle production: The China 2025 case. *Resources, Conservation and Recycling*, *122*, 114–125. doi:10.1016/j.resconrec.2017.02.005

Hou, L. (2016). Construction of Yangtze River Economic Belt and Optimization of Industrial Structure. [in Chinese]. *Journal of Nanjing University of Finance and Economics*, *1*, 39–40.

Hu, A., & Sun, J. (2014). Migration of Manufacturing Industries in China: Whether, How, and Where. [in Chinese]. *China Economic Quarterly*, *13*(4), 1533–1554.

Li, L. (2016). *China's Manufacturing Industry Development Report 2015*. Beijing: Peking University Press.

Li, L. (2017). (in press). China's manufacturing locus in 2025: With a comparison of "Made-in-China 2025" and "Industry 4.0". *Technological Forecasting and Social Change*.

Li, L., Yang, H., & Liu, J. (2014). Evaluation Study on Comprehensive Developing Ability of Regional Manufacturing Industry in China: Based on the Empirical Analysis of Manufacturing Industry in East,Middle and West China [in Chinese]. *China Soft Science*, *2*, 121–129. doi:10.3724/SP.J.1001.2013.04346

Liu, S. X. (2016). Innovation design: Made in China 2025. *Design Management Review*, *27*(1), 52–58.

Siu, K. W. M., & Contreras, G. J. (Eds.). (2016). *Design Education for Fostering Creativity and Innovation in China*. IGI Global.

Tourk, K., & Marsh, P. (2016). The new industrial revolution and industrial upgrading in China: Achievements and challenges. *Economic and Political Studies*, *4*(2), 187–209. doi:10.1080/20954816.2016.1180769

Wübbeke, J., Meissner, M., Zenglein, M. J., Ives, J., & Conrad, B. (2016). Made in China 2025: The making of a high-tech superpower and consequences for industrial countries. *Mercator Institute for China Studies, 17*.

Xia, J. (2017). A Review to the Development of Foreign Capital Manufacturing Industry in China: Looking forward to Made in China, 2025. *American Journal of Industrial and Business Management*, *07*(05), 604–613. doi:10.4236/ajibm.2017.75045

Yang, H., Li, L., & Liu, J. (2015). Impact of Home Market Scale on Technological Innovation and Its Regional Differences [in Chinese]. *Forum on Science and Technology in China*, *1*, 27–32.

Zhang, X., Peek, W. A., Pikas, B., & Lee, T. (2016). The Transformation and Upgrading of the Chinese Manufacturing Industry: Based on" German Industry 4.0. *The Journal of Applied Business and Economics*, *18*(5), 97.

KEY TERMS AND DEFINITIONS

Beijing-Tianjin-Hebei Region: The national capital region of China, which includes an economic region surrounding Beijing, Tianjin, and Hebei, along the coast of the Bohai Sea.

Green Manufacturing: The renewal of production processes and the establishment of environmentally friendly operations in the manufacturing field.

Intelligent Manufacturing: The use of production process technology that can automatically adapt to changing environments and varying production process requirements, with the capability of manufacturing various products with minimal supervision or assistance from operators.

Made in China 2025: An initiative, drafted by the Ministry of Industry and Information Technology over two and a half years, to comprehensively upgrade Chinese industry.

Pearl River Delta Metropolitan Region: A low-lying area surrounding the Pearl River estuary that mainly covers nine cities of Guangdong Province, including Guangzhou, Shenzhen, Zhuhai, Dongguan, Foshan, Zhongshan, Huizhou, Jiangmen, and Zhaoqing.

Planned Economy System: An economic system in which the government controls and regulates the economy system, including production, distribution, prices, etc.

Yangtze River Delta Region: A triangle-shaped metropolitan region where the Yangtze River drains into the East China Sea that comprises Shanghai, southern Jiangsu province, and northern Zhejiang province of China.

Chapter 2
Transformation and Upgrade of the Optical Fiber Industry in China:
Taking YOFC as an Example

Ma Huimin
Huazhong University of Science and Technology, China

Xin Dai
Huazhong University of Science and Technology, China

Changqin Yin
Huazhong University of Science and Technology, China

Ke Wang
Huazhong University of Science and Technology, China

Han Huang
Huazhong University of Science and Technology, China

Lu Xu
Rennes School of Business, France

Jie Xiong
Rennes School of Business, France

Jinlong Zhang
Huazhong University of Science and Technology, China

Yeming Gong
EMLYON Business School, France

ABSTRACT

This chapter describes the development stage of China's optical fiber manufacturing industry, and then analyses the Yangtze Optical Fibre and Cable Joint Stock Limited Company (YOFC) development stage. According to YOFC case, the authors show that continuous learning and absorption, proprietary R&D and product innovation, good use of every opportunity and favorable development policy, talent reserve and intelligence support, active transformation by sizing up the situation, independent operation, and elimination of monopolization are the implications of transformation and upgrade of the optical fiber industry.

DOI: 10.4018/978-1-5225-3468-6.ch002

INTRODUCTION

This chapter describes the historical development and evolution of China's optical fiber manufacturing industry. By a case study of Yangtze Optical Fibre and Cable Joint Stock Limited Company (YOFC), we analyze the development stages and periods of the industry leader. The development of YOFC provides a rich empirical evidence of the evolution of the fiber manufacturing industry in China. After introducing the case study of YOFC, we summarize the key successful factors: continuous learning and absorption, proprietary R&D and product innovation, seizing opportunities and favorable development policy, talent development and intelligence support, active transformation by sizing up the situation, independent operation and elimination of monopolization are the implications of transformation and upgrading of the optical fiber industry. This study may benefit the executives of high-technology companies and decision makers of other firms with ambition to reach the success of YOFC. This article also provides insights to public policy makers on how and when government can or should intervene the market development. The lessons and experiences of YOFC, in particular the transformation, offers insights to the state-own enterprises who are seeking the path of strategic renewals in China.

1. The Optical Fiber Industry in China

1.1 Made in China 2025 Policy and the Optical Fiber Industry

In order to upgrade the manufacturing industry, China's State Council have launched the "Made in China 2025" plan in March 2015. According to "Made in China" plan, integration of new-generation IT with the manufacturing industry is at the core. The Ministry of Industry and Information Technology of the China has been long committed to promoting *integration of informatization and industrialization*. Wide applications of information technology can bring a major change to the traditional manufacturing industry (Gong, 2013). "Made in China" is gradually changing from resource-driven to information-driven. Intelligent equipment in plants and workshops with powerful functions is connected with Internet or equipment wirelessly. This leads to emergence of the Internet of Things and service-oriented Internet, and promotes the integration of the physical world and the information world in the form of CPS. The interconnection within the whole plant makes cooperative work possible. The production mode has also been transformed from resource-driven to information-driven. The information-driven product manufacturing process reflects the value of intelligent manufacturing. For example, with intelligent manufacturing, production procedures can be designed more scientifically; productivity can be improved; the personalized production can be realized; the resource use can be adjusted with the most energy-efficient mode adopted. However, all the above-mentioned are based on the development of communication technology. Based on the development process of YOFC, this article analyzes the elements of fiber optic industry transformation and upgrading, and provides reference for the transformation and upgrading of other optical fiber enterprises.

1.2 Historical Development of China's Optical Fiber Industry

In recent years, we have been experienced the continuous development and increasingly wide applications of the optical fiber technology (Diao, 2017). Since emergence of the first optical fiber with practical value in the 1970s, the optical fiber technology has kept on progressing. With diversification of optical fiber and cable products, the manufacturing cost is declining, but the performance indexes are improving. So far, three key technologies, namely the optical fiber preforming bar technology, the optical fiber drawing process technology and the optical fiber manufacturing technology. It is apt to say that the composition of China's optical fiber and cable industry, after more than three decades of development, is corresponding to the key technologies, because the manufacturing process has included most manufacturing process of the cable industry, including preforming, wiredrawing, primacy coating, strength screening, coating, combining, secondary coating (including jelly filling), cabling, jacket and armor installing. Therefore, the optical fiber and cable industry, either at home and abroad, has been gradually formed an industrial constitution with the optical fiber preforming bars, optical fibers and cables at its core (Chen, 1995). Further extended, it also includes the optical fiber and cable materials. The above four parts together constitute a complete industrial chain system of China's optical fiber industry.

1.2.1 Before the Mid-1980s: Experimental and Pilot Stage

In March 1976, in a simple lab of FiberHome Technologies Group under administration of the former Ministry of Posts and Telecommunications, the first silica fiber in China—a 17m glass filament, was produced by Zhao Xinsen and his team. The test instrument showed that the optical fiber short wavelength was around 0.85mm. Calculated by the attenuation unit of the light, the attenuation was around 300 db per kilometer, which reached the international standard at that time. In 1979, Zhao Xinsen led his team to draw the first optical fiber with an attenuation of only 4db every kilometer. This was the first optical fiber with practical value in China. In 1982, Zhao Xinsen and his colleagues developed, designed, installed and launched an 8M/s cable municipal call communications project. The first practical optical fiber communications line of China spanned the whole Wuhan.

In the 1980s, when China just adopted the policy of opening-up and reform, infrastructure construction in all fields just started, and the development problems with the communication industry were particularly outstanding. Due to a weak industrial basis of China, China was still in the optical fiber R&D stage, which made it hard to realize large-scale production, let alone meet requirements of large-scale main line construction. Therefore, it was necessary to introduce foreign technologies for development of the domestic optical communication.

1.2.2 The Mid-1980s-2000: Rapid Development of China's Optical Fiber Industry Through International Joint Venture

From the early 1984, in order to change the backward development of China's communications industry, the Chinese government considered introducing foreign technologies to develop its communication industry with the offer of *exchange the market for the technology*. After several rounds of negotiation, Corning from the US, Nippon Telegraph and Telephone Public Corporation (NTTPC) from Japan, and some optical fiber manufacturers in Europe responded to China's offer, *OK, you can buy our products, but there is no way for us to develop industry with you*. At that time, only Philips from Netherlands was willing to transfer part of its technology to China.

In May 1988, the former Ministry of Posts and Telecommunications, Wuhan and Philips Netherlands jointly founded Yangtze Optical Fiber and Cable Joint Stock Limited Company (hereinafter abbreviated as YOFC). Since the 1990s, through joint venture, introduction of technologies and opening of the domestic market, China gradually set up several other optical fiber manufacturing enterprises, including

Lucent, Huaxin Tengcang, Zhongzhu, Futong Zhaohe and Xigu. They all adopted advanced technologies from world-renowned optical fiber manufacturers. Gradually, they formed China's optical fiber industry.

Popularization of the international Internet dominated the whole 1990s. Data service made great strikes. In particular, the IP service achieved explosive growth. All this contributed to rapid development of the optical fiber industry. Wide applications of other technologies, including the Fiber to the Home (FTTH) technology and the Dense Wavelength Division Multiplexing (DwDM), were also partially attributable to further development of the optical fiber industry. Along with development of the optical fiber technology, there was a greater demand for optical fiber products for communication use. By the end of 1999, the worldwide optical fiber length had reached 300 million kilometers. This meant the capacity of the backbone transmission network was redoubled every nine months. From the second half of 1999, the global fiber optical market was short of supply because of flourishing of network construction. The optical fiber and cable price of different places experienced different degrees of growth. The optical fiber preforming bars fell short of demand, and the optical fiber supply was inadequate both at home and abroad.

Meanwhile, development of China's domestic optical fiber and cable industry, driven by domestic demands, achieved rapid development. On the one hand, with entry of China into the WTO and gradual opening of China's telecommunication market, the telecommunication operators started a wave of cable construction, either in terms of business demands or in terms of capital input. Skyrocketing development of China's telecommunications, radio and television, electrical system and railway system communication and automation put forward an increasing demand of optical fibers and cables. On the other hand, cable technology was at that time easier than optical fiber technology. There were no foreign large-scale enterprises monopolizing and squeezing market share of the field in China. Therefore, domestic enterprises expanded their investment and production to their heart's content. Finally, the supply exceeded the demand in China's cable and optical fiber industry. For example, in 2001, the domestic demand of cable and optical fiber was around 12.5 million core kilometers, but the output of domestic manufacturers in that year reached 10 million core kilometers.

1.2.3 2001-2006: Government Intervention for Revival and Going-Global of China's Domestic Optical Fiber Communication Industry

After 2001, China's optical fiber and cable market bid farewell to the past rapid-development period, and started declining. The investment scale of operators suffered a dramatic shrinkage, and the competition became unprecedentedly intensified. Even cut-throat competition occurred. A major cause of the situation was supply excessively exceeding demand. On the one hand, along with production expansion of old enterprises, joining of new enterprises and location of foreign communication manufacturers in China, China's optical fiber and cable production capacity scaled a new high. On the other hand, China's telecommunication structure was adjusted, the world telecommunication industry suffered plummeting of its overall interests, and the broadband network bubble was busted. All these factors influenced the robust development momentum of China's optical fiber and cable industry. The market demand was shrinking, further sharpening the contradiction between supply and demand. The price kept falling in the domestic optical fiber and cable industry. Worse still, foreign manufacturers contended with domestic manufacturers for the profit margin in China. The cable products in domestic manufacturers mainly concentrate in areas with a low technological content, thus resulting in excessive competition in the field. In 2002, the price of the standard single mode fiber dropped by more than 50%, from 70 USD per kilometer to 30 USD per kilometer. This deprived domestic cable manufacturers of the previous price advantage.

A turnaround appeared in 2003, when YOFC and Jiangsu Fa Er Sheng Photon Co., Ltd. submitted an anti-dumping investigation application to the Ministry of Commerce on behalf of the domestic zero-dispersion displacement single mode fiber industry. On July 1, 2003, the Ministry of Commerce decided to investigate into the anti-dumping case of the zero-dispersion displacement single mode fibers imported from the US, Japan and South Korea. Later, the Ministry of Commerce also launched a questionnaire survey among stakeholders, which proved that the causality between dumping and substantive damage. On January 1, 2005, the Ministry of Commerce made an affirmative arbitration of the fiber dumping case. This alleviated the tension of dumping in the field. The fiber which with a high dumping tax rate levied on it almost stopped importing, but previously the imported products seized nearly 30% to 50% of market share.

After a severe "winter" of the optical communication had gone in China, the "spring" was back from the late 2004. China's optical fiber and cable industry gradually rose from the bottom, and embarked on the right track. In 2005, the cable sold out in China totaled at 17.5 million core kilometers, accounting for nearly 30% of the global total and ranking No. 1 in the world. This turned China into one of the major optical fiber and cable manufacturing bases in the world.

Since then, China has started exporting optical fibers and cables to the international market, and the export increases on an annual basis. For example, in 2005, China exported around 2.5 million core kilometers. In 2006, the figure increased to 3.6 million kilometers, of which more than 8 million core kilometers were exported by YOFC with a sales volume of 71.4 million USD. Fiber products of YOFC accounted for more than 10% in the foreign market, and YOFC gradually rose to be the second largest fiber manufacturer and the fifth largest cable manufacturer in the world. In 2004, FiberHome Telecommunication Technologies Co., Ltd. exported around 4,800 kilometers of fibers and 350 kilometers of cables. In 2005, they increased to 8,000 kilometers and 1,025 kilometers, respectively. In 2006, the sales of fibers dropped slightly to 6,500 kilometers, while the sales of cables skyrocketed to 7,000 kilometers. In the first half of 2007 alone, the sales of cables had reached 5,500 kilometers. From 2004 to 2007, the accumulative export sales volume reached more than 14 million USD. In 2005, Heng Tong Optic-Electric started selling its products on the international market. In the first half of 2005, 7.46 million yuan was sold out. In 2006, more than 200,000 core kilometers were exported, accounting for more than 10% of the company's total sales. In recent years, many other Chinese enterprises, such as Zhongtian, have also marched into the overseas market. In China, products of the top 10 cable manufacturers all had their independent property rights, and their product quality all reached the international advanced level. Their export growth in recent years has been maintained above 60%.

1.2.4 2007-2015: Government-Driven Demands Fueling Development of China's Domestic Optic-Electronic Industry

In 2007, the government increased issuance of 3G business license. Launch of Beijing Olympic 2008, Western Development, *Village to Village Telecommunication Project* and gradually revival of the FTTH market as well as substantive promotion of the integration of three networks—all these not only symbolized all-around applications of fibers to the traditional telecommunication lines, but also broadened the room for development of the optical fiber and cable market (Gao, 2014). Additionally, driven by the industrial informatization construction, corporate and private users kept on increasing. With promotion of *optical fiber to every household*, use of optical fiber changed from the main line to the access network and the terminal access. Either the broadcasting and television network or the telecommunication network was faced with the urgency to satisfy *optical access for replacing copper access* and *optical cable demands*. In 2016, the "Broadband China" strategy was implemented. Benefiting from scale development of 4G and favorable expectations of 5G, China's optical fiber and cable market demands grew continuously. The production capacity of Chinese enterprises accounted for more than 50% of the global total.

1.2.5 After 2015: Going Global of the Optical Communication Industry in Response to Advocacy of the Chinese Government

Currently, China is the global largest optical fiber market, and also the global largest optical fiber manufacturer. However, this does not mean that China has been a superpower in the field of optical fiber and cable. First, there are too many low-end products in China's optical fiber industry, and the production capacity of these low-end products is beyond demand. Several years ago, many Chinese optical fiber and cable enterprises blindly expanded the market by availing themselves of the robust development momentum in recent years. This not only destroyed the existing balance between supply and demand, but also resulted in a serious surplus of the production capacity. For example, the practical market demand of the cable was 80 million core kilometers, but the supply amount exceeded 120 million core kilometers. The demand and the supply were seriously out of balance. Second, innovation capability of high-end products is lacking among Chinese optical fiber and cable manufacturing enterprises. For a long time, Chinese optical fiber and cable manufacturing enterprises have concentrated on the medium- and low-end market. This directly results in a widespread lack of high-end product innovation and R&D capability. Without the essential capability, Chinese optical fiber and cable manufacturers, especially those small-and medium-sized ones, have been in a stalemate in terms of high-end product R&D level. Their retardation has dragged the overall development of the whole industry.

Along with implementation of the "Belt & Road" initiative, many optical communication enterprises have quickened their pace of "going global". Domestic optical communication giants, such as YOFC, Heng Tong Optic-Electric, Zhongtian, FiberHome, have laid out their business in countries along the "Belt & Road" (Gao, 2016). Not only do they set up optical fiber and cable manufacturing plants locally, but also they have their overseas headquartered based in these countries to further expand their overseas business. So far, China has been a manufacturing and marketing center of the global optical fiber and cable market. In the future, China will strive to become an R&D center, business consulting center and service center in the field as well.

However, during the international market expansion process, Chinese optical fiber and cable enterprises still have a lot to be desired. First, in terms of brand marketing, China should learn from international first-class enterprises to change their image of poor quality and low cost. Second, more attention should be paid to improving product quality, and creating an international quality management system. Continuous improvement of quality standards can help change overseas users' stereotyped impression of products made in China, and earn more recognition from the overseas users. Finally, Chinese and Western cultures are different. Chinese optical fiber and cable enterprises, while expanding the international market, should try to familiarize themselves with the local market culture, learn more about it, and get fully adapted to it.

2. Development Process of YOFC

2.1 Introduction of YOFC

Yangtze Optical Fiber and Cable Joint Stock Limited Company (YOFC) is a high-tech joint venture jointly founded by the former Ministry of Posts and Telecommunications, Wuhan Municipal People's Government and Philips Netherlands in May 1988. Now, Draka Comteq B.V, a Netherlandish company, also joins operation and management of YOFC. Since official launch of production in 1992, YOFC has accumulatively manufactured and sold out nearly 300 million core kilometers of optical fibers and cables with a sales volume of 5 million yuan. For 24 years in a low, the manufacturing and sales volume of the company's optical fiber and cable products ranked No. 1 in China, and even rose to the top 3 in the global fiber and cable industry. Now, YOFC has been the optical fiber and cable product and manufacturing equipment R&D and manufacturing enterprise with the most complete range of product specifications, the state-of-the-art production techniques and the largest production scale in China. The development process of the company is a reflection of the transformation and upgrade process of China's optical fiber industry.

2.2 Historical development of YOFC

2.2.1 1988-1995: Import of the Full Set of Equipment and Technology From Philips Netherlands to Form the Production Scale

In response to China's macroeconomic policy of "exchanging market for technology", the former Ministry of Posts and Telecommunications, Wuhan Municipal People's Government and Philips Netherlands jointly set up Yangtze Optical Fiber and Cable Joint Stock Limited Company (YOFC). The total investment of the company was around 1.6075 trillion NLG (or around 800 million yuan), and its registered capital was around 53.66 million NLG (around 250 million yuan). The Chinese side had 62.5% stake in the company, with the rest of 37.5% possessed by the foreign side. Thus, the Chinese side was the dominant shareholder, and the Netherlandish government provided a soft loan of 43.5 million NGL for the project. The company covered an area of 70,000 square meters, of which more than 40,000 square meters was the construction area.

In the initial development period, the two sides had signed a ten-year "Fiber Technology Transfer Contract", which clearly stipulates provision of a ten-year continuous fiber technology transfer by Philips for YOFC. Hence, from the very start, the joint venture had been manufacturing the fiber preforming bars using the internationally leading ion module technology and process, including PCE.

Based on the technology transfer, the joint venture started its production in 1992, outputting 50,000 kilometers of cable and 450 kilometers of optical fibers every year. In 1994, the company developed the G.653 single mode fiber, and the multi-mode fiber output rose to No.2 in the world. The great achievement of YOFC successfully eliminated monopolization of foreign manufacturers in the field.

In terms of the market, the joint venture in possession of the latest technology in the world had increased output of many products to No. 1 in China. Gradually, its products also started playing a role in the US market.

2.2.2 1996-2001: Skyrocketing of Production Capacity and Start of Manufacturing Informatization

In this period, growth of the international market demand and flourishing of China's communication infrastructure construction encouraged domestic manufacturers to expand their production capacity. YOFC was in the frontline.

In terms of production capacity, YOFC finished six phases of production expansion of optical fibers and cables, increasingly their respective annual production capacity to 10 million core kilometers and 5 million core kilometers respectively. The impressive performance ranked No. 3 in the world and No. 1 in China. Its production capacity of the fiber preforming bars accounted for more than 90% of China's total, and that of cables accounted for more than 40% of China's total (cn-39).

In terms of products and market, the company developed G.655 with proprietary intellectual property in 1966. The first client, Guangdong Telecommunications, put G.655 (all-02) into use the first time. In 1999, the fiber started popularizing in China's electricity departments started. The company's annual sales volume skyrocketed to around 2 billion RMB (cn-39).

In terms of informatization, the company tried making the MES system in 1995. From 1996 to 1997, the quality information system (AP1-01) was developed. In 2001, the ERP system (provided by Oracle) was introduced to further improve operation efficiency of the company.

2.2.3 2002-2007: Independent Product Development, Production Capacity Expansion and Informatization Improvement

In 2001, the Internet economy bubble was busted in the US, resulting in a significant shrinkage of the global telecommunication equipment market demands. The optical communication industry suffered an unprecedented blow. Under the condition, many manufacturers, instead of withdrawing from the market, expanded their production. This further intensified the market competition. Impacted by dumping of foreign fiber manufacturers, the fiber price plummeted in China. The increasing inventory and the slow response to market changes became two major factors restricting competitiveness of YOFC (Zhang, 2005). YOFC coped with these two challenges in the following five aspects:

1. **Anti-Dumping:** On May 7, 2003, YOFC and Jiangsu Fa Er Sheng Photon Co., Ltd. submitted an anti-dumping investigation application to the Ministry of Commerce on behalf of the domestic zero-dispersion displacement single mode fiber industry. On July 1, 2003, the Ministry of Commerce decided to investigate into the anti-dumping case of the zero-dispersion displacement single mode fibers imported from the US, Japan and South Korea. Later, the Ministry of Commerce also launched a questionnaire survey among stakeholders, which proved that the causality between dumping and substantive damage. On January 1, 2005, the Ministry of Commerce made an affirmative arbitration of the fiber dumping case. This alleviated the tension of dumping in the field. The fiber which with a high dumping tax rate levied on it almost stopped importing, but previously the imported products seized nearly 30% to 50% of market share.
2. **Development of Products with a High Technological Content:** In 2002, Corning, an American giant in the optical fiber and cable industry, launched the low water peak fiber on the market. Performance of the new product was far ahead of pervious products. It quickly occupied the market before YOFC had adequate time to respond. At the critical moment, the company leaders made a

resolute decision to organize an R&D team for concentrated technological breakthroughs. Technical backbone of the company was gathered to form the low water peak fiber technological breakthrough team (Zhang & Chen, 2006). Experiments were conducted considering product design, R&D and production, as well as equipment airtightness and raw material purity. Finally, the low water peak fiber was developed by YOFC, successfully getting rid of the foreign monopolization in the domestic fiber market. In 2005, as a part of the National Key Technology Research and Development Program of China during the "10th Five-Year Plan", the PCVD (Plasma Chemical Vapor Deposition) large-size low water peak single-mode fiber preforming bar manufacturing technology development and the fully-synthesized fiber preforming bar industrialization technology passed the expert review. The new process combined the high performance of PCVD fiber and the cost advantage of OVD process. In other words, it not only maintained the outstanding performance of the fiber, but also significantly reduced the optical fiber manufacturing cost. Many raw materials could get manufactured in China, bringing an overall improvement of the company's product competitiveness. The company also became the only possessor of the large-size preforming bar and drawing technology in China. By 2005, the company had developed the capacity to produce large-scale fibers, including G. 651, G. 652 and G. 655. The fiber output reached 9.5 million kilometers and the cable output reached 4.6 million kilometers. (Data of 2006)

3. **Improvement of R&D Technological Conditions:** In 2002, the company was recognized by four Hubei provincial committees, including Hubei Provincial economic and Trade Committee, as "Hubei Provincial Corporate Technology R&D Center". In the same year, it worked with Hubei Provincial Chemical Research Institute to set up Hubei Provincial Optical Communication Material Engineering and Research Center. In 2003, it founded the "National 863 Program Achievements Industrialization Base" with Fiber and Sensor Technology Research Center Affiliated to Wuhan University of Technology. In 2007, YOFC was approved as the "National Enterprise Technology Center", the first of its kind in the industry.
4. **Quality Management Improvement:** In 2002, the company transferred its quality management system to ISO9001: 2000 national standard. In 2004, the company officially obtained the ISO4001 issued by TUV Rhineland.
5. **Strengthening of Process Management and Informatization:** Through "system-based procedural management", the company streamlined its previous management procedures and management systems, turning to flow management. After implementation of the ERP system, the company found that its warehouse management had some problems. To cope with these problems, the company introduced the WMS (warehouse management system); the supplier management and inventory models, including TPS, AOS, MIS, and DSS; and the OA system. All these information systems were adopted to get the company rid of the information isolated island.

2.2.4 2008-2016: Expansion of Technological Advantage, Intelligent Manufacturing Transformation and Large-Scale Informatization Input

Behind rapid development of YOFC, there were a series of favorable policies, including issuance of 3G business license by the Chinese government, holding of Beijing Olympic 2008, development of the west regions, "Village to Village Telecommunication Project" and FTTH market development, integration of three networks, and "Broadband China" strategy.

a. **Expansion of Technological Advantages:** In 2009, *high efficiency electrofusion fiber manufacturing technology* of YOFC was rated by the Energy-Saving Department of the Ministry of Industry and Information as the first batch of electronic information energy-saving technological development and application plans. In 2020, YOFC was approved to build "Fiber and Cable Preparation Technological National Key Lab", and the construction result passed the acceptance check of the Ministry of Technology. Later, YOFC launched the first generation of bend-intensive single-mode filter (BI-SMF) G. 657 and bend intensive multi-module fiber (BI-OM3/OM4). The fiber which can be casually bent overcomes a shortage of the traditional fiber—the larger the fiber bending is, the higher the signal attenuation coefficient is. Meanwhile, it is tensile, compression-resistant, and compatible with outdoor fibers. Being adapting to needs of spreading fibers to households and data centers, the fiber is widely recognized to reach the international technological level. In 2013, the company joined the "FTTx China Industry Technology Innovation Strategic Alliance" (other members include Wuhan Guanxun Technology Co., Ltd., FiberHome, etc.). The "low-cost FTTx key optoelectronic device and equipment manufacturing" project assigned to it as a part of "National 12th Five-Year Plan Technological Support Program" successfully passed the review of the Ministry of Technology. The successful implementation of the project got rid of technological bottlenecks, including low cost, high performance, broad temperature range optical devices and small bending radius optical fiber, restricting industrial development for a long time, and consolidated technological advantages of YOFC. Besides, YOFC and VIA Technologies signed a cooperation agreement with each other in Wuhan, and set up their joint venture, EverPro Technologies. The joint venture, by integrating advantages of YOFC in the optical fiber and cable field and advantages of VIA Technologies in the field of core and module, will hopefully become a globally leading active optical fiber enterprise with an annual sales volume close to 3 billion RMB in three to five years.

b. **Transformation to Intelligent Manufacturing:** In 2015, YOFC became the first batch of 46 intelligent manufacturing demonstration enterprises approved by the Ministry of Industry and Information. Some of the company's projects were listed as demonstration projects. They included the optical fiber preforming bar new-type manufacturing process and equipment intelligent transformation, VAD+OVD process preparation large-size optical fiber preforming bar, fully independent intellectual property right preparation of intelligent optical fiber and preforming bar production equipment. In 2016, YOFC joined hands with Siasun, a leading Chinese robot and automatic equipment enterprise, and Wiscom System, an information system integration service provider to build a brand-new intelligent plant in Qianjiang, Hubei, and formulate industrial standards for preforming bars and fiber intelligent manufacturing. The project was invested with 780 million yuan. Based on big data, cloud manufacturing, process and production simulation, this project attempted to realize continuous technological and product upgrade. Application of the robot and automatic logistics line realized automatic logistics of the manufacturing process, and improved the technological ability of core equipment. YOFC designed and manufactured the brand-new *intertwined membrane fiber automatic packaging assembly line*. The single-disc fiber packaging time was shortened from 3 minutes under manual operation to less than 40 seconds. The single set of packaging machine could do the work of six to eight operation personnel. Meanwhile, the packaging quality was greatly improved, and the packaging cost was reduced by around 20%. After completion of the project, the productivity was expected to get increased by 20%; the product R&D period to reduce by more than 30%. In the same year, the company won the *Industrialization and Informatization Integration System Implementation Accreditation Certificate*, a national-level honor.

c. **Large-scale Information Input:** From 2008, YOFC started large-scale informatization. The tremendous efforts contributed to localization of industrial control software and high-end control equipment. Meanwhile, ERP and MAS were also localized. In particular, MAS, FAS and CAS—these information systems were all localized based on the original imported supporting systems. After location, these systems were further promoted in the domestic fiber and cable industry. Now, many Chinese fiber and cable enterprises are using the set of systems developed by YOFC.
d. **Expansion of the Management Right by Listing Itself on the Market:** In December 2014, YOFC listed itself on the Hong Kong market. The reason for its listing in Hong Kong rather than Mainland China was that YOFC has foreign shareholders. After the former Ministry of Posts and Telecommunications was revoked, the Ministry sold its shares to China Huaxin Post and Telecommunication Economy Development Center, whose held 37.5% of shares in the company. The earliest foreign shareholder, Philips Netherlands, did not involve in fiber and cable business anymore, so it transferred its shares to Draka Comteq B.V. As to the Wuhan Municipal People's Government, it sold its shares to Wuhan Yangtze Communications Industry Group Co., Ltd., which accounted for 25%. The equity structure was changed to 34%, 37.5% and 25%. There was a problem with the equity structure, that was, the one-vote veto of the foreign shareholder made YOFC lose several major development opportunities. After getting listed in Hong Kong, the foreign-held shares were reduced to 26.12%. In other words, among 11 shareholders, there were only four foreign shareholders. In this way, the four shareholders, whether arriving at the shareholders' conference or not, whether they voted for or against, would not exert a substantial influence on the company's decision-making. Therefore, since 2014, YOFC has been vigorously forging ahead. From 2014 to 2016, the company's annual sales volume increased from 20% to 30%, and the net profits increased by around 40% to 50%.

2.2.5 After 2015: International Market Development and Technological Output

Zhuangdan, President of YOFC, thought that the current global fiber and cable market is still in a short supply, and that implementation of the "Broadband China" strategy is the largest "driving force" for the growing demand (Zou, 2016). However, Chinese fiber and cable enterprises should take precautions against a rainy day. After the fever of 4G and 5G is gone, China's domestic market might be faced with the danger of shrinking. To Chinese optical and fiber enterprises, there is still a large room for their market internationalization. Therefore, YOFC has set a five-year goal, that is, to increase its overseas market income to 25% to 30% of its total income by 2020. Actions have already been taken by YOFC to realize the goal. In January 2015, YOFC set up a fiber joint venture in Indonesia. In March 2015, YOFC's fiber plant in Burma was launched. In March 2016, YOFC's joint venture in South Africa was founded.

After three decades of development, China's fiber and optical industry has been nearing the international highest level, and Chinese enterprises have the ability to go global. YOFC will actively expand the international market under the guidance of the 'Belt & Road' initiative.

Zhuangdan also mentioned that, during the international market expansion process, Chinese fiber and cable enterprises represented YOFC should learn from the leading international competitors; gradually change their image as brands with low cost and inferior quality; and pay more attention to product quality. Meanwhile, cultural differences should not be ignored. YOFC should try to get adapted to such differences; integrate its sales in both domestic and foreign markets; and finally realize the goal of strengthening and expanding its business.

3. IMPLICATIONS OF YANGTZE OPTICAL FIBER AND CABLE JOINT STOCK LIMITED COMPANY TO THE OPTICAL FIBER INDUSTRY

As the global largest preforming bar, fiber and cable manufacturer, YOFC is worth being learned by all the other Chinese fiber and cable enterprises, and provides new implications to manufacturing strategy (Yu, 2002; Gong, 2013). Below is a summary of implications of YOFC's development over the past three decades for other Chinese fiber and cable enterprises:

3.1 Continuous Learning and Absorption

During the development process of YOFC, especially during its initial development period, YOFC obtained a ten-year technology transfer from Philips Netherlands by allowing foreign capital infusion (Hu, 2002). It successfully introduced synthesized tube technology from Netherlands Plasma Fiber Company to achieve rapid development for its fiber manufacturing technologies and skills (Tian, 2012; Wang, 2005). These technologies played an important role in the initial development period of YOFC, which helped YOFC rise to the top of the domestic output in the field. Apart from the explicit technologies, the advanced management expertise introduced from foreign companies were also decisive to YOFC's success (Yang & Luo, 2001). Just as Dr. Hu from the company's R&D development said, YOFC benefited from its cooperation with the European company, Philips Netherlands. The latter provided YOFC with not only technologies, but also management expertise. This is partially attributable for YOFC's No. 1 position in the domestic cable and fiber market over the past 25 years in a row. Therefore, other Chinese fiber and cable enterprises should also think about how to make good use of technologies and management experiences from their leading partners.

3.2 Proprietary R&D and Product Innovation

A striking difference of YOFC in China's fiber and cable industry is that it has its fiber manufacturing process, equipment and software system with the proprietary intellectual property (Hu, 2005). Globally, YOFC is the only enterprise knowing three kinds of preforming bar manufacturing technologies. Apart from PCVD imported from Philips Netherlands, OVD and VAD are both developed by itself. Besides, the PCVD has been fully localized by YOFC, so it is with its high-end control equipment and software. YOFC's ERP and MES have both finished localization, or to be exact they are independently developed by YOFC (Li, 2013; Niu, 2004). All these efforts have contributed to YOFC's integration between integration and urbanization. Meanwhile, a batch of intelligent equipment and intelligent plants have been launched. That YOFC was approved as the intelligent manufacturing demonstration site and won many other relevant awards has a close bearing on YOFC's proprietary R&D. Xi Jinping, President of PRC, once said that,

YOFC has its proprietary technology. More importantly, it has the proprietary equipment. The high-end intelligent equipment of YOFC provides a firm guarantee for national information security (Xu, 2014).

Product innovation is also a linchpin to development of YOFC. In 2003, YOFC's successful R7D of the low water peak fiber helped it get out of the crisis brought by bust of the Internet economic bubble. This was a case in point. Other Chinese fiber and cable enterprises should also realize that expansion of the production capacity and lowering of the production cost alone do not work in the fiber and cable industry, where things are changing with each passing day. It is the capability of proprietary R&D and product innovation that can gain them a foothold in the market.

3.3 Seizing Opportunity and Favorable Development Policy

More than once, YOFC made use of national policies or legal means to either achieve rapid development or safeguard its legitimate rights and interests. The anti-dumping case stated above and YOFC's business expansion based on the "Belt & Road" initiative, "Broadband China" strategy and "Made in China 2025"—All this shows YOFC's adeptness at facilitating its development through different development policies (Huang, 2011). Of course, this cannot be separated from YOFC's identity as being state-owned.

3.4 Talent Development and Intelligence Support

YOFC's proprietary fiber manufacturing process, equipment and software system, and its new products with widespread influence have a close bearing on its reserve of R&D talents. Earlier in 2000, YOFC had set up the R&D Department, which in 2013 got upgraded into R&D Center. At present, YOFC had the largest fiber and cable research institute in the Asia-Pacific Region, with more than 400 resident R&D personnel, as compared with a workforce of only 2,000 of YOFC. This suggests that, without the powerful R&D team, it would be unlikely for YOFC to obtain the proprietary process and equipment, let alone develop new products which can seize more market share for YOFC.

3.5 Active Transformation by Sizing Up the Situation

Though YOFC has an unparalleled position in the domestic market, it still actively seeks transformation at critical moments. In 2011, Zhuang Dan proposed the plan of transforming China's fiber and optical industry from a global manufacturing center to *global R&D + manufacturing center + marketing center + business consulting and service center*. Later, YOFC has made unremitting efforts. So far, YOFC has made remarkable achievements in the field. The set of solution plans developed by it has already been exported to the downstream enterprises in the field. The solution plans are also applied to its plants set up abroad. This not only guarantees an important position of FOYC in the global market and the supply chain, but also stimulates YOFC to scale a new high.

3.6 Independent Operation and Elimination of Monopolization

As every coin has two sides, the joint venture is a double-edged sword. If an enterprise wants to get sustainable development in a field, it should free itself from the control of foreign investors. To the end, YOFC reduced the percentage of shares held by the foreign investor to 26.1%. In other words, among 11 shareholders, there were only four foreign shareholders. In this way, the four shareholders, whether arriving at the shareholders' conference or not, whether they voted for or against, would not exert a substantial influence on the company's decision-making. Therefore, since 2014, YOFC has been vigorously forging ahead. From 2014 to 2016, the company's annual sales volume increased from 20% to 30%, and the net profits increased by around 40% to 50%. In 2016, YOFC even got ahead of Corning to become the global largest preforming bar, optical fiber and cable manufacturer. Thus, it is important to reduce foreign investments in a company. This is necessary for an enterprise to achieve long-term development.

4. DISCUSSIONS

Comparing the development trajectories of China's optical fibre industry and YOFC, more similarities are found than deviations. YOFC, as one of the domination company in China's optical fibre industry, its development track is considered as a miniature of the whole industry's and on some certain points, it promoted the industry's growth process (Huang, 2016). The government regulations and policies shape the general industry background. And in the meantime, the growth of YOFC and the development of China's optical fibre industry complement each another.

Similar paths of development have been identified in the industry of telecommunication equipment provider industry of China (Fan, 2006; Gao, 2014) and the consumer electronics industry of China (Duysters, Lemmens and Yu, 2009,). The continuous learning and knowledge absorption provides YOFC a solid foundation to reach the leading position in the industry. This is consistent to the development of telecommunication equipment provider such as Huawei when the industry is upgrading in the global competition. And proper government interventions in the early stage of industry development of consumer electronics industry, such as Haier in China, has also been discovered in the development of YOFC. The evolution of optical fiber industry in China also shows some divergent but complement results from the existing literature, such as seizing almost all the opportunities along with its development. As companies are subject to the resource constraints, decision makers and executives of YOFC may have difficulty in judging and evaluating the opportunities. It shows that strong capabilities of the management team may complement the resource limitations and finally benefit the formulation and execution the strategy in the process of transformation and upgrading. However, this requires other important inputs such as the continuous learning and knowledge absorption.

5. CONCLUSION

China attempt to achieve the industry aims introduced by the "Made in China 2025" proposal whose goals focus on boosting manufacturing innovation and promoting domestic products to both domestic and overseas markets. Although this plan seems to be ambitious, the upgrading momentum in China's manufacturing industries may bring the credibility. China's economy locates in an important period of transition, and as manufacturing industry is considered as the pillar of the national economy, the successful transformation of the manufacturing sector plays a vital role in the development of the whole national economy. Yangtze Optical Fiber and Cable Joint Stock Limited Company as a typical manufacturing enterprise in China,has become a representative of China's optical fiber industry. After decades of developments, YOFC went through the test of growth and maturation and polished and until now has already made a luxuriant metamorphosis. Nowadays, YOFC is also a model of excellent manufacturing enterprises in China. Chinese manufacturing enterprises can learn from the development and the transformation history of YOFC.

This "Made in China 2025" plan could not miss the presence of the contribution from China's optical fiber industry whose essential referenceable development process is introduced in detail with a comparing discussion of the typical case, YOFC. Market demand plays a critical role in the upgrading process. The domestic market firstly emerged followed by developing the international market cultivation. Once a certain international market share is occupied, China's optical fiber industry took advantages of windows of opportunities which rocked its performance into the world's factory. After all those paid efforts, nowadays, China's optical fiber industry has gain significance worldwide not only of its manufacturing but also design. During that process, the solid support from the government especially on the anti-dumping issue, offered domestic company a fair market environment which guaranteed them to be competent.

As we can see from the development of YOFC, it has got rid of the habit of *being complacent and conservative*. Instead, YOFC jumped out of the low-cost and low-quality vicious circle of Chinese product. A new development path of introducing, digesting, absorbing and innovation foreign technology has been made. By cultivating their own research talents and establishing their own research team, YOFC has broken the monopoly of foreign technology, developed unique fiber technology, and achieved some technological breakthroughs in key products. Then, with the aids of the national policy on manufacturing, YOFC transformation was carried out at the critical moment, which contributed to the rapid development of itself and stabilized the market position. And in recent years, YOFC company has taken advantage of both the market and research, has been actively pursuing its own long-term development with the help of the "Made in China 2025" policy. Firstly, YOFC exerted efforts in manufacturing field with new intelligence, to achieve the transformation of enterprises; Secondly, a positive response to the national "The Belt and Road" policy call, worked in a number of countries, double the output of capital and technology, enter the world market, strode towards internationalization. YOFC now has successfully achieved the transcendence of the international giant, reached the international advanced level.

It can be said that the development process of YOFC and the progress of recent years have explained the requirements of "Made in China 2025", which reflects the strength and prospect of YOFC and become the benchmark enterprise of "Made in China 2025". YOFC case is worth leaning for China's fiber industry and even all of China's manufacturing enterprises, and is also worth to be learnt and receive attention from the world's other manufacturing enterprises and experts and scholars.

There is a long way to go before China will truly master the "Made in China 2025" objectives on the level of developed and advanced countries. However, upgrading manufacturing processes and enhance in innovation are vital to the value chain. Remaining the international competitiveness requires China to create and implement new technologies. The sophisticated manufacturing and innovative industrial upgrading is expected to lead China into an innovation economy while welcoming the success of "Made in China 2025".

ACKNOWLEDGMENT

This work is supported by The Major Project of National Social Science Foundation of China (16ZDA013) and The Project of National Natural Science Foundation of China (71772142).

REFERENCES

Chen, J. (1995). On the Formation and Function of National Innovation System from YOFC. *Science Research of Management, 3.*

Diao, X. (2017). YOFC Promote the transformation and upgrading of fiber optic cable industry. *Communications World, 10.*

Duysters, G., Jacob, J., Lemmens, C., & Yu, J. T. (2009). Internationalization and technological catching up of emerging multinationals: A comparative case study of China's Haier group. *Industrial and Corporate Change*, *18*(2), 325–349. doi:10.1093/icc/dtp006

Fan, P. (2006). Catching up through developing innovation capability: Evidence from China's telecom-equipment industry. *Technovation*, *26*(3), 359–368. doi:10.1016/j.technovation.2004.10.004

Gao, C. (2016, November 14). Intelligent manufacturing & internationalization, YOFC in the next five years to the next big move. *Communications.*

Gao, C. (2017). YOFC Qianjiang Science and Technology Park officially put into operation, Long flight integration advantages of resources, Aiming at the international market. *Communications Weekly, 6.*

Gao, X. D. (2014). A latecomer's strategy to promote a technology standard: The case of Datang and TD-SCDMA. *Research Policy*, *43*(3), 597–607. doi:10.1016/j.respol.2013.09.003

Gong, Y. (2013). *Global operations strategy: Fundamentals and practice*. Berlin: Springer. doi:10.1007/978-3-642-36708-3

Hu, L. (2005). Independent innovation, leading the future. *China Science & Technology Industry Pars, 9.*

Hu, P. (2002). *China Optical Fiber and Cable Enterprises Development Strategies Research*. Wuhan University of Technology.

Huang, H. (2011). Zhuang Dan, general manager of YOFC: China's fiber optic cable industry is facing two major opportunities. *Communications World*, *42*, 107.

Huang, Y. (2016). YOFC president Zhuang Dan: China is becoming the leading force in the global fiber optic cable market. *The People's Posts and Telecommunications*, *11*, 10.

Li, M. (2013, August 2). YOFC: Layout Global Competition. *Hubei Daily*, p. 2.

Niu, G. (2004). The Interview with Xu Xizhou, the General Manager of YOFC. Interviews With Famous Enterprises, *7.*

Tian, Q. (2012). BPR Help to Improve Enterprises High Speed Developing, Mission and Responsibility - Promoting Quality Upgrade by Quality Method. *Proceedings of the 5th China Forum on Quality and Academic Innovation.*

Wang, H. (2005). *Research on BPR Based on Business Process Modeling - A Case Study of YOFC's Inventory Management Business Process Reengineering*. Xi'an University of Technology.

Xu, S. (2014). YOFC's senior product manager Zhou Qinmin: Focus on next generation fiber. *Communications Weekly, 17.*

Xu, X. (2003). Enhance its strength to participate in international competition. *Communications World, 21*, 6.

Yang, Z., &Luo, H. (2001). On the Development of Chinese Enterprises from the Growth of YOFC. *Science & Technology Progress and Policy, 5.*

Yu, W. (2002). Current Situation and Development of China 's Fiber Optic Cable Industry. *Information System Engineering, 5.*

Zhang, G. (2005). *EIQ Analysis of Fiber Warehouse Operation of YOFC*. Huazhong University of Science and Technology.

Zhang, P., & Chen, H. (2006). VMI model implementation research of YOFC. *Journal of Wuhan Institute of Technology, 3.*

Zou, Y. (2016). *The efficient working capital- Working capital management experience of YOFC*. YOFC.

Chapter 3
Is Malaysia Ready for the Fourth Industrial Revolution?
The Automotive Sector as an i4.0 Springboard

Mathew Maavak
Universiti Teknologi Malaysia (UTM), Malaysia

Aini Suzana Ariffin
Universiti Teknologi Malaysia (UTM), Malaysia

ABSTRACT

Malaysia intends to ride on the crest of the coming i.4.0 wave. According to the 2016 GE Global Innovation Barometer study, a significant number of Malaysian executives felt positive about embracing i4.0 vis-a-vis their global peers. On the surface, Malaysia appears ready for its own i4.0 revolution. According to the WEF's Networked Readiness Index on digital readiness, Malaysia was ranked 6th in terms of having the most tech-savvy government in the world. The automotive sector is ideally suited to kickstart the i4.0 revolution as it was traditionally regarded as the "industry of industries" – particularly due to its traditional role in spearheading wider, cross-sectoral industrialisation. However, Malaysia is not yet ready to embrace the 4th Industrial Revolution. This chapter discusses the obstacles, challenges, and opportunities facing i4.0 uptake in the Malaysian automotive industry. It ends by recommending a unique pathway for i4.0 adoption in the sector.

INDUSTRY BACKGROUND

The Fourth Industrial Revolution is the culmination of centuries of technology-driven progress. Also called Industry 4.0 or i4.0, the new industrial paradigm is expected to usher in a range of new technologies that will fuse the physical, digital and biological worlds. Since it is poised to impact all disciplines, economies and industries, Brynjolfsson and McAfe (2016) have described the coming epoch as the "second machine age"; one that will feature a fully-integrated virtual dimension to industry. Using this

DOI: 10.4018/978-1-5225-3468-6.ch003

description, it can be assumed that the "first machine age" kicked off with the First Industrial Revolution which birthed new inventions and manufacturing processes during a 100-year period that ended in the mid-1800s (Landes, 1969). Industries began to be mechanized and nations that built and harnessed machines began to colonize the world.

The ensuing Second Industrial Revolution witnessed another surge in cross-sectoral inventions, notably in the transportation sector (Engelman, 2015). Mankind's technological progress could now be measured in the proliferating numbers and types of cars and aircraft. The Taylorian production process became vogue; made famous by Henry Ford's T-Model. Worldwide literacy, beginning with elementary schools, began to surge during this period, creating skills and competencies to fulfil long-term industrial and societal needs.

According to Rifkin (2011), the Third Industrial Revolution – also known as the Digital Revolution or Industry 3.0 – began in the 1980s and was marked by a steady migration from analogue to digital devices. Through the Internet, real-time multimedia interactions became possible for the first-time in history. Economies began the journey towards virtualization and international outsourcing. A high-tech job was increasingly typified by sedentary inputs on a computer screen – often half the world away from where the actual product or service was being developed or offered.

Throughout these epochs, governments had to continually tailor policies, laws and regulations to satisfy the imperatives of each new industrial paradigm. Children could no longer work in coal mines and factories, and factories were later mandated to dispose toxic effluences and by-products in a regulated manner. Environmental consciousness, sustainability and green technology soon became the global ideal *du jour.*

Rising complexities and uncertainties have however grown in tandem with ephemeralization (Fuller, 1938) forces unleashed by successive industrial revolutions. Ephemeralization describes the technological momentum where improving efficiencies to achieve greater outputs (i.e. products and services) progressively require fewer inputs (i.e. effort, time and resources). Moore's Law, which foresaw the number of transistors per square inch doubling every 18 months, epitomized both the ephemeralization process and the Digital Revolution.

Ephemeralization also initiated a race between the rapidly increasing severity and complexity of problems in a system *and the improving but nonetheless uncertain ability to anticipate, proactively solve, and constructively respond to these problems* (Homer-Dixon, T.; Walker, B.; Biggs, R.; Crépin, A.S.; Folke, C.; Lambin, E.F.; Peterson, G.D.;. Rockström, J.; Scheffer, M.; Steffen, W.; & Troell, M., 2015; p1). As systems got more connected and efficient, they became more entropy-prone and less predictable (Fuller, 1957; Heylighen, 2002).

A new industrial paradigm is therefore needed to handle complexities and uncertainties as they emerge in real-time – alongside Just-in-Time (JIT) production processes. Furthermore, twentieth century methods of running businesses and factories may no longer provide sufficient returns on investments (ROIs).

Since Industry 4.0 heralds greater efficiency, lower costs and superior products across entire value-chains, rapidly-transforming countries like Malaysia may see i4.0 as a fast-track avenue into the Developed Nations league.

SETTING THE i4.0 STAGE

The Fourth Industrial Revolution is the latest phase of an evolutionary industrial continuum. It is poised to fundamentally change the way we live, work, and relate to one another. In its scale, scope, and complexity, the transformation wrought by i4.0 will be unlike anything experienced by mankind. It will connect global stakeholders from the public and private sectors to the academia and civil society as well as production value-chains via an *internet of things, services, data and people*. The future *smart factory* will be run by greater automation, artificial intelligence (AI) and human-machine interfaces (Schwab, 2015).

While Industry 3.0 had focused on the automation of manufacturing processes, Industry 4.0 will extrapolate, integrate and inter-operationalize all aspects of the previous revolution – in addition to new modes of production. The i4.0 ecosystem will synergize cyber physical systems (CPS); big data analytics; robotics; manufacturing execution systems (MES); 3D printing; and human expertise through the Internet of Things (IoT). Unlike standalone factories of the past, productions centres, suppliers, and customers in the i4.0 ecosystem will be seamlessly interconnected as part of a global, unified value-chain (Kagermann, H., Wahlster, W., & Helbig, J., 2013; Liffler & Tschiesner, 2013).

Industry 4.0 promises the following benefits in the area of production (PWC, 2016; Kagermann, H., Wahlster, W., & Helbig, J., 2013):

- Shorter operational lead times
- Higher asset utilization
- Maximization of product quality
- Greater efficiency
- Lower costs
- Higher revenue
- Real-time information transparency
- Autonomous tasking through smart algorithms and CPS

While factories of the past had focused on the mass-production of identical or similar products, i4.0 will offer mass customization and individualization for product designers and consumers (Ramsauer, 2013). Choice will no longer be dictated by the corporate hierarchy. Henry Ford's famous tongue-in-cheek assurance that car-buyers could choose any vehicle colour they liked *as long as it was black* would be an axiom of the past (Ford & Crowther, 1922). Industries will get the agility to meet market demands anywhere in the world by tracking emerging trends and data in real time. On-demand industrial manufacturing will become a reality. Industry 4.0 will move the global industry from mass production to mass customisation at reasonable costs to the consumer (PwC, 2016).

Industry 4.0 will also empower individuals to create their own tools. Through the use of 3D printing and AI, a technician in a remote sea-based oil rig, for example, can download and "print" a component instead of waiting for days or weeks for a replacement. The days when operations were halted due to a missing cog in the machinery would soon be over.

Although Industry 4.0 is often used synonymously with the "Internet of Things" and "smart factory", the latter terms do not adequately explain the i4.0 paradigm. There are three fundamental prerequisites that categorically adumbrate Industry 4.0 (Siems, 2015):

- Horizontal and cross-company integration of the value chain – from the development of a product to its delivery.
- Vertical integration with interconnected production systems involving bi-directional flow of information between management, data scientists, machines and production floor.
- Digital consistency, including software interoperability, throughout the production process.

These prerequisites entail digital transparency and high levels of digital sentience or Digital IQ. Through integrated smart sensors, data analytics and AI, smart factories will have internal predictive abilities to monitor, diagnose and repair components and systems, leading to just-in-time maintenance and minimal downtime in the production process (PwC, 2015).

Industry 4.0 will also provide management with greater insights into the substrates-level functioning of the factory, thereby facilitating the introduction of even more efficient systems and components. In an i4.0 smart factory, the "digital twin" of a physical product or service can be created before it is analysed, tweaked or optimized via computerized systems. Digital twinning can run in parallel to the production process i.e. until the product leaves the physical factory or service enterprise (Hawes, 2016).

With millions of people getting connected to the IoT each week, there is a palpable need to improve overall productivity through streamlined asset and personnel management. In a PwC Global Industry 4.0 Survey held in 2016, around 2,000 participants from nine major industrial sectors in 26 countries anticipated i4.0 to save an average US$421 billion in costs each year over the next five years. Businesses were also expected to invest an average of US$907 billion per annum to i4.0 in order to lower costs, boost efficiency and increase revenue during the same period (PwC, 2016).

According to Espinel (2016), the emergent digital economy will permeate all aspects of society, including interpersonal interactions, business dynamics, nature of jobs, and the political process. It will generate new scientific research and breakthroughs, fuel job opportunities and economic growth as well as improve people's lives.

It is in the manufacturing sector, however, where i4.0's impact will be initially felt. A new generation of embedded smart systems will offer faster, smarter, smaller and cheaper tools, productions processes or products. Computers, smart devices and data will be endowed with the ability to communicate and learn from each other. Industries will no longer function in silos.

Developed nations, which face rising industrial competition, can resort to i4.0 to regain their global market share. For instance, while industries in the European Union (EU) traditionally generated 80% of its private innovations and 75% of exports, the region has been gradually losing market share to ascending manufacturing powerhouses in Asia. Industry 4.0 therefore may prove pivotal to the revitalization of EU industries (Travkina, 2015). Table 1 outlines the benefits of i4.0 in terms of revenue, costs and efficiency.

According to Schwab (2015), with the advent of Industry 4.0,

transportation and communication costs will drop, logistics and global supply chains will become more effective, and the cost of trade will diminish, all of which will open new markets and drive economic growth.

Industry 4.0 will also feature the *sharing economy* and blockchain technology. The sharing economy is an umbrella term that describes how individuals and organizations interact online to share or transact in goods and services. Blockchain is a digital repository of transactions that is stacked in an orderly and distributed manner. With an emphasis on trust and systems integrity, blockchain obviates the need

Table 1. Multiple Advantages of i4.0

Additional Revenue From:	Lower Cost and Greater Efficiency From:
Digitising products and services within the existing portfolio	Real-time inline quality control based on Big Data Analytics
New digital products, services and solutions	Modular, flexible and customer-tailored production concepts
Offering big data and analytics as a service.	Real-time visibility into process and product variance, augmented reality and optimisation by data analytics
Personalised products and mass customisation.	Predictive maintenance on key assets using predictive algorithms to optimise repair and maintenance schedules and improve asset uptime
Capturing high-margin business through improved customer insight from data analytics	Vertical integration from sensors through MES to real-time production planning for better machine utilisation and faster throughput times
Increasing market share of core products	Horizontal integration, as well as track-and-trace of products for better inventory performance and reduced logistics
	Digitisation and automation of processes for a smarter use of human resources and higher operations speed
	System based, real-time end-to-end planning and horizontal collaboration using cloud-based planning platforms for execution optimisation
	Increased scale from increased market share of core products

Source: (PWC, 2016)

for third-party institutions to keep records of financial, contractual or voting activities (Espinel, 2016). The digital currency Bitcoin is arguably the best-known example of blockchain technology in use today.

Highly-developed nations, armed with advanced i4.0 blueprints, are poised to enjoy first mover advantages in the smart factories of tomorrow. But where does Malaysia stand in the i4.0 calculus?

CASE DESCRIPTION: MALAYSIA AT i4.0 CROSSROADS?

Experts disagree on Malaysia's overall readiness to embrace the i4.0 revolution. According Malaysia-based technopreneur S.T. Rubaneswaran, Myanmar, Thailand and Vietnam are ahead in the regional i4.0 race. Thailand has already drawn up an i4.0 policy framework while Vietnam is on the verge of completing a similar undertaking (Ganapathy-Wallace, 2017). Rather ironically, agrarian nations may find it easier to transition to i4.0 manufacturing as compared to nations still saddled with expensively-built Industry 2.0 and 3.0 factories and infrastructure. Having a large pool of highly-skilled workers adept at tasks suited for near-obsolescent industrial paradigms may arguably pose a hindrance to the establishment of i4.0 industries.

Yet, according to the GE Global Innovation Barometer study in 2016, a significant number of Malaysian executives remained positive about i4.0 vis-a-vis their global peers. Malaysian executives generally felt more optimistic (76% vs 68% globally), excited (67% vs 61% globally) and confident (72% vs 60% globally) about the coming industrial revolution (Ahmad, 2016).

Other global studies seem to bolster such optimism. In WEF's Global Competitiveness Report 2014-2015, Malaysia was placed 20th out of 144 countries in several high criteria areas (WEF, 2014). Additionally, the WEF's 2016 Networked Readiness Index (on digital readiness) had placed Malaysia in 31st position worldwide (WEF, 2016a) as well as a notable 6th position in the specific area of government tech-savviness. The WEF based its criteria on *government efficiency in promoting information and communications technologies and providing online services to the population* (WEF, 2016c) – not on overall digital readiness per se.

As outlined in Table 2, Malaysia seems outwardly ready for its own i4.0 revolution. However, such optimism has to be counterweighed against emerging i4.0 prerequisites, including criterions associated with jobs and skills of the future.

Employment and Skill Concerns

Industry 4.0 poses various challenges for less developed nations, particularly those in Africa and Latin America. Apart from having serious infrastructural deficits, traditional competitive advantages like cheaper labour may no longer provide an edge in the i4.0 age, particularly due to the mass adoption of AI and robotics in more developed economies.

India, for example, would have faced the same dilemma if not for its formidable ICT sector, which, is currently collaborating with manufacturers and the government to digitize the native industrial landscape. The recently unveiled "Make in India" initiative intends to transform the nation into the *smart factory of the world* (Dubey, 2015). In the automotive sector alone, India's gross output is double the size of the UK's and is expected to grow qualitatively and quantitatively due to extensive investments from global auto giants and a rapidly expanding domestic market. Coupled with a growing pool of digital scientists, courtesy of its sprawling ICT sector, India may be a contender to make the *car of the future* (Hawes, 2016). However, until India's physical infrastructure catches up with its virtual sinews; native i4.0 automotive capabilities will continue to lag behind global leaders in Germany, Japan, US and UK in the short- to mid-term.

Talent, more than capital, may likely be the key differentiator in the i4.0 economy, as it may organically segregate the future job market into "low-skill/low-pay" and "high-skill/high-pay" categories. This is bound to cause social tensions (Brynjolfsson & McAfe, 2016). Schwab (2015) agrees with this observation:

Table 2. Top 10 Nations with Tech-Savvy Governments

Which Government is the Most Tech-Savvy? ***Networked Readiness Index 2016: Indicator Focus***	**Global Rank**
Singapore	1
United Arab Emirates	2
Bahrain	3
South Korea	4
Qatar	5
Malaysia	6
Japan	7
Estonia	8
Luxembourg	9
United Kingdom	10

Source: (WEF, 2016c)

As automation substitutes for labour across entire economies, the net displacement of workers by machines might exacerbate the gap between returns to capital and returns to labour.

Digital and wealth inequalities as well as underemployment represent the greatest societal concerns associated with the i4.0 revolution. The largest beneficiaries of i4.0 will be the providers of intellectual and physical capital, paralleling the ongoing wealth fractionation process worldwide. Between 2009 and 2012 in the United States alone, the incomes of the top 1% of the population grew by more than 31%, compared with less than 0.5% for the remaining 99%. Middle-class income stagnation is severely affecting youths. Around 540 million young people across 25 advanced economies face the prospect of becoming poorer than their parents (WEF, 2017).

The result is a job market with strong demand at the upper- and lower-skill ends, but with a distinctive crimping in the middle. Computerized automation can now replace humans in areas such as data entry and monitoring as well as in various number-crunching tasks. Middle-skill professionals who were traditionally considered immune to robotic competition may face the greatest employment-related disruption in the i4.0 era. Customer service jobs, for example, can be undertaken by AI-driven devices and robots while insurance claims can be settled without human intervention.

Even now, certain skilled occupations are increasingly at risk as robots gain sophistication, intelligence and work scope. Up to 35% of workers in the UK, and 47% in the US, are at risk of being displaced by technology over the next 20 years (Frey & Osborne, 2013).

But while old jobs disappear, aren't new jobs created in their stead? The WEF challenges this popular assumption. Over the next five years, global employment may not rise, but rather fall by 0.5%. Only 2 million new jobs may be created worldwide by 2021 due to technological advances while 7 million jobs, mainly involving women, may be lost (WEF, 2016b). According to a UBS report, the Fourth Industrial Revolution may not be as liberating as many assume and may instead benefit the richest segments of society (Guardian, 2016).

The displacement of human labour with robots was recently presaged at global retail giant Amazon. Kiva robots, which moved boxes around Amazon's fulfilment centres, were found to be so effective that its manufacturer was promptly bought up. Thereafter, Amazon began to deploy 1,000 Kivas in its warehouses before ramping them up to 10,000 and later 15,000 units until – at last count – it had more than 45,000 robots undertaking tasks previously done by humans (Gonzales, 2016).

Nations like Malaysia therefore must rapidly retrain their Industry 3.0 workforces to remain competitive and relevant in an i4.0-based global economy. New strategic industrial policies must be instituted to harness various i4.0 opportunities while educational institutions should focus on graduating digital scientists of the future. According to the authors, emerging nations like Malaysia face two parallel but opposing undercurrents of the i4.0 era:

- Decentralization that will localize production.
- Globalization that will outsource production to another geographic location as soon as native smart factories are found to be deficient.

Industry 4.0 skills may resolve uncertainties wrought by these contrasting undercurrents. Malaysia has realized the importance of creating an i4.0-ready workforce and has commissioned several studies in this regard.

The "Malaysia 2050" study, in particular, undertaken by the Academy of Sciences Malaysia (ASM), had singled out 95 emerging technologies that would need i4.0 adoption. These technologies were clubbed under the following umbrella sectors: nanotechnology, biotechnology, neurotechnology, green technology and digital technology (ASM, 2017). Despite identifying critical high technology areas for its future industries, Malaysian planners need to bridge prevalent disconnects between i4.0-related aspirations and the actual availability of trained manpower in Malaysia –particularly in the light of an ongoing brain-drain dilemma.

While these hi-tech sectors may need longer gestation periods to realize i4.0 goals, the domestic automotive sector could be used as a technological platform to kickstart the Fourth Industrial Revolution in Malaysia. Towards this end, the evolution of Malaysia's automotive sector needs to be briefly studied.

Market and Technological Evolution

The domestic automotive sector may be the ideal launchpad for i4.0 implementation in Malaysia. During the pre-globalization era, the automobile industry was considered the *industry of industries* due to its ability to catalyse wider industrialization in various manufacturing sectors (Dicken, 2007). Nations which developed their automotive infrastructures had either progressed to become technological trailblazers or (in the case of China and India) fast-emerging hi-tech powerhouses.

Latecomers to the automotive industry generally faced an uphill task. Since economic systems were largely confined by national borders in the previous three industrial revolutions, key automotive policy interventions in latecomer nations were either limited to joint-ventures and franchising arrangements or protectionist measures against foreign imports (Wad & Govindaraju, 2011).

The Malaysian automotive industry was birthed when Ford Malaya established the first Southeast Asian assembly plant in Singapore (then a part of Malaya) in 1926 during the British colonial era. To spur industrialization in post-independence Malaysia, a nascent automotive policy was established in 1967 to encourage the local assembly of foreign vehicles. Six assembly plants were approved, with Swedish Motor Assemblies Sdn Bhd having the honour of rolling out the first locally-assembled Volvo in December 1967 (Abdulsomad, 1999).

In tandem with a growing population, rising wealth and a waning natural resource economy, the Heavy Industrial Policy of the 1980s sought to transform Malaysia's industrial landscape. The quest to create the first national car began with the inauguration of Proton in 1983 via a joint venture between the Heavy Industry Corporation of Malaysia (HICOM), Mitsubishi Motor Corporation (MMC) and Mitsubishi Corporation (MC) of Japan. Proton, which began by assembling rebadged Mitsubishi models, gradually gained traction by increasing the local contents of its vehicles. Before long, a sprawling automotive infrastructure was created with the goal of producing internationally-competitive cars (Abdulsomad, 1999).

Backed by new protectionist measures and subsidies, the first Proton car was rolled out in 1985. Similar national automotive projects followed suit in the form of small car-maker Perodua in 1993; heavy vehicle company MTB in 1994; motorcycle manufacturer MODENAS in 1995; and light vehicle commercial manufacturer INOKOM in 1997. The Malaysian government provided additional support to original equipment manufacturers (OEMs) and suppliers through the National Automotive Policy (NAP) of 2006 (MIDA, 2006; MITI, 2009).

In Proton and Perodua, Malaysia had the distinction of having the only indigenous car marques in all of Southeast Asia. By 2002, Malaysia became the 11th country in the world to attain the capability to fully design, engineer and manufacture cars from the ground up. Nonetheless, global success proved elusive due to the inability of both domestic manufacturers to compete with established foreign brands. Proton and Perodua have not flourished beyond the domestic market, with only several thousand completely built-up (CBU) vehicles exported each year (Lim, 2017).

The local automotive sector currently hosts 27 domestic and foreign brands, and contributes RM40 billion or 4% to the nation's Gross Domestic Product (GDP). The sector includes 641 parts and components manufacturers, 53,011 after-sales businesses and a 700,000-strong workforce as of end-2016. Around 80% of domestic auto components are manufactured by Malaysian-owned companies (MAI, 2017).

Malaysia therefore has a high technology ecosystem with skilled workers engaged in vehicle and component design; manufacturing; quality management; vehicle service and repairs; and recycling and remanufacturing. The domestic automotive industry had also spurred the development of auxiliary tributaries in the education, banking, finance and logistics sectors.

CURRENT CHALLENGES FACING THE INDUSTRY

Despite having built a large industrial ecosystem over the past few decades, Malaysian technology, skills and infrastructure largely belong to the Industry 3.0 era. This is clearly apparent in the automotive sector. There is a critical need to integrate and augment extant automotive capacity through i4.0 pathways. What is missing foremost is a dedicated National Industry 4.0 policy.

Policy Evolution and Concerns

Malaysia has Industry 4.0 aspirations based on Industry 3.0 blueprints. The National Automotive Policy (NAP) exemplifies this paradox. The NAP was launched in 2006 to encourage greater efficiency, value-additions and local technology content in the domestic automotive industry. National car-makers Proton and Perodua received stricter mandates to compete at the regional and global levels. The NAP was updated in 2009 to attract foreign direct investments into both entities while another revision was made in 2014 to promote the production of energy-efficient vehicles (EEVs).

Incentives offered under the updated NAP also targeted foreign OEMs to move their operations into Malaysia. The phasing-out of imported used vehicle products and the introduction of mandatory standards for parts and components as well as fuel quality were all intended to spur the long-term development of the sector. The 2014 revision (MIDA, 2006; MITI, 2009), amongst others, introduced the following measures:

- New manufacturing licenses for EEVs.
- Incentives for foreign and local companies investing in EEVs. These included pioneer status (preferential taxation for a certain number of years); incentives for research and development; and training grants for personnel in the EEV sector.
- Lifting of equity restrictions for foreign carmakers investing in EEVs with an engine capacity of maximum 1.8 litres.
- Incentives to develop various aspects of the domestic automotive ecosystem across the production value-chain.

The following key incentives were maintained from the original 2006 NAP draft:

- 100% investment tax allowance or 10-year pioneer status for the manufacture of hybrid and electric vehicles.
- 100% pioneer status for a 10-year period or investment tax allowance for a five-year period for the manufacture of specific value-added components.

Despite the policy push for next-generation EEV and hybrid vehicle production, these incentives were met with a tepid response due to a sluggish economy and a residual *subsidy culture*. More significantly, policymakers failed to prospect the future of the global automotive industry and provide solid directions to the domestic sector. There are currently no i4.0-specific allowances, incentives and clauses in the NAP.

INDUSTRY 4.0 CHALLENGES

Industry 4.0 also comes with key challenges for the global automotive sector (Masters, 2017). In the Malaysian context, some of these challenges include:

Contractor Integration

The automotive industry relies heavily on contracted manufacturing. But integrating various contractors worldwide with end-to-end (E2E) real-time monitoring capabilities requires smart systems, high-speed data connectivity and seamless user-interfaces. Malaysian automakers lack such capabilities which, in turn, require heavy domestic investments into high-speed broadband networks, 3D printing and smart systems.

Industry 4.0 benefits from ancillary industrial synergies. Towards this end, domestic infrastructural projects such as the Mass Rapid Transit (MRT), Light Rail Transit (LRT) and new highways may be used to incubate next-generation skills in the transportation sector. The domestic smart sensor industry, in particular, will benefit from ongoing upgrades and extensions in the MRT, LRT and city traffic systems.

Data Security and Connectivity

Industry 4.0 is highly dependent on data connectivity and specialized software, and may therefore be vulnerable to cybersecurity threats. Greater interconnection of software and hardware generally increases the complexity of an i4.0 system. In the event of a breach, a few hacked vehicles can spell disaster for an i4.0 auto manufacturer. Here again, Malaysia lacks one fundamental i4.0 criterion. Decentralizing the domestic automotive infrastructure may be one way of minimizing cybersecurity risks during the nascent stages of i4.0 uptake. Malaysia's broadband infrastructure also lags behind regional counterparts in terms of cost-effectiveness and speed.

Uncertainty Management

Speed will define the smart factories of tomorrow. However as systems get more ordered, connected and efficient; they become more entropic and less predictable (Fuller, 1957; Heylighen, 2002). This is called the productivity paradox. A single defective component or software may halt production and lead to costly downtime. Uncertainties can be minimized through a complex adaptive systems (CAS) approach where business units are moderately linked within a larger smart factory structure (Eisenhardt & Piezunka, 2011). The study of complexity sciences however has yet to take off in Malaysian institutes of higher learning. In the meantime, industrial training and workshops can be conducted to increase CAS awareness at the Small and Medium Enterprise (SME) levels. Such exercises come with an advantage: they can expedite CAS insight by studying problems at the fundamental levels as they occur.

Data Steering

Different data formats used in the manufacturing and engineering sectors must be integrated and inter-operationalized. Common technical standards or IoT interoperability is needed to streamline data comparability. A Chief Digital Officer (CDO) is needed to facilitate decision-making across the automotive value-chain alongside teams of digital scientists, digital architects, operational developers and cybersecurity experts. A digital thread that connects suppliers, vehicle manufacturers and customers will bring substantial benefits to the automotive industry (Hawes, 2016). Malaysia, which had hitherto focused on building Industry 3.0 ICT capabilities, needs to retrain its workforce for i4.0 digitization and interoperability.

Employment Security

Robots and 3D printing are increasingly displacing human labour due to advances in artificial intelligence. Industry 4.0 will pose myriad challenges to the Malaysian workforce. Increasing global connectivity will induce wider outsourcing of specialized data jobs, leaving non-digital natives further behind in the employment market. An open source talent identification structure is therefore needed to detect, co-opt and train a future i4.0 native workforce.

Protectionist Legacies

Small carmaker Perodua has fared far better than Proton. Perodua's strategy of rebadging Toyota-Daihatsu city car models with incremental local componentization has paid off handsomely, at least in the domestic market. In 2016, Perodua was Malaysia's largest car-maker with 207,110 units sold comprising 35.7% of the domestic market share while Proton managed to sell only 72,290 units constituting 12.5% of the local market (MAA, 2017).

Proton's decline can be attributed to poor industrial foresight, overreliance on government support, unrealistic global ambitions and a stubborn refusal to co-opt the consumer into the vehicle design and improvement process. Irate Malaysians had long noted how "export-quality" Proton cars, packed with additional accessories, were far cheaper in the UK and Australia than in Malaysia. The Malaysian consumer was effectively subsidizing superior Proton vehicles for foreign buyers. In fact, there once existed a flourishing market for rejected export-bound cars which had minor manufacturing defects as these were still considered superior to units sold domestically.

According to a 2012 Carnegie Endowment report, for every dollar of value added at international prices, Malaysian manufacturers received the equivalent of $1.57 in the domestic market. This made the automobile industry the most protected segment in the overall Malaysian manufacturing sector (Nehru, 2012).

Proton routinely ignored complaints, feedbacks and recommendations from its buyers which were copiously available in the open source domain. The success of an i4.0 enterprise however depends on its ability to co-opt the consumer (Hoffmann & Prause, 2015; Prause, 2015). By ignoring the consumer, Proton – which began as a strategic industrial project – soon veered into a symbolically-charged national prestige boondoggle. As a result, billions of ringgit was pumped into Proton over three decades to keep it afloat before Chinese automaker Geely bought a 49% stake in the flagship national automotive undertaking (NST, 2017).

Geely is expected to retain Proton's workers and infrastructure but may likely drop many vehicle models and Industry 3.0-type projects in the pipeline. At the end of the day, the largest chunk of Malaysia's i4.0 automotive sector will be Chinese-owned and operated due to dilatory policy responses to the emerging Fourth Industrial Revolution.

Economic Challenges

Proton's slide from pole position arguably began after the ASEAN Free Trade Agreement (AFTA) took effect from 2005 onwards. Tariffs imposed on regionally manufactured automotive components were gradually eased, resulting in lower prices for locally-assembled foreign vehicles. Despite Malaysia welcoming foreign automotive investments and international competition, it is Thailand that has emerged as the regional automotive hub post-AFTA.

Both the internal and external economic environments could no longer support the local automotive sector. After six consecutive years of growth, including the highest ever total industry volume (TIV) achieved in 2015, Malaysian auto sales finally plunged by 13% in 2016 (MAA, 2017) as shown on Figure 1. This downward trend is expected to continue beyond 2020.

Figure 1. Malaysia's 40-year trend in vehicle sales (MAA, 2017)

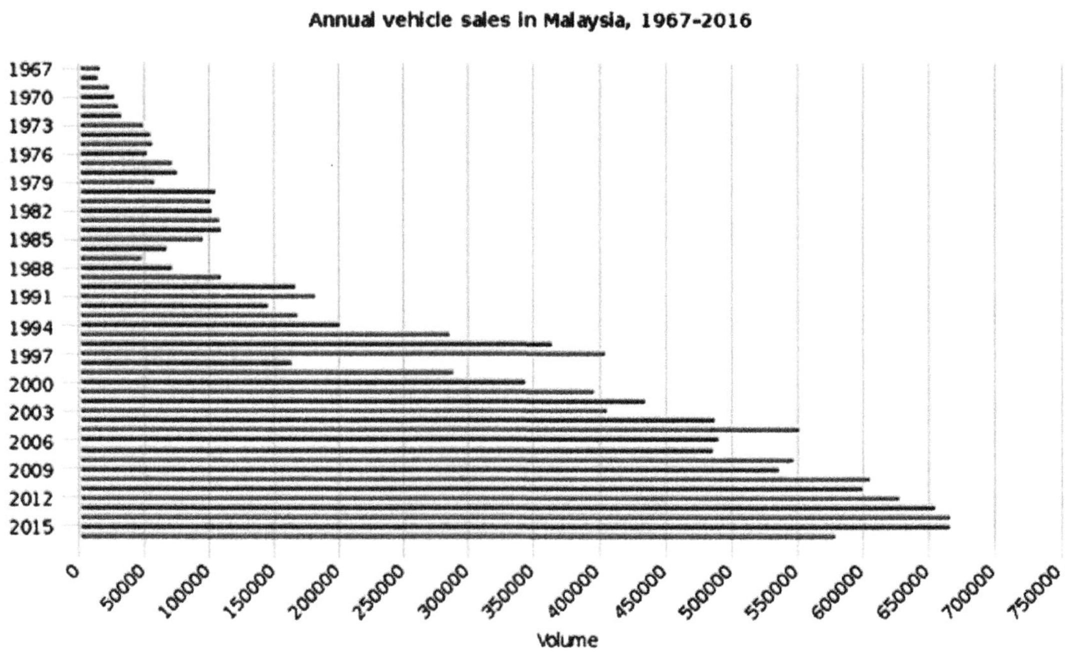

Overall consumer sentiment slumped alongside a sluggish economy. The Malaysian ringgit's slide towards becoming Asia's worst performing currency in 2015 and 2016 (Bloomberg, 2016) did not help matters. Vehicle sales were badly affected as a depreciating ringgit increased import costs for automotive tools and components. With the gradual removal of fuel subsidies, prices per litre at the pump began to surge as well despite a precipitous drop in global crude oil prices from 2014 onwards. This discouraged the purchase of new vehicles, particularly fuel-guzzling sports utility vehicles (SUVs) and pickup trucks.

The Uber and Grab phenomena – harbingers of i4.0-type services – may have also impacted auto sales as urban commuters felt a reduced need to own cars. Malaysia had the third highest car ownership rate in the world at 93%, and the highest rate of multiple car ownership with 54% of households having more than one car (Nielsen, 2014). By-lanes and streets in urban residential areas are frequently cluttered with additional household cars that cannot be accommodated inside homes and apartment compounds. This high-rate of car-ownership can be attributed to a subpar public transportation system that has festered from the late 1980s to the mid-2000s. This, in turn, forced the public to opt for Proton and Perodua vehicles as their primary modes of transport.

Malaysian household debts, which remain the highest in the region, have compounded matters further. Banks are now imposing stringent conditions on hire purchase loans for vehicles, with those earning below RM3500 per month being priced out of deposit-free car loan facilities.

It is now a make-or-break situation for the local automotive industry. The old subsidy- and tariff-driven protectionist regime and outdated industrial models can no longer prop up the sector. With regional competitors already establishing their i4.0 foundations, Malaysia needs radical new policies to overhaul its industries and orientate its workforce towards smart factories of the future.

But can the automotive sector catalyse Industry 4.0 in Malaysia the way it did with Industry 3.0 earlier?

SOLUTIONS

Industry 4.0 will fulfil the growing need for energy and resource efficiency, increased productivity and innovation as well as shorten the design-to-market developmental period for products and services. It will also facilitate end-to-end digital integration – both vertical and horizontal – across enterprise value chains (Kagermann, H., Wahlster, W., & Helbig, J., 2013). Reorientation of this scale will likely overwhelm the current capabilities of domestic industries; therefore piecemeal adaptation and localization may be an ideal way to erect the building blocks of tomorrow's smart factories. Such a staggered approach requires foresight.

Industry 4.0 Foresight

Before injecting elements of i4.0 into the Malaysian automotive sector, the government should ascertain the long-term viability of Proton and Perodua through a comprehensive foresight process (Voros, 2003). This process can begin with a series of strategic questions to triangulate the sector's long-term "possibilities" (Berkhout, F.; Hertin, J.; & Jordan, A., 2001). Such an exercise should either probe or incorporate:

Long-Term Prospects

With i4.0 being readied for adoption by global auto giants, can both national automakers compete in an increasingly borderless world? What are the long-term trends in the global transportation sector in general and the automotive industry in particular? Are there disruptive technologies or *modi vivendi* on the horizon that may render Proton and Perodua obsolete? Uber and Grab are already offering flexible transportation alternatives to commuters, reducing the need for multiple household car-ownerships. Automakers in Germany, Japan, US and UK also possess first-mover advantages in i4.0 production. Catching up via a similar developmental process would be prohibitively expensive and outright unrealistic.

Future Ownership

Should the sprawling ecosystems of Proton and Perodua be decentralized in terms of ownership? This may free up disparate entities in the value chains of both manufacturers, allowing them to engage freely with the global marketplace. This decentralizing approach may also prevent top-down political interferences of the kind that had beleaguered Proton from the 1980s to early 2000s.

Niche Focus

Should Proton and Perodua primarily focus on producing niche components and subsystems for the global automotive market and ancillary industries instead of the complete product or vehicle? This could be an ideal short-to-mid term strategy before the domestic automotive sector attains i4.0 maturity to probe longer-term horizons.

Talent Building and Retention

An i4.0 automotive ecosystem needs data scientists, algorithm architects, process experts, user interface designers and digital innovation managers, among others. Does Malaysia possess the capability to build and retain domestic experts in these areas in the coming years? Malaysia also needs to reverse its perennial brain-drain problem.

Citizen Co-Designers

The traditional industrial ecosystem was based on value-added inputs from the Triple Helix-based public, private and academic sectors. However, emerging paradigms such as Open Government, Open Innovation and Industry 4.0 require inputs from the public and consumers. Called the Quadruple Helix model, the new paradigm encourages the development of bottom-up ideas relevant to national policy-making and industrial innovation, allowing citizens and consumers to effectively co-own and propel future strategic industries (Rakhmatullin, 2014). Consumers can be co-opted as co-designers in key segments of the automotive value chain through virtual, open source channels. This will break down silos typical of prevalent enterprise planning.

Global Scanning Regimen

Firms acquire knowledge from various sources, agencies and geographical locations. These can be meshed with internal knowledge and competencies to boost innovation. Open Innovation thrives on endogenous and exogenous value additions (Chesbrough, 2003; Bartl, 2008). To thrive in the i4.0 era, domestic automotive players need to institute a permanent global technology scanning regimen to seek out, adapt and subsume the latest developments, ideas and praxis into their industries.

Incentivizing Hi-Tech SMEs

Malaysia has become complacent with its relatively profitable Industry 2.0- and 3.0-based SMEs. These SMEs in turn employ up to three million low-skilled foreign workers, amounting to 10% of Malaysia's population. There is a critical economic need to eliminate lower-skilled jobs and industries in favour of 300,000 to 400,000 unemployed Malaysians who can be incorporated into the i4.0 revolution (Ganapathy-Wallace, 2017). This move will also help maintain social and industrial stability for the foreseeable future.

Since Malaysia is a relative late-comer to the Fourth Industrial Revolution, it needs to pick and choose the right i4.0 template for local adaptation. The fractal company approach offers one such template.

The Fractal Company Model

Industries must move away from static to dynamic systems and from mechanistic to organic models of production. The single production systems of the past will soon ramify into manufacturing clusters, supply chains and collaborative organizations (Prause, 2015). Clustering creates new responsibilities and tasks as well as increased organizational complexities, necessitating the integration of information and manufacturing structures (Panetto & Molina, 2008; Raye, 2012).

An i4.0 organizational model therefore requires flexibility, environmental perceptivity and control of complexity (Shin, M.; Mun, J. & Jung, M, 2009; Koether, 2006) as the smart factory will be composed of heterogeneous resources distributed worldwide (Prause, 2015). This fragmentation of aggregate value chains may arguably create low entry barriers for SMEs and nations with lower labour costs (Dujin, A.; Geissler, C.; Horstkötter, D., 2014; Belussi & Sedita, 2010) – predicated on the condition that they incorporate i4.0 production norms.

With more than 90% of its industries composed of SMEs entailing relatively lower labour costs, Malaysia should ideally opt for the fractal company approach to kickstart its i4.0 industries. The fractal company is an open system consisting of independent units within a dynamic organizational structure. Industry 4.0 SMEs or fractal units will be characterised by a sense of self-organization, self-optimization, goal-orientation and Information and Communications Technology (ICT)-facilitated intrapreneurship (Warnecke, 1997). Such SME clusters must autonomously perceive and adapt to environmental changes and yet be able to operate within a core control architecture (Shin, M.; Mun, J. & Jung, M, 2009; Sihn, 1997).

A fractal model for Proton, for example, may consist of independent SMEs that can coordinate design and production with the national car-maker while using its available resources to pursue independent business opportunities within and outside the larger automotive realm. With technological and product multiplicity facilitated by i4.0 ecosystems, SMEs of the future will have greater adaptability, profitability and product diversity.

Building Industry 4.0 Sinews

After conducting a thorough foresight process – and if the industry's future is deemed viable – the next phase would be to study and customise i4.0 automotive templates being developed in Germany, Japan, UK and the US. Recommendations outlined by Thomas Siems (2015), congruent to the fractal company model, may act as a guidestone for the local automotive sector. These include the implementation of:

Self-Monitoring Capacity

As smart factories operate round-the-clock, equipment and product reliability will be paramount. A plethora of interconnected monitoring systems will be able to identify potential maintenance problems before they cause downtime. Embedded monitoring devices in cars, for example, will decrease the odds of unexpected breakdowns and simultaneously provide valuable feedback for maintenance interventions and future product improvements. In any case, most Malaysian industries need to invest in smart sensors and monitoring systems over the next few years, and here is where the automotive sector can take the lead.

Network Flexibility

Industry 4.0-ready automakers will be connected to manufacturing bases worldwide in order to meet the type and volume of *in situ* demand. Operations likewise can be shifted between global facilities as needed. This should prompt Malaysian auto SMEs to seek strategic tie-ups – initially in an ancillary capacity – with i4.0-ready foreign auto giants.

Capacity for Customization

Malaysian SMEs need to churn out customized products via 3D printing. Industry 4.0 not only offers mass customization prospects for the automotive industry, it will shorten delivery time for niche products. Domestic OEMs and suppliers must be attuned to changing standards and consumer demands in real-time while inventories must be kept lean to maintain market equilibrium and nimble supply chains.

RECOMMENDATIONS

To harness Industry 4.0 potentials, the Malaysian government needs to craft a robust i4.0-specific industrial masterplan. Despite having a relatively competitive workforce, Malaysian infrastructure and skills remain rooted in the Industry 3.0 paradigm. Malaysia also lacks an integrated national foresight mechanism and first-mover advantages. It is therefore pointless to plunge headlong into the i4.0 revolution without realistically assessing the current state of national readiness.

The following foundational measures may help Malaysian industries remain competitive over the next decade through the adoption of:

Open Foresight

A net-centric Open Government infrastructure must be established to include public participation in any national foresight undertaking. This will allow the public to articulate their aspirations, ideas, disagreements and suggested improvement to policies being developed by the government. The authors also recommended that an open source foresight regimen be embedded across newly-created i4.0 industrial value-chains. Smart factories cannot work without forward-thinking smart individuals. Foresight enables the identification of emerging risks and opportunities from a higher plane while smart systems can detect risks at the substrate levels of the smart factory (Maavak, 2018).

Open Foresight will also empower Malaysian industries to establish real-time synergies between smart factory clusters, thereby facilitating "smart catch-up" with global leaders in the Fourth Industrial Revolution. One of the authors of this case book chapter is currently engaged in developing a national Open Foresight model as part of his doctoral thesis.

Optimal Connectivity

Malaysia is currently ranked 16th in the world in terms of Internet penetration. Around 22 million of its 31 million citizens have access to broadband services (Yahya, 2017). However, casual social media interactions via 4G smartphones currently comprise the bulk of individual Internet usage. At the moment, Malaysian 4G infrastructure is woefully inadequate to meet the needs of Industry 4.0 which requires voluminous data flows at very high speeds. It is therefore imperative to increase fixed broadband penetration rates from the present 2.7 million subscriptions.

Malaysians are perennially overpaying for broadband services that are slower and more expensive than those available in neighbouring Thailand (Malaysian Wireless, 2016). Without world-class broadband services at affordable prices, the IoT will remain a missing backbone in Malaysia's desired smart factories.

Digital Education and Training

Digital knowledge and skills will rev the Fourth Industrial Revolution. Industry 4.0 will entail R&D and innovations in e-commerce, e-government and cybersecurity (Prause, 2015). This necessitates massive investments into Science, Technology, Engineering and Mathematics (STEM) subjects. Industry 4.0 needs smart personnel to work in tandem with smart machines which they can organically improve or co-create through integrated smart systems. Malaysia is estimated to require as many as one million science and technology workers by 2020 (ASM, 2015). Here is where i4.0-related curricula can be integrated into the national education and industrial training structures.

Cybersecurity Skills

Cybersecurity threats are surging worldwide, and may cost the world more than $6 trillion in losses by 2021. The figure was $3 trillion in 2015 (Morgan, 2016). This ominous trend cannot be ignored by i4.0 adopters as fully-digitized industries will be vulnerable to cyber-induced systems breakdowns. According to the Quann IT Security End User Study 2017, a staggering 96% of Malaysian firms had only basic or "early stage" levels of cybersecurity preparedness (Quann, 2017).

Malaysia should therefore embark on a rapid cybersecurity skills development programme without delay. One option would be to hire foreign trainers and consultants from India (another nation embarking on rapid i4.0 industrialization) on a pro-tem contingency basis.

Interoperable Software Architecture

The Malaysian government should ensure that all i4.0-related undertakings adhere to a common standard and software architecture. This will ensure integration between various SMEs in different stages of i4.0 adoption. However, the implementation of an i4.0 software architecture depends on the availability of digital scientists of the highest calibre. It is an open question whether Malaysia possesses such capabilities. An alternate approach would be to adopt software architectural templates being designed in i4.0 trailblazing nations such as Germany.

National Hybrid/EV Infrastructure

As the developed world gravitates towards hybrid and electric vehicles, Malaysia should start building a nationwide refuelling infrastructure to meet an anticipated rise in hybrid/EV machines on the road. This "halfway measure" will help transition current domestic automotive capabilities from Industry 3.0 to 4.0 levels. Such an infrastructure will also necessitate the creation of a smart electric grid which will link homes, factories, power sources, skyscrapers and fuelling stations for the multidirectional and efficient flow of electricity.

The Way Forward

While its connectivity, competency, security and inclusivity foundations are being laid down, Malaysia can begin erecting the building blocks of its i4.0 industries on a selective basis.

Instead of relying on Multinational Corporations (MNCs) to transplant their i4.0 industries and skills to Malaysia, the government can incentivize SMEs to adopt i4.0 platforms. A decentralized or fractal company approach may incentivize i4.0 uptake among SME component suppliers. As a result, a new generation of digital scientists can be gradually trained across SME horizontal value-chains. Operational missteps and production breakdowns can be minimized in relatively isolated factories during early stages of i4.0 adoption. Once these SMEs attain i4.0-level maturity, they can be steadily inducted via IoT into the larger automotive ecosystem.

It is also imperative for the government to incentivize the adoption of 3D printing among SMEs. This approach can be initially trialled on a small-scale in the automotive sector. A depreciating ringgit and a challenging employment market have caused a gradual slump in new car purchases, forcing Malaysian consumers to prolong the lifespan of their vehicles. This necessitates a larger spare parts market for older generation vehicles. However, these spare parts are relatively expensive at the moment. A set of replacement plastic door handles for a Hyundai Atos 1.1 litre (2006 production model) city car may set the owner back by RM100 in a country where the median monthly income was RM1,703 – and RM3,274 for those with tertiary education – in 2016 (DOSM, 2017).

There are lots of vehicular accessories and peripherals that can be 3D-printed and supplied by enterprising local SMEs. This leads to the question of transferring IP rights and original designs from foreign automakers. In return for the removal of remaining tariffs, the government should require foreign automakers to part with IP and design rights for basic spare parts, accessories and peripherals. The authors suggest that such a policy may release affordable spares for city cars older than 10 years; mid-range cars older than 12 years; and premium vehicles in use for more than 15 years. Since many OEMs have stopped producing original spares due to dwindling economies of scale, such components are often sourced from non-certified backyard industries in China.

From the 3D manufacture of spare parts for older vehicles, SMEs can gradually aggregate additional i4.0 capabilities to become OEM suppliers for foreign marques assembled locally. The localization of manufacture, after all, syncs with the ethos of the borderless i4.0 revolution.

An apex government body may also help oversee the development of i4.0 in Malaysia. The authors recommend the establishment of a dedicated Ministry of Industry 4.0 to institute and steer the domestic i4.0 revolution. Since the automotive industry is regarded as the "industry of industries" (Dicken, 2007), it is superbly poised to spearhead the Fourth Industrial Revolution in Malaysia.

CONCLUSION

Industry 4.0 will transform governments, industries and societies in unprecedented ways, and will empower a new generation of tech-savvy citizenry. It is poised to fundamentally change the way we live, work, and relate to one another. In its scale, scope, and complexity, the transformation wrought by i4.0 will be unlike anything experienced by mankind. It will connect global stakeholders from the public and private sectors to the academia and civil society as well as production value-chains via an *internet of things, services, data and people*.

Malaysia needs to induce a paradigm shift away from current Industry 3.0 factories and competencies to the barely-charted world of i4.0. The domestic automotive industry may be the perfect springboard for this transition, especially via a fractal company approach that focuses on i4.0 SME development.

REFERENCES

Abdulsomad, K. (1999). Promoting industrial and technological development under contrasting industrial policies: The automotive industry in Malaysia and Thailand. In K. S. Jomo, G. Felker, & R. Rasiah (Eds.), *Industrial Technology Development in Malaysia: Industry and Firm Studies* (pp. 274–300). London: Routledge.

Ahmad, H. A. (2016). *Malaysia's Performance in 2016 GE Global Innovation Barometer.* Topline Report, Malaysian Productivity Corporation. Retrieved Aug 1, 2017, from http://www.mpc.gov.my/wp-content/uploads/2016/04/Topline-2016-GE-GIB-as-at-280116.docx

ASM. (2015). *Akademi Sains Malaysia Science Outlook 2015: Action towards Vision.* Retrieved June 7, 2017, from http://mastic.mosti.gov.my/documents/10156/2d66a776-277e-4816-bce1-53a89afda5ed

ASM. (2017). *Malaysia 2050*. Policy Outline. Retrieved July 25, 2017, from http://www.akademisains.gov.my/download/Malaysia%202050%20Smart%20Communities%20Presentation%20MATRADE%2026th%20January%202017.pdf

Bartl, M. (2008). *Open Innovation!* White Paper. Munich: HYVE. Retrieved July 8, 2017, from http://www.hyve-server.de/hyveweb/cms/upload/f_1599_WhitePaper_OpenInnovation.pdf

Belussi, F., & Sedita, S. (2010). Managing the fragmented value chain of global business: Exploitative and explorative offshoring toward emerging market economies. In *The Past, Present and Future of International Business & Management, Advances in International Management* (Vol. 23, pp. 399–429). Cheltenham, UK: Emerald Group Publishing Limited. doi:10.1108/S1571-5027(2010)00000230023

Berkhout, F., Hertin, J., & Jordan, A. (2001). *Socio-economic futures in climate change impact assessment: Using scenarios as 'learning machines'*. Working Paper No. 3, July 4 2001. University of Sussex: Tyndall Centre.

Bloomberg. (2016). *Asia's Worst Currency Slump Takes Malaysian Rate Cut Off Table*. Retrieved April 25, 2017, from https://www.bloomberg.com/news/articles/2016-11-22/asia-s-worst-currency-slump-puts-malaysia-central-bank-on-guard

Brynjolfsson, E., & McAfee, A. (2016). *The Second Machine Age: Work, Progress, and Prosperity in a Time of Brilliant Technologies*. New York: W. W. Norton & Company.

Chesbrough, H. (2003). *Open Innovation: The New Imperative for Creating and Profiting from Technology*. Boston: Harvard Business School Press.

Dicken, P. (2007). *Global Shift: Mapping the Changing Contours of the World Economy*. London: Sage Publications.

DOSM. (2017). *Salaries & Wages Survey Report, Malaysia, 2016*. Department of Statistics Malaysia (DOSM). Retrieved May 27, 2017, from https://www.dosm.gov.my/v1/index.php?r=column/pdfPrev&id=U3JoKzFiekE5WFFKK0VMRWQ0a2FDQT09

Dubey, S. (2015). *How India is poised for Industry 4.0*. Retrieved June 16, 2017, from http://rvantage.net/india-poised-industry-4-0/

Dujin, A., Geissler, C., & Horstkötter, D. (2014). *INDUSTRY 4.0: The new industrial revolution*. Munich: Roland Berger Strategy Consultants.

Eisenhardt, K. M., & Piezunka, H. (2011). Complexity Theory and Corporate Strategy. The Sage Handbook of Complexity and Management. In B. McKelvey (Ed.), *The SAGE Handbook of Complexity and Management*. Sage Publications. doi:10.4135/9781446201084.n30

Engelman, R. (2015). *The Second Industrial Revolution, 1870-1914*. Retrieved July 21, 2017, from http://ushistoryscene.com/article/second-industrial-revolution/

Espinel, V. (2016). *The digital economy: What is it and how will it transform our lives?* Retrieved June 4, 2017, from https://www.weforum.org/agenda/2016/11/the-digital-economy-what-is-it-and-how-will-it-transform-our-lives/

Ford, H., & Crowther, S. (1922). *My Life and Work.* Garden City, NY: Doubleday, Page & Co.

Frey, C. B., & Osborne, M. A. (2013). *The future of employment: how susceptible are jobs to computerisation?* Working Paper. Oxford Martin School. Retrieved July 30, 2017, from http://www.futuretech.ox.ac.uk/sites/futuretech.ox.ac.uk/files/The_Future_of_Employment_OMS_Working_Paper_0.pdf

Fuller, R. B. (1938). *Nine Chains to the Moon.* New York: Anchor Books.

Fuller, R. B. (1957). A Comprehensive Anticipatory Design Science. *Royal Architectural Institute of Canada, 34.*

Ganapathy-Wallace, S. (2017). *Making Industry 4.0 a reality for Malaysia.* Retrieved Aug 31, 2017, from https://www.digitalnewsasia.com/digital-economy/making-industry-40-reality-malaysia

Gonzalez, A. (2016). *Amazon's robot army grows by 50 percent.* Retrieved Aug 25, 2017, from http://www.seattletimes.com/business/amazon/amazons-robot-army-grows/?utm_source=twitter&utm_medium=social&utm_campaign=article_left_1.1

Guardian. (2016). *Fourth industrial revolution set to benefit richest, UBS report says.* Retrieved Sept 1, 2017, from https://www.theguardian.com/business/2016/jan/19/fourth-industrial-revolution-set-to-benefit-richest-ubs-report-says

Hawes, M. (2016). *The Digitalisation of the UK Automotive Industry.* KPMG report. Retrieved Aug 18, 2017, from https://www.smmt.co.uk/wp-content/uploads/sites/2/smmt_the-digitalisation-of-the-uk-auto-industry_kpmg-apr-2017.pdf

Heylighen, F. (2002). *Complexity and Information Overload in Society: Why increasing efficiency leads to decreasing control.* Brussels: Free University of Brussels.

Hoffmann, T., & Prause, G. (2015). How to keep open-source based innovation approaches sustainable: A view from the intellectual property perspective. *Entrepreneurship and Sustainability Issues*, *2*(3), 133–141. doi:10.9770/jesi.2014.2.3(2)

Homer-Dixon, T., Walker, B., Biggs, R., Crépin, A. S., Folke, C., Lambin, E. F., ... Troell, M. (2015). Synchronous failure: The emerging causal architecture of global crisis. *Ecology and Society*, *20*(3), 6. doi:10.5751/ES-07681-200306

Kagermann, H., Wahlster, W., & Helbig, J. (2013). *Recommendations for implementing the strategic initiative INDUSTRY 4.0, White Paper.* National Academy of Science and Engineering.

Koether, R. (2006). *Taschenbuch der Logistik* (2nd ed.). Leipzig: Hanser.

Landes, D. S. (1969). *The Unbound Prometheus.* Cambridge, UK: University of Cambridge Press.

Liffler, M., & Tschiesner, A. (2013). *The Internet of Things and the future of manufacturing.* McKinsey & Company. Retrieved Nov 30, 2016, from http://www.mckinsey.com/business-functions/digital-mckinsey/our-insights/the-internet-of-things-and-the-future-of-manufacturing

Lim, A. (2017). *Holistic growth for automotive industry in 2017– MAI.* Retrieved Aug 3, 2017, from https://paultan.org/2017/01/21/holistic-growth-for-automotive-industry-in-2017-mai/

MAA. (2017). Malaysia Vehicle Sales Report for 2016. Malaysian Automotive Association (MAA) Publication.

Maavak, M. (2018). *Managing Emerging Risks through a Net-Centric Foresight Method* (Unpublished doctoral dissertation). Universiti Teknologi Malaysia, Kuala Lumpur, Malaysia.

MAI. (2017). *The Automotive Industry*. Malaysian Automotive Institute. Retrieved July 25 2017 from http://www.mai.org.my/index.php?option=com_content&view=article&id=32&Itemid=111&lang=en

Malaysian Wireless. (2016). *Average Internet Speed in Malaysia now 6.8Mbps, still slower than Thailand, Australia – Akamai.* Retrieved Aug 15, 2017, from https://www.malaysianwireless.com/2016/10/akamai-soti-malaysia-internet-speed/

Masters, K. (2017). *The Impact of Industry 4.0 on the Automotive Industry*. Flexis AG. Retrieved on Aug 14, 2017, from https://blog.flexis.com/the-impact-of-industry-4.0-on-the-automotive-industry

MIDA. (2006). *IMP3: Third Industrial Master Plan 2006-2020. Malaysia – Towards Global Competitivenes*. MITI.

MITI. (2009). *Review of National Automotive Policy*. Kuala Lumpur: MITI.

Morgan. (2016). *Cybercrime damages expected to cost the world $6 trillion by 2021*. Retrieved Aug 1, 2017, from http://www.csoonline.com/article/3110467/security/cybercrime-damages-expected-to-cost-the-world-6-trillion-by-2021.html#

Nehru, V. (2012). *Modern Industrial Policy: Lessons from Malaysia's Auto Industry*. Carnegie Endowment for International Peace report. Retrieved March 21, 2017, from http://carnegieendowment.org/2012/03/22/modern-industrial-policy-lessons-from-malaysia-s-auto-industry-pub-47625

Nielsen. (2014). *Rising Middle Class will Drive Global Automotive Demand in the Coming Two Years*. Retrieved July 17, 2017, from http://www.nielsen.com/my/en/insights/reports/2014/rising-middle-class-will-drive-global-auto-demand-in-the-coming-two-years.html

NST. (2017). *Proton would have recorded RM1 billion loss this year if not for Geely deal: Najib*. Retrieved July 30, 2017, from https://www.nst.com.my/news/nation/2017/06/245114/proton-would-have-recorded-rm1-billion-loss-year-if-not-geely-deal-najib

Panetto, H., & Molina, A. (2008). Enterprise integration and interoperability in manufacturing systems: Trends and issues. *Computers in Industry*, *59*(7), 641–646. doi:10.1016/j.compind.2007.12.010

Prause, G. (2015). Sustainable business models and structures for Industry 4.0. *Journal of Security and Sustainability Issues*, *5*(2), 159–169. doi:10.9770/jssi.2015.5.2(3)

PwC. (2015). *PwC, 2015 Global Digital IQ Survey*. Retrieved July 10, 2017 from https://www.pwc.com/gx/en/advisory-services/digital-iq-survey-2015/campaign-site/digital-iq-survey-2015.pdf

PwC. (2016). *Industry 4.0: Building the digital enterprise*. Retrieved July 11, 2017 from https://www.pwc.com/gx/en/industries/industries-4.0/landing-page/industry-4.0-building-your-digital-enterprise-april-2016.pdf

Quann. (2017). *Malaysian companies are unprepared for cyber attacks*. Retrieved May 25, 2017 from https://www.quannsecurity.com/downloads/resource/MYIDC.pdf

Rakhmatullin, R. (2014). *Triple/Quadruple Helix in the context of Smart Specialisation*. Retrieved July 19, 2017 from https://www.surrey.ac.uk/sbs/sar/centres/bcned/BCNED%20Files/1%20Ruslan_Rakhmatullin.pdf

Ramsauer, C. (2013). Industry 4.0 – Die Produktion der Zukunft. *WINGbusiness, 3/2013*, 6–12.

Raye, J. (2012). Fractal organization theory. In *Proceedings of the 56th Annual Meeting of the ISSS*. International Society for the Systems Sciences.

Rifkin, J. (2011). *The Third Industrial Revolution: How Lateral Power Is Transforming Energy, the Economy, and the World*. New York: Palgrave Macmillan.

Schwab, K. (2015). The Fourth Industrial Revolution: What It Means and How to Respond. *Foreign Affairs Magazine*. Retrieved Nov 1, 2017, from https://www.weforum.org/agenda/2016/01/the-fourth-industrial-revolution-what-it-means-and-how-to-respond/

Shin, M., Mun, J., & Jung, M. (2009). Self-evolution framework of manufacturing systems based on fractal organization. *Computers & Industrial Engineering*, *56*(3), 1029–1039. doi:10.1016/j.cie.2008.09.014

Siems, T. (2015). *Industry 4.0 in the Automotive Industry – Hype and Hurdle in One!* Retrieved July 24, 2017, from https://www.detecon.com/sites/default/files/DMR_Automotive_Hype_Siems_E_12_2015.pdf

Sihn, W. (1997). Paradigm Shift in the Corporation: The Fractal Company. *IFAC Proceedings, 30*(19), 131-136.

Travkina, I. (2015). Export and GDP Growth in Lithuania: Short-run or Middle-run Causality? *Entrepreneurship and Sustainability Issues*, *3*(1), 74–84.

Voros, J. (2003). A Generic Foresight Process Framework. *Foresight*, *5*(3), 10–21. doi:10.1108/14636680310698379

Wad, P., & Govindaraju, V. G. R. C. (2011). Automotive industry in Malaysia: An assessment of its development. *International Journal of Automotive Technology and Management*, *11*(2), 152. doi:10.1504/IJATM.2011.039542

Warnecke, H. (1996). *The Fractal Company: A Revolution in Corporate Culture*. New York: Springer-Verlag.

WEF. (2014). *The Global Competitiveness Report 2014–2015*. Retrieved July 23, 2017, from http://www3.weforum.org/docs/WEF_GlobalCompetitivenessReport_2014-15.pdf

WEF. (2016a). *Global Information Technology Report 2016*. Retrieved July 30, 2017, from http://www3.weforum.org/docs/GITR2016/WEF_GITR_Full_Report.pdf

WEF. (2016b). *The future of jobs: Employment, skills, and workforce strategy for the fourth Industrial Revolution*. Retrieved Aug 2, 2017, from http://www3.weforum.org/docs/WEF_Future_of_Jobs.pdf

WEF. (2016c). *The 10 countries best prepared for the new digital economy.* Retrieved Nov 1, 2017, from https://www.weforum.org/agenda/2016/07/countries-best-prepared-for-the-new-digital-economy/

WEF. (2017). *Global Risk Report 2017.* Retrieved Jan 20, 2017, from http://www3.weforum.org/docs/GRR17_Report_web.pdf

Yahya, B. (2017, March). *Malaysia's experience to increase broadband penetration.* Paper presented at the meeting of the Standing Committee for Economic and Commercial Cooperation of the Organization of the Islamic Cooperation (COMCEC), Ankara, Turkey.

KEY TERMS AND DEFINITIONS

Cyber Physical Systems: Describes synergistic interactions between software and physical systems, especially in a factory.

Digital IQ: The degree to which an individual or organisation understands the multifaceted nature of digital technology and weaves such knowledge into the relevant value chain.

End-to-End (E2E): Describes the beginning and end points of a method or service, eliminating as many middle levels as possible.

Internet of Things (IoT): Internet-facilitated interactions between smart devices.

Open Foresight: A quadruple helix-based foresight process that includes public participation to shape the direction of national and industrial policies.

PESTEL: A taxonomical tool used to analyse trends in the political, economic, social, technological, environmental, and legal realms.

Smart Systems: Like smart factories, smart systems may be comprised of interconnected digitized infrastructures in a non-industrial setting (e.g., sharing economy).

Taylorian Production or Taylorism: Named after Frederick Winslow Taylor (1856–1915) who promoted limited, repetitious tasking in a factory production line. The Ford Model-T was mass produced via this method.

Total Industry Volume (TIV): Total product outputs in a sector. In the automobile sector, this may include motorcycles, cars and heavy commercial vehicles.

Chapter 4
Industry 4.0 as the Last Industrial Revolution and Its Opportunities for Developing Countries

Egemen Hopali
Üsküdar University, Turkey

Özalp Vayvay
Marmara University, Turkey

ABSTRACT

In this chapter, better understanding of Industry 4.0 is presented by investigating the role of different technologies and business partners on success of Industry 4.0. Enablers for smart factory are discussed in detail, and how to match these enablers with value chain partners of Industry 4.0 are identified as a new perspective on Industry 4.0. Furthermore, the aim of this chapter is to present actions to be taken from the point of the emerging economies to sustain and increase competitive advantage by catching and implementing Industry 4.0. Consequently, Industry 4.0 can enable developing countries to get a bigger slice of the world manufacturing value chain.

INTRODUCTION

Technological developments have enabled the emerge of three main industrial era since the beginning of industrial revolution. They all increased efficiency in the industry. The recent globalization movement is challenged to meet the continuous worldwide demand for capital and consumption goods. In order to overcome this challenge, the industry should assure sustainable manufacturing.

With the fourth stage of industrialization, industry 4.0, it is expected to achieve an enlarged integration of information and communication technologies (ICT) with manufacturing. This young German term describes not only the automation of value chain items but also the integration of these instruments with

DOI: 10.4018/978-1-5225-3468-6.ch004

constant communication and real time features. This process provides an intelligent and self-adopted industry as well as, more flexible, efficient, quicker and more qualified industrial products.

Industrialization revolution started with the use of steam power at the plants in England by the end of 18th century whereas a second revolution of electricity use enabled mass production. After 1970s, third industrial revolution occurred. Thanks to this revolution, information technologies (IT) made the use automation wider in the industry. Eventually, Cyber Physical Systems (CPS) made actualization of the fourth stage of industrialization which is also known as name Industry 4.0 possible.

As a first impression, Industry 4.0 looks like the rebirth of an old paradigm, Computer Integrated Manufacturing (CIM) idea, strengthen by modern information and communication technologies (ICT). However, Industry 4.0 differentiates from CIM by its network approach which is based on the improved internet standards and ability of creating smart machines and components (Kohlberg & Zühlke, 2015).

CIM era has failed because of the challenging complexity of the required automation technology. Hence, Lean Production took part in CIM with its high effectiveness by reducing complexity and avoiding impractical or non-value-adding process steps. Therefore, Industry 4.0 vision is parallel with Lean Production and enables new implementation areas through the potential of Industry 4.0 technologies such as powerful, flexible and affordable CPS applications or extended applicability of Lean Production with various production types (Kohlberg & Zühlke, 2015).

According to three leading German associations; VDMA, Bitkom and ZVEI, contributed the definition of Industry 4.0 in spring 2014. By applying an autonomously controlled and dynamic production, Industry 4.0 should optimize the value chains. (Acatech Platform Industrie, 2014). It uses CPS instruments in order to reach increased automation. CPS is capable of working autonomously and its interaction capability with production environment makes it factory smart (Lee, 2008; Broy, 2010).

Industry 4.0 has been discovered by developed countries. The inventors of Industry 4.0 aimed to knock down competitive advantages of developing countries. By definition, developed countries where people generally have high income have a lot of industrial activities and whereas developing countries where people generally don't have high income have less industrial activities.

In this chapter, it is aimed to provide a better understanding for Industry 4.0. .How this notion was formed is presented in the following sections. The role of different technologies and business partners on success of Industry 4.0 such as cloud, intelligent robots, internet of things, simulation, big data analysis, augmented reality, cyber security; human factor is discussed and their roles in smart factory are identified by matching value chain partners with smart factory providers. It was important to match these two terms for the first time so that their roles in the smart factory system are identified. Additionally, areas of usage of industry 4.0 such as agriculture, health care, security, logistics, transportation, smart home and cities are mentioned since Industry 4.0 implementations doesn't only influence smart factories but also started to influence the daily life of people. This chapter explains how crucial Industry 4.0 is for the nation's welfare as well as its importance for daily life in many aspects. This technology proportionally grows with the market demand and the needs of customers.

The main problem is how developing countries act against the developed countries which are the inventors of Industry 4.0. This chapter mainly focuses on presenting actions to be taken by emerging economies to sustain and increase competitive advantage by catching and implementing Industry 4.0. All countries and industries are affected by this new term and they have to adopt if they are willing to save or improve their position in this competitive environment. Consequently, With Industry 4.0, developing countries like Turkey get a bigger share of the world manufacturing value chain.

VALUE CHAIN PARTNERS OF INDUSTRY 4.0

Technically, Industry 4.0 can be described as the communication between business partners, products and their environment due to increasing digitization and automation of the manufacturing as well as digital value chain creation (Lasi, H., Fettke, P., Kemper, H. G., Feld, T., & Hoffmann, M., 2014; Schmidt, R., Möhring, M., Haering, R. C., Reichstein, C., Neumaier, P., & Jozinovic, P., 2015). Therefore, production processes and simultaneous product planning increased the product quality and shortened launching time of products (Brettel, M., Friederichsen, N., & Keller M., Rosenberg, M., 2014).

Essentially, three dimensions of Industry 4.0 are required for the implementation. The horizontal integration across the entire value creation network enables customers, suppliers, and external partners to collaborate with value chain partners in a cross-company and inter-company manner (Oesterreich, T. D., & Teuteberg, F., 2016; Stock & Seliger, 2016).

The end-to-end digital integration of engineering across the entire product life cycle aims for the decrease of internal operating costs by facilitating highly customized products from the raw material acquisition to production system, and by increasing the use in production and product lifetime. Eventually, the third dimension is the vertical integration into manufacturing systems network. It aims the cross functional collaboration within different hierarchical levels of a value creation module which results in smart manufacturing (Oesterreich, T. D. & Teuteberg, F., 2016; Stock & Seliger, 2016).

Four Smart Factory providers have been identified by German Research Center of Artificial Intelligence (DKFI). Firstly, smart products recognize their production process and can communicate with smart machines. Secondly, processes can be optimized in nearly real time by Smart Planner. Furthermore, humans take a central role in the smart factory, and the innovative ICT support enables humans Smart Operators to control and supervise activities.

First advantage is the fact that smart products are intelligent items. This makes their communication with smart machines possible. In a smart factory, cyber physical devices recognize production process as opposed to old technology machines. Growing computing power and data storage skills let overall coordination through value chain partners of Industry 4.0 such as robotics, cloud or Internet of Things (IoT). On the other hand smart products are intelligent enough to plan and dispose tasks. Machine learning, machine to machine communication, human machine interaction, visualization and data analysis allow cyber physical systems to create self-learning, change production methods when necessary and to find out adequate supply of materials (Wittenberg, 2016; Neugebauer, R., Hippmann, S., Leis, & M., Landherr, M., 2016).

The way that a Smart Factory recognizes production process of cyber physical devices is handled by some value chain partners of Industry 4.0 such as intelligent robotics, cloud and IoT, which are discussed in the following section.

Robots have been widely used by manufacturers in the organizations for decades. Increasing technology and intelligent manufacturing also influenced the robotics industry. Currently, robot technology is more autonomous, flexible and prone to corporation. Furthermore, it is safer than the conventional manufacturing techniques. This situation decreases the production cost; and makes hard and subtle works easily to perform. In smart factories, improving robot technology is very convenient for the whole process of smart production. Increasing human-machine interaction is enabled by including the intelligent robots in the manufacturing process.

In the upcoming period, facilities and companies will have to share more information about products with each other. Thanks to increasing performance of cloud technology, reaction times will decrease to a level of less than seconds in the near future. Thereby, the machines and their functions in the cloud platforms will be increased and this will lead to providing a higher number of services based on the data at the manufacturing systems. Consequently, processes can be followed and control systems can be integrated with cloud which is one innovations of the Industry 4.0.

IoT was firstly defined by Kevin Ashton during a presentation in 1998.in which he mentioned that daily life objects can be combined with the sensors and Radio Frequency Identification Technology (RFID) so that these ordinary things transform to internet of things (Ashton, 2009). RFID plays a key role for IoT with its items following ability usually through Electronic Product Codes (EPC). Also, common sensor devices, barcodes and 2D codes with large scale embedded sensors can be used for IoT. Furthermore, since the items can be addressable and connected to internet, their data can flow over the computers connected to internet. These items are capable of perceiving the environment, communicating and solving the confusion. Besides, they can provide autonomous response in difficult scenarios without requiring human intervention (O'Leary, 2013; Kopetz, 2011).

Despite of the date of this definition, the first application of IoT was in 1991 with the "Trojan Room Coffee Pot" (Ashton, 2009; Santucci, 2009). Researchers inserted a video camera into a coffee machine in order to watch it when it is empty. In this way, they followed the liquid level of the coffee machine and avoided the liquid flowing upwards when the machine is empty. Thereby, this research contributed to IoT before the definition of Ashton (López de Armentia, J. & Casado-Mansilla, D., López de Ipina, D., 2012). IoT represents the immense digitization of several areas in life in the network structure. IoT assigns CPS in order to eliminate the gaps between the digital and physical domain. IoT will enable more devices, even semi-finished goods, to integrate with each other without requiring integrated data process within standard technology. Therefore, equipment in the smart factory can easily and rapidly communicate the central control systems and each other (Figure 1). Moreover, IoT applications are designed to create real time decision making processes by eliminating central control conditions of analysis and decision-making process.

IoT and its applications are crucial for successful communication between smart machines in the smart factory. Thanks to Industry 4.0 value chain partner, even millions of items can connect to each other. Therefore, it requires a flexible architecture. According to the explanation of the flexible IoT architecture, 5 layers are in conduction (Al-Fuqaha, A., Guizani, M., Mohammadi, M., Aledhari, M., & Ayyash, M., 2015). They are as follows: objects layer, object abstraction layer, service management layer, application layer and business layer (Figure 2).

In the objects layer, different information such as temperature, coordinates, humidity, mass, velocity, acceleration are obtained by sensors and actuators of several devices and then the information is collected. Plug-and-play mechanism is used in this layer in order to configure different types of items. Data is digitized and combined in the objects layer before transmitting it by secure channels to object abstraction layer. The big data which occurs based on IoT starts at this layer (Yang, Z., Yue, Y., Yang, Y., Peng, Y., Wang, X., Liu, W., 2011; Al-Fuqaha, A., Guizani, M., Mohammadi, M., Aledhari, M., & Ayyash, M., 2016).

Second layer of IoT architecture is object abstraction layer. The layer is located between objects layer and service management layer and the prior job of this layer is to safely transmit data which extracts from objects layer. Data can transmit through some technologies such as GSM, Wifi, Bluetooth, 3G besides that data management systems process and cloud computing are evaluated in this layer. Thanks to rapid

Figure 1. The Smart Factory surrounded by the IoT & Applications
Source: (Neugebauer, R., Hippmann, S., & Leis, M., Landherr, M., 2016).

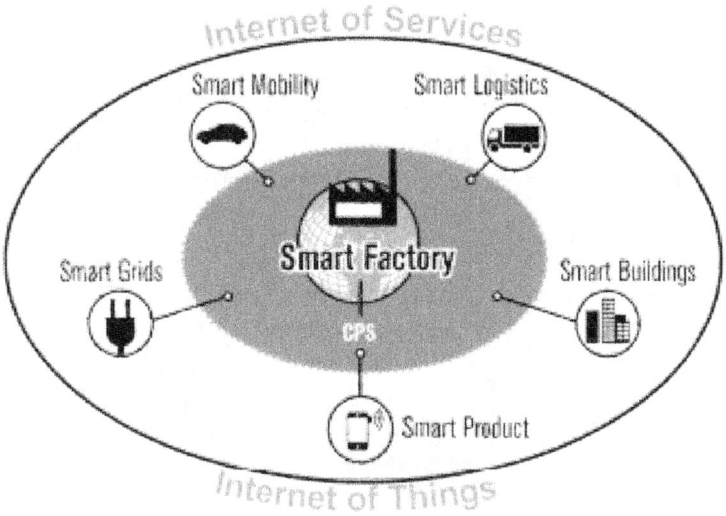

Figure 2. Five Layers of flexible IoT architecture

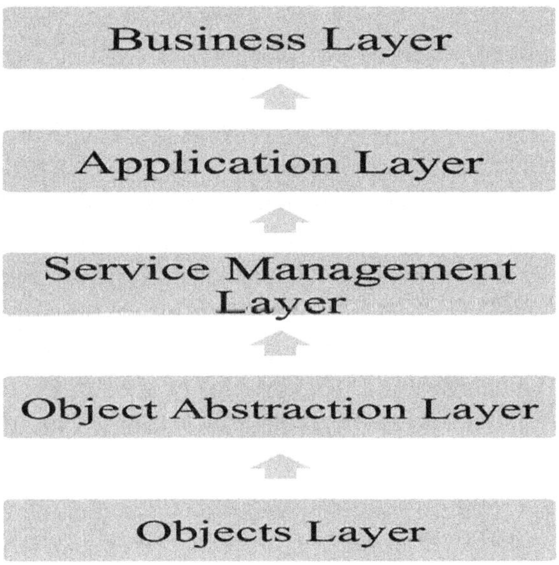

development of technology it is forecasted that 4G and 5G technology can be used in this category in the near future (Yang, Z., Yue, Y., Yang, Y., Peng, Y., Wang, X., & Liu, W., 2011; Al-Fuqaha, A., Guizani, M., Mohammadi, M., Aledhari, M., & Ayyash, M., 2016).

Service management layer is the third layer of IoT architecture. The job of this layer is to match the service based on the address and name of the service. Thus, a programmer who codes IoT applications can work with different types of things without any specific hardware platforms. Not only ease of the job of smart operators with the smart matching ability but also data processing is another feature of this layer. Through protocols and in charge of decision algorithms such as Classification and Regression Tree (CRT), Chi-squared Automatic Interaction Detection (CHAID) and Quick Unbiased Efficient Statical Tree (QUEST), information is transmitted to related services (Wu, M., Lu, T., & Ling, F., 2010; Tsai, C., Lai, C., Chiang, M., Yang, & L. T., 2014; Gubbi, J., Buyya, B., Marusic, S., & Palaniswami, M., 2013).

Fourth layer of IoT architecture is application layer. The importance of this layer for IoT is to provide users requirements by high quality into smart services. The requests of users such as humidity, velocity, acceleration are responded and provided in this layer. Service management layer caters the needs of IoT system (Wu, M., Lu, T., Ling, F., 2010; Al-Fuqaha, A., Guizani, M., Mohammadi, M., Aledhari, M., & Ayyash, M., 2016). There is a gap and ongoing debate about the description of key protocols in application layer and their scope that are being used today to apply IoT. Different needs of the communication among machines are provided by protocols such as Constrained Application Protocol (CoAP), Message Queue Telemetry Transport (MQTT), Extensible Messaging and Presence Protocol (XMPP), Representational State Transfer (RESTFUL Services), Advanced Message Queuing Protocol (AMQP), Websockets (Karagiannis, V., Chatzimisios, P., Vazquez-Gallego, F., & Alonso-Zarate, J., 2015).

Business layer locates on the top of IoT architecture layers. Fifth layer manages whole IoT activities and services as the brain of this 5 layers structure. The responsibility of constituting business model through transmitted information from application layer belongs to this layer. Previous 4 layers are monitored and managed at this layer so that decision making processes are supported and paves the way for the big data analysis. Also, business layer controls whether output, which occurs from previous layers, makes the grade or not (Yang, Z., Yue, Y., Yang, Y., Peng, Y., Wang, X., & Liu, W., 2011; Al-Fuqaha, A., Guizani, M., Mohammadi, M., Aledhari, M., & Ayyash, M., 2016).

Second enabler for the smart factory is smart planner where the process can be optimized in nearly real time. In the previous section, communication ability of smart products through robots, cloud and IoT value chain partners of Industry 4.0 is indicated. After accomplishment of this process, smart planner optimizes the data in the smart factory through other value chain partners of Industry 4.0 such as big data analysis and simulation.

The big data analysis is started applying on manufacturing systems. Its methods increase the quality of production, ease the maintenance of equipment and provide energy conservation. Not only based on manufacturing systems, but also different sources data such as corporate based and customer based are evaluated with the help of big data analysis. Thereby, this process will come to state of a standardized form in the real-time decision making. Big data analysis is linked with other value chain partners of Industry 4.0 in the smart factory. In the objects layer of IoT, data is digitized and pieced together, by this way big data starts to occur in IoT. On the other hand, big data analytics helps downstream self-organization and upstream supervisory control in the cloud. The information flow of the smart factory of Industry 4.0 as a dual closed-loop system includes big data, supervisory control terminals, interaction of big data with cloud and IoT is shown at Figure 3. If deadlocks occur in the system, load may not be balanced or the efficiency wouldn't satisfy expectations, big data analytics conducted by a programmer or a statistician should solve the problem.

Simulation is another value chain partner of Industry 4.0 is responsible for data optimization as a smart planner. 3D simulations are used in the design level of products, materials and manufacturing process. Virtual models which are constituted by real time data conduct virtual reality in order to simulate machines, products and humans in the smart factory. In this way, programmers have a chance

Figure 3. Smart Factory of Industry 4.0 Framework
Source: (Wang, S., Wan, J., Zhang, D., Li, D., Zhang, C., 2016)

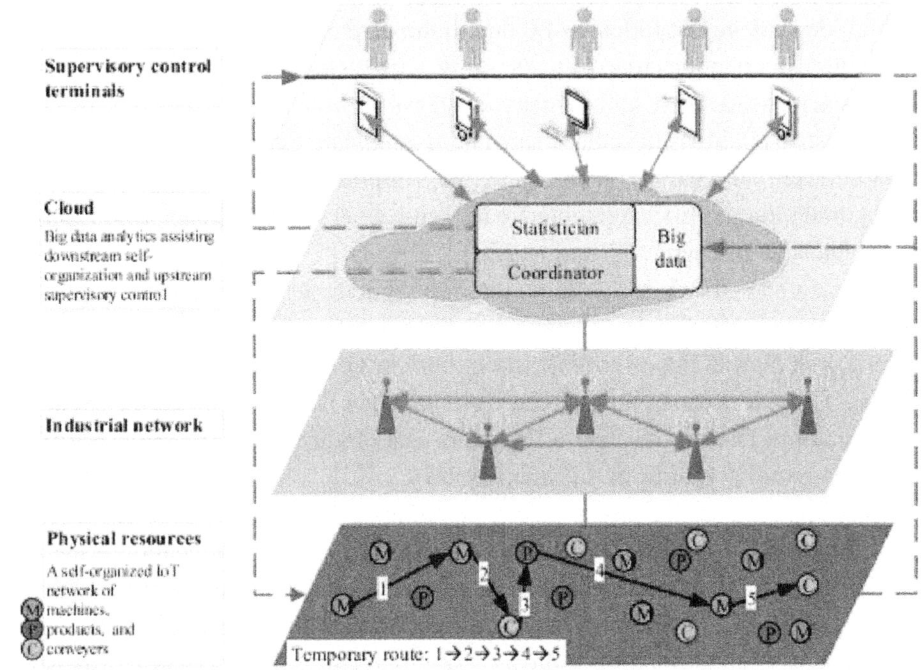

to test products at the production line before the arrangement of machine parameters by optimal data. Consequently, machine set up time decreases and the product quality increases.

If the smart factory of Industry 4.0 framework has considered, simulation programs can detect reasons of deadlock and determine appropriate strategies through verification of proposed framework and dynamic communication mechanism. Thus, the smart factory gets agile, flexible and fault-tolerance identification (Wang, S., Wan, J., Zhang, D., Li, D., & Zhang, C., 2016).

Third enabler for the smart factory is that humans take a central role in smart factory. Industry 4.0 predicts passive machines and robots take the place of labor force, which means well trained humans such as statisticians, programmers and operator will control the mechanism in the smart factory. In the first sight, the workload seems reduce but the complexity and human-machine interaction increases by Industry 4.0 (Qin, J., Liu, Y., & Grosvenor, R., 2016). The remaining tasks of operators get more complex and observing character on the account of the fact that machines undertake more tasks from operators in the smart facility. The importance of humans will be vital in the new era. The operator needs to monitor and control the whole automated production system (Wittenberg, 2016). Humans are the crucial part of the smart factory and the most important value chain partner of Industry 4.0 who is responsible for the supervisory of the systems and other value chain partners.

Fourth and the last enabler is that innovative ICT support converts humans to smart operators who control and supervise activities. ICT is one of the crucial enablers and drivers of Industry 4.0. In addition to advanced level of data storage capacity, computing power and data transmission volume, miniaturization and speed of sensor systems and integrated circuits are relatively cheap and improved enough based on the progress in hardware and software technology. This situation enables data driven production. Safety and security which are concerning data exchange and data analytics is another important aspect of ICT in data driven production. New vulnerabilities show up and they are stimulated as malicious activities based on the high dependency of Industry 4.0 due to the data exchange, digital and data driven control systems. Also, digital connections to external systems such as logistics systems, electricity suppliers or peripheral ICT systems lead safety and security concerns as well. This makes ICT is a cornerstone for the success of Industry 4.0. So as to achieve safe and trusted data exchange for data driven added value, ICT is a crucial Industry 4.0 enabler (Neugebauer, R., Hippmann, S., Leis, M., & Landherr, M., 2016). Besides, cloud, simulation and IoT; augmented reality and cyber security are another value chain partners of Industry 4.0 which are in charge of support ICT.

Currently, augmented reality is in the elementary level but in the near future augmented reality driven systems will be used more often in decision making and operation process optimization of smart factory and these systems will play an important role through improving their ability to relay real time information to employees. Operators can communicate with machines, change the parameters and get access to operational information. Thus, innovative ICT system as an Industrial 4.0 enabler makes humans smart operators who can control activities in the smart factory.

Cyber security is another value chain partners of Industry 4.0 related to ICT. Dependency of data exchange and digital control systems of required efficient cyber security precautions increases day after day. Safe and trusted communication with machines and identification of machines take an important role in order to secure critical industrial systems and production lines against cyber security threats.

Not only in the smart factory but also Industry 4.0 implementations started to influence the daily life of people through its value chain partners in different areas such as agriculture, health, security, logistics, transportation, smart home and cities (Jing, Q., Vasilakos, A. V., Wan, J., Lu, J., & Qiu, D., 2014).

In the agricultural area, Industry 4.0 can help the plant breeding by the scale of humidity and temperature and therefore provides the best conditions for the plant growth (Sato, H., Kanai, A., Tanimoto, S., & Kobayashi, T., 2016). Automatic heat and light controls in the house and offices is an Industry 4.0 benefit for the health care (Mayer, 2009). Especially, the revolution in wearable technology makes the health track easier. Industry 4.0 has the role in the design of this technology. Through the data obtained from a patient, wrong dose or wrong timing medication can be detected when the patient's past drug comparison and sudden changes perceived by wearable technology. Technology transmitted this data to the closest healthcare organization so that can prevent many damage. The data obtained from the health care services can be used to notice the illness in advanced or determine the appropriate medicine. Moreover, medical image processing analysis and biomedical signal processing are being used in order to diagnose possible illness based on electronic medical record system data (Fan, Y. J., Yin, Y. H., Da Xu, L., Zeng, Y., & Wu, F, 2014; Ukil, A., Bandyoapdhyay, S., Puri, C., & Pal, A., 2016).

Industry 4.0 contributes the smart transportation by the usage of sensors and actuators on the roads so that enables to track transportation vehicles. Additionally, it is possible to benefit from Industry 4.0 technologies in the parking systems. Sensor technologies such as camera and pressure sensors are assigned by IoT technologies so as to find and control parking space. Besides, sensors which follow the light emission of infra-red-PIR objects are in use to find parking place. These sensors collect the infrared light emission data of the cars from the interior and exterior part of parking space. This data can also be classified to detect the car. Required directive is sent out to user with SMS or a similar technology (Tsai, C., Lai, C., Chiang, M., & Yang, L. T., 2014).

Several sensors and actuators which are located in the houses and offices contribute to improve the daily life of people in different perspectives. When the owner of the house arrives to home, garage sensors perceive the car and automatically open the garage door. Automatically working coffee machines and climate control systems are such examples for smart home applications. In the smart house and office, ambient temperature can be arranged based on personal preference, hour or weather conditions automatically. Moreover, these parameters can be detected and arranged with the smart features and data mining collaboration according to habits. Smart homes and offices make the people's life easier by the help of Industry 4.0 (Mayer, 2009; Atzori, L., Iera, A., & Morabito, G., 2010). At the same time, smart environments contribute to develop industrial facility automation through proliferation of product parts which are linked to RFID tags. When the product parts arrives the processing point in the facility, tag is distinguished and read by RFID reader. Reader makes this process by the help of RFID number and other stored data. This situation stimulates machines and robots in order to make them to carry out product parts in the production line. Comparison of data obtained from RFID tag and operating system, system learns what needs to do in the following processing level. Correspondingly, under favor of mounted wireless sensors to machine monitors, product parts can be controlled whether if they surpassed the predetermined standards. If there detected surpass, smart environment makes the production stop automatically (Atzori, L., Iera, A., & Morabito, G., 2010; Spiess, P., Karnouskos, S., Guinard, D., Savio, D., Baecker, O., & De Souza, L. M. S., 2009).

Industry 4.0 has an impact on personal and social space. There are a lot of connection tools in service in order to provide the communication of people with each other and interaction between them more actively. Especially, one of the Industry 4.0 value chain partner IoT has a significant role on social network in today's world. It is possible to perceive the location of a person and share it with others. Smart applications are also evaluate the habits and suggest new places. In the same way, when people are curious about the past of ongoing activities or their personal past activities, they can use several applications like Google Calendar. Moreover, some applications such as Google Charts API make it possible to display graphs and charts about certain period of time if someone wants to see (Atzori, L., Iera, A.& Morabito, G., 2010).

Industry 4.0 not only provides innovative changes for daily life of individuals but also makes the life easier and decreases the encountered restrictions of disabled people. Industry 4.0 value chain partners especially IoT and cloud systems are in service to make disabled people's lives more comfortable. The Blind Navigation System support visually impaired people in the shopping. According to this system, supermarket separates into cells and RFID tags locates predetermined places and then these tags pin into navigation system. Individuals can use audio parsing and recognition program with the help of smart phones and state where to reach. Therefore, WLAN and Bluetooth technologies can help people, if they want to go in the supermarket. Along the same line, temperature sensors are used to get ambient temperature data. When the data exceed the predetermined value, situation is notified to a control point and then hearing impaired individuals are warned by a shining light or a vibration (Domingo, 2012; López de Armentia, J., Casado-Mansilla, D., & López de Ipina, D., 2011). New approaches are tried and experiments are made in order to improve object recognition. In this way, especially sight disabled persons can make classification on obstacles and distinguish them, recognize objects and describe from the image rapidly and accurately (Krizhevsky, A., Sutskever, I., & Hinton, G. E., 2012; Tapu, R., Mocanu, B., Bursuc, A., & Zaharia, T., 2013).

Ongoing improvement process of Industry 4.0 technologies makes the lives of individuals easier. Industry 4.0 is crucial for the nation's welfare but also it is important for the daily life within different perspectives. This technology proportionally grows based on the market demand and the needs of customers. Also, devices must be improved by matching and satisfying the customer needs with regards to their utility at any moment and anywhere (Manyika, J., Chui, M., Bughin, J., Dobbs, R., Bisson, P., & Marrs, A., 2013; Chen, F., Deng, P., Wan, J., Zhang, D., Vasilakos, A. V., & Rong, X., 2015).

INDUSTRY 4.0: A NEW CHANCE FOR DEVELOPING COUNTRIES

Industry 4.0 notion has been discovered by developed countries and in the next period, this notion and its implementations attract attention after a short time. The inventors of Industry 4.0 notion has purposed to knock down competitive advantage of Far East Countries which have low cost labor. Industry 4.0 presents an important chance to regain lost competitive advantage within years for these countries. Not only efficiency increase or high added value products, Industry 4.0 is also promise for switching traditional value chains, creating its own economy, decreasing labor force demand and increasing skilled labor.

Industry 4.0 is a convenient idea for developed countries where aging population is in the majority, they don't have enough young population to employ in the factory and these countries have educated young population who doesn't lean towards being employed in the factory. On the other hand, developing countries mostly have young population and relatively have low cost labor which provides a competitive advantage to them. If they want to save their advantageous position they have to adopt new technology. Developed countries are not only in the founder position, this new period would give them to sell their technology so that means they can be two times profitable if developing countries couldn't keep in step with.

In this new digital era, developing countries need to have talented engineers who have a comprehensive knowledge of software, able to design smart systems, not only work with robots but also produce intelligent robots so that makes them stronger and provides the fundamental but probably the powerful precaution. While the world is taking a digital shape, the countries where technology is imported instead of producing, they will become dependent of designers of digital world. For this reason, it is not enough to become suitable for Industry 4.0 and build only factories to adopt this new approach.

Emerging economies have to follow developments and if they aim for take part in the developed economies in the future, it is crucial to be one of the implementer of Industry 4.0 and avoid of losing low cost labor or logistics advantages in the new period. There are some competitive advantages in the perspective of developing economies such as low-cost labor and strategic geographic locations so that enables them currently to take part in global value chain and strengthen their exportation platforms, while there are some structural hurdles to implement Industry 4.0. Every country and each industry need to start implementing Industry 4.0, if they don't want to fall behind their rivals in the new period.

The speed and approach for implementing Industry 4.0 differs from country to country. The priority of countries, which have high product range, is that providing benefits from flexibility to increase productivity. Quality-focused approach is adopted by countries, which have influence on some industries such as pharmaceutical, health or recycling, in order to decrease deficient products. Countries where these types of industries are in the majority should focus on implement Industry 4.0 in order to optimize systems through data analysis. On the other hand, countries where labor cost is high and applying outsource activities sometimes because of the relative low cost labor of developing countries, increase automation rate in manufacturing and create demand for skilled labor. As it is seen, Industry 4.0 has to be implemented into every sector by countries if they want to have competitive advantage in the new period. Future manufacturing vision changes and the structure of factory, business, products and customers are influenced by this young term.

In the near future, old style factory will disappear and smart factory will take the place of it in everywhere. Smart factory has a conscious and intelligent structure so that enables exchange information automatically and connect the whole factory through intelligent actors such as sensors, robots, conveyors, actuators. Value chain partners of Industry 4.0 like IoT, robots, big data analysis, cloud, augmented reality allows smart factory to control this structure independently.

Industry 4.0 influences future business network through its self-organizing ability and transmission feature of real time responses among various factories, companies, suppliers, resources, customers and every kind of organizations. Whole actors can reach maximum profit with limited sharing resources by optimizing their configuration in real time (Qin, J., Liu, Y., & Grosvenor, R., 2016). Inventory problems can be a part of the history through this innovation.

Smart factory produces smart products which are embedded with sensors. This innovative product enables users to identify and follow it and processors carry information so that allow customers to benefit from functional guidance and transmit the voice of customers to manufacturers. One of the Industry 4.0 value chain partners, IoT, assigns CPS in order to close the gaps between the digital and physical domain. Therefore this technology enable more devices, even semi-finished goods, to integrate each other without doing integrated data process within standard technology. In this way, equipments in the smart factory can easily and rapidly communicate with the central control systems and each other. Furthermore, it seems that Industry 4.0 makes it possible decision-making process within real time through removing central control conditions of analysis and decision making.

In the new period, customers take advantage of Industry 4.0. Customers should order every kind of products, whenever they want without availability restriction. Furthermore, customers can know the production information of the smart products, benefit from functional guidance and could change their orders or ideas about the products any time (Qin, J., Liu, Y., & Grosvenor, R., 2016).

As we have seen, Industry 4.0 changes the aspect of factory, business, products and customers. Especially developing countries must be ready to this industrial revolution to stay competitive with developed countries. In the first sight, developed countries should focus on increase automation in manufacturing process to avoid of high cost labor. Contrary to this, developing countries have low cost labor force and this currently provides a competitive advantage. But this advantage will not continue so long. They have to take action and need to change systems to adopt Industry 4.0 for automation in order to save their competitive advantage based on low cost labor force while attempt to improve quality-focused and flexible production through Industry 4.0 to gain competitive advantage against developed countries in other industries.

There are some structural hurdles for developing countries to implement Industry 4.0. Restricted labor force is one of them; this obstacle slows down to adopt new technology. In addition to that, labor force shows changes mostly from industry to service sectors in developing countries. Also, low share of value-added products in whole production creates a drawback, while the demand for value-added products increases rest of the world.

Correct strategies and rational move can create a positive circle (Figure 4) for developing countries. Industry 4.0 is a revolution was founded and implemented firstly by developed countries but catching this revolution gives an opportunity to change global economics role of developing countries.

Figure 4. The Impact of Industry 4.0 over Developing Countries

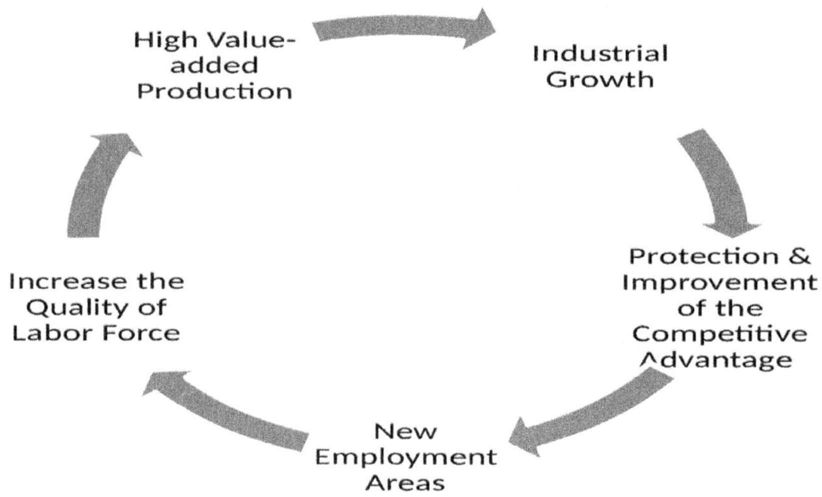

The impact of Industry 4.0 over developing countries is shown by Figure 4. Industry 4.0 creates high value-added production and it allows industrial growth years by years. Developing countries have currently an advantage based on the low-cost labor forces and Industry 4.0 is crucial to carry on this advantage against developed countries. Not only smart factory and automation features of Industry 4.0 but also other aspects of this revolution such as flexible production or quality-focused innovations will create new employment areas and increase the quality of labor force.

In the perspective of developing countries, Industry 4.0 provides the realization of economic growth. Several components such as available products, increasing demand for customized products, improving global integration and acquired revenue from global value chain stimulate this economic growth. Correspondingly this economic growth, especially local investments will increase in order to integrate Industry 4.0 technology much more into production systems. Production efficiency and customer satisfaction will increase as a result of Industry 4.0. Integrated smart machines rapidly detect the failures in production line and make the quality control of products. This process will become smarter with big data analysis.

Industry 4.0 will change the features of white color workers and oily rags. Companies need to have more competent labor force in order to manage new production technology and increase their revenue in the integrated digital world. Especially unqualified workers in the production, quality and maintenance will be replaced by automation systems. Due to the changing structure of labor force, departments which directly contacted with customers such as marketing, sales, automation, information technologies and R&D should become widespread. Especially, demand will increase for such employers who have comprehensive knowledge on software and have competence on digital systems.

Industry 4.0 technologies can be applied in the basis of companies but it is not enough for developing countries. Developing countries have to follow changes and if their goal is to take part in developed economies in the future, it is crucial to become one of the implementer of Industry 4.0 not only in company level. For this reason, it is mandatory to implement an integrative industry strategy and conversion program.

CONCLUSION

In this chapter, Industry 4.0 is investigated in detail starting from the occurrence of this young notion. Value chain partners of Industry 4.0 such as cloud, intelligent robots, IoT, simulation, big data analysis, augmented reality, cyber security and humans are discussed and their roles in smart factory are identified by matching value chain partners with enablers for smart factory. It is important that to match these two terms for the first time and so that their roles are identified in the smart factory system.

Not only in the smart factory but also Industry 4.0 implementations started to influence the daily life of people through its value chain partners in different areas such as agriculture, health care, security, logistics, transportation, smart home and cities. Ongoing improvement process of Industry 4.0 technologies makes the lives of individuals easier. Industry 4.0 is crucial for the nation's welfare but also it is important for the daily life within different perspectives. This technology proportionally grows with the market demand and the needs of customers. Also, devices must be improved by matching and satisfying the customer needs with regards to their utility at any moment and anywhere (Manyika, J., Chui, M., Bughin, J., Dobbs, R., Bisson, P., & Marrs, A., 2013; Chen, F., Deng, P., Wan, J., Zhang, D., Vasilakos, A. V., & Rong, X., 2015). Developing countries should adopt Industry 4.0 not only for its production efficiency but also for public welfare.

Industry 4.0 is a revolution discovered by developed countries. All the countries and the industries are affected by this new term and they have to adopt if they are willing to save or improve their competitive advantage. The speed and approach for implementing Industry 4.0 differs from country to country. The priority of countries changes based on their strong and weak sides. Developed countries particularly pay attention to automation in order to avoid high cost labor force, while developing countries should focus on flexible or quality-based production through improved Industry 4.0 technology. Developing countries have to adopt this revolution as soon as possible; otherwise they can lose low cost labor force advantage. But if they overcome this period quickly and they can implement Industry 4.0 technology into their systems, this industrial revolution can change the role of countries in the global economy.

Emerging economies have to decide where to implement Industry 4.0 at first. They have to consider structural hurdles and take precautions to overcome these obstacles. Low cost labor force and geographical advantages such as the logistics or market advantages must be used. By this way, Industry 4.0 can provide high value-added production, industrial growth, protection and improvement of competitive advantage, new employment areas and increases the quality of labor force. Consequently, Industry 4.0 enables developing countries to get a bigger slice of the world manufacturing value chain.

REFERENCES

Acatech-Platform Industrie 4.0. (2014). *Industrie 4.0- Whitepaper Fue Themen*. Available at http://www.acatech.de/fileadmin/user_upload/Baumstruktur_nach_Website/Acatech/root/de/Aktuelles__Presse/Presseinfos__News/ab_2014/Whitepaper_Industrie_4.0.pdf

Al-Fuqaha, A., Guizani, M., Mohammadi, M., Aledhari, M., & Ayyash, M. (2015). Internet of things: A survey on enabling technologies, protocols, and applications. *IEEE Communications Surveys and Tutorials*, *17*(4), 2347–2376. doi:10.1109/COMST.2015.2444095

Ashton, K. (2009). That 'internet of things' thing. *RFiD Journal*, *22*, 97–114.

Atzori, L., Iera, A., & Morabito, G. (2010). The internet of things: A survey. *Computer Networks*, *54*(15), 2787–2805. doi:10.1016/j.comnet.2010.05.010

Brettel, M., Friederichsen, N., Keller, M., & Rosenberg, M. (2014). How virtualization, decentralization and network building change the manufacturing landscape: An industry 4.0 perspective, Int. Mech. *J. Aerosp. Ind. Mechatron. Manuf. Eng*, *8*(1).

Broy, M. (2010). *Cyber – Physical Systems: Innovation durch softwareintensive eingebettete Systeme*. Berlin: Springer Verlag. doi:10.1007/978-3-642-14901-6

Chen, F., Deng, P., Wan, J., Zhang, D., Vasilakos, A. V., & Rong, X. (2015). Data mining for the internet of things: Literature review and challenges. *International Journal of Distributed Sensor Networks*, *2015*, 12.

Domingo, M. C. (2012). An overview of the Internet of Things for people with disabilities. *Journal of Network and Computer Applications*, *35*(2), 584–596. doi:10.1016/j.jnca.2011.10.015

Fan, Y. J., Yin, Y. H., Da Xu, L., Zeng, Y., & Wu, F. (2014). IoT based smart rehabilitation system. *IEEE Transactions on Industrial Informatics*, *10*(2), 1568–1577. doi:10.1109/TII.2014.2302583

Gubbi, J., Buyya, B., Marusic, S., & Palaniswami, M. (2013). Internet of Things (IoT): A vision, architectural elements, and future directions. *Future Generation Computer Systems*, *29*(7), 1645–1660. doi:10.1016/j.future.2013.01.010

Jing, Q., Vasilakos, A. V., Wan, J., Lu, J., & Qiu, D. (2014). Security of the internet of things: Perspectives and challenges. *Wireless Networks*, *20*(8), 2481–2501. doi:10.100711276-014-0761-7

Karagiannis, V., Chatzimisios, P., Vazquez-Gallego, F., & Alonso-Zarate, J. (2015). A Survey on Application Layer Protocols for the Internet of Things. *Transaction on IoT and Cloud Computing*, *3*(1), 11–17.

Kohlberg, D., & Zühlke, D. (2015). Lean Automation enabled by Industry 4.0 Technologies. *IFAC – PapersOnLine, 48*(3), 1870-1875.

Kopetz, H. (2011). Internet of things. In Real-time systems. Springer.

Krizhevsky, A., Sutskever, I., & Hinton, G. E. (2012). Imagenet classification with deep convolutional neural networks. *Advances in Neural Information Processing Systems*, 1097–1105.

Lasi, H., Fettke, P., Kemper, H. G., Feld, T., & Hoffmann, M. (2014). Industrie 4.0. *Business & Information Systems Engineering*, *6*(4), 239–242. doi:10.100712599-014-0334-4

Lee, E. A. (2008). Cyber Physical Systems: Design Challenges. *2008 11th IEEE International Symposium on Object Oriented Real – Time Distributed Computing (ISORC)*, 363-369.

López de Armentia, J., Casado-Mansilla, D., & López de Ipina, D. (2012). Fighting against vampire appliances through eco-aware things. *Innovative Mobile and Internet Services in Ubiquitous Computing (IMIS), 2012 Sixth International Conference*, 868-873. 10.1109/IMIS.2012.112

López de Ipiña, D., Lorido, T., & López, U. (2011). Indoor navigation and product recognition for blind people assisted shopping. *International Workshop on Ambient Assisted Living*, 33-40. 10.1007/978-3-642-21303-8_5

Manyika, J., Chui, M., Bughin, J., Dobbs, R., Bisson, P., & Marrs, A. (2013). *Disruptive technologies: Advances that will transform life, business, and the global economy*. McKinsey Global Institute San Francisco.

Mayer, R. E. (2009). *Multimedia learning*. Cambridge University Press. doi:10.1017/CBO9780511811678

Neugebauer, R., Hippmann, S., Leis, M., & Landherr, M. (2016). Industrie 4.0- From the perspective of applied research. *49th CIRP Conference on Manufacturing Systems, Procedia CIRP 57*, 2-7. 10.1016/j.procir.2016.11.002

O'Leary, D. E. (2013). 'Big Data', The 'Internet Of Things' and The 'Internet Of Signs.' *Intelligent Systems in Accounting, Finance & Management*, *20*(1), 53–65. doi:10.1002/isaf.1336

Oesterreich, T. D., & Teuteberg, F. (2016). Understanding the implications of digitization and automation in the context of Industry 4.0: A triangulation approach and elements of a research agenda for the construction industry. *Computers in Industry*, *83*, 121–139. doi:10.1016/j.compind.2016.09.006

Qin, J., Liu, Y., & Grosvenor, R. (2016). A categorical framework of manufacturing for Industry 4.0 and beyond. *Procedia CIRP*, *52*, 173–178. doi:10.1016/j.procir.2016.08.005

Santucci, G. (2009). *From internet of data to internet of things*. Paper for the International Conference on Future Trends of the Internet.

Sato, H., Kanai, A., Tanimoto, S., & Kobayashi, T. (2016). Establishing Trust in the Emerging Era of IoT. *2016 IEEE Symposium on Service-Oriented System Engineering (SOSE)*, 398-406. 10.1109/SOSE.2016.50

Schmidt, R., Möhring, M., Haering, R. C., Reichstein, C., Neumaier, P., & Jozinovic, P. (2015). Industry 4.0 - Potentials for creating smart products: Empirical research results. In W. Abramowicz (Ed.), Business Information Systems. Springer International Publishing.

Spiess, P., Karnouskos, S., Guinard, D., Savio, D., Baecker, O., & De Souza, L. M. S. (2009). SOA-based integration of the internet of things in enterprise services. *Web Services, 2009. ICWS 2009. IEEE International Conference on*, 968-975.

Stock, T., & Seliger, G. (2016). Opportunities of Sustainable Manufacturing in Industry 4.0. *Procedia CIRP, 40*, 536-541.

Tapu, R., Mocanu, B., Bursuc, A., & Zaharia, T. (2013). A smartphone-based obstacle detection and classification system for assisting visually impaired people. *Proceedings of the IEEE International Conference on Computer Vision Workshops*, 444-451. 10.1109/ICCVW.2013.65

Tsai, C., Lai, C., Chiang, M., & Yang, L. T. (2014). Data Mining for Internet of Things: A Survey. *IEEE Communications Surveys and Tutorials*, *16*(1), 77–97. doi:10.1109/SURV.2013.103013.00206

Ukil, A., Bandyoapdhyay, S., Puri, C., & Pal, A. (2016). IoT Healthcare Analytics: The Importance of Anomaly Detection. *2016 IEEE 30th International Conference on Advanced Information Networking and Applications (AINA)*, 994-997.

Wang, S., Wan, J., Zhang, D., Li, D., & Zhang, C. (2016). Towards smart factory for Industry 4.0: A self-organized multi-agent system with big data based feedback and coordination. *Computer Networks*, *101*, 158–168. doi:10.1016/j.comnet.2015.12.017

Wittenberg, C. (2016). Human-CPS Interaction – requirements and human-machine interaction methods for the Industry 4.0. *IFAC-PapersOnLine, 49*(19), 420-425.

Wu, M., Lu, T., & Ling, F. (2010). Research on architecture of Internet of Things. In *3rd International Conference on Advanced Computer Theory and Engineering (ICACTE)*, Washington, DC: IEEE.

Yang, Z., Yue, Y., Yang, Y., Peng, Y., Wang, X., & Liu, W. (2011). Study and application on the architecture and key technologies for IoT. *International Conference on Multimedia Technology (ICMT)*, 747-751.

KEY TERMS AND DEFINITIONS

Cyber Security: Safe and trusted communication among machines.

ICT: An Industry 4.0 driver that converts humans to smart operators who control and supervise activities.

IoT: Immense digitization of smart systems.

Simulation: An Industry 4.0 value chain partner responsible for data optimization as a smart planner.

Smart Factory: Awareness of manufacturing process of cyber physical devices.

Smart Product: Intelligent item that enables communication with smart machines.

Section 2

Management, Strategy, and Performance

Chapter 5
Management Challenges in the Digital Era

Radek Liska
University of Economics, Czech Republic

ABSTRACT

The chapter gives overview of factors that business leaders need to consider while leading their enterprise to new era of industry. Robotics, automation, and digitalization represent both an opportunity and a threat to any impacted company. The chapter introduces analysis of current trends in industrial world with focus on OECD countries. Also, it provides an overall summary of current changes to managerial roles and suggests how to steer transformation endeavor from multiple viewpoints. Furthermore, a set of general recommendations on reorganization matters towards agile structure is presented. Other challenges arising from i4.0 such as adjustments in education process and changes to employees' mindset are also addressed from managerial viewpoint. The final part of the chapter points out main conclusions and core message as well as areas of further research.

INTRODUCTION

Digital transformation represents a challenge to everyone in modern industry. Employees of impacted companies need to reconsider their skill sets and educate themselves to stay valuable even in an automated and digitalized process structure. Business leaders are under pressure to rebuild processes in entire companies to make them agile enough to sustain upcoming changes and later profit from such changes while redeploying the current labour force. Governments need to act and reflect changes in the structure of the desired workforce and enhance the education process accordingly to deliver technologically resourceful individuals.

Major changes such as this one, had occurred in the past. Hence, there are numerous approaches on how to deal with them. It is important to consider the nature and scale of the current changes and construct strategies that will endure rapid development and will be able to adopt emerging technologies. This chapter clarifies business and social development linked to current i4.0 transformation and gives set of recommendations on how to deal with them, while indicating possible future challenges and opportunities.

DOI: 10.4018/978-1-5225-3468-6.ch005

BACKGROUND

This chapter mergers various research findings from large-scale studies such as ones conducted by OECD, McKinley consulting company, KPMG, Harvard University, and other institutions with a wide international impact.

The topic is discussed from multiple perspectives, both at the corporate/company level as well as from the individual. Regardless of being an entry level employee or an executive responsible for taking the right course of action while considering all discussed factors, everyone is impacted.

A set of recommendations is formulated as a conclusion of this chapter to summarize the most common suggestions presented in current published research. The i4.0 phenomenon provides numerous opportunities to grow both for the companies and employees as well. If well driven, transformation to the digital enterprise can be conducted without a massive negative impact on business processes and employee base.

ERA OF DIGITAL MANAGEMENT

Most business leaders are aware of the large changes that currently impact most industries. It is crucial that company executives understand what challenges they must deal with in the upcoming years. As well as what should be considered in advance to deliver successful business transformation in a changing and innovative world.

Issues, Controversies, and Problems

The impact of digital transformation is not only limited to technical aspects of the global industry. It also brings new challenges in the field of managerial work such as leading and managing teams, companies, or organizations. Many of the arising challenges are omnipresent in the business world, however there are some specifics exclusive to i4.0 transformation.

The everchanging way to manage organizations includes new ICT trends and globalization may be easy to comprehend by many managers, hence there is a risk to not recognize the full scale of this specific era. The inability to recognize such i4.0 specific trends may prove virulent to any future company development or managerial endeavours.

There are four main areas of interest that companies are most likely to encounter in the upcoming years. Any individual with a somewhat leading role in an organization that deals with i4.0 phenomenon, should consider the following questions:

- Change in structure of teams and employee's skillset – the structure of desired education and skill background is changing in all impacted departments.
- Possible employee jobs reduction that currently occupy automatable jobs – the company leadership may face pressure from labour unions and employees themselves to stall implementation of solutions that would lead to jobs reduction.
- Lack of support/motivation among company employees – the i4.0 trends are perceived as factors representing significant change to jobs framework and could lead to outplacements.

- The company in a post i4.0 environment – How to manage a company that underwent dramatic changes in the structure of the workforce? The company itself may need a new managerial model, respecting different processes and employee structure.

These challenging managerial questions are further discussed in this chapter.

Impact of Automation and i4.0 on OECD Countries and Industry Segments

Based on an extensive research conducted across eight hundred occupations analysing over 2 000 work activates - highly structured physical activities and data collection and processing are most likely to be automated in the upcoming future. These activities account for 51% of the economic activity in the United States, delivering up to 2,7 trillion USD to the US population in wages (Manyika, J., & Chui, M. 2017). The research also suggests that half of work activities conducted by humans today could be automated by 2055. However, such long-term prediction could be influenced by economic and other factors to such an extent that mentioned state may become a reality up to twenty years later. On the other hand, variable factors may boost necessary changes and deliver expected extent of automation many years earlier.

Five selected factors determine how rapidly the automation and other i4.0 aspects are likely to be implemented into business processes in general.

1. *Technical feasibility* of solutions and its implementation. Despite the fact, that in some activates the technology can outperform human worker. There is still a necessity for further research and development to invent technical solutions for less automation prone fields of industry. Moreover, combining multiple currently available solutions may bring both speedups due to multiplied efficiency and slowdowns due to multiplied complexity (D. Pyle & C. S. Jose, 2015).
2. *Implementation and development costs* are perhaps the most visible factors that business leaders must consider while evaluating their i4.0 and automation capabilities. Depending on the industry sector, the structure of the cost and difficulty of implementation will vary extensively. The same goes for the scope of the implemented solution that stretches from basic software solutions to fully automated robotics in manufacturing facilities - with countless levels of hardware and software combining solutions in between (D. Pyle & C. S. Jose, 2015). Considering Moore's law, an exponential drop in the cost of such solution is to be expected. Hence, the implementation of i4.0 solution could accelerate rapidly in later years of the predicted timeline.
3. *Dynamics of the labour market* and its geographical diversity also represent one of the key factors that influence the potential of i4.0 implementations. Main managerial consideration should be in the matters of macroeconomics – supply x demand on the labour market and resulting wages determine when it will be cost effective to deploy automation (Douglas, D. K. 2017). Hereafter, deployment of such solutions is more likely to occur earlier in regions with high average wages compared to low wage countries (that also usually lack sufficient capital to acquire necessary technologies).
4. *Economic benefits* that are not only tied to above mentioned labour cost savings but to increased productivity, improved quality and higher safety should be considered as well. These possible savings could represent perhaps the largest benefits in the overall automation processes. Reduced maintenance cost for large-scale facilities can be the main economic driver for implementation in many sectors of advanced industrial economies.

5. *Social acceptance and regulations* as they stand today represent mostly barriers for i4.0 implementations. Starting from the reluctant response of employees arising from the fear of being replaced by machinery, to negative perception of human beings replaced by automated solutions from the customer side (especially in the service sector). However, as green technologies received subsidies by governments; it is the same case for automation and i4.0 technologies in some studied countries. Once the society fully understands and accepts the possible overall benefits, governments are likely to deploy the same process to sponsor such projects (Gates, D., & Bremicker, M. 2017).

Any responsible individual should recognize these five factors and observe their development over the longtime period to be able to provide an adequate reaction to the developing situation. Also, it is crucial to acknowledge that the ratio of influence of the above-listed factors varies depending on the selected country and industry field (Manyika, J., & Chui, M. 2017).

Most of the jobs have a partial potential to be automated, meaning that *the whole job process cannot be simply automated, but the particular activates in the job could be replaced by an automated process* to a smaller or greater extent.

Automated processes could reach the production equivalent of up to 1.2 billion of current working employees - considering the global workforce as a whole. That would also represent almost 15 trillion USD in allocated wages. Based on the methodology, the five largest economies in Europe (UK, France, Germany, Spain, and Italy) have the potential of up to 62 million full-time jobs to be automated that would equal to 1,6 trillion EUR in wages. Globally, China and India could face a challenge of about 700 million automated full-time jobs, representing the highest automation potential globally (Manyika, J. & Chui, M. 2017).

The jobs reduction that automation brings is expected to provide growth in productivity. Based on the modelling considered earlier, the production growth is expected to average from 0,8% to 1,4% annually (Manyika, J., & Chui, M. 2017).

Figure 1. Overall cumulative percent of occupations with selected technical automation potential
Source: McKinsey Global Institute (2017). A future that works: Automation, employment, and productivity. McKinsey and Company.

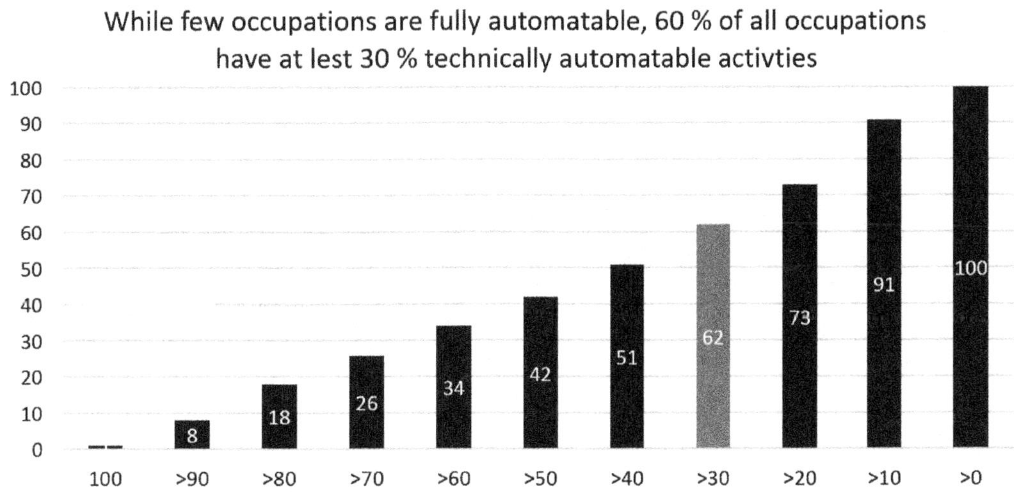

The OECD calculations presented in Figure 2 indicate which states are to be most impacted by the automation of production. Whereas, three out of the top four have one thing in common i.e., the automotive industry is the main export article of the economy: Slovakia 27%, Czech Republic 20%, and Germany 18% (CID, Harvard University, 2017). Slovakia and Czech Republic have been on top of the global list when it comes to car production per capita for a considerable number of years while Germany ranks fourth. Proving that both economies are heavily dependent on the automotive industry and car exports, making them very prone to the negative aspects and challenges that automation brings.

On the other hand, two other OECD countries with a significant automotive production industry, rank among the bottom five in the Figure 2. Japan ranks as third globally in the total number of produced cars, fifth in per capita production, creating 22% of its export revenue from the automotive industry. South Korea globally ranks as sixth in total and third in per capita car production, while automotive represents 12% of its exports (CID, Harvard University, 2017).

The risk of job loss because of automation is less substantial than sometimes claimed but many jobs will see radical change. (CID, Harvard University, 2017)

What can high-risk countries in Central Europe adopt from their Asian counterparts, to reduce possible impact of automation? Viewing the top three least automation prone EU countries, there are significant structural differences compared to the discussed automotive based nations. Estonia leads its exports with telecommunications 15%, Finland with paper production 13% and Belgium with pharmaceutical industry 11% (CID, Harvard University, 2017). An ultimate solution to reduce the risk of negative automation impact in Europe seems to be obvious, changing the structure of the economy.

However, it is obvious that such a solution is not feasible. Shifting the economy of the whole country because the currently embedded business models need to evolve is undesirable. While automation may represent a challenge in matters of technical advancements and social/employment questions, it is paramount to exploit all benefits to boost overall productivity. Therefore, impacted countries should seek other options on how to mitigate possible negative repercussions of automation and related changes. The

Figure 2. Percentage of workers in jobs at high and medium risk of automation
Note: Data for the United Kingdom corresponds to England and Northern Ireland. Data for Belgium corresponds to the Flemish Community.
Source: OECD calculations based on the Survey of Adult Skills (PIAAC) (2012) and Arntz, M. T. Gregory and U. Zierahn (2016), "The Risk of Automation for Jobs in OECD Countries: A Comparative Analysis", OECD Social, Employment and Migration Working Papers, No. 189, OECD Publishing, Paris.

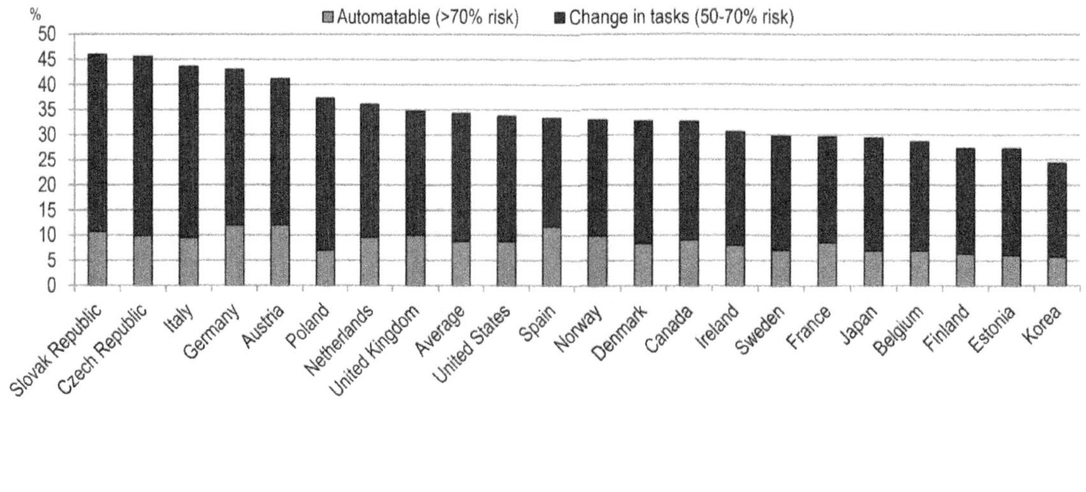

main aspects to be considered by any responsible decision maker and enterprise dealing with challenges that forth industrial revolution brings are addressed in the following sections.

Are Employees Prepared for Upcoming Changes in Work Structure?

Information and communication technology (ICT) knowledge among workers has proven to be a key success factor over the last decades. The researched trend also suggests that such ICT knowledge will gain even more importance in the future (Berger & Frey, 2016). While ICT had been marginal in many occupations some decades ago, today at least some ICT literacy is required for the majority of jobs. Based on the OECD report, up to 95% of large/corporate business employees use the internet for their work; this number drops to 85% for medium-sized enterprises and to 65% for small businesses.

Figure 3 and Figure 4 present the level of technical (ICT) skills possessed by adults in the studied OECD countries. Level 1 or lower represent most basic ICT operations skills (writing, operating basic hardware/sfotware interface). Level 2 and 3 represent more complex operations, such as online activities and operating various software solutions.

Figure 3. Percentage of 16-65 years-olds performing in each proficiency level. Most adults have low proficiency in problem solving in technology-rich environments

Notes: Individuals in Level 2 or Level 3 have more advanced ICT and cognitive skills to evaluate problems and solutions than those in Level 1 or below.

Source: OECD (2015c), Survey of Adult Skills (PIAAC) 2015

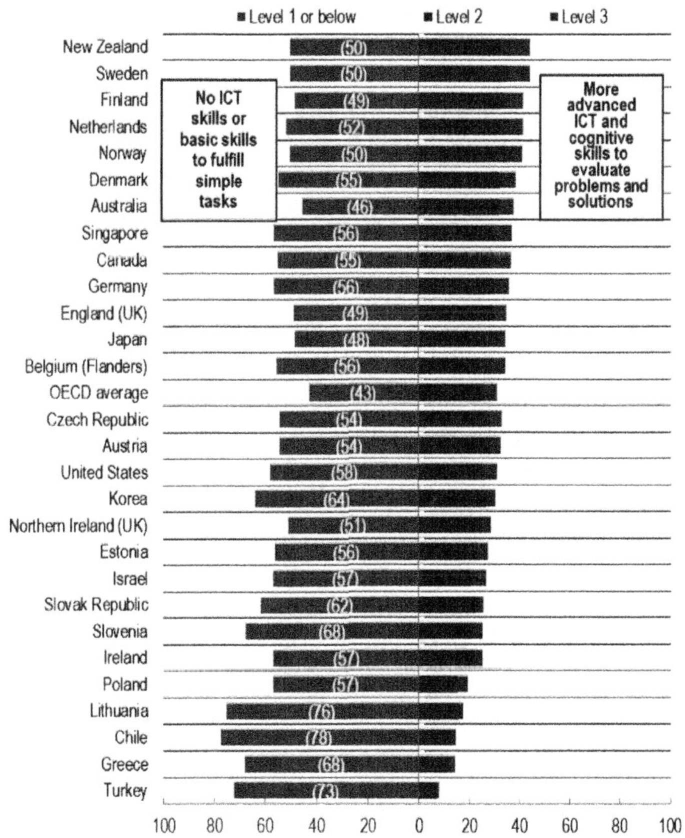

Individual readiness and willingness to adopt new technologies varies based on countless factors. There is a pattern that leads to the current situation with a knowledge/skill gap between generations. ICT knowledge was appreciated in the past three decades, and its value is growing over time. This represents a chance to significantly improve career perspectives especially for a mid-aged group of employees, that tend to master both classical organization approach and new ICT skills. While the younger generation possesses higher "problem-solving skills in technology-rich environment" (cf. Figure 4), they lack experience and managerial skills obtained by middle-aged employees through their higher level of seniority. (OECD, 2016)

Figure 3 indicates that some of the countries, even members of the EU, could face a serious shortage of ICT knowledge in the general population. While the demand for technical knowledge rises, some of the states, despite their significant population, may not be able to deliver a sufficiently qualified workforce to maintain industry requirements. A solution to such an issue could be transferred from top-ranking states in ICT skills, however considering the socio-politic situation in some of the low-ranking states, it may be difficult to execute.

The research also suggests a clear correlation between age and problem-solving skills using technology. On average, about 42% people aged 25 to thirty-four years can handle more complex tasks consisting of multiple steps and requiring application of specific technology. The percentage drops to about 10% among people aged fifty-five to 65 years.

Wages also reflect the necessity of digital skills, while considering the level of ICT skills. People with no ICT skills whatsoever tend to earn about 10% less in general, compared to people with at least some basic ICT skills. People reaching level 2 or 3 earn on average 27% more in OECD countries than those with basic ICT skills (level 1). However, there are some even more skill considering countries

Figure 4. Problem-solving skills in technology-rich environments provide strong returns
Source: OECD (2015c), Survey of Adult Skills (PIAAC) 2015.

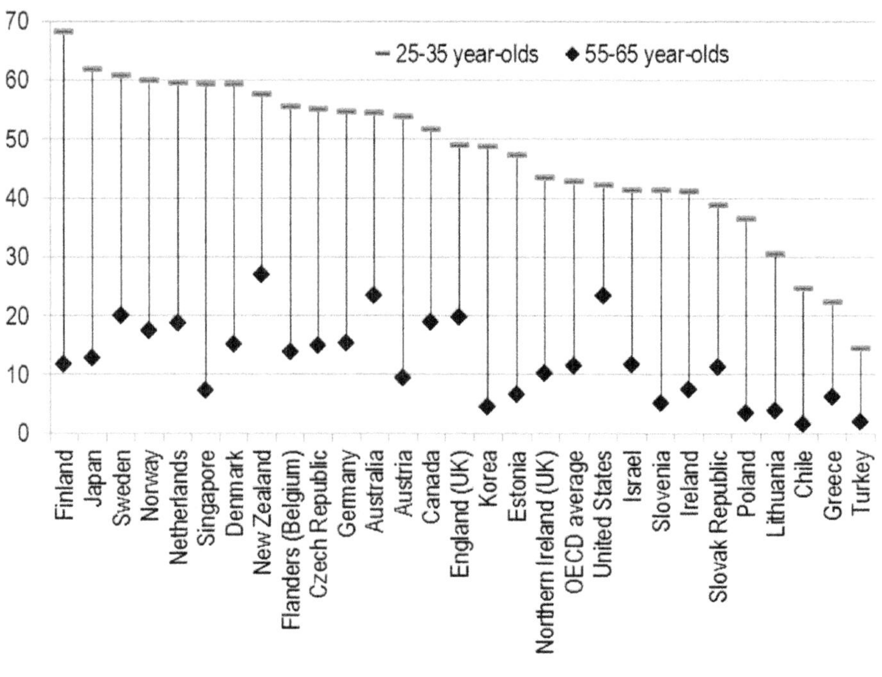

such as Singapore, USA, and The United Kingdom where high-skilled employees earn up to 50% more compared to less technically skilled ones (OECD, 2015a).

SOLUTIONS AND RECOMMENDATIONS

It is rather difficult to present a set of complex, in-depth recommendation since every business-model needs to consider numerous specifics and unique variables. Nonetheless there are somewhat general topics that must be dealt with in most companies impacted by i4.0 phenomenon.

The recommendation is the same as with any other disruptive phenomenon. It is better to adopt a proactive role rather than a reactive one. Some factors that may seem minor and easy to neglect while they emerge, may prove paramount eventually and quite difficult to catch up without previous comprehension.

On the other hand, multiple initiatives emerging from regular work unintentionally support the transition to digitalized and automated business processes. From the very nature of the idea, every simplification in any corporate processes represents a step towards automation and usually towards overall process digitalization as well (Bughin, J., 2017).

Tools Should Follow—Not Lead—New Ways of Working

Despite the effort that companies invest in the introduction of new online work tools such as, company collaboration/social platforms, the results may not meet expectations. This being primarily due to an implementation approach. Presumptions such as the selection of the right tool should be based on the various decision-making models tend to encounter pushback from end-users of the solution. Notably due to failure to deliver a perfect fit for the variety of the actual work conducted by end users. (Bughin, J., 2017).

Any collaboration platform implementation should start with adjustments to the way people work and utilize such tools. Once the necessary adjustments to the process are in place, the selection of the tool is most likely to be more successful (Bughin, J., 2017). Using a vice-versa approach may result in an undesired process change that would arise from the functionality of the tool rather than from adopting the desired changes by relevant employees.

Once the organization adopts and employees accept the new means of collaboration, further improvements towards agility are easier to implement due to the nature of the newly established framework. However, the more deeply integrated such collaboration platforms become, the more business processes tend to be dependent on them (Figure 5). Introducing a new pillar communication channel in the company should always be coordinated at all levels of the organization with wide support of all stakeholders. Despite the size of the business impact that such decision has, the single standalone solution does not implement organization transformation. It provides the necessary up-to-date digital background that enables numerous possible changes that will eventually lead to a modern, nimble, and resilient company. Digital technologies and social platforms thus adopt a supporting role in the overall transformation.

Further Growth Towards Agile Organization and Collaboration

Agile was a buzzword in business circles even before the idea of i4.0 become a broadly discussed topic. Despite that, business leaders are currently leaning towards another direction of the importance of Ag-

Figure 5. Survey results comparison - perks of instant messaging within the company
Source: McKinsey Global Institute (2017) Advanced Social technologies and the future of collaboration survey.

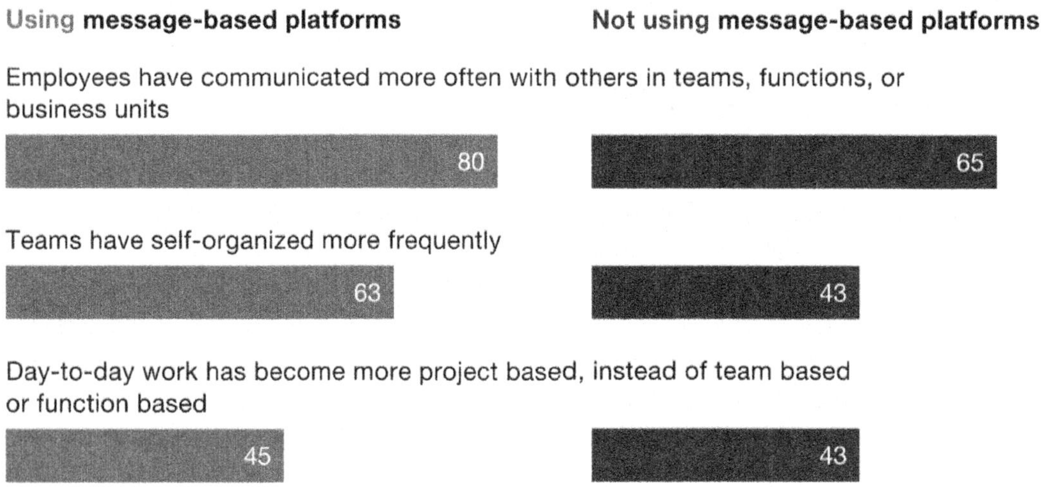

ile and is therefore, not diminishing. On the contrary, modern frameworks, in general, require different approaches towards work organization and the Agile way of working offers just that. There are many forms of Agile, but there is no "one size fits all" tendency (Bazigos M., 2015). Each organization has unique requirements and finding the right fit is perhaps the largest challenge of such implementation.

Agility is the ability of an organization to renew itself, adapt, change quickly, and succeed in a rapidly changing, ambiguous, turbulent environment.

Agility is not incompatible with stability—quite the contrary. Agility requires stability for most companies. - Aaron De Smet (2016, December, Interview transcript)

While there are countless combinations of various agile approaches, it is paramount that transformation leaders do not randomly excerpt just some principles of selected frameworks (Figure 6). It may be tempting to select the principles with the obvious and easy to interpret benefits and avoid those that at first sight represent extra effort. However, such an approach may result in a chaotic environment that encourages team members to be more creative at first. However, a delivered long-term value could be diminished by missing documentation, missing accountability for the product or by even by the complete deterioration of the established teams and their processes.

Any change or transformation of the company processes should be considered in a broad and holistic view as possible. The goal is to create a flexible structure that retains some of its organizational pillars as firm points of reference with agile surroundings. Improved collaboration and utilization of communication platforms come as supporting aspects when achieving more process-centric and product aimed organization.

Table 1. Selection of Agile work frames scaled based on difficulty

Cross-Functional Team	Innovation Hub	SCRUM
Basic application of workers uplifting from their usual teams/departments or organization structures and bringing them together, usually for specific project or purpose.	Brings together business professionals, academics, researchers and other stakeholders. Provides space for networking, idea sharing and harnessing merge of these different spheres.	Defined by its specific roles (responsibilities) and ceremonies (meetings) represents most popular strictly defined and institutionalized agile methodology.
Applicable in majority of hierarchical structures, allows to combine various skills sets and helps to speed up work pace and decision process.	Based on pillars of communal structure, self-organization and adaptability, heterogeneous knowledge base, serendipity and enabling innovation.	Originates from software development, but has wide application throughout other industries. Based on Agile manifesto and its 12 principles.

Source: Author's summary.

Pillars of Successful Agile Transformation

Business executives should pay most attention to three crucial areas of interest during any major organizational transformation towards the agile structure - processes, structure, and governance (W. Aghina, 2015).

Decision-making, and the overall *corporate governance* tend to grow alongside the size of the company. Hence the larger the company, the larger and less nimble decision-making process tends to take place. Speed and stability in decision-making are perhaps the most difficult aspects to balance. Where stability and flexibility should meet is in the empowerment of others to make decisions (Aghina, W. & Smet, A. D., 2015). If the clear mandate is given as to what extent and responsibility level an individual can decide, the decision-making process speeds up and becomes more flexible, while keeping its stability due to the given mandate.

The most sensitive topic for workers is *corporate structure* when the company is undergoing organizational change of any sort; it may signify outplacement of certain people or changes to their work positions. It is important to maintain stability to a certain degree, to avoid confusion and turbulence. Complete relocation of employees within the company structure is accompanied for the cost of losing current business ties and process in place, thus creating chaos. The flexibility and agility in the structure should be harnessed through the ability to create and dismiss ad-hoc units and teams in rapid pace. Assembling such teams permits to allocate and utilize available resources in the company to their maximum in a dynamic way (Aghina, W. & Smet, A. D., 2015). Newly created teams also allow to combine skill-sets and give team cross-functional character. Such flexible approach introduces agility when reacting to changing environment and keeps stability for employees by providing them with a clearly stated home location within the company structure.

Corporate processes are such a predominant baseline to each organization that massive changes to them could disturb the very core business strategies. The importance of stability and flexibility stands out, especially in this case. When conducting a reorganization, it is paramount to keep the stability of processes above all possible benefits of potential changes. Despite the limitation to benefits that this approach brings, the risk mitigation from keeping core business processes stable outweighs possible gains from more nimble operations. Also, if the core processes stay in place, it is easier to introduce changes to supporting processes, since people have a more positive approach towards all conducted changes if they know, that stability is still present within crucial elements.

Based on McKinsey´s organizational Health Index, the companies that focus both on speed and stability tend to rank in the top quartile regarding "organizational health." The analysis of more than 2 300 large companies from the US, identifies that the best-performing companies have acknowledged themselves as "extremely stable" (Bazigos, M. 2015). However, they also included agile features of a long-term nature that allowed the companies to adopt desired traits rapidly and deal with arising challenges. Moreover, the companies pointed out, that this characteristic enables innovation to higher extend due to easy readjustment of desired processes.

The stability is not only a matter of an organization and managerial work. The stability of ICT solutions and related infrastructure is essential as well. As ICT solutions importance grows and a higher ratio of employees become dependent on them. It is of utmost importance that ICT infrastructure receives proper attention in budget, implementation, and overall company strategy. Only the stable operating ICT infrastructure can provide a pillar for the new way of doing business. Also, while building such strategy, the current status quo of the technology should be only followed to some extent (Bughin, J., 2017). The size of reasonable "technological buffer" varies depending on the desired solution. However, not considering it, while implementing the infrastructure could prove rather expensive even in the short-term. Such a technological buffer should be represented by hardware extension capacities of the solution, but also by adding extra connectivity channels, better connections to the cloud solutions or any other business-specific features. Despite that these features may not be desired now, it would be to introduce them later as standalones.

Keeping the Transformation Reasonable

The pace of organizational change tends to accelerate over time, based on the McKinsey research conducted among global executives. Up to 60% of the respondents stated that they went through a major company reorganization in the last two years. Another 25% claimed to undergo such organizational changes three or more years ago. In comparison, one or two generations back major reorganizations would occur few times over the whole individuals career (Aronowitz, S., 2015). Also, once the companies design and implement the new structure, conditions could already be different, making the new solution obsolete in some respects. Furthermore, the reorganization itself usually takes one or two years to complete from the beginning to the end. Consequently, the situation came that far, that some companies are caught in a loop of constant reorganization on various levels (Aronowitz, S., 2015).

By combining general recommendations and best practices from already executed transformations, there is a possibility to compile a list of important target areas. Such areas of focus should be considered in the widest possible extend to deliver desired changes and expected outcomes. Factors that need to be acknowledged during design, execution and afterwards reorganization could be considerably generalized regardless of business specifications (Aronowitz, S., 2015). While it may not be feasible to integrate all the listed recommendations, the higher the number of utilized suggestions, the higher the success rate of such transformation. Out of 1 323 organizations, those following 1-2 rules had full redesign success rate of just 12%, compared to organizations following 5-6 rules that succeeded in 57% of cases. Research also states that those organizations that followed all the suggested rules reported a success rate of 86% (Smet A. D., 2014).

Even though that the rules may seem self-evident, it is crucial to communicate them and make them clear throughout the organization. Unless relevant stakeholders understand and identify with the rules, chances of successful transformation drop significantly, despite of how well the plan is executed.

- **Long-Term Strategy Comes First:** Executives often try to focus on seemingly most urgent issues in the organization. However, the most vocalized or visible issues, may not have significant impact in the long run. The frustration of teams and team managers escalates and the business leaders tend to be influenced. What should be kept to utmost importance is a long-term benefit of any organizational changes, not resolution of minor flaws. If redesign addresses only currently most visible and painful issues, it will most likely not to provide desired value for later stages of reorganization (Kaplan & Norton, 2014).
- **Research the Current Organization Thoroughly:** It is essential to know not just numbers, but also interpersonal ties, individual skillsets and the current. Up to 60% of executives stated that they did not spent enough time obtaining accurate and up to date data, hence ended up making decisions based on outdated information (Aronowitz, S., 2015). Also, the analysis of the current process should be that exhaustive that it will discover the root cause of painful or ineffective processes in the organization.
- **Don't Let Intuition Get Ahead of Reason:** If the reorganization is built on untested hypotheses or purely on intuition, it will most likely fail (respondents acknowledged that 80% of reorganizations driven purely by instinct had failed to deliver the desired outcome), (Aronowitz, S., 2015). While intuition is a desirable trait, reorganization blueprint should be based on properly selected criteria, which are properly evaluated and measured. Reduction of possible biases, political influence and other negative externalities must be ensured throughout the whole redesign process.
- **Do Not Think Just in Organizational Charts and Office Teams:** Analysing organizational charts is unlikely to reflect the actual situation in the company. It is important to understand processes within the departments and teams and base the new structure on functionalities and skillsets rather than hierarchy. Work environment also comes as a key factor; large uniform open spaces no longer provide intended collaboration traits, as the natures of work itself is changing. Transforming meeting room with casual seating to unbookable space available for ad hoc sessions and encouraging doing so, provides more collaborative workspace. The serendipity of random encounters provides great boost to innovation and cooperation within the company.
- **Design by Roles Not by People:** New structure needs to be based on roles – not the people occupying the current organizational structure. It could be tempting to fill out new positions with people that are present at the company. However, by doing so, the definition of the roles is at risk not be conducted in full. People will eventually leave the position or will be replaced, causing disruption in the structure. In contrast, if the role is clearly defined the new structure will withstand even large fluctuation spikes and remain to provide desired stability. With this rule especially – it is important not to subdue to company politics, individual ties, and peer pressure. Still, it is possible to define the role in full and offer it to someone who does not provide perfect fit (to maintain core business processes). Creating "pre-made roles" just to accommodate current skillsets that are present in the structure is undesired since it will represent an impediment to later governance.
- **Become Familiar With the Status Quo and Work with the Mindset:** Any major organization redesign is bound to encounter pushback from certain groups of employees. Knowing what beliefs, emotions, fears or hopes are present in the team adopts a key role in selecting right means of communication as well as in the selection of topics to address. During organizational change, employees represent the largest group of stakeholders, with special requirements for communication. If the processes predeceasing and following the change are not explained, the whole transformation is likely to encounter negative responses. Various forms of passive-aggressive subtleties that

may undermine the whole initiative in the long-run as at hand in such case. Desired mind-change should be conducted throughout all the departments and on all hierarchical levels. Ensuring, that every impacted individual is experiencing same shift in thinking and working habits. This rule is especially important since it is a key one when it comes to increasing employee buy-in for the transformation (Pyle, D. & Jose, C. 2015).

- **Set KPIs for Both Short-Term and Long-Term Evaluation:** Establishing a tailor-made metric for evaluation is as important as making the custom-made structure. KPIs should be defined as clearly as possible, providing up to date data about the success of the initiative (Kaplan & Norton, 2014). Well set KPIs also serve as a diagnose tool in case of lapse. Moreover, if one the metrics would exceed desired values, KPIs can serve as a failsafe to prevent collapse or breakdown of newly established processes.
- **Promote Interactive Cascade Communication:** By enabling a back and forth information exchange between employees and their direct managers. Top to bottom communication from business directors towards employees many organization levels below, does give a brand of importance to the core message. However, it is less reassuring when it comes to impact on individual organization units. Mass communication should not be used to introduce or explain operational changes. Rather a means of spreading the message to all parts of the company and encourage acceptance of changes conducted on an operational level. Interactive cascade communication helps to deliver individualalized message with the possibility of the bottom to top feedback while making everyone aware of the reasons leading to the redesign.
- **Have a Recovery Plan in Place Before Go-Live:** The preparation of large-scale reorganization requires a tremendous amount of planning for all possible outcomes. The fact that KPIs are regularly monitored and give a clear idea about the execution have zero value, once the new structure starts rapidly failing. Employee defections, interruptions to core business processes, unsettled communication channels or unaccountability for actions may emerge and cause damage the integrity of company on a massive scale. Therefore, having mitigation plans and disaster recovery scenarios in place should be one of the top priorities for responsible managers.

Most of these rules are followed during the whole reorganization process; the less painful the reorganization tends to be and the faster the implementation becomes (Smet A. D., 2014). Large-scale project such as overall business transforamtion should be mapped using software solution to track dependencies and help to manage complexity. Organization blueprint software platforms can be utilized as a single point of reference during both the design exploiting the collaboration nature of software and during the implementation (accessible, clear, and detailed plan).

BUSINESS LEADERS ACTING AS CHANGE AGENTS

Considering all the above mentioned, it is crucial for responsible individuals to take action while reflecting the rapid pace of current development. Some of the employees may perceive i4.0 changes in a very negative way, they may even try to slow down company progress towards digitalization or become indifferent due to fear of job loss (Gates, D. 2017). Role of business leaders is to make sure that inevitable transition will take place in the company that is ready for it. Ready in the matters of flexible organization structure, labour redeployed, technical solutions and with a clear strategy on how to drive changing business.

Company value can often be measured by skill sets and the knowledge base of its employees. A direct replacement of current employees could trigger process breakdown due to lack of such key knowledge. Therefore, the more sensible solution is to redeploy current labour force by providing desired kinds of training delivering such required skill set. This initiative should be conducted as a long-term plan, with clear benefits for both the company and the employees as well. Perceived value from employee viewpoint could vary strongly based on their mindset or work role. Business leaders should offer enough incentives and stress the necessity of such change in advance so that once redeployment plan is introduced, the employees would embrace it and adopt it without further delays.

Redeployment initiatives should focus not only on hard technical skills, despite that the need for such skills may be more visible and urging. Soft-skills enable to utilize technical skills to their best; employees will need to have a good level of self-control such as time and task management. Modern collaboration platforms and utilization of ICT not only empower employees but delegates larger amount of responsibility as well (Gates, D., & Bremicker, M. 2017). Same goes for communication skills, the higher the utilization of ICT, the higher the necessity to be able to implement communication in a clear and descriptive manner.

Desired structure of top-level skills tends to change; hence, it is also important to implement up-skill training to gain more mid-qualified employees that can take further training. Low and medium-skilled employees receive less training in general, and that brings the risk of having high-skilled employees in a constant loop of retraining sessions.

Companies must also deal with the lack of qualified workforce. Creating an image of a company that invests into the development of employees motivates the younger generation. The overall image of a technologically advanced company utilizing the best of current innovation is crucial when attracting the best of "Millennials" generation that sees value in such approach above other traits of the company (Douglas, D. K. 2017). Such competitive advantage could be a key differentiator in upcoming decades that will help to attract the best resources on the job market, allowing the company further growth in innovation.

The Larger Picture

As any such disruptive changes to global industry – digitalization, automation, and robotics will far exceed just companies themselves. Possible impact includes large-scale jobs loss worldwide and other negative scenarios, same as positive ones with higher productivity and more efficient industry, e.g., in matters of environment preservation.

Furthermore, basic IT skills such as programming are not sufficient among ICT employees to be considered as a specialist. The specialists need to acquire domain-specific knowledge base regarding the application of robotics, large data, machine learning, automation, and other advanced engineering areas of industry.

Major business adopters may implement necessary changes at a more rapid pace. However, standalone initiatives of companies will not solve challenges on a national level such as required adjustments to the education system, legislative matters arising from new approaches to data collection as well as RandD outside of the private sector. Most crucial role of the state is in education since changes that may take years to implement, take even longer to exploit. Business leaders should engage in defining what skillsets are to be desired in the future and try to engage their enterprises in cooperation with education institutions (Henke, N., & Bughin, J., 2016). Markets globally already face lack of specialists from various fields, and the situation will worsen with growing demand and delayed supply due to the education process.

The education process needs to involve basic ICT skills as part of common literacy, effective utilization of ICT solutions is as important as proper application of logic, numeracy, or problem-solving skills (Henke, N., & Bughin, J., 2016). Many of such skills are acquired outside of educational institutions as well; certified training centres can provide as good upskill training as many universities. Hence the state support of such non-academic establishments could lessen the education gap arising from current industry transformation.

Digitalization itself has an enormous potential to bring required education to most of the population connected to the internet. Even the basic ICT infrastructure allows attending MOOCs (massive open online courses) or OERs (open educational resources) that offer a vast selection of study materials, education videos or even custom-made interactive lectures. This trend also allows to exploit the best of hidden talents globally, that otherwise would not have access to the proper education system and hence encourages global innovation (Brynjolfsson, E. 2014). Companies usually do not recognize such courses as valid ones (in comparison to certified and publicly recognized ones), quality and cheap opportunity to develop own employees utilizing outsourced solutions or in creating own education platform.

In addition, i4.0 inspired the establishment of numerous innovation hubs, think-tanks, and start-ups that have potential to introduce other disruptive technologies or approaches that take i4.0 further. Such initiatives adopt a key role in the popularization of i4.0 a phenomenon among its audience (Henke, N., & Bughin, J. 2016). Support and collaboration with them could be beneficial from many viewpoints:

- **Corporate:** Potential employee base, possibility to agree on exclusivity to research output and even possible acquisition as part of the enterprise.
- **Government:** Cooperation during the execution of own initiatives, the attraction of more liberal-minded specialists into cooperation during government projects.
- **Academia:** Possibilities to join research projects, hosting speakers, job opportunities for students.

The more entities in the industrial world realize how disruptive changes are happening, the larger the chance that they will catch up early on. The large challenge of transferring the whole society to digital industry compatible one depends on all aspects of modern society. The sooner all concerned bring their initiatives forward and start to cooperate, the sooner everyone will relish the rewards of such a symbiosis.

FUTURE RESEARCH DIRECTIONS

All the impacted fields of business represent wide research opportunities. Narrowing the scope to the managerial viewpoint, there are main areas of interest in:

- Execution strategies regarding workforce redeployment and overall strategy of handling jobs replacement by technology
- Organizational redesign in late adapting companies considering their specific traits

- Engagement of state with companies and educational institutions and results of such endeavours
- Opportunities for emerging economies to avoid mistakes of early adopters

Further research has the possibility to bring new models of behaviour and reference case studies, that can possibly ease the transformation to all impacted entities. Also, many of ongoing studies in relevant areas will be impacted to some extent and should consider i4.0 transformation while conducting research.

CONCLUSION

Automation along with other game-changing technologies such as robotics, machine learning and artificial intelligence and overall digitalization are going to impact all the existing industries. What remains as an open question is when, to what extent, and how well prepared the markets will be for such radical change.

Even though it is not possible to give step-by-step guidelines to adopt traits of ongoing digital industrial transformation, it is possible to recommend a structured approach that business leaders should keep in mind. Such as agility of their organization, redeployment of labour, communication strategy and cooperation with other subjects.

Ongoing and future changes to the industry are not unprecedented. The world was facing similar issues in the past during previous industrial revolutions, not so long ago the internet revolution and decades back the IT revolution. Going further back, comparing years 1900 and 2000, the US faced a drop of agriculture employment ratio from 40% to just two percent (Lebergott S., 1966). Same with manufacturing jobs in the 1950s (25%) and 2010 (10%). In both cases, the structure of national employment changed radically not resulting in unsustainable unemployment but to changed employment module with new types of jobs.

As automation represents the largest *scarecrow* in matters of social impact, it needs to be considered that automated jobs will continue to produce the same value for the economy. Hence, the initiatives as universal basic income, shorter workweeks, machine taxation and others are being considered by some advanced economies (Brynjolfsson E., 2014). While these solutions need to be fully tested before actual nation-wide introduction, they prove that social unrest that world faced during the early industrial revolution is not the case today.

In the current transformation environment, it is paramount for business leaders to separate hype from reality. Massive investments without a long-term strategy, chaotic reorganizations without a clear goal, early adaptation of not finalized technologies or approaches can cause harm to later endeavors to transform the company (Gates, D., & Bremicker M., 2017). Business leaders need to consider actions of their peers and competitors and have a value-driven and resourceful approach, which enables growth of competitive advantage.

Business leaders and CEOs face challenging times, the necessity to act is urgent as well as the necessity to prepare their enterprises for upcoming changes. The fact that automation does not pose a threat will be clear once automation takes place in their very job structure – up to 25% of their workload could be automated in the upcoming years. Giving them one extra quarter of their time to invest in more productive activities (D. Pyle & C. S. Jose, 2015). Moreover, same goes for other occupations; i4.0 is not about job automation – it is about activities automation (Manyika, J., & Chui, M. 2017). Keeping that in mind, it is possible to take the right course of action and adapt to challenges that i4.0 brings.

REFERENCES

Adalet McGowan, M., & Andrews, D. (2015). *Labour Market Mismatch and Labour Productivity: Evidence from PIAAC Data*. OECD Economics Department Working Papers, No. 1209, OECD Publishing. 10.1787/5js1pzx1r2kb-en

Aghina, W. (2015, December). *The keys to organizational agility*. Retrieved August 21, 2017, from http://www.mckinsey.com/business-functions/organization/our-insights/the-keys-to-organizational-agility

Aghina, W., De Smet, A., & Weerda, K. (2015, December). *Agility: It rhymes with stability*. Retrieved August 5, 2017, from http://www.mckinsey.com/business-functions/organization/our-insights/agility-it-rhymes-with-stability

Aronowitz, S. (2015, June). *Getting organizational redesign right*. Retrieved August 17, 2017, from http://www.mckinsey.com/business-functions/organization/our-insights/getting-organizational-redesign-right

Bazigos, De Smet, & Gagnon. (2015, December). *Why agility pays*. Retrieved August 19, 2017, from http://www.mckinsey.com/business-functions/organization/our-insights/why-agility-pays#0

Berger, T., & Frey, C. (2016). *Structural Transformation in the OECD: Digitalization, Deindustrialization and the Future of Work*. OECD Social, Employment, and Migration Working Papers, No. 193. OECD Publishing. 10.1787/5jlr068802f7-en

Brynjolfsson, E. (2014). *The second machine age: Work, progress, and prosperity in a time of brilliant technologies* (1st ed.). New York: W. W. Norton and Company.

Bughin, J. (2017, July). *Advanced social technologies and the future of collaboration*. Retrieved from http://www.mckinsey.com/business-functions/digital-mckinsey/our-insights/advanced-social-technologies-and-the-future-of-collaboration

Gates, D., & Bremicker, M. (2017, May). *Beyond the hype: Separating ambition from reality in i4.0*. Retrieved from https://home.kpmg.com/xx/en/home/insights/2017/05/beyond-the-hype-separating-ambition-from-reality.html

Gates, D. K. (2017, May 11). *Industry 4.0: It's all about the people*. Retrieved August 28., 2017, from https://home.kpmg.com/xx/en/home/insights/2017/05/industry-4-0-its-all-about-the-people.html

Henke, N., & Bughin, J. (2016, December). *The age of analytics: Competing in a data-driven world*. Retrieved August 29, 2017, from http://www.mckinsey.com/business-functions/mckinsey-analytics/our-insights/the-age-of-analytics-competing-in-a-data-driven-world

Kaplan, R. S., & Norton, D. P. (2014, July 31). *How to Implement a New Strategy Without Disrupting Your Organization*. Retrieved September 26, 2017, from https://hbr.org/2006/03/how-to-implement-a-new-strategy-without-disrupting-your-organization

Lebergott, S. (1966). Output, Employment, and Productivity in the United States after 1800. NBER.

Manyika, J., & Chui, M. (2017, January). *A future that works: Automation, employment, and productivity*. Retrieved from http://www.mckinsey.com/global-themes/digital-disruption/harnessing-automation-for-a-future-that-works

OECD. (2016). *Skills for a Digital World.* Policy Brief on The Future of Work. OECD Publishing. Retrieved from http://www.oecd.org/els/emp/Skills-for-a-Digital-World.pdf

Pyle & San Jose. (2015, June). *An executive's guide to machine learning.* Retrieved September 20, 2017, from http://www.mckinsey.com/industries/high-tech/our-insights/an-executives-guide-to-machine-learning

Smet, A. D. (2014, July). *The secrets of successful organizational redesigns: McKinsey Global Survey results.* Retrieved August 22, 2017, from http://www.mckinsey.com/business-functions/organization/our-insights/the-secrets-of-successful-organizational-redesigns-mckinsey-global-survey-results

The Atlas of Economic Complexity, Centre for International Development at Harvard University. (n.d.). Retrieved from http://www.atlas.cid.harvard.edu

KEY TERMS AND DEFINITIONS

Automation: Technique or method that allows the implementation process in full without external human interaction, utilizing technical of software means.

Collaboration Platform: Category of business software allowing interactions in virtual space using ICT technologies.

Digitalization: Process of digitizing available inputs and utilizing their data value through integration with software solutions. Also, widely used as a term for integration of digital technologies to everyday life.

Key Performance Indicators (KPIs): Set of measurable values that demonstrates how effectively a measured process is conducted.

Labour Redeployment: Process of placing employees to re-education initiatives and to new workplaces instead of displacement.

Organization Agility: The capability of the business to adapt and rapidly change if needed. The overall balance of flexibility and stability of business processes.

Robotics: Interdisciplinary engineering branch dealing with design, construction, operation, and use of robots.

Chapter 6
Logistics Management and Risk Management

Kijpokin Kasemsap
Suan Sunandha Rajabhat University, Thailand

ABSTRACT

Logistics management is an important part of supply chain management and deals with the movement and storage of products and services in order to meet customer demands. Risk management is the business growth strategy that can help executives handle any crisis within company toward achieving improved business planning, reduced costs, and enhanced organizational reliability. The chapter argues that applying logistics management and risk management has the potential to enhance operational performance and gain sustainable competitive advantage in global operations.

INTRODUCTION

As a new field in the service industry, logistics is recognized as a fundamental industry in a national economy (Mu et al., 2012). Logistics industry and its service providers are affected by the changes in the global marketplace (Saatcıoglu, Denktas-Sakar, & Karatas-Cetın, 2014). Logistics service providers are able to perform their roles through vertical and horizontal cooperation with other companies and with other logistics companies (Kasemsap, 2017a). Logistics companies need to efficiently manage their supply chains, reduce cost, and improve the accuracy of process delivery toward achieving effective logistics management (Potti & Saurav, 2016).

The logistics' role in today's global and competitive markets is critical for the enterprises' viability, since it can provide the grounds for companies to become the leaders of the markets by achieving performance maximization and cost minimization (Nikolaos, Dimitris, Charisios, Dimitrios, & Nicolas, 2014). Logistics involves the integrated planning, control, realization, and monitoring of internal and network-wide material flow, product flow, and information flow (Gencer & Akkucuk, 2016). Logistics performance positively affects organizational performance (Fugate, Mentzer, & Stank, 2010) toward gaining logistics innovation in logistics industry (Grawe, Daugherty, & Ralston, 2015).

DOI: 10.4018/978-1-5225-3468-6.ch006

Risk is a consequence of uncertainties associated with the project and its execution (Anantatmula & Fan, 2013). Risk management has been affected by several happenings in the world (Acar & Acar, 2015), thus involving all activities that are performed to reduce the uncertainties associated with certain tasks (Misra, Kumar, & Kumar, 2009). Risk management is fundamental in trying to reduce the negative effects involved in its manifestation (Boghean, 2015), which may arise in the future (Brownsword & Setchi, 2012).

Risk management is the key function of project-based organizations, and its ultimate objective is to create the business value for the corporation (Khameneh, Taheri, & Ershadi, 2016). The consideration of risk is a day-to-day phenomenon used by individuals, multinational corporations, and global organizations (Brownsword & Setchi, 2012). Those related to risk need to know the methods to manage risk, to identify risk sources, and to quantify risk parameters toward effectively handling the risk (Brandon, 2006).

This chapter is based on a literature review of logistics management and risk management. The extensive literature of logistics management and risk management provides a contribution to practitioners and researchers by explaining their important aspects in global operations.

BACKGROUND

During the 1980's, Bowersox and Daugherty (1987) presented a logistics typology which postulated three dimensions of logistics strategy, including process, market, and information (McGinnis, Kohn, & Spillan, 2010). A core element of logistics management is logistics planning, which substitutes for low customer service levels, high waste, and the utilization of buffers in the execution of logistics activities (Aas & Wallace, 2012). In order to conduct logistic planning, it is necessary to have access to the relevant logistics information and a capability to transform this information into an intelligent plan (Aas & Wallace, 2012). In addition to cost savings, logistics plays an important role in improving customer service and helping companies gain competitive advantage (Xiaomin & Yi, 2017).

The technological advancements that have been developed in order to enable the coordination of logistics operations, along with the accumulated experience of supply chain consultants, constitute the most prominent factors for the existence of a supply chain integrator, whose role is to manage and coordinate both the logistics entities and the resources along the value chain (Eleni-Maria, 2013). Logistics and information technology (IT) can assist a retailer to form a logistics network with third-party firms in the supply chain, with the purpose to capture the supply chain returns through the internalization of the supply chain activities (Bourlakis & Bourlakis, 2003).

Regarding logistics industry, the risk can be mitigated through a structural adjustment in the long-distance freight transportation from road-dominated to rail-dominated perspective (Havenga, 2010). The dual nature of risk, is expressed in terms of likelihood to suffer certain economic losses (net risk), on the other hand, it is a possibility to gain a significant income under conditions of acceptable risk limits and, consequently, ensure the financial stability of the business entity under consideration (Grabovy & Orlov, 2016). Companies, that adopt risk management practices in combination with external integration, can achieve the improved results (Kauppi, Longoni, Caniato, & Kuula, 2016).

Management science, especially in the decision-making process, focuses on the identification and evaluation of skills appropriate for handling the risk (Rostek, 2016). This issue justifies the need for identifying, characterizing, and developing the strategic plans for reducing the effects of risk occurrence (Rostek, 2016). Risk management is associated with the use of market insurance to protect individuals and companies from various losses associated with accidents (Dionne, 2013). There is a positive relationship between total risk management and organizational performance in companies, which have invested higher level of intellectual capital (Mohammed & Knapkova, 2016).

As risk identification is the initial step in risk management, understanding the risks and their categories is essential to come up with an effective risk management system (Baydoun, 2016). Corporate governance failures and new legislation have emphasized the importance of enterprise risk management (ERM) in preventing the fraudulent reporting (Desender, 2011). It is necessary to take various constraints and assumptions into the consideration of risk management, such as the probability derived from the statistical analysis of historical data, the ambiguity derived from the lack of reliable information, the decision maker's subjectivity (Hasuike, 2010).

IMPORTANT ASPECTS OF LOGISTICS MANAGEMENT AND RISK MANAGEMENT

This section provides the overview of logistics management; logistics outsourcing and logistics service providers; risk management in business; risk management in the financial industry; enterprise risk management (ERM); project risk management; risk management and IT; and the issues of supply chain risk management (SCRM).

Overview of Logistics Management

The increasing competition, market differentiation, variable economic situation, and the associated risks are forcing the logistics companies to take on the new challenges and make the reasonable changes among strategic and tactical decisions in logistics industry (Cieśla, 2016). Hirschinger et al. (2015) indicated that decision makers in the transportation and logistics industry require a comprehensive understanding of the institutional business environment and factor markets in emerging economy countries to formulate the accurate supply chain strategies for the future.

As global competition intensifies, the geographic fragmentation of logistics activities creates a concentration of trade at the regional freight gateways or logistics hubs (Bolumole, Closs, & Rodammer, 2015). Public–private partnerships (PPPs) play an important role in facilitating the improvement of cross-border logistics (Davis & Friske, 2013). The transaction cost economics and the resource-based should be recognized to prove the relationships among relational governance structure, logistics customer service, and logistics performance (Leuschner, Carter, Goldsby, & Rogers, 2014).

To gain the improved logistics performance, logistics companies require the high level of organizational and interorganizational communication systems, such as radio frequency identification (RFID), electronic data interchange (EDI), and enterprise resource planning (ERP) at various levels of the logistics chain for effective coordination, planning, and decision optimization (Jhawar & Garg, 2016). Logistics personnel are positioned to play a key role in creating and maintaining a market-oriented organization as they are gaining more responsibilities in integrating cross-functional processes and implementing supply chain strategies (Fugate, Flint, & Mentzer, 2008).

Electronic commerce (e-commerce) is the important business transaction method (Kasemsap, 2016a), and focuses on information flow, capital flow, business flow, and logistics (Xiao, Liu, & Zhang, 2012), with the support of computerized networks and the Internet (Kasemsap, 2016b), toward increasing business performance and enhancing competitiveness in modern business (Kasemsap, 2018). E-commerce logistics relates to retail strategies, logistics structures, and buyer preferences (Bask, Lipponen, & Tinnilä, 2012).

The shared logistics technologies enable both manufacturers and retailers to offer the higher levels of availability and visibility of preferred brands to their end-user customers (Tokman, Richey, Deitz, & Adams, 2012). Buying company's top management championship, supplier company's designated employees, and the buyer-seller personal relationships at different levels, all have significant impacts on inter-firm collaboration, which enhances the buying company's logistics performance (Chen, Tian, Ellinger, & Daugherty, 2010).

When logistics companies develop and apply more accurate logistics forecasts in their planning and management activities, they have the potential to improve their performance across supply chain (Smith & Mentzer, 2010). To realize these improvements, companies must implement techniques, that improve forecast accuracy, and integrate more accurate forecasts into their planning activities with the support of logistics optimization (Smith & Mentzer, 2010). The scope of logistics optimization in logistics companies has expanded to address the strategic, tactical, operational, and collaborative decision making toward improving the logistics performance (Bartolacci, LeBlanc, Kayikci, & Grossman, 2012). Spreadsheets, an analytical tool familiar to logistics managers, play a crucial role in the modeling efforts of logistics companies (Bartolacci et al., 2012).

Logistics Outsourcing and Logistics Service Providers

The third-party logistics (3PL) providers have become the important players in global supply chain management as the increasing numbers of logistics companies are outsourcing their logistics activities (Lai, Li, Wang, & Zhao, 2008). With the increasing utilization of the 3PL providers by international firms seeking the integrated logistics services, many global 3PL providers form the logistics partnerships with large corporations to take care of the logistics operations in different regions (Lau & Ma, 2010). The 3PL is a special form of outsourcing various logistical activities, such as transportation, warehousing, inventory control, distribution, and audit payments (Dagiasis, 2013).

Logistics outsourcing performance involves two distinct dimensions (i.e., goal achievement and goal exceedance), which logistics managers should consider, while evaluating their logistics service providers (Deepen, Goldsby, Knemeyer, & Wallenburg, 2008). Foreign logistics service providers need to adapt to the host market environment during internationalization in order to develop their capabilities associated with competitive logistics services (Darkow, Weidmann, & Lorentz, 2015). The outsourcing of logistics activities requires creating synergetic relationship among supply chain partners with the objectives of maximizing customer value and providing a profit to each supply chain member (Carrus & Pinna, 2011). Service satisfaction is the primary driver of customer loyalty in effectively running the logistics outsourcing relationships (Cahill, Goldsby, Knemeyer, & Wallenburg, 2010).

The growth of business dynamics has caused the outsourcing of the logistics activities to increasingly gain the greater importance (Gupta, Ali, & Dubey, 2011). Outsourcing is the contracting or subcontracting of non-core activities to free up cash, personnel, time, and facilities for activities in which a company holds competitive advantage (Kasemsap, 2016c). Logistics outsourcing takes responsibility for non-core business functions, brings reductions of stocks, costs, and order-to-delivery lead-time, accelerates capital turnover, and capitalizes on the strategic synergies toward achieving the improved logistics efficiency (Grigorenco, Papadopoulos, & Rotsios, 2013).

The 3PL services can improve the core competitiveness, reduce the logistics cost, and gain the risk sharing (Huang & Yin, 2014). In the context of 3PLs, logistics-related technological adoption is critical, and the investments of information and communication technology (ICT) need to be carefully planned (Evangelista, 2013). The 3PLs are required to move from a pure operational role (e.g., transport and warehousing service providers) to a more strategic function where they may play a more important role in accelerating both physical and information flows across the supply chain (Evangelista, 2011). The 3PL importance, logistics performance, and information sharing are positively related to relationship quality, and that relationship length and the presence of a legal contract are positively related to relationship quality (Chu & Wang, 2012).

Despite of the fact that many electronic retailing companies are running virtual network by outsourcing logistics to the 3PL, there is a trend for companies to establish their own logistics channels (Lu, Liu, & Ma, 2016). Logistics service companies are pressured by the ever-increasing customer demands for higher service level at reduced costs (Evangelista, 2011). While small 3PL companies are using less expensive ICT at a tactical level mainly to cut costs and reduce errors in the day-to-day logistics operations, medium-sized and large firms have evolved to make use of more expensive ICT for various strategic purposes, such as business control, customer integration, and service differentiation (Lau & Huang, 2014).

Risk Management in Business

Traditional risk management processes are motivated by controlling risk and avoiding losses (Thekdi & Aven, 2016). A clear distinction by what is meant by low risk, moderate risk, and high risk needs to be developed and recognized toward establishing the strategic plans to reduce that risk (Smith, 2014). Achieving the alignment of risk perception, assessment, and tolerance among management teams is an important foundation upon which an effective enterprise information security management strategy can be built (Hirsch & Ezingeard, 2009). The implementation of risk management system is one of the most crucial challenges that organizations may face in the rapid changing world in order to identify, analyze, and prevent the business exposure (Almustafa & Alkhaldi, 2014).

Business continuity management is one of the most recent risk management frameworks, which can enable the organizations to improve their resilience in order to cope with the identified risks (Torabi, Giahi, & Sahebjamnia, 2016). Business processes are transformed by the radical changes in the digital economy (Ritchie & Brindley, 2009). Small businesses often face the big challenges when it comes to managing the fraud risks (Hess & Cottrell, 2016). Examples of risk in the business environments include the shortage of raw materials, increase of raw material-related purchasing prices, the decrease of product market prices, the lack/excess of demand, and the strike of labor unions (Nikbakhsh, 2012).

Embedding business processes and risk management-related best practices into the organization culture can positively affect the success of ERP system implementation (Agha, 2012). Business analyst can encounter the risks, including the exact definition of risk, the background model applied, the visualization of risks, the description of the risk management process, and the definition of the risk management limits (Toth & Sebestyen, 2016). Risk sensitivity can be easily achieved by implementing the risk-averse functional decision rules based on the risk-neutral solution (Koenig & Meissner, 2015).

Acknowledging the companies' ability to diversify, transfer, and mitigate the certain sources of risk provides the additional layer of analysis and the managerial practicability of entry mode research (Müllner, 2016). The stakeholder's attributes of power, legitimacy, and urgency play the essential roles in defining the stakeholders' proactive and reactive approaches in various risk management phases (Mojtahedi & Oo, 2017). Managerial overconfidence, which has been found to affect a number of corporate decisions, also affects corporate risk management decisions (Adam, Fernando, & Golubeva, 2015).

Risk Management in the Financial Industry

Banks play an important role in the financial systems contributing to the efficient transfers of both capital and risk between those in excess (savers) and those in need (borrowers) of money (Bergendahl & Lindblom, 2007). Banks utilize electronic banking (e-banking) as an online service to reach a wider market share, to increase customer satisfaction, and to reduce operational costs (Tsiakis, Kargidis, & Chatzipoulidis, 2015). The risks of e-banking arise as a result of uncertainty in operational risk, compliance risks, reputational risk, strategic risk, credit risk, and market risks (Ochuko, Cullen, & Neagu, 2012).

The major activity of a bank is to lend money and earn profits in the form of interest but by doing so the money is exposed to the risk of default, whereas the borrower is not able to pay the money back in specified period (Baber, 2016). Financial risks (e.g., interest rate, foreign exchange risks, and credit risks) are the significant risks for the banking operations (Bergendahl & Lindblom, 2007). The performance of financial institutions is affected by the management of risk exposure represented by an offer that includes more financial products and services than in the past (Rodriguez & Edwards, 2015). The sensitivity to direct partner risk varies in the cross-section, and is weakened by financial constraints and greater ease of monitoring foreign partners (Bodnaruk, Manconi, & Massa, 2016).

Enterprise Risk Management

ERM began to take root in the late 1990s and has become recognized as an expectation of good management and corporate governance (Fraser & Simkins, 2016). ERM has become the dominant strategic management focus of organizations primarily due to various factors, such as stakeholders' aversion to uncertainty, volatility of the current marketplace, and compliance mandates, such as the Sarbanes–Oxley Act (Arnold, Benford, Canada, & Sutton, 2015). ERM provides a holistic view that allows the sound decision making, proper prioritization, and allocation of more efficient capital toward increasing the effectiveness of corporate management (Bali & Uslu, 2017).

The utilization of an effective approach to managing the risks by a company at a different stage of the ERM maturity continuum is affected by its size, scope of operations, and legal structure (Moon, Mo, & Chan, 2014). The proper ERM requires the board and senior management to ensure that all potential threats to ERM are taken into account (Renault, Agumba, & Balogun, 2016). Managers should check the efficiency of the ERM measures adopted at the enterprise level and should review the evaluation of ERM toward keeping it updated (Renault, Agumba, & Balogun, 2016).

The evolution of risk management to the holistic view of ERM requires the destruction of barriers between organizational silos and the exchange of knowledge from different risk management areas (Rodriguez & Edwards, 2015). The operationalization of knowledge management (KM) governance formalizes, locates, and authorizes risk management as a structured response to the resolution of the structural risks and obstacles to KM strategy (Zyngier, 2008).

Project Risk Management

The project-based company is expected to manage the risks both at corporate level (macro level) and at project level (micro level) (Agarwal & Virine, 2017). At macro level, risk must be aggregated to provide the holistic view, whereas project-specific operational risk should be given priority at micro level (Agarwal & Virine, 2017). The ambitious natures of projects in terms of their burgeoning scale, value, technical novelty, compressed timeframes, and growing socio-economic significantly affect the unparalleled challenges and all against the backdrop of a legacy of failed projects, where objectives are not effectively delivered (Chapman, 2017).

The traditional risk management practices have been ineffective at helping contractors deliver the projects on time and within budget, while meeting the expectations of quality (Algahtany, Alhammadi, & Kashiwagi, 2016). Adhering to the risk management principles at a high level is a significant factor in reaching cost, schedule, and customer targets, in addition to achieving a more stable project execution (Olechowski, Oehmen, Seering, & Ben-Daya, 2016).

However, there is a strategic misalignment between projects and operational paradigm requirements due to the competing interests resulting in the risks obtained from the design, construction, and commissioning phases of projects, that are transferred to the operational phase of project life cycle (Jarman & Dreher, 2017). The risk transfer results from non-alignment of management requirements within an organization for a total view of risk profile over the full project life cycle (Jarman & Dreher, 2017).

Effective project risk management involves various variables, such as work process, organizational environment, and people (Thamhain, 2013). Risk management moderates the relationship between risk level and project success (Zwikael & Ahn, 2011). The formal risk management at the project level and integration of risk information at the portfolio level are positively associated with overall project portfolio success (Teller, Kock, & Gemünden, 2014).

Risk Management and Information Technology

Developing the effective risk management strategies requires the collection of data from various stakeholders from the enterprise's environment. Stakeholders starts to communicate the enterprise IT risk management philosophy as the method to develop a risk-oriented culture, that is able to add value to the enterprise, toward gaining the advanced solution to the IT risks (Chatzipoulidis, Michalopoulos, & Mavridis, 2016).

IT risk management includes regulatory compliance, information security, disaster recovery, and project risks (Herrod, 2008). The alignment of business strategy and IT should consider the factors of IT risk governance, project portfolio control, and risk management (Parry & Lind, 2016), particularly when applied to virtual enterprise networks (Shalan, 2010).

Distributed IT projects exhibit certain features that make them fundamentally different from traditional projects, not only involving additional decisions, but also affecting the risk management process (Prikladnicki, Evaristo, Audy, & Yamaguti, 2010). Information security risk management helps protect the IT issues in many companies and helps minimize their IT-related failure probability at reasonable costs (Fenz, 2011).

Issues of Supply Chain Risk Management

With the globalization of business operations, logistics systems are threatened by all kinds of uncertainties and disruptions (Choi, Chiu, & Chan, 2016). As companies move toward global sourcing, supply chain risk dramatically increases, which is linked to the reduced financial performance and market value (Liao, Bayazit, & Wang, 2014). Companies have reacted to the opportunities and threats of globalization through various global production practices, that have increased supply chain complexity and various forms of risks (Wiengarten, Humphreys, Gimenez, & McIvor, 2016).

Risk is an important issue that threaten the sustainability of supply chain (Kara & Fırat, 2016). Thus, companies must develop the effective supply chain risk management (SCRM) systems and integrate their risk management systems into their sustainable business strategy (Kara & Fırat, 2016). SCRM process includes various activities, focusing on the identification, measurement, evaluation, and mitigation of the main risk sources, that can affect the supply chain (Manotas-Duque, Osorio-Gómez, & Rivera, 2016). The strong cost and price risk management of a company may obstruct the adoption of green supply management, and the companies with high spend are less interested in to adopt the green supply chain management (Lintukangas, Kähkönen, & Ritala, 2016).

The suitable management of information flows is needed to create the adequate visibility level for managing the supply chain risks (Messina, Santos, Soares, & Barros, 2017). Both risk information sharing and risk sharing mechanism improve financial performance, and the effectiveness of the former is strengthened by relationship length and supplier trust, while that of the latter is strengthened by shared SCRM understanding (Li, Fan, Lee, & Cheng, 2015). SCRM culture diffusion and SCRM team support positively affect both risk information sharing and risk analysis (Fan, Li, Sun, & Cheng, 2017). Risk culture, leadership, emerging risk governance, and compliance are the essential factors in the sustainability-related risk management practices (Aziz, Manab, & Othman, 2016).

Risk management is a critical issue in complex product development, especially when suppliers are integrated (Zhao & Cao, 2015). In a networked environment, the ability to develop the supply chain relationships with suppliers is the important task for the improved organizational management (Hallikas & Lintukangas, 2016). Supply chain members should reinforce their institutional and moral views of relational governance and should manage the relational risks faced by the supply chain as a whole (Cheng & Chen, 2016).

Managing the supply chain risks becomes challenging because of the uncertainties of demand, globalization of supply chains, shorter demand cycles, and logistics outsourcing (Gupta, Meng, Goh, & de Souza, 2012). Risk management enhances the success of logistics outsourcing by securing future supply chain performance and relationships among supply chain partners (Sauvage & Haouari, 2012). The mixed strategy for the inventory management of distribution centers is suggested to improve the profits of global supply chains subject to the substantial risks (Park & Kim, 2016).

FUTURE RESEARCH DIRECTIONS

The classification of the extensive literature in the domains of logistics management and risk management will provide the potential opportunities for future research. Quality improvement is the systematic approach to the reduction or elimination of waste, rework, and losses in production process (Kasemsap, 2015a). Total quality management (TQM) presents the continuous improvement in all aspects of an organization as a process (Kasemsap, 2015b). Production planning takes place within a manufacturing business, and ensures that sufficient raw materials, staff, and other necessary items are effectively organized (Kasemsap, 2017b). Considering the correlations among logistics management, risk management, quality improvement, TQM, and production planning in global operations should be further studied.

CONCLUSION

This chapter explained the overview of logistics management; logistics outsourcing and logistics service providers; risk management in business; risk management in the financial industry; ERM; project risk management; risk management and IT; and the issues of SCRM. Logistics management is an important part of supply chain management, and deals with the movement and storage of products and services in order to meet customer demands. Risk management is the business growth strategy that can help executives handle any crisis within company toward achieving improved business planning, reduced costs, and enhanced organizational reliability. Applying logistics management and risk management has the potential to enhance operational performance and gain sustainable competitive advantage in global operations.

REFERENCES

Aas, B., & Wallace, S. W. (2012). Management of logistics planning. In J. Wang (Ed.), *Information technologies, methods, and techniques of supply chain management* (pp. 255–271). Hershey, PA: IGI Global. doi:10.4018/978-1-4666-0918-1.ch015

Acar, O., & Acar, A. B. (2015). Modern risk management techniques in banking sector. In *Banking, finance, and accounting: Concepts, methodologies, tools, and applications* (pp. 886–906). Hershey, PA: IGI Global. doi:10.4018/978-1-4666-6268-1.ch048

Adam, T. R., Fernando, C. S., & Golubeva, E. (2015). Managerial overconfidence and corporate risk management. *Journal of Banking & Finance*, *60*, 195–208. doi:10.1016/j.jbankfin.2015.07.013

Agarwal, R., & Virine, L. (2017). Integration of project risk management (PRM) into enterprise risk management (ERM). In Y. Raydugin (Ed.), *Handbook of research on leveraging risk and uncertainties for effective project management* (pp. 294–317). Hershey, PA: IGI Global. doi:10.4018/978-1-5225-1790-0.ch014

Agha, H. E. (2012). Risk management and business processes reengineering, success drivers for ERP projects: A case study. In R. Valverde & M. Rao Talla (Eds.), *Information systems reengineering for modern business systems: ERP, supply chain and e-commerce management solutions* (pp. 146–184). Hershey, PA: IGI Global. doi:10.4018/978-1-4666-0155-0.ch008

Algahtany, M., Alhammadi, Y., & Kashiwagi, D. (2016). Introducing a new risk management model to the Saudi Arabian construction industry. *Procedia Engineering*, *145*, 940–947. doi:10.1016/j.proeng.2016.04.122

Almustafa, M. M., & Alkhaldi, D. (2014). Business intelligence and agile methodology for risk management in knowledge-based organizations. In *Software design and development: Concepts, methodologies, tools, and applications* (pp. 1710–1735). Hershey, PA: IGI Global. doi:10.4018/978-1-4666-4301-7.ch082

Anantatmula, V., & Fan, Y. (2013). Risk management instruments, strategies and their impact on project success. *International Journal of Risk and Contingency Management*, *2*(2), 27–41. doi:10.4018/ijrcm.2013040102

Arnold, V., Benford, T., Canada, J., & Sutton, S. G. (2015). Leveraging integrated information systems to enhance strategic flexibility and performance: The enabling role of enterprise risk management. *International Journal of Accounting Information Systems*, *19*, 1–16. doi:10.1016/j.accinf.2015.10.001

Aziz, N. A. A., Manab, N. A., & Othman, S. N. (2016). Critical success factors of sustainability risk management (SRM) practices in Malaysian environmentally sensitive industries. *Procedia: Social and Behavioral Sciences*, *219*, 4–11. doi:10.1016/j.sbspro.2016.04.025

Baber, H. (2016). Risk mitigation practices in banking: A study of HDFC bank. *International Journal of Risk and Contingency Management*, *5*(3), 18–32. doi:10.4018/IJRCM.2016070102

Bali, S., & Uslu, Y. D. (2017). Enterprise risk management in non-profit organization. In V. Potocan, M. Üngan, & Z. Nedelko (Eds.), *Handbook of research on managerial solutions in non-profit organizations* (pp. 75–93). Hershey, PA: IGI Global. doi:10.4018/978-1-5225-0731-4.ch004

Bartolacci, M. R., LeBlanc, L. J., Kayikci, Y., & Grossman, T. A. (2012). Optimization modeling for logistics: Options and implementations. *Journal of Business Logistics*, *33*(2), 118–127. doi:10.1111/j.0000-0000.2012.01044.x

Bask, A., Lipponen, M., & Tinnilä, M. (2012). E-commerce logistics: A literature research review and topics for future research. *International Journal of E-Services and Mobile Applications*, *4*(3), 1–22. doi:10.4018/jesma.2012070101

Baydoun, M. (2016). Risk management decisions and organizational structure in the case of a development management firm: Millennium development international. In *Project management: Concepts, methodologies, tools, and applications* (pp. 1220–1237). Hershey, PA: IGI Global. doi:10.4018/978-1-5225-0196-1.ch060

Bergendahl, G., & Lindblom, T. (2007). Risk management in banking: A review of principles and strategies. In H. Rao, M. Gupta, & S. Upadhyaya (Eds.), *Managing information assurance in financial services* (pp. 26–44). Hershey, PA: IGI Global. doi:10.4018/978-1-59904-171-1.ch002

Bodnaruk, A., Manconi, A., & Massa, M. (2016). Cross-border alliances and risk management. *Journal of International Economics*, *102*, 22–49. doi:10.1016/j.jinteco.2016.05.002

Boghean, F. (2015). Risk management in the decision-making of Romanian entities. *Procedia Economics and Finance*, *32*, 1066–1074. doi:10.1016/S2212-5671(15)01569-5

Bolumole, Y. A., Closs, D. J., & Rodammer, F. A. (2015). The economic development role of regional logistics hubs: A cross-country study of interorganizational governance models. *Journal of Business Logistics*, *36*(2), 182–198. doi:10.1111/jbl.12088

Bourlakis, C. A., & Bourlakis, M. A. (2003). Logistics, information technology, and retail internationalisation: The formation of international strategic retail networks. In L. Joia (Ed.), *IT-based management: Challenges and solutions* (pp. 257–276). Hershey, PA: IGI Global. doi:10.4018/978-1-59140-033-2.ch015

Brandon, D. M. (2006). Risk planning and management. In D. Brandon (Ed.), *Project management for modern information systems* (pp. 157–182). Hershey, PA: IGI Global. doi:10.4018/978-1-59140-693-8.ch008

Brownsword, M., & Setchi, R. (2012). A formalised approach to the management of risk: A conceptual framework and ontology. In W. Lee (Ed.), *Systems approaches to knowledge management, transfer, and resource development* (pp. 263–285). Hershey, PA: IGI Global. doi:10.4018/978-1-4666-1782-7.ch018

Cahill, D. L., Goldsby, T. J., Knemeyer, A. M., & Wallenburg, C. M. (2010). Customer loyalty in logistics outsourcing relationships: An examination of the moderating effects of conflict frequency. *Journal of Business Logistics, 31*(2), 253–277. doi:10.1002/j.2158-1592.2010.tb00151.x

Carrus, P. P., & Pinna, R. (2011). Information technology and supply chain management coordination: The role of third party logistics providers. *International Journal of E-Services and Mobile Applications, 3*(4), 21–36. doi:10.4018/jesma.2011100102

Chapman, R. J. (2017). Complexity theory and system dynamics for project risk management. In Y. Raydugin (Ed.), *Handbook of research on leveraging risk and uncertainties for effective project management* (pp. 152–176). Hershey, PA: IGI Global. doi:10.4018/978-1-5225-1790-0.ch008

Chatzipoulidis, A., Michalopoulos, D., & Mavridis, I. (2016). Managing enterprise IT risks through automated security metrics. In P. Papajorgji, F. Pinet, A. Guimarães, & J. Papathanasiou (Eds.), *Automated enterprise systems for maximizing business performance* (pp. 215–243). Hershey, PA: IGI Global. doi:10.4018/978-1-4666-8841-4.ch012

Chen, H., Tian, Y., Ellinger, A. E., & Daugherty, P. J. (2010). Managing logistics outsourcing relationships: An empirical investigation in China. *Journal of Business Logistics, 31*(2), 279–299. doi:10.1002/j.2158-1592.2010.tb00152.x

Cheng, J. H., & Chen, M. C. (2016). Influence of institutional and moral orientations on relational risk management in supply chains. *Journal of Purchasing and Supply Management, 22*(2), 110–119. doi:10.1016/j.pursup.2016.01.002

Choi, T. M., Chiu, C. H., & Chan, H. K. (2016). Risk management of logistics systems. *Transportation Research Part E, Logistics and Transportation Review, 90*, 1–6. doi:10.1016/j.tre.2016.03.007

Chu, Z., & Wang, Q. (2012). Drivers of relationship quality in logistics outsourcing in China. *The Journal of Supply Chain Management, 48*(3), 78–96. doi:10.1111/j.1745-493X.2011.03259.x

Cieśla, M. (2016). Sustainable logistics strategies of transnational corporations. In T. Kramberger, V. Potočan, & V. Ipavec (Eds.), *Sustainable logistics and strategic transportation planning* (pp. 347–367). Hershey, PA: IGI Global. doi:10.4018/978-1-5225-0001-8.ch016

Dagiasis, A. P. (2013). Logistics modeling and forecasting with regression. In D. Folinas (Ed.), *Outsourcing management for supply chain operations and logistics service* (pp. 223–237). Hershey, PA: IGI Global. doi:10.4018/978-1-4666-2008-7.ch013

Darkow, I. L., Weidmann, M., & Lorentz, H. (2015). Adaptation of foreign logistics service providers' resources and capabilities to a new institutional environment. *The Journal of Supply Chain Management*, *51*(1), 27–51. doi:10.1111/jscm.12068

Davis, D. F., & Friske, W. (2013). The role of public–private partnerships in facilitating cross-border logistics: A case study at the U.S./Canadian border. *Journal of Business Logistics*, *34*(4), 347–359. doi:10.1111/jbl.12032

Deepen, J. M., Goldsby, T. J., Knemeyer, A. M., & Wallenburg, C. M. (2008). Beyond expectations: An examination of logistics outsourcing goal achievement and goal exceedance. *Journal of Business Logistics*, *29*(2), 75–105. doi:10.1002/j.2158-1592.2008.tb00088.x

Desender, K. (2011). On the determinants of enterprise risk management implementation. In N. Shi & G. Silvius (Eds.), *Enterprise IT governance, business value and performance measurement* (pp. 87–100). Hershey, PA: IGI Global. doi:10.4018/978-1-60566-346-3.ch006

Dionne, G. (2013). Risk management: History, definition, and critique. *Risk Management & Insurance Review*, *16*(2), 147–166. doi:10.1111/rmir.12016

Eleni-Maria, P. (2013). Logistics service providers: Collaboration with IFFs, 3PL, or 4PL providers? In D. Folinas (Ed.), *Outsourcing management for supply chain operations and logistics service* (pp. 52–77). Hershey, PA: IGI Global. doi:10.4018/978-1-4666-2008-7.ch004

Evangelista, P. (2011). The role of information technology in supporting supply chain coordination of logistics services providers. In I. Mahdavi, S. Mohebbi, & N. Cho (Eds.), *Electronic supply network coordination in intelligent and dynamic environments: Modeling and implementation* (pp. 113–144). Hershey, PA: IGI Global. doi:10.4018/978-1-60566-808-6.ch005

Evangelista, P. (2013). Adding value to logistics services using ICT: A case study analysis of small logistics companies in Italy. In *Supply chain management: Concepts, methodologies, tools, and applications* (pp. 924–948). Hershey, PA: IGI Global. doi:10.4018/978-1-4666-2625-6.ch054

Fan, H., Li, G., Sun, H., & Cheng, T. C. E. (2017). An information processing perspective on supply chain risk management: Antecedents, mechanism, and consequences. *International Journal of Production Economics*, *185*, 63–75. doi:10.1016/j.ijpe.2016.11.015

Fenz, S. (2011). E-business and information security risk management: Challenges and potential solutions. In E. Kajan (Ed.), *Electronic business interoperability: Concepts, opportunities and challenges* (pp. 596–614). Hershey, PA: IGI Global. doi:10.4018/978-1-60960-485-1.ch024

Fraser, J. R. S., & Simkins, B. J. (2016). The challenges of and solutions for implementing enterprise risk management. *Business Horizons*, *59*(6), 689–698. doi:10.1016/j.bushor.2016.06.007

Fugate, B. S., Flint, D. J., & Mentzer, J. T. (2008). The role of logistics in market orientation. *Journal of Business Logistics*, *29*(2), 1–26. doi:10.1002/j.2158-1592.2008.tb00085.x

Fugate, B. S., Mentzer, J. T., & Stank, T. P. (2010). Logistics performance: Efficiency, effectiveness, and differentiation. *Journal of Business Logistics*, *31*(1), 43–62. doi:10.1002/j.2158-1592.2010.tb00127.x

Gencer, Y. G., & Akkucuk, U. (2016). Reverse logistics: Automobile recalls and other conditions. In U. Akkucuk (Ed.), *Handbook of research on waste management techniques for sustainability* (pp. 125–154). Hershey, PA: IGI Global. doi:10.4018/978-1-4666-9723-2.ch007

Grabovy, P. G., & Orlov, A. K. (2016). The overall risk assessment and management: Implementation of foreign investment construction megaprojects by Russian development companies. *Procedia Engineering, 153*, 195–202. doi:10.1016/j.proeng.2016.08.102

Grawe, S. J., Daugherty, P. J., & Ralston, P. M. (2015). Enhancing dyadic performance through boundary spanners and innovation: An assessment of service provider–customer relationships. *Journal of Business Logistics, 36*(1), 88–101. doi:10.1111/jbl.12077

Grigorenco, A., Papadopoulos, P., & Rotsios, K. (2013). Does the outsourcing of logistics services keep its promise of increased efficiency?: The case of Colgate-Palmolive, Greece. In D. Folinas (Ed.), *Outsourcing management for supply chain operations and logistics service* (pp. 162–184). Hershey, PA: IGI Global. doi:10.4018/978-1-4666-2008-7.ch010

Gupta, O. K., Ali, S. S., & Dubey, R. (2011). Third party logistics: Key success factors and growth strategies. *International Journal of Strategic Decision Sciences, 2*(4), 29–60. doi:10.4018/jsds.2011100103

Gupta, S., Meng, F., Goh, M., & de Souza, R. (2012). Understanding supply chain risk management: An in-depth analysis. In M. Garg & S. Gupta (Eds.), *Cases on supply chain and distribution management: Issues and principles* (pp. 349–372). Hershey, PA: IGI Global. doi:10.4018/978-1-4666-0065-2.ch016

Hallikas, J., & Lintukangas, K. (2016). Purchasing and supply: An investigation of risk management performance. *International Journal of Production Economics, 171*, 487–494. doi:10.1016/j.ijpe.2015.09.013

Hasuike, T. (2010). Risk-management models based on the portfolio theory using historical data under uncertainty. In L. Wang & T. Hong (Eds.), *Intelligent soft computation and evolving data mining: Integrating advanced technologies* (pp. 123–146). Hershey, PA: IGI Global. doi:10.4018/978-1-61520-757-2.ch007

Havenga, J. (2010). Logistics costs in South Africa: The case for macroeconomic measurement. *The South African Journal of Economics, 78*(4), 460–476. doi:10.1111/j.1813-6982.2010.01252.x

Herrod, C. (2008). Global IT risk management strategies. In F. Tan (Ed.), *Global information technologies: Concepts, methodologies, tools, and applications* (pp. 285–298). Hershey, PA: IGI Global. doi:10.4018/978-1-59904-939-7.ch024

Hess, M. F., & Cottrell, J. H. Jr. (2016). Fraud risk management: A small business perspective. *Business Horizons, 59*(1), 13–18. doi:10.1016/j.bushor.2015.09.005

Hirsch, C., & Ezingeard, J. (2009). Aligning IT teams' risk management to business requirements. In M. Gupta & R. Sharman (Eds.), *Social and human elements of information security: Emerging trends and countermeasures* (pp. 301–315). Hershey, PA: IGI Global. doi:10.4018/978-1-60566-036-3.ch017

Hirschinger, M., Spickermann, A., Hartmann, E., von der Gracht, H., & Darkow, I. L. (2015). The future of logistics in emerging markets: Fuzzy clustering scenarios grounded in institutional and factor-market rivalry theory. *The Journal of Supply Chain Management, 51*(4), 73–93. doi:10.1111/jscm.12074

Huang, Y., & Yin, K. (2014). Research on the evaluation and selection of third-party logistics providers in B2C e-commerce mode. *Journal of Electronic Commerce in Organizations, 12*(2), 74–88. doi:10.4018/jeco.2014040106

Jarman, M. F., & Dreher, L. G. (2017). Missed opportunities from misalignment of project and operational requirements. In Y. Raydugin (Ed.), *Handbook of research on leveraging risk and uncertainties for effective project management* (pp. 363–383). Hershey, PA: IGI Global. doi:10.4018/978-1-5225-1790-0.ch017

Jhawar, A., & Garg, S. (2016). System dynamics modelling to study the effects of investment in information technology on logistics performance: A case study from India. *International Journal of System Dynamics Applications, 5*(2), 19–40. doi:10.4018/IJSDA.2016040102

Kara, M. E., & Fırat, S. Ü. (2016). Sustainability, risk, and business intelligence in supply chains. In M. Erdoğdu, T. Arun, & I. Ahmad (Eds.), *Handbook of research on green economic development initiatives and strategies* (pp. 501–538). Hershey, PA: IGI Global. doi:10.4018/978-1-5225-0440-5.ch022

Kasemsap, K. (2015a). The role of total quality management practices on quality performance. In A. Moumtzoglou, A. Kastania, & S. Archondakis (Eds.), *Laboratory management information systems: Current requirements and future perspectives* (pp. 1–31). Hershey, PA: IGI Global. doi:10.4018/978-1-4666-6320-6.ch001

Kasemsap, K. (2015b). Total quality management practices in multinational corporations. In E. Tetteh & B. Uzochukwu (Eds.), *Lean Six Sigma approaches in manufacturing, services, and production* (pp. 1–26). Hershey, PA: IGI Global. doi:10.4018/978-1-4666-7320-5.ch001

Kasemsap, K. (2016a). Advocating electronic business and electronic commerce in the global marketplace. In S. Dixit & A. Sinha (Eds.), *E-retailing challenges and opportunities in the global marketplace* (pp. 1–24). Hershey, PA: IGI Global. doi:10.4018/978-1-4666-9921-2.ch001

Kasemsap, K. (2016b). Implementing electronic commerce in global marketing. In I. Lee (Ed.), *Encyclopedia of e-commerce development, implementation, and management* (pp. 591–602). Hershey, PA: IGI Global. doi:10.4018/978-1-4666-9787-4.ch043

Kasemsap, K. (2016c). The role of strategic outsourcing in global business. In G. Alor-Hernández, C. Sánchez-Ramírez, & J. García-Alcaraz (Eds.), *Handbook of research on managerial strategies for achieving optimal performance in industrial processes* (pp. 325–357). Hershey, PA: IGI Global. doi:10.4018/978-1-5225-0130-5.ch016

Kasemsap, K. (2017a). The roles of logistics service providers and supply chain integration in global supply chain. In L. Saglietto & C. Cezanne (Eds.), *Global intermediation and logistics service providers* (pp. 265–285). Hershey, PA: IGI Global. doi:10.4018/978-1-5225-2133-4.ch014

Kasemsap, K. (2017b). Production planning: Advanced issues and implications. In U. Akkucuk (Ed.), *Ethics and sustainability in global supply chain management* (pp. 50–72). Hershey, PA: IGI Global. doi:10.4018/978-1-5225-2036-8.ch003

Kasemsap, K. (2018). The importance of electronic commerce in modern business. In M. Khosrow-Pour (Ed.), *Encyclopedia of information science and technology* (4th ed.; pp. 2791–2801). Hershey, PA: IGI Global. doi:10.4018/978-1-5225-2255-3.ch243

Kauppi, K., Longoni, A., Caniato, F., & Kuula, M. (2016). Managing country disruption risks and improving operational performance: Risk management along integrated supply chains. *International Journal of Production Economics, 182*, 484–495. doi:10.1016/j.ijpe.2016.10.006

Khameneh, A. H., Taheri, A., & Ershadi, M. (2016). Offering a framework for evaluating the performance of project risk management system. *Procedia: Social and Behavioral Sciences, 226*, 82–90. doi:10.1016/j.sbspro.2016.06.165

Koenig, M., & Meissner, J. (2015). Risk management policies for dynamic capacity control. *Computers & Operations Research, 59*, 104–118. doi:10.1016/j.cor.2014.12.004

Lai, F., Li, D., Wang, Q., & Zhao, X. (2008). The information technology capability of third-party logistics providers: A resource-based view and empirical evidence from China. *The Journal of Supply Chain Management, 44*(3), 22–38. doi:10.1111/j.1745-493X.2008.00064.x

Lau, K. H., & Huang, H. (2014). Adoption and utilization of ICT in the Chinese third-party logistics industry. In J. Wang (Ed.), *Management science, logistics, and operations research* (pp. 221–242). Hershey, PA: IGI Global. doi:10.4018/978-1-4666-4506-6.ch013

Lau, K. H., & Ma, W. L. (2010). A supplementary framework for evaluation of integrated logistics service provider. In K. St.Amant (Ed.), *IT outsourcing: Concepts, methodologies, tools, and applications* (pp. 763–781). Hershey, PA: IGI Global. doi:10.4018/978-1-60566-770-6.ch045

Leuschner, R., Carter, C. R., Goldsby, T. J., & Rogers, Z. S. (2014). Third-party logistics: A meta-analytic review and investigation of its impact on performance. *The Journal of Supply Chain Management, 50*(1), 21–43. doi:10.1111/jscm.12046

Li, G., Fan, H., Lee, P. K. C., & Cheng, T. C. E. (2015). Joint supply chain risk management: An agency and collaboration perspective. *International Journal of Production Economics, 164*, 83–94. doi:10.1016/j.ijpe.2015.02.021

Liao, K., Bayazit, O., & Wang, F. (2014). Building a natural disaster risk index for supply chain operations. *International Journal of Information Systems and Supply Chain Management, 7*(4), 20–30. doi:10.4018/ijisscm.2014100102

Lintukangas, K., Kähkönen, A. K., & Ritala, P. (2016). Supply risks as drivers of green supply management adoption. *Journal of Cleaner Production, 112*, 1901–1909. doi:10.1016/j.jclepro.2014.10.089

Lu, Y., Liu, Z., & Ma, L. (2016). Competing through logistics management: Studies on e-retailing in China. In S. Dixit & A. Sinha (Eds.), *E-retailing challenges and opportunities in the global marketplace* (pp. 256–275). Hershey, PA: IGI Global. doi:10.4018/978-1-4666-9921-2.ch014

Manotas-Duque, D. F., Osorio-Gómez, J. C., & Rivera, L. (2016). Operational risk management in third party logistics (3PL). In G. Alor-Hernández, C. Sánchez-Ramírez, & J. García-Alcaraz (Eds.), *Handbook of research on managerial strategies for achieving optimal performance in industrial processes* (pp. 218–239). Hershey, PA: IGI Global. doi:10.4018/978-1-5225-0130-5.ch011

McGinnis, M. A., Kohn, J. W., & Spillan, J. E. (2010). A longitudinal study of logistics strategy: 1990–2008. *Journal of Business Logistics, 31*(1), 217–235. doi:10.1002/j.2158-1592.2010.tb00136.x

Messina, D., Santos, C., Soares, A. L., & Barros, A. C. (2017). Risk and visibility in supply chains: An information management perspective. In G. Jamil, A. Soares, & C. Pessoa (Eds.), *Handbook of research on information management for effective logistics and supply chains* (pp. 34–57). Hershey, PA: IGI Global. doi:10.4018/978-1-5225-0973-8.ch003

Misra, S. C., Kumar, V., & Kumar, U. (2009). Project-based software risk management approaches. In M. Khosrow-Pour (Ed.), *Encyclopedia of information science and technology* (2nd ed.; pp. 3142–3146). Hershey, PA: IGI Global. doi:10.4018/978-1-60566-026-4.ch501

Mohammed, H. K., & Knapkova, A. (2016). The impact of total risk management on company's performance. *Procedia: Social and Behavioral Sciences*, *220*, 271–277. doi:10.1016/j.sbspro.2016.05.499

Mojtahedi, M., & Oo, B. L. (2017). Critical attributes for proactive engagement of stakeholders in disaster risk management. *International Journal of Disaster Risk Reduction*, *21*, 35–43. doi:10.1016/j.ijdrr.2016.10.017

Moon, K. K., Mo, P. L., & Chan, R. L. (2014). Enterprise risk management: Insights from a textile-apparel supply chain. *International Journal of Risk and Contingency Management*, *3*(2), 18–30. doi:10.4018/ijrcm.2014040102

Mu, Z., Wenli, L., Jing, L., Xiang, Y., Congying, R., & Chengjuan, W. (2012). Research on innovation mechanism and model of logistics enterprise: A Chinese perspective. In Z. Luo (Ed.), *Innovations in logistics and supply chain management technologies for dynamic economies* (pp. 227–252). Hershey, PA: IGI Global. doi:10.4018/978-1-4666-0267-0.ch014

Müllner, J. (2016). From uncertainty to risk: A risk management framework for market entry. *Journal of World Business*, *51*(5), 800–814. doi:10.1016/j.jwb.2016.07.011

Nikbakhsh, E. (2012). Supply chain risk management. In R. Farahani, S. Rezapour, & L. Kardar (Eds.), *Supply chain sustainability and raw material management: Concepts and processes* (pp. 176–204). Hershey, PA: IGI Global. doi:10.4018/978-1-61350-504-5.ch010

Nikolaos, V., Dimitris, A., Charisios, A., Dimitrios, T., & Nicolas, M. (2014). Selection of the 3rd/4th party logistics provider: A multi-criteria approach. In *Cross-cultural interaction: Concepts, methodologies, tools, and applications* (pp. 197–213). Hershey, PA: IGI Global. doi:10.4018/978-1-4666-4979-8.ch013

Ochuko, R. E., Cullen, A., & Neagu, D. (2012). E-banking operational risk management using soft computing tools. In K. Mohammed Rezaul (Ed.), *Strategic and pragmatic e-business: Implications for future business practices* (pp. 176–202). Hershey, PA: IGI Global. doi:10.4018/978-1-4666-1619-6.ch008

Olechowski, A., Oehmen, J., Seering, W., & Ben-Daya, M. (2016). The professionalization of risk management: What role can the ISO 31000 risk management principles play? *International Journal of Project Management*, *34*(8), 1568–1578. doi:10.1016/j.ijproman.2016.08.002

Park, Y. B., & Kim, H. S. (2016). Simulation-based evolutionary algorithm approach for deriving the operational planning of global supply chains from the systematic risk management. *Computers in Industry*, *83*, 68–77. doi:10.1016/j.compind.2016.09.003

Parry, V. K., & Lind, M. L. (2016). Alignment of business strategy and information technology considering information technology governance, project portfolio control, and risk management. *International Journal of Information Technology Project Management*, *7*(4), 21–37. doi:10.4018/IJITPM.2016100102

Potti, R., & Saurav, S. (2016). Logistics for global automobile manufacturing industry. In A. Dwivedi (Ed.), *Innovative solutions for implementing global supply chains in emerging markets* (pp. 129–140). Hershey, PA: IGI Global. doi:10.4018/978-1-4666-9795-9.ch008

Prikladnicki, R., Evaristo, R., Audy, J. L., & Hideki Yamaguti, M. (2010). Risk management in distributed IT projects: Integrating strategic, tactical, and operational levels. In K. St.Amant (Ed.), *IT outsourcing: Concepts, methodologies, tools, and applications* (pp. 1723–1738). Hershey, PA: IGI Global. doi:10.4018/978-1-60566-770-6.ch109

Renault, B. Y., Agumba, J. N., & Balogun, O. A. (2016). Drivers for and obstacles to enterprise risk management in construction firms: A literature review. *Procedia Engineering*, *164*, 402–408. doi:10.1016/j.proeng.2016.11.637

Ritchie, B., & Brindley, C. (2009). Risk management in the digital economy. In M. Khosrow-Pour (Ed.), *Encyclopedia of information science and technology* (2nd ed.; pp. 3298–3305). Hershey, PA: IGI Global. doi:10.4018/978-1-60566-026-4.ch525

Rodriguez, E., & Edwards, J. S. (2015). Knowledge management in support of enterprise risk management. In *Transportation systems and engineering: Concepts, methodologies, tools, and applications* (pp. 108–127). Hershey, PA: IGI Global. doi:10.4018/978-1-4666-8473-7.ch005

Rostek, K. B. (2016). Risk management: Role and importance in business organization. In D. Jakóbczak (Ed.), *Analyzing risk through probabilistic modeling in operations research* (pp. 149–178). Hershey, PA: IGI Global. doi:10.4018/978-1-4666-9458-3.ch007

Saatcıoglu, O. Y., Denktas-Sakar, G., & Karatas-Cetın, C. (2014). Logistics innovation: A service-dominant logic-based conceptual framework. In B. Christiansen, S. Yıldız, & E. Yıldız (Eds.), *Handbook of research on effective marketing in contemporary globalism* (pp. 1–26). Hershey, PA: IGI Global. doi:10.4018/978-1-4666-6220-9.ch001

Sauvage, T., & Haouari, M. (2012). Risk management: A new way to improve logistics outsourcing. In P. Evangelista, A. McKinnon, E. Sweeney, & E. Esposito (Eds.), *Supply chain innovation for competing in highly dynamic markets: Challenges and solutions* (pp. 315–331). Hershey, PA: IGI Global. doi:10.4018/978-1-60960-585-8.ch020

Shalan, M. A. (2010). Managing IT risks in virtual enterprise networks: A proposed governance framework. In S. Ponis (Ed.), *Managing risk in virtual enterprise networks: Implementing supply chain principles* (pp. 115–136). Hershey, PA: IGI Global. doi:10.4018/978-1-61520-607-0.ch006

Smith, C. D., & Mentzer, J. T. (2010). User influence on the relationship between forecast accuracy, application and logistics performance. *Journal of Business Logistics*, *31*(1), 159–177. doi:10.1002/j.2158-1592.2010.tb00133.x

Smith, K. M. (2014). Risk management in aviation: The challenge of discrimination. *International Journal of Aviation Systems, Operations and Training*, *1*(1), 35–43. doi:10.4018/ijasot.2014010104

Teller, J., Kock, A., & Gemünden, H. G. (2014). Risk management in project portfolios is more than managing project risks: A contingency perspective on risk management. *Project Management Journal, 45*(4), 67–80. doi:10.1002/pmj.21431

Thamhain, H. (2013). Managing risks in complex projects. *Project Management Journal, 44*(2), 20–35. doi:10.1002/pmj.21325

Thekdi, S., & Aven, T. (2016). An enhanced data-analytic framework for integrating risk management and performance management. *Reliability Engineering & System Safety, 156*, 277–287. doi:10.1016/j.ress.2016.07.010

Tokman, M., Richey, R. G., Deitz, G. D., & Adams, F. G. (2012). The retailer's perspective on the link between logistical resources and perceived customer loyalty to manufacturer brands. *Journal of Business Logistics, 33*(3), 181–195. doi:10.1111/j.2158-1592.2012.01051.x

Torabi, S. A., Giahi, R., & Sahebjamnia, N. (2016). An enhanced risk assessment framework for business continuity management systems. *Safety Science, 89*, 201–218. doi:10.1016/j.ssci.2016.06.015

Toth, T., & Sebestyen, Z. (2016). Project risk management process for professionals: A value-based approach. In C. Bodea, A. Purnus, M. Huemann, & M. Hajdu (Eds.), *Managing project risks for competitive advantage in changing business environments* (pp. 128–149). Hershey, PA: IGI Global. doi:10.4018/978-1-5225-0335-4.ch007

Tsiakis, T., Kargidis, T., & Chatzipoulidis, A. (2015). IT security governance in e-banking. In *Banking, finance, and accounting: Concepts, methodologies, tools, and applications* (pp. 247–281). Hershey, PA: IGI Global. doi:10.4018/978-1-4666-6268-1.ch014

Wiengarten, F., Humphreys, P., Gimenez, C., & McIvor, R. (2016). Risk, risk management practices, and the success of supply chain integration. *International Journal of Production Economics, 171*, 361–370. doi:10.1016/j.ijpe.2015.03.020

Xiao, X., Liu, Y., & Zhang, Z. (2012). The analysis of the logistics mode decision to e-commerce. *Journal of Electronic Commerce in Organizations, 10*(4), 57–70. doi:10.4018/jeco.2012100105

Xiaomin, X., & Yi, L. (2017). Customer satisfaction of the third-party logistics enterprise based on AHP: A case study. *International Journal of Information Systems and Supply Chain Management, 10*(1), 68–81. doi:10.4018/IJISSCM.2017010105

Zhao, Y., & Cao, H. (2015). Risk management on joint product development with power asymmetry between supplier and manufacturer. *International Journal of Project Management, 33*(8), 1812–1826. doi:10.1016/j.ijproman.2015.08.008

Zwikael, O., & Ahn, M. (2011). The effectiveness of risk management: An analysis of project risk planning across industries and countries. *Risk Analysis, 31*(1), 25–37. doi:10.1111/j.1539-6924.2010.01470.x PMID:20723146

Zyngier, S. (2008). Risk management: Strengthening knowledge management. *International Journal of Knowledge Management, 4*(3), 19–32. doi:10.4018/jkm.2008070102

ADDITIONAL READING

Ameknassi, L., Aït-Kadi, D., & Rezg, N. (2016). Integration of logistics outsourcing decisions in a green supply chain design: A stochastic multi-objective multi-period multi-product programming model. *International Journal of Production Economics*, *182*, 165–184. doi:10.1016/j.ijpe.2016.08.031

Aven, T. (2016). Risk assessment and risk management: Review of recent advances on their foundation. *European Journal of Operational Research*, *253*(1), 1–13. doi:10.1016/j.ejor.2015.12.023

Bakke, T. E., Mahmudi, H., Fernando, C. S., & Salas, J. M. (2016). The causal effect of option pay on corporate risk management. *Journal of Financial Economics*, *129*(3), 623–643. doi:10.1016/j.jfineco.2016.02.007

Bask, A., & Tinnilä, M. (2013). Impact of product characteristics on supply chains: An analytical literature review. *International Journal of Applied Logistics*, *4*(1), 35–59. doi:10.4018/jal.2013010103

Charwand, M., Gitizadeh, M., & Siano, P. (2017). A new active portfolio risk management for an electricity retailer based on a drawdown risk preference. *Energy*, *118*, 387–398. doi:10.1016/j.energy.2016.12.058

Damnjanovic, I., & Røed, W. (2016). Risk management in operations of petrochemical plants: Can better planning prevent major accidents and save money at the same time? *Journal of Loss Prevention in the Process Industries*, *44*, 223–231. doi:10.1016/j.jlp.2016.09.012

Derwik, P., Hellström, D., & Karlsson, S. (2016). Manager competences in logistics and supply chain practice. *Journal of Business Research*, *69*(11), 4820–4825. doi:10.1016/j.jbusres.2016.04.037

Ejrami, M., Salehi, N., & Ahmadian, S. (2016). The effect of marketing capabilities on competitive advantage and performance with moderating role of risk management in importation companies. *Procedia Economics and Finance*, *36*, 22–28. doi:10.1016/S2212-5671(16)30012-0

Fugini, M., Teimourikia, M., & Hadjichristofi, G. (2016). A web-based cooperative tool for risk management with adaptive security. *Future Generation Computer Systems*, *54*, 409–422. doi:10.1016/j.future.2015.04.015

Gao, F., & Zhao, Q. (2014). Big data based logistics data mining platform: Architecture and implementation. *International Journal of Interdisciplinary Telecommunications and Networking*, *6*(4), 24–34. doi:10.4018/IJITN.2014100103

Garschagen, M. (2016). Decentralizing urban disaster risk management in a centralized system? Agendas, actors and contentions in Vietnam. *Habitat International*, *52*, 43–49. doi:10.1016/j.habitatint.2015.08.030

Giannakis, M., & Papadopoulos, T. (2016). Supply chain sustainability: A risk management approach. *International Journal of Production Economics*, *171*, 455–470. doi:10.1016/j.ijpe.2015.06.032

Giri, B. C., & Sarker, B. R. (2017). Improving performance by coordinating a supply chain with third party logistics outsourcing under production disruption. *Computers & Industrial Engineering*, *103*, 168–177. doi:10.1016/j.cie.2016.11.022

Huo, B., Fu, D., Zhao, X., & Zhu, J. (2016). Curbing opportunism in logistics outsourcing relationships: The role of relational norms and contract. *International Journal of Production Economics*, *182*, 293–303. doi:10.1016/j.ijpe.2016.07.005

Ito, T., Koibuchi, S., Sato, K., & Shimizu, J. (2016). Exchange rate exposure and risk management: The case of Japanese exporting firms. *Journal of the Japanese and International Economies*, *41*, 17–29. doi:10.1016/j.jjie.2016.05.001

Kitagawa, N., & Okuda, S. (2016). Management forecasts, idiosyncratic risk, and the information environment. *The International Journal of Accounting*, *51*(4), 487–503. doi:10.1016/j.intacc.2016.10.002

Koutras, V. M., Koutras, M. V., & Yalcin, F. (2016). A simple compound scan statistic useful for modeling insurance and risk management problems. *Insurance, Mathematics & Economics*, *69*, 202–209. doi:10.1016/j.insmatheco.2016.05.005

Kovács, G., Tatham, P., & Larson, P. D. (2012). What skills are needed to be a humanitarian logistician? *Journal of Business Logistics*, *33*(3), 245–258. doi:10.1111/j.2158-1592.2012.01054.x

Kucukaltan, B., Irani, Z., & Aktas, E. (2016). A decision support model for identification and prioritization of key performance indicators in the logistics industry. *Computers in Human Behavior*, *65*, 346–358. doi:10.1016/j.chb.2016.08.045

Leuschner, R., & Lambert, D. M. (2016). Establishing logistics service strategies that increase sales. *Journal of Business Logistics*, *37*(3), 247–270. doi:10.1111/jbl.12133

Li, C., Ren, J., & Wang, H. (2016). A system dynamics simulation model of chemical supply chain transportation risk management systems. *Computers & Chemical Engineering*, *89*, 71–83. doi:10.1016/j.compchemeng.2016.02.019

Luo, H., Wang, K., Kong, X. T. R., Lu, S., & Qu, T. (2017). Synchronized production and logistics via ubiquitous computing technology. *Robotics and Computer-integrated Manufacturing*, *45*, 99–115. doi:10.1016/j.rcim.2016.01.008

Manikas, I., & Ieromonachou, P. (2016). Do the service priorities of companies outsourcing to 3PL providers vary by industry? *International Journal of Applied Logistics*, *6*(1), 64–96. doi:10.4018/IJAL.2016010105

Moschuris, S. J., & Velis, G. F. (2012). Customer perceptions on service satisfaction with third party logistics (3PL) service. *International Journal of Applied Logistics*, *3*(4), 33–47. doi:10.4018/jal.2012100103

Niknejad, A., & Petrovic, D. (2016). A fuzzy dynamic inoperability input–output model for strategic risk management in global production networks. *International Journal of Production Economics*, *179*, 44–58. doi:10.1016/j.ijpe.2016.05.017

Oliva, F. L. (2016). A maturity model for enterprise risk management. *International Journal of Production Economics*, *173*, 66–79. doi:10.1016/j.ijpe.2015.12.007

Paquin, J. P., Gauthier, C., & Morin, P. P. (2016). The downside risk of project portfolios: The impact of capital investment projects and the value of project efficiency and project risk management programmes. *International Journal of Project Management*, *34*(8), 1460–1470. doi:10.1016/j.ijproman.2016.07.009

Wu, Y. (2012). A dual-response strategy for global logistics under uncertainty: A case study of a third-party logistics company. *International Transactions in Operational Research*, *19*(3), 397–419. doi:10.1111/j.1475-3995.2011.00839.x

Zepeda, E. D., Nyaga, G. N., & Young, G. J. (2016). Supply chain risk management and hospital inventory: Effects of system affiliation. *Journal of Operations Management*, *44*, 30–47. doi:10.1016/j.jom.2016.04.002

Zúñiga, R., & Martínez, C. (2016). A third-party logistics provider: To be or not to be a highly reliable organization. *Journal of Business Research*, *69*(10), 4435–4453. doi:10.1016/j.jbusres.2016.03.009

KEY TERMS AND DEFINITIONS

Enterprise Risk Management: The business approach that can help individuals determine and manage any risk in the organization.

Logistics: The discipline that concerns the acquisition, collection, and transportation of resources toward destination.

Logistics Management: The practical execution of information, products, and services toward customers.

Outsourcing: The business method that allows the outside parties to organize the specific operations on a contract basis.

Project: The particular task that deals with event, duration, and cost.

Risk: The unfavorable situation that is derived from several vulnerabilities.

Risk Management: The system that indicates and manages the risk factors in any task.

Supply Chain: The connection among company, supplier, products, and services.

Third-Party Logistics: The outsourced logistics services in supply chain.

Chapter 7
Analyzing an Impact of Industry 4.0 on Logistics and Supply Chain

Petr Jirsak
University of Economics, Czech Republic

ABSTRACT

The chapter presents an impact of Industry 4.0 transformation on logistics and supply chain management. Logistics and later supply chain management discipline has gone through a number of changes in the last 50 years, namely transition among mass, lean, agile, resilient, and green. All of them are paradigm changes as each significantly reshapes the orientation of the discipline in the source of competitiveness, risk concern, customer services, productivity, process management, externalities, costs, and other aspects of the disciplines. The author presents findings gained in the exploration of these fundamental changes and provides a comparison with a previous change of paradigm. The chapter proposes a transformation that the company supply chain system has to go through to re-establish its competitive position at the time of Industry 4.0. The chapter provides a case study of 3PL perception of Industry 4.0 based on in-depth interviews conducted among the major global 3PLs operating in the Czech Republic.

INTRODUCTION

Supply chain management (SCM) is a discipline formulated in the early 1990s as a reaction to fundamental changes in logistics. The extension of logistic processes beyond company boundaries became a novelty of the past. Traditional logistics processes such as inventory management and transportation failed to provide a competitive advantage and therefore, besides these logistic processes SCM encompasses the following processes today:

DOI: 10.4018/978-1-5225-3468-6.ch007

- **Supply Chain Design:** (SCD) is a strategic discipline that defines total supply chain for each product starting from the initial supplier and ending in the final customer. In addition, it formulates processes, business partners and service levels that lead to customer satisfaction within the scope defined by delivery term (INCOTERMS).
- **Demand Planning:** (DP) was operative within the sales and marketing department but is increasingly embedded into supply SCM to integrate the sales market situation and logistic processes. The purpose of this process is to create company sales plan based on both internal and external factors e.g. inputs from sales (historical sales), marketing (promotion events), financial department (budgets and cash flow), production (production capacity), product engineering (product lifecycle), material management (stock level), procurement (supplier shutdowns), legislation (changes of taxes and regulations), weather, customer habits etc. by using quantitative and qualitative methods.
- **Production Planning:** (PP) sets a plan based on DP outputs, work-in-process and stock of finished goods to meet customer demand. SCM is accountability for production planning due to the necessity for a closer integration of PP and logistic processes to easily cope with market changes and customer requirements.
- **Supply Planning:** (SP) provides a plan of replenishment in accordance with the demand and production plans and delivery terms agreed with suppliers. The plan is an exact schedule of replenishment in push oriented strategy or a parametrization of replenishment system in pull oriented strategy.
- **Material Management:** (MM) represents replenishment process that is organized either according to a fixed plan in push or to actual consumption in pull strategy. MM is a traditional logistic process.
- **Warehousing:** (W) is a process of storing and manipulation of goods in a different form to balance supplying and production or sales process.
- **Production:** (P) is traditionally out of scope of SCM but the reduction of stock and extension of make and assembly to order leads to mutual dependency of production and logistics process. Hence, P is increasingly a common part of SCM processes.
- **Transportation Management:** (TM) covers the organization of transport, planning of roots, dispatching and fleet management. Shrinkage of customer order batch sizes increases the importance of TM in SCM. Frequent deliveries of low volumes raise the need for better integration of TM, P and MM on the process and IT level.
- **Distribution:** (D) is a process of planning and organizing of finished goods flow across warehousing and distribution facilities.
- **Packaging:** (Pkg) is a process design, sourcing, inventory management and organization of reverse flows.
- **Customer Service:** (CS) incorporates communication with customers, resolution of customer complaints about deliveries, monitoring and evaluation of logistic performances to customers.

The purpose of SCM is to link, integrate and manage the processes and necessary sources that are employed to satisfy the customer by bringing appropriate added value by means of single or multiple supply chains. The linkage quality derives from business trust among supply chain partners, set processes and implemented technology hardware and software enabling collection, processing, storing, and reporting of data on real-time bases.

SCM enhances overall performances by three fundamental drivers:

- **Structure:** Contains the spatial location of logistic and production facilities so that it meets supply chain performance that correspond with customer requirements, company strategy, and contemporary and forecasted market conditions.
- **Organization:** It is highly important that there is a specific assignment of roles to each source across all supply chain layers. Only then, does it reduce failures due to lack of clarity about the scope of accountability and responsibility of each source. Thus, organization and process boundaries are clearly defined, and their interfaces help smooth communication and coordination.
- **Processes:** Covers processes of planning, execution and controlling within the above-mentioned list of processes. In addition, change of processes due to product or customer change or improvement of processes to meet the competitive level of performance are all drivers of SCM.

SCM encompasses different layers that start from the most aggregate (L0) and end with the most detailled (L6). This typology follows the Supply Chain Operation Reference Model (SCOR), which is used worldwide for SCM process standardization and benchmarking (Zhou, H., Benton, W. C., Schilling, D. A. & Milligan, G. W., 2011).

L0 represents a set of companies that participate in the creation of a product and associated services demanded by customers. L0 outlines suppliers of all tiers, Original Equipment Manufacturer) OEM, distributors, logistics providers, IT providers and other relevant parties. L1 describes the major supply chain processes that are present in each L0 company.

These processes are: plan, source, make, delivery and return. The plan contains all planning activities of supply chain management mainly supply chain design, demand planning, production planning, supply planning, distribution planning and transport planning. Source involves procurement and material management. Make is a transformation process that is in form of production, packaging, and value-added services. Delivery encompasses order fulfilment from stock, warehousing, transportation, and cross-docking. Return is a process of organization and execution of returning products, packaging and other material that must be delivered from a customer to suppliers.

Each of the L1 processes can be managed by the pull or push the concept. Therefore, the lower level L2 recognizes process in forms of stock, to order or engineer to. To stock triggers a process based on forecast and plans, to order starts only when there is an actual demand. Engineer to is the form in which Research and Development (R&D) is a part of the customer order fulfilment as a product is an engineer-based on the actual demand. In addition, processes plan, source, make, delivery and return comprise more detailed parts: L3 sub-processes, L4 activity, L5 task and L6 act. Level of detail depends on the scope of relevant decision problem or optimization process. However, this framework enables expression of interlinkage of supply chain processes inside one company and across its supply chain.

METHODOLOGY

The chapter presents an overview of supply chain management evolution that enables the identification of fundamental differences as well as common aspects of SCM 4.0 with the preceding SCM concepts: Mass SCM, Lean SCM, Agile SCM, Resilient SCM and Green SCM. This approach answers the question how much SCM 4.0 inherits attributes from previous SCM.

The author uses critical aspects of SCM: competitive advantage, risk, customer-supplier relationship, demand orientation, productivity, lead time, added value and cost management to outline main differences among the SCM paradigms. All critical aspects are fundamental for the establishment of a competitive advantage of a company. Competitive advantage is the Holy Grail that each company seeks to be distinguished from their competitor. The source of competitiveness never persists forever but is effective only for a limited time until other companies can adapt. The effective source of competitiveness represents innovation and adherence to market and social changes. Therefore, the source of competitiveness moves from quality to price, agility, resilient, ecology, individualization to digitalization and automation.

- **Quality:** It involves the quality of production and used materials as well as compliance with functions to meet customer requirements. The medium of a competitive advantage is the product itself. The barrier of competitive advantage imitation is the owner of a unique technology and of an international patent derived from R&D. Contemporary products can have a competitive advantage solely based on the quality during a limited period of their product life cycle, particularly in the introduction phase when the appropriate technology is not available to all relevant supply players.
- **Price:** This competitive advantage comes to turn when several suppliers can provide a product of similar quality. Thus, the customer cannot distinguish between them and companies must switch to pricing to offer additional criterion of differentiation. This makes a qualification criterion of quality and transfer the decisive criterion to price. Price competition initiates a continuous price reduction to maintain a reasonable margin by the combination of the following approaches: process improvement by removal of wasted activities, reorganization of manufacturing and logistics processes, following economies of scope in procurement, production and logistics processes, reconfiguration and enhancing of supply chain processes by lean management adoption or by better negotiated terms with suppliers. Nonetheless, an effort to cost reduction cannot worsen quality of the product by using low-quality materials etc.
- **Agility:** Agility represents the ability to respond quickly and accurately to customer requirements. It is relevant as a competitive advantage when quality and prices of products sold by competitors are similar. Agility is no longer a competitive advantage entailed by-product itself, but when logistic services are a significant driver. The decisive criterion is the ability to adhere to the customer in terms of short delivery time and peaks in demanded volumes. Peaks are of both an internal and external origin and the company encourage suppliers to adjust. In addition, suppliers provide a minimum ordering quantity, web EDI, safety and efficient packaging, track, and trace etc.
- **Ecology:** Melted differences among products in terms of their functions, quality, prices, and complementary services leads to commoditization of the relevant markets. In addition, the first decade of the 21st century is typical for the promotion of environmental issues, which create a significant segment of customers that are sensitive to ecology. Hence, companies initiate green projects by which their products and operation transform into less harmful ones for the environment in terms of production, transportation, warehousing, packaging, usage, or disposal. Green can become a competitive advantage only when it exceeds regulations and is properly promoted to customers.
- **Individualization:** New source of competitiveness arises due to the disappearance of substantial differences among products regarding delivery time and the level of logistic services and increasing customer requirements. Thus, companies surpass their competitors by the provision of completely individualised products and associated services. This level of individualization is a result of the cooperative supply chain.

- **Servitization:** Increasing the value of time and work-life balance, generates a demand on the reduction of processes and activities associated with decisions about replenishment, operation, maintenance, repair, and others that people must make in both their professional and private life. Many of these activities are of a manual nature and can be automated and provided without human intervention. Automation of such routines saves time that is increasingly valuable due to lower unemployment, higher salaries, and the work-life balance attitude. The gained benefits are not the only gauge of cost but also of quality. Automation in data processing and transfer among systems decrease the probability of human errors. Therefore, servitization complements individualization of products and logistics services as competitive advantages. Companies must take over order management, maintenance, and aftermarket by using predictive techniques to provide an extraordinary imitable source of competitiveness.

The author uses the example of the 3PL approach in the Czech Republic to demonstrate the relationship of 3PL to SCM 4.0 using Czech specifics. The latter are mainly situated in the job market in which the rate of unemployment is below natural expectations. Therefore, there is a tremendous insufficient supply of both lower skilled and highly qualified individuals in the market. Furthermore, the salaries are one-third of those in leading EU countries such as, Belgium and Germany. There is also a low mobility of people in terms of the job market among the regions of the Czech Republic. This situation establishes a contradictory phenomenon as the lack of labour creates pressure on digitalization and automation, but low wages undermines the Return of Investments of the projects proposed for automation and digitalization.

Besides the labour market specifics, the Czech Republic suffers from an extremely thin vacancy rate of logistic property supply (4%) Systemy Logistiky CZ, 2016). This forces 3PL to enhance productivity to manage their operation in the current facilities. The lack of capacities in the market also reinforces developers to require a longer period of contracts unlike the period during the world economic crises of 2008 to 2014. Longer contracts provide developers the opportunity to invest in their facilities and consider more advanced technologies.

The 3PL market is decentralized in the Czech Republic which corresponds to its state in other European countries. The author discusses only 3PLs that have a subsidiary in the Czech Republic who acquire the provision of financial and knowledge support from their head office. Furthermore, global 3PLs cooperate with global customers that may initiate projects of digitalization and automation within the Czech territory.

The author uses in-depth semi-structured interviews with eight major global 3PL and provides an overview how 3PL in the Czech Republic perceive SCM 4.0.

PARADIGM CHANGE OF SCM

SCM has undergone several evolutionary maturity stages that correspond with socio-economic changes as well as with the change in the source of competitiveness. SCM evolution reflects the change of position and competences of SCM throughout time. This reflects the shift from mainly transport and warehousing to a more complex management and execution of processes of material flow and related complementary services. There are six major evolutionary stage of SCM that are considered as a paradigm change. These are Mass Logistics/SCM, Lean, Agile, Resilient, Green and SCM 4.0. A general description of these strategies follows.

Mass Logistics/SCM

Mass Logistics/SCM represents the economies of scale that aims to squeeze out the maximum productivity from machinery or labour (Liker, 2004). Mass Logistics/SCM is based on Frederick Winslow Taylor who founded scientific management at the beginning of the twentieth century. One of the fundamental principles is the division of tasks into smaller activities proved by the observation that both labour and machinery produce a higher number of activities per time. Johnson (2006) links Mass to a mechanic approach as a set of fragments that can be measured and financially appraised individually in regard to their inputs and outputs.

Hence, the orientation on a narrow scope enhances training and productivity for an activity. Such specialization induces an increasing number of workstations and batch size. Cumulation of processed material reduces the number of changeovers. Thus, such an approach spreads from production to other supply chain processes due to Taylor´s findings. Duguay (1997) formulates the fundamentals of Mass as cost reduction by increasing the volume of production, managing the functions, a direct management approach without involvement of a subordinate in decision making, a competitive attitude to internal and external suppliers and the establishment of competition among suppliers to obtain the lowest price. Besides the above-mentioned aspects of Mass, Kavanagh and Cole (2013) emphasize that Mass Logistics/SCM requires a push management strategy. The division of tasks into a simplified number of activities induces additional activities related to planning and management of these activities to accomplish the final product. This results in the implementation of new techniques and software e.g. MRP I, MRP II, DRP, ERP, APS etc. to overcome complexity.

Lean SCM

Employment of Mass SCM involves several problems that intensify with time. The main ones are the dramatic growth of work in process, an extension of lead time, the higher rigidity of SCM, too high a number of planners needed for supply chain planning, the complexity of management and lack of transparency in the organizational structure, complicated and insufficient integration of production and logistic processes. Changes in customer expectations in terms of product range and quality of complementary services worsen these consequences. An effective response provides a new paradigm, Lean SCM, which imitates the Toyota Production System (TPS). Its core concept consists of the competences in the identification and elimination of waste labelled as Muda, Mura, and Muri. Muda represents the operational waste of overproduction, waiting, non-value-added transportation, improper processes, stocks, motion, defects, insufficient employment of labour capabilities and failures in work order settings and communications. Mura covers the gaps in interfaces among processes that result in poor visibility and coordination of activities across the supply chain with consequences of high variability and Muda, waste creation. Variability cannot be simplified only to the external demand variability, which is commonly considered by demand planning. The more severe is internal random variability that is the impact of Mura and of maintenance and quality issues. Muri involves the overloading of labour which leads to dissatisfaction within the workforce, the growth of defect and human injuries. The first applications of lean within inbound logistics dates back to 1970s and within outbound to the 1980s (Carvalho, Duarte & Cruz-Machado, 2011).

A long-term practice of lean leads to the:

- Commitment of labour to process improvements across all organizational levels.
- Reduction of space for operational and administration / increase of space utilization.
- Lowering of stocks and invested capital.
- Lower number of material transactions.
- Elimination of defects.
- Reduction of touches with material.
- Decreasing number of purchasing staff.

Lean can become a competitive advantage only when it is considered as a philosophy and not only as one of the possible strategies (Bhasin & Burcher, 2006). Only then can Lean penetrate through the whole organization.

Agile

Increasing customer requirements as to shorter delivery time and the widening of the number of Stock Keeping Units (SKUs) in the 1990s is not in harmony with an excessive reduction of stock and with traditional lean tools. A common strategy to reach efficiency is the reallocation and offshoring of many productions, financial and IT processes to lower-cost regions, for instance, South East Asia, Central and Eastern Europe (CEE), Russia, South America, and North Africa during the 1990s and in the first decade of the twenty-first century. This affords companies some long-term benefits mainly in their presence in the new emerging markets, their demand and supply base and the contribution to the creation of local purchasing power through employment. Nonetheless, there are many negative effects that gradually appear connected with quality issues, delays, lack of compliance with ethical and ecological standards, international patents, extension, and rigidity of supply chains etc. Therefore, initially, the flexibility of supply chains and the incorporation of agility into lean and global supply chains brings the positioning of unified goods into critical parts of the supply chains. Consequently, the finalization of customer goods is postponed until issuance of their purchasing orders. Lean provides operational efficiency by short cycle times, one-piece flow and low variability when meeting customer requirements. When it is insufficient to meet a short delivery time, then stocks of semi-finished products and better data exchange among supply chain partners enables the fulfilment of customer service. Lean supply chain represents doing things right and the agile supply chain enhances by doing the right things (Christopher & Towill, 2000). A comparison of Lean and Agile is provided by Vonderembse et al. (2006). Agile supply chains struggle with demand variability and the shortening product lifecycle by the allocation of stock or production and logistic capacities along supply chains, increasing supply chain visibility, flexible transport and sharing of assets and organization of a quick response in supply chains (Carvalho, Duarte & Cruz-Machado, 2011).

Resilient

The relevance of resilience in supply chain grows with the globalization of supply chains in the late twenieth centruy and in the first decade of the current as well as the shift of purchasing to a more e-commerce concept. Intensified frequency and severity disturbances emerge in supply chains due to both internal and external risk (Christopher & Holweg 2011). Supply chain disturbances are mainly caused by natural disasters, an epidemic of diseases of humans or animals, the toxicity of food, hacker attacks, political and economic embargos, migration, strikes, scandals, recessions etc. Therefore, the resilient strategy aims to change structure, organization, and the operation of supply chains to mitigate vulnerability (Christopher, 2011). It means that the actions taken to prevent risk or at least curtail the negative consequences and restore ordinary performances. Chapman (2002) recognizes fundamental steps to keep l vulnerability low in the supply chains:

- Top management has cognizance of risk in the supply chain.
- Changes in corporate strategy significantly influence the risk in supply chains.
- Risk management is inevitable and an inseparable part of SCM.
- Employees are aware of the risk associated with their processes and their role in risk management.

Green

Environmental concern in supply chains is an important issue for business. Today, companies initiate discussions and projects as to the environmental impact of their operations. The proliferation of monitoring and reducing externalities in supply chains is motivated by an estimated competitive advantage and by change in legislation (Zhu, Q.; Sarkis, J. & Lai, K., 2008). The pressure of ecological agencies, politicians, and journalists to engage individuals to recognise the environmental impact of goods and their suppliers. If the balance of the negotiation power is not on the supplier side, then the certification of environmental friendliness becomes part of the tenders. Green SCM comprises the reduction of used materials, an extension of replenishment frequency, integration of reverse material and information flow into standard management, environmental risk sharing, waste minimization, reduction of low utilization of transport capacities, an increase of raw material utilization effectiveness (Carvalho, Duarte & Cruz-Machado, 2011). Companies undertake green projects that can directly reduce operational costs to lower electricity consumption or to increase sales due to a better green image.

SCM 4.0

SCM 4.0 is the maturity state of SCM that is compliant with the concept of Industry 4.0 announced in 2013 on Hanover Fair. Industry 4.0 represents the transformation of the current production and supply chain operation to a substantially more advanced level in terms of automation and digitalization. This brings a new level of efficiency and effectiveness in supply chain processes (Martinez, F., Jirsak, P. & Lorenc, M., 2016; Sommer, 2015; Daugherty, P., Banerjee, P., Negm, W. & Alter, A. E., 2015; Wang, Wan, Li & Zhang, 2016). The significant cost reduction (50%) estimated due to the impact of Industry 4.0 on SCM (Rusman, M., Lorenz, M., Gerbert, P., Waldner, M., Justus, J., Engel, P. & Harnish, M., 2015).

The main progress does not reside with the implementation of specific technologies considered to be modern although many originate from the 1970s and 80s such as, additive manufacturing and robotization. However, the fundamental is an online interconnection of autonomous sources (people, machines, material, documentation, software) to gain rapid growth of productivity through cooperation. Thus, the real-time visibility and continuous real-time optimization are the main benefits of the linkage of supply chain sources. The integration of embedded software with internal and external IT systems creates Cyber-Physical System (CPS) or virtual mirror. The main aspect of the transition to a physical cyber system is digitalization (Lasi, H., Fettke, P., Kemper, H. & Feld, T., 2014).

SCM transformation to SCM 4.0 requires extension to the scope of digitalization and automation of both administrative and physical work (Schram, H., Prockl, G., Kolar, P. (2017). Although, there is no consensus if the transition to SCM 4.0 or to Industry 4.0 is an evolutionary or revolutionary process, it is a general perception that the transition is rapid.

The major socio-technic-economic drivers for accelerating the change are:

- Change of peoples´ lifestyle and purchasing behaviour.
- Economic boom results in extremely low unemployment in industrial regions that can endanger further expansion of both the economy and companies.
- Servitization as a shift from owning a product to consuming service that reflects an unwillingness to bear the total cost of ownership for a longer time than a customer needs service.
- Promotion, education, and support of Industry 4.0 by relevant authorities: Chambers of Commerce, Ministry of Industry and Trade, industrial and trade professional associations.
- Development and rapid implementation of advanced technologies labelled as disruptive technologies.
- Extreme customization and short delivery time require a shorter time to market which is reflected in the location of production and logistic facilities.
- Increasing complexity and speed of customer satisfaction across industries results in the necessity to use CPS to collect, process, share and employ data for analyses, optimization, and decision in real time.
- Promotion of the topic by consulting companies and suppliers of technologies and services related to Industry 4.0 to extend their market.

Fundamental barriers and challenges preventing companies from rapid transformation:

- Companies are reluctant to adopt advanced technologies due to their previous high investments in machinery, robots, racking systems, transport and manipulation fleet, Enterprise Resource Planning software (ERP), Warehouse Management System software (WMS), Transport Management System software (TMS) or other investments as they have not yet been written off. Thus, previous investments must first return-back before further steps are taken. The transformation to Industry 4.0 resembles a continuous change to embed an IoT sensor in technology rather than a radical replacement of old technology by the new smart one. The different approach is in Greenfield where the past does not limit.
- The decision to rapidly implement new technologies of Industry 4.0 requires a proper knowledge base. The pitfall of technologies related to Industry 4.0 lays in their novelty for a business massive implementation. There is a lack of cases that provide sufficient data about their long-term effect on supply chain performances and their suitability for specific companies regarding size, industry, location, state of the job market, strategy etc. Therefore, a company initiating Industry 4.0 projects requires a team endowed with technical, economic and Human Resources (HR) knowledge with the ability to properly appraise the complex impact of the implementation.
- The job market situation is a factor that accelerates the transformation to Industry 4.0 as unemployment below the natural unemployment level, limits expansion and demand fulfilment in a period of economic growth. Automation and digitalization relieve individuals from heavy, harmful, routine, and tedious work and enables their reallocation to a job of higher added value. Certainly, this is relevant if the employee is capable to cope with a more sophisticated job otherwise, the employee becomes redundant. In addition, a combination of economic expansion and low unem-

ployment results in overloading of current employees. Overloading by everyday routine operation limits the ability to gather information about the essence of Industry 4.0 and possible benefits for their company.

COMPARISON OF SUPPLY CHAIN STRATEGIES: MASS, LEAN, AGILE, RESILIENT, GREEN AND SUPPLY CHAIN 4.0

The maturity stages of SCM are compared on the bases of seven critical aspects: competitive advantage, Risk, Customer-supplier relationship, demand orientation, Lead time, productivity and added value.

Competitive Advantage

Mass SCM

The competitive advantage of Mass SCM changes as a decisive criterion is of the functional and qualitative features of the product. Throughout a product lifecycle, a functional and qualitative gap among available product in the market diminishes. Hence, they become qualifiers and the competitive advantages shifts to price and unit cost. Mass SCM utilizes an economy of scale across all processes starting from procurement and ending with reverse logistics. Mass SCM is accomplished by cost-oriented strategy in which product and logistics services lack customization to meet high volumes and economies of scale.

Lean SCM

The competitive advantage of Lean SCM is in the low total cost mainly, the supply chain cost. This becomes a reaction to Mass SCM as the difference between competitors diminishes in the area typical for Mass SCM due to technological progress, globalization, and cost reduction strategy. Moreover, long-term application of economies of scope to enhance supply chain performance results in a low insular cost but the growth of the total cost because of the contradictory goals of each process owners. The qualifying criterion in tenders is a level of the logistic service corresponding to the On-Time in Full and Error free service level (OTIF) and short delivery time that meets the concept of Just in Time. However, the decisive criterion is a lower price.

Agile SCM

Market saturation, commoditization of products and consumerism reinforce demand over supply. Furthermore, the exaggeration of processes- leaning leads to skinny processes which do not have enough stock buffers or time slack to respond neither to the internal nor external operation peaks. Therefore, customers intensify their requirements on logistic services, which become decisive criterion and the competitive advantage. The qualifying criteria are quality, lead time and total cost. Total supply chains are designed so that there are safety buffers of unified outputs across a supply net. Supply chains respond to the actual demand by customization of the semi-finished goods held in stock. This is known as postponement strategy.

Resilient SCM

Resilience becomes urgent when vulnerability of global supply chains is demonstrated in numerous cases. For instance, in 2011, due to the stoppage of material flow due to the tsunami in Japan or abuse of child labour in supply chains of electronic or fashion, palm oil scandals or pirate attacks in maritime main routes. Hence, the decisive criterion is flexibility defined as the speed to return to an equilibrium after supply chain disruption. The value lays in the capability to restore operations before a natural disaster, cyber-attack, ethical scandal, attacks, strikes, the collapse of transportation etc. Supply chain total costs and lead times become qualifiers.

Green SCM

Companies achieve competitive advantage by creating the image of an ecologically friendly company in its total supply chain. Besides greater recognition, green measures are associated with the total cost savings when including even the costs induced by the liquidation of consequences of externalities and disasters. The competitive advantage and decisive criterion are the low externalities while the qualifier is service level and lead time.

SCM 4.0

Digitalization brings substantial change to customer satisfaction and therefore, digital services provide a competitive advantage. The transition from tangible product to service-oriented customer satisfaction enables better efficiency and effectiveness. There is a higher efficiency as a user hires service just during a time of need and the customer does not have to own a product. The transition is called servitization and this enables higher customization to individual customer needs. Qualifying criteria are cost, quality, service level and lead time.

Risk

Mass SCM

The risk in Mass SCM is associated with poor visibility of both internal and external processes. This is due to overstocking of a supply chain system. Mass supply chain processes encompass a high level of stocks, besides gaining economies of scale, to reduce the risk of the shortage of material due to broken machines, variability in the quality of some supplying production process, non-deliveries from suppliers, some natural disasters or any other internal or external event. Stocks enables covering and overcoming of small problems. However, continuous ignorance of small problems for instance, variability of delivery time, leads to an intensification of consequences. When the problem can be noticed, it is commonly too late to quickly resolve without significant impacts. Thus, stocks reduce risk but on a long-term basis, create more serious issues due to the concealment of problems at their start. There is a low risk of demand variability at the period of Mass.

Lean SCM

Lean SCM reduces a redundant operation and non-value added activities as well as stocks. This reveals failures and deficiencies of the supply chain and associated processes. This increases sensitivity to any failures in the supply chain processes. In addition, the transformation of Mass to Lean SCM carries risk that employees do not identify themselves with the ongoing and active search for improvements instead of hiding problems or with active participation in process improvement projects. Furthermore, there is also a risk that scientific analyses and evaluation of improvement solutions fail to replace unfounded expert judgements. There is a significant market risk in comparison to Mass in demand variability as in Lean SCM suppliers are not certain that they can sell all their planned production.

Agile SCM

Continuous pressure on the extension of demand coverage, individualization of products and services, enhancing service and reduction on costs initiates oftentimes inconsistent and system leaning of supply chain processes. Eagerness save costs from processes can result in the elimination of a buffer stock or activity securing perfect quality or outsourcing of some processes to an external partner. Thus, there is a demand for high-level services and communication and cooperation among supply chain partners. Otherwise, any internal variability in terms of lead time and quality can result in customer dissatisfaction because of no or defected delivery.

Resilient SCM

The causes of risk typical for Agile SCM persist and intensify due to the growing frequency of natural and human disruption of supply chain infrastructure and processes globally. Furthermore, there are more frequent changes in economic cycles of European economies suffering from very insignificant GDP growth. More frequent changes and downswings of aggregate demand influences demand on goods and logistics services. Unpredictable changes cause the nervous and exaggerated response to even minor fluctuations. In addition, European countries suffer from high indebtedness. Governments change policies from flat or selective cost-cutting to selective or flat subsidies. The risk of Resilient SCM is that supply chains cannot organize an operation with required performances due to external or internal disruption.

Green SCM

Green SCM contains risks of failing ecological norms either by a company or suppliers at different tiers. Companies worry of a threat that they may be linked to an ecological scandal. The negative consequence could be either rapid downswing of demand due to the ruined image or induced costs of negative effect elimination and increased insurance fees. Additionally, risks described in in Resilient SCM persist.

SCM 4.0

An increasing level of automation and digitalization assist to limit the risk of previous strategies but also opens new opportunities for risks. Firstly, SCM 4.0 works with large volumes of valuable data containing personal or confidential data. Thus, an abuse of confidential data, paralysis of the company because of a hacking information system or of low speed of data transaction are just some of the new issue that companies can challenge. Besides this, there are some other relevant risks. Building and maintenance of system encompassing high rate of automation and digitalization require knowledge and qualified staff. In addition, there is also a risk that a company pick up an inappropriate process or activity for automation and digitalization due to lack of experience and knowledge where human activity should be kept and where replaced. The novelty of automation and digitalization causes lack of experience with side effects and negative consequence in complex processes.

Customer-Supplier Relationship

Mass SCM

Mass SCM comprises short-term contracts with numerous suppliers per item or service to maintain competitiveness among the suppliers. There is an antagonistic relationship in which both parties want to gain a better negotiational power. Hence, suppliers are in a reactive position.

Lean SCM

The growth of effectiveness in Lean SCM depends on the elimination of nine sources of waste and following the14 principles. Short term contracts create many of the nine wastes for instance, overproduction, stocks, variability, and improper processes and therefore, Lean SCM transforms the customer-supplier relationship from a short-term and antagonictic orientation to a long-term partnership. Achievement of this win-win perception is a crucial aspect of cooperation as both parties do not need to search for side benefits that compensate dissatisfaction and loses. Suppliers are full-members of project teams that can influence the supplier. There is no strict recognition of a border between the supplier and customer processes in terms of scope of optimization. This is because the processes of both parties fall into one value stream that is relevant for optimization and control. Customers and suppliers cooperate in the creation and operation of vendor webs and platforms, as with Collaborative Planning Forecasting and Replenishment (CPFR) to gain mutual benefits, such as, lower safety stocks, higher utilization of fleet etc.

Nonetheless, many companies that fail to implement lean and TPS demonstrate that they are not able to overcome their perception of the supplier as the party responsible for all cost savings, failures, and other risk-related issues.

Agile SCM

Suppliers and customers cooperate as one virtual company. There is a seamless operation and optimization and changes of supply chain processes regardless of the owner of that particular part of the operation. The sustainability occurs only when the cost or possible benefits are equally distributed among all parties. There is a more intensive data interchange among the parties and a better visibility of the supply chain operation in comparison to former SCM strategies. Customers and suppliers exchange data about present demand, primary and secondary demand, status and position of goods in the pipeline, shutdowns of operations, stock level etc. Customers require flexibility, responsiveness, and quality of delivery.

Resilient SCM

In addition to the cooperation typical for Agile and lean SCM, companies across the supply chain share risk by the appropriate allocation of safety stock across the whole supply chain, selection of transport modes and routes, the contingency plan of operation and selection and monitoring of suppliers beyond the first tier. Supply chain visibility extends its scope to other tiers and deepens shared information. Decisive criteria of supplier selection are the flexibility to adjust to customer requirements, financial stability and adequate dispersion of operation facilities to prevent from complete interruption of supply chain performances. The concern with these criteria enhances the vulnerability of supply chains under conditions of disruptions of natural or human origin.

Green SCM

Suppliers and customers share data on the ecological footprint of their operation to quantify the total impact of the supply chain traced to items and pieces of goods. Furthermore, the supply chain parties exchange best practices of green logistics and collaborate on green projects as with the pooling of transport capacities. Customers implement green criteria into the selection and evaluation of suppliers. These criteria are the certification of ISO 14001, special green certificates that customers issue to their suppliers, EURO norms of vehicles, level of safety measures in warehouses, traceability of goods and associated externalities, level of reverse logistics, etc.

SCM 4.0

Digitalization brings an advanced level of visibility across global supply chains. Thus, scandals concerning issues of ethics, public danger, and other risks spread in real time globally via social networks, mass media and other information channels. This increases the concern of companies as any such scandal of one company in the supply chain that may be located far from the final market can ruin the reputation and cause significant loses to all parties in this supply chain. Digitalization improves the predictability of risk and responsiveness to negative impact mitigation as well as, leads to the pressure on all partners to select suppliers compliant with the qualitative, ethical, legal, and economic standards.

Demand Orientation

Mass SCM

Mass SCM processes start based on work orders issued on operation plans and schedules. In addition, short-term demand forecast specifies these plans and schedules. Thus, there is a lack of linkage between the actual demand and performance as production, logistic, packaging, headcount and other plans reflect the forecasts rather than the actual demand. This approach is compliant with the push concept and forecast of both external and internal demand defines the targets and plans. There are several modifications of the push concept depending on the process: engineer to stock in product development, delivery to stock purchasing, make to stock production and assembling and distribute to stock distribution. The major advantage of forecast oriented planning is that the supply chain processes are not disturbed by contemporary peaks of external or internal demand on supply chain processes and planners are able to balance the workload. Furthermore, delivery time is shorter because of the availability of goods in stock. Moreover, such a concept enables achieving economies of scope by planning the operation in cumulated volumes. However, the customer service level, as well as process efficiency, depends on demand forecast accuracy. The reliability decreases with the intensification of the external demand changes and even internal changes due to machine breakage, inadequate quality of supplied material and rescheduling of operation schedule because of customer prioritization.

Lean SCM

Lean SCM operates based on plans and schedules but unlike Mass SCM, planners create the plans based on actual demand rather than on the forecasted. The plan is created either by the Material Requirements Planning (MRP) system as with the Mass SCM or less rigidly by the Kanban system. Processes that trigger their operation based on actual customer demand have the following forms: engineer to order, replenish to order, make to order, assembly to order and distribute to order. Linkage of processes with the current market situation enables an efficient employment of resources across the supply chain because of the better adherence to customer requirements. Customer delivery time encompasses more processes and thus has a longer lead time associated with customer satisfaction. The customer is more integrated into the internal company processes in the case of labelling, packaging, production and the purchasing of material. The scope of processes executed on customer demand and those on demand forecasts is set based on the lead time of processes and level of waste reduction by using a 5S method or Kanban system. Major lead time savings are in the reduction of overproduction and storing being replaced by an intensification of delivery frequency, shrinkage of delivery quantity per item and smoothing of peaks in inbound and implant material flows. The extension of demand-oriented processes enables a better customization of products and services to customers.

Agile SCM

A better adherence to demand and flexibility to adapt to market changes resets the position of the decoupling point in which to meet demand and forecast oriented processes. Lean SCM locates the decoupling point upstream as it is possible and ideally to a supplier site. Agile SCM searches for a balance between efficiency and flexibility. Hence, the decoupling point moves forward to have a unified semi-finished product available for quick finalization and customer delivery. This initiates changes in product engineering as effective and efficient Agile SCM requires a module structured and shared parts among the product portfolio as well as a flexible and multifunction production lines and facilities. The consequence of agility is a higher work in process in comparison to the traditional Lean SCM concept and with greater flexibility.

Resilient SCM

Concerning demand orientation, Resilient SCM operates on similar principles as Agile SCM. Resilient SCM employs stocks strategically allocated across the supply chain to forestall or reduce consequential supply chain disturbances. Stocks enable the rising above insignificant supply chain disturbances without impact on the operation. Supply chain risk management embeds not only stock but better availability of online data on the operation. Thus, the decoupling point is located considering both flexibility and risk.

Green SCM

Green SCM follows previous SCM paradigms in material management and does not bring critical change in comparison to Lean SCM, Agile SCM or Resilient SCM. The concepts and technologies of Lean, Agile and Resilient SCM embed an eco-efficiency when properly implemented and operated. Nonetheless, higher sensitivity on the ecology can lead to a slow down of replenishment frequency because of better vehicle utilization. Demand-oriented supply chain processes reduce scrap rate and level of goods obsolescence.

SCM 4.0

A complete orientation on customer product customization calls for the pull concept in customer order fulfilment. Each process starts when customer order both internal and external enters. Then, CPS organizes the allocation of the order to particular work centres and manages material flow across the company. Nonetheless, the postponement concept is applied as within Agile SCM as an extremely short delivery time of a customized product and requires the location of unified semi-finished products across supply chains. Digitalization reduces the lead time of the administrative processes and leaves more time for the organization of material flow. Furthermore, digitalization enhances the visibility of supply chain beyond the boundaries of the company. Thus, a wider scope of processes is managed on pull even when delivery time is shorter within the market.

Productivity, Lead Time and Value Added

Mass SCM

Value-added for the customer are associated with the functional features of the product, which are determined in the process of research and development. Commonly, there are just minor changes, if any, during a product life cycle. Thus, the company collects and analyses customer requirements before research and development and not during the series or mass production of the goods. Product functions relate to a tangible product that arises in the manufacturing process. Thus, even added value is created within the manufacturing process. The other processes in SCM are business value added or waste. Therefore, it has consequences on the perception of productivity and targeting of a tool for productivity growth solely in the manufacturing process.

Mass SCM focuses primarily on customer delivery time and then, on the lead times of particular supply chain activities. Lead time of these activities is monitored and continually reduced to increase their productivity. Better availability of goods and high productivity is gained by increasing batch size and reducing lead times. There is no monitoring of total process lead time.

Mass SCM has an axiom about the productivity that the more a machine or human produces per time period the higher the productivity. Hence, there is the maximization of outputs perused sources. This approach leads to the decomposition of activities into more simple tasks that humans and machines execute. This simplification results in the organization of routine simple tasks that can be executed with the simplest of skills and qualifications. The expansion of this approach across the company leads to a more complex organizational structure and management. Furthermore, the new job is established to plan, coordinate and handle goods among job centres responsible for individual tasks.

The eagerness to increase productivity extends the usage of the operation in high size batches in which there is a low number of changeovers. The simple monotonous operation and high size batches produce a high number of outputs with a low number of sources per period in comparison to more frequent changes of operation of small size batches. Monitoring and evaluation of productivity in Mass SCM correspond with the general philosophy and rules of Mass SCM. This way of monitoring and measuring of productivity neglects the productivity loses associated with activities among tasks such as, internal manipulation and losses caused by new activities in the planning and coordination of individual activities.

Lean SCM

Added value extends from product functions to all aspects of the product, complementary services, and process outputs that customers consume starting from the ordering process, using a product, and ending with after-market services. Hence, customers perceive added value across supply chain processes and supply chain services significantly influence customer satisfaction and loyalty. Furthermore, customer requirements change throughout time and during phases of product life cycle. Therefore, it is obvious that companies must collect customer comments throughout the whole product lifecycle and retain a close customer relationship. Only then can a supplier dynamically adhere to individual customer requirements in terms of added value. Lean SCM monitors and analyses added value and waste in processes and impact within any proposed internal and external change. The priority of Lean SCM is to remove resources and activities that do not bring the required value to the customer or is not mandatory from directives or needed for the functioning of a company.

Lean SCM continuously reduces the overall supply chain lead time as well as of the processes. Thus, Lean SCM follows delivery time reduction along with the reduction of lead time of individual activities, waiting time of goods during the storage and time associated with planning and coordination. Hence, the full scope of lead time is measured and reduced. Such an approach contradicts the traditional silo organization structure. Therefore, productivity is measured by a value stream level that impedes the growth of productivity in one area which, in turn, would lead to the decline of productivity in the subsequent or previous process. For instance, the stock of a finished product is still in one value stream with the production process, thus the growth of production batch would be immediately reflected in the growth of the stock. Time is a major user of valuable resources in a company and it is also the major variable with which lean tools work in process optimization. The time dimension is embedded into staff training so that employees realize the correlation between time, effectiveness, and efficiency.

Unlike Mass SCM, Lean SCM recognizes as a productive output only the one demanded by the customer. Thus, productivity expresses the ratio of demanded outputs and resources needed to fulfil the demand. Productivity grows only when increased output corresponds with the added value required by the customer. Hence, there is the necessity to simplify the total process not only a certain section such as one machine or job. The productivity also grows with the reduction of variability below tolerance accepted by the client. The axiom that productivity occurs only when right things are created right the first time. The growth of productivity correlates with the production only of demanded outputs and with reduction of lead time of supply chain processes. Concerning the fact that in Lean SCM, a large scope of the processes is part of the delivery time, it is highly important that optimization targets all relevant lead times and variability of the processes. The reduction of lead time is not achieved by accelerating the work but by the elimination of those activities that do not add customer value.

Agile SCM

Agile SCM differs from the previous SCM strategy not in the perception of added value but how added value is increased, or waste reduced for customers. Agile SCM uses advanced communication and automation technologies to hasten processes and provide new logistic services related with traceability, delivery flexibility, and customization. Agile SCM follows Lean SCM, therefore, Agile SCM processes are already lean.

Agile SCM monitors and systematically reduces total supply chain lead time identically to Lean SCM but the major concern is in the delivery time which is critical for a quick response. Lead time, as well as delivery time, is reduced by the implementation of recent information and communication technologies and by the reconfiguration of the supply chain concerned with the time to market. In addition, employing automation reduces lead times and brings cost effectiveness to operations located near consumer markets. Delivery time in Agile SCM is shorter than in Lean SCM and enables a better flexibility to demand changes.

There is no difference between measuring productivity in Lean and Agile SCM, however, it differs in measures taken to enhance productivity. Agile SCM improves the visibility of demand in the final market and material flow across the total supply chain, employment of postponement strategy, strategic allocation of stock, sharing of part across product portfolio, modular structure, a combination of near-shoring and off-shoring strategy and automation implementation.

Resilient SCM

Resilient SCM extends the monitoring and enhancement of added value through performance stability and security and goods provided within the global supply chains. There is not a radical change in the added value perception, customers start to recognise the capability to minimize supply chain vulnerability. Although not directly added value, it is business value added.

Measures and actions taken to prevent or mitigate risk in the supply chain have various impacts on lead time. The location of stocks and postponement, prolong supply chain lead time unlike the engagement of a faster mode of transportation such as rail and air as a substitution to maritime transportation in some routes. Furthermore, the extended scope of sourcing from local suppliers reduces lead time due to transportation lead time and higher frequency of replenishment.

There is a difference in measuring productivity between Resilient SCM and Agile SCM. The formula measuring productivity is reformulated by adding added value for customers gained from the reduction of risk to the nominator and placing induced costs because of the employment of sources used for risk prevention and mitigation. Hence, resilient productivity encompasses efficiency, effectiveness and on top of that also risk-effectiveness. Resilient SCM uses, aside from measures of productivity typical for Lean and Agile SCM, also creates a knowledge base of gathering, analysing, and evaluating information on possible risks associated with external and internal factors of the supply chain. Moreover, preparedness for a continuous assessment of contingency plans and their adaptation to changing conditions are also critical aspects of productivity management.

Green SCM

Customers extend perceived added value by the ecological footprint of their supply chains and products they purchase and use. Social pressure and public awareness encourage individuals to increase their concern on the environmental aspects of purchasing goods, their suppliers and supply chains. Such concerns create the ecological aspect as an inevitable part of the added value perceived by customers. Added value grows with increasing the environmental friendliness of related goods and supply chain as with the provision of services. These services are associated with the measuring, controlling, and reporting of operations on the environment and with reverse logistics. Lead times and even delivery times extend with the lowering of delivery frequency so that there is a higher utilization of loading and space limits of the cargo vehicle capacity. Furthermore, the transition from road to rail transportation leads to prolonging the transportation lead time unless high volumes equal to block trains are shipped.

SCM 4.0

Added value shifts from a tangible product to services in comparison to the previous SCM concepts. Moreover, digital services are part of the added value. Companies diagnose differently added value required by their customers within the previous concepts:

- **Mass SCM:** Specialised suppliers are convinced that they know fully their customer´s needs and added value
- **Lean SCM, Agile SCM:** Research among customers as to their needs and added value
- **Resilient SCM, Green SCM:** Monitoring of external factors (legislation, politico-economic situation, natural disasters, strikes etc.)

SCM 4.0 continuously collects and analyses data about customer behaviour and various data of external factors. Big data are filtered to smart data and provide an opportunity to dynamically parameterize provided added value for individual customers regarding their need for time and circumstance. Thus, the customer does not have to explicitly express a needed added value but through their behaviour, data produced defines this. This eliminates the problem when a customer is not aware of what brings the added value and expresses varied requirements.

A better visibility in the supply chain enables a higher velocity of stocks and shorter storage time. In addition, an integrated information platform in parallel with distributive decision-making enables reducing lead time of planning, which is one of the main inefficiencies in the current operation. Lean SCM targets commonly on material flow and the planning processes are commonly overlooked or avoided because of functional silos that are rarely changed. SCM 4.0 establishes an integration of technologies, which results in the redundant capacity in planning and the flatting of the organizational structure. SCM 4.0 provides an early identification of the variability of the customer or process owner toleration, diagnoses of the situation, re-planning and rescheduling the operation and addressing the most suitable measures for rectification. Hence, total planning lead time shrinks. Furthermore, the application of modern technologies, for instance additive manufacturing, leads to locating production facilities and the supply base closer to the market which shortens lead time.

Digitalization provides on-time monitoring of overall productivity and overall equipment effectiveness, total time effectiveness. This brings not only on-time performance data but also permits predictive analyses so that early identification of the overall equipment effectiveness decline can prevent the production defects or severe equipment damage. That is certainly relevant beyond the production process and thus, the gap between expected and actual productivity is continuously monitored and assessed. Hence, the staff is allocated based on the actual performance and bottlenecks. Besides the above-mentioned enhancement of productivity, there is another critical impact of digitalization on productivity. Unlike the previous SCM strategies, digital services, the accuracy of data collection, processing and reporting become an integral part of productivity. Internet of Things (IoS) cannot operate without IoT and accurate and real-time data. Productivity grows with an increasing level of human routine operations by automation or when visualization and robotization provide significant assistance to the staff in to minimize quality defects, accidents, and to hasten production, administrative and logistic processes within SCM.

Cost Management

Cost management is a relevant aspect of assessing SCM concepts as costs are a major factor that influences motivation, management, and optimization of SCM processes. There are four main aspects that are considered: orientation on costs, revenues, or both; method of cost minimization; reporting of costs, and consideration of external costs.

Mass SCM

Mass SCM takes decisions based on minimum unit costs. They are calculated as cost per unit in a single production or logistic activity. The calculation involves the assignment of overhead costs to a unit based on a key (process time etc.) and adding variable costs. It is obvious that minimum cost is gained by following scale economics. Hence, cost accounting explicitly favours the accumulation of lots and division of labour to small and simple tasks. Total cost is the sum of unit costs and does not cover all relevant costs as there is no consideration of hidden cost (planning, storing, handling, reworking etc.). An orientation on the minimum unit cost leads to inefficiencies of the total supply chain, as cost reduction of one or a low number of activities can induce much greater cost rise in other parts of the supply chain. However, the Mass SCM cost management system cannot detect it. Mass SCM decisions are taken solely based on internal data. There is no consideration of externalities or the possible negative impacts on business partners.

Lean SCM

Lean SCM calculates costs per value stream in which decisions are made based on total costs. In addition, there is an evaluation of relevant consequences on the total supply chain including costs. Lean SCM associate cost with lead time and therefore, all lean tools and approaches work with lead time. Concerning the above mentioned on the Lean SCM, it is obvious that Lean SCM cost management supports reduction of non-value-added activities and therefore, the reduction of costs associated with resources used on non-value-added activities. It supposes that cost management of Lean SCM is more data intensive in terms of collection, processing, and reporting. Nonetheless, it is not true, as Lean SCM uses several axioms of TPS and many costs are not evaluated as there is long-term proof of experience about their benefits and impacts. Analogically, the fact that 1<2 is not repeatedly proved always when required.

Agile SCM

Cost management in Agile SCM is similar to the Lean SCM.

Resilient SCM

Cost management in Resilient SCM incorporates principles of cost management in Lean SCM. In addition, there is a calculation of costs associated with risk actions in supply chains, such as late or non-deliveries of material to a production process from the suppliers.

Green SCM

Cost management in Green SCM incorporates principles of cost management in Lean SCM. Besides, cost management contains costs of environmental externalities of supply chain operations.

SCM 4.0

Digitalization provides visibility of cost drivers along the supply chain. Furthermore, simulation embedded in SCM 4.0 provides cost calculation of different scenarios of the operation. The cost management follows the principles of Lean SCM and cost-effectiveness is associated with the relationship between cost and time. IoT and numerous sensors enable accurate monitoring and in real-time, lead time of individual customer order replenishment and consumed resources.

CASE STUDY FROM THE CZECH REPUBLIC ABOUT THE PERCEPTION OF INDUSTRY 4.0 BY 3PL

The attitude of 3PL to Industry 4.0 reflects the requirements of 3PL customers on contracted logistics. Thus, it is the customer-driven approach. Customers commonly do not set a specific method of customer satisfaction but define the service requirements. It is then up to the 3PL to establish a process, assign suitable technologies and staff to meet needs with a reasonable profit. However, the requirements and prices of logistic services determine the implementation of digitalization and automation.

Besides the traditionally high level of OTIF that oscillates between 96% and 99,9% based on information obtained during interviews. regarding a sector, there is pressure to enhance traceability from the pallet level to the distribution box and even piece level. In addition, customers expect on-line data from their 3PL about operations related to their goods. These requirements associated with investments into digitalization, as the transformation to a paperless operation is a fundamental aspect. Furthermore, the 3PL major concern is the better integration of ERP, WMS and TMS in a platform with an interface for new disruptive technologies for example, augmented reality, drones, additive manufacturing, and big data analytics. The development or customization and implementation are associated with tremendous effort and investment. Apart from traceability, customers expect sufficient flexibility from their 3PL in terms of processing and dealing with a high variability of volumes. This becomes extremely important with the growth of the e-commerce sector that is typical of demand variability, short delivery time to a specific window and of higher dispersion of demand.

However, these attributes are mainly associated to qualitative aspects of the contemporary logistic market. There is also a continuous emphasis on price reduction, therefore, 3PL companies must continuously work to enhance their efficiency. The price reduction is either explicitly mentioned in a contract specifying % of costs that 3PL must annually reduce or through the regular organization of the tenders, oblige 3PL to do so. This contradicting behaviour of customers creates both a positive and negative effect on the development of Industry 4.0 among 3PL companies.

The length of the 3PL contract has decreased with the time. Common contracts are between 3-5 years which is caused by the organization of regular tenders every three years. The contract length follows the length of the product lifecycle that equally has diminished. Furthermore, a contract length between lessor and 3PL as a lessee has shortened to a common duration of 3 years. A short-term contract influences the motivation of 3PL to invest into operational innovation.

Another aspect of the transformation to SCM 4.0 is corporate governance as the level of autonomy plays a significant role in the ability to respond to business changes. Obviously, belonging to a global corporation brings both positives and negatives for transformation to SCM 4.0. 3PL subsidiaries in the Czech Republic take advantage to employ a knowledge base on advanced technologies that is researched and tested in centres of excellence. Not each of the global 3PL has such a centre dedicated to research and proof of concept of Industry 4.0 disruptive technologies used in SCM 4.0. Some, have only centres that develop knowledge in process excellence e.g. Lean and Six Sigma or within the scope of traditional technologies. However, when there is such research centre, then the Czech subsidiary uses the outputs of research, proof of concept and if available, pilot projects. This provides significant benefits and provides a better market position, especially with lessons learnt about the implementation of advanced SCM 4.0 technologies. What the Czech market lacks is experienced implementers that guarantee the suitability of the business solution. There exists an abundance of marketing bulletins about the testing of some advanced technology in supply chain operations. However, as commercial literature they lack sufficient detail in such areas as 3D printing, 4D printing, drones, virtual reality and in specific settings of operational and customer service. It then becomes that this knowledge is shared among the subsidiaries. Nonetheless, SCM 4.0 is not something that can be implemented as a package solution neither is its technology portion. Local subsidiaries must tailor the solution to specifics of the individual customer. In addition, the local subsidiary may benefit from financial support to develop a SCM 4.0 solution to showcase. Without investments from headquarters, the local subsidiary cannot afford the solution.

Job market conditions are a major driver of digitalization and automation in the Czech Republic. An extreme deficiency of logistic operators, warehouse personnel, and drivers within the job market tends to be the higher concern of 3PL rather than digitalization and automation. The fact that it is impossible to hire an employee in most of the regions of the Czech Republic either full time or temporary, makes 3PL the only option. The Czech labour cost level is one-third of the leading EU countries such as, Germany and Belgium. This disqualifies the advanced level of automation and digitalization in terms of acceptable ROI. However, a limited supply of labour results in the growth of wages by 10% annually based on interviews. and thus, it remains cheaper to conduct work by humans rather than through automation or digitalization. Nonetheless, when the current economic prosperity continues, the breaking point will be achieved, and automation will be inevitable. Waiting for the breaking point provides enough time for innovation leaders to transform towards SCM 4.0. Current labour cost level determines that it is still convenient to extend delivery time and locate logistics facilities in the Czech Republic rather than locating closer to the centre of gravity in western Europe. Hence, this situation is still convenient for the Czech Republic.

The current situation in the Czech Republic favours digitalization rather than hard automation which does not provide a reasonable ROI. Digitalization is associated with lower investments and requires less radical changes within the company than in case of automation. Moreover, companies have a long-term experience with implementation of new software and the integration, however, the creation of environments and cultures to work with a collaborative robot is more intensive.

3PL implements SCM 4.0 to increase their productivity. They use Lean or Lean Six Sigma management to optimize their processes to increase annual productivity. Nonetheless, the processes are so optimized that it becomes increasingly difficult to reach annual cost savings required by the 3PL clients by incremental process improvements. Therefore, 3PLs are challenged to search for a completely new approach and SCM 4.0 offers new opportunities to achieve this. The establishment of paperless communication, automation of routine work, and digital support of humans in their processes, create new SCM systems that can rapidly increase productivity. However, SCM 4.0 follows the previous SCM concepts and is a consequence of evolution and ideas on how currently available advanced technologies support and change SCM processes.

FUTURE RESEARCH DIRECTIONS

The presented findings outline the current perception of SCM 4.0. It is evident that there are many attributes SCM 4.0 inherits from previous SCM paradigms and thus, SCM 4.0 is an evolutionary continuance of the past. However, SCM 4.0 also brings radical changes to the business model, HR, cooperation in supply chain and the value of data. The identified obstacles impeding transformation to SCM 4.0 maturity is still an insufficient interest and demand from customers on services of SCM 4.0 as described in case study of 3PLs. The findings outline that customers use price as the decisive criterion in tenders that disqualify an advanced level of automation among 3PLs within the Czech Republic. In addition, low wages prolong ROI of many SCM 4.0 innovations and disqualify them. Furthermore, short term period orientation of global corporations hinders innovation and transformation to SCM 4.0. The last major obstacle is the unclear impact of innovation on society in general and company employees.

The future research targets at the identification as to how to establish a road map to achieve progressive innovation with sustainability in terms of customers, suppliers and employees. Particularly, the author uses an in-depth semi-structured interviews and field research to formulate lessons learnt from the transformation to SCM 4.0 in terms of the challenging obstacles identified above.

CONCLUSION

SCM 4.0 is a transformation of SCM regarding the concept of Industry 4.0. The topic is abused by professionals as a marketing tool to convince customers about the advanced maturity of the supplier. Thus, it is not the exception, that simply the implementation of one dimensional code (1D) barcodes or Autonomous Guided Vehicle based on induction is promoted to be a project of SCM 4.0 or Industry 4.0. The age of SCM 4.0 is at its beginning, therefore, it remains unclear as to the most suitable transformation process, the suitability of application of advanced technologies or new changes in HR. This chapter demonstrates that SCM 4.0 is an evolutionary new stage of SCM that inherits many attributes from previous SCM concepts, especially from Lean SCM.

There is a reshaping of the business models as SCM 4.0 shifts competitive advantage from tangible products to services and extends servitization. SCM 4.0 extends the data about supply chain operation that customers and suppliers can use to better customize product and supply chain services.

SCM 4.0 limits risk through better traceability and visibility of processes but there is a new issue of risk about data security. Placing sensors along the supply chain enables the collection of big data that are very sensitive and can be exposed to cyber-attacks. There is an extremely high dependency on data in SCM 4.0, therefore, companies take measures to secure their data from possible external and internal intruders. The data collection, processing, storing, and reporting are dependent on electricity thus, contingency plans for blackouts are in place.

Advanced ICT enables to achieve the goals of previous SCM concepts especially, Resilient SCM and Green SCM in terms of customer-supplier relationship. There is a complete visibility in operations across the total supply chain. SCM 4.0 is the demand-oriented concept and by advanced technologies in production and SCM reduces time to market and extends the scope of customization.

SCM 4.0 provides monitoring of customer behaviour and thus, can dynamically respond to customer needs and adjust order management. Supplier detects demanded goods and services based on a collection of big data about the customer. Order management is automated. Productivity is enhanced by the reduction of non-value-added activities related to undigitized processes. Digitalization establishes a paperless administration and automates planning and administration. Furthermore, automation of routine task saves human capacities for jobs in which automation is not viable due for the heterogeneity of operation. Digitalization and integration of IT provide better visibility to monitor actual online productivity such as OEM. SCM 4.0 uncovers traditionally hidden cost drivers and provides a real-time allocation of cost to task and goods. Therefore, their costs are evaluated more on the performance-based concept and more scope is variabilized.

Companies recognize opportunities of Industry 4.0 and SCM 4.0. Concerning 3PL in the Czech Republic, their activities can be divided into two categories. First, the global 3PLs intensify research activities in applied research, proof of concept and pilot projects of the disruptive technologies in cooperation with research centres that are shared for local subsidiaries by the parent company. They have available results about the suitability of a wide range of advanced technologies for supply chain processes. Second, they search for customers that would be willing to pay for the services based on advanced technologies. However, customers value price as the decisive criterion and consequently, traditional SCM operation is still more efficient than SCM 4.0 in the Czech Republic. Therefore, innovators hesitate with SCM 4.0 and express that SCM 4.0 is not still an issue. Innovation leaders are preparing at a technological and strategic level by defining the roadmap of transformation to SCM 4.0. However, there is still a lack of consideration of changes needed in talent management, hiring, and corporate culture.

ACKNOWLEDGMENT

This paper is one of the research outputs of the project IGA VŠE No. IP305027 financially supported by University of Economics, Prague

REFERENCES

Bhasin, S., & Burcher, P. (2006). Lean viewed as a philosophy. *Journal of Manufacturing Technology Management*, *17*(1), 56–72. doi:10.1108/17410380610639506

Carvalho, H., Duarte, S., & Machado, C. (2011). Lean, agile, resilient and green: Divergencies and synergies. *International. Journal of LEAN Six Sigma*, *2*(2), 151–179. doi:10.1108/20401461111135037

Chapman, P., & … . (2002). Identifying and Managing Supply Chain Vulnerability. *Logistics & Transport Focus*, *4*(4), 59–70.

Christopher, M., & Holweg, M. (2011). Supply Chain 2.0: Managing supply chains in the era of turbulence. *International Journal of Physical Distribution & Logistics Management*, *41*(1), 63–82. doi:10.1108/09600031111101439

Christopher, M., & Towill, D. R. (2000). Supply chain migration from lean and functional to agile and customised. *Supply Chain Management*, *5*(4), 206–213. doi:10.1108/13598540010347334

Daugherty, P., Banerjee, P., Negm, W., & Alter, A. E. (2015). *Driving Unconventional Growth through the Industrial Internet of Things, s.l.* Accenture.

Duguay, C. R., Landry, S., & Pasin, F. (1997). From mass production to flexible/agile production. *International Journal of Operations & Production Management*, *17*(12), 1183–1195. doi:10.1108/01443579710182936

Johnson, H. T. (2006). Lean Accounting: To become Lean, Shed Accountings. *Cost and Management*, *20*(1), 6–17.

Kavanagh, S., & Cole, J. (2013). *LEAN Achieving Critical Mass. Government Finance Review*, *29*(3), 12–20.

Lasi, H., Fettke, P., Kemper, H., Feld, T., & Hoffmann, M. (2014). Industry 4.0. *Business & Information Systems Engineering*, *6*(4), 239–242. doi:10.100712599-014-0334-4

Liker, J. K. (2004). *The Toyota way: 14 management principles from the world's greatest manufacturer*. New York: McGraw-Hill.

Martinez, F., Jirsak, P., & Lorenc, M. (2016). *Industry 4.0. The end Lean Management?* Prague: VSE.

Rusman, M., Lorenz, M., Gerbert, P., Waldner, M., Justus, J., Engel, P., & Harnish, M. (2015). *Industry 4.0. The Future of Productivity Growth in Manufacturing Industry*. Retrieved from http://www.zvw.de/media.media.72e472fb-1698-4a15-8858-344351c8902f.original.pdf

Schram, H., Prockl, G., & Kolar, P. (2017). About Claims and Realities of Digitization in Current Maritime Transportation Chains. In *Annual conference of the International Association of Maritime Economists (IAME) 2017*. Graduate School of Management, Kyoto University.

Sommer, L. (2015). Industrial Revolution – Industry 4.0: Are German Manufacturing SMEs the first Victims of this Revolution? *Journal of Industrial Engineering and Management.*, *8*(5), 1512–1532. doi:10.3926/jiem.1470

Systemy-Logistiky, C. Z. (2016). *Trh industrialnich nemovitosti: shrnuti 2016 a vyhled 2017*. Retrieved Jully 14, 2017, from http://www.systemylogistiky.cz/2017/01/13/trh-industrialnich-nemovitosti-v-cr-shrnuti-2016-a-vyhled-2017/

Vonderembse, M. A., Uppal, M., Huang, S. H., & Dismukes, J. P. (2006). Designing supply chains: Towards theory development. *International Journal of Production Economics*, *100*(2), 223–238. doi:10.1016/j.ijpe.2004.11.014

Wang, S., Wan, J., Li, D., & Zhang, C. (2016). Implementing Smart Factory of Industrie 4.0: An Outlook. *International Journal of Distributed Sensor Networks.*

Zhou, H., Benton, W. C. Jr, Schilling, D. A., & Milligan, G. W. (2011). Supply Chain Integration and the SCOR Model. *Journal of Business Logistics*, *32*(4), 332–344. doi:10.1111/j.0000-0000.2011.01029.x

Zhu, Q., Sarkis, J., & Lai, K. (2008). Confirmation of a measurement model for green supply chain management practices implementation. *International Journal of Production Economics*, *111*(2), 261–273. doi:10.1016/j.ijpe.2006.11.029

KEY TERMS AND DEFINITIONS

Cyber-Physical System: Integrated system that provides a digital mirror to the real state that enables decentralized decision making within SCM processes.

ERP: Enterprise resource planning is a software with a fundamental that enables software support of critical company functions: sales, marketing, production, logistics, finance, etc.

ROI: Return on investment measures the time needed to return the investment provided to innovate, change, etc.

SCM 4.0: Supply chain management with completely digitalized processes using advanced technologies in operation and management.

Stock: Goods stored for a certain time. It is a synonym for inventory from a supply chain operational perspective.

TMS: Transport management system is a software that enables the organization of transport of goods and fleet management.

WMS: Warehouse management system is a software enabling the management of warehousing processes such as planning, monitoring, delegation of jobs, evidence, and others.

Chapter 8
Balancing Exploration and Exploitation Through Customer Development Model:
Leveraging Industry 4.0 for Sustainable Performance

Krishna Raj Bhandari
University of Vaasa, Finland

ABSTRACT

Balancing exploration and exploitation in entrepreneurial ventures enabled by Industry 4.0 has not been the focus of the existing literature. It is because the phenomenon is emerging and the focus has been to use practitioners' best practices in studying such phenomenon. In this chapter, the author combines the literature in balancing exploration and exploitation with the practitioners' best practices such as customer development model and lean startup. The author proposes that the existing models are good in principle but in order to really solve the problem in such an uncertain environment driven by big data, cloud computing, internet of things (IoT), and artificial intelligence, managers need to embed optimization algorithms in their decision making.

INTRODUCTION

The recent developments triggered by the accelerated pace of technological change famously labeled as Industry 4.0 (i4.0) is becoming a new economic and social force. Not only that a new paradigm is emerging where old business models are being transformed, strategies are becoming more and more real-time and fact-based, and all new processes based on optimization algorithm are taking place. Bughin, Chui & Manyika (2015) argued that the major differentiating factor in competition would come from the Internet of Things (IoT). This changing landscape in competitive strategies triggered by IoT and in general from Industry 4.0 (i4.0) demands that senior leaders and board members must think at the system level to solve the challenges created by the technological disruption. The opportunities are

DOI: 10.4018/978-1-5225-3468-6.ch008

many but gathering data together from different IoT systems may not be enough. This triggers analytical challenge for which developing or purchasing, customizing, and then deploying analytical software to get insights for decision-making is highly important. IoT enabled new business models would be the norms rather than exceptions.

The implications of i4.0 are tremendous for companies like Alibaba.com from China and 'sharing economies' such as Uber and Airbnb. All of these new enterprises are transforming traditional business models and enabling entrepreneurship at the mass level. Balancing exploration and exploitation (March, 1991) in this emerging landscape becomes even more important. Exploration means searching for new business models and experimenting the future. But the only exploration will not make one successful, one needs to exploit or capture the value in the emerging phenomenon. One of the processes used in navigating such a changing landscape is called customer development model (Blank, 2013). The customer development model has four steps: customer discovery, customer validation, customer creation, and company building (or scaling up the company). The balance of exploration and exploitation, however, depends on how fast a build-measure-optimize-learn (BMOL) loop is executed in the pursuit of customer development.

Key terms used in this chapter are exploration, exploitation, i4.0, customer development model and build-measure-optimize-learn (BMOL) loop. Exploration is defined as activities related to search, experiment, explore, innovate and aspire. This is good for long-term but detrimental in short-term as perpetual search trap leads to firm failure. Exploitation is defined as activities related to efficiency, productivity, and optimization. This is good for short term but bad for a long term as success trap leads to firm failure (March, 1991). Loosely defined i4.0 is an umbrella concept where internet of things, automation, cloud computing, 3D printing, digitalization, and mobile technologies that enable new business models and drive innovation and efficiency at the same. Taken from Blank (2013), customer development model has four phases: customer discovery, customer validation, customer creation and company development. Based on Ries (2011) BML loop is the development cycle to experiment and learn. But in this chapter BMOL loop with extra O as optimization is used. The unit of progress is validated learning. Managing under uncertainty needs dynamic capabilities (Teece, D. J., Pisano, G., & Shuen, A. 1997; Teece, 2007) where sensing, seizing and reconfiguring activities are important for sustainable performance. Marr (2016) illustrated that how the technological waves shaped our life in the human history. From steam engine and the first machines that improved productivity to electricity which enabled assembly line and mass production. The third wave came from the computers that enabled automation. Now is the i4.0 wave with robotics connected remotely to computer systems and machine learning algorithms which can learn and control the robotics as the realization of "smart factory".

Based on the *McKinsey Quarterly Industry 4.0* has become more than just a popular discourse at least in the manufacturing sector (Baur & Wee, 2015). There is a growing convergence of trends and technologies with a potential to change the manufacturing landscape. Executives have started to understand that it is no more a hype as it reveals the power of disruption in the way factories work. Some authors have called it the next industrial revolution. Thus, executives must embrace this change and plan for actions to sail the ship in the right direction. This could be achieved by learning the new possibilities but at the same time exploiting the certainties in the current realities. March (1991) coined the term balancing exploration and exploitation for a winning mindset.

The latest systematic literature review by Liao, Deschamps, Loures and Ramos (2017) on the fourth industrial revolution suggested that there are top 5 keyword clusters emerging in the existing literature such as industry 4.0, cyber-physical system, manufacturing, smart factory, and the internet of things.

This disruption will enable horizontal integration, vertical integration, and end-to-end digital integration. Amidst the buzz around i4.0, there is a lack of understanding how to manage such an uncertainty. This chapter is an attempt to solve that puzzle by bringing proven theoretical construct from the academic literature and merging that with the recent development in practices in entrepreneurial ventures. Earlier these concepts were used in startups but with the onset of use by *General Electric* in their whole organizations, it is becoming a mainstream agenda as well.

This chapter is divided into following sub-chapters. First, the background of the chapter is presented followed by the main focus of the chapter with an eye to delve into issues, controversies, and problems. Then the subsequent chapter provides solutions and recommendations.

FOCUS OF THE CHAPTER

Issues, Controversies, Problems

There are three general questions explored in this chapter. First, how to avoid success trap or perpetual search trap? Second, how can a firm leverage customer development model for the innovation triggered by i4.0? Third, how to accelerate the pace of innovation in i4.0?

How to avoid success trap?

The latest dissertation (Bhandari, 2017) finding provides a plausible solution for an "*Innovator's Dilemma*", a ground-breaking book by *Harvard University* professor Clayton Christensen. Firms should be "ambidextrous" in reaping short-term profits, called exploitation; and innovating for long-term success, called exploration at the same time. The term "ambidexterity" means balancing both efficiency and innovation at the same time.

If the relative ratio between exploration and exploitation is in the very low range or very high range, it is not beneficial for the firm. However, gaining an optimum range in the middle helps firms to avoid success trap or in that matter exploitation trap. Such a trap exists due to the relentless pursuit of profits (e.g. Nokia) at the expense of innovation and experimentation for new products and services. However, there are perpetual search traps as well as Xerox once was in this trap. Following overall cost leadership, however, did not have an impact when balancing exploration and exploitation but differentiation and hybrid strategies were important. Thus in the i4.0 era firm's attention towards what is emerging in the long term and what could be exploited for the short term profit is even greater than before. This is due to the fact that as discussed earlier i4.0 is a different phenomenon as it will enable new business models and change the competitive landscape completely. In this transformation ecosystem and the platform-based economy is in the forefront. Earlier knowledge and skills would not be sufficient as it demands the knowledge of new technologies and software that drives the innovation.

Over forty years of empirical research has failed to resolve a basic strategy question in strategic management literature. How to operate in extreme conditions of uncertainty? A solution-oriented approach would be to ask how can a firm leverage customer development model for the innovation triggered by i4.0? As evident from the startup related literature, customer development model (Blank, 2013) suggests that under the conditions of uncertainty such as created by i4.0 technologies, search for a new business model is crucial. The search happens first with customer discovery and the customer validation. Here the goal is to experiment with the customer to test the value proposition so that getting quick feedback and doing iteration is possible. Once the customer need is validated then the scalability is needed. Here the goal is to create the customer first and build the company at large. In the search phase, validated learning is the only unit of progress to measure it in accounting terms. Each customer development models could be iterated by build-measure-learn (BML) loop suggested by Ries (2011) in his book *Lean Startup*. Higher the uncertainty, faster the loop should be the focus. As mentioned earlier the unit of progress is validated learning. Most theorists believe strategic purity—the extent to which a business pursues one type of generic strategy over another—contributes to better performance. However, the latest findings (Krishna, 2017) suggest that pursuing both cost-plus differentiation strategy called hybrid strategy is feasible.

Third, how to accelerate the pace of innovation in i4.0?

As evident from the literature, it took forty years to understand the hybrid strategies in strategic management literature, over 50 years of research in international business (IB) literature has failed to resolve a basic internationalization question: how to scale up a venture in the condition of uncertainty? The extant literature since fifty years has been inconclusive. Based on the latest literature, a conclusion is reached that rather than using multiple theories, it is good to focus on the dynamic capabilities-based view (DCV) (Teece, D. J., Pisano, G., & Shuen, A., 1997; Teece, 2007, 2014) to streamline the theoretical contribution. However, dynamic capabilities are dynamic by nature and tracing them in innovation and scaling activities is extremely challenging. Another implication is that earlier realization was that the resource-based view (RBV) (1991) and DCV are siblings. However, recent realization after the immersion into theoretical framework and operationalization is that the resource position barrier as advocated by the RBV needs to be leveraged to realize the sense, seize, and orchestrate notion of the DCV. Entrepreneurial management and empowering innovations are only possible from the DCV perspectives and the scaling of innovation under extreme uncertainty created by i4.0 is moving from advantage-seeking mode to opportunity-seeking mode now. Explaining the firm-specific advantages would be easier from the DCV perspective as well. Thus, a clear theoretical rationale for navigating the business model generated by i4.0 and for the discussions in this chapter is DCV.

The emerging literature in i4.0 is more focused on global value chains and international business (Strange, Strange, Zucchella & Zucchella 2017). This emerging worldview tracks the widespread adoption of new digital technologies such as internet of things, big data & analytics, robotic systems, and additive manufacturing. One of the important aspects of this phenomenon is to see the impact on the location and organization of activities within the global value chains (GVCs). In studying these implications for GVCs the interesting part is to explore how these emerging technologies create new configurations involving suppliers, firms, and customers. For this to be successful Teece (2014) argued that recombination of resources and capabilities is very important. Concurring this Strange, Strange, Zucchella & Zucchella (2017) found that the i4.0 related technologies are on the cusp of disrupting how and where activities are located and organized within GVCs. Not only the disruption the goal is to figure out who captures the value created within those GVCs. Implications for strategy are huge to make sure that the company is able to capture the value created by this disruption. A new competitor may come completely from a new industry as digitalization has enabled many conglomerates such as FANG (Facebook, Apple, Netflix, and Google). However, to safeguard against the cyber-risks and implications for the privacy of individuals extra attention to security must be placed. This means regulation is just lagging with the pace of change.

SOLUTIONS AND RECOMMENDATIONS

A practical solution to understand the underlying puzzle triggered by i4.0 is to create a map of the balancing exploration and exploitation with customer development model and role of lean startup thinking mainly represented by build-measure-optimization-learn (BMOL) loop as shown in Figure 1.

Balancing Exploration and Exploitation in the Age of i4.0

Based on author's early career at Nokia and its evolution, the motivation to explore what makes a firm sustainable in the long-run has been the focus of the research. While at Nokia, the focus was on exploiting the GSM technology fullest but the exploration and for that matter exploitation of the 3G innovation emerging fast was missing. However, the firm was good at the exploration of new technologies by then also. Reading emails in Nokia communicator long before Apple came with touchscreen iPhone was possible. After few years, it was visible that Nokia missed the biggest disruption in the mobile industry and Nokia mobile phones had to be sold. So, it raised a question, why the giants fail? Or in other words what makes a company successful in the long-run – the broader research question of this chapter. However, the scope of this chapter has been limited to the key antecedents and moderating variables of sustainable performance in the age of i4.0.

Following the collapse of Nokia has been interesting even after leaving Nokia. Vuori and Huy (2016) found that distributed attention and shared emotions were critical in losing the smartphone battle. In this qualitative study from 2005-2010 when one of the world's best brands collapsed into the rumble, they found that top and middle managers' shared emotions in the smartphone innovation process triggered a multitude of behaviors which resulted into the demise of the giant. However, one important part of this equation is organizational attention triggering fear among managers. Top managers were scared of external competitors and shareholders but middle managers were afraid of internal groups, including superiors and peers. There were a communication bias and interpretation bias between top managers and middle managers. Therefore, attention towards balancing exploration and exploitation was clouded by the shared emotions and distributed attention.

March (1991) suggested that in order to succeed in the long run balancing exploration and exploitation trade-off is crucial. Exploration implies search, experimentation, development, and innovation related activities which have the performance impact in the long run. If a firm is geared towards short-term financial gains indicated by firm's stock price, they do not invest in exploration activities. This results in exploitation trap or success trap or learning myopia. Figure 1 shows the map where balancing act of exploration and exploitation results into multiple business model innovations. There are two performance curves depending on what type of build-measure-learn (BML) loop (Reis, 2011) capability the firm has. At a weaker BML loop of execution, the balance curve is lower while at a stronger BML loop the performance curve is higher. For i4.0 related innovation, the breakthrough is normally in changing the business model. Therefore, understanding the relative exploration measured as the ratio of exploration divided by the sum of exploration and exploitation would be an interesting index to understand the balance of exploration and exploitation. The following section elaborates the existing literature on the balancing of exploration and exploitation and compares it with my conceptualization.

Thus, this chapter has implication for theory and practice. The chapter counters the resource fungibility (Penrose 1959) based on the resource immobility logic of the RBT (Barney, 1991) to create sustainable competitive advantage. Rather than assuming linear impact on performance, our premise is to seek the optimum level of derived valuable information from the big data that becomes the cornerstone of strategic decision-making. The digitalization improves functional capabilities, shapes the industrial innovation, and enables learning breakthroughs (Mazzei & Noble, 2017) all leading to performance improvement. However too much or too little of digitalization is not beneficial. There is a need to tune in to the optimum level of digitalization.

Wade and Hulland (2004) assessed the RBV and information systems research. In their assessment of effects of information technology on firm performance, they found mixed results (see their table 5 page 125 for more details). A large body of researchers saw a direct and positive impact on firm performance while Warner (1987) was the only study reporting for negative impact. Per Wade and Hulland (2004), the RBV treats information assets and systems differently.

The former is asset-based, while the latter comprises a mixture of assets and capabilities formed around the productive use of information technology. It is our contention that the RBV, through its focus on attributes and its recognition of the importance of resource complementarity, will uncover an enhanced role for information systems in sustained firm competitiveness (Wade & Hulland, 2004:132).

Thus, following the similar tone and view of digitalization, the focus of this chapter is to reconcile these mixed findings. One of the major aspects of digitalization is driven by big data. Per Mazzei and Noble (2017), there are three tiers of the impact of big data. First, big data could be just a tool in the traditional value chain. Second, big data could be a stimulus for new ventures and industry development. And the third tier argues for big data as a driver of competitive strategy. As evident in this discussion anchored in the RBT and organizational learning perspectives, the expected relationship between digitalization and long-term performance is curvilinear.

As discussed in Wade and Hulland (2004), a few authors found information system (IS) has no effect on performance but a large majority of authors suggested that there are contingent effects of other constructs such as top management commitment to IS. Attention is a scared resource and as per Ocasio (1997), studying the RBV in tandem with the Attention-based View (ABV) is the right approach for sustainable competitive advantage. However, this chapter does not elaborate on the ABV as such to limit the scope.

Comparing Relative Exploration-Performance With Similar Studies

One of the similar studies to Bhandari (2017) is by Kim and Huh (2015) as shown in Table 1. By using organizational longevity (lifespan of each firm in IT-related industries) as a dependent variable and exploration as an independent variable, authors reported an inverted U-shaped relationship. However, the focus of this chapter is on the balance of exploration and exploitation measured as relative exploration and dependent variables are Tobin's Q and ROA in contrast to organizational longevity used by Kim and Huh (2015). On a key contribution, the authors checked the moderating effect of competitive strategies and environmental dynamism.

Departing from the orthogonal aspect of measuring the exploration and exploitation trade-off, this chapter focused on the measure as two ends of a continuum in terms of innovation context. Bhandari (2017) also followed this school of thought. Therefore, comparing current findings with their findings is

Figure 1. Balancing exploration and exploitation in innovation process through customer development model
Source: Synthesis by the author

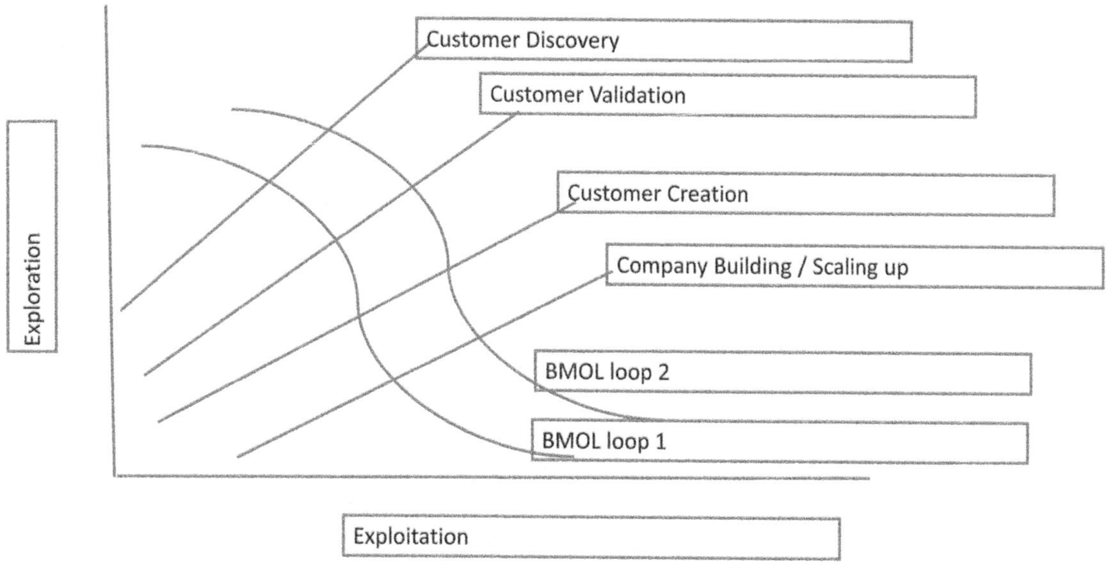

possible. The key difference between Kim and Huh (2015) and current work is on the way of measurement of exploration and exploitation plus the dependent variable. On the measurements, the Bhandari (2017) follows Uotila et al. (2009) to use a key approach through the keyword counts from the annual reports by computer-aided text analysis (CATA) in contrast to the level of patents.

On the analysis and research design, the study by Kim and Huh (2015) also suffers from the existing problem in the literature— common method variance (CMV), endogeneity and unobserved heterogeneity. Kim and Huh (2015) fall into the replication category without furthering the theoretical discourse. However, the common thread linking current study with Kim and Huh (2015) is the inverted U or curvilinear relationship between independent variable and dependent variable. This notion supports the balance of exploration and exploitation (March 1991) for the long-term performance. The moderating effect of competitive strategies (cost and differentiation but not the hybrid) are equally comparable. The moderating effect of hybrid strategy on the relationship between balancing exploration and exploitation and performance is, therefore, unique contribution this study.

The strategy is called *stuck in the middle* when the emphasis on all dimensions are low or at the average level. This means one is focusing on both cost and differentiation but not having full potential achieved. The efforts are low or at the average level. On a similar thought-provoking and groundbreaking concept Porter (1985) claimed that as differentiation is costly as achieving both cost and differentiation is a paradox. I concur, unlike the existing literature, all three forms of strategic choices—cost, differentiation and hybrid (cost plus differentiation). In the current operationalization, hybrids are the strategies when both cost and differentiation are combined in each dimension (lower the mean representing the cost leadership and above mean for differentiation). This is similar operationalization as reported by Spanos et al. (2004) and Gabrielsson et al. (2016).

Based on these findings, as conceptually plotted in Figure 1 the balance of exploration and exploitation has an optimum level when financial performance is at its best. As evident the strategic choices could be thought of balancing both cost-plus differentiation, that is, hybrid and differentiation only. However, cost leadership approach would not be successful in the long run.

Customer Development Model

Most of the startup entrepreneurial ecosystem targeting industry 4.0 is recommended to follow customer development (Blank, 2013) together with Business Model Canvas. The four steps to epiphany are that there are four steps in customer development model: discovery, validation, creation, and scale. During the customer discovery phase, the key hypotheses should test the customer/problem fit. Similarly, during the customer validation phase, the key hypotheses should test the problem/solution fit. During the customer creation phase, the key hypotheses should test the solution/customer fit. Finally, during the scaling phase solution/channel fit, related hypotheses are tested. This hypothesis-driven development is the secret recipe of great innovations coming from entrepreneurial ecosystems or in the Silicon Valley as a starting point.

Artificial intelligence, internet of things (IoT), cloud computing, big data, and automation summarized together as digitalization or for that matter need for exploration and related changes in the business model have triggered a new industrial wave called Industry 4.0 (i4.0). To understand such a phenomenon, the existing conceptualization of exploration as suggested by March (1991) is valid. I extended March's (1991) definition of exploration and exploitation where exploration is described by activities such as explore, search, experiment while exploitation is described by activities such as exploit, refine, efficiency etc.

Though the change wave has just started, CEOs are required to focus their attention on best honesty for the long-run future of the company on this new emerging paradigm (Porter & Heppelmann, 2015). A note of caution is that 'smart, connected products' are not synonymous with the Internet of Things. In the new era, products themselves are enabling the revolution by unlocking new value and transforming both companies and competition. Earlier waves of digitalization change were focused on value-chain automation and integration. The current paradigm is different as it embeds into products, creating benefit

Table 1.

	Key hypotheses	Findings
Bhandari (2017)	-inverted U shape between Relative Exploration and performance	-there is an inverted U-relationship between Relative Exploration and Tobin's Q
	-Moderating effect of cost, differentiation and hybrid strategies	-Cost leadership did not have a positive moderating effect but differentiation and hybrid support the hypothesis.
Kim and Huh (2015)	-inverted U-shaped relationship between exploration and longevity	-there is an inverted U-relationship between exploration and organizational longevity.
	-the moderating effect of internal and external contexts.	-Differentiation strategy has a positive moderating effect. No test of hybrid.
Uotila et al. (2009)	-inverted the U-shaped relationship between relative exploration and performance.	-there is an inverted U-relationship between relative exploration and performance (Tobin's Q)

and changing the locus of competition (Porter & Heppelman, 2015). Strategic management literature discusses dynamic capabilities to "sense", "seize", and "orchestrate" resources (Teece, 1997) as the cornerstone of maneuvering in such a dynamic environment for sustainable competitive advantage.

As a summary, as evident from the history of transformation from automation to integration to smart-connected products will change the game in the competition and its value chains and value networks. Industry boundaries are fading and platform plus ecosystem economy is on the rise. The only exploration will not take us to the sustainable future, please remember, one needs to balance both exploration and exploitation. Easier said than done, perhaps it is an art rather than science.

Build-Measure-Optimize-Learn (BMOL) Loop

Build-measure-optimize-learn (BMOL) loop as shown in Figure 2 is the execution loop in hypothesis-driven development and essence of searching for a business model and later execution of business model as well. In *Lean Startup* thinking only BMOL loops were discussed but to be successful in i4.0, the loop must have an 'optimize' stage. As discussed earlier under the high level of uncertainty created by i4.0 it is important to understand that this loop needs to be faster enough. However, a new thinking to BMOL loop needs to be taken into consideration that the algorithm based systems optimizing loops are more important and the model can predict the future as well. Thus, predictive analytics becomes a holy grail of the innovation management (both searching for a business model and scaling the company).

BML loop in Figure 2 shows that the higher the speed of execution the better the balance of exploration and exploitation. The first BML curve shows the lower level of execution while the second BML curve shows the higher level of execution.

Figure 2. Build-measure-optimize-learn loop
Source: Modified from Ries (2011)

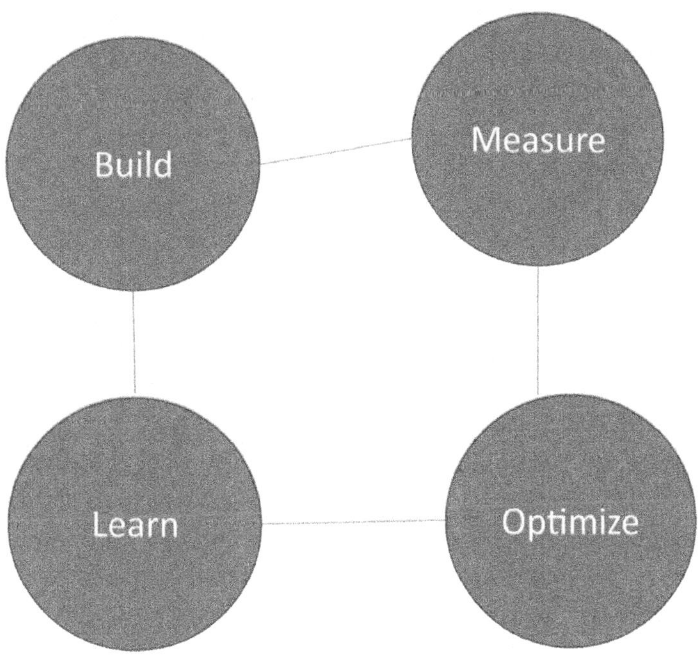

Implications for i4.0 Research and Implementation

Liao et al. (2017) is a good point to start discussing further research. As discussed in Figure 1 and Figure 2, in order to make i4.0 successful, following Liao et al.'s (2017) recommendations to go for horizontal integration, vertical integration and end-to-end digital integration must be realized. As the industry is just evolving there are eight priority areas for action suggested by Liao et al. (2017) and I concur to those recommendations such as developing standardization and reference architecture, managing complex systems, delivering a comprehensive broadband infrastructure and giving safety and security a priority. Similarly, a new innovative work organization and design, training and continuing professional development, regulatory framework and resource productivity and efficiency must be taken seriously for the realization of ubiquitous applications enabled by i4.0.

Implications of i4.0 on Globalization, Economic Nationalism or Populism

The exploration led to the international business (IB) literature, strategic adaptation literature, and competitive strategies literature. As a surprise, the academic literature reported mixed findings as discussed earlier on the benefits of internationalization or scaling i4.0 innovation in the global market. One school of thought says that there is a diversification discount (Denis, Denis & Yost 2002), while, the other says globalization is beneficial due to the flexibility it creates (Chang, Kogut & Yang 2016). The theoretical rationale behind such arguments is that flexibility in reconfiguring resources outweighs the diversification discount associated with it, resulting in diversification premium (Chang et al. 2016).

For the last century, the globalization has been seen as a bane and a boon at the same time. Globalization enabled economic integration but at the same time created political marginalization and cultural homogenization. Recent publications in the *Economist* suggested that globalization is in retreat. Populists are giving slogans such as "our country first" and "immigration is evil". And spreading these messages have been easier than said—thanks to Facebook and other media outlets. There is unease in the cultural realm. Per Contractor, there is an emerging sense of "global consciousness" and sensitivity to noble thoughts and fear and nationalism at the same time. Driven by this global phenomenon this chapter took a stance at the firm level to understand whether internationalization or in that matter scaling a company as per customer development model is good for the companies in the long-run.

At this point in the history of time, this generation is witnessing a great revolution triggered by technologies such as AI, cloud computing, IoT, big data, and a new generation of technologies in the mobile industry. Even though there are opposing views on globalization, the collective conscience of Y-generation may be on the cusp of embracing the openness. China is optimistically forging ahead with One Belt, One Road initiative to connect China with Europe and Southeast Asia. Similarly, India is welcoming FDI to leverage its demographic dividend with a young workforce ready for new challenges.

Levinthal and March (1993) argued that learning has many virtues. However, learning process is far from perfect. In an organization, learning has to balance trade-offs on developing new knowledge that is exploration, and exploiting current skills and capabilities. This inherent tension might be even higher in the case of i4.0 as disruption demands more exploration at the expense of exploitation. There are three forms of learning myopia *the tendency to overlook distant times, distant places, and failures.* In simpler terms, short-termism or success trap or exploitation trap is too strong in modern management thinking driven by quarterly results and share price. Thus, managers need to build ambidextrous (both exploration and exploitation) competencies to survive in the long-run.

FUTURE RESEARCH DIRECTIONS

The recommendation suggested above could be possible by opting a new dependent variable or measure of success. The IB literature and also the strategic management literature uses return on assets (ROA) and Tobin's Q (market value/book value) or similar dependent variables based on accounting standards. ROA is the generally used measure of success in the business where relentless pursuit of profit is the mantra. However, Tobin's Q is a better measure as it has implications for the market taken into considerations. Even then, the short-term myopia is dominant in the corporate world, basically driven by quarterly results and share price. In order, not to fall prey to this myopia, one needs to focus on a new measure of success.

A Recent publication by Nobel laureate Oliver Hart and Zingales (2017) is proposing that *Companies Should Maximize Shareholder Welfare Not Market Value*. This is somehow challenging albeit differently the Milton Friedman doctrine of 1970:

Conduct the business in accordance with [shareholders'] desires, which generally will be to make as much money as possible while conforming to the basic rules of the society, both those embodied in law and those embodied in ethical custom.

The outcry is where is the morality in business? In fact, one of the future researches one should undertake will be precise to establish a link between moral philosophy, investment policy, prosocial investor's *invest & engage* approach as suggested by Hart and Zingales and corporate policy.

The CEO's honesty and attention are mainly driven by Principal-Agent theory. As per the theory, they have been rewarded for maximizing shareholder's value. Majority of the stock-trading volume comes from institutional investors such as hedge funds and pension funds. On average they own the stock for a year or so. They are only exploiting the company in the short-term. They are not investing for the long-run as suggested by exploration orientation in the chapter. Capitalism needs to fix this conundrum, before having a success in establishing sustainable companies. CEO's must be rewarded for long-term company health, employee prosperity, and societal and environmental impact. A new dependent variable must be developed and practiced. Thus, I propose that a new dependent variable must measure success in terms of social impact, environmental return, and finally for sure economic return: 3PS (PEOPLE, PLANET, AND PROFIT).

CONCLUSION

The beauty of capitalism is that it creates its own path to correct the course and sail again.

Globalization is not at a retreat, or is it? However, it needs to correct itself for its anomalies and forge ahead. *Occupy Wall-Street* movements and riots in front of G20 meetings are crying for change. While *World Economic Forum* is busy in press releases, *World Social Forum* is raising its concerns as well. Unless and until the concerned authority listens to these genuine voices, capitalism will falter. Choices are the symbols of what the generation belongs to. Respecting the other side of the table and building harmony where dignity, peace, and prosperity could be possible in this lifetime. Celebrating the 'global consciousness' must be the focus of the new generation.

The technological innovation in automation and efficiency innovation is taking away around 70% of jobs and globalization the rest. This is creating abundant capital resulting in cost of capital close to zero. Unless and until we invest on empowering innovation as suggested by Professor Christensen from *Harvard*, which creates jobs and uses capital, we are heading towards stagnation, as it is evident in Japan since a long time and Unite States is facing the same problem. Due to the onset of i4.0 a new multinationals or meta-nationals will emerge and benefit from this change would be the main focus of the policymaking. Are we racing against machines or we are co-opting machines to build a safer and freer world?

REFERENCES

Barney, J. (1991). Firm resources and sustained competitive advantage. *Journal of Management, 17*(1), 99–120. doi:10.1177/014920639101700108

Baur, C., & Wee, D. (2015, June). Manufacturing's next act. *McKinsey Quarterly.*

Bhandari, K. (2017). *Internationalization and Organizational Ambidexterity for Sustainable Performance: Moderating Effects of Firm-specific Advantages and Competitive Strategies.* Acta Wasaensia 379, Vaasan yliopisto, University of Vaasa.

Blank, S. (2013). *The four steps to the epiphany: successful strategies for products that win.* BookBaby.

Bughin, J., Chui, M., & Manyika, J. (2015). An executive's guide to the Internet of Things. *The McKinsey Quarterly.*

Chang, S., Kogut, B., & Yang, J. S. (2016). Global diversification discount and its discontents: A bit of self-selection makes a world of difference. *Strategic Management Journal, 37*(11), 2254–2274. doi:10.1002mj.2574

Denis, D. J., Denis, D. K., & Yost, K. (2002). Global diversification, industrial diversification, and firm value. *The Journal of Finance, 57*(5), 1951–1979. doi:10.1111/0022-1082.00485

Gabrielsson, M., Seppälä, T., & Gabrielsson, P. (2016). Realizing a hybrid competitive strategy and achieving superior financial performance while internationalizing in the high-technology market. *Industrial Marketing Management, 54,* 141–153. doi:10.1016/j.indmarman.2015.07.001

Hart, O., & Zingales, L. (2017). *Companies Should Maximize Shareholder Welfare Not Market Value.* Academic Press.

Kim, G., & Huh, M. G. (2015). Exploration and organizational longevity: The moderating role of strategy and environment. *Asia Pacific Journal of Management, 32*(2), 389–414. doi:10.100710490-014-9399-3

Lasi, H., Fettke, P., Kemper, H. G., Feld, T., & Hoffmann, M. (2014). Industry 4.0. *Business & Information Systems Engineering, 6*(4), 239–242. doi:10.100712599-014-0334-4

Levinthal, D. A., & March, J. G. (1993). The myopia of learning. *Strategic Management Journal, 14*(S2), 95–112. doi:10.1002mj.4250141009

Liao, Y., Deschamps, F., Loures, E. D. F. R., & Ramos, L. F. P. (2017). Past, present, and future of Industry 4.0-a systematic literature review and research agenda proposal. *International Journal of Production Research*, *55*(12), 3609–3629. doi:10.1080/00207543.2017.1308576

March, J. G. (1991). Exploration and exploitation in organizational learning. *Organization Science*, *2*(1), 71–87. doi:10.1287/orsc.2.1.71

Marr, B. (2016). What Everyone Must Know About Industry 4.0. *Forbes Magazine*. Accessed on 31.07.2017 from https://www.forbes.com/sites/bernardmarr/2016/06/20/what-everyone-must-know-about-industry-4-0/#5ed8a614795f

Mazzei, M. J., & Noble, D. (2017). Big data dreams: A framework for corporate strategy. *Business Horizons*, *60*(3), 405–414. doi:10.1016/j.bushor.2017.01.010

Ocasio, W. (1997). Towards an attention-based view of the firm. *Strategic Management Journal*, *18*(S1), 187–206. doi:

Penrose, E. T. (1959). *The theory of the growth of the firm*. New York: Sharpe.

Porter, M. E., & Advantage, C. (1985). *Creating and Sustaining Superior Performance*. Academic Press.

Porter, M. E., & Heppelmann, J. E. (2015). How smart, connected products are transforming companies. *Harvard Business Review*, *93*(10), 96–114.

Ries, E. (2011). *The lean startup: How today's entrepreneurs use continuous innovation to create radically successful businesses*. Crown Books.

Spanos, Y. E., Zaralis, G., & Lioukas, S. (2004). Strategy and industry effects on profitability: Evidence from Greece. *Strategic Management Journal*, *25*(2), 139–165. doi:10.1002mj.369

Strange, R., Strange, R., Zucchella, A., & Zucchella, A. (2017). Industry 4.0, global value chains and international business. *Multinational Business Review*, *25*(3), 174–184. doi:10.1108/MBR-05-2017-0028

Teece, D. J. (2007). Explicating dynamic capabilities: The nature and microfoundations of (sustainable) enterprise performance. *Strategic Management Journal*, *28*(13), 1319–1350. doi:10.1002mj.640

Teece, D. J. (2014). A dynamic capabilities-based entrepreneurial theory of the multinational enterprise. *Journal of International Business Studies*, *45*(1), 8–37. doi:10.1057/jibs.2013.54

Teece, D. J., Pisano, G., & Shuen, A. (1997). Dynamic capabilities and strategic management. *Strategic Management Journal*, *18*(7), 509–533. doi:

Uotila, J., Maula, M., Keil, T., & Zahra, S. A. (2009). Exploration, exploitation, and financial performance: Analysis of S&P 500 corporations. *Strategic Management Journal*, *30*(2), 221–231. doi:10.1002mj.738

Vuori, T. O., & Huy, Q. N. (2016). Distributed attention and shared emotions in the innovation process: How Nokia lost the smartphone battle. *Administrative Science Quarterly*, *61*(1), 9–51. doi:10.1177/0001839215606951

Wade, M., & Hulland, J. (2004). The resource-based view and information systems research: Review, extension, and suggestions for future research. *Management Information Systems Quarterly*, *28*(1), 107–142. doi:10.2307/25148626

KEY TERMS AND DEFINITIONS

Build-Measure-Optimize-Learn (BM/OL) Loop: BML loop is the development cycle to experiment and learn. The unit of progress is validated learning. In this chapter, the conceptualization adds optimization in the loop and the BML loop becomes BMOL loop.

Customer Development Model: Driven by the logic of business model search and execution, it has four phases: customer discovery, customer validation, customer creation, and company development. The first two phases are helping to search for a business model while the latter two phases are for business model execution.

Exploration: Exploration is defined as activities related to search, experiment, explore, innovate, and aspire. This is good for the long term but detrimental in the short term. Perpetual search trap leads to firm failure as well. In the history of innovating firms, Xerox fell into this trap. Therefore, balancing exploration and exploitation should be our focus.

Exploitation: Exploitation is defined as activities related to efficiency, productivity, and optimization. This is good for the short term but bad for the long term as success trap leads to firm failure. Nokia and Kodak fell into this trap. Therefore, balancing exploration and exploitation needs to be the focus of the strategist.

Industry 4.0 (i4.0): Loosely defined it is an umbrella concept where internet of things, automation, cloud computing, 3D printing, digitalization, and mobile technologies that enable new business models drive innovation and efficiency at the same. The focus of this chapter is on the implications of i4.0 in helping to balance exploration and exploitation.

Chapter 9
Incorporating Industry 4.0 in Corporate Strategy

Anirudh Agrawal
Copenhagen Business School, Denmark

Sebastian Schaefer
TechQuartier, Germany

Thomas Funke
TechQuartier, Germany

ABSTRACT

Knowledge tells us that increase in productivity decreases margins in a competitive market and increases margins in a growing market. Not much is known about Industry 4.0 and its position within the corporate strategy and its possible impact on corporate performance. This chapter discusses the position of Industry 4.0 within the corporate strategy and how it may impact corporate performance. The main points include that corporates have to reflect on their core resources, leadership, and knowledge portfolio to take advantage of the Industry 4.0 platform. The corporates engaging in cost and volume strategies and those engaging in fast new product development strategies may benefit greatly with Industry 4.0. The services of Industry 4.0 may be outsourced but with added risks. Finally, the increased productivity with Industry 4.0 under constraint market growth may lead to the potential risk of market failure and large-scale layoffs.

INTRODUCTION

The primary mission of any corporation is to maximize profitability on behalf of its shareholders (Friedman, 2009) and to provide the best value to its stakeholders (Freeman, 1984). The development of technologies such as the big data and data analysis, IoT, artificial intelligence (AI), flexible robotics, 3D printing, augmented reality, 3D holographic scanning smarter sensors, greater miniaturization, cloud computing, customer feedback and Customer management software (CMS), location detection technologies such as radio-frequency identification (RFID), natural language programming, and chang-

DOI: 10.4018/978-1-5225-3468-6.ch009

ing global social-political environments are all driving human productivity toward a new industrial revolution (Herter & Ovtcharova, 2016; Reinhard, Jesper, & Stefan, 2016). These new technologies are consequently increasing the productivity of the corporations and changing the market equilibrium. The more these technologies evolve and are accepted by the industry, consequently, the industrial productivity shall proportionately increase. However, as the productivity of the corporation increases, it may or may not proportionately increase the performance and profitability.

Contrary to popular understanding, any impulsive investment in technology may increase the corporate debt and, consequently, decrease the corporate performance. Technology adoption and subsequent productivity change may also distort the market equilibrium, which, will force the competitors to engage in similar cost/volume strategies, lowering the overall margins per unit of production (Porter, 1979) for the whole industry. With these possible consequences in mind, it is important to logically weigh where in the value chain would the Industry 4.0 platform technology increase the value for the corporation and how these technologies would contribute to the competitiveness in the long run.

In the background of the evolving Industry 4.0 technological environments, this chapter provides a framework on how the corporations can increase their performance by reflecting on the role of Industry 4.0 on the overall corporate strategy. While most of the literature on Industry 4.0 is on automation (Mrugalska & Wyrwicka, 2017), productivity, benefits, and business models (Man & Strandhagen, 2017), this chapter tries to create a dialogue between academics of the Industry 4.0 and those who study the corporate strategy and corporate performance. A clearer understanding of Industry 4.0 and its position in corporate strategy will help us in understanding better how to develop business models and strategize the "may or buy" decision on Industry 4.0 technology.

The chapter is structured in the following way: First, it briefly reviews Industry 4.0. Next, this is followed by an assessment of corporate strategy and strategy landscape. Finally, the chapter discusses the position of Industry 4.0 in corporate strategy landscape and how and where it brings value to corporate performance. The chapter presents eleven propositions that give strategy-level perspectives on Industry 4.0.

LITERATURE REVIEW

The motivation of this chapter is to provide a slightly different perspective on Industry 4.0 where the authors contextualize it in the corporate strategy. Most of the scholarships around Industry 4.0 are on the disruptive increase in productivity, automation, new market alpha, and industry digitalization, but the research rarely makes any conversation on corporate strategy. It is in this context that this chapter adds value.

A BRIEF OVERVIEW OF INDUSTRY 4.0

Industrial revolutions have always been accompanied with a disruptive increase in productivity. The increase in productivity has also increased wages and, subsequently, the quality of life of the citizens. The evolution of Industry 4.0 is incremental, yet its effect will have a disruptive impact on corporate performance, productivity and overall markets and industries. One can understand it better when studying all the different stages of industrial revolutions (Figure 1).

Industry 1.0 was the first generation of industrial revolution that started around late 18th century. During this generation, it was the first time that machines, instead of animals, started to support humans in manufacturing and production. The invention of water turbines and steam engines helped the people–machine interface by increasing their productivity substantially. The factories owned the energy-generation systems. The management structures of these manufacturing and production units were highly pyramidal and feudal. The productivity was higher than before, and the degree of human intervention was very high.

Industry 2.0 evolved from the first generation after the introduction of electricity in the 1890s. The electrical energy-driven machines further changed the outlook of the industry. It increased industrial productivity. In this era, the productivity was higher and easier, leading more corporations to engage in production and manufacturing activities. With limited market capacity, this led to increased competition. The competition also led to a faster innovation, resulting in the division of labor and the structuring of the study of business and management into a more specialized field. This was also the era, when the European firms were aggressively looking for newer markets especially in third would countries. The theories of scientific management were formulated during this time. This was also the period when business schools started to emerge and management as a field of inquiry started to take structure.

Industry 3.0 evolved from the second generation of industrial revolution. It started around the 1970s when information technology (IT) integrated management systems were introduced. IT significantly reduced transaction costs and control costs of managing and running a corporation. IT-based management systems also enabled the decoupling of organizations' core strength from manufacturing. Post Industry 3.0, the organizational core competency and core value proposition were decoupled from manufacturing and production. For example, Nike, Zara, General Motors, Apple, and Dell are globally renowned for their products. These companies own the brand, research and development (R&D), and the intellectual rights of the products but they do not own the manufacturing. The generation of Industry 3.0 enabled production as a service. This was one major change over Industries 1.0 and 2.0. The organizational design was divided into more specialized functions such as marketing, finance, manufacturing, corporate Entrepreneurship, R&D, and IT. Management research became more scientific and started using more advanced methods for innovation. Consequently, management study was further classified into more specialized fields of study.

Industry 4.0 is an incremental innovation over Industry 3.0 but with the integration of AI and IoT, the disruptive impact on productivity will be far greater than the previous generations of revolution. The term was first used among German manufacturing associations and corporations who were the first ones to rapidly adopt the Industry 4.0 technologies. Industry 4.0 platform is a German government-funded think tank that disseminates information on Industry 4.0. According to them, Industry 4.0 represents a further integration of computing, IT, robotics, Internet, big data, blockchain, and decentralized independent AI based machines which can take corrective decisions while manufacturing. In the world of Industry 4.0, people, machines, equipment, logistics systems, and products communicate and cooperate with each other directly. Production and logistics processes are integrated intelligently across company boundaries to make manufacturing more efficient and flexible (Schweichhart, 2016). According to the McKinsey and Company, the Industry 4.0 is the integration of the manufacturing sector with the IoT framework using the latest sensors, integrating production systems with the back-end supply chain and with the front-end market demand functions using analytic powers, and further reducing contractual risks by using blockchain technologies and the latest manufacturing techniques, eliminating human intervention all together (Wee, Kelly, Cattel, & Breunig, 2015). Management structures during Industry 4.0 are imagined to be more decentralized and flatter, albeit more specialized. Newer organizational functions such as expertise in data analytics are prominently getting updated into management.

Industry 4.0 is an outcome of the integration of a series of innovative technologies of productivity, creativity, and Industry 3.0 into a single platform. The main scope of Industry 4.0 lies in the reorganization of industrial production methods by incorporating internet of things (IoT), Information and Communications Technology (ICT), big data and AI technologies, robotics, and RFIDs and integrating them with customer feedbacks in order to be (a) more green and sustainable in the industrial processes and supply chains, (b) create a new strategic advantage in the market, (c) reduce costs by using autonomous machines, and (d) ensure faster product development.

For example, initially the RFIDs inside the warehouse were primarily used for tracking the inventory and optimizing warehouse management. However, now the scope of RFID has expanded. They have been tried, tested, and integrated with production systems. This integration has reduced the dependence on assembly line worker and increased the control and monitoring of assembly line production machines. The RFID attached to the work parts are designed to send the problem to the machine and, accordingly, the machine processes the parts into a finished product. The machined parts are then transported to another workstation by autonomous robots, eliminating the need of a fixed assembly line. Earlier, there was a dedicated staff to program and supervise the machines, fix the assembly line, and set the tools in workstations. However, now all these steps are automated, eliminating human interventions. With RFID and autonomous robots, the product design to manufacturing time has been significantly reduced (Whelan, 2016) .

Most research on Industry 4.0 is focused on the RAMI 4.0 framework (Schweichhart, 2016). The conversation is around how to implement Industry 4.0 business models and how these will increase the productivity; however, there is still no discussion on the strategic impact on the corporations post industry 4.0 implementation. Unlike in the previous generations where human intervention was high, in the ideal case, it is assumed that human intervention in the system of production would be completely eliminated. How would the corporations strategize this new trend? What capabilities would the corpora-

Figure 1. Evolution of Industry 4.0
Source: See also (Reinhard, G., Jesper, V., & Stefan, S., 2016; Wee, D., Kelly, R., Cattel, J., & Breunig, M., 2015).

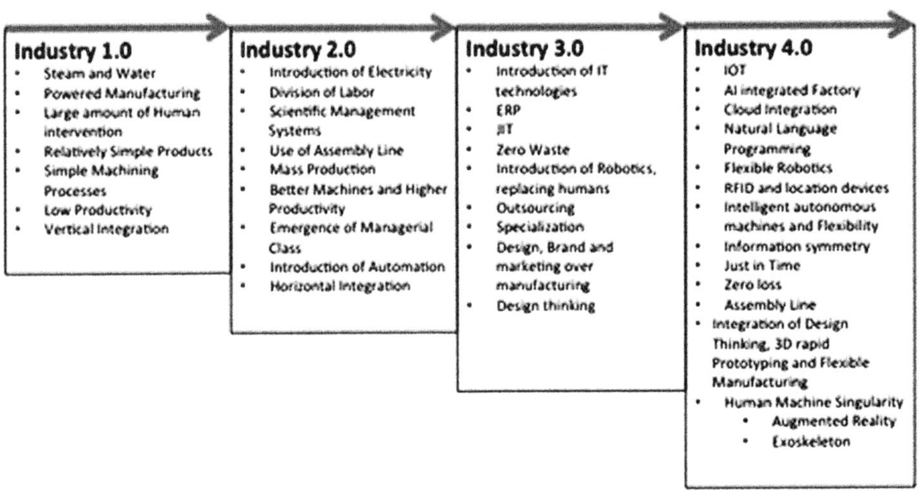

tions require in order to manage this? How would the market change subsequently? It is presumed that the overall strategic impact on corporates would change disruptively post Industry 4.0. This also calls for a deeper study at the social, corporate, and technology levels of the overall impact of Industry 4.0.

CORPORATE STRATEGY AND CORPORATE PERFORMANCE

The Corporate Strategy is a set of guidelines and drivers that direct the decisions and actions of a corporation in order to improve the corporate performance in the short and long run under conditions of uncertainty (Porter, 1980a; Tallman, 1991). There are many corporate strategies such as market strategy, cost strategy, volume strategy, new product strategy, wage arbitrage, new market strategy, and non-market strategy all of which are undertaken to increase a corporations' performance. The corporation engages with all these strategies at multiple levels to enhance the corporate performance. The role of a strategy is not limited to just increasing the revenues or decreasing the input cost. It also includes creating brand value and brand recall—New Market Entry, Credit Rating, ability to attract government subsidy, ability to win government projects such as Lock-Heed Martin or EADS, and greater market access. Thus, the corporate performance is not narrowly dependent on profitability but also includes wider measures such as profitability, survivability, credit rating, longevity, ability to attract public funding, brand value, and increasing market access and market penetration (Rao, 1994).

Corporate strategies are driven by two critical antecedents (Grøgaard, 2012). First, the portfolio of resources it possesses forms a major driver of corporate strategy (Morgan, Vorhies, & Schlegelmilch, 2006). Corporate resources include tangible resources such as the reputation of the top management team, learning capabilities, patent portfolio, cash reserves, credit rating, market width and penetration, product development /manufacturing flexibility, and market knowledge. Second, the corporate strategy is developed by environmental characteristics, institutional norms, market cycles, and international and national trade treaties (Freeman, 1984; Tallman, 1991).

Figure 2 represents a framework of corporate strategy and corporate performance. The role of corporate strategy is to take into account the present resources, understand the external market environment and corporate resources, evaluate the market dynamics, and develop strategies to manage the sustainability of corporate performance over short- and long-term in the changing market – industrial environment. As corporations adopt Industry 4.0, how would corporate strategy change and how would corporates strategize in a dynamic competitive environment?

POSITION OF INDUSTRY 4.0 WITH RESPECT TO CORPORATE STRATEGY AND CORPORATE PERFORMANCE

The ability of any corporation to improvise upon its capabilities and strategize tend to help it survive longer (Ruiz-Ortega & García-Villaverde, 2008). Successful corporations such as IBM, GE, and BMW have shown remarkable ability to learn, survive, and grow. On the other hand, corporations (such as Nokia and Kodak), which were market leaders at some point in time but lacked the ability to iterate and strategize based on the changing market and technological environments ended in eventual failure (Binns,

Figure 2. Antecedents, Actions, and Outcomes of Corporate Strategy
(Strategy Landscape) (Authors' Source)

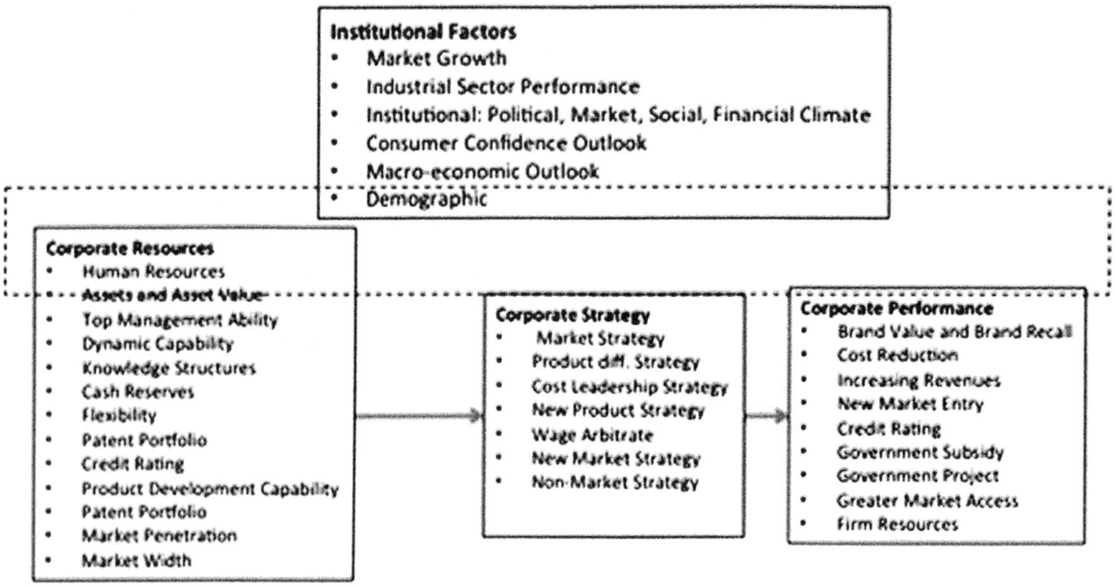

Harreld, & Tushman, 2014). While blindly absorbing a new technology may increase the risks of investment failure, failing to timely adopt will also lead to complete irrelevance in the market. Given the high impetus on the promise of Industry 4.0, many corporations are making substantial capital investments to strategize the future. The risk of irrelevance because of the lack of timely adoption outweighs the initial capital expenditure (Sosna, Trevinyo-Rodríguez, & Velamuri, 2010). Consequently, it is important for the corporations to reflect on their capabilities, their ability to learn and subsequently, prioritize actions accordingly. In this section, the chapter presents how the implementation and absorption of Industry 4.0 are dependent on the corporations's capabilities. Further, the chapter shows how Industry 4.0 supports the corporate strategy and how it positively improves the corporate performance.

Impact of Corporate Resources on Industry 4.0

As has been observed in the previous industrial revolutions, each stage of the revolution brought new organizational designs and the requirement of a new type of a skill set. The complexities of Industry 4.0 would require new organizational capabilities and resources. Organizational resources and capabilities of production are closely interlinked in order to create a long and lasting shareholder value. The capabilities of production have to be holistically aligned with the corporate resources and corporate strategy in order to create sustainable competitive corporate performance (Arthurs & Busenitz, 2006). Before integrating Industry 4.0, corporations have to reflect upon their existing capabilities, market environment, and corporate strategy. Corporation's capability to learn emerging technologies and map changing industrial and market landscape would greatly help in the successful absorption of Industry 4.0 technology.

Proposition: 1

Successful Implementation and Absorption of Industry 4.0 Is Highly Dependent on the Dynamic Capabilities of the Corporation

In a highly competitive market, corporations would engage aggressively to seek leading positions. Industry 4.0 platform of technologies is a certain enabler in that direction. One of the reasons why Silicon Valley scores highly on creating and adopting technologies is that they have an easier access to highly trained human resources. One needs highly valued and qualified skilled human resources to drive, produce, and maintain the Industry 4.0 systems (Gatewood, Shaver, & Gartner, 1995). Corporations that are able to secure trained human resources would be better positioned in the competitive landscape. Thus, the successful implementation and absorption of Industry 4.0 platform of technologies are highly dependent on the human resources. The industry and governments need to work together to create human resources flexible for Industry 4.0 standards and requirements.

Proposition: 2

Successful Implementation and Absorption of Industry 4.0 Is Highly Dependent on the Human Resources of the Corporation

The Upper Echelon Theory clearly says that the success of an organization is highly dependent on the cognitive and leadership capabilities of the top management teams (Carmeli, Schaubroeck, & Tishler, 2011; Mueller & Barker Iii, 1997). The more acceptable and adaptable the top management teams are toward implementing emerging technological advances, the probability to succeed in accepting the change would greatly increase. Thus, the successful implementation of Industry 4.0 platform of technologies is not only highly dependent on the corporate strategy and evolving market dynamics but also on the cognitive and leadership capabilities of the top management. For example, Kodak was once a market leader but soon found that its leaders could not adopt the existing business towards the changing technological landscape. Subsequently, the board had to reconfigure the top management team from outside the group (Gavetti, Henderson, & Giorgi, 2003). The mélange of new culture brought by the new leadership and the existing work culture among the incumbent managers created tensions within the organization. Eventually, Kodak lost its market share and position.

Proposition: 3

Successful Implementation and Absorption of Industry 4.0 Is Highly Dependent on the Cognitive and Leadership Ability of the Top Management Team

The market width and depth greatly influence the corporations' ability to learn from multiple (strong and weak networks) sources and hedge market risks. The weak ties framework suggests that corporations which capitalize their discerning knowledge sources faster tend to learn and adapt faster (Granovetter, 1983; Liu & Duff, 1972). They also tend to manage uncertainty and risks faster. The weak ties help corporations to identify the opportunities, resources, and expectations much earlier. In order to forge weak ties, they must have diversified portfolios and ability to forge asymmetric complementary ties at different levels. Both market depth within a given service/product point and market width across various domains may help them to identify opportunities early. Similarly, the breath and debt of market access help the them to manage the market risks and uncertainty better. Using similar logic, Industry 4.0 requires knowledge and resources from various domains including IoT, robotics, IT, manufacturing and blockchain. Corporations, which have the ability to identify the emerging technologies and opportunities early from the various discerning market sources, tend to learn faster and compete better. The Samsung Group is a highly diversified group operating in traditional logistics business as well as cutting-edge mobile technology business. Until 2008, Nokia (focused mobile technology firm) was a market leader and Samsung was a distant fourth. However, by 2012, Samsung was able to take over the market share of Nokia. Among the many reasons cited, diversified market and product strategy helped Samsung the most to outcompete Nokia.

Proposition: 4

Successful Implementation and Absorption of Industry 4.0 Is Highly Dependent on the Market Width and Market Depth of the Corporation

While conducting a cost-benefit analysis, if the cost of incorporating the Industry 4.0 technologies turns out to be more than the potential increase in overall benefits to the corporation, then, the corporation may engage with industry 4.0 service providers. Hence, it is best for the corporations to observe, learn, and outsource their requirements than to develop in-house. If the asset specificity of Industry 4.0 technology is very high such that the capital expenditure and market risk outweighs the potential benefits, then the corporation should engage with Industry 4.0 service providers instead of buying and installing them within their own factory premises (Hendrikse & Veerman, 2001; Susarla, Barua, & Whinston, 2009). The cost and organizational dynamics of outsourcing the Industry 4.0 capabilities may have an entirely different effect on the corporate strategy (Englander, 1988; Grover & Malhotra, 2003). The risks of outsourcing the capabilities to industry 4.0 services providers may also be very high. While, the in-house development of industry 4.0 capabilities may significantly increase the costs, but, buying the industry 4.0 services may significantly weaken proprietary capabilities.

Proposition: 5

Successful Implementation and Absorption of Industry 4.0 Are Highly Dependent on the Asset Specificity, Frequency of Use, and Market Risk

Impact of Industry 4.0 on Corporate Performance

The product differentiation strategy of any corporation is a strategy where it sells diversified range of products. For example, Mercedes sells different range and quality of cars. Subsequently, the diversified range of products increases the production and the marketing costs for the corporation. The biggest difference in Industry 4.0 generation and its predecessors is that it provides a higher degree of control, customization, and decentralized collaboration during production. The larger impact of these capabilities would be customer-centric products at lower costs (Wee, D., Kelly, R., Cattel, J., & Breunig, M., 2015). Corporations would be able to produce high quality, highly customized products to customers at a lower cost. Using Industry 4.0 capabilities, Corporations like Mercedes would be able to produce multiple ranges of models at a far lower production costs. The lower cost of production for Corporations would directly impact its financial bottom-line and increase its capabilities to provide a diversified range of products, therefore positively impacting corporate performance (Porter, 1980b, 1980c, 1985). Adoption of Industry 4.0 platform of technologies clearly provides a strong competitive edge to corporations engaging in product differentiation strategies and diversified product portfolios. Therefore, the chapter concludes that the Industry 4.0 platform of technologies greatly enhances the corporate performance.

Proposition: 6

Industry 4.0 Will Increase the Corporate Performance if It Is Coupled With the Product Differentiation Strategy of the Corporation

If a corporation's initial core strategy is cost leadership strategy, which involves selling a large number of products at lower prices, in that case, it would make strategic sense for it to invest in building resources that increase the output at a reduced price (Porter, 1980b, 1980c, 1985). The increases in production efficiency and volume strategy have a very high connection with increased corporate performance. Industry 4.0 capabilities are positioned to greatly reduce production costs. Thus, it makes strategic dexterity for the corporations to invest in Industry 4.0 capabilities. Corporations engaging in volume strategy must engage in cost-benefit analysis while making decisions on Industry 4.0 platform of technologies.

Proposition: 7

Industry 4.0 Will Increase the Corporate Performance If It Is Coupled With the Cost Leadership Strategy of the Corporation

New product development requires design thinking, customer feedback, market study, and customer profiling. It also requires strong, flexible, and rapid prototyping capabilities such as 3D printing, cad-cam design, and flexible machining capabilities. These are some of the capabilities that Industry 4.0 introduces to the current production systems (Qin, Liu, & Grosvenor, 2016). Industry 4.0 significantly enhances the ability to launch a product by integrating the *design to prototype any product or service* through customer requirements, market research, and, consequently, reducing the product development life-cycle time and cost considerably (Qin, J., Liu, Y., & Grosvenor, R., 2016). Data has shown that when the corporations launch new products at a higher rate they tend to have stronger performance over competitors (Pujari, Wright, & Peattie, 2003). Increased product development will positively impact the corporate performance (Rubera, Chandrasekaran, & Ordanini, 2016). Hence, accordingly, the corporate performance shall increase if Industry 4.0 is strategically integrated with the new product development strategy of the corporation.

Proposition: 8

Industry 4.0 Will Increase the Corporate Performance if It Is Coupled With the New Product Development Strategy of the Corporation

The implementation of Industry 4.0 is positioned to massively increase the productivity and reduce the overall costs of the corporation (Wee, D., Kelly, R., Cattel, J., & Breunig, M, 2015). As the Corporation engages in more aggressive actions, its competitors would also engage in similar actions. Higher productivity in a competitive market will put pressure on the overall margins. Higher pressure on margins will make everyone worse off. Consequently, corporations would be forced to aggressively engage in actions and strategies to explore and exploit newer markets (March, 1991; Rodan, 2005). The new market exploration and exploitation strategy of the corporation will have a positive impact on its performance. Hence, in the long run, if a corporation chooses to aggressively engage with the Industry 4.0 platform of technologies, it will also have to invest and couple Industry 4.0 with the new market development strategies. Failing to do so may increase the risks of underutilization of production systems or may increase the inventory costs.

Proposition: 9

Industries 4.0 Will Increase the Corporate Performance if It Is Coupled With the New Market Development Strategy of the Corporate

The prominent non-markets strategies of any Corporation include corporate social responsibility (CSR) expenditure, support to public projects and goods, social value creation through community engagement, investment in industry associations, strategic lobbying with the government, and strategically managing different social and political groups (de Figueiredo, 2010; Sandel, 2012). These strategic investments are executed to create trust with the public and the government. Industry 4.0 is there to increase the productivity at the employee and organizational levels. It does not share any common characteristic with the non-market strategies of the corporation. The non-market strategies have no commonalities with the Industry 4.0 technology. Consequently, incumbent corporations must not replace their focus on non-market strategies with an increased focus on Industry 4.0. Rather, the current media narrative against automation and digitalization, the corporations digitalizing must invest more on non-market strategies to manage their public relations.

Proposition: 10

Industry 4.0 Will Have No Impact on the Corporate Performance if It Is Coupled With the Non-Market Strategies of the Corporation

Industry 4.0 will drastically increase labor productivity. It will also decrease the cost of organizational control. Consequently, the increased productivity may lead to a decreased requirement of manpower. The decreased requirement of the workforce may lead to an increased possibility of large-scale layoffs. The layoffs may create stress in the markets. Increased productivity will also lead to commodification, reduced margins, and higher stress in the markets. Consequently, this will lead to social, political, and economic tensions in the business-social environment, which will result in adverse consequences for the corporation (Flanagan & O'Shaughnessy, 2005). The negative spillovers because of increased productivity will also lead to reduced fund allocations and reduced tax incentives from the government. It can also lead to an increased governmental scrutiny of the enterprise's activities. On the other hand, engaging the government and public about Industry 4.0 and its greater impact on market equilibrium may lessen these fears. Autonomous vehicles are one example of Industry 4.0 (Beede, Powers, & Ingram, 2017). It is a disruptive innovation but it also threatens millions of jobs (drivers and transporters) that are dependents on vehicles. The recent tests by Google and Uber have not only attracted interest from tech enthusiasts but also raised concerns about the future of jobs.

Proposition: 11

Industry 4.0 Implementation May Have a Negative Impact on the Corporate Performance if It Drastically Increases the Probability of Employee Layoffs or Market Competition

Using the 11 propositions developed in the chapter, the authors propose a diagram describing the position of Industry 4.0 within the corporate strategy landscape (Figure 3). The current available scholarship on Industry 4.0 is limited to conceptual definitions, adaptation in the industry, and operationalization within the manufacturing plant. The eleven propositions presented here, therefore, provide a perspective on how the corporate strategy and thereby corporate performance might get influenced while adopting Industry 4.0 enabling technologies. It also adds value to the current literature on Industry 4.0 by bringing in the strong corporate strategy perspective. The authors also hope to create a dialogue between Industry 4.0 solution providers/creators, corporations and policymakers.

CONCLUSION AND FUTURE OUTLOOK

This chapter looks not only at the changing technologies disrupting the current industrial sector but also at the corporate strategy and where and how Industry 4.0 adds value to the corporate performance. Corporations that learn and adapt faster tend to survive longer. They are generally more profitable while those, which are slow, tend to lose out to the competition. Industry 4.0 is an upcoming platform of technologies that is revolutionizing the rate of productivity per employee. It also has the promise to

Figure 3. Position of Industry 4.0 within corporate strategy landscape
Source: (Authors' Source)

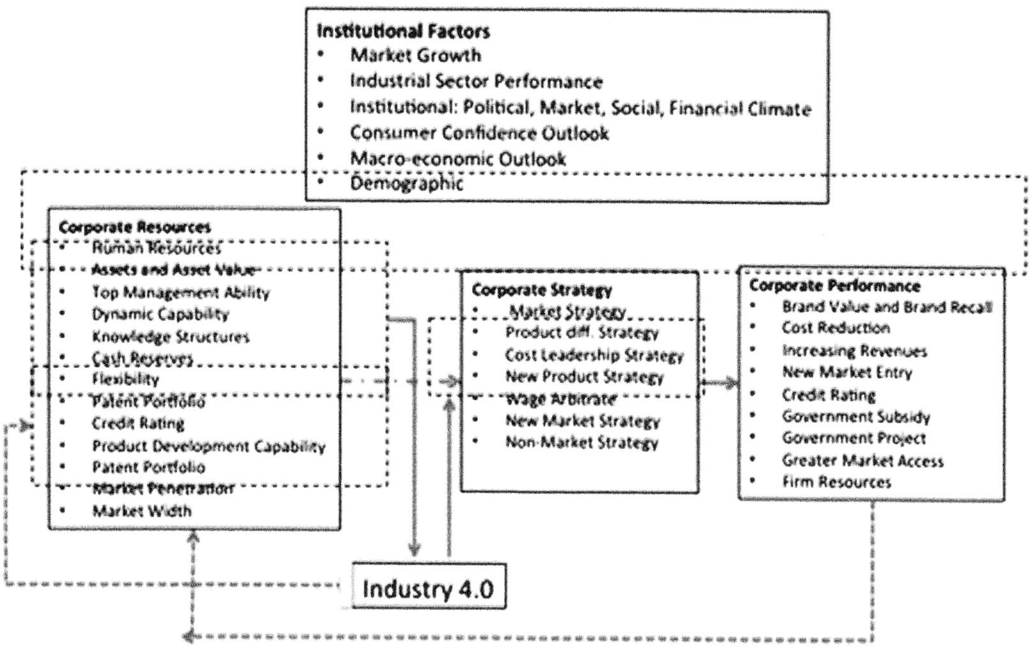

dramatically reduce the cost of controlling and compliance incurred by corporations. Therefore, the future outlook of Industry 4.0 looks promising. However, governments and the civil society have yet to take into account the socio-political-economic spillovers. For instance, if the productivity of existing employees increases substantially with Industry 4.0, it would also require for the market demand to grow equally. In case of limited growth into the market demand, there will be a very high risk of an economic crash, market failure, and possible large-scale unemployment as was witnessed during the Great Depression in the 1930s and in 2007–2008. In order to manage uncertainty that might arise due to higher productivity and, therefore, unplanned layoffs, policymakers should study Industry 4.0 from different positions. They must study the consequential spillovers on the socio-economic equilibrium, labor productivity, market equilibrium, and the plan for any major market failure. They might also consider reorganizing schooling and training curriculums to help people secure employment.

This study is primarily at the organizational level and discusses the position of Industry 4.0 within the broader corporate strategy. However, the study found that there is very little critical literature on the in-depth research on the growth of Industry 4.0 in the long run from a public policy perspective. Industrial revolution 1.0 and onward have greatly changed the productivity of corporations and consequently enhanced their profitability. The strategic resources of the corporations changed dramatically post Industry 3.0. In this era, the intellectual resources of the firm were decoupled from manufacturing. Industry 4.0 will now further change the outlook of intellectual resources, manufacturing and supply chains. Industry 4.0 would further reduce human intervention and decrease costs of controlling and monitoring. Given the lowering of wages, the rising unemployment in northern countries, and rising wages in southern countries, multinational companies are already restructuring their supply chains and manufacturing strategies. However, it is still to be seen how these restructuring would impact the labor markets in North and South. Presently, China is the production engine of the world, which exports goods to the rest of the world at very competitive prices. Will Industry 4.0 change this trend? Similarly, as Industry 4.0 gains further acceptance, the labor force of the new industrial age would be highly productive and will have higher wages compared to the present worker, given our knowledge of the previous industrial revolutions. How will the rise in wages impact the current economic equilibrium at the country and international trade levels? As industries adopt Industry 4.0 technology the uncertainties over employment, trade secrets, and core strength continue to persist. The research calls for further studies on Industry 4.0 and its impact on outsourcing. In order for the corporation to successfully absorb Industry 4.0 technology, they also need a highly skilled workforce. The research calls policymakers to relook at the technical education to incorporate the requirements of the new industrial revolution.

REFERENCES

Arthurs, J. D., & Busenitz, L. W. (2006). Dynamic capabilities and venture performance: The effects of venture capitalists. *Journal of Business Venturing*, *21*(2), 195–215. doi:10.1016/j.jbusvent.2005.04.004

Beede, D., Powers, R., & Ingram, C. (2017). The employment impact of autonomous vehicles. Washington, DC: Office of the Chief Economist, U.S. Department of Commerce Economics and Statistics Administration.

Binns, A., Harreld, J. B., III, & Tushman, M. L. (2014, December). The art of strategic renewal. *MIT Sloan Management Review*.

Carmeli, A., Schaubroeck, J., & Tishler, A. (2011). How CEO empowering leadership shapes top management team processes: Implications for firm performance. *The Leadership Quarterly*, *22*(2), 399–411. doi:10.1016/j.leaqua.2011.02.013

de Figueiredo, J. R. J. P. Jr. (2010). A tribute to Oliver Williamson: Institutions, politics, and non-market strategy. *California Management Review*, *52*(2), 123–131. doi:10.1525/cmr.2010.52.2.123

De Man, J. C., & Strandhagen, J. O. (2017). An Industry 4.0 research agenda for sustainable business models. *Procedia CIRP*, *0*, 721–726. doi:10.1016/j.procir.2017.03.315

Englander, E. J. (1988). Technology and Oliver Williamson's transaction cost economics. *Journal of Economic Behavior & Organization*, *10*(3), 339–353. doi:10.1016/0167-2681(88)90054-6

Flanagan, D. J., & O'Shaughnessy, K. C. (2005). The effect of layoffs on firm reputation. *Journal of Management*, *31*(3), 445–463. doi:10.1177/0149206304272186

Freeman, E. R. (1984). *Strategic management: A stakeholder approach*. Boston: Cambridge University Press.

Friedman, M. (2009). *Capitalism and freedom*. University of Chicago Press.

Gatewood, E. J., Shaver, K. G., & Gartner, W. B. (1995). A longitudinal study of cognitive factors influencing start-up behaviors and success at venture creation. *Journal of Business Venturing*, *10*(5), 371–391. doi:10.1016/0883-9026(95)00035-7

Gavetti, G. M., Henderson, R., & Giorgi, S. (2003). Kodak (A) Case. Harvard Business School.

Granovetter, M. (1983). The strength of weak ties: A network theory revisited. *Sociological Theory*, *1*, 201–233. doi:10.2307/202051

Grøgaard, B. (2012). Alignment of strategy and structure in international firms: An empirical examination. *International Business Review*, *21*(3), 397–407. doi:10.1016/j.ibusrev.2011.05.001

Grover, V., & Malhotra, M. K. (2003). Transaction cost framework in operations and supply chain management research: Theory and measurement. *Journal of Operations Management*, *21*(4), 457–473. doi:10.1016/S0272-6963(03)00040-8

Hendrikse, G. W. J., & Veerman, C. P. (2001). Marketing cooperatives and financial structure: A transaction costs economics analysis. *Agricultural Economics*, *26*(3), 205–216. doi:10.1111/j.1574-0862.2001.tb00064.x

Herter, J., & Ovtcharova, J. (2016). A model based visualization framework for cross discipline collaboration in Industry 4.0 scenarios. *Procedia CIRP*, *57*, 398–403.

Liu, W. T., & Duff, R. W. (1972). The strength in weak ties. *Public Opinion Quarterly*, *36*(3), 361–366. doi:10.1086/268018

March, J. G. (1991). Exploration and exploitation in organizational learning. *Organization Science, 2*(1), 71–87. doi:10.1287/orsc.2.1.71

Morgan, N. A., Vorhies, D. W., & Schlegelmilch, B. B. (2006). Resource-performance relationships in industrial export ventures: The role of resource inimitability and substitutability. *Industrial Marketing Management, 35*(5), 621–633. doi:10.1016/j.indmarman.2005.05.018

Mrugalska, B., & Wyrwicka, M. K. 2017. Towards lean production in Industry 4.0. *Procedia Engineering, 182*, 466–473.

Mueller, G. C., & Barker Iii, V. L. (1997). Upper echelons and board characteristics of turnaround and nonturnaround declining firms. *Journal of Business Research, 39*(2), 119–134. doi:10.1016/S0148-2963(96)00147-6

Porter, M. E. (1979). How competitive forces shape strategy. *Harvard Business Review, 57*(2), 137–145. PMID:18271320

Porter, M. E. (1980a). *Strategy toward buyers and suppliers*. Academic Press.

Porter, M. E. (1980b). Industry structure and competitive strategy: Keys to profitability. *Financial Analysts Journal, 36*(4), 30–41. doi:10.2469/faj.v36.n4.30

Porter, M. E. (1980c). *Industry Evolution*. Academic Press.

Porter, M. E. (1985). *Competitive advantage*. New York: Free Press.

Pujari, D., Wright, G., & Peattie, K. (2003). Green and competitive: Influences on environmental new product development performance. *Journal of Business Research, 56*(8), 657–671. doi:10.1016/S0148-2963(01)00310-1

Qin, J., Liu, Y., & Grosvenor, R. (2016). A categorical framework of manufacturing for Industry 4.0 and beyond. *Procedia CIRP, 52*, 173–178. doi:10.1016/j.procir.2016.08.005

Rao, H. (1994). The social construction of reputation: Certification contests, legitimation, and the survival of organizations in the American automobile industry: 1895-1912. *Strategic Management Journal, 15*(Winter), 29–44. doi:10.1002mj.4250150904

Reinhard, G., Jesper, V., & Stefan, S. (2016). Industry 4.0: Building the digital enterprise. *2016 Global Industry 4.0 Survey*.

Rodan, S. (2005). Exploration and exploitation revisited: Extending March's model of mutual learning. *Scandinavian Journal of Management, 21*(4), 407–428. doi:10.1016/j.scaman.2005.09.008

Rubera, G., Chandrasekaran, D., & Ordanini, A. (2016). Open innovation, product portfolio innovativeness and firm performance: The dual role of new product development capabilities. *Journal of the Academy of Marketing Science, 44*(2), 166–184. doi:10.100711747-014-0423-4

Ruiz-Ortega, M. J., & García-Villaverde, P. M. (2008). Capabilities and competitive tactics influences on performance: Implications of the moment of entry. *Journal of Business Research*, *61*(4), 332–345. doi:10.1016/j.jbusres.2007.07.029

Sandel, M. J. (2012). *What money can't buy: The moral limits of markets*. New York: Farrar, Straus, and Giroux.

Schweichhart, K. (2016). *Reference Architectural Model Industrie 4.0*. RAMI 4.0.

Sosna, M., Trevinyo-Rodríguez, R. N., & Velamuri, S. R. (2010). Business model innovation through trial-and-error learning: The Naturhouse Case. *Business Models*, *43*(2–3), 383–407.

Susarla, A., Barua, A., & Whinston, A. B. (2009). A transaction cost perspective of the "software as a service" business model. *Journal of Management Information Systems*, *26*(2), 205–240. doi:10.2753/MIS0742-1222260209

Tallman, S. B. (1991). Strategic management models and resource-based strategies among MNEs in a host market. *Strategic Management Journal*, (12), 14–69.

Wee, D., Kelly, R., Cattel, J., & Breunig, M. (2015). *Industry 4.0—how to navigate digitization of the manufacturing sector*. McKinsey & Company.

Whelan, R. (2016). Fully autonomous robots: The warehouse workers of the near future. *The Wall Street Journal*. Retrieved from https://www.wsj.com/articles/fully-autonomous-robots-the-warehouse-workers-of-the-near-future-1474383024

KEY TERMS AND DEFINITIONS

Corporate Competitiveness: Corporate competitiveness is the ability of the business to provide products and services as or more effectively and efficiently than relevant competitors.

Corporate Performance: Corporate performance is how effectively and efficiently a given business organization is achieving the objectives written in the strategy document of the business.

Corporate Productivity: Productivity is a measure used in many contexts. In this chapter, productivity is related to business performance. It is the ratio of output to input used in the production process.

Corporate Strategy: Corporate strategy is a set of statements that guides the corporation's decisions and actions to ensure its competitive position in the given industry and market.

Industry 4.0: Industry 4.0 is also known as "Smart Factory." It is a platform for increasing the productivity by systematically using multiple innovations in data science, automation, IoT, big data, robotics, modular manufacturing, and decentralized decision making by machines.

Institutional Factors: Institutional factors are social structures (rules, culture, routines, norms, and conditions) formed by the government, markets, and society that influence the organizational behavior and functioning.

Labor Market: Labor market refers to the supply and demand for labor in which employees provide the supply and employers the demand. It is a major component of any economy and is intricately tied in with markets for capital, goods, and services.

Labor Productivity: Labor productivity is equal to the ration between a measure of output volume (gross value added) and a measure of input use (total number of hours worked).

Market Forces: Market forces are the factors that influence the price and availability of goods and services in a market economy. Market forces push prices up when supply declines and demand rises, and drive them down when supply grows and demand contracts.

Market Uncertainty: Market uncertainty is the situation where the current state of knowledge is such that (a) the order and nature of things are unknown, (b) the consequences, extent, or magnitude of circumstances, conditions, or events is unpredictable, and (c) credible probabilities to possible outcomes cannot be assigned.

Chapter 10
Embracing Cybersecurity Risk Management in the Industry of Medical Devices

Maria Lai-Ling Lam
AJ-Great Limited, China

Kei Wing Wong
Calvin College, USA

ABSTRACT

The promises of Industry 4.0 in the medical device industry needs to be built on sound cybersecurity infrastructures, polices, and practices. During 2011-2017, the authors interviewed many manufacturers of medical devices in China, Germany, Israel, Japan, Taiwan, and U.S. about their attitude towards cybersecurity. Many manufacturers are not committed to cybersecurity risk management because they pursue lower cost and shorter product life cycles; do not have sufficient knowledge of operating environments of hospitals; have defensive attitude toward vulnerability disclosure; and reap quick benefits from the low-trust level among stakeholders and unequal power between manufacturers and distributors. Only a few large U.S. manufacturers of medical devices have set up robust secure platforms and interoperable optimal standards which benefit the users. As cybersecurity is a shared responsibility, many small and medium-sized enterprises need to be empowered through the support of international organizations and local government policies.

INTRODUCTION

Industry 4.0, the fourth industry revolution, allows intelligent data gathering, data storage, data distribution, and real-time responses through many heterogeneous cyber-physical systems and internet of things [IoT] (General Electric, 2017; Siemens, 2016). Some promising examples of industry 4.0 in the medical device industry are robotics in health care, fitness apps, tele-medicine, smart home care, and real-time processing through data analytic and data mining. Industry 4.0 empowers but also disrupts the current manufacturing sector of medical devices. Manufacturers not only can digitally manage the entire lifecycle

DOI: 10.4018/978-1-5225-3468-6.ch010

of products and production processes through the IoT, cyber-physical systems, powerful sensors and big-data analytics, but also predict the maintenance of their smart products (Chiu et al., 2017; Loffler & Tschiesner, 2013; Sogeti, 2017). When an operating system and an information technology system are integrated in the manufacturing process, cyber security is an on-going significant challenge in the heterogeneous environments constructed by industry 4.0 (Woodside Capital Partners, 2017). The manufacturers must comprehend the complexity of managing cybersecurity of diverse devices and systems when new medical devices are added to the existing system of health care providers. They are called to design their new devices with the in-depth knowledge of the users' operation system and be open to any vulnerability report from the community (Food and Drug Administration [FDA], 2016; Fu, 2014; National Institute of Standards and Technology [NIST], 2017; Schwartz, 2016).

The promise of industry 4.0 in the medical device industry needs to be built on sound cybersecurity infrastructures, policies, and practices. Manufacturers must know how to design and implement a secure embedded system *that typically must provide multiple functions, security features, and real-time guarantees at a minimum cost* (Sadeghi et al., 2015). When they want to realize the benefits of industry 4.0, they must assure the cybersecurity of their own systems and also the systems that support the health care providers and other stakeholders. These manufacturers must monitor the performance of their smart products in the hand of health care providers and are willing to take predictive maintenance and the assessment of the vulnerability of the devices when they are installed in the system of health care providers (Kobes, 2014; Schwartz, 2016). Unfortunately, cyber security is not treated as the first priority in the design process of many manufacturers of medical devices (Cooper, 2016). The practice of industry 4.0 in the entire medical device industry also challenges our existing social and legal systems (Doehmann, 2016). Its impact may become greater in our existing embedded health care systems and networks which are not equipped with updated software.

Cybersecurity risk management is regarded as shared responsibility among stakeholders, including manufacturers, users, information technology vendors, and health care delivery organizations. Manufacturers are expected to have industry-self-regulations which monitor the cybersecurity of the entire smart product life-cycle process (FDA, 2016). The entire medical device ecology is described by a key representative of FDA as very complex, complicated, uncertain, intensive, diverse, and evolving rapidly (Schwartz, 2016). Many manufacturers of American medical devices are criticized for lagging behind other industries in terms of cybersecurity management and standard setting (Cooper, 2016). A recent survey of about 242 medical device manufacturers finds that even though these manufacturers, an average, spend approximately U.S. $4 million in the security of their devices, only 34% of respondents follow the FDA published Secure Development Life Cycle process for medical devices (Ponemon Institute, 2017). Many small and medium enterprises are expected to comply with FDA cybersecurity guidelines much less than those respondents. Why do many companies not comply with the FDA cybersecurity guidelines? Are FDA cybersecurity guidelines not effective?

A few global American manufacturers have developed their strategies toward 4.0 and tend to focus on the cybersecurity of their smart production process rather than the entire product life-cycle of the smart products (General Electric, 2017). They can easily ignore the fact that one medical device can still function but can be used to break down the users' operating system. For example, Class 1 products which are exempted from the FDA approval, can be the entry point of cyberattack (Wellington, 2014). As the authors see it, there are two essential research questions: (1) What factors led these manufactures not to invest in cybersecurity management? (2) Under what conditions will these manufacturers develop their cybersecurity capabilities and increase their digital global competitive advantages? This chapter proceeds with four sections. The first section describes the complexity of the medical device ecology and cybersecurity risk management in the industry 4.0 and the second section describes the methodology. The third section answers the research questions and the fourth section describes the implications to manufactures and distributors in the era of industry 4.0. The fifth section addresses future research questions.

THE INDUSTRY OF MEDICAL DEVICES AND CYBERSECURITY RISK MANAGEMENT IN INDUSTRY 4.0

The medical device industry is highly regulated, concentrated, and diversified in terms of channel members' relationships. Thirty percent of multinational medical device firms control 70% of the global market share. The U.S. medical device market accounts for half the global market. There are more than 6500 medical device manufacturers in the U.S. and many are small and medium-sized enterprises (Trade Department, 2016). There are more than 500,000 medical devices in the industry. They are intrinsically diverse in their designs, usages, implementations, and applications. The product life cycle of each device can be significantly different from others. The industry is diversified and ranges from simple cotton to complicated implantable cardioverter defibrillators. The following section will review the definitions and classifications of medical devices, FDA cybersecurity risk management, the opportunities and challenges of manufacturers in the cybersecurity risk management in the industry 4.0.

Definitions and Classifications of Medical Devices

World Health Organization [WHO] (n.d.) lists the brief definition of medical devices as,

an article, instrument, apparatus or machine that is used in the prevention, diagnosis or treatment of illness or disease, or for detecting, measuring, restoring, correcting or modifying the structure or function of the body for some health purpose. Typically, the purpose of a medical device is not achieved by pharmacological, immunological, or metabolic means.

The FDA also adopts this definition and keeps on refining its regulatory tools to ensure manufacturers to address cybersecurity issues in the premarket [PMA] and post-market lifecycle phases of all medical devices (FDA, 2016).

FDA classifies medical devices into three class levels according to the risks associated with these devices (FDA, 2015). Class I devices are used to be simple in designs and have low risks. An example of Class I devices is dental floss. They are mainly subjected to manufacturers' quality control and many are exempted from regulatory controls. Class II medical devices that have higher risks than Class I devices are more concerned about *its safety and effectiveness*. An example of Class II devices is insulin pumps. Class III medical devices have the highest risk level and need most regulatory controls. An example of Class III devices is cardiac defibrillators. Most Class II devices and three-fourths of Class III devices receive FDA's 510 (k) treatment. Only 25% of Class III devices need to undergo premarket review. The classification can be misleading. Wellington (2013) criticized, *The current medical device classification does not always reflect the cyberattack risk posed by a particular device* (p.186). Some Class I devices with mobile apps or mobile related applications can constitute a cyber-threat and easily be exempted from regulatory control. For example, the storage of the tremendous medical data system can be classified as a Class I device, but it can be used as the entry point to attack the entire health care operating system. The cybersecurity risks associated with the Class I device is seriously underestimated by regulators. When industry 4.0 is adopted, many Class I devices can be mass-produced at a lower cost without much regulation.

FDA Cybersecurity Risk Management

According to the FDA guidelines, managing cybersecurity risks must start from the design process of medical devices and be implemented throughout the entire product life cycle. FDA Guidance (2014) defines cybersecurity as,

the process of preventing unauthorized access, modification, misuse or denial of use, or the unauthorized use of information that is stored, accessed, or transferred from a medical device to an external recipient (p. 3).

When the FDA requested the U.S. manufactures to have pre-review processes in 2014 and then issued the post-review guidelines on Dec. 28, 2016 (FDA Guidance, 2016), it showed that the government could only persuade the manufacturers of medical devices to identify, detect, and prevent the cybersecurity risk for the entire product life cycle.

FDA Guidance (2016) states,

Cybersecurity risk management is a shared responsibility among stakeholders including the medical device manufacturer, the user, the Information Technology (IT) system integrator, Health IT developers, and an array of IT vendors that provide products that are not regulated by the FDA (p. 6).

Manufacturers are requested to initiate the design and collaborative process with many stakeholders. They must build security and balance the need for access control and credential management control in the equipment, systems, and networks even beginning with the first step of the design process. It means that the devices cannot be easily used by unauthorized users and can be accessed by health care providers at different locations. Healey et al. (2015) recommended, *Manufacturers need to work with the security industry and regulators to develop a comprehensive risk model to follow during product innovation, design, and delivery* (p.13). They encouraged manufacturers to collaborate with FDA and many stakeholders such that the device will be a robust secure platform for additional technologies and services.

However, many stakeholders are not capable of following the FDA's cybersecurity advice. A recent survey including 242 medical device manufacturers and 262 health care delivery organizations illustrates that only about 50% of the respondents complied with the FDA guidelines to mitigate or reduce inherently security risks in their medical devices. Only 37% of manufacturers are confident that security vulnerabilities in their devices can be detected. Only 25% of manufacturers are confident that the security protocols or architecture designed built inside devices adequately protects clinicians (users) and patients (Ponemon Institute, 2017). Many lack confidence in the security of medical devices, even though they are designed and manufactured by them. Many respondents perceive that building secure service is challenging and they are not the only party to be held accountable for the security of these devices. The FDA cannot command the medical device manufacturers to follow the published Secure Development Life Cycle.

In Kobes' dissertation about security implications of implantable medical devices, Class III products, he analyzed each stakeholder's capacities and obstacles in the process of practicing cybersecurity management (Kobes, 2014). Manufacturers of medical devices know the design of the devices and are capable of upgrading the design. Unfortunately, they do not treat security as their first priority and also do not possess adequate knowledge concerning the users' software systems. On the other side, health care providers know the context in which the devices operate and the relationships of devices with patients. However, hospitals do not keep track a record of security, have limited knowledge of the cybersecurity threat, and even do not have much knowledge of proprietary technology. Software developers know the technology but do not understand health care systems and mainly focus on the speed of introducing a new technology. In summation, the accountability of the security of medical device manufactured or used is found to be wanting, even much lower in the Class I products. Thus, many manufactures' commitment to cybersecurity risk management of the users is even worse when Class 1 products are perceived to have the lowest risk.

Although the government has regulatory authority, it cannot foresee the consequences of emerging technology. In 2016, the U.S. National Institute of Science and Technology (NIST) has facilitated manufacturers to manage their cybersecurity risk by adopting the NIST framework for improving critical infrastructure cybersecurity (i.e. identify, protect, detect, respond, and recover) (NIST, 2016). NIST collaborates with the Department of Homeland Security's Critical Infrastructure Cyber Community (C^3) Voluntary Program to promote the implementation of cyber security framework among small and medium enterprises (Romie, 2017). The framework seems to provide common standards across all industries and allows users to grade their cyber risks and choose specific security controls. According to an informative speech of Suzanne Schwartz, a key representative of FDA, she requested the need to develop a trusted environment for information sharing with a "whole of community" approach. Manufacturers need to treat cyber hygiene as paramount and adopt a vulnerability disclosure and coordinated policy to improve the security culture of the entire medical device ecology (Schwartz, 2016). She endeavors to persuade the manufacturers to be self-regulated for the greater common good. Unfortunately, the existing American legal system is not sufficiently prepared to prevent those cyberattacks on medical devices and hospital networks (Wellington, 2013).

The distributors and original equipment manufacturers [OEM] outside the U.S. just comply with the FDA requirements although these regulations are not the best mechanisms to prevent cyberattack. The local government outside the U.S. must implement innovative public health policies to enable her people to access appropriate and safe medical devices (World Health Organization [WHO], 2010). These devices work only if they are used properly by health care providers and users in particular health care delivery settings. The safety, efficacy, and effectiveness of the medical devices highly depend on the skills and expertise of the users. The value of education and the actual impact of the medical devices on the health care settings can easily be ignored (International Society for Pharmacoeconomics and Outcomes Research [ISPOR], 2016).

Opportunities and Challenges of Manufacturers in the Cybersecurity Risk Management in the Industry 4.0

When medical device manufacturers' business processes and factories are automated in the industry 4.0, they can gain a benefit in machine-to-machine communication, predictive maintenance, and engagement from clients (Sogeti, 2017). They also can be empowered to manage the cybersecurity of their smart products from the material suppliers to consumers. They can predict the maintenance of their smart product. Some medical device manufacturers, such as General Electric and Siemens, are shifting their strategy toward industry 4.0 (CNBC, 2014; General Electric, 2016; Siemens, 2013). They anticipate providing more customized and safe medical devices at much lower costs to many people around the world. The CEO of Siemens claimed to be very close to industry 4.0 through the recent acquisition of software companies including LMS, CD-adapco, Polarion, and Mentor Graphics (Ogewell, 2017). General Electric also acquired several software companies in 2016 and moved from a manufacturing products to a service-oriented business when it moved toward industry 4.0. According to Woodside Capital Partners (2017), it stated,

Immelt <CEO of General Electric> has stated his ambition to become one of the world's top ten software firms with sales of programs and services worth $15bn as early as 2020 (p.2).

When manufactures adopt the strategy toward 4.0, they must need to invest much time and resources to develop a secure embedded system given the current vulnerability in the production process. Doehmann (2016) reminds us of the cybersecurity issue and the imbalance of power in the industry 4.0 environment. Digital networked medical devices can improve the quality of health care at a much lower cost but also can create cybersecurity risks (The Economist, 2017). More benefits can also result in more risks. For example, insulin pumps, heart monitors, and x-ray communication systems can be easily abused by cybercriminals to attack the health care networks (Higgins, 2015). The growing threat of cyberattack on medical devices and hospital networks is real and the stake of failure of cybersecurity is very high. In 2017, cybersecurity is regarded as one of the top ten issues in the medical device industry (Kalorama Information, 2017). The recent "Wannacry" cyberattack revealed how emergency care service at many hospitals were disrupted because of malware. More than 200,000 victims in more than 150 countries were affected (Dwoskin & Adam, 2017).

There is a serious vulnerability of current industrial internet of things [IoT]. It means that medical device manufactures have to balance availability and security management when they adopt industry 4.0. They must prevent any interruption in production and any system failure. They must know how to preserve certain security and privacy aspects of the lifetime of smart production processes and smart products. The need for more cybersecurity in the industry 4.0 is more critical now than when more devices and networks are more vulnerable to attack in the industry 4.0. The strategy toward industry 4.0 not only considers the cybersecurity of the manufacturers' production systems but also users' operation system which supports the function of the smart products. Medical device manufacturers not only need to focus the security of their smart production systems but also the security of the systems that enable the devices to have proper functions when they want to realize the benefits of industry 4.0. The choices of the practice of industry 4.0 will depend on how well cybersecurity is managed in the industry. Sadeghi et al. (2015) concluded,

However, existing security solutions are inappropriate since they do not scale to large networks of heterogeneous devices and cyberphysical systems with constrained resources and/or real-time requirements (para. 29).

In summation, the medical device manufactures who adopt industry 4.0 strategy, can track the performance of the smart products from the distributors to consumers. Manufacturers must maintain the cybersecurity of their production systems and also users' operation system in the entire product life cycle and the global supply chain. With the usage of advanced technology in the industry 4.0, it is possible to make entire product life-cycle to be transparent and to hold all stakeholders to be accountable to cybersecurity. The FDA's classification of medical devices does not fully take into account the cybersecurity risk of Class I devices which have mobile apps or mobile medical data systems. Manufacturers usually do not pay attention to the cybersecurity risks of Class 1 products when they have been exempted from regulations.

METHODOLOGY

The authors used induction methods to summarize the decades of their professional experience in the medical device industry and reviewed the literature related to the U.S. medical device industry, FDA cybersecurity guidelines, voices of medical device manufacturers, industry associations and relevant consultant companies. During 2011 to 2017, the authors also interviewed many manufacturers of medical devices and representatives in the medical trade shows and tours in China, Germany, Israel, Japan, Taiwan and U.S. They also interviewed the business executives and experts in the medical device industry in Hong Kong about their responses toward the 2017 European Union and FDA regulations on medical devices. During medical exhibitions, they asked different companies' representatives to explain the functions of many medical devices including medical beds, incubators, air mattresses, refrigerators, wheelchairs, recliners, and other Class I medical devices. They asked how the electronic control panels and mobile apps provided safety to patients and health-care providers. They also asked whether these companies' products earned certificates from Europe and FDA approvals. No one mentioned how the design of these products was resilient to cybersecurity attacks. They also asked manufacturers whether they knew the progressive FDA pre-review and post-review guidelines. All manufacturers seemed not to know the stringent FDA requirements and did not intend to prepare to be proactive. As Class I medical devices are used to be exempted from the pre-review and post-review processes, these manufacturers were not aware that the mobile apps with these Class I devices could be the entry point to attack the entire operating system of users. The authors also asked manufacturers and representatives in numerous medical exhibitions whether their organizations took steps to prevent cyberattack.

The authors also visited an OEM (Original Equipment Manufacturer) factory of international medical devices in Taiwan and asked whether cybersecurity management technology has been transferred from some international manufacturers or practiced in the factory. The answer was surprisingly "No." During 2012 to 2017, they analyzed the reports of several U.S. medical device innovators and their activities in cybersecurity conferences. Only a few key medical device manufacturers have developed collaborative activities with key stakeholders. From the published literature, the authors also examined the consolidation processes of a few medical device companies when they publicly announced the strategy toward Industry 4.0. They also examined the reports of many cybersecurity consultancy services and insurance services of medical devices. The authors interviewed the distributors in Hong Kong and examined whether they considered themselves to have the responsibility of cybersecurity risk management of the medical devices they carried. These distributors' main job were to sell the devices to the Hospital Authority in Hong Kong through the government tender process. They provided the products according to the specifications of the Hospital Authority. The authors had examined the specifications of Class 1 products, such as several intelligent air mattresses, and found there were no concerns about using these products as an entry point for cyberattack. It seems that the Hospital Authority is not aware of the level of vulnerability of those intelligent Class I medical devices in the users' operating systems. They continued to interview those who know the operating systems of hospitals in Hong Kong and understood the phenomenon of not engaging in cybersecurity risk management in Hong Kong. They also interviewed distributors and asked whether the manufacturers requested them to take up the responsibility of cybersecurity risk management. The answer was "No." Thus, the buyers, the suppliers, and distributors in the global supply chain were not well-prepared for the cybersecurity risk management.

FINDINGS

What Factors Led These Manufactures Not to Invest in Cybersecurity Management?

Cybersecurity management is not the highest priority among many manufacturers, OEM suppliers, distributors, and users in the entire global supply chain. In the authors' interviews, 75% of respondents' organizations did not take any step to prevent cyberattack. There are unequal powers of the manufacturers and distributors in the global context. In particular, those distributors of American made devices in developing countries are accustomed to cover a high proportion of hidden costs and make the products to be effective in the local settings. Many manufacturers are not committed to cybersecurity management because of these following reasons: pursue lower cost and shorter product life cycles; do not have sufficient knowledge of operating environments of hospitals; have defensive attitude toward vulnerability disclosure; and reap quick benefits from the low-trust level among stakeholders and unequal power between manufacturers and distributors.

Pursue Lower Cost and Shorter Product Life Cycles

Many American manufacturers of medical devices focus on innovative products and only comply with the safety and privacy legal requirements established by FDA. Kalorama Information (2017), a research company, stated,

It costs over $200,000 for a standard business to launch a new device with the FDA and $4700 for a "shortcut" or a 510 (k) application off a previously approved device (para. 2).

The manufacturers of medical devices will keep the cost down and not upgrade their software. They even don't want to change the malware when these devices have been approved by FDA. They also need to invest cybersecurity in the entire process of the product life-cycle and will do less if the cycle is expected to be made shorter. It is very expensive for manufacturers of medical devices to upgrade their software or make the software be compatible to the users. Many American manufactures of medical devices do not have the culture of cyber-hygiene and knowledge about cybersecurity (Cooper, 2016). One distributor in the authors' study said, *doctors always ask us to provide new products*. New products can increase the prestige of health-care providers and pride of users. However, these new products with updated software may be downgraded to adapt to a non-updated network system of a particular health care provider. The effectiveness of medical devices is bounded by the contextual environment in which the devices are used. The demand of new products from users and the supply of many new products from many start-up companies also lead many manufacturers to be more short-term focused and determine the product to be obsolete earlier. One manufacturer in a medical exhibition said,

At this moment, we do not think how to solve the problem of cyberattack because our team only focuses on the invention of new medical products.

Cybersecurity is not incorporated in the development of new medical products. Some companies perceive that medical device technology is changing faster than their capabilities to ensure their devices to be secure (Ponemon Institute, 2017). It is better to fulfill the government's standards and quickly sell the product without much investment in cybersecurity. One manufacturer said,

The manufacturers of medical devices product only need to learn how to fulfill the FDA and CE standards and to sell the product. We don't need to concern about cybersecurity.

Many medical device manufacturers are under extreme pressure to release their products without much quality assurance and testing procedures (Ponemon Institute, 2017). The investment in Industry 4.0 may also motivate the manufactures to cut costs in designing secure and sustainable smart products when there is keen competition on the speed of launching new products in the market.

Do Not Have Sufficient Knowledge of Operating Environment of Hospitals

Many U.S. manufacturers do not have sufficient knowledge of the hospital environment, in particular those users from developing countries. It is also difficult to transfer knowledge from one hospital to another hospital as each one is unique. Many medical devices are connected to hospital networks or internet without passwords or encryption. The outbreak of WannaCry ransomware infected medical devices and led a few key manufacturers to learn how to mitigate the risk. For example, Bayer AG has to update the security of all devices in the U.S. when its radiology equipment was infected from the network to the Window-based devices (Kuchler, 2017).

Many medical devices do not even match the need of the users in developing countries (WHO, 2010). Many U.S. manufactures of medical devices just treat developing countries as revenue from their low-quality and high-volume products. Many U.S. manufacturers and OEM suppliers in China and buyers of health care devices are not aware of how these medical devices increase the vulnerabilities of the entire system of health care providers. One device can still function but can be used to break down the entire system. The data collected in the hospitals in mainland China is under the control of People's Republic of China and can be used for political surveillance. Although there is one country and two systems and rules of law in Hong Kong, China, the cybersecurity management in the hospitals is much lower than that in the finance industry in Hong Kong. One chief information officer in Hong Kong said, *You can get a lot of patients' information from the medical devices in any hospital.* Another information technology researcher said,

there is only protection (i.e., firewall) outside the entire hospital, but there is no protection among medical devices inside the patients' rooms.

The Hospital Authority in Hong Kong has defined the standard of the firewall protocols but the entire hospital system can easily be attacked by many simple devices. However, the Authority is not aware the risk level and does not specify cybersecurity management in her procurement process.

Have Defensive Attitude Toward Vulnerability Disclosure

When cybersecurity researchers announce the vulnerabilities of certain devices to the media, medical device manufactures become defensive and regard them as disruptive agents. An insightful historical review of cybersecurity of medical device by Dr. Kevin Fu, a well-known cybersecurity expert, commented that many vendors were unprepared to receive vulnerability reports (Fu, 2014). Thus, the disclosure of vulnerabilities by the third party has not yet been regarded as a way for managing cybersecurity risks. Furthermore, many cyber researchers have signed non-disclosure contracts with particular manufactures when they designed the products for these manufactures. The exploitation of vulnerabilities of medical devices in a particular system and the impact on a patient's health can be excused and not addressed by the binding non-disclosure contracts among manufactures, designers and even health-care providers. There is a long expanse of time for many U.S. medical device manufactures to manage coordinated vulnerabilities throughout the entire product life cycle. The cost is too high and the speed of market is too fast. The hidden cost of cybersecurity management in different contexts is too high for manufacturers, OEM suppliers, and distributors to bear. It is easier to be tempted to ignore the risks and keep on creating new products to make the existing products obsolete at a faster speed. Medical device manufacturers can easily attribute the security problems to other stakeholders when there are a lot of obscurities in the building and the assurance of secure medical equipment in the complex systems. One interviewee said,

The responsibility of medical cybersecurity is not in the hands of the manufacturer of medical products. It should be the software company or IT company. The IT company can improve the security in the cloud and firewall.

Reap Quick Benefits From the Low-Trust Level Among Stakeholders and Unequal Power Between Manufacturers and Distributors

There are many competing interests among stakeholders in the highly complex and uncertain medical device ecology. The trust level among stakeholders in the U.S. medical device ecology is criticized as being low (Schwartz, 2016). When customers and governments demand high quality at a lower cost, the manufacturers are tempted to cut many hidden costs including cybersecurity management. Many interviewees are very concerned about the threat of cybersecurity regulations and the cost of complying with many regulations in different countries. Whoever initiates the harmonization of different regulations and the mobilization of the participation of different stakeholders for better cybersecurity management will increase the operating costs of leaders. The more powerful stakeholders will enjoy different economic and political benefits from the harmonization of standards. Who should take up the responsibility to help small or less powerful agents in the global supply chain to be well-equipped with the new cybersecurity requirements cannot be easily identified. There are many negotiations, conflicts, and struggles among stakeholders when cybersecurity management or new regulations are adopted. The local government can never regulate all unexpected behaviors and must rely on self-regulations among members in the global supply chain.

The hidden cost of training, education, service, and maintenance about particular devices in developing countries can easily be borne by the local distributors outside the United States when there are unequal posers between American manufacturers and local distributors. Many companies are reluctant to share information or data in order to sustain their competitive advantages even though these data can improve the design and cybersecurity management in the entire product life cycle which is situated in different social, economic, political, and legal contexts. The medical device life cycle also has significant differences in various contexts. Large companies can use their power in the global supply chain to ask small companies to absorb the extra cost of implementing cybersecurity management while these large companies can access capital and expertise at a lower cost when they improve their efficiency by using industry 4.0. One medical device distributor said, *Asking us to do cybersecurity management is like to put a knife on our neck.* The distributor is afraid of adding to the cost if there is security by product design throughout the entire product life cycle process. Many distributors will not initiate an assessment of their vulnerability of their users' operating systems and their role in reducing cybersecurity when their suppliers do not pay for that additional cost. Also their users do not pay attention to the cybersecurity risk in their specifications in the procurement process. Thus, many distributors will not spearhead the manufacturers to become aware of the problems of cyber vulnerability even though they have collected some evidence about cyber risks when they interact with the users.

Under What Conditions Will These Manufacturers Develop Their Cybersecurity Capabilities and Increase Their Digital Global Competitive Advantages?

Only a few large U.S. manufacturers of medical devices initiated many collaborative workshops with the government, researchers, insurance companies, consultants, and competitors to develop their cybersecurity capabilities. These key innovators have enough resources and expertise to grow and experiment various external and internal cybersecurity policies. They have greater access to capital and lower cost of production when they move toward industry 4.0. They develop their social capacities for resilience and reflections through collaboration and information sharing with stakeholders (Lam, 2000, 2007, 2009a, 2009b, 2010a, 2010b, 2010c, 2011a, 2011b, 2011c, 2012a, 2012b, 2012c, 2014, 2017; Vaill, 1997). They leverage on the open data and technology provided by the Industry 4.0. They set up learning platforms and experiments on how to incorporate medical devices as fully as possible into the current evolutionary flow of infrastructure security capabilities (Grimes, 2016). The more they increase users' awareness of cyber hygiene, the more they can provide better service from their robust platforms. Through numerous negotiations, the key manufacturers of medical devices can develop optimal standards which benefit software providers and health care providers. The standards are shared among different operation systems of material suppliers, production, and end users. Consequently, their competitive advantages and their capabilities to sense, seize, and transform opportunities in the industry 4.0 are enhanced through sound cybersecurity structures, policies, and practices (Teece, 2007). They also control the robust platforms and flourish when there are more informed consensus how to share data and to be proactive to cybersecurity issues in an open space. Many research findings can be reproduced and errors can be detected before these products are used by customers. The information about the security risks can also be openly available to clinicians and patients while the privacy of the users is endorsed.

Here are the best practice of Medtronic and Johnson & Johnson:

Medtronic employees participated in many cybersecurity management workshops. Medtronic has gradually shifted from making medical devices to making robust secure platforms for different technologies and services. For example, Medtronic's Global Privacy and Security Office organized a Product Security Symposium on November 5, 2014. The company was dedicated to *establish industry-leading security measures and safeguards* through extensive collaborative work between their employees and external experts (Medtronic, 2015:45). In 2015, the company approved a companywide Global Product Security Policy, *which provides guidance on integrating security into product development* (Medtronic, 2015:45). The company keeps on investing in the cybersecurity management and develops its capabilities through many internal processes and external collaborations with government and external organizations working on product security. The company invests in general-purpose know-how in the area of cybersecurity and broadens its capabilities for the coming industry 4.0 (Pisano, 2015). It also generates revenue by providing cybersecurity services to its customers, distributors, suppliers, and other stakeholders when they are included in the embedded secure system that provides multiple intelligent functions at real time processing in different locations when it adopts industry 4.0 strategy.

Johnson & Johnson cautioned customers about the hacking threat. It warned more than 100,000 diabetes patients of a flaw in their insulin pump. Kuchler (2017) reported that the director of product security and research development at Johnson and Johnson has taken cybersecurity as an integral part of product safety and a normal part of the product development process. The company has adopted more proactive and integrative approaches toward cybersecurity. It also collaborates with the Yale Open Data Access Project (YODA) to increase its clinical data transparency (Waldstreicher, 2016). It is preemptive and uses Yale's open data platform to increase the security of its products, production system, and the users' operating system. It also works toward publishing the list of software companies in its devices such that the hospitals can check their vulnerabilities. Johnson & Johnson shows its ability to update its devices and to notify the hospitals in advance how long it will support the devices.

In summation, these key innovators have practiced cybersecurity risks assessment for the entire product life cycles and initiated the post-market review process before FDA proposed the post-market review guidelines. They have organized and restructured their internal design process. They have developed, implemented, and refined their cybersecurity management policies. They practice cyber hygiene, adopt coordinated vulnerability management, and deploy mitigation earlier by being transparent and open to their stakeholders in advance. They are proactive in the cybersecurity management and make the process of reviewing devices' vulnerabilities be a part of organization routine. Their devices are made to be kept updated on the health care providers' networks as many common standards have been established through information sharing and open collaborative activities.

IMPLICATIONS

Industry 4.0 provides possible solutions for many U.S. medical devices manufactures to address the cybersecurity of smart products when the current problems of embedded secure system is solved. These

U.S. manufacturers will also address the cybersecurity risks of Class I products and investigate their vulnerability when these Class 1 products are connected to mobile applications. They also can address the vulnerability of the medical data system and distributed data operating system of their customers when they are willing to invite the public to address the weakness of the devices and disclose their design of the devices to their customers.

When the key innovators adopt strategy toward industry 4.0, they have already developed robust platforms for multiple products and services planned to generate more revenue from proving cybersecurity services and standards in their trustworthy platform. They are proficient to know how to improve the process of design and increase the abilities of users to upgrade the system through their common standards, robust platforms, and NIST (National Institute of Standards and Technology) cyber framework. They are skillful to know how to build security and demand security into their devices throughout the entire product life cycle, starting from the design process. Their experience of having transparent collaborative activities with multiple stakeholders can be shared among other stakeholders. Their expertise of managing cybersecurity risks can enable other stakeholders to know how to fully utilize the opportunities provided by industry 4.0 and improve patients' lives through effective, usable, affordable, and secure medical devices in the world. Thus, their existing interoperable standards can be extended to sustain trust, innovation, and effectiveness of their medical devices in the coming industry 4.0. They need to cultivate trust among stakeholders in the community and mobilize other stakeholders to be committed to cybersecurity management as a shared responsibility. Any compromised practices of cybersecurity by small and medium-sized enterprises will affect their entire global supply chain. These key innovators are recommended to take these actions to improve the security culture of the entire medical device industry: develop industry self-regulations in the cybersecurity practices; provide open-data sharing with their stakeholders; adopt vulnerability disclosure and coordinated policies; provide certifications and contracts for small and medium enterprises that fulfill the cyber-hygiene requirements that are attainable, affordable, and accreditable.

On the other hand, the development of industry 4.0 may strengthen the power of a few large innovative medical device manufacturers at the expense of many small and medium-sized enterprises. Several key U.S. medical device manufacturers will consolidate the industry through merger and acquisition and aggressively market their adoption of industry 4.0. There will be more integration between the business system and factories through automation and concentration of power of these few key medical device manufacturers. The practices among key U.S. medical device manufacturers may enhance the U.S. cybersecurity infrastructure and demand more compliance from OEM suppliers and distributors from those countries that are different from the U.S. cybersecurity standards. Many small and medium-sized manufacturers inside the U.S. or outside the U.S. may be marginalized when they cannot mobilize their strategies toward industry 4.0 and work seamlessly with these strong key U.S. medical device manufacturers. They perceive to bear heavy costs to comply with the interoperability of the standards that strengthen the few key innovators in the global supply chain.

As there is no complete expertise in the industry 4.0, it is vital to prepare unanticipated problems and develop social capacities for resilience and reflections through the security by design and active involvement of all stakeholders in the global supply chain. Those distributors in different countries need to be better equipped to meet their new roles to provide cybersecurity services to the users and suppliers and to inform their representative associations to affect their local government policy about new regulations on the medical devices industry. The hidden cost of providing new cybersecurity services may create tremendous barriers for these small enterprises. Those international organizations such as WHO (World Health organizations), WTO (World Trade Organizations), WIPO (World Intellectual Property Organizations) have to negotiate with these few prominent manufactures of medical devices to enhance the accessibility of affordable and secure medical devices in the world when the industry 4.0 is to be effectively implemented. Furthermore, these international organizations should provide more education about medical devices to the local people and train the local government to know how to evaluate the impact of these medical devices to the local health care system.

The local government inside or outside the U.S. has to set up policies to empower these small and medium-sized medical device manufacturers and distributors to be aware of cybersecurity risks in the design process of the products and provide incentives for these manufactures to develop strategy toward industry 4.0. The local government may learn from the best practices of other governments. For example, U.K. government has mandated that all public-sector contracts must be granted to enterprises with cybersecurity certifications and has driven some small and medium-sized enterprises to be equipped with cybersecurity practices (European Union Agency For Network and Information Security [ENISA], 2016). The local government also needs to harmonize the regulations and addresses the inequality issue. For example, members of Hong Kong Productivity Council have equipped their selected members to upgrade their capabilities to meet new legal standards coming from the U.S. and Europe through harmonizing the regulations and doing voluminous consultation work. Those small enterprises in Hong Kong which earnestly need more resources to meet the new regulations may not be supported as their failure rate to earn the certificates that meet the new standards is much higher than those that need less resources to be well-equipped. It is a justice issue of whom should be supported by the Hong Kong Productivity Council to meet the new standards.

Small and medium-sized enterprises must gain benefits from cybersecurity programs which allow them to be worthy partners in the global supply chain. They may get demonstrable certifications from governments or their supply chain when they fulfill the standards that are affordable, attainable, and accreditable. Some small and medium-sized enterprises are also trained to know how to do vulnerability disclosure and reduce the cyber risk in the entire global supply chain. It is better for them to visualize their roles in providing cybersecurity in the equipment, systems, and networks. They can understand how they contribute to the cybersecurity infrastructure and increase their competency when their partners are adopting industry 4.0 and need strong cybersecurity infrastructure.

In the industry 4.0, a social movement led by white hackers, consumers, and community members will emerge when more and more medical devices have been adopted by individual consumers in their homes. More and more consumers can use the open sources or crowdsourcing to publish many reports related to the vulnerability of medical devices. These civil journalists may lead many manufacturers, distributors, and health care providers to be more responsive and accountable to the security needs of their consumers and professionals in the community. Thus, many manufacturers must need to meet the cybersecurity needs of individual consumers and develop their dynamic capabilities and social capabilities for resilience through managing cybersecurity risks in the smart production and smart consumption processes in the industry 4.0. Hopefully, companies moving toward industry 4.0 will also share their standards, best practices, and guidelines with other stakeholders to ensure trust, innovation, and effectiveness in the complex, complicated, uncertain, intense, diverse, and evolving medical devices industry.

FUTURE RESEARCH

Medical device cybersecurity is a shared responsibility among stakeholders. Security by design in the entire production process in the product life cycle and the user's operation system will be an extremely high value-added service and a key differentiator in the medical device industry. The future research consists of three areas: (1) How do the key innovators shape the cybersecurity behavior of other stakeholders when they move toward industry 4.0? (2) What are the effective coping mechanisms with FDA and European Union regulations? (3) What are the ethical issues of availability, accessibility, and ownership of data in the processes of cybersecurity management when these manufacturers are moving toward industry 4.0? The extended research questions are described as follows:

Influence of Key Innovators on Cybersecurity Behavior of Other Stakeholders

In the industry 4.0, key American medical device manufacturers are capable to implement an overarching set of security standards starting from the design process in the entire product life cycle. Will these standards be embraced by members in the global supply chain? What will non-coercive initiatives of American device manufacturers do for the best enhancement of the cybersecurity infrastructure of members, including distributors outside the U.S.?

When companies progress in the industry 4.0, what kinds of partnerships will be effective for cybersecurity risk management? What factors determine the success of partnerships with competitors, local and international non-government organizations, and local governments in the medical devices industry?

Will the company have more shared valued sector or a systematic sustainable shared value business model when the company focuses the security of the smart production process but also the security of the system that enables the medical devices to have proper functions when it wants to realize the benefits of industry 4.0?

The practice of industry 4.0 in the entire medical devices industry will be affected by the cybersecurity infrastructure and result in the accumulation of power of key innovative medical device manufacturers. Will the cloud sourcing among final users encourage more stakeholders to treat cyber-hygiene as their first priority in the medical devices industry? When multinational medical device manufacturers have adopted industry 4.0 technology, how do they balance availability and security management in the entire product life cycle? What are the impacts of those medical devices manufactured or distributed by industry 4.0 on each country's health care system? Will the impact be measured in terms of Unite Nations sustainable development goals?

Effective Coping Mechanisms With FDA and European Union Regulations

More and more firms from developed countries will use OEM manufacturers from the developing countries while those medical devices have adopted IoT and powerful cyber-physical systems. Many medical devices firms are catching up with the industry 4.0 trend and learning how to comply with more stringent industry regulations set by European Union 2017. How do these key medical device companies follow their codes of conduct when they have to rely on OEM manufacturers and distributors from developing countries to implement those demanding regulations? Some governments from developing countries claim to own the data of all medical devices while the manufactures of these devices promise to have data protection for their final users. How do these manufacturers reconcile the conflicts about the accessibility, availability, and ownership of data in different countries? How do external reporting guidelines set by European Union, Global Compact, Sustainability Index, affect the industry self-regulated practices in the area of cybersecurity? Regulators are used to lag behind the technological changes of the devices when these manufactures adopt 4.0 strategy. What kinds of self-regulating mechanism will be effective in the industry?

When industry 4.0 is adopted, it is necessary that many states need to contemplate on how to share open data with citizens and firms in and outside their own countries. How do various professional industry organizations visualize many open data in various industries in different countries to empower various stakeholders, including manufacturers, distributors, health care providers, and patients to increase their capacities to provide secure service in a world with a network of interconnected medical devices? How does the development of e-governance in each country relate to the cybersecurity risk management of the medical device industry? What kinds of institutional factors will empower their members in the medical device industry to embrace cybersecurity risk management as opportunities rather than threats? What kinds of programs should be adopted to enhance the capability of small and medium-sized enterprises inside and outside the U.S. to comply with cybersecurity guidelines in the global supply chain?

Ethical Issues of Availability, Accessibility, and Ownership of Data

With the prevalent use of cloud computing and open data research in the industry 4.0, there are many ethical issues that have not been discussed by the philosophers who were trained at least ten years ago. Multinational medical device enterprises must reexamine their privacy policy and transparency requirements. Data then should be interpreted by existing social norms or algorithms to be relevant information that may affect the reputations of organizations or individuals. These third parties can be ranking agencies, hospital authority agencies, or user representatives from developing countries. They have specified the criteria for data protection. How do multinational medical device companies maintain their brands' reputations and fulfill the specifications required by the third parties in other countries? How do multinational medical devices leverage on the expertise of their distributors from developing countries to deliver their data protection promises to the final end customers?

Many ethical issues about data ownership, data protection, data interpretation, data regulations, and data security need to be discussed widely within an organization and in the community. There is always incomplete expertise about the technology used in the Industry 4.0. There is the time gap between the cause and effect when more and more complex technologies are adopted. Each organization actor needs to set its privacy and transparent codes while it also develops social capacities for reflection and resilience. It also needs to develop trusting relations with its stakeholders as the vast amount of stakeholders' data are used for selected objectives. The choice of data and algorithms are not a political neutral process, and can be location specific. The algorithm used to interpret the data collected may be controlled by the key powerful manufacturers. How do medical device manufacturers frame their process of data collection from their distributors and users in different countries? How do organizations protect customers' personal data and still be transparent to customers about the usage of their data? When companies move toward industry 4.0, how do they change their data protection policies? Are there any changes in the external and internal policies dictating data protection policies? Are there any changes in the organization posting data protection within the company? Nevertheless, it seems evident that the development of industry 4.0 will give rise to a number of challenges about data protection and each stakeholder's ethical responsibility in the area of cybersecurity.

ACKNOWLEDGMENT

The author thanks Dr. Martha J.B. Cook, Alice Lam, Carman Lam, five anonymous reviewers, and participants in this project.

REFERENCES

Chiu, M., Ganesan, V., & Patel, M. (2017, July). Taking the pulse of enterprise IoT. *McKinsey & Company Internet of Things*. Retrieved September 1, 2017, from http://www.mckinsey.com/global-themes/internet-of-things/our-insights/taking-the-pulse-of-enterprise-iot

CNBC. (2014). *Philips: How the internet of things could affect health care*. Retrieved March 16, 2017, from http://www.cnbc.com/2014/01/23/how-the-internet-of-things-could-affect-healthcare.html

Cooper, T. (2016). *Medical devices cybersecurity: From best practices to standard*. Retrieved Jan. 5, 2017, from http://ceitcollaboration.org/docs/Cyber-Security-Part-II.pdf

Doehmann, I., & Sp, G. (2016). *Industry 4.0: legal systems, the social contract and health care*. Retrieved Jan. 5, 2017, from http://www.scl.org/site.aspx?i=ed47630

Dwoskin, E., & Adam, K. (2017, May 14). More than 150 countries affected by massive cyberattack, Europol says. *The Washington Post*. Retrieved from https://www.washingtonpost.com/business/economy/more-than-150-countries-affected-by-massive-cyberattack-europol-says/2017/05/14/5091465e-3899-11e7-9e48-c4f199710b69_story.html?utm_term=.7cd4bbf6aa42

European Union Agency for Network and Information Security (ENISA). (2016). *Review of cyber hygiene practices*. Retrieved August 17, 2017, from https://www.enisa.europa.eu/publications/cyber-hygiene

Food and Drug Administration (FDA). (2015). *What does it mean for FDA to "classify" a medical device?* Retrieved from March 20, 2017. https://www.fda.gov/AboutFDA/Transparency/Basics/ucm194438.htm

Food and Drug Administration (FDA) Guidance. (2014). *Content of premarket submissions for management of cybersecurity in medical devices*. Retrieved from https://www.fda.gov/downloads/MedicalDevices/DeviceRegulationandGuidance/GuidanceDocuments/UCM356190.pdf

Food and Drug Administration (FDA) Guidance. (2016). *Postmarket management of cybersecurity in medical devices*. Retrieved from https://www.fda.gov/downloads/MedicalDevices/DeviceRegulation-andGuidance/GuidanceDocuments/UCM482022.pdf

Fu, K. (2014, April 29). *Medical devices cyber security: the first 164 years* [Video file]. Retrieved Jan. 5, 2017, from https://www.youtube.com/watch?v=QKgdvmomopw

General Electric. (2017). *The industrial internet*. Retrieved from March 16, 2017. https://www.ge.com/digital/industrial-internet

Grimes, S. (2016). *Best practices for medical device cybersecurity management*. Retrieved from Jan. 5 2017, http://ceitcollaboration.org/docs/Cyber-Security-Part-II.pdf

Healey, J., Pollard, N., & Woods, B. (2015). *The healthcare internet of things: rewards and risks*. Washington, DC: The Atlantic Council of the United States. Retrieved from http://www.atlanticcouncil.org/images/publications/ACUS_Intel_MedicalDevices.pdf

Higgins, K. (2015). *Hospital medical devices used as weapons in cyberattacks*. Retrieved March 16, 2017, from http://www.darkreading.com/vulnerabilities---threats/hospital-medical-devices-used-as-weapons-in-cyberattacks/d/d-id/1320751

International Society for Pharmacoeconomics and Outcomes Research (ISPOR). (2016). *Assessing the value of medical devices—Choosing the best path forward: Where do we go from here* [PowerPoint slides]. Retrieved from https://www.ispor.org/sigs/Assessing_Value_of_Medical_Devices_2016DC-IssueP.pdf

Kalorama Information. (2017, January 3). Research firm announces top ten medical device trends to watch. *PR Newswire*. Retrieved Jan. 15, 2017, from http://www.prnewswire.com/news-releases/research-firm-announces-top-ten-medical-device-trends-to-watch-2017-300384787.html

Kobes, S. D. (2014). Security implications of implantable medical devices. *Graduate These and Dissertations*. 13683. Retrieved from http://lib.dr.iastate.edu/etd/13683

Krumholz, H. M., & Waldstreicher, J. (2016). The Yale Open data Access Project: How Johnson & Johnson is leading the way on clinical data transparency. *The New England Journal of Medicine*, *375*, 403–405. doi:10.1056/NEJMp1607342 PMID:27518657

Kuchler, H. (2017, Aug. 2). Medical device makers wake up to cyber security threat. *Financial Times*. Retrieved from https://www.ft.com/content/00989b9c-7634-11e7-90c0-90a9d1bc9691

Lam, M. (2017). Empathetic Leadership as an Alternative Paradigm for Responsible Supply Chain Management. In N. Meunjohn & A. McMurray (Eds.), *The Palgrave Handbook of Leadership in Transforming Asia* (pp. 295–314). Palgrave Macmillan. doi:10.1057/978-1-137-57940-9_16

Lam, M. L. L. (2000). *Working with Chinese expatriates in business negotiations: Portraits, issues, and applications*. Westport, CT: Quorum Books.

Lam, M. L. L. (2009a). Beyond credibility of doing business in China: Strategies for improving corporate citizenship of foreign multinational Enterprises in China. *Journal of Business Ethics*, *87*(S1), 137–146. doi:10.100710551-008-9803-3

Lam, M. L. L. (2009b). Sustainable development and corporate social responsibility of multinational enterprises in China. In J. R. McIntyre, S. Ivanaj, & V. Ivanaj (Eds.), *Multinational Enterprises and the Challenge of Sustainable Development* (pp. 230–244). Cheltenham, UK: Edward Elgar. doi:10.4337/9781849802215.00023

Lam, M. L. L. (2010a). Beyond legal compliance: Toward better corporate citizenship of foreign multinational enterprises in China. *Journal of Biblical Integration in Business*, *13*, 100–109.

Lam, M. L. L. (2010b). Managing corporate social responsibility as an innovation in China. In L. Al-Hakim & J. Chen (Eds.), *Innovation in business and enterprise: Technologies and frameworks* (pp. 224–238). Hershey, PA: IGI Global. doi:10.4018/978-1-61520-643-8.ch015

Lam, M. L. L. (2010c). Political implications of the corporate social responsibility movement in China. *The Journal of International Business Research and Practice*, *4*, 125–134.

Lam, M. L. L. (2011a). Becoming corporate social responsible foreign multinational enterprises in China. *The Journal of International Business Research and Practice*, *5*, 47–61.

Lam, M. L. L. (2011b). Challenges of sustainable environmental programs of foreign multinational enterprises in China. *Management Research Review*, *34*(11), 1153–1168. doi:10.1108/01409171111178729

Lam, M. L. L. (2011c). Successful strategies for sustainability in China and the global market economy. *International Journal of Sustainable Development*, *3*(1), 73–90.

Lam, M. L. L. (2012a). A best practice of corporate social responsibility: Going beyond words on a page and a check. Advances in Sociology Research, 13, 157-164.

Lam, M. L. L. (2012b). An alternative paradigm for managing sustainability in the global supply chain. *International Journal of Social Ecology and Sustainable Development*, *3*(4), 1–12. doi:10.4018/jsesd.2012100101

Lam, M. L. L. (2012c). Corporate social responsibility movement in China: What can foreign corporations' corporate social responsibility programs in China do to universal values? In K. Wang (Ed.), *Dialogue among Cultures: Peace, Justice and Harmony* (pp. 221–234). Beijing, China: Foreign Language Press.

Lam, M. L. L. (2014). Empathy as a Major Contributing Factor to Sustainability in the Global Supply Chain. In M. Khosrow-Pour (Ed.), *Inventive approaches for technology integration and information resources management* (pp. 53–67). Hershey, PA: IGI Global Publications. doi:10.4018/978-1-4666-6256-8.ch002

Loffler, M., & Tschiesner, A. (2013, June). The internet of things and the future of manufacturing. *McKinsey & Company Digital McKinsey*. Retrieved September 1, 2017, from http://www.mckinsey.com/business-functions/digital-mckinsey/our-insights/the-internet-of-things-and-the-future-of-manufacturing

Medtronic. (2015). *Integrated Performance Report: Governance and engagement*. Retrieved Jan. 25, 2017, from http://www.medtronic.com/content/dam/Medtronic/US/Citizenship/mdt_2015_integrated_report.pdf

National Institute of Standards and Technology (NIST). (2016). *Framework for improving critical infrastructure cybersecurity*. Retrieved from https://www.nist.gov/sites/default/files/documents/cyberframework/Cybersecurity-Framework-for-FCSM-Jan-2016.pdf

Ogewell, V. (2017, April 27). Is industry 4.0 realistic? Face to face with Siemens CEO Tony Hemmelgarn—TV report. *Engineering.Com Websites*. Retrieved from June 15, 2017 http://www.engineering.com/PLMERP/ArticleID/14814/Is-Industry-40-Realistic-Face-to-Face-with-Siemens-CEO-Tony-Hemmelgarn-TV-Report.aspx

Pisano, G. (2015). *A normative theory of dynamic capabilities: connecting strategy, know-how, and competition*. Harvard Business School Working Paper, No. 16-036.

Ponemon Institute. (2017, Mau 27). Medical device security: An industry under attack and unprepared to defend. *Ponemon Institute Research Report*. Retrieved August 11, 2017, from https://www.synopsys.com/content/dam/synopsys/sig-assets/reports/medical-device-security-ponemon-synopsys.pdf

Romie, C. (2017). Small business cybersecurity: federal resources and coordination. *National Institute of Standards and Technology*. Retrieved August 17, 2017, from https://www.nist.gov/speech-testimony/small-business-cybersecurity-federal-resources-and-coordination

Sadeghi, A., Wachsmann, C., & Waidner, M. (2015). Security and privacy challenges in industrial internet of things. *Proceedings of the 52nd Annual Design Automation Conference (DAC '15)*. 10.1145/2744769.2747942

Schwartz, S. (2016, May 26). *Medical devices and cybersecurity* [Video file]. Retrieved Jan. 15, 2016, from https://www.youtube.com/watch?v=d9RUHXWWiO8

Siemens. (2016, Feb. 21). *Spirit of innovation: The fourth industry revolution* [Video file]. Retrieved March 16, 2017, from https://www.youtube.com/watch?v=0Sj6miQif6s

Sogeti. (2017). *The fourth industrial revolution: Things to tighten the link between IT and OT.* VINT research report 3. Retrieved March 16, 2017, from https://www.sogeti.com/explore/reports/vint-research-3-things---the-fourth-industrial-revolution/

The Economist. (2017, March 2). Wonder drug: A digital revolution in health care is speeding up. *The Economist*. Retrieved from https://www.economist.com/news/business/21717990-telemedicine-predictive-diagnostics-wearable-sensors-and-host-new-apps-will-transform-how

Trade Department. (2016). Medical technology industry United States. *SelectUSA.gov Websites*. Retrieved Jan. 15, 2017, from https://www.selectusa.gov/medical-technology-industry-united-states)

Vaill, P. B. (2007). Organizational epistemology: Interpersonal relations in organizations and the emergence of wisdom. In E. Kessler & J. Bailey (Eds.), *The handbook of managerial and organizational wisdom* (pp. 327–355). Thousand Oaks, CA: Sage. doi:10.4135/9781412982726.n15

Wellington, K. B. (2014). Cyberattacks on medical devices and hospital networks: legal gap and regulatory solutions. *Santa Clara High Technology Law Journal*, *30*(2), 139-198. Retrieved from http://digitalcommons.law.scu.edu/chtlj/vol30/iss2/1

Woodside Capital Partners. (2017). The industrial internet of things: Making factories "smart" for the *next* industrial revolution. *Silicon Valley London*. Retrieved June 15, 2017, from http://www.woodsidecap.com/wp-content/uploads/2017/04/WCP-IIoT-Report-Spring-2017-1.pdf

World Health Organization (WHO). (2010). *Barriers to innovation in the field of medical devices*. Retrieved Jan. 10, 2017, from http://apps.who.int/iris/bitstream/10665/70457/1/WHO_HSS_EHT_DIM_10.6_eng.pdf

World Health Organization (WHO). (n.d.). *Medical Devices*. Retrieved Jan. 23, 2017, from http://www.who.int/medical_devices/definitions/en/

KEY TERMS AND DEFINITIONS

Cyber-Hygiene: Simple routine measures to minimize the risks from cyber threats.

Cybersecurity: The process of preventing unauthorized modification, misuse, or denial of use information that is transferred from one device to an external recipient.

Digital Networked Medical Devices: Medical devices are connected by internet of technology and provide real-time data processes to decision makers. There are four categories of networked medical devices: consumer products for health monitoring; wearable, external medical devices; internally embedded medical devices; stationally medical devices.

E-Governance: The integration of information and communication technology in all process to enhance government's ability to serve the needs of the public.

Social Capacity for Resilience and Reflection: Social assets cope with uncertainties and adversaries created by a system of interconnected technologies.

Social Movement: Social and group actions to increase the awareness of risks and take proactive actions.

U.N. Sustainable Development Goals: United Nations has set up 17 sustainable goals to end poverty, protect the planet, and ensure prosperity for all by 2030.

Vulnerability Disclosure: The policy publishes the details of security problems of a computer system, network, or software to the users and invite public scrutiny on security issues.

Section 3
Frameworks

Chapter 11
Industry 4.0 From the Systems Engineering Perspective:
Alternative Holistic Framework Development

Vladimír Bureš
University of Hradec Králové, Czech Republic

ABSTRACT

Systems engineering focuses on design, development, and implementation of complex systems. Not only does the Industry 4.0 concept consist of various technical components that need to be properly set and interconnected, but it is also tied to various managerial aspects. Thus, systems engineering approach can be used for its successful deployment. Overemphasis of technological aspects of Industry 4.0 represents the main starting point of this chapter. Then, collocation analysis, word clusters identification, selection and exemplification of selected domain in the business management realm, and frequency analysis are used in order to develop a holistic framework of Industry 4.0. This framework comprises six levels – physical, activity, outcome, content, triggers, and context. Moreover, the information and control level is integrated. The new holistic framework helps to consider Industry 4.0 from the complex systems engineering perspective – design and deployment of a complex system with required parameters and functionality.

INTRODUCTION

Systems engineering represents a discipline that deals with radical improvement or design, modelling and development of complex artificial systems. In the past, there were three main leaps that significantly influenced construction of complex systems. We call them industrial revolutions. We are told that the fourth one has been taken place for several years in the advanced economics. The first industrial revolution was based on mechanical production plants based on water and steam power at the end of the 18th century. The second industrial revolution was tied to mass labour production based on electrical energy at the beginning of the 20th century. Automatic production based on electronics and internet technology

DOI: 10.4018/978-1-5225-3468-6.ch011

is a specific feature of the third industrial revolution that we noticed during 1970s. Nowadays, the fourth industrial revolution is the subject of interest any various technological or economic fora, congresses, conferences, or blogs written by experts. This topic can be found in headlines in both professional and research journals. Thus, the buzzword "Industry 4.0" represents a magic formula for both research initiatives, and practical implementations. This term was coined in Germany, the biggest European economy, while comparable initiatives outside Europe are called "Advanced Manufacturing Partnerships" for the USA or "Made in China 2025" for China (Dujin, Geissler & Horstköter, 2014; Kagermann, Wahlster, & Helbig, 2013). Its main principle mechanisms, technologies, tools or methods have already been implemented in various types of organisations ranging from healthcare industry, precision agriculture or retail industry, to transportation, manufacturing, energy, construction or public administration (Attaran, 2017).

Introduction of Industry 4.0 into an enterprise is a complex task. Thus, techniques and methods that originated in the systems engineering field of study can be very helpful. Technological side of systems engineering represents its integral component and is mostly perceived as systems engineering itself. From this perspective, the connection of systems engineering and Industry 4.0 is quite clear and straightforward. However, there is the other side of the coin. All industrial revolutions were associated also with human, process, economic or social facets. Pure technological change would be useless if higher objectives was not achieved. Industry 4.0 is not an exception. Therefore, a higher level of operational efficiency, a higher level of automatization and productivity are considered to be the main objectives of Industry 4.0 (Thames & Schaefer, 2016). Achievement of these objectives is associated with five major features, namely 1) digitisation, optimisation, and customisation of production; 2) automation and adaptation; 3) human machine interaction ; 4) value-added services and businesses; 5) automatic data exchange and communication (Roblek, Meško, & Krapež, 2016; Posada, J., Toro, C., Barandiaran, I., Oyarzun, D., Stricker, D., Amicis, R. de, … Vallarino, I. Jr., 2015). Furthermore, application of modelling and simulations of economic systems can be added as the sixth feature (Bureš & Tučník, 2014; Tučník & Bureš, 2013).

Industry 4.0 is currently explored from many points of view and is associated with phenomena such as Big Data, Cloud Computing, Internet of Things, Cyber-Physical Systems, or Smart Factory Automation. Although this list is definitely not complete and enumeration could continue with tens of other concepts and terms, it is clear that the concept is grounded in technological progress and application of advanced technological systems. Surprisingly, implementation of Industry 4.0 in practice is not as complicated as it may seem. The reason is that complexity and requirements in the manufacturing industry have steadily increased for last decades. Introduction of the Industry 4.0 concepts has only strengthen this trend. As cited by Hofmann and Rüsh (2017):

the implementation starts with small steps here and there, there won't be a big bang that is going to introduce Industry 4.0. On the contrary, it will come step by step. But if we look back in ten years we will see that the world has changed significantly.

The crucial question here is, whether we can talk about industrial revolution when changes will come slowly, step by step. Should we talk about evolution? Answer to this question can be found in analysis of both underlying ideas and components of Industry 4.0 and managerial approaches and consequences that will be brought by Industry 4.0 introduction in practice.

According to Thuemmler and Bai (2017) there are four main Industry 4.0 components. These can be described in the following way (Hermann, Pentek, & Otto, 2015):

1. **Cyber-Physical Systems (CPS):** Industry 4.0 is characterised by an unprecedented connection via the internet or other distributed ledgers that bring the physical and the virtual world together (Akanmu & Anumba, 2015). In the manufacturing context, this results in high synchronisation of information related to the physical shop floor and the virtual computational space. This enables a higher degree of control, surveillance, transparency and efficiency in the production process. CPS realise the integration of networks through the use of multiple sensors, actuators, control processing units and communication devices.
2. **Internet of Things (IoT):** The term "internet of things" became popular in the first decade of the 21st century and can be considered an initiator of Industry 4.0. Some authors use it as a synonym to the Industry 4.0 concept (Roblek, V., Meško, M., & Krapež, A., 2016). Nolin and Olson (2016) stress that the IoT:

seems to envisage a society where all members have access to a full-fledged Internet environment populated by self-configuring, self-managing, smart technology anytime and anywhere (p. 361).

A wide range of definitions for the IoT can be found in literature. Alongside with definition, specific technologies, tools, or devices that belong under this umbrella concept are listed.

3. **Internet of Services (IoS):** Internet of services is related to so-called "service society" (Andersson & Mattsson, 2015). This type of society is characterised by its emerging nature and is based on the idea that services are made easily available through web technologies, enabling companies and individuals to combine, create and offer new kind of value-added services. From the technological point of view, concepts such as service-oriented architecture (SOA), software as a service (SaaS) or business process outsourcing (BPO) are closely related to the IoS (Hofmann & Rüsch, 2017). Nevertheless, Barros and Oberle (2012) propose a broader definition of the term service, namely

a commercial transaction where one party grants temporary access to the resources of another party in order to perform a prescribed function and a related benefit. Resources may be human workforce and skills, technical systems, information, consumables, land and others (p. 6).

4. **Smart Factory:** Smart factory is built on the idea of a decentralised production system, in which *human beings, machines and resources communicate with each other as naturally as in a social network* (Kagermann, H., Wahlster, W. & Helbig, J., 2013). Previously mentioned components – CPS, IoT and IoS – are somehow embedded in this last competent. That is way some authors consider smart factories as another key feature of Industry 4.0. In the smart factory, products find their way independently through production processes and are easily identifiable and locatable at any time, pursuing the idea of a cost-efficient, yet highly flexible and individualised mass production.

Hofmann and Rüsch (2017) define Industry 4.0 with the help of the following characteristics:

- Products and services are flexibly connected via the internet or other network applications like the blockchain (consistent connectivity and computerization).
- The digital connectivity enables an automated and self-optimised production of goods and services including the delivering without human interventions (self-adapting production systems based on transparency and predictive power).
- The value networks are controlled decentralised while system elements (like manufacturing facilities or transport vehicles) are making autonomous decisions (autonomous and decentralised decision making).

Dominance of technological approach to Industry 4.0 is apparent and understandable. Glas and Kleemann (2016) argue that Industry 4.0 is not limited to the technical dimension of digitalizing modern businesses (Felser, 2015), as it is rather the complete new organization and network coordination of value and supply chains. They are convinced that other concepts, e.g. "Smart Factory", "Internet of Things and Services" or "Cyber-Physical Systems", are sub-systems or sub-elements of the overarching Industry 4.0 concept. Particular technologies represent facilitators of required changes and progress. However, underestimation other perspectives can jeopardise implementation of the whole concept. As Kagermann et al. (2013) noted:

smart factories will make the increasing complexity of manufacturing processes manageable for the people who work there and will ensure that production can be simultaneously attractive, sustainable in an urban environment and profitable" (p. 21).

Therefore, some authors endeavour to define Industry 4.0 in a more complex and holistic way. Therefore, two studies introducing holistic view are presented here. First, Schaefer (2017) perceives Industry 4.0 as a four-level complexity. Its basic level is represented by security issues which are considered as the main prerequisite for further development and successful implementation in practice. Next level comprises any technology that can be applied, e.g. representation of the cyber-physical system. The third level emphasise that application of relevant technologies can lead to innovation and new types of product service systems. As a consequence, new business models suitable for Industry 4.0 have to be developed and implemented (see the Result section).

Second, authors of the RAMI 4.0 developed a 3D model which represents all different manually interconnected features of Industry 4.0 from the technical to economic perspectives (Zezulka, Marcon, Veselý, & Sajdl, 2016). The RAMI 4.0 represents and a tiny elaboration of the SGAM - Smart Grid Architecture Model (Trefke, J., Rohjans, S., Uslar, M., Lehnhof, S., Nordstrom, L., & Saleem, A., 2013). In the RAMI 4.0 architecture, assets are represented by physical parts like sensors, actuators, mechanical parts, documents etc. This layer is connected with virtual presentation with the help of the Integration layers, which provides digitally processable information about the fundamental layer. Communication layer standardises communication with the help of universal data formats directed to the Information layer. Information layer has various functionalities, e.g. conducts runtime of data pre-processing, performs execution of rules, maintains data integrity, or provides structured data. Functional layer provides platform for horizontal functional integration. It contains environment for modelling of services and support of business processes. Business layer support integrity of functions in the flow of value and enables mapping of business models. It contains regulative and legislative conditions and represents an interface among various business process (Zezulka, Veselý, & Braun, 2017). From the RAMI 4.0 perspective, this chapter pays attention to the highest layer in which several business processes are performed. However, it is clear that they both take advantage of and are limited by underlying layers.

It is not surprising that a plethora of articles and papers focused on practical issues addresses the opportunities of Industry 4.0 and present technological solutions or tools that should enable implement selected aspects of Industry 4.0 in practice. Authors attempt to motivate or even urge companies to participate in the initiative (Hofmann & Rüsch, 2017). Although the idea of Industry 4.0 roots back to the high-tech strategy presented by German authorities and thus has obtained a lot of attention recently, a comprehend and holistic research on managerial perspective is difficult to find and the technological perspective prevails (Lu, 2017; Liao, Deschamps, Loures, & Ramos, 2017) (see also methodological section below). This situation has to be considered unsatisfying, especially from a scientific point of view.

Considering the all aforementioned information, the main research question of this chapter is stated as follows: How to support design, development and implementation of Industry 4.0 from holistic perspective? The answer is based on a set of methods described in the next section.

METHODOLOGY AND MAIN OBJECTIVE

It is apparent from approaches presented above that managerial perspective represents quite significant part of Industry 4.0. Therefore, this chapter focuses on managerial perspective. The aim is to, based on the literature review, find out to which extent the managerial point of view is stressed in the current scientific literature. Furthermore, the main domains from the business management realm are identified. This chapter is based on systematic review of information resources tied to Industry 4.0. There are various approaches to a process of review development originated in different disciplines (Webster & Watson, 2002; Smith, Devane, Begley, & Clarke, 2011; Khan, Kunz, Kleijnen & Antes, 2003). However, this chapter follows systematic review as defined by Shamseer et al. (2015).

In this study, selection of resources is grounded in the PRISMA model (Moher, Liberati, Teztlaff, & Altman, 2009). The PRISMA Statement consists of a 27-item checklist and a four-phase flow diagram (see Figure 3). The aim is to assist authors in order to improve the reporting of systematic reviews and meta-analyses. Although PRISMA was initially focused on randomized trials, it can also be used as a basis for reporting systematic reviews of other types of research. PRISMA may also be useful for critical appraisal of published systematic reviews. However, the PRISMA checklist is not a quality assessment instrument to gauge the quality of a systematic review (Moher, D., Liberati, A., Tetzlaff, J., Altman D.G., & The PRISMA Group, 2015). Nevertheless, this procedure is slightly modified in this chapter as duplication is not observed, only merging of resources is performed. Eligibility criteria are the following:

- Written in English (although there is a lot of German publications e.g. in ZWF Zeitschrift fuer Wirtschaftlichen Fabrikbetrieb, which however cannot be evaluated properly due to the language barrier),
- Recent publications, i.e. no older than 5 years (from 2012),
- Returned on the search term "industry 4.0" (as papers from early 1990's in Web of Science or even from 1928 in Scopus were returned during the database search),
- Paper type: original research (reviews and reference works are excluded for context description and introduction into the concept),
- Papers indexed in Scopus and Web of Science,

- Abstract available,
- Focus on arbitrary I4.0 related aspect,
- Business and economic focus.

Amount of publications included into the PRISMA selection process is presented in Figure 1.

In order to outline the current state of the business management-oriented publications, descriptive statistical results of the dataset available in the Scopus and Web of Science databases can be briefly presented. Figure 2 and Table 1 quite clearly confirm that the Industry 4.0 concept originated in Germany. From the managerial perspective, the vast majority of publications was produced in this country. Furthermore, two thirds of publications indexed in Web of Science are published in three countries only – Germany, Czech Republic, and China. Figure 3 and Table 2 reveal that Industry 4.0 is related to plethora of disciplines. Moreover, it supports findings presented by (Glas & Kleemann, 2016) who found out that although Industry 4.0 has acquired broader media coverage and attention of practitioners and public recently, search results in academic publications (Science Direct or EBSCO Business Source Premseeier) mostly analyse Industry 4.0 from an information technology perspective (e.g. Posada, J.,

Figure 1. PRISMA flow diagram
Source: (Author's own work)

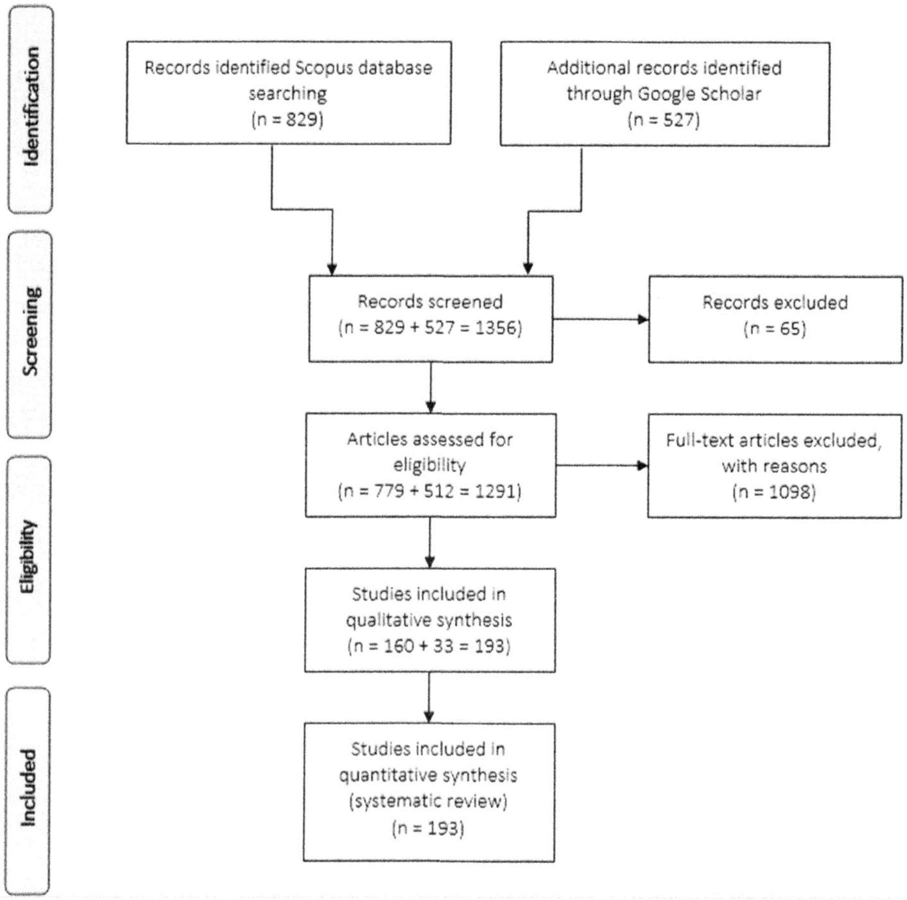

Toro, C., Barandiaran, I., Oyarzun, D., Stricker, D., Amicis, R. de, … Vallarino, I. Jr., 2015). Other perspective are somehow neglected. Results obtained from the databases also justify the necessity to acquire resources from more databases. Scopus and Web of Science, thought respected databases indexing high-quality journal papers, offer only fragment of selected available works which cannot be considered as representative. That is also why other databases than used by Posada et al. (2015) are used in this study.

To make the issue even more obvious Table 3 presents keywords associated with documents identified when the simple search phrase "Industry 4.0" was used in the Scopus database. Unfortunately, these keywords do not properly depict the content of particular paper. Although managerial keywords are included, papers are mostly technical and managerial aspects are mentioned only marginally.

Therefore, the collocation analysis and identification of word clusters are performed with the help of freely available application KH coder. The main purpose is to better identify the main managerial concepts used in publications. Due to outcomes from the preliminary analysis, the main objective of this chapter is to both verify findings made by (Glas & Kleemann, 2016) based on analysis the existing information resources in which way their work will be significantly extended and synthesise acquired outcomes in a form of general model, holistic framework, which would establish context for managerial approach to Industry 4.0 based on the latest research topics.

RESULTS

Single authors consider Industry 4.0 from various perspectives that are mutually interrelated. Moreover, they present Industry 4.0 applications in several domains ranging from healthcare to automotive industry

Figure 2. Business-related Industry 4.0 publications (Scopus database, August 28, 2017)
Source: (Author's own work)

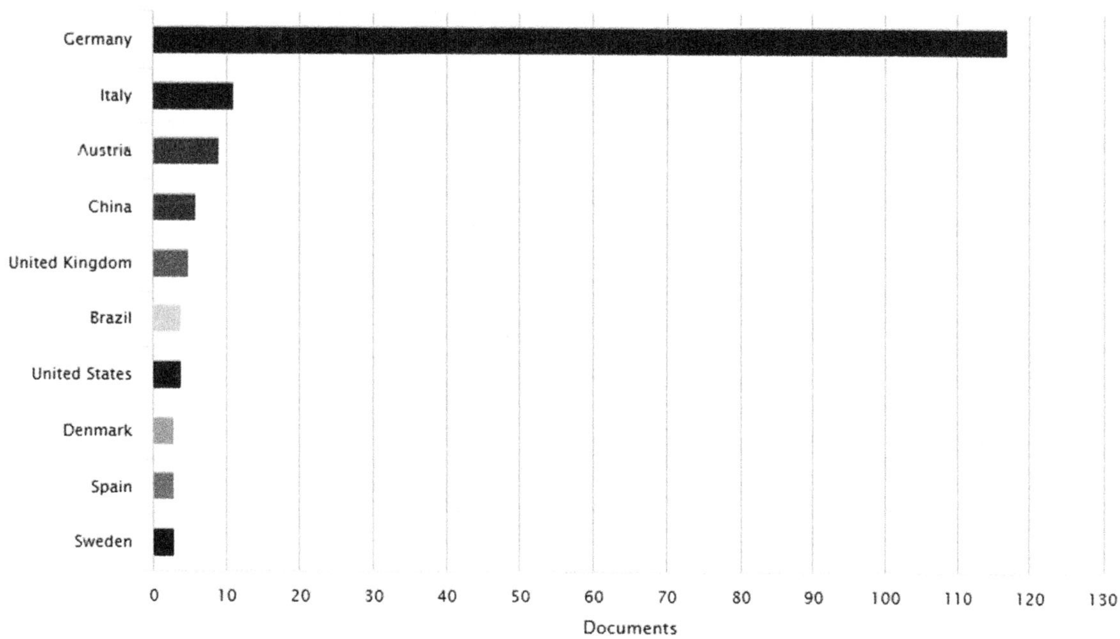

Table 1. Territories in Web of Science (August 28, 2017)

Complete List of Records			Business and Economics		
County / Territory	**Record Count**	**% of 562 Records**	**County / Territory**	**Record Count**	**% of 33 Records**
Germany	229	40.747	Germany	9	27.273
Peoples Republic of China	74	13.167	Czech Republic	7	21.212
Spain	29	5.160	Peoples Republic of China	7	21.212
England	25	4.448			
Austria	21	3.737			
USA	21	3.737			
Czech Republic	19	3.381			
Italy	17	3.025			
Taiwan	16	2.847			
France	15	2.669			
Norway	14	2.491			
Poland	11	1.957			
Sweden	11	1.957			
Australia	10	1.779			

Source: (Author's own work)

Figure 3. Categories of publications indexed in Scopus (complete list of records, August 28, 2017)
Source: (Author's own work)

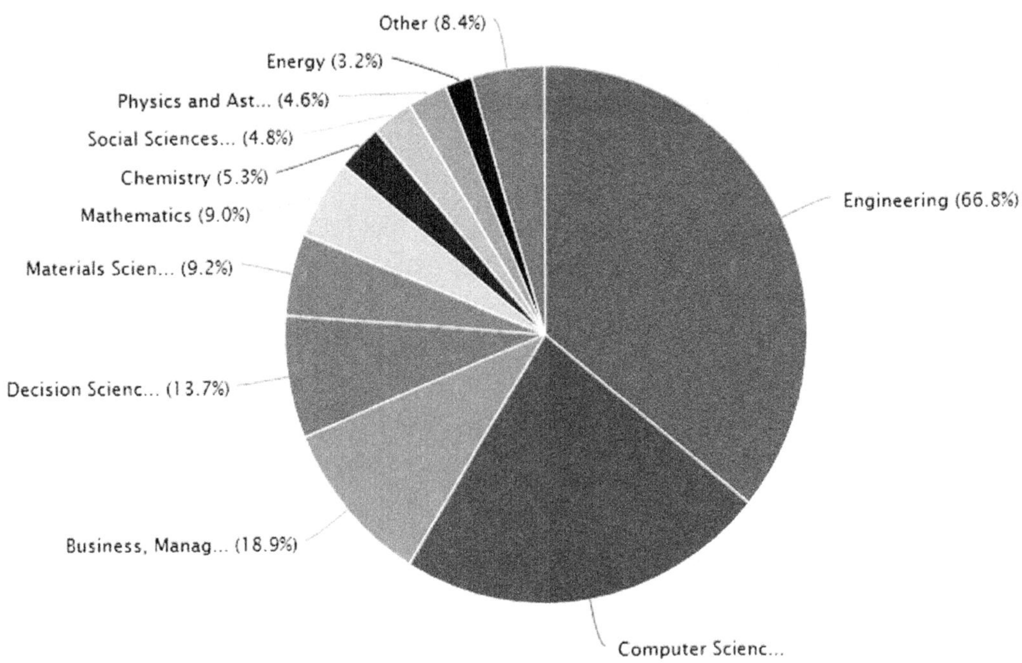

Table 2. Categories in Web of Science (complete list of records, August 28, 2017)

Research Areas	Record Count	% of 562 Records
Engineering	320	56.939
Computer science	175	31.139
Automation control systems	68	12.100
Operations research	38	6.762
Telecommunications	37	6.584
Business Economics	***34***	***6.050***
Education/Educational research	20	3.559
Material science	19	3.381
Instruments	16	2.847
Robotics	15	2.669
Social sciences / Other topics	15	2.669
Food science and technology	10	1.779
Chemistry	8	1.423
Science technology	8	1.423
Physics	6	1.068
Remote sensing	5	0.890

Source: (Author's own work)

or security. However, little is said about specific managerial functions. Therefore, this section presents selected domains, which are currently discussed in the research papers. Namely, business model innovation; procurement, logistics and supply chains; human resources; and knowledge management are exemplified.

As Industry is mostly perceived as the process of automation, robotisation or digitalisation, which has been taking place for several years now, little is written about specific steps or strategies how to execute the process of Industry 4.0 implementation in practice. Very likely, these procedural analyses were presented in the past and are not subject of interest at the moment. Apparently, this statement is speculative and needs to be verified by analysis of different dataset. However, there are some exceptions (Kagermann, H., Wahlster, W. & Helbig, J., 2013). For instance, Erol, Shumacher and Sihn (2016) describe three main stages in which Industry 4.0 has to be introduced:

- Within the "Envision" stage a company gets familiar with the concepts of the Industry 4.0. It develops its own understanding and aligns Industry 4.0 ideas with company strategy, specific objectives and stakeholders' needs.
- The "Enable" stage deals with breaking down the long-term Industry 4.0 vision into a more specific business model and to develop principal strategies towards its successful implementation (Chesbrough, 2007). Strategies answer the question of what has to be done to achieve the desired outcome.

Table 3. Frequency of selected keywords related to Industry 4.0 in Scopus (various version of the same concept merged, August 28, 2017)

Technical	Managerial
Cyber Physical Systems (218)	
Manufacture (205)	
Embedded Systems (166)	
Internet Of Things (92)	
Automation (82)	
Big Data (70)	
Industrial Revolutions (66)	
Internet (46)	
Industrial Research (45)	Decision Making (50)
Production System (44)	Life Cycle (35)
Engineering (36)	Information Management (33)
Factory Automation (35)	Management (29)
Smart Factory (34)	Production Control (28)
Smart Manufacturing (33)	Product Design (25)
Artificial Intelligence (32)	Manufacturing Process (23)
Manufacturing Industries (29)	Process Control (23)
Internet Of Things (IOT) (26)	Production Process (23)
Distributed Computer Systems (25)	Competition (19)
Virtual Reality (25)	Quality Control (18)
Robots (24)	Engineering Education (17)
Industrial Production (21)	Supply chain (<15)
Information Systems (21)	Enterprise resource planning (<15)
Optimization (21)	E-learning (<15)
Robotics (21)	Education (<15)
Data Handling (20)	Knowledge management (<15)
Augmented Reality (19)	
Cloud Computing (19)	
Complex Networks (19)	
Multi Agent Systems (19)	
Design (18)	
Machinery (18)	
Data Acquisition (17)	
Human Computer Interaction (17)	

Source: (Author's own work)

- Eventually, the "Enact" phase focuses on transforming strategies into single projects with their own goals, teams and principal milestones. As any other business project, these projects are evaluated and prioritised against the resources available, potential risks and expected impact on the overall mission.

Analysis of word clusters on sample of papers reveals that, from the managerial perspectives, production and manufacturing are the main topics covered by analysed publications. This is not surprising as Industry 4.0 is focused mostly on implementation of technologies used in manufacturing (see Table 4). Moreover, the existing technologies already applied in practice are related to automation or digitalisation of manufacturing (Trappey, A.J.C, Trappey, C.V., Hareesh Govindarajan, U., Chuang, A.C., & Sun, J.J., 2017; Thoben, Wiesner, & Wuest, 2017).

Table 4. Top Word Clusters related to production or manufacturing in Industry 4.0

Word Cluster	Score
Smart manufacturing	7472.757
Industrial production	7067.566
Production process	6613.978
Production systems	6554.996
Manufacturing industry	4725.358
Manufacturing systems	2428.183
Production planning	1712.902
Intelligent manufacturing	1513.426
Production control	1317.390

Source: (Author's own work)

Identification of world clusters associated with the term "business" reveals that "business model", "business models", "business process model" and "new business model" represent four concepts from the list of top-5 (together with "business processes"). Other related clusters can be identified in the list of top-20 ("business model development" or "new business models for smart factories"). Collocation analysis confirms this results. It shows that the term "business" is associated almost merely with "model". More specifically, "business model" is the most used concept with overall Z-score 23.227 due to 49 occurrences. When we look for the second highest collocation in text, we find "new business" with Z-score 9.432 and overall 25 occurrences. The third in a line are "business media" with overall 4 occurrences. Thus, it is apparent that from the managerial point of view, business models and related topics play the most significant topic. When considering the term "management" plethora of associated words are identified (slot management, resolution management, failure management, energy management or even brewery management). Mostly, technical concepts can be found and managerial collocations such as chain management, inventory management or logistics management are in minority and do not protrude. The only exception is "management system" with 28 total occurrences. However, this term is too abstract that it can mean anything in the economic system at the national level. Nevertheless, it is helpful for establishment of a new framework in the synthetic part of this chapter.

Results acquired from the quantitative semantical analysis indicate only main prevailing concept – business model. Other managerial domains have significantly lower occurrence in texts. Thus, only three other domains are selected and exemplified in order to highlight specifics and main topics – namely human resources management, supply chain management, and knowledge management. The aim is to summarise and present content already published, not to elaborate or add new ideas focused on connection of Industry 4.0 with selected domains. The main added value of this chapter is based on generalisation of these exemplified domains for the purpose of constructing a new Industry 4.0 holistic framework.

Business Models Innovations

While implementation procedures do not represent research mainstream in this topic, business models do. Business models describe rationales how companies create, deliver and capture value and the process of constructing a business model is part of the business strategy (Hummel, Slowinski, Matthews, & Gilomnt, 2010). Teece (2010) define a business model as a management hypothesis about what customers want, how they want it, and how the enterprise can organize itself to best meet these needs, get paid for doing so, and make a profit. A business model is composed of different elements or components (Osterwalder, Pigneur, & Tucci, 2005), which have been conceptualised at different levels of aggregation. As already stated in the introductory section, business models are quite frequent subject of discussions in Industry 4.0 debates (Schaefer, 2017). Hence, not surprisingly, this represents the first aspects that is discussed in many publications – the implementation process outlined by Erol, Schumacher and Sihn (2016) presented above can serve as an example. Moreover, they are considered as the cornerstone and main presumption of success in the Industry 4.0 domain. The idea is that we can discuss any stage of implementation only if the proper business model is selected and prepared for its establishment.

Attaran (2017) argues that the technology provides us with two distinct opportunities:

1. Transform business processes (Predictive maintenance; Better asset utilization; Higher productivity)
2. Enable new business models (Remote monitoring, e.g. Telemedicine, Smart Home, Drones; Enables anything-as-a-service)

Transformation of business processes and implementation of Industry 4.0 have significant impact on an organisation. As stated by Gerlitz (2015) innovations are rather new adaptations or transformations by using technologies, which to some level are already developed (see Figure 4). They refer to smart specialisation and structural evolution, which is not driven by radical innovations, but instead by adaptation to radical transformation. Gerlitz differentiates between incremental and radical innovations. Whereas the former implies the level, which improves a certain technology as compared to a previous level, i.e. continuous improvement, the latter has very far-reaching impact. She claims that industry 4.0 can be understood as incremental process, which may enable either sustainable or radical disruptive innovations for the market and proposing new values for businesses. Nevertheless, specifics associated with particular regions needs to be carefully considered (Hájková & Hájek, 2011).

Prause (2015) connects Industry 4.0 with the concept of a fractal company. A fractal enterprise is characterised by self-similarity, self-organization, self-optimization, goal-orientation, and dynamics as winning attributes of flexible and adaptable manufacturing organizations. There are five properties, which have been pointed out by Warnecke (1993) which are also compatible with characteristics of the Industry 4.0. Prause (2015, p. 161) states that:

the process of building a fractal structure is based on relations between material, personal and information whereby inside a fractal structure these relations are closer and more intensive than on the outside, so that fractal building is comparable to mathematical cluster process based on the relationship and weights of the resources.

In the context of Industry 4.0 due to the increasing importance of information, internet, cross-company interconnectivity in online operations and supply chain management the weight of information gains

Figure 4. Comparison of traditional and Industry 4.0 innovation process
Source: (Gerlitz, 2015)

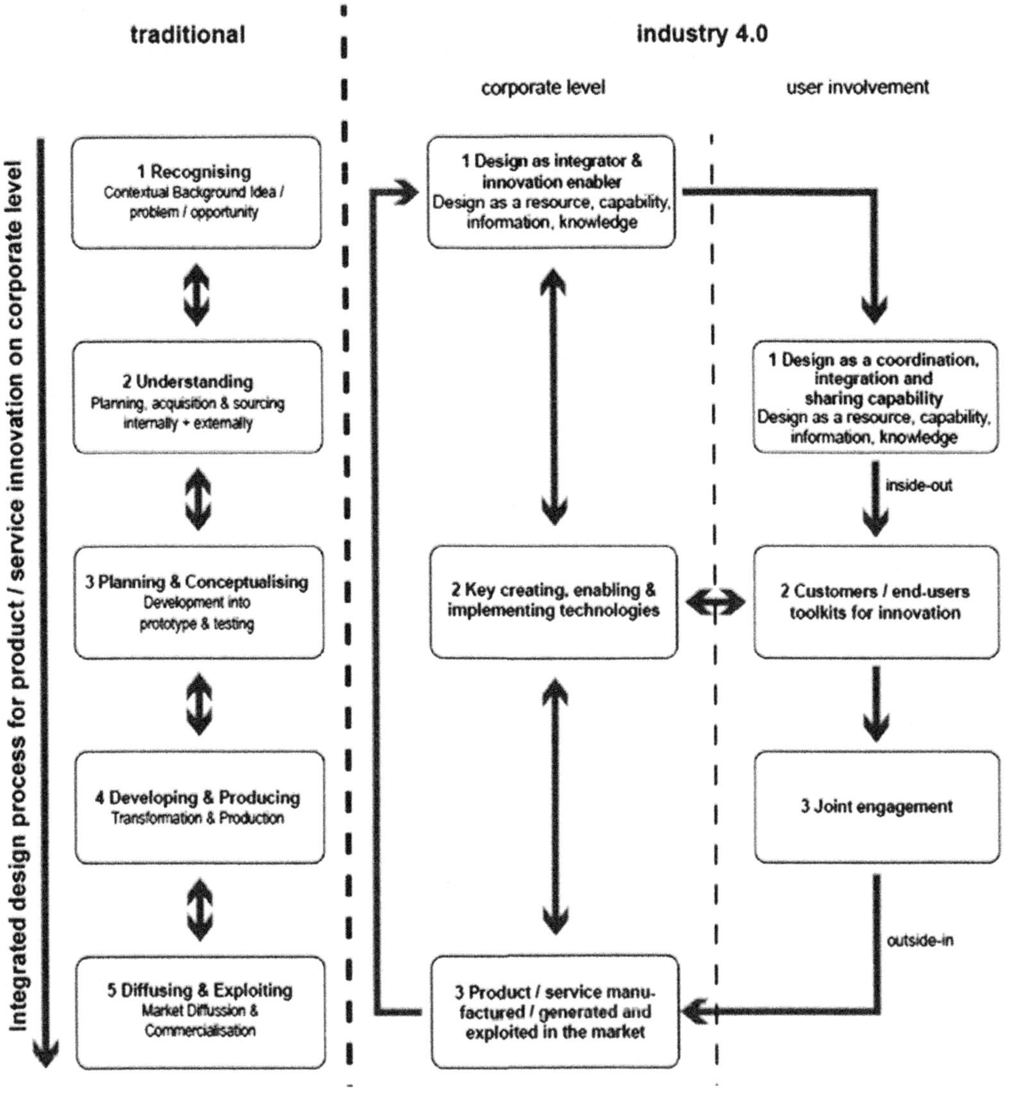

significant importance in the clustering process whereby the supply chain comprises the entire product life-cycle process including product design and development, operations management and logistics (Koether, 2006). Based on these findings Prause (2015) differentiate two basic models:

- **Open Innovation Models:** Innovation approach is in line with the internet and network orientation of the Industry 4.0 concept and it embraces collective concepts. Open innovation is referred to as a concept, which underscores the way of going beyond the corporate boundaries, i.e. an active strategic deployment of environmental clout or external factors of influence to increase its own innovation potential. Crucial determinants of such concepts are the shift from the industrial society to the network-based knowledge and communication society like it is facilitated in Industry 4.0 in innovation, especially all kinds of open innovation thinking.

- **Service Design Models:** Industry 4.0 paves the way for new business models covering also new sustainability concepts of product life cycles. Derived sustainable business models can deliver marketing advantages for sustainable products even if they are related with higher prices. service design represents sustainable design since not the material product stands in the focus of the business model but the service, which is realized by the product, which poses new challenges since successful service design solutions have to be connected to a strong and coherent brand identity and a smart business model.

Burmeister, Luettgens and Piller (2016) present a study which aim is to contribute with exploratory insights to a better understanding of how new business models are being designed, implemented, and supported, using the paradigm shift of Industry 4.0. First, they identified a number of changes expected in a firm's business model as a result of Industry 4.0. Second, they analysed current approaches to business model innovation and derived best practices regarding process, organizational structure, and tools, suggesting a contingent relationship between the design of a business model innovation process and the inherent characteristics of the business model it aims to innovate. Figure 5 summarised acquired results. By highlighting significantly supportive and promising practices for developing Industry 4.0 business models (marked as "X" in particular table cells), they identify key business model innovation competencies with relevance along most dimensions.

Human Resources

Not surprisingly, at the micro level lack of studies deals with human resources main functions such as motivation, evaluation, hiring etc. Shamim, Cang, Yu and Li (2016) outline ways in which Industry 4.0 influence traditional human resources management functions. Namely, they focus on training, staffing, compensation, performance appraisal, and job design. Authors consider they study as one of the initial attempts to draw the attention towards the important role of management practices in industry 4.0. They offer a viewpoint on suitable managerial practices that can promote the climate of innovation and learning in the organization.

At the macro level, the Industry 4.0 concept is mostly criticised for possible job loss and growing unemployment. For instance, (Brynjolfsson & McAfee, 2014) postulated a technological unemployment that arises when jobs are replaced by intelligent machines. However, the opposite is true. The most robotised economies like Japan, South Korea, Singapore, or Germany have the lowest unemployment rates. Problems with productivity can be identified in economies like Spain of Greece which received cheap money related to the access to the European Union (Challe, Lopez, & Mengus, 2016). Apparently, the unemployment is very weakly associated with digitalisation and robotisation and it has to be created by the market forces rather than subsidies.

It is important to understand that not only production processes but also the roles of employees are expected to change dramatically. Spath et al. (2013) expect employees to enjoy greater responsibility, to act as decision makers and to take on supervising tasks instead of driving forklifts, for instance. In the same context, some critics have recently pointed out that the automated and self-regulating nature of the smart factory might cause severe job destruction. However, hardly any reliable study supports that fear. Although primarily technical aspects have been considered so far, it is to be expected that the Industry 4.0 will also bring about a revolution in the working world (Schoenthaler, Augenstein, & Karle, 2015).

Figure 5. Business models innovation
Source: (Burmeister, C., Luettgens, D., & Piller, F.T., 2016)

I40 BM Characteristics		Business Model Innovation: Observed Best Practices																	
		Process (incl. trigger)						Organization						Resources and Tools					
		• Agile and iterative BMI process	• Proactive + open BMI process front-end	• Systematic VP (alternatives) design based on customer/market requirements	• Rapid prototyping/realization of minimal viable solutions	• Feedback loops with customers	• Early evaluation and decision gates	• Top-management sponsorship, management and directions	• Defined responsibilities and capacity for BMI lead/support	• Dedicated BMI or I40 team with interdisciplinary staffing (incl. IT + Ops)	• Inter-departmental and cross-entity collaboration	• Open organization with dedicated partnership mgmt.	• Entrepreneurial culture with freedom and responsibility	• Dedicated BMI toolkit incl. BM structuring + VP modelling framework	• Ecosystem analysis methodology tools and networking skills	• BM evaluation method with qualitative + quantitative criteria	• IT support for BMI (front end, collaboration tool, monitoring etc.)	• Intra-industry knowledge transfer	• Aligned performance mgmt. system to account for BMI + long-term performance
VP	• High product/service differentiation/customization	X	X	X	X	X	X	X		X	X	X	X	X	X	X	X	X	X
	• End-customer focus, B2B2C	X	X	X	X	X		X		X	X	X	X	X	X		X	X	X
	• Comprehensive Service business	X	X	X		X		X		X	X	X	X	X	X			X	X
	• Synchronized product/service combinations/VAS	X	X	X		X	X	X	X	X	X	X	X	X	X	X		X	X
VCr	• Value chain integration, consolidated control	X	X				X	X	X	X	X	X	X	X	X		X	X	X
	• Flexible and dynamic VCr networks	X						X	X	X	X	X	X	X	X		X	X	X
	• Connected information flows	X	X			X			X	X	X	X		X	X		X	X	X
	• Close (End-)customer relations, B2B2C	X	X	X		X			X	X	X	X	X	X	X		X	X	X
	• Short time-to-market	X	X	X	X	X	X	X	X	X	X	X	X	X		X		X	X
	• High efficiency						X	X	X	X	X	X				X			
	• High scalability									X	X	X			X				
	• High availability, preventive maintenance								X	X	X							X	
VCa	• Value appropriation from data/digital structures	X	X	X		X		X		X	X	X	X	X	X	X	X	X	X
	• Variabilization of prices and costs	X									X	X	X			X			
	➔ I40 Business Model Patterns ➔																		
	Goal	• Increase flexibility of the process and overcome experience-gap • Reduce development time • Market relatedness						• Extension of roles and skills • Openness • Pragmatism • Entrepreneurial thinking						• Optimal process support • Structuring guide • Decision support					

VP = Value Proposition, VCr = Value Creation Layer, VCa = Value Capture Layer
X = Identified practices that are significantly supportive or even critical for this issue

It will create new jobs and other jobs will change considerably. Industry 4.0 requires new skills that were previously have not necessarily promoted in our current education systems, but perhaps even inhibited:

- Advanced requirements for working independently and self-organized.
- Ability to collaborate intensively and effectively with external partners.
- Business transaction processing is replaced by approval, monitoring, planning, simulation tasks.

Hence, the task of the people development in the companies is to insure the correspondence between the requirements of the companies and the competence offers and development potentials. This task in general is not new but the discussion about industry 4.0 have shown that in some aspects it has become a quite new challenge. Decker (2016) relates this challenge with so called Generation Y (Bureš, Tučník, Mikulecký, Mls & Blecha, 2016). As Decker notices, the leadership and the operational level will become more and more integrated. We are speaking about "grey collar staff". Managers need to be able to understand the details of the processes to support the systems and optimise the results in order to achieve sustainable control of complex cyber physical systems. Very often it has been seen that highly automated systems where people are more or less totally separated from the process, deliver less quality than people-based systems (Decker, 2016). Therefore, it is expected that people will come back into the automated processes as a new kind of partner of the digitalized machinery and the robots.

Supply-Chain Management

The literature review revealed that three main domains are investigated. First, the overall concept of supply chain management is studied. Second, logistics and its relation to Industry 4.0 is analysed. Last, procurement as a self-standing activity in the supply chain management is presented. Hofmann and Rüsch (2017) show different Industry 4.0 opportunities in terms of decentralisation, self-regulation and efficiency. Improved demand assessment or shortened cycle times can be expected. With respect to Just in Time systems, reduced bullwhip effects, highly transparent and integrated supply chains as well as improvements in production planning represent the most promising benefits. They see majority of implications on the operative level of logistics management. Moreover, their scenarios also show the significance of Industry 4.0 with respect to cross-organisational logistics, particularly in terms of real time information flows, end-to-end supply chain transparency and improvements in flexibility, thus helping companies to optimise value-creation. However, they conclude that Industry 4.0 potentials need be evaluated situationally due to the complex nature of logistics management.

According to Roblek et al. (2016) Industry 4.0 represents progress, among other areas, in linking manufacturing sites in a comprehensive supply chain. They state that distribution and procurement will increasingly be individualized. Glas and Kleeman (2016) point out that usage of advanced information technologies nothing new in the context of procurement. The concept of electronic procurement (eProcurement) is already well established (Brenner & Wenger, 2007). Related to concept such as eBusiness, Internet and Supply Chain Management, the technology use was bigger than ever and (Essig & Arnold, 2001) this was the relatively easy integration of a company with suppliers. However, taking into consideration the paradigms of Industry 4.0 one key aspect however seems to be the emphasis on "smart" IT systems. It means that manual work associated with eProcurement is expected to be automated in the entire procurement processes. Glas and Kleeman (2016) outline the following procedure - smart systems automatically recognize demand for a certain material and from that, independently generate an order that is transmitted to the respective supplier without any necessary human interference. The actual automation therefore can be seen as a distinction of "Procurement 4.0" versus eProcurement.

Another implication related to procurement and implementation of Industry 4.0 technologies can be derived from the organizational paradigm in Industry 4.0. The step from "exchanging information" to the "free flow of information" between connected products, services and consequently, and organisations has to be considered as a significant change. However, the "free flow" implies a much higher degree of exchangeability of data itself, a higher degree of automation of the information exchange and possibly even the integrated use of the data under the concept of "big data analytics" (Lee, Kao, & Yang, 2014).

Supply chain structures in industry 4.0 are characterized by flexible processes and high efficiency which should be not only cost saving but also supposed to offer benefits like improved management for complex products, reduced time to market, and production on demand. Normally, differentiation and cost leadership are considered as contradictory competition strategies, but industry 4.0 has the challenge to enable them simultaneously (Shamim, S., Cang, S., Yu, H., & Li, Y., 2016).

Knowledge Management

Knowledge economy which represents the context of knowledge management initiatives in an enterprise is partially based on digitalisation (Bureš, 2006a; Brunet-Thornton, & Bureš, 2010). This process also represents one aspect of Industry 4.0. Apparently, these domains are mutually interrelated. Knowledge management deals with knowledge of various types. Product-related knowledge represents one of the main intellectual assets that a company possesses.

Relationship of knowledge management with Industry 4.0 can be presented with the help of well-known SECI model which represents a cycle of knowledge transformation from its tacit to explicit form. It may seem that Socialisation as a process of tacit knowledge exchange will be suppressed. The opposite is true. Robotization enables more intensive social interaction as for instance hard work in noisy environments is conducted by machines and people can be shifted to other environments more suitable form mutual conversations, chats etc. While Internalisation and Externalisation will very likely remain at the same level since they are related to training and specific abilities of individuals, Combination as an exchange of explicit knowledge can be again supported by Industry 4.0. Digitalisation and automation can be apparently associated with representation of knowledge and its embodiment into Industry 4.0 technical systems. Industry 4.0 is tied to cyber physical systems production, based on heterogeneous data and knowledge integration (Lu, 2017). Hence, knowledge management represents a specific domain, which has been tied to Industry 4.0 principles for several years. Industry 4.0 enables extension of this knowledge base by smart concepts that are extensively used and implemented worldwide (Schmidt, R., Möhring, M., Härting, R.C., Reichstein, C., Neumaier, P., & Jozinović, P., 2015). Similarly, the concept of Ambient Intelligence which is related to application to various knowledge technologies and sensor systems supports Industry 4.0 and its implementation in organisations (Bureš, 2006b). Adamczewski (2016) notices that dynamic development of ICTs in recent years has popularised SMAC (Social, Mobile, Analytics, Cloud) platform. It enables to create a unique eco-system of IT solutions that enables organizations to develop their businesses. The constantly growing quantity of data provided by mobile devices, social media, browsers, and other technologies creating a new business model based on information generated by the business environment. It this way, basic principles of knowledge management need to be applied in order to avoid information overload.

Connections between knowledge management and Industry 4.0 can be seen not only at the contextual or technological level. Roblek et al. (2016) offer comparison of classical Knowledge Processes and knowledge processes associated with Industry 4.0 (see Table 5).

Holistic Framework

Outcomes from the analytical stage presented in previous sections serve as an input for the synthesis stage, in which holistic framework for managerial perspective on Industry 4.0 is developed. If we take frameworks mentioned in the theoretical section, main terms revealed by the sematic analysis and four exemplified managerial disciplines, one coherent whole can be created in order to outline Industry 4.0 in one rich picture. In order to make the framework more solid, results from the frequency analysis of main concepts is added.

The framework contains six levels. Each level is based on main concepts (nouns) and activities related to these concepts (verbs):

1. **Physical Level:** This level comprises main technological devices, machines, gadgets or any hardware that is used in Industry 4.0. These entities need to be applied, implemented or introduced in order to enable realisation of the higher level.
2. **Activity Level:** At this level, devices from the physical level are proactively and purposefully used. However, their pure employment is mostly complicated. Therefore, they need to integrated and introduced into the existing functions such as research, development, manufacturing, applications, or production.
3. **Output Level:** This level brings the main desired output – product and services. However, this narrow view wouldn't be sufficient for holistic approach. The problem is that newly delivered products or services need to be created in environment with specific traits and characteristics if we want the business to be sustainable.
4. **Content Level:** At this level more abstract concepts are established. Basic business models or business processes are designed. They have to be explicitly demonstrated and allow.

Table 5. Comparison of classical knowledge processes and Industry 4.0 knowledge processes

Classical Knowledge Processes	Internet 2.0 Based Knowledge Processes	IoT Knowledge Processes
Knowledge based on the data acquired from the intranet. Customer relationship management. Data are saved in local servers.	Information is accessed and stored via clouds and platforms such as Google and Facebook.	Big data acquired directly from the things and customers. Analysed and saved in clouds.
Local time and personal limited access.	Business or private content is available on any device, any place, any time.	Real time. Content is available online. No limitations for sharing information between people or things.
Organisation limited networking: information sharing and discussion via email or intranet.	Internet 2.0 provides online relations between the customer and supplier. The discussion is limited to the matter of content and physical data entry.	Information sharing and collaboration via wireless communications between people, between people and things, and between things.

*Source: (*Roblek, V., Meško, M., & Krapež, A., *2016)*

5. **Triggers Level:** This level is characterised by the Industry 4.0 concept itself. This level is conceptual and mostly represents starting point when Industry is discussed in a company. Pioneers with enthusiasm operate at this level and help to promote associated ideas, experiences, or lessons learnt.
6. **Context Level:** This level represents the main system in which the shift to Industry 4.0 principles are perform. This context can be considered differently by distinct individuals. For somebody it can be company, for somebody else it can be a whole industry. Nevertheless, this level bounds all lower levels.

In fact, there is also another, the seventh, level. It deals with information transmission and control functions. They have to be enabled and realise in order to ensure interrelationship among levels and existence of feedback so crucial for successful development of Industry 4.0 in a company. The holistic framework is presented in Figure 6.

CONCLUSION

Prause (2015) emphasises that Industry 4.0 has ambitions, which are going beyond the development and use of cyber-physical systems and dynamic production networks. Industry 4.0 aims also for energy and resource efficiency, increased productivity, shortening of innovation and time-to-market cycles together with a horizontal and vertical integration through value networks and an end-to-end digital integration of engineering across the entire value chain. He is convinced that internet–linked production facilities and networked manufacturing systems open up a machine-to-machine communication and interaction, which allows to name, identify and trace single products during their whole creation process and later on during their life time, which generates new perspectives for the entire supply chain including product design and development, operations management and logistics (Brettel, Friederichsen, Keller, & Rosenberg, 2014).

Economic outlooks connect Industry 4.0 with growing productivity and overall success bringing happiness to all stakeholders regardless the type of industry. For instance, a new report conducted by the World Economic Forum - The Future of Jobs - estimates that nearly half a million construction jobs will be taken by robots before 2020. The report outlined that more than 5.1 million jobs will be handed

Figure 6. Holistic framework for Industry 4.0
Source: (Author's own work)

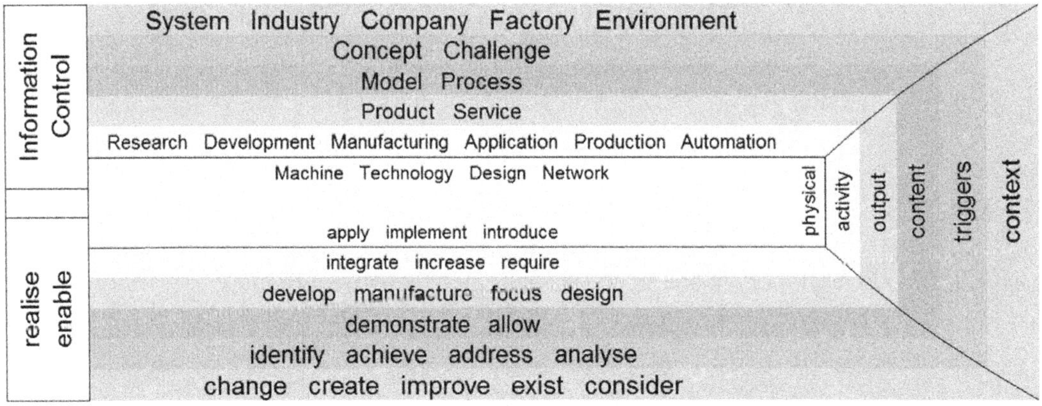

over to robots with 10 percent of those in the construction industry in 15 of the world's largest economies (Can, 2016). The technological changes that are expected to revolutionise the industry are mobile construction workers that can efficiently lay bricks as well as mobile 3D printers that can respond to environmental changes (Miley, 2017). However, specific feature of the construction industry is that it suffers from record low productivity which has not significantly risen for a long time (Judy, 2016). Vast majority of large construction projects are over budget and the industry is a huge contributor to environmental and material waste (Babaev, Sukhonos, Starostina, & Beletsky, 2016). Therefore, it seems that outlined development is little bit overemphasised at the moment. Gordon (2012) reminds that it was possible to double the standards of living in 30 years during the mid of the last century. Currently, this progress can be done in approx. 100 years. Thus, low pace of productivity growth is not an issue on in the construction industry only. It represents a global problem going across industries and a reason why some economists consider Industry 4.0 movement as a "disgrace" (Kovanda, 2017).

Implementation of Industry 4.0 technologies can be studied from the systems engineering point of view. The fundamental task is to design and implement a complex system in which various socio-technical subsystems are incorporated. The main objective of this chapter was to develop a framework that can help to introduce Industry 4.0 into an enterprise. Inclusion of managerial facet and emphasis on holistic perspective represent the main added value of the new framework. It is grounded on sematic analysis of recent research outcomes. Its creation is also based on exemplification of four domains in the business management realm. These domains range from those which experience the most intensive debate in the scientific literature to marginal topics that are awaiting for their rise. Lastly, the frequency analysis helped to incorporate systemic approach. Eventually, all acquired outcomes serve as an input for design of a new holistic framework of Industry 4.0 that takes into consideration experience of practitioners and ideas of researcher. It is built on conviction that the productivity problem outlined in the previous paragraph can be better grasped and handled if managerial perspective is not neglected and holistic approach is applied. This statement is based on existing gap between intensity of work devoted to technological aspects of Industry 4.0 and managerial issues. In general, appropriate management approaches play crucial role in to systems engineering. Implementation of Industry 4.0 is not an exception. They play a vital role in the development of productivity, dynamic capabilities, and effective learning and innovation climate during the time of fourth industrial revolution.

ACKNOWLEDGMENT

The financial support of the Faculty of Informatics and Management, University of Hradec Králové (FIM UHK) Specific Research Project "Autonomous Socio-Economics Systems" is gratefully acknowledged. Author would like to thank Tomáš Nacházel for his helpfulness during data gathering stage.

REFERENCES

Adolphs, P. (2015). RAMI 4.0: An architectural Model for Industrie 4.0. In *Object Management Group meeting* (pp. 1–31). Berlin, Germany: OMG.

Akanmu, A., & Anumba, C. J. (2015). Cyber-physical systems integration of building information models and the physical construction. *Engineering, Construction, and Architectural Management, 22*(5), 516–535. doi:10.1108/ECAM-07-2014-0097

Andersson, P., & Mattsson, L. G. (2015). Service innovations enabled by the internet of things. *IMP Journal, 9*(1), 85–106. doi:10.1108/IMP-01-2015-0002

Attaran, M. (2017). The internet of things: Limitless opportunities for business and society. *Journal of Strategic Innovation and Sustainability, 12*(1), 10–29.

Babaev, V., Sukhonos, M., Starostina, A., & Beletsky, I. (2016). Improving the processes of cost management in the construction and energy projects. *Eastern European Journal of Enterprise Technologies, 4*(3-82), 10-17.

Barros, A., & Oberle, D. (2012). *Handbook of Service Description*. New York, NY: Springer. doi:10.1007/978-1-4614-1864-1

Brenner, W., & Wenger, R. (2007). *Elektronische Beschaffung: Stand und Entwicklungstendenzen*. Berlin: Springer. doi:10.1007/978-3-540-34018-8

Brettel, M., Friederichsen, N., Keller, M., & Rosenberg, M. (2014). How Virtualization, Decentralization and Network Building Change the Manufacturing Landscape: An Industry 4.0 Perspective. *International Journal of Mechanical, Aerospace, Industrial and Mechatronics Engineering, 8*(1), 37–44.

Brunet-Thornton, R., & Bureš, V. (2010). Meeting Czech Knowledge Management Challenges Head-On: KM-Be.At-It. In M. Al-Shammari (Ed.), *Knowledge Management in Emerging Economies: Social, Organizational and Cultural Implementation* (pp. 20–46). Hershey, PA: IGI Global.

Brynjolfsson, E., & McAfee, A. (2014). *The Second Machine Age – Work, Progress, and Prosperity in a Time of Brilliant Technologies*. New York, NY: W. W. Norton & Co., Inc.

Bureš, V. (2006a). Knowledge Management and its Implementation. In *Proceedings of the 2nd International Conference on Web Information Systems and Technologies WEBIST 2006* (pp. 115-118). Setubal, Portugal: INSTICC.

Bureš, V. (2006b). Systems Thinking as a Basis for Ambient Intelligence. In *Proceedings of 11th conference on Information Technologies in Computer Science - ITiCSE06* (pp. 318). Bologna, Italy: ACM.

Bureš, V., & Tučník, P. (2014). Complex Agent-based Models: Application of a constructivism in the Economic Research. *E+M. Ekonomie a Management, 17*(3), 152–168. doi:10.15240/tul/001/2014-3-012

Bureš, V., Tučník, P., Mikulecký, P., Mls, K., & Blecha, P. (2016). Application of ambient intelligence in educational institutions: Visions and architectures. *International Journal of Ambient Computing and Intelligence, 7*(1), 94–120. doi:10.4018/IJACI.2016010105

Burmeister, C., Luettgens, D., & Piller, F. T. (2016). *Business Model Innovation for Industrie 4.0: Why the 'Industrial Internet' Mandates a New Perspective on Innovation*. RWTH-TIM Working Paper.

Can, O. (2016). *Five million jobs by 2020: the real challenge of the fourth industrial revolution*. World Economic Forum. Retrieved September 1, 2017, from https://www.weforum.org/press/2016/01/five-million-jobs-by-2020-the-real-challenge-of-the-fourth-industrial-revolution/

Challe, E., Lopez, J. I., & Mengus, E. (2016). *Southern Europe's Institutional Decline*. HEC Paris Research Paper No. ECO/SCD-2016-1148.

Chesbrough, H. (2007). Business model innovation: It's not just about technology anymore. *Strategy and Leadership*, *35*(6), 12–17. doi:10.1108/10878570710833714

Decker, J. (2016). Business 4.0 and Generation Y/Z: Challenges and Opportunities for Human -Resources Management. In *TAKE 2016 – Theory and Applications in the Knowledge Economy* (pp. 770–785). Aveiro, Portugal: Eduardo Tomé.

Dujin, A., Geissler, C., & Horstkötter, D. (2014). *Industry 4.0: The new industrial revolution*. Munich: Roland Berger Strategy Consultants.

Erol, S., Schumacher, A., & Sihn, W. (2016). Strategic guidance towards Industry 4.0 – a three-stage process model. In *International Conference on Competitive Manufacturing* (pp. 495-500). Stellenbosh, South Africa: University of Stellenbosh.

Essig, M., & Arnold, U. (2001). Electronic Procurement in Supply Chain Management: An Information Economics-Based Analysis of Electronic Markets. *The Journal of Supply Chain Management*, *37*(4), 43–49. doi:10.1111/j.1745-493X.2001.tb00112.x

Gerlitz, L. (2015). Design for product and service innovation in Industry 4.0 and emerging smart society. *Journal of Security and Sustainability Issues*, *5*(2), 181–198. doi:10.9770/jssi.2015.5.2(5)

Glas, A. H., & Kleemann, F. C. (2016). The impact of industry 4.0 on procurement and supply management: A conceptual and qualitative analysis. *International Journal of Business and Management Invention*, *5*(6), 55–66.

Gordon, R. (2012). *Is US economic growth over? Faltering innovation confronts the six headwinds*. CEPR Policy Insights, n. 63. Retrieved September 5, 2017, from http://cepr.org/sites/default/files/policy_insights/PolicyInsight63.pdf

Hájková, V., & Hájek, P. (2011). Typology of regional innovation systems in Europe - A neural network approach. *International Journal of Mathematical Models and Methods in Applied Sciences*, *3*(5), 463–471.

Hermann, M., Pentek, T., & Otto, B. (2015). *Design Principles for Industrie 4.0 Scenarios: A Literature Review*. Working Paper No. 01/2015, Technical University of Dortmund.

Hofmann, E., & Rüsch, M. (2017). Industry 4.0 and the current status as well as future prospects on logistics. *Computers in Industry*, *89*, 23–34. doi:10.1016/j.compind.2017.04.002

Hummel, E., Slowinski, G., Matthews, S., & Gilomnt, E. (2010). Business Models for collaborative Research. *Research Technology Management*, *53*(6), 51–54.

Judy, S. (2016). Construction owners face extended workers gap, productivity impacts. *Engineering News-Records, 275*(8).

Kagermann, H., Wahlster, W., & Helbig, J. (2013). *Recommendations for implementing the strategic initiative INDUSTRY 4.0*. Berlin, Frankfurt: National Academy of Science and Engineering.

Khan, K. S., Kunz, R., Kleijnen, J., & Antes, G. (2003). Five steps to conducting a systematic review. *Journal of the Royal Society of Medicine*, *96*(3), 118–121. doi:10.1177/014107680309600304 PMID:12612111

Koether, R. (2006). *Taschenbuch der Logistik*. Leipzig: Hanser.

Kovanda, L. (2017). *Disgrace named Industry 4.0* (in Czech language). Retrieved September 5, 2017, from http://finmag.penize.cz/ekonomika/326099-blamaz-jmenem-prumysl-4-0

Lee, J., Kao, H. A., & Yang, S. (2013). Service innovation and smart analytics for Industry 4.0 and big data environment. *Procedia CIRP*, *16*, 3–8. doi:10.1016/j.procir.2014.02.001

Liao, Y., Deschamps, F., de Freitas Rocha Loures, E., & Pierin Ramos, L. F. (2017). Past, present and future of Industry 4.0 - a systematic literature review and research agenda proposal. *International Journal of Production Research*, *55*(12), 3609–3629. doi:10.1080/00207543.2017.1308576

Lu, Y. (2017). Industry 4.0: A survey on technologies, applications and open research issues. *Journal of Industrial Information Integration*, *6*, 1–10. doi:10.1016/j.jii.2017.04.005

Miley, J. (2017). *New Report Says Robots Will Take Over Construction Industry by 2020*. Retrieved September 5, 2107, from https://interestingengineering.com/new-report-says-robots-will-take-over-construction-industry-by-2020

Moher, D., Liberati, A., Tetzlaff, J., & Altman, D. G. (2009). Preferred Reporting Items for Systematic Reviews and Meta-Analyses: The PRISMA Statement. *PLoS Medicine*, *6*(7), e1000097. doi:10.1371/journal.pmed.1000097 PMID:19621072

Moher, D., Shamseer, L., Clarke, M., Ghersi, D., Liberati, A., Petticrew, M., ... Stewart, L. A. (2015). Preferred Reporting Items for Systematic Review and Meta-Analysis Protocols (PRISMA-P) 2015 statement. *Systematic Reviews*, *4*(1), 1. doi:10.1186/2046-4053-4-1 PMID:25554246

Nolin, J., & Olson, N. (2016). The internet of things and convenience. *Internet Research*, *26*(2), 360–376. doi:10.1108/IntR-03-2014-0082

Osterwalder, A., Pigneur, Y., & Tucci, C. (2005). Clarifying Business Models: Origins, Present, and Future of the Concept. *Communications of the Association for Information Systems*, *16*, 1–25.

Posada, J., Toro, C., Barandiaran, I., Oyarzun, D., Stricker, D., Amicis, R., & de. (2015). Visual Computing as a Key Enabling Technology for Industrie 4.0 and Industrial Internet. *IEEE Computer Graphics and Applications*, *35*(2), 26–40. doi:10.1109/MCG.2015.45 PMID:25807506

Prause, G. (2015). Sustainable business models and structures for Industry 4.0. *Journal of Security and Sustainability Issues*, *5*(2), 159–169. doi:10.9770/jssi.2015.5.2(3)

Roblek, V., Meško, M., & Krapež, A. (2016). A complex view of Industry 4.0. *SAGE Open*, *6*(2), 2158244016653987. doi:10.1177/2158244016653987

Schaefer, D. (2017). *Industry 4.0 – A holistic perspective*. University of Bath.

Schmidt, R., Möhring, M., Härting, R. C., Reichstein, C., Neumaier, P., & Jozinović, P. (2015). Industry 4.0 - Potentials for Creating Smart Products: Empirical Research Results. *Lecture Notes in Business Information Processing*, *208*, 16–27. doi:10.1007/978-3-319-19027-3_2

Schoenthaler, F., Augenstein, D., & Karle, T. (2015). Design and governance of collaborative business processes in Industry 4.0, In *Proceedings of the Workshop on Crossorganizational and Cross-company BPM (XOC-BPM)* (pp. 1-8). Lisbon, Portugal: IEEE.

Shamim, S., Cang, S., Yu, H., & Li, Y. (2016). Management approaches for Industry 4.0: A human resource management perspective. In *2016 IEEE Congress on Evolutionary Computation* (pp. 5309-5316). Vancouver, Canada: IEEE. 10.1109/CEC.2016.7748365

Shamseer, L., Moher, D., Clarke, M., Ghersi, D., Liberati, A., Petticrew, M., … The PRISMA-P Group. (2015). Preferred Reporting Items for Systematic Review and Meta-Analysis Protocols (PRISMA-P) 2015: Elaboration and explanation. *BMJ 2015*, *349*, g7647.

Smith, V., Devane, D., Begley, C. M., & Clarke, M. (2010). Methodology in conducting a systematic review of systematic reviews of healthcare interventions. *BMC Medical Research Methodology*, *11*(1), 15. doi:10.1186/1471-2288-11-15 PMID:21291558

Spath, D., Ganschar, O., Gerlach, S., Hämmerle, M., Krause, T., & Schlund, S. (2013). *Studie: Produktionsarbeit Der Zukunft – Industrie 4.0*. Retrieved June 8, 2015, from http://www.iao.fraunhofer.de/images/iao-news/produktionsarbeit-der-zukunft.pdf

Teece, D. J. (2010). Business Models, Business Strategy and Innovation. *Long Range Planning*, *43*(2-3), 172–194. doi:10.1016/j.lrp.2009.07.003

Thames, L., & Schaefer, D. (2016). Software-defined cloud manufacturing for Industry 4.0. *Procedia CIRP*, *52*, 12–17. doi:10.1016/j.procir.2016.07.041

Thoben, K. D., Wiesner, S. A., & Wuest, T. (2017). "Industrie 4.0" and smart manufacturing – a review of research issues and application examples. *International Journal of Automotive Technology*, *11*(1), 4–16. doi:10.20965/ijat.2017.p0004

Thuemmler, C., & Bai, C. (2017). Health 4.0: Application of industry 4.0 design principles in future asthma management. In C. Thuemmler & C. Bai (Eds.), *Health 4.0: How Virtualization and Big Data are Revolutionizing Healthcare* (pp. 23–37). Cham: Springer. doi:10.1007/978-3-319-47617-9_2

Trappey, A. J. C., Trappey, C. V., Hareesh Govindarajan, U., Chuang, A. C., & Sun, J. J. (2017). A review of essential standards and patent landscapes for the Internet of Things: A key enabler for Industry 4.0. *Advanced Engineering Informatics*, *33*, 208–229. doi:10.1016/j.aei.2016.11.007

Trefke, J., Rohjans, S., Uslar, M., Lehnhof, S., Nordstrom, L., & Saleem, A. (2013). *Smart Grid Architecture Model use case management in a large European Smart Grid project. In 4th IEEE/PES Innovative Smart Grid Technologies Europe* (pp. 1–5). Lyngby, Denmark: IEEE.

Tučník, P., & Bureš, V. (2013). Inclusion of Complexity: Modelling Enterprise Business Environment by Means of Agent based Simulation. *International Review on Modelling and Simulations*, *6*(5), 1709–1717.

Warnecke, H. (1993). *The Fractal Company: A Revolution in Corporate Culture*. Berlin: Springer. doi:10.1007/978-3-642-78124-7

Webster, J., & Watson, R. T. (2002). Analyzing the past to prepare for the future: Writing a literature review. *Management Information Systems Quarterly*, *26*(2), xiii–xxiii.

Zezulka, F., Marcon, P., Vesely, I., & Sajdl, O. (2016). Industry 4.0 – An Introduction in the Phenomenon. *IFAC PapersOnline*, *49*(25), 8–12. doi:10.1016/j.ifacol.2016.12.002

Zezulka, F., Veselý, I., & Braun, V. (2017). Introduction to Industry 4.0 and fundamental models (in Czech language). *SystemOnLine, 1-2*.

KEY TERMS AND DEFINITIONS

Business Model: A business model is a company's plan for how it will generate revenues and make a profit. It explains what products or services the business plans to manufacture and market, and how it plans to do so, including what expenses it will incur. Simply stated, all it really means is how you plan to make money.

Framework: A real or conceptual structure intended to serve as a support or guide for the building of something that expands the structure into something useful.

Innovations: The process of translating an idea or invention into a good or service that creates value or for which customers will pay. To be called an innovation, an idea must be replicable at an economical cost and must satisfy a specific need. Innovation involves deliberate application of information, imagination and initiative in deriving greater or different values from resources, and includes all processes by which new ideas are generated and converted into useful products. In business, innovation often results when ideas are applied by the company in order to further satisfy the needs and expectations of the customers.

Internet of Things: Concept of basically connecting any device with an on and off switch to the internet (and/or to each other). This includes everything from cell phones, coffee makers, washing machines, headphones, lamps, wearable devices, and almost anything else one can think of. This can also be applied to components of machines, for example, a jet engine of an airplane or the drill of an oil rig.

Knowledge Management: Knowledge management is the systematic management of an organization's knowledge assets for the purpose of creating value and meeting tactical and strategic requirements; it consists of the initiatives, processes, strategies, and systems that sustain and enhance the storage, assessment, sharing, refinement, and creation of knowledge. Knowledge management therefore implies a strong tie to organizational goals and strategy, and it involves the management of knowledge that is useful for some purpose and which creates value for the organization.

Systems Engineering: An interdisciplinary approach and means to enable the realization of successful systems. It focuses on defining customer needs and required functionality early in the development cycle, documenting requirements, then proceeding with design synthesis and system validation while considering the complete problem.

Chapter 12
Towards a Framework for Assessing the Maturity of Manufacturing Companies in Industry 4.0 Adoption

Luca Scremin
Politecnico di Milano, Italy

Fabiano Armellini
Polytechnique Montréal, Canada

Alessandro Brun
Politecnico di Milano, Italy

Laurence Solar-Pelletier
Polytechnique Montréal, Canada

Catherine Beaudry
Polytechnique Montréal, Canada

ABSTRACT

The recent introduction of new disruptive technologies aimed at monitoring, controlling, optimizing, and automating production systems is shifting the manufacturing landscape towards a fourth industrial revolution. In this new industrial paradigm, manufacturing companies face complex challenges requiring the development of new organizational and technological capabilities. With this context in mind, this chapter is intended to provide a maturity assessment framework to understand the transformation process in manufacturing companies transitioning to Industry 4.0. The proposed framework is applied to 10 in-depth industrial case studies in Canada and Italy, two countries with increasing awareness of the Industry 4.0 revolution. A comparative case analysis revealed four different standards, or archetypes, for Industry 4.0 adoption, which are discussed and analyzed, highlighting a relationship between a company's manufacturing configuration and its path towards Industry 4.0 adoption.

DOI: 10.4018/978-1-5225-3468-6.ch012

INTRODUCTION

The world is undergoing a new technological revolution, brought about by a convergence of disruptive digital technologies such as intelligent machinery and robotics, big data analytics, Cyber Physical Systems (CPS) and the Internet of Things (IoT). The impact and integration of these new technologies on and within production systems is what drives the fourth industrial revolution, also known as Industry 4.0 (I4.0), Smart Manufacturing or the Industrial Internet of Things (IIoT).

Even though Industry 4.0 is still in its infancy, German and US companies are some steps ahead in the adoption of smart manufacturing technologies, mainly because of the presence of national strategic plans for Industry 4.0 introduction. Other countries are becoming more and more aware of the relevance of Industry 4.0, and catch-up initiatives are emerging, which is the case of Italy and Canada. At the end of 2016, the Italian government officially presented its national plan for investments, productivity and innovation, titled "Piano Nazionale Industria 4.0," which has been in operation since mid-2017. Although a few Canadian provinces, such as Quebec, Ontario and Alberta, have begun to show an interest in Industry 4.0 via grant programs and research studies, the Canadian Government has not yet devised a national plan. Since Italian and Canadian companies are currently stepping up the pace of Industry 4.0 implementation/adoption, albeit not as fast as would be required, a cross-country study on the introduction of smart systems in manufacturing companies is timely.

The need for an instrument to assess the benefits of the adoption process established by companies in their transition to Industry 4.0 emerged during the problem definition. Accordingly, we designed a framework, the Adoption Maturity Model (AMM), composed of a series of indicators on the requirements and concepts for ideal Industry 4.0 adoption to identify the various maturity stages required.

Prior to the design phase, a comprehensive literature review was performed in order to define the concept of Industry 4.0 and consider its challenges, trends and enablers. The critical comparative analysis of scientific contributions to existing maturity models, determining their strength and weaknesses, helped us build the framework underlying our case studies. This framework served as a basis for developing the interview guide to assess the Adoption Maturity Model applied to 10 industrial organizations, five Italian and five Canadian.

The 10 case studies focused on the adoption of Industry 4.0 in the manufacturing industry through the lens of the framework designed. Lastly, this research performed a comparative analysis of the different approaches developed by the companies selected in order to provide new insights on the introduction of Industry 4.0.

The goals of this chapter are thus to review the emerging literature about Industry 4.0 in order to build a framework to assess the maturity of manufacturing companies as concerns its adoption, and then to test this framework with real in-depth case studies.

To meet these goals, the remainder of the chapter is organized as follows. The next section reviews the literature on Industry 4.0, its definition and the measurement of the maturity necessary for its adoption. Then, the methodological approach used in the research is presented, followed by the discussion of the framework (AMM) developed from the literature review. Afterwards, brief section addresses how the case studies were built. The results from these case studies are then presented and discussed, followed by the chapter's conclusions.

LITERATURE REVIEW

The concept of Industry 4.0 was first coined in Germany in 2011 when the government passed the High-Tech Strategy Action Plan for the implementation of the High-Tech Strategy 2020 (MacDougall, 2014). This new concept is internationally, and often indiscriminately, known as *Industry 4.0, Industrial Internet of Things* (IIoT) (Arnold, Kiel, & Voigt, 2016) and *Smart Manufacturing* (Kang, H. S., Lee, J. Y., Choi, S., Kim, H., Park, J. H., Son, J. Y., … Noh, S. Do., 2016; Miragliotta, G., Macchi, M., & Terzi, S.., 2016a). Miragliotta et al. (2016b) define Smart Manufacturing as:

a vision of the future in which manufacturing companies, thanks to the adoption of digital technologies, will increase their efficiency and competitiveness through the interconnection and the co-operation among their resources (plants, people and information), both internal and distributed along the value network.

According to the Acatech working group (Kagermann, Wahlster, & Helbig, 2013), the creation of global networks encompassing machinery, warehousing systems and production facilities in the shape of Cyber-Physical Systems (CPS) will enable the autonomous exchange of information, and trigger actions and independent control. These improvements involve industrial manufacturing, the engineering supply chain and life-cycle management transforming new facilities in smart factories, pursuing the following three types of integration:

1. **Horizontal Integration Through Value Networks:** Refers to the connection of IT systems used at several different stages of the manufacturing process, either within the organization or throughout its supply chain networks (Zhou, 2015);
2. **Vertical Integration and Networked Manufacturing Systems:** Are IT systems communicating between different hierarchical levels of the company to share information and facilitate decision making company-wide (Leyh, Schäffer, Bley, & Forstenhäusler, 2016);
3. **End-to-End Digital Integration of Engineering Across the Entire Value Chain:** Consists in the integration of all engineering activities, from design and R&D, to the deployment and delivery of final products, from within the company and across the entire value chain (Leyh, Schäffer, Bley, & Forstenhäusler, 2016).

Since the adoption of far-reaching technologies in manufacturing has attracted the interest of academia and industry, most public institutions in developed countries have recognized the relevance of a competitive manufacturing sector in relation to national economic strength (Miragliotta, G., Macchi, M., & Terzi, S., 2016b). Given that Industry 4.0 refers to the growing trend among manufacturing companies to adopt a series of enabling smart manufacturing technologies, there is no unique classification, even though the degree of similarity between categorizations is high. This study took into consideration the technology classification presented in Italy by the "Piano Nazionale Industria 4.0" (National Plan Industry 4.0), which is similar to the categorization used in a Boston Consulting Group report (Michael, R., Markus, R., Philipp, G., Manuela, W., Jan, J., Pascal, E., & Harnisch, M., 2015).

The several challenges posed by Industry 4.0 can be grouped in different areas. In a new configuration linked to Smart Manufacturing, new systems will generate data in various ways (Khan & Turowski, 2016). Especially with respect to production environment, data are collected from different machines, sensors, plants, partners and infrastructure. Such an amount of information requires the development of new algorithms, models, products and visualization techniques to use and to gain benefits from their use (Weyer, Schmitt, Ohmer, & Gorecky, 2015). Moreover, following the concepts of horizontal and vertical integration, companies must exchange data within factories or departments and ensure real-time availability of data for other processes, which also include external partners, in order to keep processes optimized.

Companies are requiring new competencies in terms of training and skills development, and face a shortage of skilled staff to meet this need (Khan & Turowski, 2016). For this reason, essential changes in the way IT experts, unskilled and skilled workers are trained are fundamental. In this direction, some research has been carried out to identify the skills required need to master Industry 4.0 (Dworschak, B., Helmut, B., & Achtenhagen, C., 2013; Hartmann & Bovenschulte, 2013).

Also a top concern, cybersecurity will be the major preoccupation in the future for industries. Smart factories have greater security issues than traditional companies (Wang, Wan, Li, & Zhang, 2016). On the one hand, organizations must protect information about customers, suppliers, business strategies and know-how (industrial secrets), which is generally stored in the public cloud rather than a private data centre, thereby increasing the risk of disclosure in a cyber attack. On the other hand, thanks to the I4.0, machines, organization networks and human resources are increasingly connected to the cloud. In this hyper-connected world, the threat of cyber attacks rises exponentially (Cisco, 2017).

Hermann et al. (2016) put forward four design principles of Industry 4.0: interconnectivity, information transparency, decision decentralization and technical assistance. The introduction of these principles as new design paradigms is expected to produce a number of changes and benefits within companies that will impact every sphere of their business. Some of the transformations the literature highlights include the autonomous optimization of production, the increase in flexibility (Arnold, C., Kiel, D., & Voigt, K.-I., 2016), the creation of value through new services (Park, 2016), the enhancement of products through the incorporation of digital technologies (Leyh, Schäffer, Bley, & Forstenhäusler, 2016), the transformation of companies' business models, and increased energy efficiency (Stock & Seliger, 2016).

In these current and future scenarios, maturity and readiness models can help companies rigorously evaluate their own status respecting the implementation of Industry 4.0 (Wendler, 2012), and thus allow them to better position their organization as well as help them find better positions for change. Despite its importance, to the best of our knowledge, no such model has as yet been addressed in the literature. In fact, the models in the literature have different foci: some provide a tool for self-assessment for companies (Geissbauer, Vedso, & Schrauf, 2016b; Lichtblau, K., Volker Stich, Bertenrath, R., Blum, M., Bleider, M., Millack, A., … Schröter, M., 2015; Schumacher, Erol, & Sihn, 2016); others identify a general approach to understanding Industry 4.0 (Rockwellautomation, 2014). Those connected to maturity in some way have other goals, such as the technological evaluation of parts of the company (Leyh, Schäffer, Bley, & Forstenhäusler, 2016) or the identification of general maturity stages (Beaudoin, J., Lefebvre, G. L., Normand, M., Gouri, V., & Skerlj, A., 2016; Jodlbauer, H., Schagerl, M., & Brunner, M., 2016). Appendix 1 provides a comparison of the several maturity models found in the literature, based on the analysis by De Bruin et al. (2005).

METHODOLOGY

This research project is exploratory, aimed at obtaining a better comprehension of the new concept of Industry 4.0. Considering the novelty of the subject, the study was designed as a cross-sectional research project relying on qualitative methods for data collection. In order to analyze and evaluate the Industry 4.0 adoption process, the study was conducted through the creation of 10 case studies, made up of companies located both in Italy and in Canada, a satisfactory sample size for case study-based research (Eisenhardt, 1989).

The methodology used in this work is founded on semi-structured interviews conducted in companies involved in the research. Prior to the company interviews, information was gathered and analyzed by desk research, using multiple observations, company websites and archival sources. The research framework was structured to explore manufacturing companies' adoption of Industry 4.0 using a proper maturity model following a step-by-step process. The following steps were used to achieve the goals set out in the beginning of the chapter.

Step 1: Firstly, a *literature review* was carried out covering Industry 4.0, enabling technologies and existing maturity models.

Step 2: Next, a *maturity model framework* for Industry 4.0 adoption was proposed to assess the adoption process. Based on the literature review performed, the model comprises 35 maturity items, divided into 8 maturity indicators.

Step 3: The *interview guide* for data collection was then created. To ensure a connection between the guide and the framework, a consistency check was implemented to link questions to maturity items.

Step 4: Next, data were collected using the interview guide: manufacturing managers of 10 companies, 5 Italian and 5 Canadian, were contacted to participate in semi-structured interviews about their experience with Industry 4.0 adoption.

Step 5: With the data from the interviews in hand, the next step was the elaboration of the *case studies* for each interviewed company to summarize the interview using a uniform structure. The case studies include an introduction of the company, its motivations for adopting Industry 4.0, the implementation process, the major challenges it faced during the implementation process, an explanation of the system in place, and the performances obtained.

Step 6: Through the information gathered from the case studies, and using the reference maturity model developed in step 2, the *thresholds for each maturity item* were determined to validate the model and evaluate the cases.

Step 7: Next, the *adoption maturity indicators* for each case study were calculated and represented using appropriate radar charts, which enabled the assessment of the cases.

Step 8: This quantitative assessment also allowed for a cross-case comparative analysis, in which a comparison matrix was developed to confront the different case studies in each implementation step.

Step 9: Finally, through analyzing the comparison matrix along with the individual maturity assessment, *archetypes were identified* and *conclusions on Industry 4.0 adoption* were formulated.

Procedure Model for Developing the Framework

The development of a maturity model for the evaluation of the introduction process of Industry 4.0 in manufacturing companies was based on Becker's step-by-step approach for the development of maturity models (Becker, J., Knackstedt, R., & Pöppelbuß, J., 2009). This framework methodology has a strong theoretical foundation in the rigorous method set out in the design science approach of Hevner et al. (2004). Moreover, with a view to strengthening this development methodology, the main phases of generic maturity model development proposed by De Bruin et al. (2005) were assessed. A specific feature of this development is the inclusion in its final step of the goal of continuously tracking the model's evolution and development to ensure its relevance and level of generalizability over time.

In accordance with the previously mentioned development procedure, the Adoption Maturity Model (AMM) was designed in several steps:

- **Problem Definition/Scope:** The AMM aims at providing the maturity level of the process put in place by manufacturing companies when introducing Industry 4.0 in their organizations. This model has been designed to evaluate the maturity level of companies that have already, or partially, moved towards I4.0. The development of the model is intended for researchers, who could use it to evaluate and identify trends and insights respecting the introduction of the fourth industrial revolution, and for practitioners from inside or outside the organizations. The model is also useful for managers and executives to assess the implementation process with a view to identifying the areas that have not already been addressed by the change or those that require more effort to achieve a better maturity level. Furthermore, external entities, such as consultants and I4.0 solution providers, would employ the AMM to communicate the need for and scale of intervention to their clients, using an impartial and reliable maturity framework.
- **Comparison of Existing Maturity Models:** Seven maturity models addressing Industry 4.0 were identified during the literature review. The comparison process then performed highlighted the lack of a model that could express the maturity level of the entire Industry 4.0 adoption process put in place by the organization.
- **Determination of Development Strategy/Design:** The comparison of existing maturity models and the literature review suggest a design strategy that combines some parts and features of the existing models, with the addition of new indicators and stages that are missing in the evaluation of the adoption process. At this stage, the principal features of the new framework were decided upon to facilitate its development in the further steps (De Bruin, T., Freeze, R., Kaulkarni, U., & Rosemann, M., 2005). Since the expected benefits stemming from the use of the model can be linked to both internal and external figures, such as executives and consultants, the method of application relies on the use of a semi-structured interview. Accordingly, the model can be adopted as a self-assessment tool or by third-party entities. The respondents must be part of management because, in order to identify the maturity evaluation of the process put in place for the transition to Industry 4.0, the interviewer must interact with someone in a managerial role who has been involved in the change process or who is aware of the impact of the process at all layers of the company. In addition, it was decided how maturity stages can be reported to the audience (the company involved in the evaluation). Each maturity indicator and item has five maturity stages, from zero to four, where zero represents a poor maturity evaluation and four stands for full accomplishment. Five stages were chosen, without considering the non-existent stage because, as previously mentioned, the model is applied to companies that have already taken some initiatives in introducing I4.0.
- **Iterative Maturity Model Development/Populate:** The design process of the model has undergone different iterations. Based on the literature review of existing maturity models, enablers, challenges and trends, a first version of the model was drafted, including maturity indicators and items. Starting from the first architecture, the model was shown to an extended research team involving experts in the fields of IoT, project management and innovation management. A brainstorming session was held to foster the generation of new items and indicators for the maturity

framework. After this stage, the literature review was extended to include the research papers suggested by the research team. The information gathered from the brainstorming and the publications enabled the creation of the final structure of the Adoption Maturity Model.

- **Concept of Transfer and Evaluation:** Implementation of transfer media/test: The AMM was tested using several interviews, creating the related case studies. Before the data was collected, the interview guide was developed and the companies selected, in accordance with the process of building theories from case studies research.
- **Evaluation/Deploy:** The case studies were used to evaluate the adoption maturity levels of 10 manufacturing companies that brought Industry 4.0 into their processes. This stage was used to verify the extent of the model's generalizability to provide acceptance and improve its standardization.

THE ADOPTION MATURITY MODEL

The iterative development of the maturity model led to the identification of 35 "maturity items," which form the basic "building blocks" to evaluate the maturity of the Industry 4.0 adoption process. These items are grouped into eight maturity indicators, which are, in turn, organized along three axes as follows: strategy, maturity and performance.

Strategy Axis

It is imperative for companies to establish a clear and precise strategic roadmap for the introduction of Industry 4.0 (Erol, Schumacher, & Sihn, 2016). The three indicators belonging to the Strategy Axis (business strategy, technology strategy, and networking and integration) assess the maturity and awareness shown by the company management while formulating strategic implementation plans, deploying proper decision-making processes to achieve the planned objectives, and identifying intervention areas in the change process.

- **Business Strategy Indicator:** This indicator is used to assess the alignment between the company's business strategy and its implementation of Industry 4.0. To face this new technological shift, a company must develop its own vision and strategies to prepare appropriate *roadmaps* for Industry 4.0 implementation (Erol, S., Schumacher, A., & Sihn, W., 2016). To make this transition, the company needs to plan for adequate *investments* in resources dedicated to the transition to I4.0 (Erol, S., Schumacher, A., & Sihn, W., 2016; Geissbauer, R., Vedso, J. V., & Schrauf, S., 2016). Moreover, the tailored strategy for smart manufacturing should consider the possibility of *improving existing products and services* (Zhou, 2015), or the development of *new business opportunities* arising from the growing pervasiveness of digital technologies (Kagermann, H., Wahlster, W., & Helbig, J., 2013; Rennung, Luminosu, & Draghici, 2016).
- **Technology Strategy Indicator:** The purpose of this indicator is to assess the *decision-making model* designed by the company during the selection of *infrastructure, standards and technologies* related to I4.0. Indeed, the implementation of I4.0 in the organization through integration with existing technologies may lead the company to choose certain types of platforms and standards. These choices are particularly critical during the initial phases of the implementation process due to the multitude of available turnkey solutions and standards (Miragliotta, Macchi, & Terzi, 2016).

The choice of the wrong standard or platform could affect the further internal development of the system, resulting in poor performance, the potential limitation of integration possibilities and the consequent loss of enthusiasm and commitment of employees and management. Thus, the need to consider the choices made. Moreover, there is also the growing threat of cyber risk in today's hyper-connected world (Cisco, 2017), a major issue in the development of solutions in Industry 4.0. Since IoT implies physical objects like smart machines connected to cloud platforms and other infrastructures, they are becoming potential targets for malicious attacks that can sabotage industrial facilities and/or steal precious information (Sniderman, Mahto, & Cotteleer, 2016). Although it is not possible to guarantee 100% data security, companies must adopt effective practices to *manage cyber risk* (Helu, Morris, Jung, Lyons, & Leong, 2015).

- **Networking and Integration Indicator:** This indicator assesses the scope of the introduction of I4.0 in an organization. Considering the literature review, the establishment of a fully integrated I4.0 system is the result of the following three different levels of integration (Kagermann, H., Wahlster, W., & Helbig, J., 2013): (1) Horizontal integration through value networks; (2) Vertical integration and networked manufacturing systems; and (3) End-to-end digital integration of engineering across the entire value chain. This indicator aims at assessing the maturity level in terms of these three integration dimensions.

Maturity Axis

Since Industry 4.0 encompasses the introduction of new platforms, infrastructure, technologies and competencies in the organization, this axis helps evaluate the degree of maturity regarding both the extent of smart technologies implemented and the capability of exploiting them to improve performances, through three indicators: (1) Infrastructure for I4.0; (2) Analytical Skills; and (3) Absorptive Capacity.

- **Infrastructure for I4.0 Indicator:** This indicator aims to assess the *enabling infrastructure* available to the company, given the requirements of Industry 4.0. To assess the maturity of the company embracing I4.0, the model provides an evaluation of the smart *technologies adopted*, the *ICT* (Information and Communication Technology) *systems* that enable their integration, and the cyber *security system* that the company installed or developed to ensure a high level of safety in data management and integrity (Cisco, 2017; Kobara, 2016).
- **Analytical Skills Indicator:** New infrastructure and smart technologies are useless unless the company is able to use them effectively. From this perspective, existent maturity reference models are unanimous in identifying Data Analytics as one of the most important skills for this purpose, even though it is not normally part of the set of basic skills of manufacturing companies (Wang, S., Wan, J., Li, D., & Zhang, C., 2016). Several items are used to measure this indicator. Firstly, companies must be *aware of the importance of analyzing massive data* coming from the new systems. Secondly, the infrastructure should be mature enough to allow an automatic and *digital collection of information* (Zhou, 2015). Furthermore, the *ability to analyze big data* (Herterich, Uebernickel, & Brenner, 2015; Lee, Kao, & Yang, 2014), and the establishment of a *self-assessment system* for the purpose of continuous improvement (Bagheri, Yang, Kao, & Lee, 2015; Weinberger, Bilgeri, & Fleisch, 2016) are two other maturity items that define the indicator.

- **Absorptive Capacity Indicator:** This indicator reflects the company's ability to recognize and assimilate new information, practices and processes related to a specific topic (Cohen & Levinthal, 1990), in this case Industry 4.0. The new manufacturing paradigm will lead to significant changes in the way people work, creating new jobs and skills profiles and making others obsolete (Lorenz, Rüßmann, Strack, Lueth, & Bolle, 2015). For these reasons, and considering the rising average age of the workforce (Khan & Turowski, 2016), companies need to develop a profound *awareness of the skills required for Industry 4.0* in order to re-train their employees to fill the knowledge and skills gaps arising from the introduction of new far-reaching technologies and work practices (Dworschak, B., Helmut, B., & Achtenhagen, C., 2013; Dworschak & Zaiser, 2014), and, if necessary, to acquire new external specialized skills (Lorenz, M., Rüßmann, M., Strack, R., Lueth, K. L., & Bolle, M., 2015). The model therefore verifies whether a company has implemented *training systems* aligned with the new Industry 4.0 requirements and whether a *knowledge management system* linked to the smart manufacturing system is in place (El Said, 2015; Roblek, Meško, & Krapež, 2016).

Performance Axis

A model evaluating the maturity of the adoption of new technologies, competencies and processes should include in the overall assessment the performance and impacts deriving from their introduction. This axis thus examines the benefits of Industry 4.0 implementation by means of two indicators.

- **Benefits of Industry 4.0 Adoption:** This indicator aims to assess the impact of the introduction of Industry 4.0 on the company's overall results, including external impacts on the business. The expected benefits that could derive from the transition to I4.0 were broken down into:
    - **Economic Benefits:** Such as an increase in revenues due to the development of new business opportunities (Arnold, C., Kiel, D., & Voigt, K.-I., 2016; Geissbauer, R., Vedso, J. V., & Schrauf, S., 2016a) and increased competitiveness thanks to the reduction in cost (Lee, J., Kao, H. A., & Yang, S., 2014);
    - **Social Benefits:** Impact on the quality of labour, employee empowerment, among other social benefits for the company and society (Stock & Seliger, 2016);
    - **Environmental Benefits:** Such as lower emissions, energy consumption, waste and other residues, among other possible benefits (Stock & Seliger, 2016).
- **Impact on Efficiency:** The second performance indicator embraces several conventional parameters for measuring business efficiency, which is expected to be impacted by the introduction of smart manufacturing technologies. The study of the expected impacts on performance was carried out in the literature review leading to the identification of 12 selected Key Performance Indicators (KPIs): (1) Employee efficiency; (2) Number of breakdowns; (3) Order fulfillment rate; (4) Average machine downtime; (5) Cost reduction; (6) Lower decision-making time; (7) Lead time reduction; (8) Impact on inventory requirements; (9) Energy consumption reduction; (10) Time-to-market reduction; (11) Defect rate reduction; and (12) Forecast accuracy.

Figure 1 summarizes the three axes, the eight indicators and their respective items.

Figure 1. I4.0 maturity assessment framework

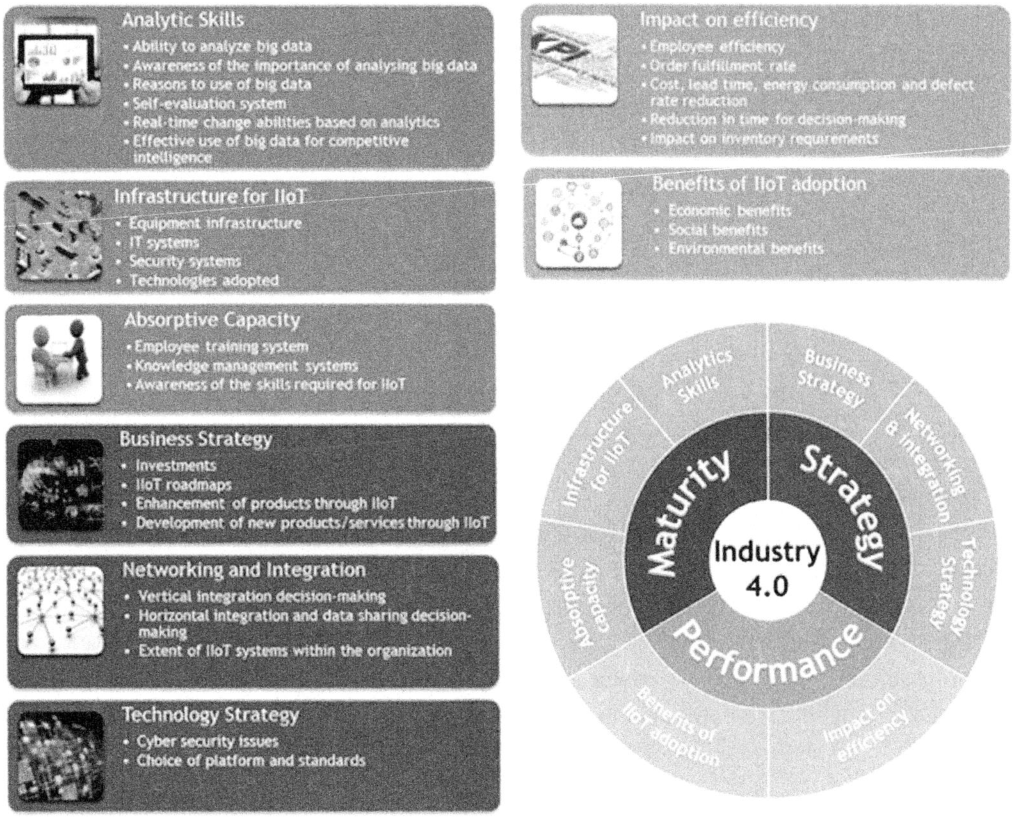

CASE STUDIES

Ten manufacturing companies were selected for the interviews, five in Italy and five in Canada. The selection process for Italian companies was carried out with the collaboration of ANIMA (Federation of Italian Associations of Mechanical Industry), which facilitated the participation of associated companies in the research. Canadian companies were selected thanks the support of ISED (Innovation, Science and Economic Development Canada), the Canadian ministry for economic development. Selected companies were asked to agree to a personal interview between a researcher and the company's manufacturing manager.

With the goal of creating case studies on Industry 4.0 adoption, the process for selecting companies focused on identifying manufacturing companies that had already applied (at least to a certain extent) Industry 4.0 in their organizations.

To understand the relationship between their perceptions about Industry 4.0 and their effective adoption, the selected companies were first asked if they considered themselves an Industry 4.0 company or if they were applying such concepts. To participate in this study, the company was asked to identify a manager who was seriously involved in the decision-making process on the introduction of the new smart systems, so that s/he could provide a cogent view of the motivations, steps required, technologies adopted, impacts, etc. Interviews, of a maximum duration of 90 minutes, were conducted either in

Table 1. Summary of case studies

Case	Country	Revenues	Employees	Business sector
C1	IT	>1000 M€	>10K	Engine manufacturer
C2	IT	>1000 M€	>10K	Ship manufacturer
C3	IT	50 M€	170	Industrial machinery manufacturer
C4	IT	300 M€	500	Forklift truck manufacturer
C5	IT	200 M€	600	Heating system manufacturer
C6	CAN	52 MCAD	150	High precision machinery
C7	CAN	7 MCAD	65	High precision machinery
C8	CAN	10-25 MCAD	100	High precision machinery
C9	CAN	5-10 MCAD	60	Material sorting and transformation
C10	CAN	>100 MCAD	1K	Heating system manufacturer

person or via video conference (Skype), depending on the company's location, and were recorded for more accurate transcripts.

The entire process followed an interview protocol (as per the interview guide in Appendix 2), supporting the interviewers during the collection of data needed for the maturity indicators evaluations. At the end of each interview, the respondent was asked to fill in a performance table, which gave the researcher access to quantitative information on the impacts of Industry 4.0 on performance indicators.

To enable comparison among different case studies, they were structured in a standardized fashion, as presented in Table 2.

After preparing the transcripts of all interviews, every single sentence or paragraph was analyzed and colour-coded, to be able to refer each piece of information to the relevant section. Thanks to this coding, all the information was sorted into six sections. Finally, the key information was synthesized

Table 2. Case Studies Structure

Section	Topics Covered
Introduction	• Brief company description. • Introduction on I4.0 experience.
Motivations and Industry 4.0 Strategy	• Motivations for implementing an I4.0 system. • Strategy developed for I4.0 implementation.
Implementation process	Steps required during the adoption of the new system
Challenges and Obstacles	• Cybersecurity • Employee training • Technological challenges • Resistance to change
Industry 4.0 system in place	Structure of the system implemented with focus on technologies implemented and integration level.
Performance and Impact	• Benefits and efficiency impact due to I4.0. • Impact on company's operations and processes.
Maturity Indicators	Table provides a summary of the key characteristics of the case study according to the eight maturity indicators.

in a synoptic table at the end of each case study, divided into eight maturity indicators belonging to the Adoption Maturity Model.

A quantitative assessment of the maturity of Industry 4.0 adoption for the 10 case studies was required to relate collected information to possible "maturity stages" for each indicator and item. A maturity stage is a description of a maturity state, that is, it expresses the maturity level reached by the company in respect of a certain indicator or item (Kohlegger, Maier, & Thalmann, 2009). Since the model was developed as a framework for qualitative data analysis, the various stages provide a series of thresholds describing "what" a company should have done, "how" it should have done it or "to what extent" to obtain a certain evaluation. Maturity stages were identified using extant maturity models and the results from the literature review, and were validated through the data collected during the analysis of the 10 case studies. Each indicator has five maturity stages, ranging from zero to four, where zero represents a poor maturity evaluation and four, a full accomplishment. Each item belonging to the axes Maturity and Strategy were assessed using the dedicated table of maturity stages, and the maturity evaluations of the indicators were calculated through the average value of the indicator's items. Table 3 provides an example for the item "Industry 4.0 and Roadmaps."

As concerns the performance axis, maturity stages were identified by looking at the number of KPIs impacted for the indicator "Impact on Efficiency," while for "Benefits of the I4.0 Adoption," a Benefit Score was calculated for each case study. This score was obtained by adding points in the case of positive benefits (+2 for economic benefits and +1 for environmental and social benefits) or subtracting points in the case of negative impacts (-2 for economic benefits and -1 for environmental and social benefits), as shown in Table 4.

Table 3. Example of maturity stages for the item "Industry 4.0 and Roadmaps"

	Industry 4.0 Roadmaps
0	Industry 4.0 is not part of the business strategy/strategic process. No roadmaps developed.
1	Industry 4.0 (focused on technology development) is part of the general strategy of the company. No roadmaps developed.
2	Industry 4.0 is part of the business strategy of the company. Roadmaps may be developed but the action plan is not well defined.
3	Industry 4.0 is part of the business strategy of the company. Roadmaps developed. Long-term action plans are still not clear.
4	Industry 4.0 is part of the business strategy of the company. Roadmap developed with short-, medium- and long-term plans regarding the introduction of technologies and infrastructure, employee training and external/internal integration.

Table 4. Composing economic, efficiency and social benefits for scoring the impact of Industry 4.0

Stage	**Impact on Efficiency**	**Benefits of I4.0 Adop.**
0	Negative impacts due to the system integration are more numerous than positive impacts.	Benefits Score <=0
1	Positive impacts are present in few indicators (<=30%). Most KPIs have remained unchanged. Possible presence of negative impact.	2<= Benefits Score >0
2	The number of positive impacts (around 50%) is similar to stable indicators. The probability of negative impacts is low.	4<= Benefits Score >2
3	Positive impacts are more numerous (>50%) than stable indicators. No negative impacts.	6<= Benefits Score >4
4	Most of KPIs have improved thanks to the introduction of the new system (>80%).	Benefits Score > 6

Once all maturity stages were defined, the maturity levels of the eight indicators were assessed based on the information contained in the tables "maturity indicators" at the end of each case study. A synthesis of the eight maturity levels was in turn included in the overall evaluation of Industry 4.0 adoption.

DISCUSSION AND RESULTS

The elaboration of the case studies, followed by their integration in maturity charts, allowed the researcher to gather a rich set of information to assess Industry 4.0 readiness and maturity in the sample of companies under study (Tsang, 2014). From the comparative analysis of the case studies (Eisenhardt, 1989), through the lens of the framework developed, it was possible to identify some trends in terms of Industry 4.0 adoption in relation to the companies' size, motivations and other descriptive characteristics.

Maturity

Given the average maturity level of the sample selected, the maturity axis can be considered to be the most developed axis within the AMM. Even though I4.0 adoption processes are not yet fully completed, all interviewed companies upgraded their facilities with new infrastructure and technologies to enable Industry 4.0. The analysis of case studies showed that organizations that implemented I4.0 adopted such systems in varying degrees, as noted in the literature review (Bangemann, T., Riedl, M., Thron, M., & Diedrich, C., 2016).

The level of adoption was affected by the capacity to consider big data and analytics as a competitive asset (analytic skills), that is, to recognize the importance of the actual IT infrastructure (I4.0 infrastructure), as well as the internal capacity to absorb and implement the knowledge and skills that come with I4.0 (absorptive capacity).

Analytics Skills

Awareness of (and reasons for) the necessity to be able to make use of big data is the starting point for building an effective I4.0 system within an organization (Khan & Turowski, 2016; Koch & Kuge, 2014; Wang, S., Wan, J., Li, D., & Zhang, C., 2016). Therefore, it is not surprising that the companies presenting a high motivation and awareness of the importance of data analytics (C1, C3, C7, C8) were found to be the most mature with regard to their ability to analyze it. Although these enterprises practice real-time decision making based on big data, they do not consider their decision-making process to be autonomous. While the real-time data that is collected and analyzed by the information system serves as a helpful support, the final decision relies on people.

In the remaining companies, management and operators could also rely on real-time information gathered from their data collection systems, but had a low capacity to analyze massive data.

It can be seen that the digital collection of data is performed with varying degrees of maturity in all companies, thanks to the introduction of new machinery ensuring the collection of this type of information. Lastly, it was noted that the maturity of the self-evaluation systems in place is strictly related to the three other items of the axis.

In analyzing these cases through the lens of the capacity level framework developed by CEFRIO (Beaudoin, J., Lefebvre, G. L., Normand, M., Gouri, V., & Skerlj, A., 2016), it was observed that the companies analyzed in this report fall under the first three levels of the model- "monitoring," "control" and "optimization." In addition, most cases came under the first two levels. Even though the high-performance machinery of C7 could carry out some optimization autonomously, no companies' systems have yet reached full "optimization" or come even close to the "autonomy" levels as defined by the CEFRIO.

Infrastructure for Industry 4.0

Two different trends in the establishment of the Industry 4.0 infrastructure could be distinguished in the case studies.

- **Adoption of Turnkey Solutions:** In these cases, a solution provider was in charge of the installation of IT infrastructure and hardware devices within the company. The provider then supports the customer in all the processes and in future development stages.
- **Internal Development of the I4.0 Solution:** The company builds the competencies internally to manage and structure its own system. A further difference between firms that adopted this configuration was found. In some cases enterprises decided to develop their Industry 4.0 systems with the help of external experts on both infrastructure and technologies. The companies maintained the *supervision of the adoption process*, deciding which technologies and standards they wanted to have in their plant based on a benchmark analysis, while most of the design and installation process were performed by external entities. However, some companies preferred to *develop and design* their systems *internally* and to perform the physical integration of new technologies.

While each option has its advantages and disadvantages, the choice must be aligned with the strategic goals of Industry 4.0 implementation. Table 5 presents a comparison of these options. Generally speaking, the turnkey solution is faster and simpler, but allows less room for flexibility and future modifications. It may be a better choice for the companies that see I4.0 adoption as a one-time decision rather than an ongoing process. The internal development of I4.0 changes relies intensely on knowledge acquisition and absorption, which might be useful for "personalizing" these technologies to fit the company's specific future needs.

Looking at the characteristics of each case study and their infrastructure choices, it seems that *larger companies tend to adopt internal development* rather than rely on turnkey solutions. The fully integrated solutions provided by external suppliers are often not compatible with the dimensions of these organizations' structures. Moreover, bigger companies tend to have more heterogeneous skills within their organizations than do small firms, enabling the development of in-house solutions. Our results do not clearly show what led to the decision to fully design an I4.0 system internally or to supervise its conception with the help of an external provider. This decision could be related to the availability of specialized skill or, as some interviewees claimed, it could be because they wanted to maintain total control and understanding over their I4.0 system so that they could remain independent of specific providers. More data is needed to understand this issue.

Counter to this finding, C7, despite being the smallest company in the sample, decided to design its own systems internally, with very good results compared to the other organizations. In fact, it has one of the most mature adoption profiles. C10 instead, having a significant organizational structure, preferred to rely on a solution provider, which in the end did not provide the expected benefits due to the introduction of a partial system.

Table 5. Internal development vs. turnkey solutions

Factor	Turnkey solution	Internal development	
		Process Supervision	**Internal Design**
System Scaleability	To be assessed from case to case	High	
Required competencies	Provided by solution provider	To be developed inside the organization	
Hiring employees	Usually not necessary, or necessary only during the implementation and transition phases	The company must identify its needs for specialized profiles to supervise the process and provide training to acquire these competencies – hiring might be necessary	The company must identify its needs for specialized profiles to supervise the process and provide training to acquire these competencies – hiring new specialized skills is highly recommended
Training required	Mainly focused on operations	Need to develop digital competencies, as well as for operations	
Installation process	Provided by solution provider	Provided by external/internal actors but always supervised internally	Provided internally
Installation duration	Usually some weeks (often shorter than internal development)	Uncertain due to competency development and pilot launch (often longer than turnkey solutions)	
External actors involved	Solution provider	External consultants and technology providers	External consultants might be approached
System ownership	Solution provider	Company	
Absorptive capacity	Limited due to the system ownership	Strategic functions, if well managed	Strategic functions

Companies must carefully evaluate the *scaleability* of the solution offered by the provider. On the one hand, if the system developed by the supplier responds to the company's needs, upgrading the manufacturing facilities to a smart system can be done relatively quickly, mainly through learning by doing by the solution provider. In C8 for instance, the system had been previously tested in other companies prior to its implementation. On the other hand, if the company is not able to properly evaluate the scaleability of the system for its manufacturing processes, the risk of low system exploitation could lead to a failure of the implementation, or an impact below expectations (C10).

If the market is not able to satisfy the organization's needs, that is, no available system can respond to its requirements, internal development, followed by a continuous improvement approach, is the only possible way to implement a suitable Industry 4.0 solution. The decision-making process is more time and resource consuming than the turnkey solution, but if it is well developed the resulting system will meet the company's real needs. Moreover, internal development also guarantees the continuing improvement of competencies, the advancement of knowledge that can be used for further refinement of the system, and independence from any specific solution provider for upgrades and modifications.

For example, C7 felt that it was better to rely on experts to develop good personalized software, but did not want to be dependent on them, because it would have been expensive in the long term. For this reason, the company employed IT specialists to maintain the level of control and knowledge internally. In the end, their I4.0 solution is run by their employees. Considering the technologies and infrastructure selected during the implementation process, even in this case it is possible to make a distinction between the choice of relying on a turnkey solution or internal development.

Starting from the introduction of technologies provided by specialized suppliers, three enterprises (C8, C9 and C10) have adopted similar technologies even though the providers were different. The installation process involved specialized software to manage the self-assessment system and the data collection and analysis. It was located on a cloud platform in C9 and internally hosted on dedicated servers in C8 and C10 to manage the self-assessment system and the data collection and analysis. Moreover, the supplier provided the connection for the production department and the software thanks to the use of proper devices to allow communication between the machinery and the software. A series of human-machine interfaces, such as screens and tablets for entering production data and monitoring, were provided. This configuration is similar is to that proposed by Bagheri et al. (2015), a 5-level architecture of CPS. At the moment, the last layers (cognition and configuration) cannot be performed, although the providers are aiming in this direction.

Furthermore, the cybersecurity standards and procedures were entirely entrusted to the providers of the smart systems. In terms of the companies that chose to develop their I4.0 systems internally, different technologies were selected according to their needs. C1 and C2 decided to establish a strong I4.0 foundation, developing a data warehouse and restructuring the databases already present in their organization. In general, the technologies adopted by the companies were new machinery enabling IoT (C1, C2, C6, C7) devices to connect to old machines (C6, C7), visual boards to enable system self-assessments (C1, C2, C4, C6, C7), wearable solutions (C1, C2) and simulation systems (C2). Cybersecurity systems and policies were developed internally (C1, C2, C3) by companies that were seriously concerned about this issue, while the remaining organizations did not design or consider them, since the integration of their I4.0 configuration remains focused on internal operations only.

Absorptive Capacity

Where internal development was favoured, the awareness of skills required for I4.0 was, on average, well identified. C5 is an exception to this trend. In fact, the company showed a strong lack of awareness about the concept of Industry 4.0. If the paradigm shift is not properly identified and analyzed, strategic and operational plans cannot match the I4.0 requirements, preventing the company from fully understanding the skills profiles required for the fourth industrial revolution. Therefore, beyond the infrastructure choice, a *correlation between the "business strategy" and the "absorptive capacity" indicators* was found. By the way of example, it was noted that the companies that obtained a lower evaluation in the strategic indicator, have lower I4.0 awareness (C2, C5, C9, C10) than the others.

Furthermore, in the case of a turnkey solution, the provider transfers only part of its own knowledge to the customer, involves the firm's employees during the implementation and start-up and assists in the operation phases. Even though this training enables companies to use the system according to their original requirements, some companies (C8, C9, C10) realized that they were not using the I4.0 system to its full potential, and, even more, that they lacked the capacity to manipulate the system (Dworschak & Zaiser, 2014).

More globally, two training approach trends were recognized in relation to the infrastructure choices presented in the previous indicator. Internal development of the Industry 4.0 system enabled the design of specific training programs to create and foster new digital and decision-making competencies, with the exception of C5, which created only internal training on the job to facilitate the use of the new automated systems installed. In addition, especially in the cases of internal design, the companies recognized the need to bring specific new knowledge to the organization through the acquisition of new IT talent and/or specialists. Some enterprises felt that in some ways they were no longer simply manufacturing companies, but had also become more and more IT oriented with a fully operating IT team. Many of their most recent hires were IT specialists rather than operators and machinists, which was something quite new for these companies.

When a turnkey solution was selected, the training sessions were structured with a view to "compliance." Since the specific knowledge of the system's development and installation is provided by solution providers, the needs of the companies' operators are more focused on the proper use of new systems and technologies than on developing digital competences that could enable them to modify the I4.0 system. To further expand the system, the company will have to decide whether to acquire the competencies lacking through hiring or employee training, or to involve the system supplier in the process.

Finally, the lowest indicator of the axis is whether the Knowledge Management System in place is suitable for an Industry 4.0 system. This result seems strictly connected to the maturity item "Ability to analyze massive data." In fact, the limited capability of big data analysis can affect the company's ability to create new knowledge from its processes. In the sample analyzed, the generation of insights derived from using the new smart systems is still strictly tied to real-time data analysis and results-sharing through direct training. In a mature I4.0 scenario, it would also be expected that this data be used for enhancing the company's knowledge to create new products, services and processes benefiting from integrated IT sharing organization-wide (Deloitte, 2015; El Said, 2015).

Strategy Axis

It is essential that the implementation of an I4.0 solution be aligned with the firm's strategy and that top management believe in its benefits. While this observation may seem obvious, our cases showed that it is not always true.

Business Strategy

Awareness of the potential of I4.0 and the establishment of an ad hoc strategy to adopt its enabling technologies is the first step in structuring a solid shift towards a new manufacturing configuration. In accordance with Erol et al. (2016), the case study investigation showed that strategic plans and roadmaps facilitate and clarify the change process. C1, C3, C7 and C8 are the enterprises that developed appropriate strategic plans, resulting in the case studies that attained the higher maturity evaluations in the sample. Once again, the partial failure of the smart system in C10 is a good example of what could happen if the plan is not clearly defined and supported by top management – and understood by all employees.

In addition to the development of a strategic plan for the introduction of Industry 4.0, the companies *must develop their own understanding of Industry 4.0*, which should then be transformed into an Industry 4.0 strategic vision. The lack of awareness of this paradigm can lead to contradictory choices respecting the implementation process. Of the case studies analyzed, C5 is a clear example of a lack of awareness of Industry 4.0. The new manufacturing paradigm has not been appropriately approached to identify the main features, opportunities and steps that could have been implemented.

In terms of investments, it was observed that the companies mainly used investments to finance the acquisition of technologies, development of infrastructure, training of employees and installation of facilities. Italian enterprises relied on internal funding since the national funding plan for Industry 4.0, "Industria 4.0," was not available at the time of the interviews. The Canadian companies received financial support from provincial and federal governments, which was used for the integration of I4.0 systems with machinery, infrastructure and training. But even with this assistance, companies complained about the availability of financial resources. Grant initiatives were mainly focused on the initial introductory phases of new systems, technologies and upfront training rather than on the maintenance and upgrades phases. C10 exemplifies the problems that can arise if a company chooses to only partially implement an I4.0 system, a decision reached because of a lack of the necessary financial resources.

In the opinion of the management of the Canadian companies visited, which was also expressed in discussions with other experts, the government should help more and provide support beyond the introductory phases of these technological advancements, that is, for their later exploitation in order to use the full capabilities of I4.0 technologies and thus achieve increased competitiveness over time. This assistance should include not only actual tax incentives, but also investments – for example, real money.

Not all companies have taken advantage of the opportunity to develop or enhance new products and services through the utilization of I4.0.

Analysis of the case studies offers two possible explanations. The first relates to manufacturing configuration. Companies that produce products for final customers (C1, C2, C3, C4, C5, C10) seem to be facilitated in the design of additional features and services linked to I4.0. Others, such as manufacturers of high precision machining, do not have the possibility of applying changes or services to the production outcome since they do not own the items produced (they are often outsourcing suppliers). The second possible explanation could be the lack of integration of the systems in place with the external value networks.

The opportunity to exploit new business opportunities through I4.0 can be analyzed by examining the motivations expressed by the companies' managers during the interviews. Those firms specialized in high precision machining and C9 were focused on efficiency and process improvement rather than on the search for new business opportunities. In contrast, C1, C2, C3 and C4 were influenced not only by internal motivations, for example, increased efficiency and quality, but also by external factors like client requests. This topic will be further analyzed in the following subsection, which presents the companies' archetypes on Industry 4.0 adoption.

Networking and Integration

Of all the indicators, "Networking and Integration" was the most critical in the strategic axis. In all the companies interviewed, I4.0 was not thoroughly implemented within the organization.

It was found that emphasis was given to internal vertical operation, which seems to be the initial motivation for I4.0 implementation. However, in almost half the cases (C4, C5, C9, C10), evaluation of the vertical integration remains low. These companies adopted new technologies and infrastructure only in a limited area of the organization, that is, the production department. Instead of introducing the new smart system in multiple layers throughout the organization, they preferred to implement it only in the department that ensured a rapid gain in efficiency compared to the other areas.

Although horizontal integration was also noted in some cases, it was often limited, with few or no iterations with partners outside the company. Moreover, little evidence of engineering end-to-end integration was observed, with the exception of C1, C3 and C4. Collaboration among value networks is essential for a company wishing to boost the performance of its supply chain and, accordingly, to offer value-added products and services to its customers (Herterich, M. M., Uebernickel, F., & Brenner, W., 2015; Lee, J., Kao, H. A., & Yang, S.,2014; Rennung, F., Luminosu, C. T., & Draghici, A., 2016).

This lack of integration may be justified by the I4.0 maturity level of the value networks. In fact, some companies were planning to share information with their clients or customers, but were not yet ready (C1, C7) or the infrastructure in place allowed only static communication via email (C8, C9). This lack of integration may also be explained by the type of activities of some of the companies under study, which may be, by their nature, reactive to such integration rather than to their orchestrators.

Technology Strategy

Two contradictory trends were observed respecting the companies' concern about cybersecurity and the introduction of I4.0.

A number of companies (C1, C2, C3 and C4) were seriously concerned about cyber issues. These enterprises had identified potential issues during the introduction of smart technologies, through the formulation of the roadmap for I4.0 or a proper risk management process. Since they belong to large corporations (C1, C2, C4) and are used to collaborating with large customers (C3) requiring a set of security standards, the companies are more sensitive to cybersecurity.

In the second group, cybersecurity tied to the introduction of I4.0 was not considered a major concern, even though some enterprises were aware of the potential threats. For example, cybersecurity concerns prompted firm C7 to locate its servers inside a locked room in its plant. The fact that cybersecurity did not seem to be viewed as a major threat clearly contrasts with the best practices identified in the literature review (Cisco, 2017; Kobara, 2016). The lack of external horizontal integration throughout the value network may explain this lack of concern about security since there is no direct sharing of information outside the boundaries of the companies. However, external cyber attacks can happen despite the absence of outbound information flows. Research by the SANS institute (Shackleford, 2015) found that up to 80% of data breaches originated in the supply chain.

To prevent such attacks, organizations should develop cybersecurity systems embedded in their I4.0 configuration. Cybersecurity should therefore be considered at the first stage of I4.0 conception. Even though a company may not at present see the need for cyber protection, it is much easier and cheaper to include security features during the system's conception than at later stages.

As concerns the maturity item *Decision-making process with respect to the choice of platforms and standards*, a good average evaluation was noted in almost all the companies, with the exception of C9 and C10, which chose to engage a turnkey solution provider.

As already observed in the previous section on "infrastructure for I4.0", companies must carefully evaluate the scaleability of the solution that third parties provide. The selection process was properly carried out in C8, resulting in a satisfactory I4.0 transition. In contrast, the other two companies (C9 and C10) were unable to describe the decision-making process that led them to select one provider over another.

Performance

This last theme examined the benefits resulting from the implementation of I4.0 solutions inside, and in some ways, outside the enterprise using two indicators: "benefits of I4.0 adoption" and "impact on efficiency." The data were difficult to collect for many reasons, mainly because implementation of I4.0 was relatively new (C3, C9), in progress (C1, C2), partial (C5, C10), or in continuous improvement

(C8). Even though it was not possible to obtain the exact details requested, one conclusion emerges: all companies saw an improvement in their production and processes.

Benefits of I4.0 Adoption

Although the adoption of I4.0 among the companies interviewed was incomplete in most of the cases, many benefits from these systems were observed. From an economic point of view, an increase in company competitiveness, due to cost reduction for instance, is common to all the cases studied. Moreover, in fewer cases, companies benefited from an increase in revenues for the following reasons: (1) the introduction of new services linked to Industry 4.0 introduction (C1, C4, expected for C3); (2) the development of new enhanced products that include smart technologies (expected for C3, C4); and (3) the acquisition of a new market share due to increased efficiency and the subsequent cost reduction (higher competitiveness, lower price, higher sales volumes).

It seems that companies that provide the market with final products for which they own their design and production processes have more opportunities to develop new services and products by integrating I4.0 in their plant (See section "Companies' Archetypes").

From an environmental perspective, the benefits of I4.0 implementation were the saving of energy and the reduction of waste, even if most of the companies considered the environmental impact on their systems negligible (7 out of 10). Although this impact was poorly assessed in the companies selected, two approaches to this theme are worthy of note. C1 has integrated the roadmap for I4.0 implementation with a series of actions aimed at reducing the environmental impact during the last stages of the introduction process, relying on the installation of new smart-heating systems and renewing the company's lighting. Firm C6 has already implemented a smart heating system; connected thermometers indicate when the plant requires or does not require heating. It turned out that the heat did not need to be turned on for the greater part of the winter, although it had always been turned on in previous years. This led to better energy efficiency and savings for the company; in other words, a win on both the economic and the environmental front.

These two examples show that companies should re-evaluate the potential environmental benefits of introducing IoT, since the reduction of resources and emissions leads to an increase in company competitiveness (cost reduction) and visibility (Ford, 2016; Stock & Seliger, 2016).

Finally, from a social perspective, the companies experienced positive social impacts from establishing Industry 4.0. In some cases (C1, C4, C7, C8), management observed a natural empowerment of the operators owing to the greater accountability involved in using the new systems. In the new configurations, the operators are responsible for making decisions that had been centralized before the transition to I4.0. This reflects the information in the literature (Kagermann, H., Wahlster, W., & Helbig, J., 2013) and is opposed to theories positing that the fourth industrial revolution will bring contradictory effects in the work environment (Hirsch-Kreinsen, 2016). Another social benefit was the improvement of communications between management and operators in C9, which enabled the sharing of strategic and operational plans with the workforce and thus increasing their commitment and efficiency.

Impact on Efficiency

In terms of efficiency gains, the systems in place impacted different strategic KPIs and no common development path in the companies' performances could be identified. Some companies had problems conveying the real impacts of the I4.0 system according to the KPIs used in the maturity model adopted for this study (C6, C7, C10), which suggests that these firms are not measuring KPIs. For an effective rating of I4.0 implementation, companies should develop, in addition to their implementation roadmaps, *appropriate scorecards* to evaluate their progress, identifying specific targets to drive performance improvement (Farooq & Hussain, 2011; Jung, Morris, Lyons, Leong, & Cho, 2015).

DISCUSSION: THE ARCHETYPES OF I4.0 ADOPTION

From the analysis of the case studies, similar objectives and trends on the Industry 4.0 adoption process were observed as regards the manufacturing classification of each company. The enterprises were grouped according to the definitions of discrete (De Oliveira Gomes & Trabasso, 2016) and process manufacturing (Qian, Zhong, & Du, 2017). The discrete group was further broken down into two different clusters, depending on the nature of the discrete product, differentiating between companies that own the final product and those providing manufacturing services. The three classifications were combined with the results gained from the case studies to obtain a set of archetypes respecting the 10 companies interviewed during this project.

- **X – Product Based Manufacturing Companies (C2, C5, C10):** This group includes enterprises belonging to the discrete manufacturing configuration that own the product design. In this classification, the companies have not exploited the opportunities of introducing additional services thanks to the adoption of Industry 4.0. The enterprises that are part of this cluster are focused on the optimization of their processes and efficiency gains. For the eventual enrichment of the company's offer, exploiting I4.0 will lead to a transition towards the archetype Product & Service Based Companies.
- **Y – Service Based Manufacturing Companies (C6, C7, C8):** This cluster belongs to the discrete manufacturing configuration, even though it differs from the previous one. These enterprises offer their customers a series of manufacturing services such as machining operations and product/component design. Their manufacturing configuration leads to a continuous improvement of both internal efficiency and supply chain performance. I4.0 is considered an opportunity to increase company competitiveness through enhancing productivity and decreasing cost structure.
- **XY – Product & Service Manufacturing Companies (C1, C3, C4):** These companies belong to the discrete manufacturing classification that offers the market both products and related services. New services are developed thanks to the introduction of Industry 4.0. In addition to the increased efficiency and effectiveness of their processes, these companies aim at offering new solutions to the market through new features and services, enabled by the integration and use of smart technologies in their final products. In this cluster, the creation of new business models is crucial in order to align the new value proposition with the appropriate revenues streams (Weinberger, M., Bilgeri, D., & Fleisch, E., 2016).
- **Z – Process Manufacturing Companies (C9):** The firm in this archetype relies almost entirely on I4.0 for the achievement of internal efficiency and process optimization, given the fact that the nature of the products does not allow for the enhancement of production via smart technologies (Qian, F., Zhong, W., & Du, W., 2017).

In the light of these considerations, the archetypes' trends can be summarized as follows: A transition towards archetype XY (Product & Service Based Companies) is expected for X (Product Based Manufacturing Companies). The ownership of product design and production processes can facilitate the introduction of additional embedded features and services in the product offered to the market. C1, C3 and C4, which are currently classed in archetype XY, have directly tackled the Industry 4.0 paradigm, exploiting these opportunities.

In the cluster Product & Service Based Companies unusual behaviour was noted for C3 and C4. In fact, the two companies preferred to focus Industry 4.0 mainly on final products/installations rather than on internally achieving efficiency gains and creating comprehensive I4.0 solutions that can be integrated in their customers' plants. C3 seems to be shifting from being a purely manufacturing company *to becoming an Industry 4.0 provider.* In contrast, the other two archetypes are expected to remain in their clusters to pursue the aforementioned objectives.

CONCLUSION

The present research contributes to the literature on the relevance gap of existing maturity models on Industry 4.0. A new framework is proposed for evaluating the maturity of the adoption process established by manufacturing companies towards the fourth industrial revolution. This *Adoption Maturity Model* (AMM) fills the gaps highlighted during the comparison of the existing frameworks (Beaudoin, J., Lefebvre, G. L., Normand, M., Gouri, V., & Skerlj, A., 2016; Jodlbauer, H., Schagerl, M., & Brunner, M., 2016; Leyh, C., Schäffer, T., Bley, K., & Forstenhäusler, S., 2016; Schumacher, A., Erol, S., & Sihn, W., 2016), since it incorporates elements describing the evaluation of the maturity of Industry 4.0 configuration (e.g. Infrastructure for I4.0) and the elements representing the maturity of the process deployed (Technology Strategy and Performances).

Also, through case studies, the research provides in-depth insights on the motivation, challenges and outcomes faced by manufacturing companies that have implemented Industry 4.0 technologies in their plants. The comparative analysis provides several contributions towards identifying similar steps related to the development of Smart Manufacturing, enriching the current scientific literature. One key aspect is the importance of the formulation of a strategic vision supported by proper action plans (Erol, S., Schumacher, A., & Sihn, W., 2016), which was highlighted by the strong influence that the "Business Strategy" indicator had on the majority of other AMM sections. The lack of support from senior management leads to incomplete and unsatisfactory 4.0 implementation, either because it is not well adapted to the enterprise's own processes or because a partial implementation does not allow for the full use of the potential and promises inherent in I4.0. This means that the development of a sound understanding of Industry 4.0 is the foundation on which to base further technological and organizational choices, from defining training sessions, to the skills to be developed and the infrastructure to be implemented. The descriptive analysis of the data reveals a relationship between company size and the decision-making process for the definition of the systems architectures: in fact, in our sample, the use of turnkey solutions in smaller companies seems to be preferred due to the lack of resources and internal competences.

Moreover, further analysis of the companies' traits led us to identify four company archetypes, highlighting the existence of relationships between the enterprises' manufacturing configurations and relative Industry 4.0 adoptions and trends. It was noted that discrete and process manufacturing companies applied a different approach to the deployment phase towards the fourth industrial revolution. In addition, the discrete cluster has been further broken down based on the nature of the product offered. The characteristics of their value propositions seem to influence the motivations and objectives of switching to an Industry 4.0 configuration. Unlike companies offering only manufacturing services, those that own the design and/or the production processes, express different needs from the development of their smart manufacturing configurations, since they see the opportunity to improve internal efficiency and external competitiveness through new business models (considering both the offer of enhanced products and the development of additional services due to I4.0), while the former perceive potential business opportunities mainly in greater competitiveness due to operational excellence.

The contribution of the present study has relevant implications in both scientific and managerial areas. In terms of its scientific advancements, the development of a conceptual model of maturity for the implementation of Industry 4.0 enables the collection of data on the state of progress of manufacturing companies across different industries, as well as the identification of success factors, new insights and best practices for the effective implementation of Industry 4.0. Researchers could also use the model to refine research on the companies' archetypes that were noted during the comparative analysis of case studies.

Some implications of the Maturity Framework developed can be considered relevant even for business practitioners, either internal or external to the organization, involved in the transition to Industry 4.0. The "Scope and Problem Definition" phase performed during the development of the framework considered the target audience for which this model was designed (Becker, J., Knackstedt, R., & Pöppelbuß, J., 2009; Wendler, 2012). Specifically, management and executives can use the framework presented to effectively manage the company's transition process towards the fourth industrial revolution. Through the use of the maturity stage items identified during the AMM design process, the model offers a reference framework to plan the implementation of smart manufacturing in companies' processes. Moreover, the model can be used as a self-assessment tool, with a view to assessing the current implementation maturity level, identifying the areas that have not yet been addressed by the change, or those that require more effort to attain a higher stage of maturity. Considered from an external perspective, practitioners like consultants and I4.0 solution providers can employ the Adoption Maturity Model to provide customers with specific implementation roadmaps by relying on an impartial and reliable framework.

During the current research, some limitations were noted. The first is tied to the size of the sample of companies selected. In fact, even though 10 case studies are considered a sufficient number to perform case study research (Eisenhardt, 1989), a cross-industry study should consider a higher number of respondents, aiming at strengthening the framework validation and gaining greater insight from the different adoption processes implemented. There is also the issue of the generalizability of the archetypes found, due to the small sample (Tsang, 2014). Only one enterprise fits into the category "Process Manufacturing Companies," and the other clusters include too few enterprises, thus making it difficult to conduct a comprehensive study of their characteristics.

In terms of the methodology used to design the Adoption Maturity Model (De Bruin, T., Freeze, R., Kaulkarni, U., & Rosemann, M., 2005), and because Industry 4.0 was quite new for the enterprises visited, it was not possible to address the last development phase, "Maintain." The continuing relevance of the framework will be guaranteed only by maintaining the model over time and ensuring its suitability in relation to any possible alteration that could affect Industry 4.0.

Lastly, the methodology followed to establish the maturity stages of the Performance Axis also has some limitations. Based on the literature review, a number of benefits (economic, environmental and social) and KPIs that could be affected by the introduction of Industry 4.0 were identified. Since the research addressed a cross-industry study, the selection of these parameters, particularly those tied to efficiency performances, were grouped together without considering the company configuration under assessment. Moreover, for the purpose of calculating the performance indicators, the numerical impact of the various items was not considered. Only the qualitative effects (negative, positive or constant impact) were taken into consideration.

In light of the limitations and the results of this study, the data used in the present study open avenues for further research. First, more case studies should be conducted to collect more data that could confirm not only the various archetypes, but also the relevance of the AMM. It would be interesting to see whether there is any variation among countries and manufacturing sectors. More valuable instruments should be offered to managers and practitioners who are in charge of implementing innovative and high-performing systems within the industrial economic context. Adding cases would also help identify the best practices and best policies to help manufacturing enterprises transit to the fourth industrial revolution. In addition, it would be interesting to revisit the enterprises studied to conduct a maturity assessment review in order to study the evolution of their awareness of Industry 4.0. This would provide an opportunity to test the Adoption Maturity Model over time and thus increase its relevance.

REFERENCES

Arnold, C., Kiel, D., & Voigt, K.-I. (2016, June). How industry 4.0 changes business models in different manufacturing industries. *ISPIM Innovation Conference*, 1–20.

Bagheri, B., Yang, S., Kao, H. A., & Lee, J. (2015). Cyber-physical systems architecture for self-aware machines in industry 4.0 environment. *IFAC-PapersOnLine*, *28*(3), 1622–1627. doi:10.1016/j.ifacol.2015.06.318

Bangemann, T., Riedl, M., Thron, M., & Diedrich, C. (2016). Integration of Classical Components into Industrial Cyber-Physical Systems. *Proceedings of the IEEE*, *104*(5), 947–959. doi:10.1109/JPROC.2015.2510981

Beaudoin, J., Lefebvre, G. L., Normand, M., Gouri, V., & Skerlj, A. (2016). *Prendre Part à la Revolution Manufacturière?* CEFRIO.

Becker, J., Knackstedt, R., & Pöppelbuß, J. (2009). Developing Maturity Models for IT Management - A Procedure Model and its Application. *Business & Information Systems Engineering*, *1*(3), 213–222. doi:10.100712599-009-0044-5

Cisco. (2017). *Cisco 2017 Annual Cyber Security Report. WD info*. Cisco.

Cohen, W. M., & Levinthal, D. A. (1990). Absorptive capacity: A new perspective on learning and innovation. *Administrative Science Quarterly*, *35*(1), 128–152. doi:10.2307/2393553

De Bruin, T., Freeze, R., Kaulkarni, U., & Rosemann, M. (2005). Understanding the Main Phases of Developing a Maturity Assessment Model. *Australasian Conference on Information Systems (ACIS)*, 8–19.

Deloitte. (2015). *Industry 4.0. Challenges and solutions for the digital transformation and use of exponential technologies*. Deloitte.

Dworschak, B., Helmut, B., & Achtenhagen, C. (2013). Future skills needed for the Internet of Things in industrial production as part of the early identification initiative of the German Federal Ministry of Education and Research. *Frequenz (Bern)*.

Dworschak, B., & Zaiser, H. (2014). Competences for cyber-physical systems in manufacturing-First findings and scenarios. *Procedia CIRP*, *25*(C), 345–350. doi:10.1016/j.procir.2014.10.048

Eisenhardt, K. M. (1989). Building theories from case study research. *Academy of Management. The Academy of Management Review, 14*(4), 3–36.

El Said, G. R. (2015). Understanding Knowledge Management System antecedents of performance impact: Extending the Task-technology Fit Model with intention to share knowledge construct. *Future Business Journal, 1*(1–2), 75–87. doi:10.1016/j.fbj.2015.11.003

Erol, S., Schumacher, A., & Sihn, W. (2016). Strategic Guidance towards Industry 4.0 - a Three-stage Process Model. *International Conference on Competitive Manufacturing, 9*, 495–501.

Farooq, A., & Hussain, Z. (2011). Balanced scorecard perspective on change and performance: A study of selected Indian companies. *Procedia: Social and Behavioral Sciences*, *24*, 754–768. doi:10.1016/j.sbspro.2011.09.043

Ford, S. (2016). *Additive manufacturing and sustainability: an exploratory study of the advantages and challenges*. Academic Press.

Geissbauer, R., Vedso, J. V., & Schrauf, S. (2016a). *Industry 4.0: Building the Digital Enterprise Transportation and logistics key findings*. PWC - 2016 Global Industry Survey.

Geissbauer, R., Vedso, J. V., & Schrauf, S. (2016b). *The Industry 4.0: Digital Operations Self Assessment*. Academic Press.

Helu, M., Morris, K., Jung, K., Lyons, K., & Leong, S. (2015). Identifying performance assurance challenges for smart manufacturing. *Manufacturing Letters*, *6*, 1–4. doi:10.1016/j.mfglet.2015.11.001 PMID:26783512

Hermann, M., Pentek, T., & Otto, B. (2016). Design principles for industrie 4.0 scenarios. *Proceedings of the Annual Hawaii International Conference on System Sciences,* 3928–3937. 10.1109/HICSS.2016.488

Herterich, M. M., Uebernickel, F., & Brenner, W. (2015). The impact of cyber-physical systems on industrial services in manufacturing. *Procedia CIRP*, *30*, 323–328. doi:10.1016/j.procir.2015.02.110

Hevner, A. R., March, S. T., Park, J., & Ram, S. (2004). Design Science in Information Systems Research. *Management Information Systems Quarterly*, *28*(1), 75–105. doi:10.2307/25148625

Hirsch-Kreinsen, H. (2016). Digitalisierung industrieller Arbeit: Entwicklungspfade und Perspektiven. *Journal for Labour Market Research*, *49*(1), 1–14. doi:10.100712651-016-0200-6

Jodlbauer, H., Schagerl, M., & Brunner, M. (2016). Reifegradmodell Industrie 4.0. *Industrie 4.0 Management, 5*(32), 49–52.

Jung, K., Morris, K. C., Lyons, K. W., Leong, S., & Cho, H. (2015). Mapping strategic goals and operational performance metrics for smart manufacturing systems. *Procedia Computer Science, 44*(C), 184–193. doi:10.1016/j.procs.2015.03.051

Kagermann, H., Wahlster, W., & Helbig, J. (2013). *Securing the future of German manufacturing industry: Recommendations for implementing the strategic initiative INDUSTRIE 4.0. Final report of the Industrie 4.0 Working Group. National Academy of Science and Engineering (ACATECH).* Federal Ministry of Education and Research.

Kang, H. S., Lee, J. Y., Choi, S., Kim, H., Park, J. H., Son, J. Y., ... Noh, S. D. (2016). Smart manufacturing: Past research, present findings, and future directions. *International Journal of Precision Engineering and Manufacturing - Green Technology, 3*(1), 111–128.

Khan, A., & Turowski, K. (2016). A Perspective on Industry 4.0: From Challenges to Opportunities in Production Systems. *Proceedings of the International Conference on Internet of Things and Big Data*, 441–448. 10.5220/0005929704410448

Kobara, K. (2016). Cyber physical security for Industrial Control Systems and IoT. *IEICE Transactions on Information and Systems, E99D*(4), 787–795.

Koch, V., & Kuge, S. (2014). *Opportunities and challenges of the industrial internet.* Strategy PwC.

Kohlegger, M., Maier, R., & Thalmann, S. (2009). Understanding maturity models results of a structured content analysis. *Proceedings of IKNOW '09 and ISEMANTICS '09*, 51–61.

Lee, J., Kao, H. A., & Yang, S. (2014). Service innovation and smart analytics for Industry 4.0 and big data environment. *Procedia CIRP, 16*, 3–8. doi:10.1016/j.procir.2014.02.001

Leyh, C., Schäffer, T., Bley, K., & Forstenhäusler, S. (2016). SIMMI 4.0 – A Maturity Model for Classifying the Enterprise-wide IT and Software Landscape Focusing on Industry 4.0. *Proceedings of the Federated Conference On Computer Science and Information Systems, 8*, 1297–1302. 10.15439/2016F478

Lichtblau, K., Volker Stich, Bertenrath, R., Blum, M., Bleider, M., Millack, A., ... Schröter, M. (2015). Industrie 4.O readiness. *IMPULS - Foundation for Mechanical Engineering, Plant Engineering and Information Technology.*

Lorenz, M., Rüßmann, M., Strack, R., Lueth, K. L., & Bolle, M. (2015). Man and Machine in Industry 4.0. *The Boston Consulting Group, 18.*

Michael, R., Markus, R., Philipp, G., Manuela, W., Jan, J., Pascal, E., & Harnisch, M. (2015). Industry 4.0: The Future of Productivity and Growth in Manufacturing Industries. *The Boston Consulting Group.* Available online: http://industry.gov.au/

Miragliotta, G., Macchi, M., & Terzi, S. (2016a). Smart manufacturing: tecnologie e quadro applicativo. *Osservatorio Industria 4.0/Smart Manufacturing.*

Miragliotta, G., Macchi, M., & Terzi, S. (2016b). Smart Manufacturing in Italia: Stato dell'Arte e Stima di Mercato. *Osservatorio Industria 4.0/Smart Manufacturing.*

Park, S. (2016). Development of Innovative Strategies for the Korean Manufacturing Industry by Use of the Connected Smart Factory (CSF). *Procedia Computer Science, 91*, 744–750.

Qian, F., Zhong, W., & Du, W. (2017). Fundamental Theories and Key Technologies for Smart and Optimal Manufacturing in the Process Industry. *Engineering, 3*(2), 154–160. doi:10.1016/J.ENG.2017.02.011

Rennung, F., Luminosu, C. T., & Draghici, A. (2016). Service Provision in the Framework of Industry 4.0. *Procedia: Social and Behavioral Sciences, 221*, 372–377. doi:10.1016/j.sbspro.2016.05.127

Roblek, V., Meško, M., & Krapež, A. (2016). A Complex View of Industry 4.0. *SAGE Open, 6*(2), 215824401665398. doi:10.1177/2158244016653987

Rockwell Automation. (2014). The Connected Enterprise Maturity Model. *Rockwell Automation, 12*. Available online: http://www.rockwellautomation.com/

Schumacher, A., Erol, S., & Sihn, W. (2016). A Maturity Model for Assessing Industry 4.0 Readiness and Maturity of Manufacturing Enterprises. *Procedia CIRP, 52*, 161–166. doi:10.1016/j.procir.2016.07.040

Shackleford, D. (2015). Combatting Cyber Risks in the Supply Chain. *A SANS Whitepaper*. Available online: https://www.sans.org/reading-room

Sniderman, B., Mahto, M., & Cotteleer, M. (2016). *Industry 4.0 and manufacturing ecosystems: Exploring the world of connected enterprises*. Deloitte University Press.

Stock, T., & Seliger, G. (2016). Opportunities of Sustainable Manufacturing in Industry 4.0. *Procedia CIRP, 40*, 536–541.

Tsang, E. W. K. (2014). Generalizing from research findings: The merits of case studies. *International Journal of Management Reviews, 16*(4), 369–383. doi:10.1111/ijmr.12024

Wang, S., Wan, J., Li, D., & Zhang, C. (2016). Implementing Smart Factory of Industrie 4.0: An Outlook. *International Journal of Distributed Sensor Networks*.

Weinberger, M., Bilgeri, D., & Fleisch, E. (2016). IoT business models in an industrial context. *Automatisierungstechnik, 64*(9), 699–706. doi:10.1515/auto-2016-0054

Wendler, R. (2012). The maturity of maturity model research: A systematic mapping study. *Information and Software Technology, 54*(12), 1317–1339. doi:10.1016/j.infsof.2012.07.007

Weyer, S., Schmitt, M., Ohmer, M., & Gorecky, D. (2015). Towards industry 4.0 - Standardization as the crucial challenge for highly modular, multi-vendor production systems. *IFAC-PapersOnLine, 28*(3), 579–584. doi:10.1016/j.ifacol.2015.06.143

Zhou, K. (2015). Industry 4.0: Towards Future Industrial Opportunities and Challenges. *12th International Conference on Fuzzy Systems and Knowledge Discovery (FSKD)*, 2147–2152. 10.1109/FSKD.2015.7382284

KEY TERMS AND DEFINITIONS

Big Data: Extremely large sets of non-structured data that have the potential, through the employment of advanced computational analytical methods, to reveal patterns, trends, and associations, especially relating to human behaviour and interactions.

Cyber Physical Systems (CPS): Systems that typically comprise mechanical, electrical, and software elements that are controlled by computer-based algorithms integrated with the internet (or a local network), thus allowing virtual operation and monitoring by users.

Cybersecurity: A term to designate the collection of principles, policies, tools, devices, concepts, guidelines, risk management methods, actions, training, best practices, and technologies that can be used to protect the cyber environment and organization and users' assets from cyber attacks, so to assure the availability, integrity, and confidentiality of data and systems.

Data Analytics: The process of examining data sets, using formal procedures, methods, and tools in order to draw conclusions about the information they contain.

Industrial Internet of Things (IIoT): The use of internet of things (IoT) technologies within manufacturing applications.

Industry 4.0 (I4.0): A term introduced by the German government in 2011 to designate the fourth industrial revolution: a new era of industrial manufacturing systems consisting of connected automated systems that allow interoperability, information transparency, technical assistance, and decentralized decisions.

Internet of Things (IoT): A global dynamic information network comprised of objects connected to the internet, by the incorporation of radio-frequency identification devices, sensors, and actuators, as well as other intelligent instruments and devices that allow any physical object to become an integral part of the internet.

Maturity Model: Every tool or framework that allows the measurement of an organization's capacity for continuous improvement in a particular discipline on a number of areas and axes.

APPENDIX 1

Table 6. Existing maturity models

Model Name / Source	What Is It Used For?	How Is the Model Designed?	Where Do Assessment Data Come From?	Method of Goal Benchmarking	Number of Stages	Existing Stage	Tool Supported
"A maturity model .... maturity of manufacturing enterprises" (Schumacher et al., 2016)	Self - assessment company's Industry 4.0	62 maturity items divided into 9 company dimensions	Measurement of maturity items through questionnaire	Each maturity item is ranked from 1 to 5, then each maturity dimension is obtained using a proper formula	5 levels for each item from 1 to 5	No	Calculation of maturity level SW supported
IMPULS – Industrie 4.0 Readiness (Lichtblau et al., 2015)	Online self-check tool for Industry 4.0 readiness	18 maturity items divided into 6 indicators	Questionnaire	Each dimension is ranked from 1 to 5 for each indicator, then the final value is obtained multiplying each indicator for a coefficient	6 stages from 0 to 5	Yes	Online tool
SIMMI 4.0 (Leyh et al., 2016)	classification of company's IT system landscape in the context of the Industry 4.0 requirements	4 Maturity dimensions	Interview/self-assessment	Qualitative evaluation	5	No	No
Industry 4.0 / Digital Operations Self-Assessment (Geissbauer et al., 2016b)	Industry 4.0 self-assessment	6 maturity dimensions	Questionnaire	No details	4	No	Online tool
Four levels of I4.0 capability (Beaudoin et al., 2016)	Identification of four consecutive implementation stages for Industry 4.0	4 levels of Industry 4.0 capability	Self-assessment	N/A	4	No	No
The Connected Enterprise Maturity Model (Rockwell automation, 2014)	Five-stage approach to achieve Industry 4.0	five-stage implementation process	N/A	N/A	5	No	No
I4.0 Reifegradmodell (Jodlbauer et al., 2016)	Model to help company applying Industry 4.0	13 maturity items divided into 3 dimensions	Interview/self-assessment	Qualitative evaluation	10	Yes	No

APPENDIX 2

Table 7. Interview guide

	Introduction
1	**Can you describe your business briefly? (History, products, size, customers, suppliers)?**
2	**Do you know what big data is?**
2a	Did it affect your decision to implement an I4.0 system? How?
2b	Do you consider the use of massive data is important for your business? Why?
	Industry 4.0 in the Business
3	**What were the reasons that led to the implementation of an I4.0 system within your company?**
3a	Is it part of the business strategy adopted by your company?
3ai	If yes, could you describe it?
3aii	If yes, do you have a roadmap for the I4.0? Could you briefly describe it to me?
3b	What was the decision-making process with respect to the implementation of the I4.0 like? Who was involved?
4	**Can you briefly describe your I4.0 system?**
4a	How integrated is it in your business? (Only in the workplace, in all departments, some departments, etc.)
4ai	If integrated in at least two departments: How are communication and decision making structured among these departments?
4b	Does your system communicate with partners located outside the company?
4bi	What other companies are connected? What type of information is exchanged?
4bii	(If connected to a business partner), does it influence decision making? How?
5	**How do you handle cybersecurity issues related to I4.0?**
5a	Can you briefly describe your cybersecurity system? Why did you choose it?
6	**How does I4.0 fit into your current business strategy?**
7	**What was the level of investment required to implement the I4.0 system?**
7a	What was the investment used for? Infrastructure? Hiring Employees? Licences? Training? Others?
7b	Was it difficult to obtain the financing? Why?
7c	What were the sources of funding?
	Before I4.0 Adoption
8	**Which technologies have you chosen to implement I4.0?**
8a	Could you describe the decision-making process that led to the selection of these technologies?
8b	Why these technologies over others?
8bi	Was this related to the infrastructure that you had installed?
8bii	Has your Information Technology System influenced the choices of I4.0 technologies? If yes, how? Otherwise, why not?
9	**How did you prepare the implementation of I4.0 within your company?**
9a	What is your standard employee training procedure like?
9b	How do you make sure that the company retains the knowledge that is absorbed by its employees?
9c	Were there particular issues that have slowed or required additional effort prior to the implementation? (Ex. Technology in place, employee competence, ability to use the data, cyber-security)
9d	How did you prepare your employees during the transition to the I4.0 configuration?

continued on following page

Table 7. Continued

10	**Did you have external support for the implementation of the I4.0?**
10a	If yes, what precisely?
10b	Did your provincial government support you in your efforts? How?
10c	Did the federal government support you in your efforts? How?
	During Adoption
11	**Could you describe the I40 implantation?**
11a	What were the main challenges?
11ai	How did you solve these problems?
11b	On the other hand, what was easy during the implementation?
12	**Did the implementation of I4.0 require a modification of your infrastructure? Equipment? Computer systems? Others?**
12a	What were the changes?
	After I4.0 Adoption
13	**How do you use all data that are now available through the I4.0 system?**
13a	How does it affect your decision making in everyday life?
13b	What uses do you make of the data that are now available?
13c	Are you satisfied with your use of the available data? Why?
14	**In your opinion, what are the benefits due to the implementation of the I4.0 system for your company?**
14a	What are the economic benefits?
14b	What are the environmental benefits?
14c	What are the social benefits?
15	**How did I4.0 affect your efficiency in production? (Using "Performance table")**
16	**On the other hand, have you identified limitations or disadvantages from the implementation of the I4.0 system? (E.g. compared with employees, customers, headquarters, IT security issues, etc.)**
	Looking Back on Experience
17	**Overall, are you satisfied with the I4.0 implementation within your company? Why?**
17a	What can you do now that you were not able to do before, thanks to I4.0?
17b	Are you satisfied with the technological choices? Why?
18	**Has I4.0 implementation created new business opportunities for your company? (Improved product, new markets and products, etc.)**
18a	If yes, could you describe them?
19	**Looking back, do you think that your company was ready to implement an I4.0 system when you did so? Why?**
19a	What would you have done differently?
20	**Would you recommend other companies implement an I4.0 system? Why?**
20a	(If yes) What would be your advice to them to succeed in the implementation in their manufacturing?
21	**Do you have any suggestions to the government to be able to help companies like yours during the implementation of an I4.0 system?**
22	**Do you have anything to add, a question or a comment that you believe to be important that has not been addressed in the interview?**

Section 4

Knowledge Transfer and Education

Chapter 13
Knowledge Transfer and Introduction of Industry 4.0 in SMEs:
A Five-Step Methodology to Introduce Industry 4.0

Dominik T. Matt
Free University of Bolzano, Italy

Erwin Rauch
Free University of Bolzano, Italy

Michael Riedl
Fraunhofer Italia Research, Italy

ABSTRACT

Industry 4.0 is for most companies and especially for small and medium sized enterprises (SMEs) one of the major challenges after the wave of lean management. The aim of this chapter is to provide a methodological guidance for the practical use of the Industry 4.0 vision and principles in production system design in the specific context of SMEs. Based on the analysis of literature, a procedure model for the target-oriented introduction of Industry 4.0 principles in SMEs is proposed. A first practical evaluation of the approach is carried out based on two industrial case studies. The experiences made in the industrial cases show that Industry 4.0 is not limited to the application in large enterprises but is very suitable also for SME. This chapter contributes, with its case-study-based methodology, to the existing sparse knowledge on the introduction of Industry 4.0 in SME production systems.

INTRODUCTION

Many companies in various industries have reorganised their production in the recent past, following the principles of lean production or even taking advantage of novel production strategies such as agile manufacturing and mass customisation (Brettel, M., Friederichsen, N., Keller, M., & Rosenberg, M.,

DOI: 10.4018/978-1-5225-3468-6.ch013

2014), and thereby increasing flexibility and achieving significant progress in productivity and in readiness for delivery. However, the demands are growing: the trend towards individualisation of products is increasing, efficiency-enhancing serial or even mass-production concepts are increasingly being pushed back, and classic approaches to automation are failing in the demand for a production up to the 'lot size 1'. Industrial production is faced with a profound change and the question of the quadrature of the circle: *Is automation of individuality possible?* (Matt D. T., Rauch E., & Fraccaroli D., 2016). A popular term, 'Industry 4.0' is currently broadly debated both by researchers and practitioners as a visionary concept that promises to resolve this conundrum. Industry 4.0 technologies also facilitate the fabrication of customised products and, thus, the concept of mass customisation (Matt & Rauch, 2017). However, the majority of small and medium-sized enterprises (SME) are still quite sceptical regarding this vision and many of them doubt the benefits (Matt D. T., Rauch E., & Fraccaroli D., 2016). Industry 4.0 represents a special challenge for businesses in general and for SMEs in particular. The readiness of SME to adapt to Industry 4.0 concepts and their organisational capability to meet this challenge exists only in part. The smaller SMEs are, the higher the risk that they will not be able to benefit from this revolution (Sommer, 2015). SMEs are conscious about the knowledge in adaption deficits and this opens the need for further research and action plans for preparing them for Industry 4.0.

This chapter proposes a methodology for an efficient transfer of knowledge in the context of Industry 4.0 and the related cyber-physical production systems, and is derived from a careful literature research and evaluated through two industrial case studies, wherein Industry 4.0-relevant knowhow and concepts were transferred from research into the industrial practice of small and medium-sized enterprises. The case analysis shows that Industry 4.0 is not only accessible for large high-tech-enterprises. However, the implementation must be gradual along a clearly defined strategy. Thus, the purpose of this chapter is to propose a methodological guidance from a focused knowledge transfer to the practical implementation of the Industry 4.0 vision and principles in production system design and in the specific context of small and medium-sized enterprises. It should serve as a starting point for broader and more detailed study regarding research on how to implement Industry 4.0 in industrial enterprises and, especially, in SMEs.

The chapter is structured as follows: after the initial introduction in Section 1, the authors analyse the state of the art in the implementation of Industry 4.0 principles and the Smart Factory concept in SMEs. Section 3 describes the research methodology, the objectives of this research and the proposed implementation approach consisting of five successive steps. In Section 4, the authors describe the application of the 5-step implementation approach in two industrial case studies. In Section 5, a critical discussion follows and shows the advantages, but also the current limitations, of the proposed approach. This section addresses future direction for further research. Finally, the chapter ends with a brief summary and conclusion.

THEORETICAL BACKGROUND

This literature review section is organised in three parts. First, the terms 'Industry 4.0', 'Smart Factory' and 'Cyber-Physical System' are explained to provide a basic knowledge of these concepts. The second part describes the extension of the Smart Factory concept in small and medium-sized enterprises, while the third part highlights the importance of knowledge transfer in Industry 4.0 competencies and then formulates the objective of this research.

Industry 4.0 and Smart Factory

Based on advanced digitalisation within factories, the combination of Internet technologies and future-oriented technologies in the field of 'smart' objects (machines/products) is likely to result in a new paradigm shift in industrial production, known as Industry 4.0 (Lasi, H., Fettke, P., Kemper, H. G., Feld, T., & Hoffmann, M., 2014). Following the mechanisation, electrification and computerisation of industrial production, we are now on the verge of the fourth industrial revolution with the arrival of the Internet of Things and Services. The term 'Industry 4.0'was first introduced at the Hannover trade fair in 2011 (Kagermann, H., Lukas, W. D., & Wahlster, W., 2011) as an expression for the so-called 'fourth industrial revolution' and essentially addresses the technological integration of Cyber-Physical Systems (CPS) in the production process which enables (Internet-based) networking with all partners in the value chain (Schröder, 2016). To date, the term has been mainly used in popular science and has not been broadly established in the scientific literature (Brettel, M., Friederichsen, N., Keller, M., & Rosenberg, M., 2014). A review of most recent scientific literature identifies four key components of Industry 4.0: Cyber-Physical Systems, Internet of Things (IoT), Internet of Services (IoS) and Smart Factory (Hermann, M., Pentek, T., & Otto, B., 2015). In the following, these terms are explained to facilitate a better understanding of Industry 4.0 and the related topics.

A cyber-physical system (CPS) is a combination of computers and physical systems. CPS is about the intersection, not the union, of the physical and the cyber. It combines engineering models and methods with the models and methods of computer science (Lee, 2015). Connecting physical world objects (made of atoms) with information (packaged as bits) may segue to another revolution, predicted by many, including Neil Gershenfeld, the director of MIT's Center for Bits and Atoms (Datta, 2015). CPS positively affects manufacturing in the form of Cyber-Physical Production Systems (CPPS) in process automation and control (Monostori, 2014). Cyber-Physical Systems are also enablers for changing business logic and value chains, with the conjunction of cyber-physical systems and the development of new business models, facilitating the creation of disruptive innovations (Rauch, E., Seidenstricker, S., Dallasega, P., & Hämmerl, R., 2016).

CPS have to be synchronised one with another and with the external world to share information and trigger actions, first by homogenising and integrating the communication systems through necessary hardware and middleware, and, second, by constructing a centralised backbone network where all valuable information is collected for further big data analysis (Rojas, R., Rauch, E., Vidoni, R., & Matt, D. T., 2017). Thus, the Internet of Things (IoT) plays a major role in the implementation of Industry 4.0. The Internet of Things, also known as the Internet of Objects, refers to the networked interconnection of everyday objects, which are often equipped with ubiquitous intelligence. IoT will increase the ubiquity of the Internet by integrating every object for interaction via embedded systems, leading to a highly distributed network of devices communicating with human beings as well as other devices (Xia, F., Yang, L. T., Wang, L., & Vinel, A., 2012). Regarding the introduction in the context of Industry 4.0, the term has been extended to the Industrial Internet of Things (IIoT). IIoT includes emerging technologies such as industrial wireless networks (IWNs), big data, and cloud computing, which will bring great opportunities for promoting industrial upgrades and even allow the introduction of the fourth industrial revolution (Wan, J., Tang, S., Shu, Z., Li, D., Wang, S., Imran, M., & Vasilakos, A. V., 2016). IIoT combines physical manufacturing and value creation with information processing, providing physical objects that traditionally lie in industrial environments with cognitive, perception or actuation, communication and autonomy capabilities (Törngren, M., Bensalem, S., Cengarle, M. V., Chen, D.-J., McDermid, J., Passerone, R., Sangiovanni-Vincentelli, A., & Runkler, T., 2014).

The Internet of Services (IoS) presents a paradigm in which everything is available as a service on the Internet. It can also be viewed as networked services or systems across the real and virtual worlds over the Internet. In the IoS, services – as encapsulated functional entities containing interaction processes by service providers and customers – are redistributed, virtualised and converged over the Internet to meet the requirements of and create value for customers (Xu, X., Sheng, Q. Z., Zhang, L. J., Fan, Y., & Dustdar, S., 2015). An example of IoS is cloud computing. Cloud computing will play a major role in the future Internet of Services, enabling on-demand provisioning of applications, platforms and computing infrastructures (Moreno-Vozmediano, 2013).

With Industry 4.0, companies will cross-link their products, machines, storage, handling and transport systems as well as other operating equipment such as cyber-physical systems (CPS) in a worldwide network of so-called 'Smart Factories' (Kagermann, H., Wahlster, W., & Helbig, J., 2013). The term Smart Factory is not consistently defined. Radziwon et al. (2014) identify several interchangeable expressions, such as U-Factory (ubiquitous factory) (Yoon, J. S., Shin, S. J., & Suh, S. H., 2012), Factory-of-Things (Lucke, D., Constantinescu, C., & Westkämper, E., 2008), Real-Time Factory (Zuehlke, 2010), or Intelligent Factory of the Future (Hameed, B., Durr, F., & Rothermel, K., 2011). In the Smart Factory, a completely changed production logic is applied: the products themselves become 'smart'. Such 'smart objects' are not only able to store data and information about their location, their current state and their surroundings (e.g. via radio frequency identification - RFID), but also provide them with real-time decision-making logic, which allows them to independently find the way through their production and logistics environment. They are, thus, clearly identifiable and localisable; they know their history, their current state and their target state, as well as alternative ways to achieve it. In doing so, they must interact with their production and logistics environment. Products need to communicate with machines, and these machines and other resources must, in turn, exchange information and subsequently initiate processes autonomously (Einsiedler, 2013; Distefano, S., Banerjee, N., & Puliafito, A., 2016).

Based on the literature review and the definitions of CPS, IoT, IoS and Smart Factory, the authors derive the following definition of Industry 4.0:

Industry 4.0 is a collective term for technologies and concepts of value chain organisation. Within the modular structured Smart Factories of Industry 4.0, CPS monitor physical processes, create a virtual copy of the physical world and make decentralised decisions. Over the IoT, CPS communicate and cooperate with each other and humans in real time. Via the IoS, both internal and cross organisational services are offered and utilised by participants of the value chain (Hermann, M., Pentek, T., & Otto, B., 2015).

Industry 4.0 and the comprehensive IT integration in production are regarded as the central theme for the intelligent factory of the future (Bauer, W., Schlund, S., Marrenbach, D., & Ganschar, O., 2014). The theoretical approaches and necessary technologies are now widely available. The competition will take place through the integration into industrial practice, the development of economic applications and the definition of new business models (Gausemeier, 2015). These productivity potentials cannot be achieved by simply by the purchase of emerging Industry 4.0 technologies, but require an individual adaptation to the specific conditions in the company and the connectivity between each of the technologies. For the efficient adaptation and integration of cyber-physical production systems into industrial practice, a broad scientific knowledge base is necessary. This is due, on the one hand, to the complex interrelations involved in the implementation of cyber-physical systems and, on the other, to the high degree of specialisation of companies, particularly in the case of small and medium-sized enterprises (Moore, J., Loughran, A., McCusker, E., Solvang, W. D., Sziebig, G., Yu, H., Ericson, A., Holmqvist, J., Wenngren, J., Pieska, S., Vahasoyrinki, J., & Kaartinen, H., 2016). Industry 4.0 is setting new standards for production systems and machines: they must be smart, efficient and highly adaptive, as the products to be manufactured can constantly change. In other words, production in Industry 4.0 should be more individual, flexible, efficient and faster (Matt D. T., Rauch E., & Fraccaroli D., 2016). This vision of the Smart Factory sounds equally as adventurous for SMEs. But how far are we actually from that?

Smart Factory: An Extension to SMEs

This question cannot be answered generally, as companies are very differently prepared for the development of 'smart networking'. This is shown by the example of a recent study by the Association of German Mechanical and Plant Engineering Companies VDMA (Lichtblau, K., Stich, V., Bertenrath, R., Blum, M., Bleider, M., Millak, A., Schmitt, K., Schmitz, E., & Schröter, M., 2015), according to which, every fifth mechanical and plant engineering company in Germany deals with 'Industry 4.0'. In fact, only 5.6% of the surveyed companies are among the pioneers of the Industry 4.0 implementation, while 17.9% consider themselves as newcomers in the subject and the overwhelming majority of 76.5% have not yet taken any systematic steps towards Industry 4.0. And this despite it being unquestionably integral to the self-understanding of the German mechanical and plant engineering sector showcase itself as an industry and technology leader in this issue. This is in consideration that, in Germany, the mechanical engineering industry is the industry with the highest number of employees, even before the electrical and the automotive industry, with mainly small and medium-sized enterprises and an average company size of about 173 employees (VDMA, 2014).

Radziwona et al. (2014) assert that one of the main handicaps of a Smart Factory vision is the lack of concepts that are applicable in SMEs. Most SMEs have a need for automation solutions in manufacturing to optimise operations. Apart from the related necessary investments, practical experience shows that productivity potentials cannot be realised by the mere purchase of technologies, but often require an individual adaptation to the specific conditions in the company. Experience also shows that, for the efficient adaptation and integration of cyber-physical production systems into industrial practice, a broad scientific knowledge base is necessary. This is due in part to the complex interrelations involved in the implementation of cyber-physical production systems, but also to the high degree of specialisation of companies, especially in the case of small and medium-sized enterprises (Riedl, M., Garcia, D., Rauch, E., & Matt, D. T., 2016).

Moreover, many elements of the Smart Factory have not yet left the research laboratories. There is also no uniform concept for the Smart Factory that can be applied to any industrial operation (Hermann, M., Pentek, T., & Otto, B., 2015). Each company must analyse its situation and its individual needs and then choose those approaches that promise the best prospects for achieving the goals set. In this respect, certain parallels to 'lean production' and to the associated integration approach of the so-called holistic production systems can be recognised. A holistic production system is by no means a rigid conception frame with fixed methods and tools, rather it is the result of a company-specific, cooperative development process between executives, experts and employees. Despite a wide variety of variants and design variants in operational practice, almost all holistic production systems are based on similar basic objectives: the improvement of competitiveness by simultaneously increasing flexibility and efficiency by means of the systematic and continuous reduction of waste in all processes along a strictly customer needs-oriented value chain. In order to achieve these goals, work-organisational approaches from the lean-method-toolkit have been the focus of attention so far.

Now, Industry 4.0 opens up new technological perspectives. The Smart Factory concept is, therefore, a logical technological step into the future: from data will come knowledge, from knowledge will come benefit. According to Mrugalska et al. (2017), lean production and Industry 4.0 can coexist and support each other. The Smart Factory does not replace lean production, rather it provides new technological tools that enable the lean principles to further develop (Matt D. T., Rauch E., & Fraccaroli D., 2016): physical kanban cards, whiteboards and other lean tools are gradually being replaced with modern technologies of the real-data processing and visualisation, rather like small evolutionary steps. According to Sanders et al. (2016), Industry 4.0 is capable of implementing lean principles – committing to Industry 4.0 makes a factory lean as well as smart. Through integrated information and communication systems, the shortcomings of conventional practices can be overcome to improve productivity and eliminate waste. Industries now have the combined benefits of real-time integration of the entire factory along with the assurance of minimal waste generation (Sanders, A., Elangeswaran, C., & Wulfsberg, J., 2016). New possibilities from information and communication technologies are matching with lean environments. For companies, Industry 4.0 offers an estimated benefit by stabilising lean processes with Industry 4.0 technologies (Wagner, T., Herrmann, C., & Thiede, S., 2017).

However, application-oriented research needs to be developed pertaining to the criteria of implementing lean manufacturing (Sanders, A., Elangeswaran, C., & Wulfsberg, J., 2016). This is corresponding directly to the practical experience of the authors in closely following and supporting SMEs in their specific development processes towards the Smart Factory. The two use cases at the end of this chapter can, therefore, be seen as examples for the application of a reference architecture presented by the authors in the following paragraphs.

Knowledge Transfer: Industry 4.0 as a Competence

In order to transfer approaches from the Internet of things, mobile robotics or the mobile Internet to the production halls in the form of short-term and medium-term solutions, both knowledge in the field of production technologies, mechatronics and a strong understanding of ICT are prerequisites. In this context, Industry 4.0 must be understood not so much as a product, but rather as a competence. Furthermore, the learning capacity of not just the single worker, but of the whole company is a crucial aspect. Based on this, the question naturally arises as to how these competencies can be transferred to practice. The challenge is to understand the concepts from an information technology-linked view of production and to apply it to one's own tasks. In order to make this potential available to small and medium-sized enterprises in the context of applied research, appropriate approaches for a transfer of knowledge from applied research into practice are needed (Riedl, M., Garcia, D., Rauch, E., & Matt, D. T., 2016).

Knowledge differs from pure information through the background or context and the individual experience of its intermediary or recipient. Knowledge can, therefore, be understood and interpreted differently (Nonaka & Takeuchi, 1995). From the combination of approaches based on technologies and company organisation, different conceptual models for a holistic transfer of knowledge have been developed in the past (Grimpe & Hussinger, 2008). These can be seen as a paradigm of learning organisations. Companies, with their internal structure, are receptive to new trends and proactively support the learning process of their employees. These companies are in a position to constantly develop and change, as well as to react dynamically to internal and external effects, thus successfully competing. Knowledge in an organisation can be broadly classified into two categories (Groever & Froese, 2016): explicit and tacit knowledge. Explicit knowledge is that which can be measured, captured, examined and easily be passed on to others in a codified format - a formal and systematic language. Tacit knowledge, on the other hand, is highly personal, context-specific and comes from one's experience. It is hard to measure, capture or examine. That might be too narrow in the light of new cyber-physical systems as self-organising and decision-capable technical entities (Gronau, 2015). In the era of Industry 4.0 and digitalisation, companies can also manage tacit knowledge. In the future, at least some of the competencies to make decisions will lie with technical actors (Gronau, N., Thim, C., Ullrich, A., Vladova, G., & Weber, E., 2016).

Knowledge transfer in organisations can be defined as the process through which one unit (e.g., group, department, or division) is affected by the experience of another (Argote & Ingram, 2000). According to Argote and Ingram (2000), knowledge transfer in organisations manifests itself through changes in the knowledge or performance of the recipient units. Thus, knowledge transfer can be measured by measuring changes in knowledge or changes in performance. Experience in the field of knowledge transfer has demonstrated knowledge transfer to be a phenomenon that inherently involves interdependencies and asymmetries between providers and recipients of knowledge, and difficulties during different knowledge transfer stages (Caloghirou, Y., Kastelli, I. & Tsakanika, A., 2004; Wehn & Montalvo, 2016).

Figure 1 shows a simplified version of the 5-step model of transfer of knowledge in companies as described by Gilbert and Cordey-Hayes, (1996) and which is often used in literature. It shows the process or the successive steps for a consistent transfer of knowledge leading to successful technological innovation.

The first step corresponds to the basic identification of knowledge in the sense of a knowledge acquisition. As the basis of the knowledge transfer, this can also be understood as the identification of important trends or the identification of potentially useful findings from basic research. On this basis, the communication of knowledge takes place in verbal or written form. In essence, this step serves as a first dissemination of knowledge within the company. In order to maintain the knowledge acquired and communicated in the following, concrete application in the company is indispensable. The results of the application of knowledge enable the company to learn and build new competencies. In the case of successful application, this leads to an acceptance of knowledge or new knowledge in the company. This essential step ensures that the new knowledge is compatible with the basic orientation of the company and often takes place at an individual level. The key to a successful transfer of knowledge lies, ultimately, in the assimilation of knowledge. The results from applied knowledge are firmly integrated into the company and its corporate philosophy. This step is crucial to anchoring the knowledge in the core business processes in the long term and is, thus, essentially different from the often only project-based first application of knowledge (Riedl, M., Garcia, D., Rauch, E., & Matt, D. T., 2016).

Figure 1. Simplified version of the 5-step model for the transfer of knowledge in companies
(Gilbert & Cordey-Hayes, 1996)

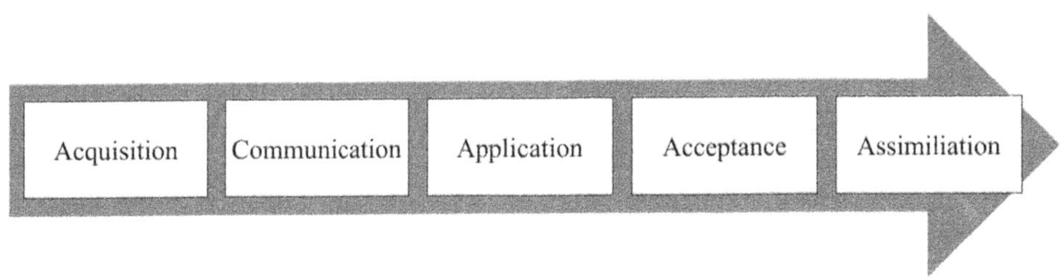

In particular, implicit expert knowledge is only successfully transferred if the recipient is able to work with this knowledge independently of the source. The knowledge is, thus, integrated into the company and its processes so that an independent problem solution is possible. An on-site training methodology and proactive support in the initial application of knowledge (Szulanski, 2000), for example, through coaching with the aim of supporting knowledge dissemination, directly correcting and directly reporting back, can be supported by knowledge-based educators.

In principle, different channels are possible for the above-mentioned process of transferring knowledge from research into industry. These can be distinguished with regard to their relative importance (Bekkers & Freitas, 2008). The authors conclude in their experimental investigation that the different weighting of channels of knowledge transfer depends on the following factors:

1. Basic characteristics of specific knowledge (such as implicit / explicit knowledge, systemic knowledge or expected breakthrough).
2. Subject-specific background of knowledge.
3. Individual and organisational characteristics of those involved in the process of knowledge transfer (experience, publications and patents, entrepreneurship and research environment).

In particular, the importance seems to be independent of the industrial sector in which knowledge is transferred. Table 1 shows an overview of channels of the knowledge transfer divided into higher-ranking groups, as well as their typical characteristics (according to Bekkers & Freitas, 2008).

The authors of the study cited also note that joint research and contract research is well suited to transfer knowledge, which is characterised by many interrelationships. Clearly, each of the different channels of knowledge transfer is obviously suitable for a specific context. Formal technology transfer, for example, through joint research and contract research, and informal technology transfer, for example, through workshops or exchanges of workers, influence each other and are complementary to one another by, for example, informal contacts supporting the quality of a formal technology transfer (Grimpe & Hussinger, 2008).

In addition to the distinctive qualities of knowledge itself (Argote & Ingram, 2000; Chen, 2004), the key factors in the successful knowledge transfer are the trust between the two partners (Szulanski, 2000; Szulanski, G., Jensen, R. J., 2004), the organisational structures of knowledge exchange (Szulanski, 1996), the motivation (Bock & Kim, 2002; Kuo & Shih, 2014) and the commitment of the partners (Amesse & Cohendet, 2001). For a successful transfer of knowledge, both appropriate skills for acquiring knowledge on the part of the receiving partner as well as for knowledge dissemination on the other hand are required (Martin & Salomon, 2003; Schulze, A., Brojerdi, G., & von Krogh, G., 2014).

On-site training is an appropriate measure for the understanding of important contextual information, especially for knowledge with interchanges (Carlile & Rebentisch, 2003). In addition, the decontextualisation of knowledge (Cummings & Teng, 2003) and the support for the application of knowledge (Schulze, A., Brojerdi, G., & von Krogh, G., 2014), especially on the spot (Szulanski, 2000), support a successful transfer of knowledge to industry. Implicit expert knowledge is often based on many years of experience and forms the basis, which can be passed on in a knowledge transfer. At the same time, however, the ability of the knowledge-imparting partner is also essential to recognise the significance of the relevant knowledge for the specific field of application (Szulanski, G., Jensen, R. J., 2004). The more understanding is available for the application, the more efficiently knowledge can be obtained, for example, using suitable analogies, well-understood examples and appropriate metaphors (Hashweh, 2005).

Table 1. Channels of the knowledge transfer divided into superordinate groups, as well as their typical characteristics

Superordinate Groups of Knowledge Transfer		Characteristics
Scientific publications, conferences and workshops	• Scientific publications or professional publications and reports. • Participation in conferences and workshops. • Personal contacts (informal).	Important, especially if the knowledge is well-written and many interrelationships, especially for IT.
Exchange of labour	• Graduates as employees. • Students as trainees. • University staff as employees in industry. • Employees with simultaneous employment in research and industry. • Temporary exchanges of workers.	Important, especially, when breakthroughs are to be expected and the knowledge is difficult to document or publish.
Joint and contract research	• Collaborative projects in the area of R&D (in the context of funding programs). • Contract research. • Financing of PhD. projects. • Consultancy services by university staff.	Important, especially to transfer published knowledge as well as systemic knowledge and knowledge with many interchanges, especially with large companies and universities as well as with regard to the IT sector.
Contact via alumni or professional associations	• Personal contact through memberships in professional associations. • Personal contact through alumni organisations.	Important, especially for basic research and the area of economics and business models, as well as electrical engineering.
Organisation of specific activities	• Contractual in-business training and training measures. • Spin-offs of the university. • Specific activities through university technology transfer agency. • Shared facilities (for example, laboratories, equipment, offices).	Less important for the transfer of knowledge in the field of mechanical engineering. Especially important to transfer systemic knowledge and knowledge with many interchanges.
Patents and Licensing	• Patents (Patent Office or Patent Databases). • Licensing patents of the university or 'know-how' licenses.	Important in the case of a large number of published patents and knowledge with many interchanges.

Source: (According to Bekkers & Freitas, 2008)

In particular, in the transfer of knowledge between companies, the aim is to identify the area of knowledge which is helpful for the other partner, but, at the same time, to find the compromise of not having to give up its own advantage with regard to specialisation in the market and in the competition. The ability to find the right balance is a key part of the successful transfer of knowledge between companies (Schulze, A., Brojerdi, G., & von Krogh, G., 2014). For this, the cooperation of very heterogeneous partners can be very helpful, e.g. with regard to core competencies or industry sectors. The better the knowledge-imparting partner understands the motivation and abilities of the other partner's knowledge, the better he can select adequate channels and tools for efficient knowledge transfer (Martin & Salomon, 2003). It is important to decouple and abstract the knowledge of the original topic area, while, at the same time, embedding it in sufficient background information, so that a successful application in the new topic area becomes possible. Carlile & Rebentisch (2003) note that, in particular, the process of knowing knowledge with the knowledge-imparting partner can be of decisive importance in many situations. It is necessary to create a common language, a common understanding among all partners of the knowledge transfer (Schulze, A., Brojerdi, G., & von Krogh, G., 2014). Schulze et al. (2014) emphasise, in particular, the possible collaborative character of a knowledge transfer. Also, for the knowledge-imparting partner, effects arise from which it can profit, e.g. through a deepening insight into a new field of application of knowledge.

A possible approach of Industry 4.0 knowledge transfer in SMEs is presented by Ganzarain and Errasti (2016). In their stage process model, companies are guided in knowledge transfer and finding new opportunities for diversification and optimisation in areas within Industry 4.0. The stage process model is structured in three main stages:

1. **Stage 1:** Vision
2. **Stage 2:** Roadmap
3. **Stage 3:** Projects

In the first stage, internal and external partners are involved to understand what is Industry 4.0. In addition, the company analyses its own capacity and resources in introducing Industry 4.0. At the end of the first stage, a vision for Industry 4.0 should be defined. The second stage is dedicated to developing a roadmap for implementing Industry 4.0 in SMEs. The given approach of Ganzarain and Errasti (2016) is a more strategy-oriented approach and aims to define an Industry 4.0 strategy for SMEs. There can be found elements for knowledge transfer, but the focus lies in defining a vision, strategies and a roadmap for implementation. In the following, the authors present a 5-step methodology that is more focused on the process of knowledge transfer as well as the identification of own competencies in Industry 4.0 and the resulting potential in its introduction.

5-STEP METHODOLOGY TO FACILITATE THE KNOWLEDGE TRANSFER OF INDUSTRY 4.0 PRINCIPLES TO SMES

Based on the above described general scientific fundamentals and the long-term experience of the authors in introducing lean production systems and flexible automation in small and medium-sized enterprises (Matt, 2008; 2009; 2013), as well as based on Ganzarain and Errasti (2016), a 5-step approach has been developed which is suitable for Smart Factory concepts in SMEs. The proposed approach is illustrated in Figure 2.

While Steps 3, 4 and 5 can be used for every type of industrial company to implement Industry 4.0, the first two steps of the proposed methodology are important for SMEs. The main difficulty of SMEs is to understand what is Industry 4.0 and how these new technologies can improve productivity in their company. Many SMEs don't have enough qualified staff and, therefore, need the first step to train their people and to generate the awareness that Industry 4.0 is of crucial importance for the future of the company. Further, the second step should help SMEs to organise their ideas and needs regarding Industry 4.0. While many of the emerging Industry 4.0 technologies and tools can be applied in large companies, this does not apply for SMEs. In the following, the above shown five steps of the proposed methodology are explained in detail.

Step 1: Information and Awareness

In the context of Industry 4.0, Smart Factory, Cyber-Physical-Systems, etc., there is currently a conceptual diversity and a definition jungle in which SMEs are often not able to cope with the issue and, thus, have a certain scepticism. At the same time, there is often a lack of direct reference to one's own entrepreneurial reality, as well as suitable case studies, which could facilitate the projection of theoretical

Figure 2. 5-step methodology for the introduction of Smart Factory concepts in SMEs

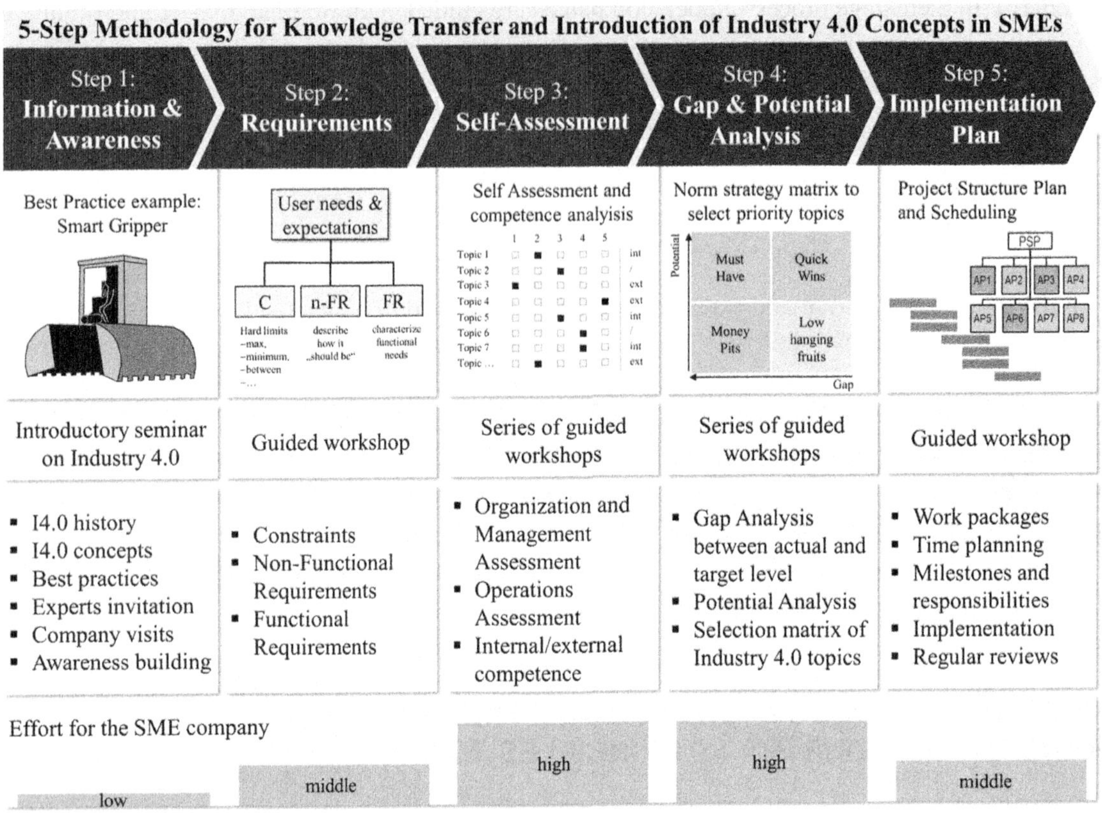

approaches and laboratory concepts into their own productive environment. Therefore, an introductory seminar will explain the most important terms and concepts of Industry 4.0 and Smart Factory.

For example, the often very abstract term 'cyber-physical system' (CPS) becomes immediately more comprehensible if there are illustrative examples behind it. Figure 3 shows an example of the application of CPS using an intelligent gripper for wood chips in an industrial heating system. Equipped with suitable sensors for the measurement of moisture, ash content and granularity of the wood chips, this CPS collects measured data. Through the collected data, the system composes - depending on the respective operating state of the burner communicated directly to the gripper (M2M - machine2machine) - the right mixture of different wood chips, thus minimising CO2 emissions (Garcia, D., Riedl, M., Niedermayr, F., Waid, S., & Matt, D. T., 2015; Niedermayr, F., Waid, S., Garcia, D., Riedl, M., & Matt, D. T., 2015).

In combination with the introductory seminar, SMEs should have the opportunity to see some best practice examples from other companies. This is possible in three ways: a) integrating examples of implementations in other SMEs, as in Figure 3, b) inviting experts from industrial practice to speak about their best practices or c) visits to best practice companies.

In this phase, it is important to generate awareness that the world does not stand still and processes as well as systems are changing. Therefore, companies also have to change according to this new trend of Industry 4.0. In this phase, the first to steps in the knowledge transfer model of Gilbert and Cordey-Hayes (1996) – see also Figure 1 – are fulfilled.

Figure 3. Smart Gripper: Sensors and intelligent control algorithms for optimising the emissions of an industrial heating system
(Garcia, D., Riedl, M., Niedermayr, F., Waid, S., & Matt, D. T., 2015)

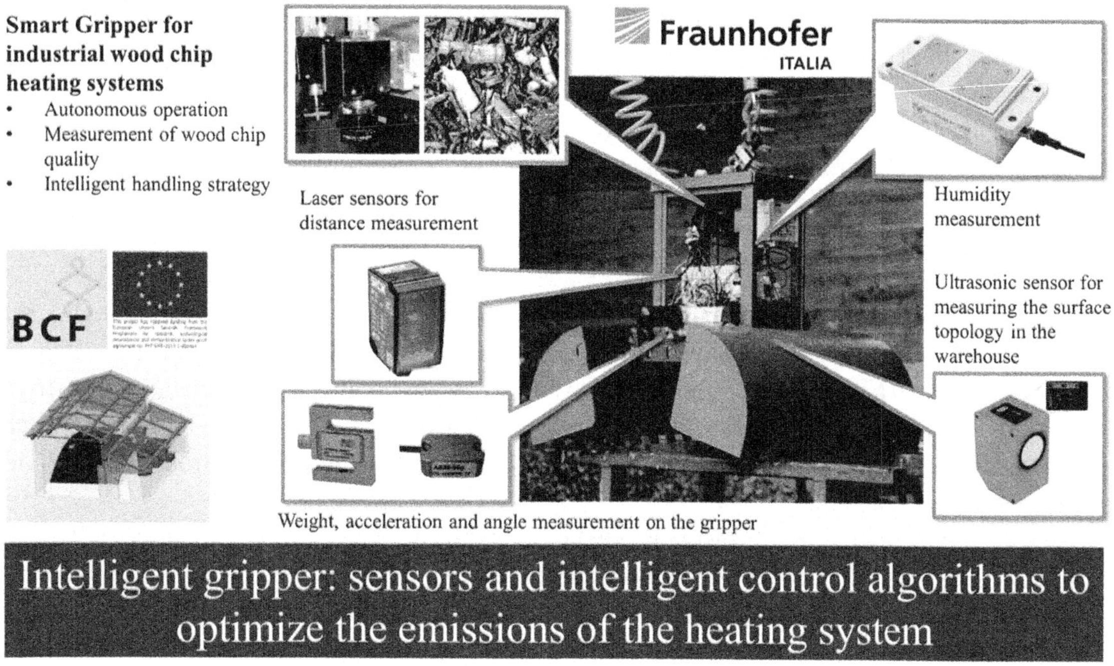

Step 2: Requirements

In a second step, the requirements for the introduction of Industry 4.0 have to be defined in a workshop. In this phase, the participants of the workshop are informed about the principles of Industry 4.0 and should express a 'wish list' of expectations regarding Industry 4.0 in their company. This initial collection of desires, user needs and requirements should be used to define the limitations for investigation as well as the constraints for the initiative. Axiomatic Design Theory is used for the categorisation of requirements. Axiomatic Design was developed by Nam P. Suh (Suh, 1990) as a design method whereby a designer starts from the collection of customer requirements or needs, translating them into functional requirements. Based on the functional requirements, possible design solutions are derived in a systematical top-down decomposition. In our research, we do not use the whole Axiomatic Design approach, but only the initial phase of collecting requirements in order to categorise the requirements in a reasonable way. In Axiomatic Design theory (Suh, 1990; Thompson, 2013), customer requirements are differentiated into the following categories:

- **Constraints:** The determination of a hard limit usually indicates the presence of a constraint, defined as follows. Constraints can be a defined number of minimum or maximum. An example for a constraint is when space in production is limited to a certain number of square metres or that the budget for the introduction of Industry 4.0 is limited to a certain value, due to the financial limits of the firm.

- **Non-Functional Requirements:** Non-functional requirements focus on 'how' the artefact should be, in order to meet the standards set by the involved stakeholders. Their omission can compromise functional requirements. Non-functional requirements can be distinguished by the use of the form 'should be', together with an adjective that aims to influence stakeholders' awareness In case of a smart manufacturing system for SMEs, a non-functional requirement could be that the production system should be productive with moderate production costs.
- **Functional Requirements:** Functional requirements help the designer in the determination of the sub-levels requirements and related design solutions. They should be de independent from each other to reduce complexity of the system design and characterise the functional needs of the artefact.

The moderator in this workshop has to collect, as a first step, all customer needs through a brainstorming round. In the next step, the individual customer needs should be discussed and categorised according to the three types of requirements shown above. This supports the participants to keep in mind what are the limitations, the main expectations and what functional topics need to be worked. Usually, customer attributes have to be rewritten or reformulated, when categorised as constraint, non-functional requirement or functional requirement.

Where possible, tangible and measurable targets should be defined in this stage. If requirements are measurable, the greater the acceptance in the management and the workforce, which, in turn, considerably facilitates and accelerates implementation. In addition to business-oriented requirements (such as productivity, inventories, flexibility, delivery service level, etc.), other objectives can also be incorporated, for example, improved ergonomics or 'demographic-free' jobs.

Step 3: Self-Assessment

Based on the defined requirements in the form of constraints, non-functional requirements and functional requirements, the actual situation should be discussed together to self-assess the actual competence and achievements in Industry 4.0 concepts and principles.

Such a self-assessment and competence analysis should be conducted on two levels: a) organisation and management and b) operations. Therefore, groups should be divided in two parts, one working on more management and strategy-oriented topics and the other group working on operational tasks.

Organisation and Management Assessment

The analysis of the organisation consists of an assessment if companies are Industry 4.0 ready and if they only apply Industry 4.0 concepts in their management structure or processes. While much Industry 4.0-related literature gives recommendations about technological changes, very few describe also the organisational challenges in the introduction of Industry 4.0. The following are the main dimensions to be analysed in this group, according to Anderl et al. (2015) and Schuhmacher et al. (2016):

1. **Strategy:** Vision, strategy, roadmap, business models.
2. **Leadership:** Management competence, central coordination of Industry 4.0.
3. **Governance:** Data security management, protection of intellectual property, labour regulations for Industry 4.0.

4. **Supply Chain Network:** Digital competence of customer and supplier, digitalisation of processes along the supply chain.
5. **Culture:** Knowledge-sharing, open innovation, awareness of Industry 4.0.
6. **People:** ICT competencies of people, willingness and openness of employees.
7. **Process Digitalisation:** ICT tools for digitalisation, mobile devices, real-time communication.

Operations Assessment

This can be done most systematically along the value chain of the company. A previous value-stream design is suitable as a method to support this phase and to better understand the material and information flow. Many SMEs are already familiar with this instrument from the lean toolkit and very often already have a current state map of their value stream. Thus, it can be applied without many explanations. In the case of the collective discussion of the value stream (or the value streams), the actual state of competence in Industry 4.0 implementation in operations can be investigated. In addition, initial ideas of potential areas for improvement and application can be identified. The following are the main dimensions to be analysed in operations according to Anderl et al. (2015) and Schuhmacher et al. (2016):

8. **Product:** Individualisation of products, digitalisation of products, product intelligence, integration of sensors, connectivity of products
9. **Production Control:** Decentralisation in production planning and control, use of modern tools like Manufacturing Execution Systems (MES), connectivity of systems.
10. **Shop Floor Management:** Big data analytics for production, use and evaluation of data, monitoring, visualisation of shop floor data.
11. **Operator 4.0:** Changing role of the operator, competencies and skills of operators, willingness and openness of employees.
12. **Technologies:** ICT in production and logistics, man-machine interaction, automation, advanced manufacturing processes, predictive maintenance.

In both, the organisation and management assessment as well as the operations assessment, the participants should discuss the actual state in the achievement of the above described dimensions and elements. In order to manage a self-assessment or an assisted assessment through external partners or experts, every element in the dimensions has to be evaluated using a rating scale. There are different possibilities to define such a rating scale. One possibility is to evaluate the elements on a Likert scale reaching from 'not implemented' to 'fully implemented' (Schumacher, A., Erol, S., & Sihn, W., 2016). Another possibility is to define formulated and clearly defined stages of maturity for each element, with practical examples (Anderl, R., Picard, A., Wang, Y., Fleischer, J., Dosch, S., Klee, B., & Bauer, J., 2016), in order to facilitate an assessment by the group of participants. In the second case, one maturity stage could be closer to the other. Both possibilities are illustrated in Figure 4. Therefore, in our case, we suggest the use of a Likert scale to guarantee a neutral rating.

Further, it helps to document in the workshops whether competencies in the above described dimensions and elements are available and, if so, on which of the two following levels:

- **Internal Competence:** Competence in own organisational structure and own staff – e.g. experienced specialists in robotics or in vision systems, as well as successfully implemented projects.

Figure 4. Assessment of Industry 4.0 elements based on a) Likert scale or b) maturity stages

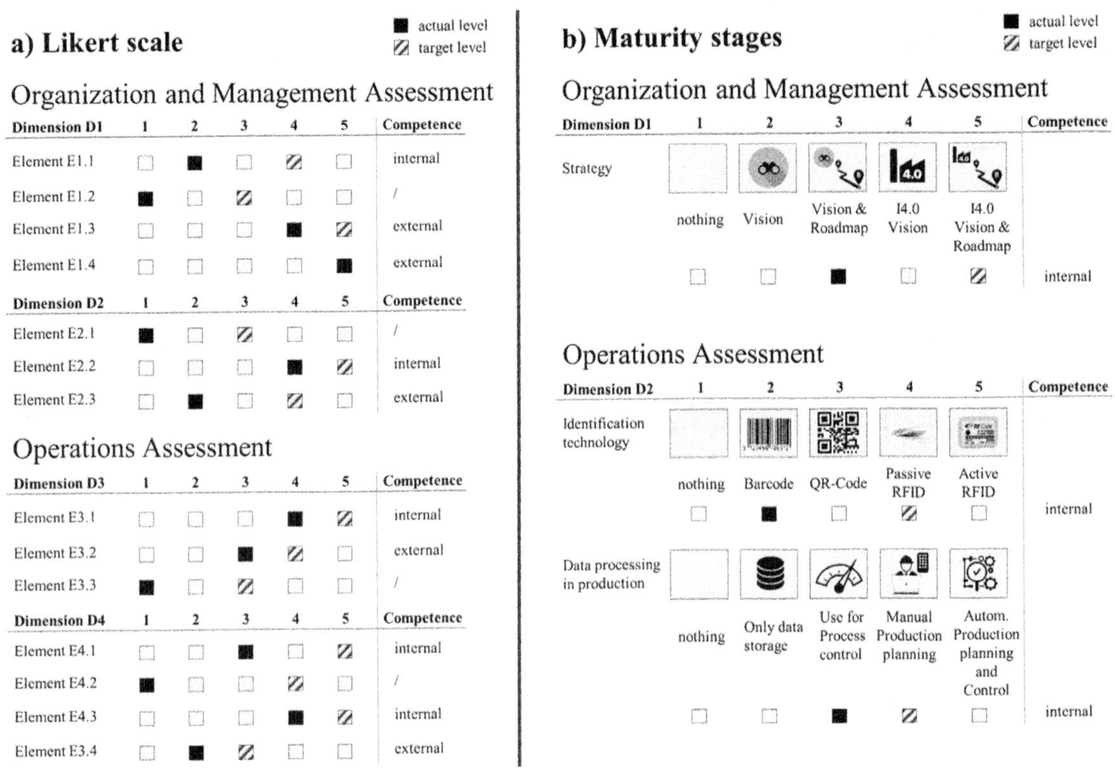

- **External Competence:** Access to competencies through an experienced and qualified supplier in the supplier network - e.g. a supplier with a high expertise in sensors.

Step 4: Gap and Potential Analysis

The previous self-assessment and competence analysis summarises the current situation of a company dealing with the introduction of Industry 4.0. In a next step, a gap analysis should be done to identify where Industry 4.0 topics are already implemented and where gaps are significant. According to the requirements defined in Step 2, the single dimensions and elements have to be discussed in order to define the target level of competence to be achieved and the resulting gap between actual level and needed or requested level (see Figure 5).

Depending on the defined requirements, some dimensions and elements can be more important than others. For example, for a firm, traceability and identification of the product along the production flow can be highly important, while automation or man-machine interaction are less or not important. In this case, the gap in both examples could be the same, but the expected potential is different. Thus, gap analysis should be followed by the determination of importance or potential through implementation of an Industry 4.0 element. In a similar case described in Schuhmacher et al. (2016), the authors propose a factor for evaluating the potential with a Likert scale reaching from 'no potential' (rating = 1) to 'very high potential' (rating = 5). The evaluation of the potential could be determined by individual evaluation of every participant in the groups and then calculating the average overall.

Figure 5. Strategies for selection of Industry 4.0 topics to implement - matrix with gap on x-axis and potential on the y-axis

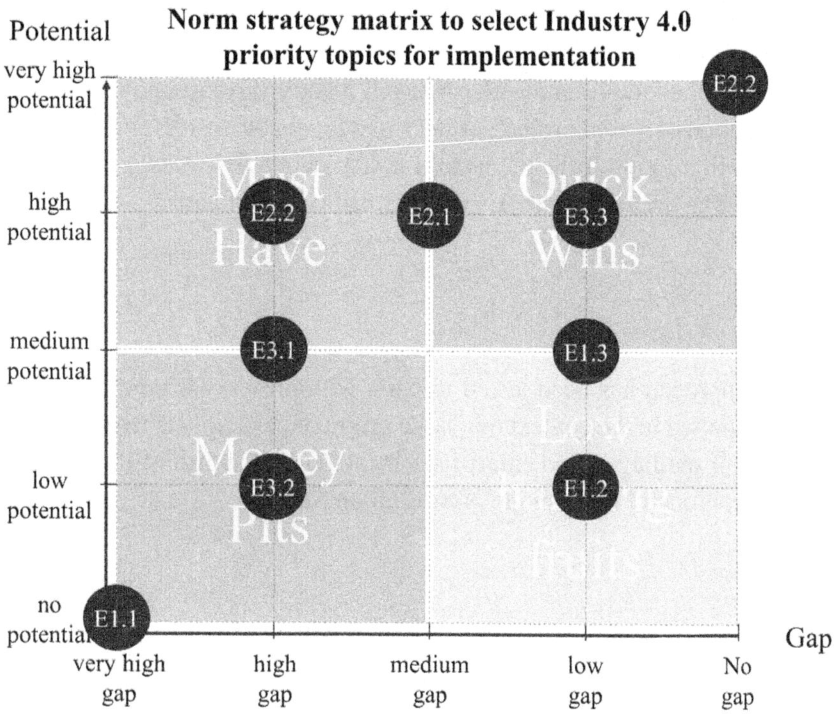

Based on the evaluation of the gap and the potential in implementing these elements or concepts, a matrix can be designed in order to select those concepts with most potential and to determine also the needed effort and time for implementation. Figure 5 shows the structure of such a matrix. If the elements in Figure 5 show a high potential and only a low gap to achieve it, we speak about so called 'quick wins' and, thus, Industry 4.0 concepts with a high priority in implementation combined with a short-term implementation. If the elements show a lower potential and only a low gap, then these are called 'low hanging fruits' and can be categorised as short-term concepts of lower priority. Elements with a high potential combined with a high effort to overcome a high gap are called 'must have' and need a well-defined medium-term planning of time and resources. In the fourth case, a combination of low potential and a high gap, we speak of 'money pits' and the company should try to avoid them and not invest in the implementation of these Industry 4.0 concepts.

Step 5: Implementation Plan

Based on the results from Figure 5, the areas of actions are selected and detailed in a further workshop, involving further employees and skilled workers, where work packages are derived and then, subsequently, organised in an implementation plan. In the implementation plan, the teams, deadlines and responsibilities are defined and documented. This implementation plan is then used as roadmap for a step-by-step conversion and monitoring of the progress in each work package.

Before concluding the phase of work package definition, the project team should check whether all constraints, and non-functional as well as functional requirements, are represented and respected in the work packages. If there are any inconsistencies, the project team can react and adapt the implementation plan before the kick-off of the operative implementation phase.

In the case of extensive and important work packages, it could be reasonable to start with smaller pilot projects. The implementation of pilot projects creates first touchable results and, therefore, acceptance of employees. Through such pilot projects, the last three steps in the knowledge transfer model of Gilbert and Cordey-Hayes (1996) – see also Figure 1 – can be fulfilled (Application, Acceptance, Assimilation).

CASE STUDIES

The above described approach has been tested in parts within two case studies. In Case Study A, the procedure model was applied in the context of a large group of participants from several different industries, all of them small or medium-sized enterprises located in the North of Italy. Case Study B reports the application of the approach in one single North Italian SME.

Case Study A

The methodology described in the previous section was carried out in collaboration with several companies from Northern Italy within the framework of a six-month series of events. A total of 40 participants from the industry participated in the event and scientific support was provided by an interdisciplinary team of scientific staff. The companies involved had a very heterogeneous industrial background. Figure 6 shows the applied steps of the Five-Step Methodology, while Table 2 shows the key data of the case study.

Step 1: As the initial step of Case Study A, an introductory seminar with speakers, bringing together scientific and practical knowledge, was held for the participants. To prepare the Self-Assessment in Step 3, the participants had to fill in a template asking for specific requirements for their company as an exercise after the seminar (Step 2). For the Self-Assessment, the group of participants was divided into two working groups. In these working groups, the participants completed the subsequent steps of Self-Assessment (Step 3) and Gap & Potential Analysis (Step 4) with scientific assistance.

At this point, the main results of the working groups are summarised, since these can be regarded as the most important component and result of the intended knowledge transfer. The workshops in this case study covered only the operational analysis and, thus, topics on different levels of operations in the

Figure 6. Applied steps of the Five -Step Methodology for Knowledge Transfer and introduction of Industry 4.0 Concepts in SMEs in Case Study A with a set of 40 North Italian SME.

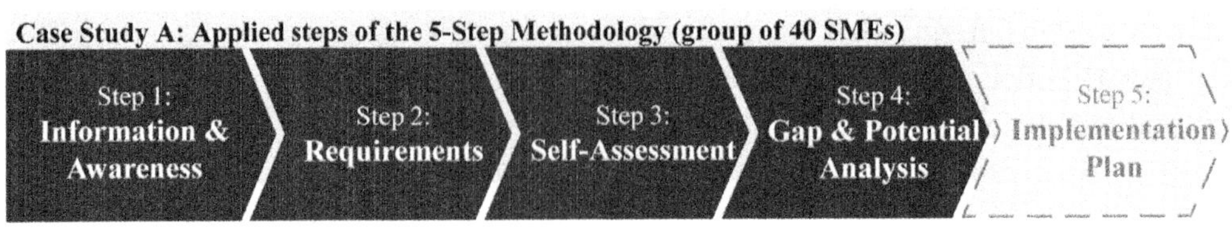

company from the supply chain to the operational level, through planning and monitoring tasks at the process level up to individual production modules and workstations. The following list gives an overview of the treated use cases:

- Process monitoring and remote maintenance.
- Smart maintenance.
- Transparent order management and prioritisation of orders.
- Self-diagnosis and self-optimisation in production processes.
- Virtual production paper: dynamic work instructions.
- Smart workstation: assistance in assembly and logistics processes.

Table 3 shows an example of some of the project ideas elaborated in the working groups and provides an overview of the thematic scope and the first steps of applying the acquired knowledge by the participants with corresponding Gap & Potential assessment (Step 4).

In a concluding round of feedback, the participants positively evaluated both the approach of the transfer of knowledge as well as the results. The following selection of individual comments from the participants gives an impression:

I found the contact with other companies and the overview of the current status in other companies particularly helpful.

The discussion in the working groups and the exchange taking place were a great added value for the whole event.

The focus of the seminar series and workshops on CPPS supports the development of the first pilot applications in the company.

The exchange of ideas and openness in the discussions and working groups are seen as a great benefit. Looking beyond the boundaries of one's own business can help identify important trends and identify

Table 2. Key data of the case study

Key Data	
Participants	40 participants with a majority of engineering background and several years of industrial experience.
Industries	• Automation technology. • Automotive. • Battery technology. • Domotics and building automation. • Industrial gases. • Metal processing. • Utilities in the field of energy and telecommunications. • measuring systems. • Agrochemistry. • Medical technology.
Size and Turnover of Companies	SMEs with 50 to 250 employees, as well as revenues between €5 and €50 million.

Table 3. Exemplar excerpt from the project ideas worked out during the workshops, including a short qualitative assessment

Selection of Worked Out Project Ideas (Qualitative Assessment)	
Digitalisation on the Shopfloor: Assistance functionalities for employees during assembly processes. ➔Idea: Smart workstations to increase quality in assembly.	Gap: medium-high Potential: high Time-line: medium-term
Relevant and mobile Information: Lean, Industry 4.0 and problem management ➔Idea: Provide relevant information and work instructions dynamically on mobile devices	Gap: low Potential: high Time-line: short-term
From Rocket Science to Shopfloor Reality: Lean, Industry 4.0 and prioritisation in order management ➔Idea: Electronic tagging in internal processes (analogous to supermarket)	Gap: low Potential: medium-high Time-line: short-term
Communication and Information Management in Industry 4.0: Lean, Industry 4.0 and holistic information management ➔Idea: smart sensors and information in real time	Gap: medium Potential: medium-high Readiness: medium-term
Intelligent Products to stay competitive: Innovative products through integration of Internet-of-Things approaches and additional services ➔Idea: Support of life cycle management through networked products	Gap: medium Potential: medium-high Time-line: medium-term
Improve Machine & Process Control with better data & connection: Optimisation of process control ➔Idea: Efficient response to digital traceability issues	Gap: medium-high Potential: high Time-line: medium-term

the necessary knowledge that a company should adopt in the future. Although the workshops are seen as great added value in the individual companies, some participants judged the time for the effective elaboration of the project ideas as too short.

Case Study A addressed the first four stages of the five-stage model with a special focus on operations. However, this did not happen at the company level, but rather as part of an awareness raising of the company's own knowledge bearers, which can subsequently bring this new knowledge into the company.

This is the reason why the last step of the 5-step methodology presented in this chapter was not executed as part of the case study carried out with this group of companies. Organised on project level, the scientific monitoring had to stop after Step 4' nevertheless, participating companies stated their interest to proceed with implementation plans, but, unfortunately, on their own. Confidentiality regarding participating competitors was mentioned as the main reason for these decisions. As described by Gilbert and Cordey-Hayes (1996), the acceptance of new knowledge takes place after the successful application, especially at the individual level. In particular, the accompanying workshop corresponds to the approach described by Szulanski (2000) for effective on-site training and proactive support in the first application by the scientific coaches.

The channels used in the described method for the transfer of knowledge and, in particular, the contents to be transferred with regard to the topic Industry 4.0, correspond to the respective characteristics according to Bekkers and Freitas (2008); see also Table 1. At the same time, however, it becomes clear that the described methodology can only be a first step for the transfer of knowledge into the company. Further scientific support in the application or integration into the company or its processes is very important for the sustainability of the results. According to Grimpe and Hussinger (2008), this would seem to be a suitable complement to the already implemented steps to raise awareness and to anchor the new knowledge within the company.

Case Study B

The second case study reports the application of the approach in one single medium-sized company. It is taken from a (still ongoing) project with an Italian medium-sized manufacturer of sanitary articles. Figure 7 shows the applied steps of the Five-Steps Methodology in case study B.

The company has always strategically positioned itself as a 'flexibility leader' and describes itself as an 'industrially organized craft enterprise'. All articles are produced just-in-time on customer orders, 40% of which are custom-made. The company has always strived to achieve the highest degree of flexibility in terms of variants and volumes without compromising productivity. As a result, a holistic production system was introduced as early as 2001 according to the principles of lean production and, from then on, continuously improved. In 2009, product identification and tracking using RFID (Radio Frequency Identification) was introduced. RFID technology is an important building block or even the prerequisite for entry into many Industry 4.0 applications. Products and components can be clearly identified and tracked by radio. Firstly, the RFID identification was used primarily for tracking the production order, for automatically labelling the packaged products, for monitoring inventory levels, and for checking the completeness of shipments. However, this is only a fraction of the possibilities offered by this technology in the context of the Smart Factory.

The now cramped space conditions at the old production site have prompted the company management to build a new 'greenfield' plant, which is to be ready for the middle of 2018. In the course of this factory-planning project, the opportunities are now also being taken of planning the new factory according to the principles of Industry 4.0.

Therefore, a project team consisting of internal and external specialists and executives was compiled and the Smart Factory 2018 project was launched. The 5-step approach described above was applied to identify and implement Industry 4.0 technologies and solutions. Corresponding to Step 1 of the presented methodology, an introductory training in the principles of Industry 4.0 and in requirements analysis, the value chain of the company 'from ramp to ramp' was carried out. In comparison to Case Study A, this initial step was tailored to the demands and specific already existing knowledge of the company, coming, in particular, from past individual experiences (see above). Therefore, experts with scientific and practical background sensitised the participants in a series of seminars. Two working groups of company employees defined the individual requirements in an iterative process – the organisational and management oriented requirements on the one hand and the operational perspective on the other (Step 2).

As result of Step 3, these working groups identified the following topics of interest for future development: 1) order processing (information flow from customer order to delivery note and invoice); 2) goods receipt and warehouse; 3) component manufacturing; 4) picking and material supply, assembly; 5) packaging and dispatch.

Figure 7. Applied steps of the Five-Step Methodology for Knowledge Transfer and introduction of Industry 4.0 Concepts in SMEs in Case Study B with an SME from the manufacturing sector.

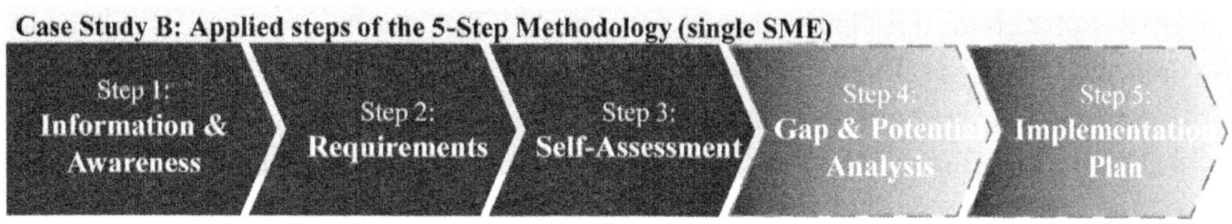

As the first approach to Step 4 (and subsequently Step 5) of the methodology, the gap and potential of possible solutions were analysed on the basis of a macro value stream plan. At the time of writing this chapter, these phases are still work in process; therefore, final results will be reported in future publications of this case study. Nevertheless, the potential of the methodology in general was perceived by the participants, e.g. 79 ideas and applications for Industry 4.0 concepts were recently developed and validated in this project. As part of the ongoing Step 5 of the methodology, these ideas were grouped together into a total of eight work packages, where they were further concretised. For each of the eight defined work packages, a separate project team was set up, which first carried out concept elaboration with investment planning and an accurate profitability analysis for the measures within the work package.

In the meantime, the planning phase for the new and smart greenfield factory is nearly concluded and the results are very promising. The research team will also continue to assist the company in the implementation phase in order to collect more information and data that might deliver valuable inputs for the further research work in this field.

DISCUSSION AND OUTLOOK FOR FUTURE RESEARCH

However, the described application of the developed methodology for knowledge transfer and introduction of Industry 4.0 principles in the case study has different boundary conditions, which must be taken into account when the described results are transferred. In principle, of course, findings obtained from the consideration of only one case study are not easily transferable to other circumstances. In this context, the discussed case studies have a quite contrasting character. While Case Study A is implementing the presented methodology on a higher, more general level, while also integrating some aspects of open innovation approaches, Case Study B is focusing more on the specific conditions and individual experience of one SME. Nevertheless, the first analysis of results seems to prove the compatibility of the presented methodological approach to both situations. In addition, the development of the methodology along with the implementation and evaluation of the case study were carried out by the same research team. Therefore, the described methodology can be used and analysed in other case studies. For further discussion of the approach, it is important to record a larger set of results. This also applies to the specific background of the company involved in the case study and its employees. In the further tests of the methodical approach of the transfer of knowledge, it will be of crucial importance to test this in various industrial contexts. At the same time, it is not unlikely that there are significant regional differences in the academic, industrial and political frameworks that influence the successful transfer of knowledge from the industry to cyber-physical production systems. Therefore, the initial starting point of an SME must be kept in consideration and the fact that this topic can be addressed on various levels: the contents have to be adapted to these specific requirements of the company. This is true not only for the initial situation, but also for mid- and long-term changes, as the contents of the Smart Factory will change in future, hand-in-hand with continuous technological advances. This suggests that the capability to learn and adapt will be crucial for companies on different levels in the future (as it was in the past). A potential methodological approach for this challenge was presented by the authors and partly validated in practice during the presented use cases. In order to overcome the given limitations and further develop the methodology, the authors will carry out, over the next four years, the collaborative research project SME 4.0 – Industry 4.0 for SMEs, financed by the European Commission within the H2020-MSCA-RISE-2016 program (grant n° 734713 – www.sme40.eu), which involves international research and industry partners from Europe, Asia and the USA. The aim of this research project is to analyse, in the first two years, the specific requirements of SMEs in the introduction of Industry 4.0 solutions. In the following two years, the research team will be working on concepts and solutions for smart SME manufacturing, smart SME logistics and organisational models and implementation strategies for smart SMEs.

CONCLUSION

The concept of the Smart Factory, based on the approaches and technologies of Industry 4.0, is currently being discussed intensively in research as well as in industrial practice. The proposed 5-step approach for knowledge transfer and the introduction, as well as implementation, of Industry 4.0 concepts is aimed primarily at SMEs in order to help them with a methodological guidance to access the potentials of Industry 4.0 in a step-by-step procedure towards the planning, design and implementation of a Smart Factory.

Within this research, a methodology of an efficient transfer of knowledge in the context of Industry 4.0 was derived from a careful literature research and evaluated by the promising experiences made in two industrial case studies, wherein Industry 4.0-relevant knowhow and concepts were transferred from research into industrial practice. The methodology serves, above all, to sensitise small and medium-sized enterprises to the possible potentials of the so-called Industry 4.0. The first results from the case studies suggest that the use of complementary channels of informal knowledge transfer within the framework of seminar events and collaborative on-site training methods enables industry participants, within a short time, to be able to develop suitable project approaches for the use of Industry 40 applications in their own company.

REFERENCES

Amesse, F., & Cohendet, P. (2001). Technology transfer revisited from the perspective of the knowledge-based economy. *Research Policy*, *30*(9), 1459–1478. doi:10.1016/S0048-7333(01)00162-7

Anderl, R., Picard, A., Wang, Y., Fleischer, J., Dosch, S., Klee, B., & Bauer, J. (2015). *Leitfaden Industrie 4.0-Orientierungshilfe zur Einführung in den Mittelstand [Guideline Industry 4.0-Guidance for the introduction into middle sized enterprises]*. Frankfurt, Germany: VDMA Verlag.

Argote, L., & Ingram, P. (2000). Knowledge transfer: A basis for competitive advantage in firms. *Organizational Behavior and Human Decision Processes*, *82*(1), 150–169. doi:10.1006/obhd.2000.2893

Bauer, W., Schlund, S., Marrenbach, D., & Ganschar, O. (2014). *Industrie 4.0 –Volkswirtschaftliches Potenzial für Deutschland [Industry 4.0-Economic potential for Germany]*. Berlin, Germany: BITKOM.

Bekkers, R., & Freitas, I. M. B. (2008). Analyzing knowledge transfer channels between universities and industry: To what degree do sectors also matter? *Research Policy*, *37*(10), 1837–1853. doi:10.1016/j.respol.2008.07.007

Bock, G. W., & Kim, Y. G. (2002). Breaking the myth of rewards: An explanatory study of attitudes about knowledge sharing. *Information Resources Management Journal*, *15*(2), 14–21. doi:10.4018/irmj.2002040102

Brettel, M., Friederichsen, N., Keller, M., & Rosenberg, M. (2014). How Virtualization, Decentralization and Network Building Change the Manufacturing Landscape: An Industry 4.0 Perspective. *International Journal of Mechanical, Aerospace, Industrial. Mechatronic and Manufacturing Engineering*, *8*(1), 37–44.

Caloghirou, Y., Kastelli, I., & Tsakanika, A. (2004). Internal capabilities and external knowledge sources: Complements or substitutes for innovative performance. *Technovation*, *24*(1), 29–39. doi:10.1016/S0166-4972(02)00051-2

Carlile, P. R., & Rebentisch, E. S. (2003). Into the black box: The knowledge transformation cycle. *Management Science*, *49*(9), 1180–1195. doi:10.1287/mnsc.49.9.1180.16564

Chen, C. J. (2004). The effects of knowledge attribute, alliance characteristics, and absorptive capacity on knowledge transfer performance. *R & D Management*, *34*(3), 311–321. doi:10.1111/j.1467-9310.2004.00341.x

Cummings, J. L., & Teng, B. S. (2003). Transferring R&D knowledge: The key factors affecting knowledge transfer success. *Journal of Engineering and Technology Management*, *20*(1-2), 39–68. doi:10.1016/S0923-4748(03)00004-3

Datta, S. P. A. (2015). Dynamic socio-economic disequilibrium catalyzed by the Internet of Things. *Journal of Innovation Management*, *3*(3), 4–9.

Distefano, S., Banerjee, N., & Puliafito, A. (2016). Smart Objects, Infrastructures, and Services in the Internet of Things. International Journal of Distributed Sensor Networks.

Einsiedler, I. (2013). Embedded Systeme für Industrie 4.0. *Production Management*, *18*, 26–28.

Ganzarain, J., & Errasti, N. (2016). Three stage maturity model in SME's toward industry 4.0. *Journal of Industrial Engineering and Management*, *9*(5), 1119–1128. doi:10.3926/jiem.2073

Garcia, D., Riedl, M., Niedermayr, F., Waid, S., & Matt, D. T. (2015, September). *Analysis and simulation of handling algorithm for intelligent movement of a woodchip gripper*. Paper presented at 10th Conference on Sustainable Development of Energy, Water and Environment Systems, Dubrovnik, Croatia.

Gausemeier, J. (2015, February). *Szenario-basierte Entwicklung von Zukunftsoptionen für Industrie 4.0* [Scenario-based development of future options for industry 4.0]. Paper presented at Industry 4.0-Forum Science and Research, Hasso Plattner Institute, University of Potsdam, Germany.

Gilbert, M., & Cordey-Hayes, M. (1996). Understanding the process of knowledge transfer to achieve successful technological innovation. *Technovation*, *16*(6), 301–312. doi:10.1016/0166-4972(96)00012-0

Grimpe, C., & Hussinger, K. (2008). Formal and Informal Technology Transfer from Academia to Industry: Complementarity Effects and Innovation Performance. *ZEW Discussion Papers*, No. 08-080.

Gronau, N. (2015). The influence of Cyber-Physical Systems on the creation of production systems [in German]. *Industrial Management (Des Plaines)*, *3*, 16–20.

Gronau, N., Thim, C., Ullrich, A., Vladova, G., & Weber, E. (2016). *A Proposal to Model Knowledge in Knowledge-Intensive Business Processes.* BMSD.

Grover, R., & Froese, T. M. (2016). Knowledge management in construction using a SocioBIM platform: A case study of AYO smart home project. *Procedia Engineering*, *145*, 1283–1290. doi:10.1016/j.proeng.2016.04.165

Hameed, B., Durr, F., & Rothermel, K. (2011). *RFID based Complex Event Processing in a Smart Real-Time Factory, Expert discussion: Distributed Systems in Smart Spaces*. Retrieved February 19, 2017, from https://www.tk.informatik.tu-darmstadt.de/fileadmin/user_upload/Group_TK/filesDownload/hameed.pdf

Hashweh, M. Z. (2005). Teacher pedagogical construction: A reconfiguration of pedagogical content knowledge. *Teachers and Teaching*, *11*(3), 273–292. doi:10.1080/13450600500105502

Hermann, M., Pentek, T., & Otto, B. (2015). *Design Principles for Industrie 4.0 Scenarios: A Literature Review*. TU Dortmund, Working Paper No. 01 / 2015. Retrieved March 11, 2017, from http://www.snom.mb.tu-dortmund.de/cms/de/forschung/Arbeitsberichte/Design-Principles-for-Industrie-4_0-Scenarios.pdf

Kagermann, H., Lukas, W. D., & Wahlster, W. (2011). Industrie 4.0: Mit dem Internet der Dinge auf dem Weg zur 4. industriellen Revolution [Industry 4.0: With the Internet of Things on the Road to the 4th Industrial Revolution]. *VDI-Nachrichten*, *13*, 2–2.

Kagermann, H., Wahlster, W., & Helbig, J. (2013). *Deutschlands Zukunft als Produktionsstandort sichern. Umsetzungsempfehlungen für das Zukunftsprojekt Industrie, 4.0* [Germany's future as a production site. Implementation recommendations for the industrial sector, 4.0]. Retrieved February 20, 2017,https://www.bmbf.de/files/Umsetzungsempfehlungen_Industrie4_0.pdf

Lasi, H., Fettke, P., Kemper, H. G., Feld, T., & Hoffmann, M. (2014). Industry 4.0. *Business & Information Systems Engineering*, *6*(4), 239–242. doi:10.100712599-014-0334-4

Lee, E. A. (2015). The past, present and future of cyber-physical systems: A focus on models. *Sensors (Basel)*, *15*(3), 4837–4869. doi:10.3390150304837 PMID:25730486

Lichtblau, K., Stich, V., Bertenrath, R., Blum, M., Bleider, M., Millak, A., … Schröter, M. (2015). *Industrie 4.0 – Readiness*. Frankfurt, Germany: Impuls-Stiftung für den Maschinenbau, den Anlagenbau und die Informationstechnik.

Lucke, D., Constantinescu, C., & Westkämper, E. (2008). Smart factory - a step towards the next generation of manufacturing. In M. Mitsuishi, K. Ueda, & F. Kimura (Eds.), *Manufacturing Systems and Technologies for the New Frontier* (pp. 115–118). London, UK: Springer. doi:10.1007/978-1-84800-267-8_23

Martin, X., & Salomon, R. (2003). Knowledge transfer capacity and its implications for the theory of the multinational corporation. *Journal of International Business Studies*, *34*(4), 356–373. doi:10.1057/palgrave.jibs.8400037

Matt, D. T. (2008). Template based Production System Design. *Journal of Manufacturing Technology Management*, *19*(7), 783–797. doi:10.1108/17410380810898741

Matt, D. T. (2009). Design of Lean Manufacturing Support Systems in Make-to-order Production. *Key Engineering Materials*, *410-411*, 151–158. doi:10.4028/www.scientific.net/KEM.410-411.151

Matt, D. T. (2013). Design of a scalable assembly system for product variety. *Assembly Automation*, *33*(2), 117–126. doi:10.1108/01445151311306627

Matt, D. T., & Rauch, E. (2017). Designing assembly lines for mass customization production systems. In V. Modrák & D. Mourtzis (Eds.), *Mass Customized Manufacturing: Theoretical Concepts and Practical Findings* (pp. 15–35). Boca Raton, FL: CRC Press Francis & Taylor.

Matt, D. T., Rauch, E., & Fraccaroli, D. (2016). Smart Factory für den Mittelstand: Gestaltung eines ganzheitlichen Produktionssystems nach der Industrie 4.0 Vision in kleinen und mittelständischen Unternehmen (KMU) [Smart Factory for small and medium-sized enterprises: design of a holistic production system according to industry 4.0 vision in small and medium-sized enterprises (SMEs)]. *ZWF*, *111*(1-2), 52–55. doi:10.3139/104.111471

Monostori, L. (2014). Cyber-physical production systems: Roots, expectations and R&D challenges. *Procedia CIRP*, *17*, 9–13. doi:10.1016/j.procir.2014.03.115

Moore, J., Loughran, A., McCusker, E., Solvang, W. D., Sziebig, G., Yu, H., . . . Kaartinen, H. (2016, June). *Developing a Toolbox of supports for small and medium sized manufacturing companies*. Paper presented at 2016 International Symposium on Small-scale Intelligent Manufacturing Systems (SIMS), Narvik, Norway. 10.1109/SIMS.2016.7802907

Moreno-Vozmediano, R., Montero, R. S., & Llorente, I. M. (2013). Key challenges in cloud computing: Enabling the future internet of services. *IEEE Internet Computing*, *17*(4), 18–25. doi:10.1109/MIC.2012.69

Mrugalska, B., & Wyrwicka, M. K. (2017). Towards Lean Production in Industry 4.0. *Procedia Engineering*, *182*, 466–473. doi:10.1016/j.proeng.2017.03.135

Niedermayr, F., Waid, S., Garcia, D., Riedl, M., & Matt, D. T. (2015, September). *Design of a scalable and robust woodchip handling control system*. Paper presented at 10th Conference on Sustainable Development of Energy, Water and Environment Systems, Dubrovnik, Croatia.

Nonaka, I. A., & Takeuchi, H. A. (1995). *The knowledge-creating company: how japanese companies create the dynamics of innovation*. Oxford, UK: Oxford University Press.

Radziwona, A., Bilberg, A., Bogers, M., & Madsen, E. S. (2014). The Smart Factory: Exploring Adaptive and Flexible Manufacturing Solutions. *Procedia Engineering*, *69*, 1184–1190. doi:10.1016/j.proeng.2014.03.108

Rauch, E., Seidenstricker, S., Dallasega, P., & Hämmerl, R. (2016). Collaborative Cloud Manufacturing: Design of Business Model Innovations Enabled by Cyberphysical Systems in Distributed Manufacturing Systems. Journal of Engineering.

Riedl, M., Garcia, D., Rauch, E., & Matt, D. T. (2016). Industrie 4.0: Wissenstransfer von der Forschung in die Praxis [Industry 4.0: Transfer of knowledge from research to practice]. In C. M. Schlick (Ed.), *Megatrend Digitalisierung – Potenziale der Arbeits- und Betriebsorganisation?* (pp. 111–129). Berlin, Germany: Gito.

Rojas, R., Rauch, E., Vidoni, R., & Matt, D. T. (2017, June). *Enabling Connectivity of Cyber-Physical Production Systems: A Conceptual Framework*. Paper presented at 27th International Conference on Flexible Automation and Intelligent Manufacturing, Modena, Italy. 10.1016/j.promfg.2017.07.184

Sanders, A., Elangeswaran, C., & Wulfsberg, J. (2016). Industry 4.0 implies lean manufacturing: Research activities in industry 4.0 function as enablers for lean manufacturing. *Journal of Industrial Engineering and Management.*, *9*(3), 811–833. doi:10.3926/jiem.1940

Schröder, C. (2016). *The Challenges of Industry 4.0 for Small and Medium-sized Enterprises*. Retrieved January 13, 2017, from http://library.fes.de/pdf-files/wiso/12683.pdf

Schulze, A., Brojerdi, G., & von Krogh, G. (2014). Those Who Know, Do. Those Who Understand, Teach. Disseminative Capability and knowledge Transfer in the Automotive Industry. *Journal of Product Innovation Management*, *31*(1), 79–97. doi:10.1111/jpim.12081

Schumacher, A., Erol, S., & Sihn, W. (2016). A Maturity Model for Assessing Industry 4.0 Readiness and Maturity of Manufacturing Enterprises. *Procedia CIRP*, *52*, 161–166. doi:10.1016/j.procir.2016.07.040

Sommer, L. (2015). Industrial revolution-industry 4.0: Are German manufacturing SMEs the first victims of this revolution? *Journal of Industrial Engineering and Management*, *8*(5), 1512–1532. doi:10.3926/jiem.1470

Suh, N. P. (1990). *The principles of design*. New York: Oxford university press.

Szulanski, G. (1996). Exploring internal stickiness: Impediments to the transfer of best practices within the firm. *Strategic Management Journal*, *17*(S2), 27–43. doi:10.1002mj.4250171105

Szulanski, G. (2000). The process of knowledge transfer: A diachronic analysis of stickiness. *Organizational Behavior and Human Decision Processes*, *82*(1), 9–27. doi:10.1006/obhd.2000.2884

Szulanski, G., & Jensen, R. J. (2004). Overcoming stickiness: An empirical investigation of the role of the template in the replication of organizational routines. *Managerial and Decision Economics*, *25*(6–7), 347–363. doi:10.1002/mde.1195

Thompson, M. K. (2013). A Classification of Procedural Errors in the Definition of Functional Requirements in Axiomatic Design Theory. In *Proceedings of the 7th International Conference on Axiomatic Design* (pp. 107-112). Worcester, MA: Worcester Polytechnic Institute.

Törngren, M., Bensalem, S., Cengarle, M. V., Chen, D.-J., McDermid, J., Passerone, R., ... Runkler, T. (2014). *CPS State of the Art, EC FP7 Project 611430 CyPhERS*. Tech. Rep. Deliverable D5.1.

VDMA. (2014). *Maschinen- und Anlagenbau* [Mechanical engineering and plant engineering]. Retrieved March 10, 2017, from http://www.berufsstart.de/unternehmen/branchen/maschinen-anlagenbau/verband.php

Wagner, T., Herrmann, C., & Thiede, S. (2017). Industry 4.0 Impacts on Lean Production Systems. *Procedia CIRP*, *63*, 125–131. doi:10.1016/j.procir.2017.02.041

Wan, J., Tang, S., Shu, Z., Li, D., Wang, S., Imran, M., & Vasilakos, A. V. (2016). Software-defined industrial internet of things in the context of industry 4.0. *IEEE Sensors Journal*, *16*(20), 7373–7380.

Wehn, U., & Montalvo, C. (2016). Knowledge transfer dynamics and innovation: Behaviour, interactions and aggregated outcomes. *Journal of Cleaner Production*.

Xia, F., Yang, L. T., Wang, L., & Vinel, A. (2012). Internet of things. *International Journal of Communication Systems*, *25*(9), 1101–1102. doi:10.1002/dac.2417

Xu, X., Sheng, Q. Z., Zhang, L. J., Fan, Y., & Dustdar, S. (2015). From big data to big service. *Computer*, *48*(7), 80–83. doi:10.1109/MC.2015.182 PMID:27110033

Yoon, J. S., Shin, S. J., & Suh, S. H. (2012). A conceptual framework for the ubiquitous factory. *International Journal of Production Research*, *50*(8), 2174–2189. doi:10.1080/00207543.2011.562563

Zuehlke, D. (2010). Smart Factory - towards a factory-of-things. *Annual Reviews in Control*, *34*(1), 129–138. doi:10.1016/j.arcontrol.2010.02.008

KEY TERMS AND DEFINITIONS

Cyber Physical System: The combination of physical and digital (cyber) systems with its advantages compared to the only physical or digital system.

Industry 4.0: The fourth industrial revolution after mechanization, electrification, and computerization dealing with internet of things, big data, and cyber physical systems.

Knowledge Transfer: The ability to transfer knowledge and competences from a skilled person or group to another less-skilled group.

Maturity Model: A model that describes different stages of maturity of a system.

Self-Assessment: A system or approach to assess and evaluate the own capabilities and competences.

Smart Factory: The holistic combination of all Industry 4.0 concepts in a factory to become intelligent.

SME: Small and medium-sized enterprises between 50 and 250 employees according to the European Commission.

Chapter 14
Positioning Theoretical Perspective in Academic Writing:
Teaching Culture Theory in International Business Studies in the Context of Industry 4.0

Cheryl Marie Cordeiro
University of Gothenburg, Sweden

ABSTRACT

A main challenge for academic writing for students at master thesis level is to find the right perspective from which to launch the argument of the thesis. In the context of international business (IB) studies, the eclectic theoretical paradigm of the field offers students myriad frameworks from which to frame their research questions. The purpose of this chapter is to illustrate how perspective in academic writing can be taught and learnt in a systematic manner. Taking the example of the teaching of culture theory in international business (IB) studies, this chapter illustrates how the deictic or "pointer" function of the pronoun system in language can be used to help perspective research position and research design.

INTRODUCTION

Paradigm Shift Towards Systems Thinking in Pedagogy

Our young are our future. The skills taught to them today are what will carry them through for the management of the society and living of tomorrow. What is different today than just about thirty years ago is the increased complexity in society and living, much to the development of new technologies.

Graduating master students of international business (IB) studies face the challenge of entering a world of interconnectivity and complexity in the era of Industry 4.0 (i4.0). The twin learning goals for

DOI: 10.4018/978-1-5225-3468-6.ch014

students of IB are theoretical understanding and application of theory in practice. As part of their higher education programme, master level students often find themselves doing internships in large multinational enterprises (MNEs) before graduating whilst completing their thesis work. This internship period is part of their building of their social network and capital. The time spent at MNE not only allows for them to make industry contacts but to collect data for their thesis research and writing. In the era of i4.0, network and flows seem to be key concepts (Capra, 2015) not just in digital infrastructure but in the social circles, and understanding different perspectives becomes crucial.

Advances in the physical and social sciences made in the past thirty years have contributed towards an increased interest from scholars and practitioners towards the study of complex systems in the form of interrelated networks. Students who graduate from higher education learning at universities and who enter the global labour talent pool either as entrepreneurs or as employees in a company face a reality and work environment that is today far more technologically interconnected and complex than previous decades. Driving innovation and progress in organisations and in society will depend increasingly upon implementing processes based on an understanding of ecology and a systems perspective of management, organization and living. Keeping pace with this evolution of interconnectedness were ideas set forth by organismic biologists during the first half of the twentieth century. From an object-oriented perspective, scholars began to think in terms of processes, connectedness, relationships, patterns and context (Capra, 2015; Capra & Luisi, 2014). The move towards a holistic understanding of systems from the academic circles within the physical and social science has also led to current interest in the pedagogical formulation of integrated frameworks of theory and methods to be applied in various fields that fall broadly under the management of organizations and of society, from corporate strategy formulation to national / regional policy making (Theisens, Hooge & Waslander, 2016; Jacobson & Wilensky, 2006; Bar-Yam, 1997).

Education in i4.0: Positioning Perspective in Research Design

A primary concern for students at master thesis level in the process of formulating their thesis is research design and finding the right perspective within which their thesis research questions are framed. Greater complexity has increased the need to perspectivise, to be able to view issues, events and challenges in multiple facets in order to facilitate progress. Part of managing a complex system is the task of situating point of view, or perspective in terms of theoretical conceptualisation and framework of analysis to their academic writing is important because it acts as a scaffold upon which their research can be designed and research questions framed (Alvesson & Sandberg, 2011; Sandberg & Alvesson, 2011). IB studies, which provides foundational theories and tools of organization and management has inherent vocational underpinnings. This means that students of IB studies are not only exposed to a variety of theoretical conceptualisations for their chosen topic in their thesis work, but they will need to be able to apply that knowledge in order to acquire appropriate empirical data for their written analysis. Their thesis findings should ideally be transferable/generalizable to the real world working contexts of multinational corporations in the form of project management, corporate research and development (R&D) proposals, and/or executive education training programmes for example.

The challenge of finding a research perspective and a relevant theoretical framework is increased by the fact that theories within the field of IB studies are influenced from various disciplines that include economics, economic geography, sociology, psychology and political science to name but a few (Meyer & Peng, 2016). The process of having to choose between the numerous IB theories as conceptual framework to their thesis project, of perspectivising, and grounding their point of view in a theoretical framework that eventually bolsters their research design and questions, can be a daunting task, especially if the theories seem to present a contradictory point of view (Fuerst, 2010; Cecil, 2004). Point of view and the teaching of perspective in academic writing in higher education (Hathaway, 2015; Goatly, 2000) is however, not a unique pedagogical question to the field of IB studies. Some other fields of inquiry include corpus linguistics for learning specialized academic writing (Flowerdew, 2017), language and ideology (Simpson, 1993), special needs education (Gardner & Wolfe, 2015) and medical education (Skinner & Gormley, 2016).

Purpose and Focus

The theoretical foundations of IB studies are eclectic. The focus of this paper is to illustrate how framing of research questions and research perspective in academic writing can be accomplished in a systematic manner using applied linguistics of the Pronoun system in language in use. The paper shows how a four-quadrant model, named the Götheborg IV or G4 model, can be applied as framework and tool for both supervisor and student, to situate the choice of research perspective using the deictic function or 'pointer' function of pronouns in language in use (Cordeiro 2016a, 2016b). Beginning with theoretical concepts related to the choice of topic by the student, grounding a theoretical perspective can be viewed as the student's launching platform of the research design and research question asked. Perspective helps shape how the thesis is eventually formulated in rhetorical structure bolstered by empirical field studies that they set out to collect and analyse.

This paper is presented in three sections. It begins by explaining how the basic elements of the Pronoun system in grammar found in most languages of the world, *I (You), We (They), It/Its,* can be mapped into a four-quadrant model, the G4 model, and used to unfold various perspectives and different types of knowledge zones. This systematic mapping of perspectives can be used to help individuals ground their research perspective in theory and framework of analysis. In a second section, the teaching of the theory of culture in IB is taken as an example of how this knowledge and model of perspectivising can be applied in practice, in the field of IB and management. A background and literature review of the research and teaching of culture in IB studies is presented. Here, dominant and seemingly dichotomous conceptualisations of culture are reconciled into a systems / emergent view of culture. The final section of the paper contains the concluding thoughts and observed limitations of the application of the G4 model as a learning tool for theoretical perspectivising for master level thesis writing.

MAPPING KNOWLEDGE ZONES

Using the Pronoun System of Language to Map Knowledge Zones and Methods of Inquiry

75% of the world's language typology includes a *subject, verb* and *object* in its sentence construction (Crystal, 1997, 1990). The pronoun perspectives of *I, We, It* and *Its* fulfil a 'pointer' function that directs the attention of the user towards a certain perspective. The difference in perspective is reflected in the use of language because inherent in the structure of language are its multiple levels of construct reflected in its patterns of use (Halliday & Matthiessen, 2014; Halliday, 1994). In language, the use of noun, noun-phrases and pronouns in Subject position renders the various perspectives of agents and actors of happenings/events, while noun, noun-phrases and pronouns in Object position denotes who/what is affected by the agent of a verb in a sentence. These perspectives can be mapped in a four-quadrant model illustrated in Figure 1.

The perspectives from the quadrants are holons, moving from narrower to broader perspectives, with each broader perspective encompassing the narrower perspectives. The Individual Interior perspective is expressed in the Upper Left quadrant (UL, *singular subjective*) which are *I (intra) / You (extra).* The Collective Interior perspective is expressed in the Lower Left quadrant (LL, *plural intersubjective*) which are *We (intra) / They (extra).* It is in the LL quadrant that many anthropological and ethnographical research studies of culture are designed and framed. Crossing diagonally over from bottom left to top right, the Individual Exterior perspective is expressed in the Upper Right quadrant (UR, *singular objective*), which are *It (intra) / It (extra).* Many statistical empirical studies on culture in IB would fall in this quadrant in research design and framing, of which the dimensional theory of culture can be efficiently applied. In this quadrant of research frameworks, scholars / students can for example, study from an objective point of view, the combined effects of elements from the UL and LL quadrants in terms of human behaviour exhibited in relation to their environment. If a student was interested in studying networks of behaviours,

Figure 1. The grammatical function from the system of pronouns in language, "I", "We", "It" and "Its", translates into four perspectives that render four different types of knowledge zones
(Wilber 2000)

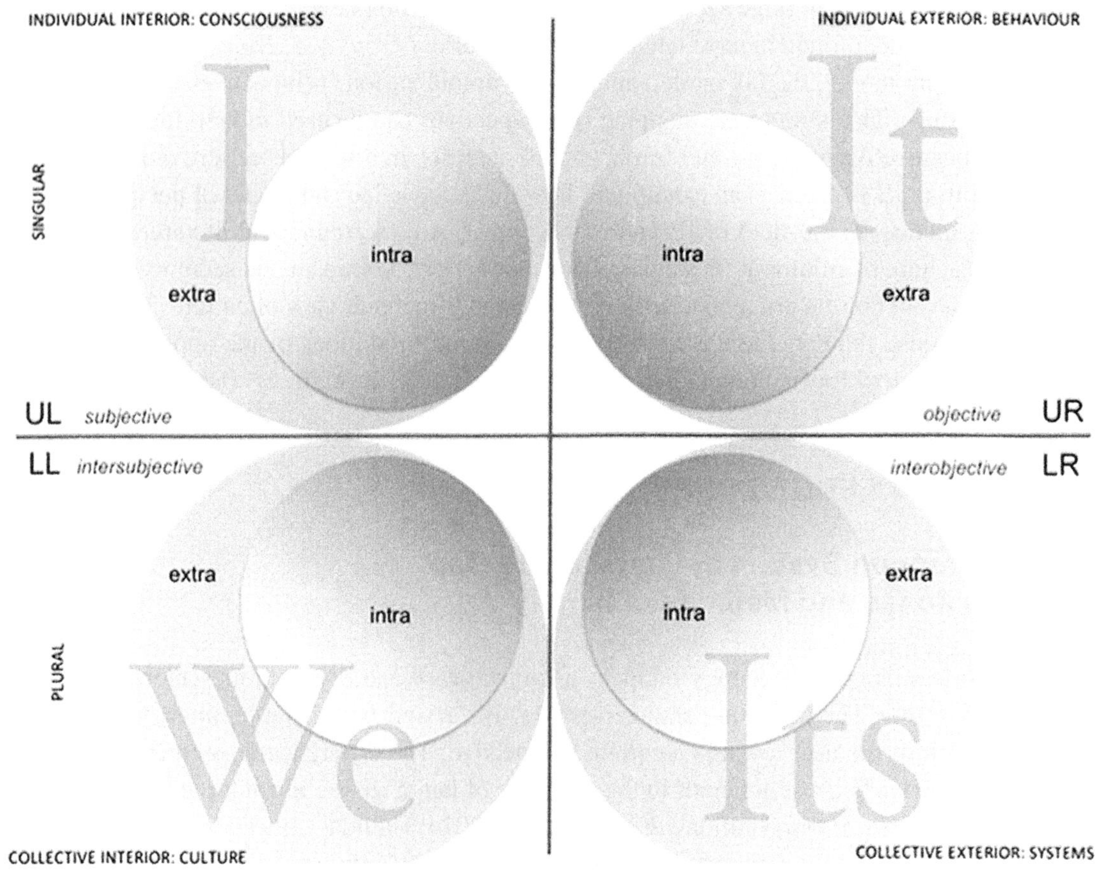

then this could be framed in the Collective Exterior perspective, expressed in the Lower Right (LR, *plural interobjective*). The LR quadrant would be the broadest perspective, encompassing all other perspectives. This quadrant frames system-of-systems type studies or the effect of network relation/s type studies.

Figure 1 not only maps various perspectives, but the quadrants render four different types of knowledge zones. Taking into account that each perspective can have an intra- or extra-, a singular or plural positioning, a resulting eight knowledge zones and methodologies can be mapped onto a four-quadrant model as shown in Figure 2 (Wilber 2006:36-40). Figure 2 shows some examples of disciplines or knowledge paradigms that broadly define and are defined by the methodologies in the four quadrants. 'I' studies for example, are heavily empiricism oriented.

EVOLVING CULTURE THEORY IN INTERNATIONAL BUSINESS STUDIES

An aspect of international business and trade that is ubiquitous in the context of i4.0 is the fabric of heterogeneous culture. The continuous meeting and exchange of ideas from people of differing cultural backgrounds characterises meetings and living. Yet culture has never been an easy concept to decipher

Figure 2. The grammatical function of pronouns, "I", "We", "It" and "Its" translates into four perspectives that render four different types of knowledge zones
(Wilber 2006:36-40)

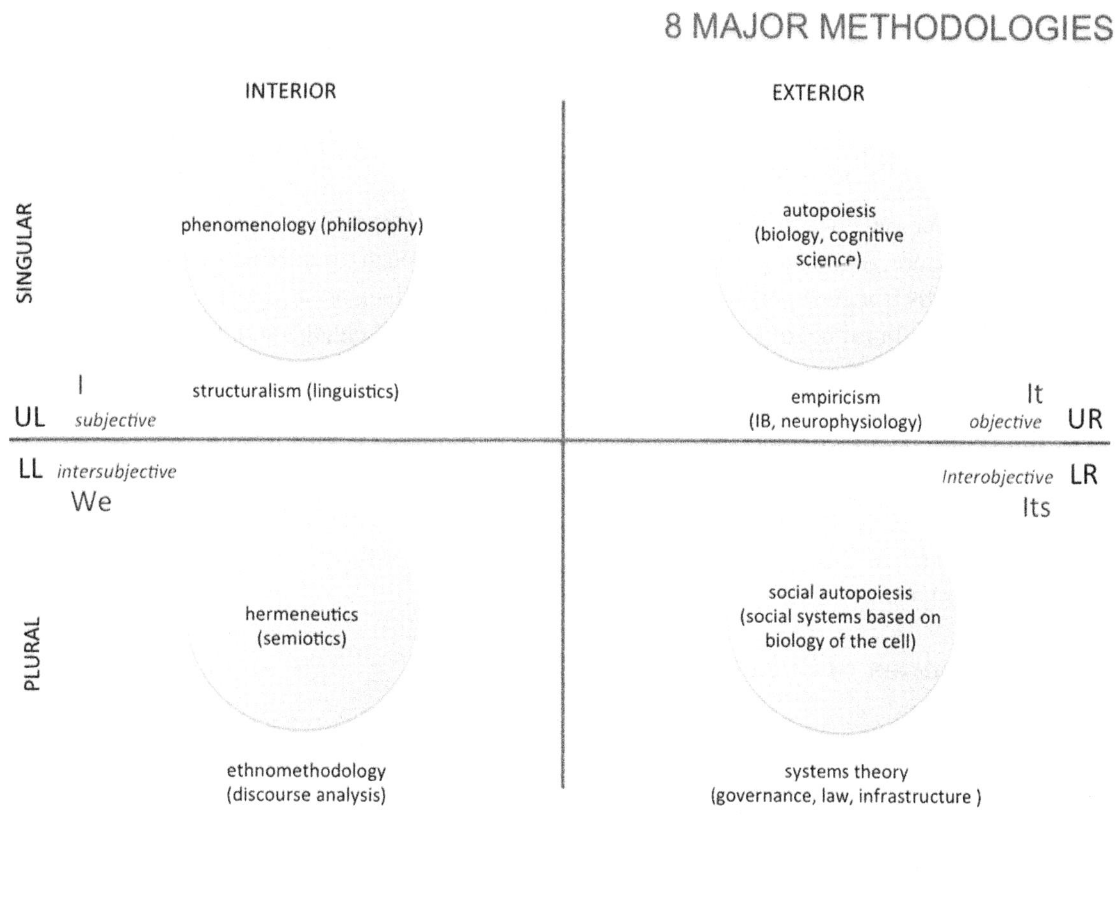

or measure and even those in academia tend to need to define how they use the term 'culture' in their own studies. Culture is a shared set of assumptions and behaviour, tacit knowledge of social norms that is inherent feature of groups of individuals. This shared assumptions and group knowledge manifests in various dimensions and at different levels of society (Steers, Sánchez-Runde & Nardon, 2013; Schein, 1990) that in cumulation gives rise to ideology, defined as the beliefs and value-systems that are collectively shared (Rosenmann, 2017; van Dijk, 2006; Simpson, 1993).

New technologies redefine the everyday contexts within which people work, live and interact with each other. Advancing developments in cyber physical systems, where wireless technology and social media platforms on the Internet allow for the forming of virtual groups with instant contact that further dissolve the concrete geographic boundaries of groups of individuals. Social media platforms for example literally connect individuals from various remote locations in virtual space in real-time, no physical border crossing necessary. These globalising processes put increasing pressure on academics and practitioners to re-conceptualises theories of culture as they are currently being applied in research studies and practice. As such, the past thirty years have seen advances made in the various fields of sciences that set the context for the current academic discussion and teaching of culture theory in the field of IB. New ways of seeing and new discoveries in science will also have bearing on how the subject of culture is being taught at universities in the context of higher education. Executive education in corporate in-house management training programmes might also meet with new ideas on culture theory in IB studies.

Already in 1952, Kroeber and Kluckhohn had uncovered 164 definitions of 'culture'. Culture is a product of the mind through shared meanings and symbols:

Culture consists of patterns, explicit and implicit, of and for behaviour acquired and transmitted by symbols, constituting the distinctive achievements of human groups, including their embodiments in artefacts; the essential core of culture consists of traditional (i.e. historically derived and selected) ideas and especially their attached values; culture systems may, on the one hand, be considered as products of action, and on the other as conditioning elements of further action. (Kroeber & Klulckhohn, 1952)

More definitions and conceptualisations of culture exist in the literary canon today. But scholars and practitioners alike are generally positive in mindset. There has been an interest in scholastic literature since the late 1990s, for new perspectives of culture and its influence on the normative dimensional construct in cross-cultural negotiations, dynamics in organizational change and multicultural team settings (Shenkar, 2012a, 2012a; Sackmann & Phillips, 2004; McSweeney, 2002; Holden, 2002; Salk & Brannen, 2000; Schein 1990).

The following sections trace the development of this new perspective of culture in IB studies by presenting two constructs of culture, followed by a discussion of how these views can be reconciled in perspective. This is done so that readers might understand how the conceptualisation of culture in the field of IB can be taken as an example of teaching the situating of theoretical perspective in academic writing at master level for students in IB studies.

Teaching Theories of Culture

The theoretical conceptualisations of culture in IB studies began in the 1930s with studies in cultural anthropology in relation to organization (Richardson & Walker, 1948; Warner & Low, 1947; Roethlisberger & Dickson, 1939; Mayo, 1933) human psychology, human development and national cultures (Gelfand,

Chiu & Hong, 2014; Bird & Fang, 2009; Fang, 2005-2006, 2003; Osland, J. S., Bird, A., Delano, J. & Jacob, M., 2000). Two broad theoretical frameworks on culture have thus far been presented and taught in higher education syllabuses to students, the (1) dimensional and; (2) emergent constructs.

A Normative (Dimensional) Perspective

The manner in which culture is conceived and taught in higher education in the field of IB is rapidly evolving. Theoretical development in cultural studies at both national and organizational levels took ground during the 1970s with the expansive work of Geert Hofstede (2001, 1984, 1980). Covering more than 70 countries with IBM employee value scores collected between 1967 and 1973, his efforts culminated in a book in 1980, *Culture's Consequences*, which outlined how values at the workplace were influenced by national culture. He identified four dimensions with which to describe national culture: individualism-collectivism, masculinity-femininity, power distance, and uncertainty avoidance. His later research added a fifth dimension – Confucian dynamism (short-term vs. long-term orientation).

Not unawares of the limitations of the dimensional framework he constructed for the study of culture (Hofstede 1980:43), the dimensional construct gained considerable popularity within a short period of time with scholars applying it in study of both private corporations and government institutions (Trompenaars & Hampden-Turner, 1998; Triandis, 1995a, 1995b, 1993, 1990, 1988). These published works became part of the canonical literature that defined and laid foundation to further the dimensional theory of culture in relation to a delineated geographic region with a tendency towards an 'either/or' perspective that placed emphasis on similarities and differences between cultures.

The success of the dimensional theory to culture was to large extent due to that it not only enabled a nebulous concept like culture to be measured and analysed, but it provided researchers with a systematic framework within which large scale (thus generalizable) cultural studies can continue to be researched and compared. From organization leadership to cross-cultural teamwork, the dimensional construct proved useful even in the context of measuring predicted success in foreign direct investment (FDI) (Kogut & Singh, 1988). An underlying feature that characterises the dimensional construct studies is an assumed averaged collected set of values that are generalized to form the basis of a particular 'national culture' which can then be compared to another set of collected values (Tipton, 2009; Luo, 2007; Todd, 2006; Zander, 2004; House, R., Javidan, M., Hanges, P., & Dorfman, P., 2002; Hofstede, 2001, 1980).

But the dimensional construct is not without critique in its applications in IB studies and teaching. Scholars have acknowledged that the appeal of the dimensional framework is illusory even at national / country level comparison because it assumes too much internal homogeneity. The contextual and circumstantial symmetry between two nations / cultures are also overly generalized, seemingly discounting culture as a living entity that learns and evolves over time (Venaik & Brewer, 2013; Shenkar, 2012a, 2012b; McSweeney, 2009, 2002; Shenkar 2001). If taught in this dimensional construct and 'static' manner to students, students will be at the disadvantage of having too limited a perspective on how to further research culture as a topic of choice for their thesis writing for example.

An Emergent Perspective

In this conceptualisation, culture is seen as a living entity, as both product and process. This more fluid and dynamic view has been reflected from studies in the fields of anthropology and human behavioural psychology from the early 1900s when the concept of 'organization climate' was discussed as 'group norms' (Lewin, Lippitt & White, 1939). Twenty years on in the 1950s, the focus of scholarly attention was the idea of 'cultural ecology' where culture was conceptualized in anthropology as a phenomenon that evolved in response to the natural environment (Steward, 1955). Culture was anchored in the context of social life (Geertz, 1973) and seen as an adaptive system with an ecological aspect as well as an ideational aspect (Keesing, 1974). In this parallel evolution of cultural theory to the dimensional construct in management science, roles, norms, attitudes and values of organizations were studied but not explicitly referred to in terms of an 'organizational culture' (Katz & Kahn, 1978). Instead, the discourse of management and organization is laced with distinct metaphors of biomorphic, anthropomorphic and sociomorphic flavours (Allaire & Firsirotu, 1984).

The emergent perspective of culture in IB, where culture is viewed as a dynamic product and process, rests upon an understanding of non-reductionistic dialectical thinking capabilities of the human mind and the orientation of human values (Fang, 2012, 2005-2006; Peng & Nisbett, 2000, 1999). In the context of higher education, one of the goals of the master level education programme is to have students be able to exhibit independently, non-reductionisitc dialectical thinking, as reflected in their thesis writing.

'Non-reductionistic' in this context refers to the capacity of the human mind to think dialectically in problem solving. The resolution of contradiction in the human mind is to be understood in its broadest sense, in terms of the formalities of logic as well as in its semantic and interpretive meaning. Studies have shown that mature human cognition has the ability to perspectivise and reconcile both logical as well as psychological contradictions into a holistic view (Jeste, D. V., Ardelt, M., Blazer, D., Kraemer, H. C., Vaillant, G. & Meeks, T. W., 2010; Staudinger, 2008; Wilber, 1980; Graves, 1970).

RECONCILING AND OPERATIONALIZING OPPOSING THEORIES OF CULTURE

From the findings to the critical literature review in the above sections, the dichotomy in the theoretical constructs in the study of culture becomes apparent. In academic writing practice, this disparity of perspective from prominent scholars in the field tend to pose a challenge for students. Students struggle with reconciling the complexities of the two theoretical perspectives of culture, and have difficulty in framing their method of inquiry and research design.

Within the field of IB studies, a multidimensional phenomenon that requires an understanding of culture at various levels of management science is firm internationalization / globalization. Since firm globalization theory focuses on the emergent qualities of the processes of globalization, crossing borders and cultures, the modelling of such a theory can be used as an example to illustrate and operationalize the dialectical relations between dimensional and emergent theories of culture.

Firm Globalization Theories: Example of the Uppsala Model

Studies of culture in IB often take the perspective of the dimensional construct of culture when accounting for the globalization processes of a firm. These studies often focus on various aspects of managerial competencies, dyadic business relationships and networks, studying such as the geographical configuration and coordination capacities of the firm applied to different industries from fashion retailing to information communication technology (Michael Clark, J. N., Quast, L., Jang, S., Wohkittel, J., Center, B., Edwards, K., & Bovornusvakool, W.,2016; Almodóvar & Rugman, 2015; Childs & Jin, 2014; Steenkamp & Geyskens 2012; Forsgren & Hagström, 2007). As such it would be interesting to see how an applied linguistics approach (using the Pronoun system of language) can help in the unfolding of research perspectives and contextualise more concretely, the study of culture in the context of studying firm internationalisation processes.

The most prominent of internationalization models grounded in an evolutionary/emergent perspective in the field of IB studies is the Uppsala Model (UM) by Johanson and Vahlne (2009, 1977). Widely cited and critiqued (Carneiro, Rocha & Silva 2008; Oviatt & McDougall, 1994; Andersen, 1993; Langhoff, 1977), the first publication of the UM in the late 1970s was conceived for the purpose of explaining the internationalization processes of the firm. It was developed on the idea that knowledge was lacking about the processes of firm internationalization that posed a barrier to further organization growth. Culture and organizational psychology feature as underlying elements in internationalization processes because of *the increasing involvement of the firm in the individual foreign country, and [the] successive establishment of operations in new countries* (Johanson & Vahlne, 1977). The firm encompassed not just a widely dispersed engagement in foreign markets (defined as 'internationalization'), but it also had a network of differentiated units that could exploit advantages of specialization on location (defined as 'globalization') (Ghoshal & Bartlett, 1990). Empirical data for the UM was obtained from the study of Swedish multinational enterprises (MNEs).

Elements in the UM can be applied to both firm internationalization and globalization processes because the mechanisms of the model are sufficiently general to allow for its application for most managerial processes characterised by emergence such as uncertainty, ambiguity and complexity (Vahlne, Ivarsson & Johanson, 2011). A large part of the workings of the processes of globalization are human relations across different cultures, and the capacity to manage people across differing cultural contexts. In the UM, the aspect of Time and Culture is implied in globalization processes, but not made explicit as referenced elements in either state or change variables.

In the later developed UM in 2009 and 2014, the MNE is also referred to as 'the firm as a whole', as reflected in the lines found in Vahlne and Ivarsson's study,

in order to grow and improve on their effectiveness, multinational enterprises (MNEs) reconfigure their widely dispersed value chains and develop their coordination systems to make the different units specialize, integrate and operate towards the overall best for the firm as a whole (Vahlne & Ivarsson, 2014).

The duo directions of globalization, inherent in the UM, indicate a need for a non-ambiguous use of the word 'firm'.

The disambiguation of the word 'firm' is an important first step in operationalizing the unfolding of the different Pronoun system perspectives that turns the UM (Figure 1) into the G4 model (Figure 3). This applied linguistics approach, of using the Pronoun system in language that disambiguates the word 'firm' into 'main enterprise' and 'subsidiary' in the UM allows for the unfolding of perspectives in firm globalisation research studies.

An Applied Linguistics Approach to Unfolding Theoretical Perspectives: The Götheborg IV (G4) Model

Using the mapping in Figure 1, Figure 3 illustrates the G4 model as a reconfiguration of elements of firm globalization found in the UM. The G4 model is based on the functional use of pronouns inherent in the structure of language. The empirical data to the G4 model is derived from the combined data collected

Figure 3. The Götheborg IV (G4) Model mapping the 4 different knowledge zones of the UM, that renders 8 perspectives of the interior and exterior of enterprise (Hn) and firm (H1), and the knowledge gaps. The LL quadrant illustrates the dialogic relations between Hn and H1 and the knowledge zone gap to be complemented from the UM. The G4 model itself illustrates the dialectic reconciliation of the different research strategies of culture, in its dimensional and emergent constructs.

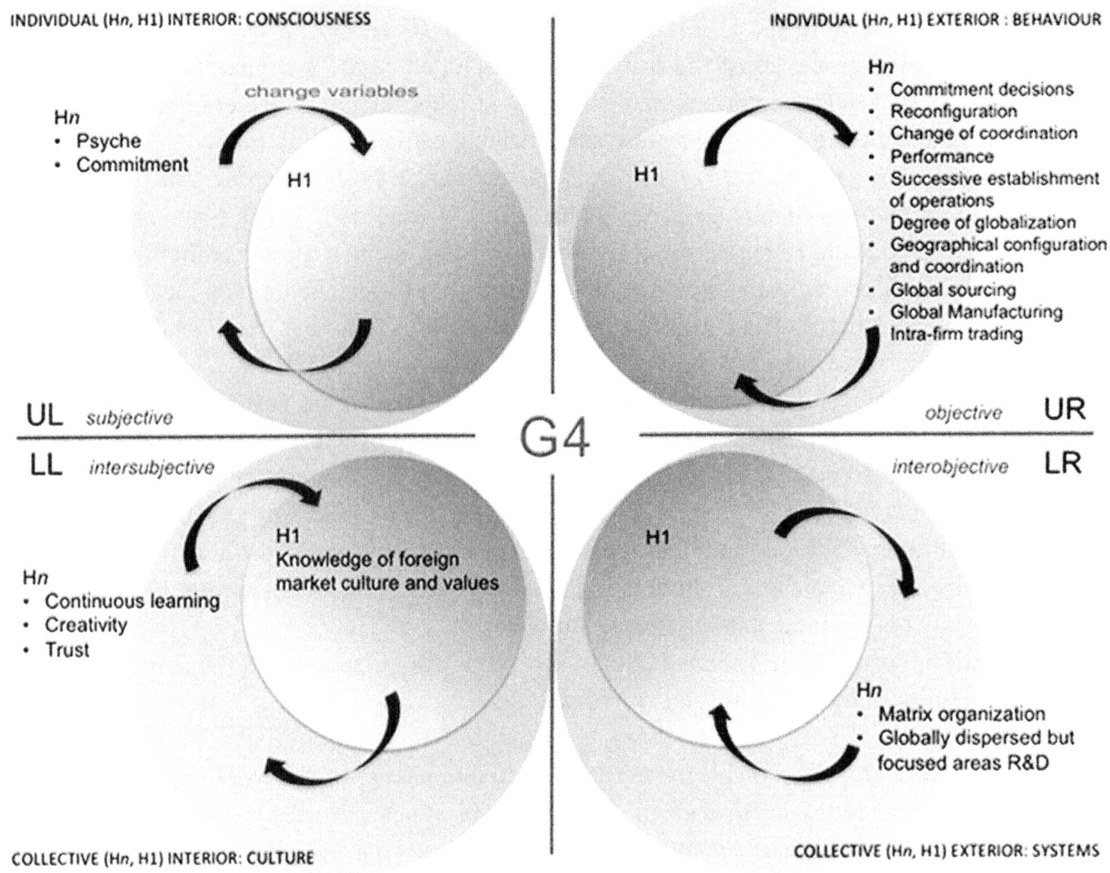

from the UM studies and studies on the Swedish management style in Swedish managed organizations (Cäker, Andersson & Wickelgren, 2011; Cordeiro-Nilsson, 2010, 2009; Birkinshaw, 2002; Källström & Solli, 1997; Lindell & Arvonen, 1996; Jönsson, 1995). The focus of the G4 model is on the qualitative aspects of the globalization processes of the firm. Such aspects include management in uncertainty in relation to knowledge of foreign market culture, values, continuous learning, creativity and trust-building that is implicitly referred to but seldom explicitly analysed in the UM (Vahlne & Ivarsson, 2014).

The element of Time, which is reflected in change variables in the UM, is reflected differently in the G4 model. In the G4 model, Time is reflected not as an element in any specific zone of knowledge located in any quadrant, but rather, Time exists in the background fabric of globalization processes. Without Time, there will be no such anthropic processes.

Different from the UM, the G4 model makes two fundamental distinctions in the processes of firm globalization. The first distinction is made in the consideration of the perspectives of *I*, *We* and *It/Its* in language. This renders and translates into a four-quadrant model reflecting four broad knowledge zones in each quadrant. It is within this four-quadrant model that elements of the firm globalization processes are then placed. The G4 model makes explicit a further distinction of the UM's duo directions of globalization by disambiguating the use of the words 'enterprise' and 'firm'. The word 'enterprise', as referred to by the UM model will be denoted by the capital letter, H, in the context of the G4 model. Because an enterprise can contain an unknown number of subsidiary units, denoted by *n*, within its network, the MNE or 'firm as a whole' (as termed by Vahlne & Ivarsson, 2014) is denoted as H*n*. The word 'firm', is taken as a singular example of a unit within the MNE, denoted by H1. Taking the enterprise ('firm as a whole', H*n*) and firm subsidiary (H1) as singular holons, 8 perspectives can be derived from the G4 model. Thus unfolding the elements of the UM into interior and exterior H*n* and H1 perspectives of the globalization processes, placed in the four-quadrants of the G4 model.

In the G4 model, the multi-levelled function and role of culture in both dimensional and emergent theories become more explicit in visualisation. These eight interior and exterior perspectives provide the operationalizing framework upon which the dialectics of culture from Individual to Group and Groups of Groups (culture as system and network), can be studied systematically from quadrant to quadrant.

As a point of clarification the G4 model is not meant to be a replacement or improvement of the UM, but rather, the G4 model can be described as an applied linguistics perspective of the elements of the UM. Both models are dynamic in theoretical construct, but the G4 model reconfigures the UM by applying the system of pronouns found in language use to the elements of the UM. In so doing, the G4 model helps unfold the relativity in perspective in firm globalization processes, enabling firm globalisation processes to be studied at different levels even within a single enterprise. So the study of culture for example, of a single MNE can be studied at subsidiary, network of subsidiaries (national/regional) or enterprise levels.

Pedagogic Value of the Götheborg IV Model

The pedagogic value for the master thesis student is that the G4 model is a way for the students to systematically position their research questions in the study of the various aspects of firm globalization processes, including placing the study of culture within this model.

The G4 model unfolds a novel perspective to the processes of firm globalization by overtly situating the role and function of language within the firm's globalization processes. It also reveals knowledge gaps that can be identified for further research and thesis work. It illustrates for students (as well as teachers/supervisors), how the grammatical functions of language can be used as a tool to help uncover the agency of the firm globalisation processes that operate in symbiosis with the local environment for its sustained development. The study of culture materialises in these contexts mainly through the management strategies and styles of top-level managers (Cordeiro-Nilsson, 2010, 2009; Jönsson, 1995). This application can also be done in practice for managers in project management purposes, where knowledge gaps can be identified and filled as part of project scoping.

Practical Application of the Götheborg IV Model

The four-quadrant visualisation of perspectives enables an unveiling of point-of-view when studying culture in organization at any targeted level from Individual to Group, Organization to Networks of Organizations.

The UL quadrant is the zone of H*n* and H1 knowledge pertaining to the consciousness and ideology of the Individual Interior of the firm and enterprise. In the UM, this is where the 'Commitment' behind the 'commitment decisions' is represented. The LL quadrant is the zone of knowledge of H1 and H*n* pertaining to the Collective Interiors of firm and enterprise culture. These interior knowledge zones are then expressed in the exterior quadrants, the actions of which can be observed exteriorly. The UR quadrant is the zone of H1 and H*n* knowledge pertaining to Individual Exteriors of firm and enterprise behaviours, and the LR quadrant is the zone of H1 and H*n* knowledge pertaining to Collective Exteriors of firm and enterprise structures and systems.

Research studies, questionnaires and surveys can be designed by using the quadrant structure as a tool that can be used to systematically target the quadrant of knowledge needed and the level of analysis required. The four-quadrants also help in identifying knowledge gaps, uncovering whose / which perspectives are lacking (*I, We, It/Its*), and it can help indicate where possible solutions might be found by looking at the inter-connectivity of processes in the four-quadrants.

A study of the processes of globalization that adopts a wide systemic perspective would thus encompass a study of the interior and exterior perspectives of H*n* and H1, and how they operate at various socio-cultural levels in a continuous dialogic synchrony towards the sustained development of H*n* in relation to its larger collective socio-cultural context. Research design at this level will necessarily need to reconcile and take into consideration both the dimensional and emergent theories of culture in order to render a deeper, more comprehensive understanding of firm processes based on human motivation and action.

As a measure of impact of ideas transferred or how much the students understand how to perspectivise their own research questions, Figure 4 and Figure 5 can be said to be examples of the application of the deictic function of pronouns found in Figure 1 and Figure 3, unto a topic of interest for research in thesis writing. The two figures appear in the authors' finalised version of their master thesis project.

In Figure 4, the authors Dehghani and Strandberg (2015:26) illustrate in multiple over-layering of perspectives, the thematic findings of how language can be viewed as empowering of disempowering at a multinational corporation studied.

In Figure 5, the authors Bälter and Dennermyr (2016:79) illustrate the barriers and facilitators for knowledge transfer in a shared language setting, where culture features as part of their studied factors in a likewise four-quadrant model as the G4 model.

Important in Figures 4 and 5 is the illustration of an understanding of complexity and its manner of visualisation in the thesis work. The figures in general, reflect an applied comprehension that practicalities and realities often occur simultaneously, in the same space. Solving challenges in such an environment will need a comprehensive perspective, one situated in an understanding of relativity of context of situation.

Observed Challenges Faced by Students in the Unfolding of Perspectives Seminar Session

The main challenge for students in theoretical perspectivising that in turn affects their research design and questions is abstractness even with explicit teaching and the use of models as visualisation tools. While one purpose of the teaching of perspectives in research methods is for the students to apply that knowledge over a broad area of research topics and research design, the example of culture and firm globalization processes may not interest all students. The result is that students, when stressed for time with concluding other term essays and project work, tend to take a reductionist approach to learning, and simply discard what they deem is an irrelevant example for their own immediate work. The idea

Figure 4. An application of a perspectivising technique as illustrated in the Götheborg IV model unto the concept of language as empowering or disempowering in a study of a multinational corporation by Dehghani and Strandberg (2015)

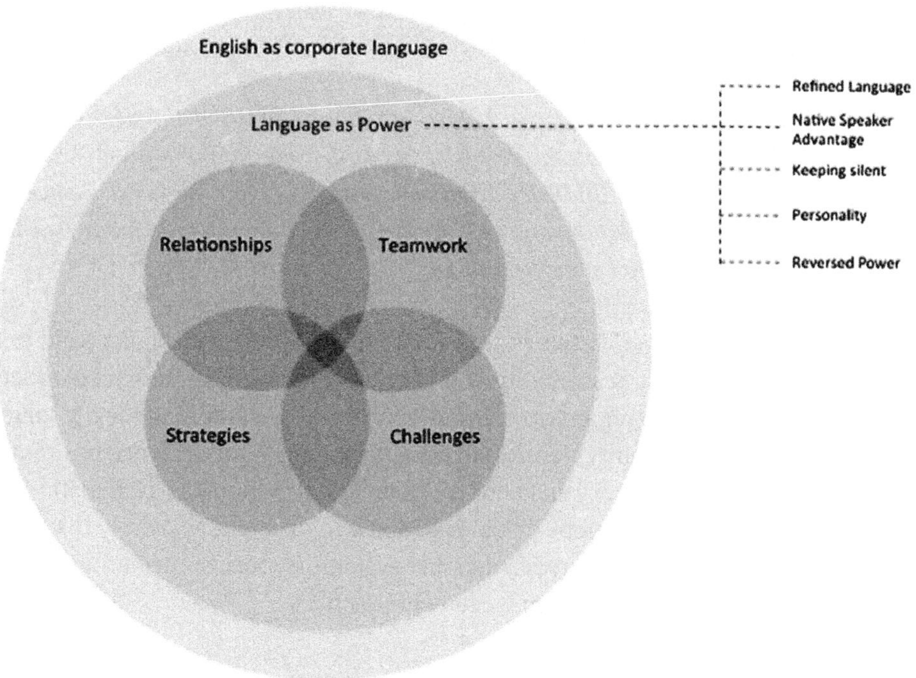

Figure 5. An application of a perspectivising technique as illustrated in the Götheborg IV model unto the concept of knowledge transfer by Bälter and Dennermyr (2016)

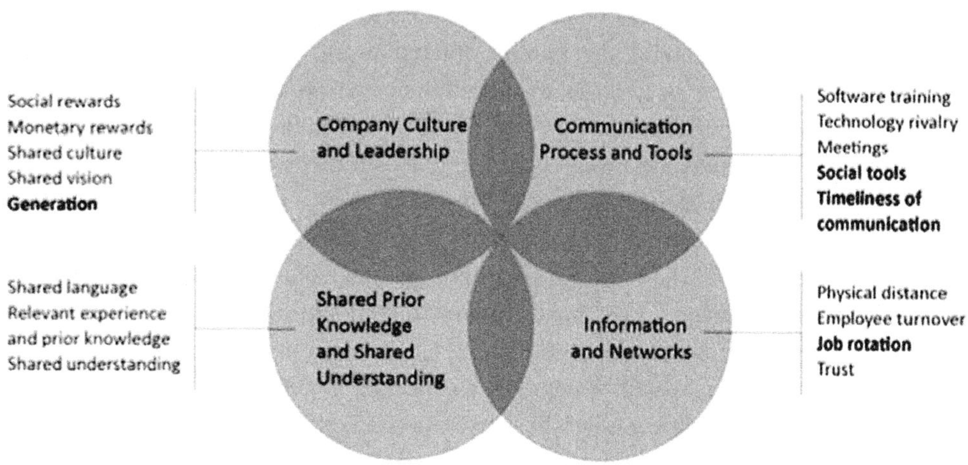

is that if they are not studying organization culture or firm globalization processes, the perspectivising method is not needed for them to graduate. As a counter measure to these challenges, groups of students have been encouraged to apply the perspectivising model as a tool towards other topics of interest, apart from organization culture that is used as a class example.

The Götheborg IV Model and Future Research Directions Towards Industry 5.0

Whilst i4.0 puts cyber physical technology at centre stage, building up digital infrastructures, networks and inter-connectivity, Industry 5.0, that will be enabled by advances in biotechnology and synthetic biology (Sachsenmeier, 2016), puts the human factor back at centre stage alongside technologies:

From previous industrial paradigm shifts, we have— post hoc—learned the necessity of an engaged academic and public dialogue. Industry 4.0 has already triggered a debate about what it will be like to live alongside robots in the future. Industry 5.0 discussions touch on the very essence of humanity's existence, physical integrity, and relationship with nature. At the moment this debate seems theoretical, yet it will soon come to the fore (Sachsenmeier, 2016).

As such, it seems that from a qualitative research aspect, the ability for scholars and practitioners in the near future to perspectivise their research study will become increasingly crucial in order to engage in academic and public dialogue with regards to international business, trade, and the continued refining of an integral eco-perspective of humanity's co-existence with nature. Whilst science has shown repeatedly that all things are interconnected, theory and concept seem to fall behind in a systematic perspectivising of activities and happenings. Applications of the G4 model in different academic disciplines could be seen as complementing knowledge acquired from other systems studies, contributing towards the building of an integral worldview for better life management practices.

CONCLUSION

The purpose and focus of this article has been to address a fundamental challenge faced by master thesis students when about to formulate their thesis writing project, which is the question of theoretical perspectivising, and launching their own research point of view. An example of the study and teaching of culture in IB studies was presented, that can be situated as part of the process of firm globalization taught to students in the field of IB, as a means to find their own theoretical perspective and grounding for their writing. When placed in the broader context of i4.0, it can be seen that the ability and capacity to perspectivise research position and research design makes for a crucial element in being able to take part in scholastic and public dialogue on important issues pegged at different levels, from international business and trade to knowledge about the management of new technologies and bio-sciences.

The G4 model, which applies the Pronoun system of language in use unto the elements of the UM in firm globalization theory, presented a systematic manner for students to reconcile the two dominant (and seemingly opposing) theoretical constructs of culture. Culture is a ubiquitous human entity that varies across different peoples and thus would be a good reflection of the different values to be negotiated for a common global vision. The G4 model shows that there exists no real dichotomy between the dimensional and emergent theories of culture, both perspectives are needed as part of a developing integral worldview.

REFERENCES

Allaire, Y., & Firsirotu, M. E. (1984). Theories of organizational culture. *Organization Studies*, *5*(3), 193–226. doi:10.1177/017084068400500301

Almodóvar, P., & Rugman, A. M. (2015). Testing the revisited Uppsala model: Does insidership improve international performance? *International Marketing Review*, *32*(6), 686–712. doi:10.1108/IMR-04-2014-0142

Alvesson, M., & Sandberg, J. (2011). Generating research questions through problematization. *Academy of Management Review*, *36*(2), 247–271.

Andersen, O. (1993). On the internationalization process of firms: A critical analysis. *Journal of International Business Studies*, *24*(2), 209–231. doi:10.1057/palgrave.jibs.8490230

Bälter, M., & Dennermyr, E. (2016). *Shared language, shared knowledge? Investigating barriers and facilitators to knowledge transfer in a common language context: The case of European multinational corporations*. Master Degree Project, Graduate School, University of Gothenburg. Available at http://hdl.handle.net/2077/48362

Bar-Yam, Y. (1997). *Dynamics of complex systems*. Reading, MA: Addison-Wesley.

Bird, A., & Fang, T. (2009). Editorial: Cross cultural management in the age of globalization. *International Journal of Cross Cultural Management*, *9*(2), 139–143. doi:10.1177/1470595809335713

Birkinshaw, J. (2002). The art of Swedish management. *Business Strategy Review*, *13*(2), 11–19. doi:10.1111/1467-8616.00205

Cäker, M., Andersson, T., & Wickelgren, M. (2011). Formal incentive systems in organizations with a Swedish management style: Conflict or interaction? In *Conference: The Actor-Reality Perspective*. Gothenburg University Publications (GUP). Retrieved from http://bit.ly/1xjBUi7

Capra, F. (2015). The systems view of life a unifying conception of mind, matter, and life. *Cosmos and History: The Journal of Natural and Social Philosophy*, *11*(2), 242–249.

Capra, F., & Pier Luigi, L. (2014). *The systems view of life: A unifying vision*. Cambridge, UK: Cambridge University Press. doi:10.1017/CBO9780511895555

Carneiro, J., Rocha, A., & da Silva, J. F. (2008). Challenging the Uppsala internationalization model: A contingent approach to the internationalization of services. *BAR - Brazilian Administration Review*, *5*(2), 85–103. doi:10.1590/S1807-76922008000200002

Cecil, K. (2004). Walking a maze of views to the center: Teaching point of view. *English Journal*, *93*(5), 54–59. doi:10.2307/4128936

Childs, M. L., & Jin, B. (2014). Is Uppsala Model valid to fashion retailers? An analysis from internationalization patterns of fast fashion retailers. *Journal of Fashion Marketing and Management*, *18*(1), 36–51. doi:10.1108/JFMM-10-2012-0061

Cordeiro, C. M. (2016a). An integrated perspective of a 'World Without Verona Walls': the Götheborg IV model. In Gränsöverskridande: Vänbok till Claes G. Alvstam. Centrum för Europaforskning vid Göteborgs Universitet (CERGU), skrift nr. 30. University of Gothenburg, Kompendiet, Göteborg, Sweden.

Cordeiro, C. M. (2016b). The Gotheborg IV (G4) Model and the Function of Language in the Globalization Process of the Firm: The Case of Swedish MNEs. In M. Khan (Ed.), *Multinational Enterprise Management Strategies in Developing Countries* (pp. 215–236). Hershey, PA: Business Science. doi:10.4018/978-1-5225-0276-0.ch011

Cordeiro-Nilsson, C. M. (2009). *Swedish management in Singapore: A discourse analysis study* (Doctoral dissertation). Gothenburg University Publications (GUP), University of Gothenburg. Available at https://gup.ub.gu.se/publication/93669

Cordeiro-Nilsson, C. M. (2010). A discourse analysis study of assimilation and integration of management style: The case of Swedish managers in Singapore. *The New English Teacher*, *4*(1), 13–53.

Crystal, D. (1990). *Linguistics* (2nd ed.). Harmondsworth, UK: Penguin.

Crystal, D. (1997). *The Cambridge encyclopedia of language* (2nd ed.). Cambridge University Press.

Dehghani, J., & Strandberg, M. (2015). *Well said, well done! Language as a source of power in multinational teams* (Master thesis project). Graduate School, University of Gothenburg. Available at http://hdl.handle.net/2077/39894

Fang, T. (2003). A critique of Hofstede's fifth national culture dimension. *International Journal of Cross Cultural Management*, *3*(3), 347–368. doi:10.1177/1470595803003003006

Fang, T. (2005-2006). From 'Onion' to 'Ocean': Paradox and change in national cultures. *International Studies of Management & Organization*, *35*(4), 71–90.

Fang, T. (2012). Yin Yang: A new perspective on culture. *Management and Organization Review*, *8*(1), 25–50. doi:10.1111/j.1740-8784.2011.00221.x

Flowerdew, J. (2017). Corpus-based approaches to language description for specialized academic writing. *Language Teaching*, *50*(1), 90–106. doi:10.1017/S0261444814000378

Forsgren, M., & Hagström, P. (2007). Ignorant and impatient internationalization? The Uppsala Model and internationalization patterns for internet-related firms. *Critical Perspectives on International Business*, *3*(4), 291–305. doi:10.1108/17422040710832559

Fuerst, S. (2010). The development of international business theory: implications for international business teaching and research in Colombia. *Cuadernos de Administración,* 33-51.

Gardner, S. J., & Wolfe, P. S. (2015). Teaching students with developmental disabilities daily living skills using point-of-view modeling plus video prompting with error correction. *Focus on Autism and Other Developmental Disabilities*, *30*(4), 195–207. doi:10.1177/1088357614547810

Geertz, C. (1973). *The interpretation of culture*. New York: Basic Books.

Gelfand, M. J., Chiu, C., & Hong, Y. (2014). *Advances in culture and psychology* (Vol. 2). Oxford, UK: Oxford University Press.

Ghoshal, S., & Bartlett, C. A. (1990). The multinational corporation as an interorganizational network. *Academy of Management Review, 15*(4), 603.

Goatly, A. (2000). *Critical reading and writing: An introductory coursebook.* London: Routledge.

Graves, C. W. (1970). Levels of existence: An open system theory of values. *Journal of Humanistic Psychology, 10*(2), 131–155. doi:10.1177/002216787001000205

Halliday, M. A. K. (1994). *An introduction to functional grammar* (2nd ed.). London: Edward Arnold.

Halliday, M. A. K., & Matthiessen, C. (2014). *Halliday's introduction to functional grammar* (4th ed.). Abingdon, UK: Routledge.

Hathaway, J. (2015). Developing that voice: Locating academic writing tuition in the mainstream of higher education. *Teaching in Higher Education, 20*(5), 506–517. doi:10.1080/13562517.2015.1026891

Hofstede, G. (1980). *Culture's consequences: International differences in work-related values.* Los Angeles, CA: Sage.

Hofstede, G. (1984). National cultures and corporate cultures. In L. A. Samovar & R. E. Porter (Eds.), *Communication between cultures.* Belmont, CA: Wadsworth.

Hofstede, G. (2001). *Culture's consequences: Comparing values, behaviours, institutions and organizations across nations* (2nd ed.). Thousand Oaks, CA: Sage.

Holden, N. J. (2002). *Cross-cultural management: A knowledge management perspective.* Harlow, UK: Financial Times/Prentice Hall.

House, R., Javidan, M., Hanges, P., & Dorfman, P. (2002). Understanding cultures and implicit leadership theories across the globe: An introduction to project GLOBE. *Journal of World Business, 37*(1), 3–10. doi:10.1016/S1090-9516(01)00069-4

Jacobson, M., & Wilensky, U. (2006). Complex systems in education: Scientific and educational importance and implications for the learning sciences. *Journal of the Learning Sciences, 15*(1), 11–34. doi:10.120715327809jls1501_4

Jeste, D. V., Ardelt, M., Blazer, D., Kraemer, H. C., Vaillant, G., & Meeks, T. W. (2010). Expert consensus on characteristics of wisdom: A Delphi method study. *The Gerontologist, 50*(5), 668–680. doi:10.1093/geront/gnq022 PMID:20233730

Johanson, J., & Vahlne, J. (1977). The internationalization process of the firm: A model of knowledge development and increasing foreign market commitments. *Journal of International Business Studies, 8*(1), 23.

Johanson, J., & Vahlne, J. (2009). The Uppsala internationalization process model revisited: From liability of foreignness to liability of outsidership. *Journal of International Business Studies, 40*(9), 1411–1431. doi:10.1057/jibs.2009.24

Jönsson, S. (1995). *Goda utsikter: Svenskt management.* Göteborg: Bokförlaget BAS.

Källström, A., & Solli, R. (1997). *Med takt och taktik: Om den ekonomiska krisen, våra kommuner och det kommunala ledarskapet*. Göteborg: Bokförlaget BAS.

Katz, D., & Kahn, R. L. (1978). *The social psychology of organizations* (2nd ed.). New York: Wiley.

Keesing, R. M. (1974). Theories of culture. *Annual Review of Anthropology*, *3*(1), 73–97. doi:10.1146/annurev.an.03.100174.000445

Kogut, B., & Singh, H. (1988). The effect of national culture on the choice of entry mode. *Journal of International Business Studies*, *19*(3), 411–432. doi:10.1057/palgrave.jibs.8490394

Kroeber, A.L. & Kluckhohn, C. (1952). Culture: A critical review of concepts and definitions. *Harvard University Peabody Museum of American Archeology and Ethnology Papers 47.*

Langhoff, T. (1997). The influence of culture differences on internationalization processes of firms: an introduction to a semiotic and intercultural perspective. In I. Bjorkman & M. Forsgren (Eds.), *The Nature of the International Firm*. Copenhagen: Handelshojskolens Forlag.

Lewin, K., Lippitt, R., & White, R. K. (1939). Patterns of aggressive behavior in experiementally created "social climates". *The Journal of Social Psychology*, *10*(2), 271–299. doi:10.1080/00224545.1939.9713366

Lindell, M., & Arvonen, J. (1996). The Nordic management style in a European context. *International Studies of Management & Organization*, *26*(3), 73–91. doi:10.1080/00208825.1996.11656689

Luo, Y. D. (2007). From foreign investors to strategic insiders: Shifting parameters, prescriptions and paradigms for MNCs in China. *Journal of World Business*, *42*(1), 14–34. doi:10.1016/j.jwb.2006.08.009

Mayo, E. (1933). *The human problems of an industrial civilization*. New York: Macmillan.

McSweeney, B. (2002). Hofstede's model of national cultural differences and their consequences: A triumph of faith – a failure of analysis. *Human Relations*, *55*(1), 89–118. doi:10.1177/0018726702551004

McSweeney, B. (2009). Dynamic diversity: Variety and variation within countries. *Organization Studies*, *30*(9), 933–957. doi:10.1177/0170840609338983

Meyer, K. E., & Peng, M. W. (2016). Theoretical foundations of emerging economy business research. *Journal of International Business Studies*, *47*(1), 3–22. doi:10.1057/jibs.2015.34

Michael Clark, J. N., Quast, L., Jang, S., Wohkittel, J., Center, B., Edwards, K., & Bovornusvakool, W. (2016). GLOBE Study culture clusters: Can they be found in Importance ratings of managerial competencies? *European Journal of Training and Development*, *40*(7), 534–553. doi:10.1108/EJTD-03-2016-0016

Osland, J. S., Bird, A., Delano, J. & Jacob, M. (2000). Beyond sophisticated stereotyping: cultural sensemaking in context [and executive commentaries]. *The Academy of Management Executive (1993-2005)*, *14*(1), 65-79.

Oviatt, B., & McDougall, P. (1994). Toward a theory of international new ventures. *Journal of International Business Studies*, *25*(1), 45–64. doi:10.1057/palgrave.jibs.8490193

Peng, K., & Nisbett, R. E. (1999). Culture, dialectics, and reasoning about contradiction. *The American Psychologist*, *54*(9), 741–754. doi:10.1037/0003-066X.54.9.741

Peng, K., & Nisbett, R. E. (2000). Dialectical responses to questions about dialectical thinking. *The American Psychologist*, *55*(9), 1067–1068. doi:10.1037/0003-066X.55.9.1067 PMID:11036717

Richardson, F., & Walker, C. (1948). *Human relations in an expanding company*. New Haven, CT: Yale University Press.

Roethlisberger, F. J., & Dickson, W. J. (1939). *Management and the worker: An account of a research program conducted by a western electric company, Hawthorne Works, Chicago*. Cambridge, MA: Harvard University Press.

Rosenmann, A. (2017). Mapping lay perceptions of contemporary global culture and its ideological and political correlates. *Political Psychology*, *38*(2), 351–369. doi:10.1111/pops.12316

Sachsenmeier, P. (2016). Industry 5.0 – The relevance and implications of bionics and synthetic biology. *Engineering*, *2*(2), 225–229. doi:10.1016/J.ENG.2016.02.015

Sackmann, S. A., & Phillips, M. E. (2004). One's many cultures: A multiple cultures perspective. In N. A. Boyacigilller, R. A. Goodman, & M. E. Phillips (Eds.), *Crossing Cultures: Insights from Master Teachers* (pp. 38–47). New York: Routledge.

Salk, J. E., & Brannen, M. Y. (2000). National culture, networks, and individual influence in a multinational management team. *Academy of Management Journal*, *43*(2), 191–202. doi:10.2307/1556376

Sandberg, J., & Alvesson, M. (2011). Ways of constructing research questions: Gap-spotting or problematization? *Organization*, *18*(1), 23–44. doi:10.1177/1350508410372151

Schein, E. H. (1990). Organizational culture. *The American Psychologist*, *45*(2), 109–119. doi:10.1037/0003-066X.45.2.109

Shenkar, O. (2001). Cultural distance revisited: Towards a more rigorous conceptualization and measurement of cultural differences. *Journal of International Business Studies*, *32*(3), 519–535. doi:10.1057/palgrave.jibs.8490982

Shenkar, O. (2012a). 2011 Decade Award Winning Article. Cultural distance revisited: Towards amore rigorous conceptualization and measurement of cultural differences. *Journal of International Business Studies*, *43*, 1–11. doi:10.1057/jibs.2011.40

Shenkar, O. (2012b). Retrospective. Beyond cultural distance revisited: Switching to a friction lens in the study of cultural differences. *Journal of International Business Studies*, *43*, 12–17. doi:10.1057/jibs.2011.42

Simpson, P. (1993). *Language, ideology and point of view*. London: Routledge. doi:10.4324/9780203312612

Skinner, J., & Gormley, G. J. (2016). Point of view filming and the elicitation interview. *Perspectives on Medical Education*, *5*(4), 235–239. doi:10.100740037-016-0278-0 PMID:27438056

Staudinger, U. M. (2008). A psychology of wisdom: History and recent developments. *Research in Human Development*, *5*(2), 107–120. doi:10.1080/15427600802034835

Steenkamp, J., & Geyskens, E. (2012). Transaction cost economics and the roles of national culture: A test of hypotheses based on Inglehart and Hofstede. *Journal of the Academy of Marketing Science*, *40*(2), 252–270. doi:10.100711747-011-0266-1

Steers, R. M., Sánchez-Runde, C., & Nardon, L. (2013). *Management across cultures: Developing global competencies* (2nd ed.). Cambridge, UK: Cambridge University Press.

Steward, J. H. (1955). *Theory of culture change: The methodology of multilinear evolution*. Urbana, IL: University of Illinois Press.

Theisens, H., Hooge, E., & Waslander, S. (2016). Steering dynamics in complex education systems. An agenda for empirical research. *European Journal of Education*, *51*(4), 463–477. doi:10.1111/ejed.12187

Tipton, F. B. (2009). Modeling national identities and cultural change: The western European, Japanese and United States experiences compared. *International Journal of Cross Cultural Management*, *9*(2), 145–168. doi:10.1177/1470595809335722

Todd, J. (2006). Introduction. *Nationalism & Ethnic Politics*, *12*(3), 315–321. doi:10.1080/13537110600882320

Triandis, H. C. (1988). Collectivism vs. individualism: A reconceptualization of a basic concept in cross-cultural social psychology. In G. K. Verma & C. Bagry (Eds.), *Cross-cultural studies of personality, attitudes and cognition*. London: Macmillan. doi:10.1007/978-1-349-08120-2_3

Triandis, H. C. (1990). Cross-cultural studies of individualism and collectivism. In J. Berman (Ed.), *Nebraska symposium on motivation, 1989* (pp. 41–133). Lincoln, NE: University of Nebraska Press.

Triandis, H. C. (1993). Collectivism and individualism as cultural syndromes. *Cross-Cultural Research*, *27*(3-4), 155–180. doi:10.1177/106939719302700301

Triandis, H. C. (1995a). *Individualism and collectivism*. Boulder, CO: Westview.

Triandis, H. C. (1995b). Motivation and achievement in collectivist and individualist cultures. In M. L. Maehr & P. R. Pintrich (Eds.), *Advances in motivation and achievement: Culture, motivation and achievement, 9* (pp. 1–30). Greenwich, CT: JAI Press.

Triandis, H. C., Brislin, R., & Hui, C. H. (1988). Cross-cultural training across individualism- collectivism divide. *International Journal of Intercultural Relations*, *12*(3), 269–289. doi:10.1016/0147-1767(88)90019-3

Trompenaars, F., & Hampden-Turner, C. (1998). *Riding the waves of culture: Understanding Cultural Diversity in Global Business* (2nd ed.). New York: McGraw-Hill.

Vahlne, J., & Ivarsson, I. (2014). The globalization of Swedish MNEs: Empirical evidence and theoretical explanations. *Journal of International Business Studies*, *45*(3), 227–247. doi:10.1057/jibs.2013.60

Vahlne, J.-E., Ivarsson, I., & Johanson, J. (2011). The tortuous road to globalization of Volvo's heavy truck business - extending the scope of the Uppsala model. *International Business Review*, *20*(1), 1–14. doi:10.1016/j.ibusrev.2010.05.003

Van Dijk, T. A. (2006). Ideology and discourse analysis. *Journal of Political Ideologies*, *11*(2), 115–140. doi:10.1080/13569310600687908

Venaik, S., & Brewer, P. (2013). Critical issues in the Hofstede and GLOBE national culture models. *International Marketing Review*, *30*(5), 469–482. doi:10.1108/IMR-03-2013-0058

Warner, W. L., & Low, J. (1947). *The social system of the modern factory: The strike, a social analysis*. New Haven, CT: Yale University Press.

Wilber, K. (1980). *The atman project: A transpersonal view of human development*. Wheaton, IL: Theosophical Publishing House.

Wilber, K. (2000). *Sex, ecology, spirituality: The spirit of evolution* (2nd ed.). Boston: Shambhala.

Zander, L. (2004). Editorial: Dialogue on identifying culture. *International Journal of Cross Cultural Management*, *4*(3), 275–290. doi:10.1177/1470595804047812

KEY TERMS AND DEFINITIONS

Complex Systems: A complex system is one that is composed of many interacting components. In many cases it is useful to represent these components as nodes linked by their interactions. Examples of complex systems are global climate, computer networks, multinational enterprises, and ecological systems. Complex systems can be characterised by non-linearity and emergence.

Holon: A holon is an entity that is both part and whole at the same time, defined as a whole in a whole, the larger of which is more than the sum of its parts. Coined by Arthur Koestler in his book *The Ghost in the Machine* published in 1967, holons are defined as hierarchies of sub-wholes that can exist simultaneously as self-contained wholes in relation to other subordinate parts. Complex systems can be said to be constitute of holons.

Integral: The word integral used in this paper can be defined as "whole." However, many ideas in this paper including that of complex systems and holons parallel that of integral theory, which refers to a meta-theory that draws together a number of existing theories in separate knowledge paradigms into a single framework.

Götheborg IV (G4) Model: The Götheborg IV or G4 model is a research/project design framework and tool that helps users to situate a perspective for research and project design in a systematic way. It uses the deictic (pointer) function of the Pronoun System in language in use, *I/You, We/They, It*, and *Its*, mapped unto four quadrants. These four quadrants also represent different types of knowledge zones.

Section 5
Process and Value

Chapter 15
Siemens' Customer Value Proposition for the Migration of Legacy Devices to Cyber-Physical Systems in Industrie 4.0

Diana Claudia Cozmiuc
University of the West Timisoara, Romania

Ioan I. Petrisor
University of the West Timisoara, Romania

ABSTRACT

Industry is transforming from Industrie 3.0, automation, to Industrie 4.0, digitalization. Siemens intends to be a key player in Industrie 4.0, whose customer value proposition will shape manufacturing industries at customers. This chapter analyzes Siemens' customer value proposition for cyber-physical systems as manufacturing equipment and products in terms of this technology's impact on value. The goal is to identify concrete value drivers which cyber-physical systems technology in Industrie 4.0 brings. The statements about these value drivers belong to Siemens and are compared to operations' management literature. Cyber-physical systems negotiating as peer-to-peer in Industrie 4.0 will bring a new level of complexity. Manufacturing complexity builds complex products. Cyber-physical systems peer-to-peer negotiation decides manufacturing scheduling and brings unprecedented levels of complexity and flexibility. Manufacturing complexity enables new business models, one of which is mass customization.

INTRODUCTION

Within the context of digital disruption, Industrie 4.0 is a vision for the digital disruption in manufacturing. This vision involves a proposal of technology to be developed, cyber-physical systems, as manufacturing equipment. This chapter explores, analyzes, induces, critiques Siemens' research and development strategy

DOI: 10.4018/978-1-5225-3468-6.ch015

for cyber-physical systems as manufacturing equipment, as products, the manufacturing processes they perform, their capabilities and performance achievements, the smart factories they are part of and the new business models they enable. The ground of this research is the advent of Industrie 4.0 at Siemens, competitors and customers (manufacturing industries). The research methodology for the literature review follows the main topics proposed by the Industrie 4.0 project in the journal databases. For the empirical study, the research relies on a large body of evidence about Siemens that covers all publicly available communications about Siemens in annual reports, on the Siemens Web site, in Siemens Pictures of the Future, Siemens the Magazine, in press releases, other reports and Google searches by key words. As Siemens is researching and developing cyber-physical system technology, this chapter expounds how Siemens complements cyber-physical systems technology with its key value drivers.

BACKGROUND

The Industrie 4.0 proposal

Industrie 4.0 is the name for the fourth technology generation in manufacturing history, which is attributed to a technology revolution. Whereas Industrie 1.0 was driven by steam and lasted between 1700-1860, Industrie 2.0 means the assembly line and spanned 1870-1969, Industrie 3.0 involves automation technology during 1969-2020 and Industrie 4.0 refers to manufacturing based on cyber-physical systems to take place after 2020 (Kagermann et al, 2013; Toro, Barandiaran & Posada, 2015).

Industrie 4.0 is a German name, which originates in 2011 from a project in the high-tech strategy of the German government, Zukunftsprojekt Industrie 4.0 and an initiative which promoted the idea as an approach to strengthening the competitiveness of the German manufacturing industry. Industrie 4.0 is a pillar for Germany's competitiveness in manufacturing. The key promoters of the idea are the Industrie 4.0 Working Group and the Plattform Industrie 4.0, and describe the vision, the basic technologies the idea aims at, and selected scenarios (Kagermann et al, 2013; Plattform Industrie 4.0, 2014). Industrie 4.0 is part of the Horizon 2020 research project CREMA launched in 2015 (CREMA, 2015). Industrie 4.0 is a topic of debate for the European Parliament (2015), which calls it *digitalization for productivity and growth*. This involves debates at the European Parliament organized with Angela Merkel, Germany's Chancellor, among others. The European Parliament (2015) relates cyber-physical systems technology with value drivers such as increased flexibility, mass customization, speed, quality, productivity, new business models. Industrie 4.0 has trigerred investment in future manufacturing technology in countries around the world. According to an expert quoted by the European Parliament, investment in the Industrial Internet cyber-physical systems create is to shift from 20 billion USD in 2012 to 500 billion USD in 2020. The investment will shift value added from 23 billion USD to 1300 billion USD in 2020. Countries around the world follow. In USA, the National Network for Manufacturing Innovation is funded with 1 billion USD (European Parliament, 2015). In Asia/ Pacific, companies are expected to invest 60 billion USD in Industrie 4.0 by 2020 (European Parliament, 2015).

Industrie 4.0 is a collective term for technologies and concepts of value chain organization (Hermann, Pentek, & Otto, 2015). Within the modular structured smart factories of Industrie 4.0, cyber-physical systems monitor physical processes, create a virtual copy of the physical world and make decentralized decisions. Over the Internet of Things, cyber-physical systems communicate and cooperate with each other and humans in real time. Via the Internet of Services, both internal and cross organizational services are offered and utilized by participants to the value chain. Industrie 4.0 is *a new level of value chain organization and management across the lifecycle of products* (Plattform Industrie 4.0, 2014). In the Plattform Industrie 4.0 publication, Kagermann et al. (2013) describe their vision of Industrie 4.0 as follows: "In the future, businesses will establish global networks that incorporate their machinery, warehousing systems and production facilities in the shape of cyber-physical systems. In the manufacturing environment, these cyber-physical systems comprise smart machines, storage systems and production facilities capable of autonomously exchanging information, triggering actions and controlling each other independently. This facilitates fundamental improvements to the industrial processes involved in manufacturing, engineering, material usage and supply chain and life cycle management. The smart factories that are already beginning to appear employ a completely new approach to production. Smart products are uniquely identifiable, may be located at all times and know their own history, current status and alternative routes to achieving their target state. The embedded manufacturing systems are vertically networked with business processes within factories and enterprises and horizontally connected to dispersed value networks that can be managed in real time – from the moment an order is placed right through to outbound logistics. In addition, they both enable and require end-to-end engineering across the entire value chain.". In a nutshell, this means Industrie 4.0 will virtualize products, manufacturing equipment, logistics equipment modularly as cyber-physical systems and enable them to make and negotiate decisions about the manufacturing schedule in smart factories across the Internet of Things and smart supply chains across the Internet of Services.

Industrie 4.0 may be, via technology innovation and business model innovation, digital disruption in manufacturing (Plattform Industrie 4.0, 2017). The digital technology Industrie 4.0 focuses on is cyber-physical systems and their interaction across the Internet (Kagermann et al., 2013).

MAIN FOCUS OF THE CHAPTER

Issues, Controversies, Problems

Industrie 4.0 is a proposal to make manufacturing in high-cost countries, particularly Germany and later the European Union, earn a high return on investment in manufacturing. This is accomplished via technology innovation in cyber-physical systems, which brings a new metric in manufacturing, complexity, which at its turn enables new, unprecedented, performance indicators and new, unprecedented, business models. This chapter builds a case example on how Siemens intends to meet technology innovation (cyber-physical systems technology) for Industrie 4.0 and its business sense, value. Siemens intends to lead Industrie 4.0 (Siemens, 2013c). Since 2013, Siemens has communicated its plans for Industrie 4.0 and this is to develop the envisioned technology with concrete value benefits to customers. Cyber-physical systems are not only researched and developed as technology per se, but also as process owners and parts of systems of systems such as the smart factory and the smart supply chain. They bring new types of performance and value drivers, which my be the pillars of new business models. This chapter is case study about how technology, cyber-physical systems, and its capabilities, the main of which is complexity, create value.

Industrie 4.0: Production Based on Cyber-Physical Systems

According to Monostori et al (2016), Mosterman and Zander (2016), Toro, Barandiaran, and Posada (2015), Ivanov, Sokolov, and Ivanova (2016); Lee, Bagheri, and Kao (2015); Qin, Liu, and Grosvenor (2016), cyber-physical systems are one of the most significant advances in the development of computer science, information and communication. Cyber-physical systems are defined by Lee as orchestrations of computers and physical systems. Embedded computers control physical processes, usually with feed-back loops, where physical processes affect computations and vice-versa (Lee, 2012; Lee, 2017).

Cyber-physical systems are adapted to Industrie 4.0. According to Toro, Barandiaran, and Posada (2015), cyber-physical systems are

systems of collaborating computational entities which are in intensive connection with the surrounding physical world and its ongoing processes, providing and using, at the same time, data accessing and data processing services available on the Internet.

Cyber-physical systems may be production equipment. Cyber-physical production systems rely on the latest, and the foreseeable further developments of computer science, information and communication technologies on one hand, and of manufacturing science and technology, on the other. They may lead to the 4th industrial revolution, Industrie 4.0. Cyber-physical systems are central to the Industrie 4.0 vision and are furthermore entitled to be part of smart machines, storage systems and production facilities able to exchange information with autonomy and intelligence (Toro, Barandiaran, & Posada, 2015).

Cyber-physical systems is a technology proposal to the world, adapted to manufacturing by the Industrie 4.0 working group. Research is being conducted in order to bring cyber-physical systems to reach the Industrie 4.0 proposal. An important component of Industrie 4.0 is the convergence of the physical and the virtual worlds (Kagermann, 2013) made possible by cyber physical systems. Powerful, autonomous microcomputers (embedded systems) are increasingly being wirelessly networked with each other and with the Internet of Things. This is resulting in the convergence of the physical world and the virtual world (cyberspace) in the form of cyber-physical systems (Kagermann, 2013). Industrie 4.0 relies on concepts such as vertical integration, end-to-end engineering, horizontal integration, cyber-physical systems, smart factories, smart supply chains (Cozmiuc & Petrisor,). This chapter relies on 2017 research about cyber-physical systems (Shafiq, Sanin, Szczerbicki, & Toro, 2017), which shows that the convergence of the physical world with the virtual world in manufacturing takes place at three levels: the first is resource/object level, the second is the process level and the third is the factory/system level.

Research and Development Topic for Cyber-Physical Systems and Industrie 4.0 Level 1: Cyber-Physical Systems as Resources

A virtual engineering object (Shafiq, Sanin, Szczerbicki, & Toro, 2017) is knowledge representation of an engineering artefact and it has three main features: (1) the embedding of the decisional model; (2) a geometric representation, and; (3) the necessary means to relate this virtualization to the physical object being represented. In manufacturing, cyber-physical systems are cyber-physical products which negotiate with cyber-physical factory equipment their design needs (Qin, Liu, & Grosvenor, 2016). Treating cyber-physical systems as manufacturing resources entitles them to be part of smart machines, storage systems and production facilities able to exchange information with autonomy and intelligence

(Toro, Barandiaran, & Posada, 2015). In Industrie 4.0, cyber-physical systems are key, and designing cyber-physical systems to create flexible and reconfigurable manufacturing systems is called vertical integration (Kagermann et al, 2013). Vertical integration is one of key topics in Industrie 4.0 (Kagermann et al, 2013). Vertical integration and networked manufacturing systems describe

the intelligent cross-linking and digitalization within the different aggregation and hierarchical levels of a value creation module from manufacturing stations via manufacturing cells, lines and factories, also integrating the associated value chain activities such as marketing and sales or technology development (Acatech: Umsetzungsstrategie Industrie 4.0 Ergebnisbericht der Plattform Industrie 4.0. acatech, 2015, cited by Stock & Seliger, 2016).

The proponents of the Industrie 4.0 model (Kagermann et al, 2013) cite Siemens as reference for making this recommendation. As far as vertical integration is concerned, the Industrie 4.0 intends to use this to design cyber-physical systems that create flexible and reconfigurable manufacturing systems (Kagermann et al, 2013).

From a technology perspective, an essential view to cyber-physical systems is the 5C architecture (Lee, Bagheri, & Kao, 2015; Qin, Liu, & Grosvenor, 2016), an example for guiding the development of Industrie 4.0 depending on cyber-physical system attributes. This architecture is divided into five levels: connection level, conversion level, cyber level, cognition level, and configuration level. The connection level focuses on hardware development, which is accomplished by the sensor network and wireless communication. At the connection level, the device is embedded with sensors, free communication and plug and play capability. On the conversion level, raw data is transformed into useful information by using data analysis technologies. The cyber level controls the entire network via the cyber-physical system. The cyber level involves clustering for similarity in data mining, time machine for variation identification and twin model for components and machines. This is the generally accepted cyber-physical level. The cognition level and configuration level engage artificial intelligence in the network, which are considered as future attributes of manufacturing. The cognition level involves collaborative diagnostics and decision making, remote visualization for human and integrated simulation and synthesis. Decision on priority of tasks to optimize the maintaining process can be made. This level belongs to decision support systems. Condition based monitoring,

involves self-optimization for disturbance, self-adjustment for variation and self configuration for resilience. The configuration level is the feedback from cyber space to physical space and acts as supervisory control to make machines self-configure and self-adaptive. This stage acts as resilience control system to apply the corrective and preventive decisions, which has been made in cognition level, to the monitored system." (Lee, Bagheri, & Kao, 2015).

This level belongs to resilient control systems. This view about cyber-physical systems has been argued as essential to Industrie 4.0 by authors previously (Cozmiuc & Petrisor,), who find it the most useful theoretical match for Siemens technology presentations.

In the Industrie 4.0 interpretation by CapGemeni, cyber-physical systems are smart products (CapGemeni, 2014). CapGemeni assesses smart products have a huge potential for growth. Smart products will drive revenue growth by enhancing the user experience and improving the total cost of ownership, which significantly intensifies the customer relationship and interaction: they will enable completely new value propositions and business models.

Research and Development Topic for Cyber-Physical Systems and Industrie 4.0 Level 2: Processes Orchestrated by Cyber-Physical Systems

A virtual engineering process (Shafiq, Sanin, Szczerbicki, & Toro, 2017) is a knowledge representation of a manufacturing process/process planning of an artefact that gathers and stores entire shop-floor-level information regarding the operations required, their proper sequence, and the resources (virtual engineering objects) needed to manufacture it. The virtual engineering process selects the necessary manufacturing operations and determines their sequences, as well as selecting the manufacturing resources needed to transform a design model into a physical component economically and competitively. In addition to this, information of all the virtual engineering object of the resources associated with the process is also linked in virtual engineering processes.

In Industrie 4.0, processes should be integrated end-to-end. End-to-end engineering across the entire product life cycle describes

the intelligent cross-linking and digitalization throughout all phases of a product life cycle: from the raw material acquisition to manufacturing system, product use, and the product end of life (Acatech: Umsetzungsstrategie Industrie 4.0 Ergebnisbericht der Plattform Industrie 4.0. acatech, 2015, Stock & Seliger, 2016).

The proponents of the Industrie 4.0 model (Kagermann et al, 2013) cite Siemens as reference. In the Industrie 4.0 vision, end-to-end digital integration throughout the engineering process serves the purpose that digital and real worlds be integrated across a product's entire value chain and across different companies whilst also incorporating customer requirements.

Cyber-physical systems make and negotiate decisions about schedule coordination (Ivanov, Sokolov, & Ivanova, 2016). According to Mosterman and Zander (2016), machine-to-machine technology is key to Industrie 4.0. Machine-to-machine communication in the Internet of Things is subject to research about Industrie 4.0 (Gazis, 2015). Similar research comes from Mosterman and Zander (2016), Ismail and Kastner (2016), Thoben, Busse, Denkena, and Gausemeier (2014), Brettel et al, 2016. According to Hehenberger et al (2016), designers of cyber-physical systems should focus not only on the separate physical and computational components, but also on their integration and interaction.

Researchers focus on the capabilities provided by current manufacturing technology and the gap necessary to reach Industrie 4.0 (Qin, Liu, & Grosvenor, 2016). Studies show existing production technology has a gap to the desired functionality of cyber-physical systems. Researchers focus on the capabilities provided by current manufacturing technology and the gap necessary to reach Industrie 4.0 (Qin, Liu, & Grosvenor, 2016). Manufacturing progressive concepts such as digitalization, communication, standardization, flexibility, customization, real-time responsibility, predictive maintenance will move to Industrie 4.0, which involves decision making, early aware, self-optimization, self-configuration (Qin, Liu, & Grosvenor, 2016). Further research needs to be conducted to meet decision making, early aware, self-optimization and self-configuration attributes of Industrie 4.0 (Qin, Liu, & Grosvenor, 2016). Manufacturing attributes that still need to be developed to reach Industrie 4.0: decision making, early aware, self-optimization and self-configuration will enable cyber-physical systems to make and negotiate decisions at an unprecedented high level of complexity. With respect to schedule coordination, research is conducted to increase machines' capability to manage complexity (Lee & Jung, 2016) and for the self-optimization of production systems (Brettel et al, 2016).

The core capability of Industrie 4.0 is a historically unprecedented level of high complexity in manufacturing (Kagermann et al., 2013). Research about Industrie 4.0 highlights the same feature: complexity. According to a report by Acatech (2011, cited by Schuh et al, 2014), cyber-physical systems can be characterized by five constitutive dimensions that lead towards "increasing openness, complexity and intelligence of systems": merger of the physical and virtual world; dynamic formation of system-of-systems; context-dependent and autonomously operating systems; cooperative systems with decentralized control; extensive human-system-collaboration. Complexity is a new metric for manufacturing (Kumari & Kulkarni, 2016). Modern manufacturing systems are largely characterised by growing complexity, which is evident not only in manufacturing systems, but also in the products, processes, and company structures (Kumari & Kulkarni, 2016). Among the various attempts made to model complexity in the past decade, the focus has been on complexity of manufacturing systems configurations (ElMaraghy, Kuzgunkaya, & Urbanic, 2005 cited Kumari & Kulkarni, 2016), complexity of mixed-model assembly lines (Hu, Zhu, Wang, & Koren, 2008 cited by Kumari & Kulkarni, 2016) and the complexity that arises due to product variety (Wang & Hu, 2010 cited by Kumari & Kulkarni, 2016). Further research remains to be performed (Kumari & Kulkarni, 2016). Production systems are modelled as complex networks, where cyber-physical systems lead to decentralized factory decisions (Becker & Wagner, 2016).

A key metric related to complexity is flexibility (Brettel, Klein, & Friederichsen, 2016). There has been a growing interest for flexible manufacturing and mass customization in the recent years. Literature has focused on various aspects of the topic like definitions of manufacturing flexibility, dimensions, classifications and taxonomies, measurement of flexibility, the relationship between uncertainty, flexibility and performance, or the dimension of supply-chain flexibility (Brettel, Klein, & Friederichsen, 2016). One definition of flexibility may be the ability to work with a high number of product requirements and production scenarios (Shewchuck & Moodie, 1998). This may be extended to complex product design. It is called operational flexibility and is measured as the greater is the ability to utilize the elements of the manufacturing system in alternative ways (Shewchuck & Moodie, 1998). Range flexibility is the total envelope of capability or range of states which the production system or resource is capable of attaining (Shewchuck & Moodie, 1998). One production system is more flexible than another if it can exhibit a wider range of states or behaviors; for example, make a greater variety of products, manufacture at different output levels or delivery lead times, and so on. Response flexibility is the ease in terms of cost, time, or both with which changes can be made within the capability envelope (Shewchuck & Moodie, 1998). Action flexibility is defined as the capacity to take new action to meet new circumstances (Shewchuck & Moodie, 1998). This corresponds to an early definition of manufacturing flexibility (Beach, Muhlemann, Price, Paterson & Sharp, 2000) is provided by Gupta and Goyal in 1989 as the ability of a manufacturing system to cope with changing circumstances or instability caused by the environment. Cox (1989) defines manufacturing flexibility as the quickness and ease with which plants can respond to changes in market conditions (Beach, Muhlemann, Price, Paterson & Sharp, 2000). Another similar definiion is the ability to change or react with little penalty in time, effort, cost or performance (Upton, 1994, cited by Beach, Muhlemann, Price, Paterson & Sharp, 2000).

CapGemeni points to decentralized production control in smart factories enabled by cyber-physical systems as a pillar for Industrie 4.0 (CapGemeni, 2014). Manufacturing schedule will be decided as price is on a market: decentralized production control transforms the production floor into a marketplace of capacity and production needs (CapGemeni, 2014). As each production module will be able to obtain the information needed to make decisions autonomously, the shop floor will consist of a network of locally optimizing decision-making agents. Based on a multi-agent system, the production environment will organize itself. This could be realized through a market mechanism on shop floor level: the capacity of production systems

represents the offer, while demand arises from the orders to be fulfilled. The business impact is mastering the complexity of individualized production without any additional cost, flexibility. Implementing decentralized control mechanisms will be the only way of managing the complexity of individualized industrial production (CapGemeni, 2014).

Research and Development Topic for Cyber-Physical Systems and Industrie 4.0 Level 3: Cyber-Physical Systems as Smart Factories

In this section, the extension of the virtual engineering object – virtual engineering process (Shafiq, Sanin, Szczerbicki, & Toro, 2017) concept to the factory level (i.e., virtual engineering factory) is discussed, and a unified architecture covering all three aspects of a manufacturing unit is proposed. A manufacturing factory is a collection of integrated equipment and human resources whose function is to perform one or more processing and/or assembly operations starting with a raw material, part, or set of parts. Horizontal integration across the entire value creation network describes

the cross-company and company-internal intelligent cross-linking and digitalization of value creation modules throughout the value chain of a product life cycle and between value chains of adjoining product life cycles (Acatech, 2015, cited by Stock & Seliger, 2016).

The proponents of the Industrie 4.0 model (Kagermann et al, 2013) cite Siemens as reference. In the original Industrie 4.0 proposal (Kagermann et al, 2013), horizontal integration will enable cyber-physical systems to support business strategies, new value networks and new business models.

Industrie 4.0 involves a high level of collaboration through production networks – also requires high level of information technology integration to support collaborative product development, collaborative manufacturing and all other value adding processes (Mourtzis, 2010; Neuberta et al., 2004, cited by Veza, Mladineo, & Gjeldum, 2015). It can be realized through vertical integration called production networks (Sturgeon, 2002 cited by Veza, Mladineo, & Gjeldum, 2015), or through horizontal integration called manufacturing networks (Markaki et al., 2013, cited by Veza, Mladineo, & Gjeldum, 2015). Production networks are seen as one of three key elements of Industrie 4.0. According to Veza, Mladineo, and Gjeldum (2015), since Industrie 4.0 is based on factories that are smart factories, these factories already have preposition to achieve information exchange in real-time across enterprises borders. It allows creation of flexible value chain that can have innovative product development and agile and smart manufacturing, so it can be called innovative production network. An innovative production network may be called temporary virtual alliance, a virtual extended enterprise.

In the CapGemeni interpretation of Industrie 4.0, cyber-physical systems form smart factories with decentral production control (CapGemeni, 2014) and smart supply chains with agile collaboration networks (CapGemeni, 2014).

ORGANIZATION BACKGROUND

Siemens is the largest European engineering corporation, with business in manufacturing, energy, building management, healthcare, transportation, smart cities on international markets. Siemens' history dates back to its founder Werner Won Siemens in 1847, with Siemens an international conglomerate active in a variety of businesses throughout time. Siemens currently has 79.6 billion Euros sales and employs 349 000. Siemens intends to lead all its markets based on technology and technology related innovation, particularly related to core technology in electrification, automation and digitalization. The most important of these markets is manufacturing industries, where Industrie 4.0 is a model proposal for digitalization in manufacturing, the technology, its capabilities, its performance, business models, strategy.

SETTING THE STAGE

Research and innovation are undertaken for cyber-physical systems. These are physical devices with a cyber-copy of their physical selves, the digital twin, which together with technology such as semantics, self capabilies allows cyber-physical systems to make unprecedented complex decisions about manufacturing, logistics and form smart factories around the Internet of Things and smart supply chains around the Internet of Services. Industrie 4.0 means production based on cyber-physical systems, a technology still being researched and developed. Siemens is more than a technology supplier to manufacturers: Siemens' solutions bring capabilities, the key of which is complexity, and concrete performance stipulations stemming from complexity, such as flexibility, that are included in contracts. Siemens has announced its intention to lead it in several progressive steps that will transform its customers' technology, its capabilities, its performance, business models and strategy in the entire supply chain.

CASE DESCRIPTION

Industrie 4.0 at Siemens: A New Capability, Unprecedented High Complexity Management Transforms Manufacturing

Siemens conceives Industrie 4.0 as a substantial increase in manufacturing complexity (Siemens, 2013d), that was not possible with previous technology. Since 2013, Siemens has announces its intention to lead Industrie 4.0, which Siemens summarizes as the algorithmicized "production chess" within cyber-physical systems (Siemens, 2013d, pp. 5; Siemens, 2013c). In Siemens' vision for Industrie 4.0, decentral cyber-physical systems (CPS) interact via embedded Internet-based technologies (Siemens, 2013d). The product to be manufactured contains all necessary information on its production requirements. Integrated production installations self-organize considering the entire value chain. Industrie 4.0 leads to flexible decisions on production process on the basis of the current situation. In the Industrie 4.0 vision, communities of machines organize themselves, supply chains automatically cooperate with each other, and unfinished products send data needed for their processing to the machines that will turn them into merchandise (Siemens, 2013c, pp. 54-55). Products and machines will communicate with one another and exchange commands. The factories of the future will optimize and control their manufacturing processes largely by themselves, thus increasing industrial productivity (Siemens, 2013c). Siemens sees Industrie 4.0 as a chess computer, an algorithm to determine the optimal move in any situation, by analyzing and comparing future game scenarios. According to Siemens, this is precisely what happens in Industrie 4.0: all the parameters and data used to develop and manufacture products in order to predict optimal production paths and then reevaluated after each step (Siemens, 2013c). Such flexible, optimized manufacturing processes will slash time to-market, for example, by speeding up the construction of production facilities. They will also make it possible to manufacture product variants and even single customized products easily and at low cost (Siemens, 2013c).

Siemens' solutions for Industrie 4.0 at customers come in several steps. The first is the Digital Enterprise (Siemens, 2016d; Cozmiuc & Petrisor,). It comprises Product Lifecycle Management, automation solutions and Digital Services. Siemens is the world leader in automation manufacturing technology (Siemens, 2017). Siemens intends to expand its number one market position in manufacturing and use it as basis for digitalization (Siemens, 2017). Siemens is also a leader is digitalization, for Product Lifecycle Management software and Mindsphere for digital services (Siemens, 2017). Siemens is to take a step by step approach to Industrie 4.0, where the Digital Enterprise is the first step and is already achieved. The future predictible step is migrating customers' production equipment to cyber-physical devices and creating smart products (Cozmiuc & Petrisor) and is already achieved in pilot plants at Siemens. Gradually, manufacturing will evolve until the self-optimization of cyber-physical systems anticipated for 2030 (Siemens, 2016d).

Complexity is the key capability in Industrie 4.0, and works as a response to market requirements for manufacturing industries. It is the high level of complexity managed by cyber-physical systems that sets Industrie 4.0 apart from its predecessors, Industrie 3.0, Industrie 2.0, Industrie 1.0. According to Siemens, delivering market leading innovation is driving manufacturers to more complexity (Siemens, 2014d) and generates risk. Siemens intends to turn complexity into competitive advantage for customers (Siemens, 2014d). Siemens intends to master complexity to maximize innovation and minimize risk (Siemens, 2014d). Complexity comes from complex products, complex processes, complexity in managing people (Siemens, 2014d). Manufacturing processes achieve complexity via decisions made by cyber-physical systems, digitalization. According to Siemens, digitalization is the only way to plan and optimize complex industrial processes (Siemens, 2014a).

This chapter is about complexity as a key capability in manufacturing and the performance it enables.

Cyber-Physical Systems Research Topic Level 1: Cyber-Physical Systems as Resources

Transforming Legacy Manufacturing Equipment to Cyber-Physical Systems

Siemens has already achieved Industrie 4.0 in its own prototype plants (Strategy + Business, 2016). Siemens provides solutions for its customers, which include the world leading share of automated manufacturers, to do the same. Industrie 4.0 means production based on cyber-physical systems (Siemens, 2016d; Siemens, 2013d). The migration of customers' legacy devices to cyber-physical systems achieves Industrie 4.0 (Cozmiuc & Petrisor). Siemens points to a huge number of legacy systems, the 300 000 customer devices currently connected to the Web of Systems for digital services, to be converted to Industrie 4.0 (Siemens, 2016e). Siemens intends to migrate customers' existing asset base to cyber-physical systems (Siemens, 2015g).

Siemens' approach for the Internet of Things bridges automation to digitalization (Siemens, 2015g). Today's automated devices are Web enabled smart devices which provide local automation, analytics and other services; they provide local decision making at the point of influence for operation fidelity, scalability and data ownership protection (Siemens, 2015g). Via several software technologies, these smart automated systems will be migrated to cyber-physical systems, that is distributed interacting autonomous devices which negotiate and coordinate processes. Siemens calls its approach to the Web of Systems *a device centric and system aware approach* (Siemens, 2015g). Intelligent and smart mechatronic objects make decisions independently (Siemens, 2013d).

The technology used by Siemens to migrate existing devices to cyber-physical devices is called by Siemens "Web of Systems Joiner" and makes legacy devices smart web objects (Siemens, 2015g). The Web of Systems "Joiner" helps migrating legacy devices of the installed base to the Web of Systems (Siemens, 2015g). This solution has several characteristics: high acceptance, wide distribution, better cost efficiency (Siemens, 2015g). High acceptance means it is well-introduced through numerous existing web services, easy to deploy and use. Wide distribution means independent from computing platforms and inherently network-enabled; can be deployed even down to very constrained devices. Better cost efficiency means reuse and integration of existing resources, reduced implementation costs and time-to-market. Siemens has already constructed first examples of cyber-physical systems in the Web of Systems: optimizing water networks IceWater (Siemens, 2015g); smart freight wagon (Siemens, 2015g); smart grid (Siemens, 2015g). Software is the main enabler for improvement and innovation (Siemens, 2013d).

A cyber-physical system (CPS) is a system of collaborating computational elements controlling physical entities (Siemens, 2013d). There are several technologies that are used to transform current physical devices to cyber-physical systems (Cozmiuc & Petrisor). These technologies are the digital twin, semantics, self capabilities (Cozmiuc & Petrisor, in press a). Cyber-physical systems are systems of collaborating computational elements controlling physical entities (Siemens, 2013d). This technology means cyber-physical systems have a virtual copy of themselves, the digital twin. This is similar to the cyber-level in the 5C architecture (Lee, Bagheri, & Kao, 2015). In the fourth level of the 5C architecture, cyber-physical systems are apt to make and negotiate decisions (Cozmiuc & Petrisor), and these decisions are related to the virtual copy of their physical selves: their design requirements or the processes they are capable of. Beyond the digital twin technology and decision making capabilities, cyber-physical systems at Siemens have "self" capabilities (Siemens, 2013c): self-organization, self-configuration, self-learning, self-healing, self-optimization, self-protection, self-explaining.

This intelligence in machines, which Siemens calls the chess algorithm in production, allows cyber-physical systems to make and negotiate unprecedented highly complex decisions. This leads to performance. Additional intelligence, which for cyber-physical systems means highly complex decision making or cognition, increases flexibility and performance in production (Siemens, 2013d). Cyber-physical systems provide maximum structural flexibility and robustness in complex, large-scale distributed systems (Siemens, 2015g). They are application empowered and provide highest functional flexibility and evolution over device and system lifetime (Siemens, 2015g). They focus on functional profiles and systems synthesis, lifecycle management and eco-systems (Siemens, 2015g).

Cyber-Physical Systems as Systems: Smart Complex Products

Whereas Industrie 4.0 can only achieved when manufacturing equipment is cyber-physical, the concept also involves cyber-physical products. In Industrie 4.0, the smart product has a digital twin that moves across the product lifecycle, creating the digital thread. The digital or cyber twin of the physical product begins with product design and is progressively enriched with information about production processes required, production engineering required, production execution performed and service needs (Siemens, 2014d). Products are growing more complex fast (Siemens, 2015e). Siemens cites Roland Berger Strategy Consultants, according to whom product complexity has more than doubled in the last 15 years until 2015 (Siemens, 2015e). Designing cyber-physical products moves progressively to the virtual world, where Siemens is seeking a full digital twin of complex individualized products that are realizable (Siemens, 2017). In order to achieve the chess algorithm, the product to be manufactured contains all necessary information on its production requirements (Siemens, 2013b).

Smart innovation, the name for all Product Lifecycle Management software solutions, the strategy to design and plan products, means customers will develop and produce with maximum flexibility (Siemens, 2014d). Product innovation makes products complex and smart (Siemens, 2015e). Smarter products are accelerating every industry (Siemens, 2015e). Smart products go beyond incremental to transformational innovation (Siemens, 2016i). Siemens argues in favor of smart innovation that in a world of smart, connected products, where entire markets can vanish with a single innovation, manufacturers must take a new approach to business. Next generation product design enables product complexity, modularity and reuse, performance and quality (Siemens, 2016d). The digital enterprise realizes complex products (Siemens, 2016d), as production based on cyber-physical equipment makes complex products and many production variants achievable (Siemens, 2014a). Product complexity also means individualized product variants (Siemens, 2014a).

Cyber-Physical Systems Research Level 2: Processes Orchestrated by Cyber-Physical Systems

New Production Scheduling That Meets Unprecedented Complexity

Production scheduling is decided by cyber-physical systems as products negotiating with cyber-physical systems as manufacturing equipment and logistics equipment. Cyber-physical production equipment knows the manufacturing processes it is capable of. Products are also cyber-physical and can negotiate the processes it needs. The product to be manufactured has all the necessary information for every step of its production (Siemens, 2013d). Machines and products exchange information for self optimization (Siemens, 2013d). The negotiation between the production processes required by the product and provided by the production equipment will make autonomous production decisions (Siemens, 2013d). The migration of legacy devices to cyber-physical systems enables digital manufacturing processes, which in Industrie 4.0 compared to Industrie 3.0 bring a new capability that is key to the others: complexity management (Siemens, 2013d). In Siemens' view, digitalization is really the only way to plan and optimize complex industrial processes (Siemens, 2014a). The automobile industry is a good example of that: it is not only characterized by tough competition and high cost pressure – due to their slight depth of manufacturing, carmakers also have to stay in command of a wide-ranging network of parts suppliers (Siemens, 2014a).

Siemens defines digitalization as a networked world of complex and heterogeneous systems (Siemens, 2016h). Complexity may refer to production processes in the factory or the entire value chain (Siemens, 2013d). It is a minimum pre-requisite for Industrie 4.0 that production equipment is cyber-physical and able to schedule production. Furthermore, complexity may refer to product design. Siemens designs cyber-physical systems to replace top-down automation production control, the cloud, with the fog (Siemens, 2015b). As cyber-physical systems are growing together, there is a need for a distributed architecture, a shift for IT platforms towards less hierarchical structures (Siemens, 2015b). Siemens proposes minimal invasiveness and peer to peer negotiation in place of the classical technical central solution (Siemens, 2015b). The central classical solution coordinates all units top-down. The minimal invasive peer-to-peer solution involves negotiation among intelligent units, such as building automation systems and power grids, where each cyber-physical unit gets to keep its own data (Siemens, 2015b). By placing functionality on lower layers, security is non-negotiable, direct access is given for for on-top applications, model complexity is limited, reliability and predictability are brought, enginering effort is reduced, self-contained modules and proprietary are brought, optimization of own business is allowed, and so are technical possibilities (Siemens, 2015b). Minimal invasiveness brings new complexity metrics (Siemens, 2015b). Minimal invasiveness allows business model innovation (Siemens, 2015b). This relies on intelligent devices being able to make and negotiate decisions (Siemens, 2016f; Siemens, 2016g).

Production Based on Cyber-Physical Systems Promises to Achieve Value Drivers to Customers

The value drivers sought by Industrie 4.0 for Siemens' customers are: integrating product and production, with shorter innovation cycles (given by product design), more complex products, larger data volumes (a product design issue), flexible production, individualized mass production, the ability to face volatile markets; these come along with high productivity, quality and efficiency (Siemens, 2016d). All these value drivers will be achieved together. Referring to product performance, Siemens proposes customers more complex products, individualized mass production, the ability to face volatile markets, quality. These value drivers will be enabled by cyber-physical systems as products. Production based on cyber-physical systems is able to achieve complex processes needed for complex product design, where managing product model complexity by cyber-physical systems is an issue researched by Siemens (Siemens, 2015b). This research predicts cyber-physical systems will achieve new complexity metrics (Siemens, 2015b). By achieving the digital twin of the product design, quality is enhanced (Siemens, 2013a). Individualized mass production is achievable, as evidenced; cyber-physical systems will support new business models (Siemens, 2015b).

Algorithmicized "production chess" means decentral cyber-physical systems (CPS) interact via embedded Internet-based technologies (Siemens, 2013b). This brings several types of flexibility, the first of which is modularity. Machines and products exchange information for self optimization (Siemens, 2013d). After OPC UA, this means production equipment offers information about the production processes it is capable of, and products offer information about the production steps they require (Siemens, 2014b). Products know their own production systems (Siemens, 2013a). Modular production units provide optimized organization of networked production facilities taking into account the entire value chain (Siemens, 2014b). Cyber-physical systems are modular production units with complete and consistent virtual image (Siemens, 2014c). The classic static production line in manufacturing is being complemented by modular designs (Siemens, 2015c).

Modularity is a pre-requisite for flexibility. Moving from automation, Industrie 3.0., to digitalization, Industrie 4.0. will bring previously unaimagined complexity in products, processes and people (Siemens, 2013b; Siemens, 2013c; Siemens, 2014d). Siemens' vision for Industrie 4.0 is based on the chess algorithm in production: complexity (Siemens, 2013c; Siemens, 2013b). Siemens calls this algorithmicized "production chess" within cyber-physical systems (Siemens, 2013b), which means decentral cyber-physical systems interact via embedded Internet-based technologies. Cognition in machines leads to decisions; in Industrie 4.0, these decisions are to derive required actions, to sequence actions, to schedule actions (Siemens, 2016f; Siemens, 2016g), that is, to schedule production. Production steps are configured as follows: cyber-physical systems simulate and compare production options on the basis of instructions; cyber-physical systems propose compliant "optimal" production paths; an optimal production path is selected; production is implemented (Siemens, 2013b). The chess algorithm means decisions consider a significantly larger number of options than previously possible. Processes are decided considering all past actions and future scenarios for the optimal production schedule. Production is autonomous with embedded inteligence (Siemens, 2015c). These decisions are flexible on the basis of the current situation (Siemens, 2013b), considering the entire value chain (Siemens, 2013b). Cyber-physical systems form autonomous production facilities, with optimized organization of networked production facilities taking into account the entire value chain (Siemens, 2013d). In this new organization, production steps are configured flexibly in response to changing situations. As intelligent cyber-physical systems make decisions independently, additional intelligence increases flexibility and performance in production, manages complexity and increases the speed of changes (Siemens, 2013d). Artificial intelligence in cyber-physical systems enables them to sequence actions with higher flexibility and resilience and schedule actions with increased productivity, that is availability and efficiency (Siemens, 2016f). Industrie 4.0 (Siemens, 2013d) involves process optimization in dynamic networks. The production network involves flexible value chains with information available in realtime across company boundaries (Siemens, 2014c). Processes are optimized in dynamic networks (Siemens, 2014c). Complexity means a great number of options referring to production processes and product design in the factory or the entire value chain. Complexity in production processes brings flexible production (Siemens, 2016d).

Complexity (Siemens, 2014a) leads to a trend toward increasingly individualized products. Individualized production is a form of flexibility (Siemens, 2014c). According to Siemens, on account of the many features offered, trillions of versions of an automobile are possible, which is why practically no two cars leaving the assembly line are now alike (Siemens, 2014a). Despite that fact, all parts delivered by the suppliers have to be available on the line at the right time and in the right order (Siemens, 2014a).

As flexibility increases, so does the capability to face volatile markets. Siemens pilot projects Engineering Apps for Advanced Manufacturing Engineering Apps4AME and Skillpro aim to take stes towards developing manufacturing flexibility in the face of shorter industry cycles (Siemens, 2014a). Siemens aims to respond to customers' business environment, which means that the faster customer preferences change and the shorter product lifecycles become, the faster the production facilities needed to make those products will age. Siemens's response is modularity in manufacturing: to be able to update equipment regularly, inexpensively, and rapidly by replacing individual modules. With the "plug and produce" approach, new equipment can be inserted in a production system without a lot of expense and effort for installation, as part of the Engineering Apps for Advanced Manufacturing Engineering Apps4AME project (Siemens, 2014a). Another Siemens project called Skillpro will examine how individual components of complex production systems can quickly be added to, removed, modified, and networked together (Siemens, 2014a).

According to Siemens, higher flexibility is also required for another reason: despite the increasing variety of products and processes, production must not consume more time, energy, and resources than previously (Siemens, 2015a). Additional value drivers are high productivity (and efficiency). Artificial intelligence in cyber-physical systems enables them to schedule actions with increased productivity, that is availability and efficiency (Siemens, 2016f). Additional intelligence also increases performance

(Siemens, 2013d). Peer-to-peer negotiation of cyber-physical systems with the power grid makes them capable to manage energy efficiency (Siemens, 2015b).

Siemens has built pilot plants for Industrie 4.0 (Strategy+business, 2016), for example in Amberg, other parts of Germany and in China. Siemens achieves Industrie 4.0 in its factory in Amberg. In an interview with Strategy+Business (Strategy+business, 2016), Siemens CEO Joe Kaeser describes the prototype Industrie 4.0 factories Siemens has built in Amberg, other parts of Germany and China. He claimed to achieve machine-to-machine manufacturing schedule coordination, Industrie 4.0. This brings mass customization, almost full quality, and an eightfold increase in productivity over the past five years. Siemens' vision for the Amberg plant is:

the real and the virtual production worlds will be more closely intertwined in the future. By 2030, products, components, and machines may be able to communicate among themselves and, in addition to controlling their own manufacturing, also be able to optimize it. Products subject to individual requirements could then be manufactured at the same speed and with the same quality and cost-efficiency as those that come off the assembly line. Experts say that cyber-physical systems (CPSs) could serve as the basis for self-organized and self-optimized manufacturing. (Siemens, 2014a, pp. 40).

This means that, int he future, in the Amberg facility, production will no longer be organized as a production line for each product type, but each production line will be able to manufacture each type of product (Siemens, 2014a, pp. 40). This means, in a vision that for 2014 was still far future, each of the 19 production lines will be available to manufacture a new production order (Siemens, 2014a).

Cyber-Physical Systems Research Level 3: Cyber-Physical Systems as Smart Factories

Smart Factories Formed by Cyber-Physical Systems

Digitalization means that the physical world and the cyber world converge in smart factories across the Internet of Things and the Internet of Services (Siemens, 2013d). Cyber-physical systems will communicate owning all information as digital model (Siemens, 2013d). Siemens intends to move Web 2.0 to what Siemens calls the Web of Systems (Siemens, 2015g). The Web of Systems combines web technologies with smart networked devices and domain context (Siemens, 2015g). Web 2.0 combines ubiquitous communication: Internet, Web 2.0 technologies with smart networked devices: autonomous, interacting, local analytics, application enabled and domain-specific requirements, cross-domain integration, semantics (Siemens, 2015g). Siemens is a primer of the semantic web (Siemens, 2016e). Context driven interaction among cyber-physical systems is given by semantic technologies (Siemens, 2016e). The Web of Systems refers to the smart grid, to Industrie 4.0 and to smart cities (Siemens, 2015g). The Web of Systems is a new business model (Siemens, 2015a).

The Web of Systems is a device centric and system aware approach to the Internet of Things (Siemens, 2015g). Its basis is applying proven and widely used Web 2.0 technology and semantics within and across domains (Siemens, 2015g). The Web of Systems puts devices, machines and their interactions in the center of digitally networked industries. Devices process data locally and make decisions. Owners decide what happens with their data. Devices organize themselves and communicate with each other. New functionalities can be installed as with apps on smartphones. The installed base can be digitalized with the Web of Systems. Siemens delivers infrastructure and industry solutions characterized by: reliability, durability, data security (Siemens, 2016h; Siemens, 2015a). Siemens believes the Internet of Things has tremendous potential (Siemens, 2016e). In critical infrastructure, customers have much higher requirements regarding reliability, service life and data protection; for this reason, in a Web of Systems devices process data locally in place of the cloud (Siemens, 2016e). This ensures that the knowledge and the intellectual property of customers remain protected (Siemens, 2016e).

New Business Models for Smart Factories Enabled by Complexity in Manufacturing

According to Siemens, digitalization provides four different, yet mutually dependent levers to innovate business models in the manufacturing industry (Siemens, 2016d): products, value chain disruption, sales, services. Industrie 4.0 brings new business models. Although Siemens envisions a variety of business models, the most popular one is mass customization, where highly individual and complex customer orders trigger the production and logistics processes in the entire supply chain (Siemens 2014a; Siemens, 2014d; Siemens, 2015c). The innovation industries are challenged by high mix, high volume and high complexity (Siemens, 2016b). Siemens is seeing how thanks to the existing technical possibilities, entirely new business models are emerging (Siemens, 2014a). Siemens claims digitalizationis the only way to manage complex industrial processes and that, once this is achieved, it will lead the way to a command of networks that changes business models (Siemens, 2014a). Siemens notes a trend which Siemens claims digitalization enables, a trend toward increasingly individualized products: because of the many features offered, trillions of versions of an automobile are possible, which is why practically no two cars leaving the assembly line are now alike. This impacts manufacturers and suppliers. Customers place individual orders online: in many cases, innovative products are completely individualized items that customers configure online and that are then produced on demand (Siemens, 2015c). Since publicly tackling the Industrie 4.0 proposal in 2013, Siemens mentions individualized mass production as a key value driver (Siemens, 2013b; Siemens, 2014b; Siemens, 2015c).

CURRENT CHALLENGES FACING THE ORGANIZATION

Siemens competes by offering customers technology and a concrete value proposition for it in products, solutions, services and expertise. Success will depend on the quality of both technology and its customer value proposition.

SOLUTIONS AND RECOMMENDATIONS

Siemens works well towards providing customers with the technological and value innovations they need to manage digital disruption. Siemens' statements about value are general and work needed to be done to induce these trends from a variety of presentations. Siemens is concrete about value provided by existing technology, Product Lifecycle Management, which is return on investment and Mindsphere, which is enhancing specific performance. Siemens tends to be less concrete when it comes to cyber-physical systems, which is a tew technology in an uncertain highly competitive environment. In order to keep its advantage, Siemens might consider to co-create solutions for customers' specific issues rather than provide the direction to value in an otherwise blurry environment.

FUTURE RESEARCH DIRECTIONS

Research and development effort is conducted worldwide to reach the cyber-physical capabilities: digital twin, semantic protocols, self capabilities. The same goes for meeting complexity in manufacturing, which is the goal of Industrie 4.0. As the goal of this technology is not per se, the highlight of this research will be to make it create value.

CONCLUSION

Industrie 4.0 means production based on cyber-physical systems, and reaches a historically unprecedented level of high complexity. Industrie 4.0 brings new types of products as cyber-physical systems. These products are complex, intelligent, innovative, individualized. Industrie 4.0 means processes, that is manufacturing schedule, are decided based on peer-to-peer negotiation of cyber-physical systems. This enables highy complex decisions and manufacturing flexibility at the same cost and resource consumption as the assembly line. Flexibility is driven by modularity, peer-to-peer negotiation of cyber-physical systems, brings the ability to face volatile markets, and makes it possible to manufacture at the same level of quality, cost and energy consumption as in the past. Intelligent factories work with new business models such as mass customization. Industrie 4.0 brings innovative technology and previously unattainable value drivers that make investment in this innovative technology appeal to customers. In the Siemens offer to customers, Industrie 4.0 may be the digital disruption in manufacturing it is expected to be.

REFERENCES

Beach, R., Muhlemann, A., P., Price, D, H., R., Paterson, A, & Sharp, J., A. (2000). A review of manufacturing flexibility. *European Journal of Operational Research, 122*(2000), 41-57.

Becker, T., & Wagner, D. (2015). Identification of Key Machines in Complex Production Networks. *Procedia CIRP, 41*(2016), 69 – 74.

Brettel, M., Fischer, F. G., Bendig, D., Weber, A. R., & Wolff, B. (2016). Enablers for self-optimizing production systems in the context of Industrie 4.0. *Procedia CIRP*, *41*, 93–98. doi:10.1016/j.procir.2015.12.065

Brettel, M., Klein, M., & Friederichsen, N. (2016). The relevance of manufacturing flexibility in the context of Industrie 4.0. *Procedia CIRP*, *41*, 105–110. doi:10.1016/j.procir.2015.12.047

CIMData. (2016). *Siemens PLM Software's Simcenter: Predictive Engineering Enables Systems-Driven Product Development*. Retrieved on March 15th, 2017, from http://www.cimdata.com/en/component/docman/cat_view/43-complimentary-reports/45-commentaries?start=30

Cozmiuc, D., & Petrisor, I. (n.d.a). Industrie 4.0 at Siemens – steps made next. *Journal of Cases on Information Technology*, *20*(1).

Cozmiuc, D., & Petrisor, I. (n.d.b). Industrie 4.0 at Siemens – steps made today. *Journal of Cases on Information Technology*, *20*(2).

CREMA. (2015). *Providing Cloud-based Rapid Elastic Manufacturing based on the XaaS and Cloud model*. Retrieved on May 25th, 2016, from www.crema/project.eu

European Parliament. (2015). *Industry 4.0 Digitalisation for productivity and growth*. Retrieved on May 25th, 2016, from http://www.europarl.europa.eu/RegData/etudes/BRIE/2015/568337/EPRS_BRI(2015)568337_EN.pdf

Gazis, V. (2017). A Survey of Standards for Machine-to-Machine and the Internet of Things. *IEEE Communications Surveys and Tutorials, 19*(1).

Hehenberger, P., Vogel-Heuser, B., Bradley, D., Eynard, B., Tomiyama, T., & Achiche, S. (2016). Design, modelling, simulation and integration of cyber physical systems: Methods and applications. *Computers in Industry*, *82*, 273–289. doi:10.1016/j.compind.2016.05.006

Hermann, M., Pentek, T., & Otto, B. (2016). *Design Principles for Industrie 4.0 Scenarios*. Retrieved on January 10th, 2017, from http://ieeexplore.ieee.org/document/7427673/?arnumber=7427673&newsearch=true&queryText=industrie%204.0%20design%20principles

Ismail, A., & Kastner, W. (2016). Co-Operative Peer-to-Peer Systems for Industrial Middleware. *IEEE World Conference on Factory Communication Systems (WFCS)*. 10.1109/WFCS.2016.7496497

Ivanov, D., Sokolov, B., & Ivanova, M. (2016). Schedule Coordination in Cyber-Physical Supply Networks. *IFAC-ChaptersOnLine, 49*(12), 839–844.

Kagermann, H. (2013). *Recommendations for implementing the strategic initiative Industrie 4.0: Final report of the Industrie 4.0 Working Group*. Retrieved on January 13th, 2017, from http://www.acatech.de/fileadmin/user_upload/Baumstruktur_nach_Website/Acatech/root/de/Material_fuer_Sonderseiten/Industrie_4.0/Final_report__Industrie_4.0_accessible.pdf

Kagermann, H. (2014). Chancen von Industrie 4.0 nutzen. Bauernhansl.

Kumari, M., & Kulkarni, M. S. (2016). A complexity based look-ahead mechanism for shop floor decision making. *Procedia CIRP*, *41*, 63–68. doi:10.1016/j.procir.2015.12.032

Lee, E. A. (2010). CPS Foundations. *Proc. of the 47th Design Automation Conference (DAC)*, 737-742.

Lee, E. A. (2012). *Cyber-physical systems*. Retrieved on April 10th, 2017, from http://cyberphysical-systems.org/

Lee, E. A., & Seshia, S. A. (2017). *Introduction to Embedded Systems — A Cyber-Physical Systems Approach*. MIT Press.

Lee, J., Bagheri, B., & Kao, H. (2015). A Cyber-Physical Systems architecture for Industry 4.0 based manufacturing. *Manufacturing Letters*, *3*, 18–23. doi:10.1016/j.mfglet.2014.12.001

Lee, O. & Jai, J. E. (2016). Sequence Clustering-based Automated Rule Generation for Adaptive Complex Event Processing. *Future Generation Computer Systems, 66*(2017), 100–109.

Monostori, L. (2016). Cyber-physical systems in manufacturing. *CIRP Annals - Manufacturing Technology, 65*(2016), 621–641.

Mosterman, P. J., & Zander, J. (2016). Industry 4.0 as a Cyber-Physical System study. *Software & Systems Modeling, 15*(1), 17–29. doi:10.100710270-015-0493-x

Plattform Industrie 4.0. (2014). *Plattform Industrie 4.0, 2014: Industrie 4.0. Whitechapter FuEThemen*. Retrieved on January 13th, 2017, from http://www.plattformi40.de/sites/default/files/Whitechapter_Forschung%20Stand%203.%20April%202014_0.pdf

Plattform Industrie 4.0. (2017). *Shaping the Digital Transformation Within Companies –Examples and Recommendations for Action Regarding Basic and Further Training*. Retrieved on January 13th, 2017, from https://www.plattform-i40.de/I40/Redaktion/EN/Downloads/Publikation/digital-transformation-training.pdf?__blob=publicationFile&v=3

Qin, J., Liu, Y., & Grosvenor, R. (2016). A Categorical Framework of Manufacturing for Industry 4.0 and Beyond. *Procedia CIRP, 52*, 173–178. doi:10.1016/j.procir.2016.08.005

Schuh, G., Potente, T., Varandani, R., Hausberg, C., & Fränken, B. (2014). Collaboration Moves Productivity To The Next Level. *Procedia CIRP, 17*, 3–8. doi:10.1016/j.procir.2014.02.037

Shafiq, S. I., Sanin, C., Szczerbicki, E., & Toro, C. (2017). Towards an experience based collective computational intelligence for manufacturing. *Future Generation Computer Systems*, 66.

Shewchuk, J. P., & Moodie, C. L. (1998). Definition and Classification of Manufacturing Flexibility Types and Measures. *International Journal of Flexible Manufacturing Systems, 10*(4), 325–349. doi:10.1023/A:1008062220281

Siemens. (2013a). *Future of manufacturing, View on enabling technologies*. Retrieved on April 10th, 2017, from http://www.bicc-net.de/workspace/uploads/subfeatures/downloads/bicctalk_cps-ictlabs_2013_hahn-524ad62786aaf.pdf

Siemens. (2013b). *Shaping the Future of Production with Siemens: On the way to Industry 4.0*. Retrieved on April 10th, 2017, from http://www.siemens.com/press/pool/de/events/2013/industry/2013-04-hannovermesse/presentation-russwurm-e.pdf

Siemens. (2013c). *Siemens annual report*. Retrieved on April 10th, 2017, from https://www.siemens.com/annual/13/en/download/pdf/Siemens_AR2013.pdf

Siemens. (2013d). *Siemens – Industries 4.0 et smart mechatronics objects*. Retrieved on April 10th, 2017, from http://www.emm-mechatronics.eu/sts/www-emm-mechatronics-eu/img/ht/files/emm2014/ppt/siemens-caisson.pdf

Siemens. (2014a). *Digitalization of manufacturing*. Retrieved on April 10th, 2017, from https://www.siemens.com/content/dam/internet/siemens-com/customer-magazine/old-mam-assets/print-archiv/2/industry-journal/industry-journal-1-2014-en.pdf

Siemens. (2014b). *Future of Manufacturing*. Retrieved on April 10th, 2017, from https://opcfoundation.org/wp-content/uploads/2014/09/3_140805_OPC_Foundation_Redmond_v7a_incl_Siemens_Slides_20140731.pdf

Siemens. (2014c). *Industry 4.0, What is it, and what does it mean for us?* Retrieved on April 10th, 2017, from https://www.iica.org.au/upload/education/Siemens_Industry4_0_IICA.pdf

Siemens. (2014d). *Maximizing PLM Value in an Innovation Economy*. Retrieved on April 10th, 2017, from http://media.plm.automation.siemens.com/se_se/plm-connection/Hemmelgarn-Nordic-PLM.pdf

Siemens. (2015a). *Combining the Virtual and Physical Worlds*. Retrieved on April 10th, 2017, from http://www.siemens.com/press/pool/de/events/2015/corporate/2015-11-innovation/presentation-digitalization-automation-e.pdf

Siemens. (2015b). *Cyber-Physical Systems - contradicting requirements as drivers for innovation*. Retrieved on April 10th, 2017, from http://www.slideshare.net/heisss/cyberphysical-systems-49324556

Siemens. (2015c). *The digital twin*. Retrieved on April 10th, 2017, from https://www.siemens.com/content/dam/internet/siemens-com/customer-magazine/old-mam-assets/print-archiv/advance/adv152-en-screen.pdf

Siemens. (2015d). *Industrie 4.0 – Digitalization strategy*. Retrieved on April 10th, 2017, from https://community.plm.automation.siemens.com/siemensplm/attachments/siemensplm/tecnomatix-forum@tkb/163/1/29_Dr_Ulrich_Rossgoderer_Siemens_Industry_4_0_Siemens_Plant_Simulation_Usermeeting_2015_approved.pdf

Siemens. (2015e). *Innovation for the Future*. Retrieved on April 10th, 2017, from https://www.siemens.com/press/pool/de/events/2015/corporate/2015-09-analyst-conference/presentation-grindstaff-e.pdf

Siemens. (2015f). *Siemens Digitalization Strategy & Sinalytics Platform*. Retrieved on April 10th, 2017, from https://www.siemens.com/digitalisierung/public/pdf/Sinalytics-and-Digital-Services-Presentation.pdf

Siemens. (2015g). *Web of systems for a digital world*. Retrieved on April 10th, 2017, from http://www.siemens.com/press/pool/de/events/2015/corporate/2015-12-internet-of-things/presentation-iot-russwurm_web-of-systems-e.pdf

Siemens. (2015h). *Web of Systems – From research to real world*. Retrieved on April 10th, 2017, from http://www.siemens.com/press/pool/de/events/2015/corporate/2015-12-internet-of-things/presentation-iot-stephan-from-research-to-real-world-e.pdf

Siemens. (2016a). *Agile Global Manufacturing Networks are Critical for Your Industry 4.0 Strategy*. Retrieved on April 10th, 2017, from http://camstar.industrysoftware.automation.siemens.com/en/the-essential-role-of-mes-in-industry-4-0/blog/agile-adaptive-manufacturing-networks-making-industry-4-0-real/

Siemens. (2016b). *Defects: A Vanishing Species?* Retrieved on April 10th, 2017, from http://camstar.industrysoftware.automation.siemens.com/en/the-essential-role-of-mes-in-industry-4-0/industry-4-0-ready/

Siemens. (2016c). *Keys to success in the age of smart innovation.* Retrieved on April 10th, 2017, from https://www.plm.automation.siemens.com/en_us/about_us/facts_philosophy/smart-innovation-portfolio/#lightview%26url=/en_us/Images/Siemens-PLM-Smart-Innovation-Info-graphic-Part-3_tcm1023-237750.pdf%26title=Infographic: Keys to Success in the Age of Smart Innovation%26description=The same forces changing what you innovate are changing how you innovate.%26docType=pdf

Siemens. (2016d). *Industrie 4.0 from both a user's and a vendor's perspective.* Retrieved on April 10th, 2017, from http://www.sysint-conference.org/uploads/media/SysInt2016_Keynote_Volkwein.pdf

Siemens. (2016e). *Innovation for the Future.* Retrieved on April 10th, 2017, from http://web.stanford.edu/class/archive/ee/ee392b/ee392b.1166/lecture/may17/Siemens.pdf

Siemens. (2016f). *Sinalytics enables Digitalization: Industrial Data Analytics.* Retrieved on April 10th, 2017, from https://indico.cern.ch/event/524996/contributions/2193648/attachments/1287431/1915652/SiemensSinalytics-Roshchin.pdf

Siemens. (2016g). *Semantics-related Challenges in Data Analytics Applications @ Siemens.* Retrieved on April 10th, 2017, from http://dbonto.cs.ox.ac.uk/workshop16/Stephan_Siemens.pdf

Siemens. (2016h). *Siemens Digitalization Strategy & Sinalytics Platform.* Retrieved on April 10th, 2017, from https://m.siemens.com/en/about/core-topics/digitalization/media/pdf/Sinalytics-and-Digital-Services-Presentation.pdf

Siemens. (2016i). *The new age of smart innovation.* Retrieved on April 10th, 2017, from https://www.plm.automation.siemens.com/en_us/about_us/facts_philosophy/smart-innovation-portfolio/#lightview%26url=/en_us/Images/Siemens-PLM-Smart-Innovation-Infographic-Part-1_tcm1023-236310.pdf%26title=Infographic: The New Age of Smart Innovations%26description=Smart Innovation Portfolio Infographic Series, Part 1%26docType=pdf

Siemens. (2017). *Siemens Vision 2020 – Focus on profitable growth.* Retrieved on April 10th, 2017, from https://www.siemens.com/investor/pool/en/investor_relations/financial_publications/speeches_and_presentations/170110_presentation_commerzbank_conference.pdf

Stock, T., & Seliger, G. (2016). Opportunities of sustainable manufacturing in Industry 4.0. *Procedia CIRP, 40*, 536–541. doi:10.1016/j.procir.2016.01.129

Strategy+business. (2016). *Thought Leaders. Siemens CEO Joe Kaeser on the Next Industrial Revolution.* Retrieved on January 13th, 2017, from http://www.strategy-business.com/chapter/Siemens-CEO-Joe-Kaeser-on-the-Next-Industrial-Revolution?gko=efd41

ten Hompel & Vogel-Heuser (Eds.). (2014). Industrie 4.0 in Produktion, Automatisierung und Logistik. *Anwendung, Technologien und Migration*, 603–614.

Thoben, K.-D., Busse, M., Denkena, B., & Gausemeier, J. (2014). Editorial: System-integrated Intelligence - New Challenges for Product and Production Engineering in the Context of Industry 4.0. *Procedia Technology, 15*, 1–4. doi:10.1016/j.protcy.2014.09.028

Toro, C., Barandiaran, I., & Posada, J. (2015). A perspective on Knowledge Based and Intelligent systems implementation in Industrie 4.0. *Procedia Computer Science*, *60*, 362–370. doi:10.1016/j.procs.2015.08.143

Veza, I., Mladineo, M., & Gjeldum, N. (2014). Managing Innovative Production Network of Smart Factories. *IFAC-ChaptersOnLine, 48*(3), 555–560.

Wu, D., Liu, S., Zhang, L., Terpenny, J., Gao, R. X., Kurfess, T., & Guzzo, J. A. (2017). A fog computing-based framework for process monitoring and prognosis in cyber-manufacturing. *Journal of Manufacturing Systems*, *43*, 25–34. doi:10.1016/j.jmsy.2017.02.011

Zukunftsprojekt Industrie 4.0. (2017). *Digitale Wirtschaft und Gesellschaft*. Retrieved on January 13th, 2017, from https://www.bmbf.de/de/zukunftsprojekt-industrie-4-0-848.html

KEY TERMS AND DEFINITIONS

Cyber-Physical Systems: Orchestrations of computers and physical systems; embedded computers control physical processes, usually with feed-back loops, where physical processes affect computations and vice-versa.

Industrie 4.0: A research and development project for production based on cyber-physical systems with the goal of making manufacturing in high-cost countries in Europe earn a high return on capital.

Manufacturing Complexity: A high number of manufacturing processes and their permutations.

Manufacturing Flexibility: The manufacturing system's ability to absorb large-scale variety or changes, such as in volume, capacity, or capability.

Manufacturing Resilience: The manufacturing system's ability to absorb large-scale changes, such as in volume, capacity, or capability, particularly facing disruption and over the long term.

Virtual Engineering Factory: A collection of integrated equipment and human resources whose function is to perform one or more processing and/or assembly operations starting with a raw material, part, or set of parts; factory or supply chain level; level 3 of cyber-physical system research and innovation; business model level.

Virtual Engineering Object: Cyber-physical system; level 1 of cyber-physical system research and innovation; also known as system level; the technology that supports products, production equipment in Industrie 4.0.

Virtual Engineering Process: A knowledge representation of a manufacturing process/process planning of an artefact that gathers and stores entire shop-floor-level information regarding the operations required, their proper sequence, and the resources (VEOs) needed to manufacture it; level 2 of cyber-physical system research and innovation; the technology that supports manufacturing processes and logistics processes in Industrie 4.0.

APPENDIX

Evaluation Number 1

Smart innovation is the strategy to innovate products for Siemens' customers. Siemens supports customers to innovate, this is the main meaning of innovation here. Also, cyber-physical systems technology is a technology innovation, treated as such in a related article (Cozmiuc & Petrisor, n.d.a).

Evaluation Number 2

The reference list has been corrected. The data analysis is now focused on the value drivers the new technology enables. Siemens researches cyber-physical systems as core technology and adapts them to manufacturing. Not only at Siemens, but in the original proposal, this is what Industrie 4.0 is – digital technology, possibly disruption, in manufacturing. The issues with the references come with the adobe files – they show several page numbers and I had trouble choosing. They are now corrected. There is a lot to say about Industrie 4.0 strategy and digital disruption and it is hard to decide what to focus on in 10000 words. The chapter focuses on cyber-physical systems alone – when Industrie 4.0 means more than cyber-physical systems. This was the original intention of the chapter. I made the choice to focus on this technology and its customer value proposition in light of the additional literature review needed for Siemens's strategy for Industrie 4.0 in general, which involves several technologies, an analysis of the timeframe and many more details about the Industrie 4.0 business landscape. If this had been possible in 10000 words I would have done it. I hope that with the new data analysis, the chapter suits its title and intention and evaluation requirements. Cyber-physical systems and their value proposition are the critical part of Industrie 4.0 and of Siemens' strategy. It is cyber-physical systems technology and value proposition that may create digital disruption and that causes Industrie 4.0 to be a revolution when compared to Industrie 3.0. Unless they create value the revolution will not make sense.

Chapter 16
Process Excellence and Industry 4.0

Felipe Martinez
Independent Researcher, Czech Republic

ABSTRACT

The process excellence discipline comprises several philosophies, approaches, and techniques with different headings and origins. The history of the industrial revolutions is related with the beginnings and development of these process excellence approaches. Therefore, the aim of this chapter is to explore the evolution of process excellence throughout these four industrial revolutions in order to propose recommendations to successfully cope this new revolution from the process excellence perspective. The chapter reviews publications about the history of the industrial revolutions, technologies of the fourth industrial revolution, and it includes the outputs from a roundtable with Industry 4.0 experts. The chapter concludes that the concept of process and process excellence is essential to implement this new revolution and that the current practices of process excellence most be review in with the perspective of Industry 4.0.

INTRODUCTION

Process excellence involves several philosophies, approaches and techniques such as Quality Management System (QMS), Toyota Production System (TPS), Theory of Constraints (TOC), Business Processes Reengineering (BPR), Lean Management (LM), Six Sigma (SS) and much more. Regardless of the heading or origin, all of them aim to improve organizations by exploring their processes and determining specific changes.

The history of these approaches relates with the industrial revolutions. Each revolution brings into the scene new characteristics and aspects that influence these process excellence approaches and consequently, it is expected similar scenario from this current revolution.

Therefore, the aim of this chapter is to explore the evolution of process excellence throughout these four industrial revolutions. The chapter explores milestones in the process excellence philosophy, techniques and tools. The chapter proposes recommendations to cope this new revolution from the process excellence perspective.

DOI: 10.4018/978-1-5225-3468-6.ch016

The chapter reviews publications in the topic to determine theoretical perspective. This includes the outputs of professional and academic conferences on the topic and the outputs from a roundtable with industry 4.0 experts (Martinez, Jirsak, & Lorenc, 2017).

The main conclusions of the chapter are that the concept of process is essential to implement i4.0 initiatives and that the industry 4.0 provides process excellence methodologies with new aspects that enhance its activities and therefore the organizational improvement.

PROCESS EXCELLENCE AND ITS METHODOLOGIES

The relationship between i4.0 and process excellence has little presence in the current literature. It relates with the technological aspects, but it has less attention to processes excellence. The analysis of abstracts of i4.0 related papers shows some keyword occurrence of main process excellence concepts such as process (40%), Value (8%), Waste (1%) and Continuous Improvement (18%) but it illustrates low correlation with i4.0 keywords within these papers (Martinez, Jirsak, & Lorenc, 2016). Therefore, this chapter focuses on the comparison of the process excellence approaches throughout the four industrial revolutions. This timeline perspective contributes to determine the importance of process excellence to develop i4.0.

Processes are inherent to organizational performance. The pursuit of process excellence belongs to the strategy and management of organizations that continually seek to achieve better results. Early organizational theories introduce the importance of time in processes to manage and control organizations (Taylor, 1911). Henry Fayol publishes in 1916 "the administration theory" which summarizes fourteen principles of management. This also includes activities to achieve goals (Fayol, 1967). The creation of Ford Motor company in 1903 (Henry Ford Heritage Association, 2017) utilizes the manufacture model of Henry Ford (1863-1947) which increases process productivity with mass production.

Contemporary models also include processes among their elements. The "7S" model contains the organizational processes in the element "systems" (Peters & Waterman, 1982). The mechanisms for collaboration and the workflow determine the element "processes" in the "Star Model" (Galbraith & Kates, 2008, p. 17). The "Six Box" model (Weisbord, 1987, p. 9) present similar element: "Helpful Mechanism". The congruence model observes the entire organization from a process approach (Nadler & Tushman, 1980). Other models such as "Holonic Enterprise" (Ulieru & Este, 2004) and "Fractal Web" (McMillan, 2004, p. 170) also employ elements of the process approach.

These different organizational performance approaches develop several definitions and understandings of the concept of process in organizations. The mechanisms to achieve goals; activities to perform; interconnected activities that allow the functioning of the organization; time measuring for performance and others are attempts to define processes in organizations. Contemporary definitions of the term involve these elements. Hammer, et al. (1993) defines process as *a collection of activities that takes one or more kinds of input and creates an output that is of value to the customer*. Similar, Rosing, et al. (2015) understand the concept of process as

a collection of interrelated task and activities that are initiated in response to an event which aims to achieve a specific result for the consumer of the process.

Moreover, the International Standards Association (ISO) presents a general and specific definition of process that combines all these elements in a simple sentence: *A set of interrelated or interacting activities, which transforms inputs into outputs*, it has a process owner and it has process parameters that allow measure its performance (ISO, 2015).

These five elements (Outputs, Activities, Inputs, Owner and Parameters) summarize the definition of process (Figure 1). The Outputs are the most important element of the definition. They align the other elements. The Outputs contains customer's requirements such as amount of units, delivery time, design, etc. In other words, Outputs are what the customer needs. The understanding of the outputs determines the necessary Activities to obtain the customer's requirements. This comprise manufacture, services, marketing, finance and other tasks that in combination and synchronization create the desire output for the customer. The element Inputs refers to all material, tools, people and others necessary to perform the Activities. The process Owner is responsible for the correct functioning of the process. This person knows the process and knows how it works. Process parameters include time and other factors that allow the process Owner to manage and improve the process. The understanding of these elements facilitates the venture to pursuit process excellence.

The definition of the word Excellence stands: *The quality of being outstanding or extremely good* (Oxford Dictionaries, 2017). This definition together with the ISO9001:2015 definition of process declare that process excellence is outperforming set of activities, which transforms inputs into outstanding outputs for the customer. The Output is the result of outperforming set of activities that exceptionally coordinate different inputs. It has a brilliant process Owner that always guarantee the excellent level of performance based on parameters that always provide truthful data. Is not this a utopia? Yes, it is, but the pursuit of excellence is not. Then, process excellence is about to constantly work to be closer to this utopia. This is continuous improvement. The systemic repetitive implementation of tools, techniques and methodologies allow the organization to obtain long-term results (Gonzalez Aleu & Van Aken, 2016).

The process excellence discipline contains several approaches. The principles and evolution of these approaches are very similar. Some authors include some of the approaches as tools of the others or as complementary methodologies. This chapter only includes six of them: QMS, TPS, TOC, BPR, LM and SS.

Figure 1. Process definition
Source: Author's own work from the definition of process ISO 9001:2015 (ISO, 2015)

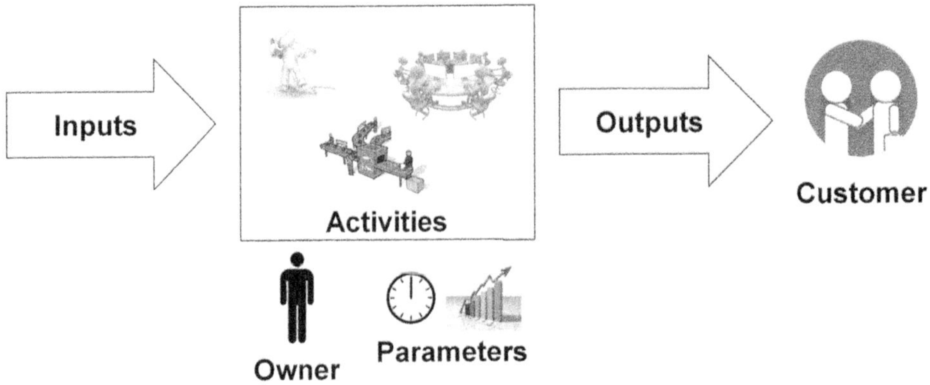

Quality Management System

This approach influences the organizational performance (Kaynak, 2003) and it has great emphasis in the organizational process excellence. The QMS introduces the concept of quality: *The degree to which a set of inherent characteristics fulfil requirements* (ISO, 2015). The approach aims to develop an organization that fulfils customer's requirements. QMS follows the PDCA cycle (Plan-Do-Check-Act) first discussed by Walter A. Shewhart (1939) with further development by Deming (1950) who also included the 14 points of Total Quality Management (TQM). The PDCA cycle is one of the main sources to argue continuous improvement in the pursuit of process excellence. The first step, Plan, includes the recognition of an opportunity to change in the organization and the creation of a plan that allows this change. The second phase, Do, realize the change in small-scale study. Then, it is necessary to verify the consequences of the change, Check, and learn from it. The last step, Act, implements the change if the results of the previous step are positive. Nevertheless, if the results are not satisfactory, it is necessary to come back and repeat the cycle from the first step. In both cases, the lessons learnt are input to the next use of the cycle (Tague, 2005).

Apart from the PDCA cycle, QMS implements the use of seven tools to achieve quality: The flowchart illustrates a graphical representation of the process as a flow of connected activities or sub processes. Cause-and-effect diagram (also called Ishikawa or fishbone chart) search for the root causes that create a specific problem or situation. The data checklist is a structured form to capture the needed data for a small-scale study or measurement. Control charts illustrate the changes over the time of a certain process parameter. Histogram is a statistical graphical tool that shows the occurrence of each different value within a data set. Pareto chart and Lorenz curve facilitate the establishment of priority factors. Scatter diagram explores the relationship of two variables. Stratification complements the tool when the mean of the data is unclear (Tague, 2005).

The ISO9001:2015 is the standard for QMS. The content of the standard includes context, leadership, planning, support, operations, evaluation and improvement (ISO, 2015). Context is about the organizational scope towards quality. This includes the organizational definition, expectations, stakeholders and the QMS documents system. Leadership refers to the activities and actions that the organization does to ensure a culture focused on quality and customers. This embraces the quality policy and the roles and responsibilities for the quality assurance. Planning involves risk management, objectives, plan performance and QMS control. The support element of the standard comprises all the activities and actions in order to provide the QMS with the necessary resources and competent people. Additionally, support explains the involvement of people with the QMS, the QMS communication and its documentation. Operations specify processes, products and services. This involves the development, implementation, control and monitoring of internal and external processes. It also includes the process to design products and services, its requirements, operation management practices, production control and procedures related with nonconforming outputs. The section evaluation concentrates on the practices to monitor, measure, analyze and assess the QMS performance. This includes QMS audit (internal and external) and management reviews. The last element develops improvements that the organization use to detect improvement opportunities, the procedures to reduces the occurrence of nonconformities, and the practices to enhance the effectiveness and efficiency of the QMS (ISO, 2015).

Toyota Production System

Toyota has become a reference of quality and process excellence. The books "The Machine That Changed the World" (Womack, Jones, & Roos, 1990) and "The Toyota Way" (Liker, 2004) have become a reference to the TPS practices. Moreover, the main reference author to the TPS system is Taiichi Ohno with publications such as "Just-In-Time for Today and Tomorrow" (Ohno, 1988), "Toyota Production System: Beyond Large-Scale Production" (Ohno, 1988) and "Workplace Management" (Ohno, 1988). Nevertheless, it origins involve the work of Eiji Toyoda (1913 – 2013) and Taiichi Ohno (1912 – 1990). The Toyota corporate website summarizes the key aspects of the TPS (Toyota Corporation, 2017).

The Figure 2 graphically explains TPS. This approach has a strong philosophical essence. The TPS goal is high quality, low cost and shortest lead-time. The term quality refers to the fulfilment of the customer's requirements. All the activities at the TPS must be performed with lower cost and as fast as possible but without compromising the high quality of the outcome.

Two pillars support the TPS. First is Jidoka. A Japanese word refers to automation with human element. The system separates the machine work from the human work but it combines both when necessary, for example, in the recognition of nonconformities. The system is able to detect the defects during manufacturing. Then, it has procedures to repair the issues or take out the piece (sometimes even stop the production line) and finally, it explores the causes of the abnormality and it develops solutions in order to improve the process.

The second pillar is Just in Time (JIT). It seeks for a continuous manufacturing flow. It means that the manufacturing process runs without any interruptions and does what it should. The concept of Takt Time allows the recognition of the continuous flow. The takt time from the customer's side is the rate of the customer's demand while the takt time from the production line is the rate of process output. The pull system activates manufacturing processes based on demand. Then, just in time is a system that allows the manufacture of the needed product at the right moment in the right place.

The base of the TPS includes tools such as heijunka, standardization and kaizen. Production levelling or heijunka facilitates the manufacturing process avoiding unevenness. Standardization allows the

Figure 2. TPS conception
Source: Adaptation of TPS house (Lean Enterprise Institute, 2017)

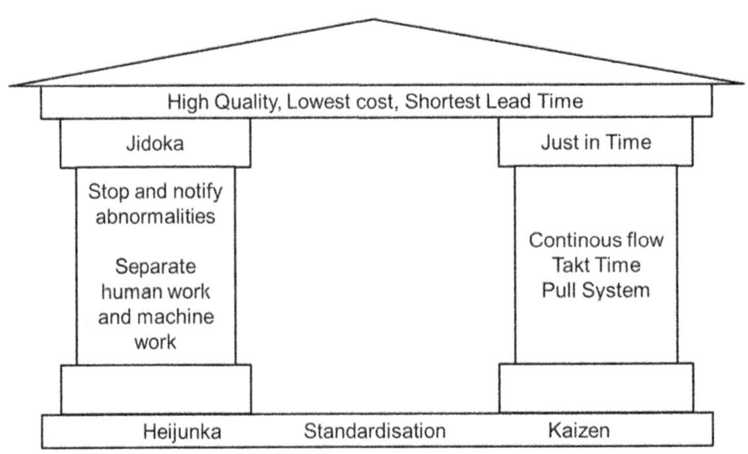

system to assess the performance of process and facilitates the improvements. The philosophical element of Kaizen refers to continuous improvement.

The TPS argue three types of system deficiencies that every modern, sophisticated manufacturing system should avoid. These are Muda, Mura and Muri. Muda (Waste) is an activity that consumes resources without creating value for the customer. TPS argue eight types of waste (Womack & Jones, 1996).

The next system deficiency is Mura. It comprises the activities that create unevenness, inconsistencies and irregularities. These changes lead to an unbalanced situation and generate production flow interruptions.

Finally, Muri refers to overburden, unreasonable, impossible or overdoing. It includes the activities with disproportionately consumption, burden and efforts of workers, materials or equipment.

Theory of Constraints

This theory searches activities, processes, actions or any other elements that prevent the organization to achieve its goals (Constraints). The TOC argues that "a chain is no stronger than its weakest link" and therefore managing constraints allow the organization to achieve their goals (Goldratt E. M., 1984). The author of the theory is Eliyahu Goldratt (1947 – 2011) an Israeli physicist that dedicated his life to teach organizations and managers principle of cause and effect in manufacturing and business (Goldratt Marketing Group, 2017). The most important book that explains TOC is "The Goal" (Goldratt E. M., 1984). The book is a novel for managers. It argues that the organizational goal is "to make money". Moreover, Goldratt (1998) explains that "make money" is the goal for a profit organization and the instrument to achieve goals for a non-profit organization. The TOC proposes three measurements to assess organizational performance. First is throughput or the rate that the organization needs to generate money by sales. Second is inventory or the money that the organization uses to purchase elements that allow them to sell. The third is operational expenses or the money needed to transform inventory into throughput (Goldratt E. M., 1998; Goldratt E. M., 1984).

The TOC implements the five-step procedure to improve the organizational processes (Goldratt E. M., 1998; Goldratt E. M., 1984). The procedure starts with the identification of system's constraints. The next step concentrates in exploit constraint rather than search solutions for its elimination. This means that the analysis focuses on activities and actions that allow the process constraint to work as much as possible. The third step subordinates all other process activities to the constraint in order to permit the constraint work at its maximum. It means that the process is as good as its weakest part: the constraint. Just after these three steps, the procedure searches for solutions that elevate the possible work of the constraint. At the implementation of any of the previous steps, the constraint can to move to other part of the system. Then, it is necessary to start over again at the first step and always prevent inertia. This last step introduces continuous improvement principle to the theory.

Business Processes Reengineering

The QMS and TPS are approaches based on continuous improvement. The combination of several individual projects at specific processes creates a process excellence system. However, there are organizations with archaic and ancient processes that needs a totally and radical redesign. This is the approach of BPR also called Reengineering. It takes the few acceptable things at the operation and strongly introduces process approach to develop new processes almost from scratch (Knights & Willmott, 2000). The origins of the BPR relates with the articles of Davenport and Short (1990) and Hammer (1990) and the book on reengineering (Hammer & Champy, 1993). The intention is to show that the total redesign of the organizational processes is worth more than small adjustments with long-term effect. Its application is radical and controversial, but it obtains great results in the short term (Knights & Willmott, 2000). The approach reviews the organizational goals, their processes and introduces IT solutions to the new processes.

The methodology generally follows four steps. The first step of the cycle is the identification of processes for reengineering. The best candidates are those processes with outdated fundamentals and obsolete principles. The process review aims to understand the purpose of the process in the organization. This includes the analysis of the customers and their needs together with the organizational goals. Then, the new process arises with new fundamentals and principles. It usually involves IT solutions. The final step tests the redesigned process and makes its implementation to the system. Notice that the reengineering fails to provide a continuous improvement approach since the process identification search for archaic processes. Then, the next process improvement arrives when the redesigned process become outdated. Moreover, additional work to the methodology introduces the Process Reengineering Life Cycle that provides consideration to the continuous improvement (Guha, Kettinger, & James, 1993).

Lean Management

The definition of the word Lean is: *(of a person or animal) thin, especially healthily so; having no superfluous fat* (Oxford Dictionaries, 2017). The use of this word is both a conscious and strategic choice (Womack & Jones, 1996). It indicates an organization with less waste (fat) in their processes and more value (muscles) for customers (Womack & Jones, 1996; Norlyk, 2011). The origins of Lean management refer to the book "The Machine That Changed the World" (Womack, Jones, & Roos, 1990). This book explores the implementation of TPS around the world and creates an enhanced version using different tools from TPS and QMS. Toyota Motor Corporation (2016) argues that Lean has become a fundamental component of Toyota's success.

The usual description of Lean management refers to waste reduction (Matawale & Datta, 2015; Matawale, Datta, & Mahapatra, 2014; Alemi & Akram, 2013; Vinodh & Balaji, 2011; Vinodh & Chintha, 2011). Moreover, Lean management is a methodology that creates value to the customer by reducing waste in a continuous improvement environment (Hines, Holwe, & Rich, 2004). The usual improvements delivered by Lean management implementations are more productivity, flexibility, performance and cost reduction. In general, the outcome on Lean management implementation is better processes. This includes efficiency, effectiveness, shorter lead, cycle times, lower inventories, and others achievements related with the TPS Muda, Mura and Muri.

Lean frequently uses tools from different approaches. For example, Kanban, SMED and 5S are tools from TPS while FMEA, DFMA and APQP arrive from QMS and automobile sector. Kanban belongs to JIT and creates a smoothly production flow (Ohno, 1988). Usually, the tools relates with cards and boards on the factory, but Kanban means the signal that informs the moment to start the production of a certain amount of pieces or products.

Single Minute Exchange of Die (SMED) is a tool that reduces setup machine time and therefore, it is possible to manufacture different types of products within the same working hours (Shingo, 1985).

The 5S is a five-step tool that guides the workers to organize their workplace (George, Maxey, Rowlands, & Price, 2005). It eliminates from the workplace all unnecessary elements (sort). It places the needed elements in best possible layout to develop an effective and efficient work (straighten). It cleans the workplace to increase the possibility to identify abnormalities (shine). It determines standards of the new designed workplace (standardize). Finally, the tool defines mechanisms to keep the workplace in excellent conditions in the long term (sustain) (George, Maxey, Rowlands, & Price, 2005).

The tool Failure Mode and Effects Analysis (FMEA) aims to prevent possible problems and issues in the process and product even before they exist (Mikulak, McDermott, & Beauregard, 2008). It is consider an essential part of any QMS (ISO, 2015). The tool explores any possible failure modes, its causes and effects. Then, it assesses their probability of occurrence (P), the severity of the impact to the system is failure happens (S) and the capability of the system to detect the occurrence of the failure (D). The risk level is a combination of the three assessments (P*S (+D)). The risk level determines the failure modes priority in order to create actions to prevent the occurrence of the failures.

The Design For Manufacture and Assembly (DFMA) is a tool for the design the easiest manufacture process and the respective assembly process. FMEA and DFMA are essential tools for the implementation of Advanced Product Quality Planning (APQP). The aim of APQP is to introduce quality in the product from its very beginning. The majority of nonconformities arise from a design that fails to introduce quality (AIAG, 2008).

Moreover, the implementation Lean management and its tools is beyond automobile manufacturing. There are several examples of Lean implementation in services (Piercy & Rich, 2009), higher education (Comm & Mathaisel, 2005), health care (Kimsey, 2010), human recourses (Higgins, 2007) or even the application of Lean in entrepreneurship knows as Lean StartUp (Ries, 2011). Then, Lean management prove that process excellence is relevant in a diverse type of processes at manufacturing systems but also in systems that outside these industries.

Six Sigma

The implementation of Lean management determines standards that the organization follows to create customer value. However, probability of nonconformities or systems errors occur. The Six Sigma methodology focuses in this phenomenon. It deeply explores individual processes to determine their variability and reduce the probability of occurrence (Brue, 2015).

The origin of the methodology refers to a group of engineers from Motorola Company in the min-1980s (Tennant, 2001). They observed and studied the Japanese quality techniques and realized that quality variability in the process outcomes is their major challenge. Moreover, the company General Electric is one of the major promoters of the Six Sigma methodology.

The methodology introduces the DMAIC cycle (Define, Measure, Analyze, Improve and Control) which guide the development of the process improvement projects (George, Maxey, Rowlands, & Price, 2005). It is similar to the PDCA cycle and it provides the methodology with the continuous improvement philosophy (Sahno, Shevtshenko, Karaulova, & Tahera, 2015). Furthermore, Six Sigma introduces other important tools such as SIPOC (Supplier, Inputs, Process, Outputs and Customer) which facilitates the specification of processes or the concept of "Voice of the Customer" (VoC) that aims to determine customer's requirements. This last one is a great complement of the Quality function deployment (QFD) tool or House of Quality from QMS.

THE FOUR REVOLUTIONS OF INDUSTRY

The description and background of these process excellence approaches (QMS, TPS, TOC, BPR, LM and SS) determine the timeline milestones to review approaches appearance and development throughout the four industrial revolutions. These four phases belongs to the i4.0 concept (Schwab, 2016). Additionally, the economic and industrial revolutions comprise challenges and determine the new context for organizational performance (Perez, 2010). Therefore, this chapter explores the evolution of process excellence throughout these four industrial revolutions.

The first industrial revolution relates with the major historical and economical milestone of our era (Deane, 1979). The industrial revolution at the end of the eighteen century. It was a change in the production systems of the nations. Industrial machine products replace agriculture and handcraft goods. The development of waterpower and steam power machines facilitates goods manufacture at higher volumes.

The use of machines increases productivity but sometimes this substitution (manual vs. machines) is insufficient. Process analysis is required. That is one of the contributions of Frederick Taylor (1856 – 1915). He deeply analyses the production processes and develops several techniques to increase efficiency (Dixit, Hazarika, & Davim, 2017). These techniques establish work standards of better working methods based on the time limit of the production activities. It means that the coordination of the times among machines and human work need balance to optimize the production output.

The understanding of organizations as system of processes regulated by time permits the development of mass production. The system implements the conveyor belt. The origin of this technology dates back to the beginning of the first industrial revolution when Oliver Evans (1755 - 1819) assembly a primitive form of band conveyor for flour mill (Walker, 2012). His work also includes several water and steam machines. However, Henry Ford (1863-1947) implements the conveyor belt for the Model T manufacture process (Henry Ford Heritage Association, 2017). Then, the factory behaves as a unique large process on which sub processes feed the main process in coordination with individual machine times.

Machines and production systems increase their productivity with electric power. Therefore, the characteristic of the second industrial revolution is the introduction of electricity to the production processes (Schwab, 2016). The electrification of industry increases flexibility, lowers costs, enhances workers moral, improves quality, is cleaner, more silent and handier (Tugwell, 1927). Electricity is the next step that Henry Ford uses to increase productivity and quality at affordable prices (Beaudreau, 2005). He is convinced that make the best possible goods quality at lowest cost paying highest wages is possible and it is the best combination to avoid situations such as the great depression (Beaudreau, 2005). The word Quality appears in the industry lexicon during those days. Books such as "Economic Control of Quality of Manufactured Product" (Shewhart W. A., 1931) and tools such as PDCA (Shewhart & Deming, 1939) evidence the importance of quality in the production processes. Moreover, just after the Second World War the concept of quality develops in organizations mainly in Japan based on Deming's work (1900-1993) and the introduction of the 14 points of Total Quality Management (TQM) (1950). Then, Toyota Corporation reviews the work and philosophy of Eiji Toyoda (1913 – 2013) and implements TQM and other approaches to develop TPS (Ohno, 1988). Moreover, the introduction of computers and robots to the manufacturing systems creates new challenges.

Computers and production processes automation define the third industrial revolution (Schwab, 2016). The first commercial available microprocessor developed by Intel in 1971 (Reilly, 2003) begins this revolution. Computer science professionals begin the development of better machines for industry such as Computer Numeric Control (CNC) or industrial robots mainly for the automobile industry. Toyota also develops their own robots since 1980s (Ota, 2012). Moreover, authors such as Eliyahu Goldratt (1947 – 2011) warns that the implementation of automation in specific manufacturing cell might increase the productivity of the cell but destroys the productivity of the entire factory (Goldratt E. M., 1984). TOC challenges automation with process approach. The automation should follow the factory logics of the five-step procedure on which the constraint determines the place of the system for automation. Then, the automation of manufacturing processes is far beyond the installation of computers, CNCs and robots in the factory. It is about process improvement by technology implementation.

Since industrial processes automation requires integral analysis, then it could be easier to start a new factory with new technology and close the old one (Green field vs Brown field). This is the approach of BPR (Hammer & Champy, 1993). There are major economic, political and social changes in the 1990s (Fukuyama, 1993). The organizations structures are outdated to challenge the new markets, politics, economy, systems, etc. Globalization speedup (Wesseling, 2009) and Information and Communication Technologies (ICT) add to the equation more challenges for the manufacturing facilities (Frenkel, 1990). Then, the BPR approach arrive as an excellent answer to design and implement process excellence in new manufacturing systems that cope these major changes with the support of ICT.

Moreover, the radical system improvement needs continuous improvement (CI) to increase performance (Davenport & Short, 1990). Figure 3 illustrates this combination.

Therefore, CI methodologies such as Lean management and Six Sigma still have the opportunity to provide the industry with techniques and tools for process improvement. In one hand, Lean management approach facilitates standards implementation while Six Sigma helps to reduce their variability. Then, the combination of all process excellence approaches allow manufacturing facilities to improve and perform in accordance with their strategies.

Today the industry faces Industry 4.0 (Baur & Wee, 2015). The main characteristics of this revolution are cyber-physical systems, real-time connectivity, big data analytics and others new technologies throughout the entire supply chain (Lasi, Fettke, Kemper, Feld, & Hoffmann, 2014). This includes concepts such as Internet of Things (IoT) (Islam, Kwak, Kabir, Hossain, & Kwak, 2015) or smart factories (Rashid, Sayin, Oureshi, Shami, & Khan, 2011).

An important milestone for i4.0 is Internet and its spread use among people and companies. People around the world are in constant use of emails, social media and other technologies (Haigh, Russell, &

Figure 3. Combining BPR and CI
Source: (Greasley, 2009, p. 277)

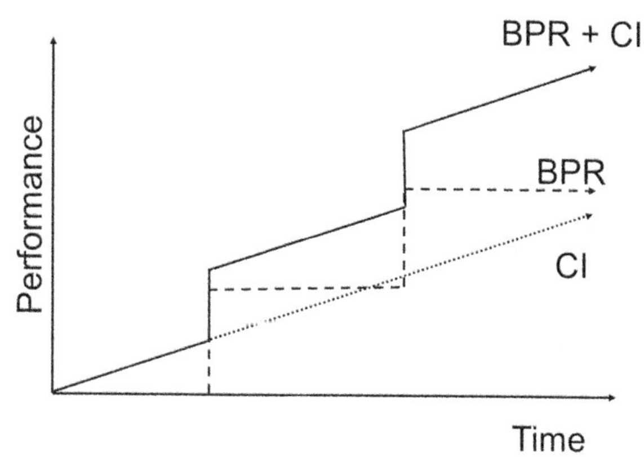

Dutton, 2015). This connectivity facilitates the creation and evolution of new business such as Uber or Airbnb. These organizations provide better services with less infrastructure thanks to the possibilities of internet and the social connectivity. The business expectations for this new generation of business is more than 11 trillion USD for 2025 and the 70% of these possibilities are at industry (Manyika, James; Chui, Michael; Bisson, Peter; Woetzel, Jonathan; Dobbs, Richard; Bughin, Jacques; Aharon, Dan, 2015).

Several new technologies facilitate the development of this revolution. Augmented reality introduces new possibilities in maintenance (Zhu, Ong, & Nee, 2013) or artificial intelligence facilitates the development of human-technology teamwork (Norman, 2017). Process excellence approaches need to understand and use these technologies in order to provide organizations with tools and techniques for their improvement.

The Figure 4 and Table 1 summarize the timeline analysis of the four industrial revolutions and the development of these six process excellence methodologies.

The fourth industrial revolution promises higher manufacturing processes flexibility, faster and precise processes, error rates reduction, accurate data and others benefits (Schwab, 2016). However, the systematic literature review reveals that the majority of publications on i4.0 dedicates to explain and present specific technologies and its benefits and so far the inclusion of i4.0 as a next step in process excellence is poor (Martinez, Jirsak, & Lorenc, 2016). Then, it is necessary to determine the aspects that process excellence approaches need to develop in order to provide organizations with successful implementation of this new revolution.

IMPLEMENTING PROCESS EXCELLENCE IN I4.0

The fourth industrial revolution has just begun. Governments and companies promote it by presenting benefits in conferences and submits. However, it is still complicated to find an entire successful i4.0

Figure 4. Process excellence methodologies and industrial revolutions
Source: Author's own work

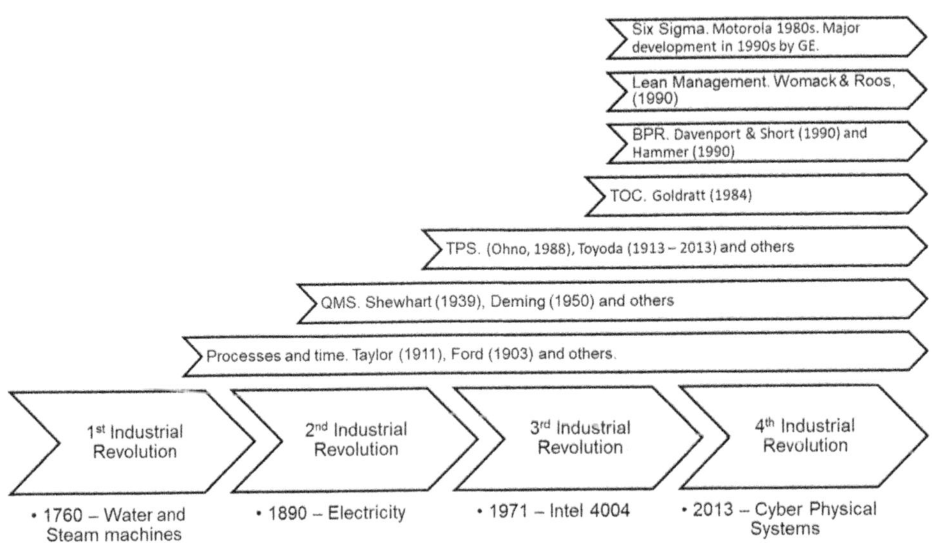

Table 1. Process excellence methodologies and industrial revolutions

Industrial Revolution	Process Excellence
1st industrial revolution. Machines, steam machines. A major change from an agriculture based economy to an industry-based economy.	Manufacture processes speed up. The measure of production time and productivity become the first parameter of process excellence (Taylor, 1911).
2nd industrial revolution. Electricity allows the machines and manufacture systems to improve their performance.	Mass production increases the volume of products and manufacture speed. Time measurement still basic for process management and improvements but product defects occur and it is important to manufacture without them. Beginnings of QMS and TPS.
3rd industrial revolution. Electronics and computer-based machines allow the manufacturing systems to create better products and balanced processes. Customers want more individualized products.	The introduction of IT in business introduces several possibilities to create new processes BPR. This period consolidates QMS and TPS and it develops TOC and Lean management. Process variability is an issue that Six Sigma covers.
4th industrial revolution. Cyber-physical systems, big data, smart factories, smart products.	More data from machines. Less people working at the shop floor. Complex interactions of IT systems with machine and human systems. High individualization of products. Connectivity throughout the entire supply chain.

Source: Author's own work

implementation on which scholars and practitioners might obtain best practices to develop new methodologies or techniques. Moreover, this section of the chapter presents possible changes for process excellence approaches based on new technologies understanding possible applications in the i4.0 framework.

The review of the history of the four revolutions and processes excellence approaches (Figure 4 and Table 1) illustrates that the principles of process excellence were valid, are valid and will remain valid. However, the new revolution challenges process excellence with higher complexity but at the same time, it brings new technologies that provide insights to improve current techniques and tools or to create new ones.

The principles of process excellence are processes and continuous improvement. Organizations are collection of processes. Outputs, inputs, activities, owner and parameters remain as the framework to understand the mechanisms that organizations use to perform (Figure 1). However, there are more subjects in the process approach. The first industrial revolution concentrates in manufacturing processes. The subjects are materials, work in progress and final goods. The second revolution introduces electricity. The ICT brings in to the business context communication as new subject. Today, approaches such a Lean management introduces new subjects such as customer experience in services (Piercy & Rich, 2009), learning process in higher education (Comm & Mathaisel, 2005), operational processes in health care (Kimsey, 2010), recruitment and carrier path in human recourses (Higgins, 2007) or time and money in entrepreneurship (Ries, 2011). Nevertheless, these new subjects enhances the validity of process approach and the introduction of i4.0 brings new subjects to it. Then, from this historical perspective, the concept of process contributes with i4.0 development.

Organizational continuous improvement is the second process excellence element that remains during history. Steam machines, electricity and then electronics demonstrate that each revolution searches for improvements. Kaizen is one of the basis of TPS (Figure 2) and the combination of CI and BPR provides better results (Figure 3). Today i4.0 is a great opportunity to improve business and organizations dramatically (Dolejs, 2016). It brings the possibility to create new business based on new technologies (John, 2016). The German government pioneers with i4.0 to improve their industry (Germany Trade & Invest, 2014). Then i4.0 is about improvements. It is the willing to be better that determine excellence.

Process excellence is the continual and persistent thinking about new and better mechanisms to provide the customer with the required or better product or service. This principle still valid and provide i4.0 with a long-term background.

Process excellence has excellent elements for i4.0 development such as DMAIC or PDCA tools. These comprise activities that guide the development of process excellence implementations. However, i4.0 challenges these current procedures. These tools require an enhancement within the i4.0 context. The following lines explore the current practices of process excellence and possible changes of these tools under the i4.0 context.

Process Identification

This activity is an essential part of QMS and TPS. It is about the definition of each process element (Figure 1). The PDCA cycle, ISO 9001:2015, DMAIC and others have process identification as one of the first activities to develop and it is usually the first. For example, Six Sigma utilizes SIPOC. A tool for process identification. Voice of the Customer (VoC) complements the identification. Process mapping outcomes from flowcharts, layouts, process diagrams, among others illustrate the process in different perspectives (Damelio, 2011).

Process identification requires process knowledge. It is necessary to meet with the people related with the processes and visit the process itself. Brainstorming sessions and gemba walks provide information from the people in order to define the process (Gesinger, 2016). Documentation is other source to understand the process. The collection of this information facilitates the process mapping (Damelio, 2011). It is usual to develop several versions of the process mapping outcomes until these graphical representations have all needed characteristics to be useful for the respective improvement.

Virtual reality, augmented reality, simulations, virtual communication are technologies that have the possibility to enhance process identification. For example augmented reality present several applications (Carmigniani, Furht, Anisetti, Ceravolo, & Damiani, 2011). The knowledge of the people related with the process is important for process identification. Then, real-time communications technologies allow the development of brainstorming session without the need to visit the process. Virtual reality and augmented reality have the potential to replace gemba walks. Simulations and real-time data develop better outcomes from process mapping tools. Moreover, since customers' requirements rapidly change, real-time data to determine VoC accelerates the DMAIC or PDCA cycles.

Measurement

The process identification determines the parameters that allow process management but also its improvement. The concept of Critical To Quality (CTQ) complements the decision on the variables to measure. Therefore, it is necessary to establish mechanisms to capture data about those parameters. The activity measurement consolidates those mechanisms and aims for accurate and usable data. Time, distances, temperature, pressure or number of nonconformities are some of usual process parameters needed for its management or improvement.

The usual representation of these measurements are tools that allow their interpretation and analysis to determine actions on the process. For example, QMS has the seven basic quality tools for process improvement. These are Cause-and-effect diagram, Check sheet, Control charts, Histogram, Pareto chart, Scatter diagram and Flowchart (AIAG, 2008). Then, it is necessary to verify the accuracy of the collected data. The tool Measurement System Analysis (MSA) validates the procedure of data collection and calculates the uncertainty of devices and systems (Taghizadegan, 2013). However, data caption from a high-end technology machines is paper written form from the machine's high-tech screen (Bares, 2016).

The fourth industrial revolution is also about data. Chronometers, measuring tapes, pressure gauges, thermometers, radio-frequency identification (RFID), small parts counters, traffic counters among others are instruments able to extract the required data from processes. Industrial wireless networks are a good example (Li, Xiaomin ; Li, Di; Wan, Jiafu; Vasilakos, Athanasios V; Lai, Chin-Feng; Wang, Shiyong, 2017). Clouds, networks and internet provide real-time data. The installation of sensors at the machines and other parts of the process facilitates the measurement but it also creates large and complex amount of data (Bares, 2016). Then, the progress on big data fits requirements to develop i4.0.

Data Analysis

The aim of data analysis is the transformation of the raw data into information that provide insights about possible process improvements or signals about process behavior for its management. The raw data comes from measurement. However, it is necessary to review it with tools and statistics. This exploration reveals information that determines the actions to perform. These actions manage the process or introduce improvement for better performance.

The seven quality tools of QMS are instruments for data caption and analysis. Further statistical analysis of the data complements the outcomes from these tools. Analysis of variance (ANOVA), hypothesis test of the mean (t-test), chi-square method and others provide additional information about the process parameters and their relationships. Statistical software facilitates the implementation of these tools and methods.

Big data analytics promises to support i4.0 implementation (LaValle, Lesser, Shockley, Hopkins, & Kruschwitz, 2011). Data visualization, scenarios, simulations, regression and mathematical models are part of the big data features. In this perspective, it seems like there is nothing new but the problem is that there are "piles of data" that nobody seems to use or barely understands (Bares, 2016). Then, decision makers fail to take advantage of the possibilities offer by big data analytics.

Process Management and Control

The completion of process identification, measurement and analysis provide the necessary information to take management or improvement actions.

Operations management takes decisions about the amount of units to manufacture (Loading), the arrangement of the manufacture orders in the productions lines (Sequencing), the specific times to begin manufacture (Scheduling) and the mechanisms to track the processes (Monitoring & Controlling) (Slack, Chambers, & Johnston, 2010).

Machines with automation systems like Jidoka or communication systems like Andon had already overtaken the activities of process monitoring and controlling. Moreover, real-time detection systems facilitate the caption, analysis and presentation of data for further decision-making (Hsu, Wang, Jiang, & Wei, 2015). The digital twins approach replicates the real factory in virtual system (Bares, 2016). Statistical process control (SPC) is a robust method that provide the elements for real-time monitoring of processes (Young, Bond, & Wiedenbeck, 2007). Technologies such as artificial intelligence (AI) have the possibility to overtake the decisions on operations management tasks. In a pull system, the demand sets loading and real-time demand information determine the production loads. Real-time capacity analysis facilitates sequence of orders and its scheduling. For example, the quality by design of pharmaceutical companies have developments with AI (Aksu, Buket; Paradkar, Anant; de Matas, Marcel; Özer, Özgen; Güneri, Tamer; York, Peter, 2013).

Process Improvement

The improvement actions utilize several tools and methods that introduces changes on the process to increase their performance. For example, 5S method organizes the machines, tools and people in a specific layout. Single Minute Exchange of Die (SMED) reduces the machine setup time or change over time. Cellular flow creates special work units to develop different assembly jobs. Kanban a TPS method, facilitate the material and products flow together with JIT and JIS. Pull principle changes the principles of factory logics since the manufacture start production based on demand.

Process improvement within i4.0 is a big challenge. The knowledge on process improvement is open. TPS itself promotes the open source as a mean for continuous improvement of the system itself. Therefore, AI technologies have the possibility to compare the information from processes with previous improvements to determine the necessary changes in the process. Cognitive technologies such as Doctor Watson uses the current knowledge and learn from its own cases to provide solutions (IBM Watson Health, 2017).

The Table 2 summarizes some of the possibilities that the new technologies bring to the current practices of process excellence approaches. Digital twins, big data analytics, augmented realty or RFID are technologies from the new revolution already installed in some manufacture facilities. Furthermore, there are others technologies that gives some positive insights but still under development. Moreover, the importance for process excellence is that the introduction of i4.0 brings new technologies that change manufacture processes and therefore, there are changes in the procedures used by the discipline to provide organizations with improvements.

FUTURE RESEARCH DIRECTIONS

The introduction of i4.0 opens new perspectives in research of process excellence in organizations. The main premises is that the concept of process still valid. Organizational performance growth depends on

Table 2. Possible i4.0 process excellence practices

Activity	Some Current Practices	Possible i4.0 Practices
Process Identification	Brainstorming sessions, gemba walks, process mapping.	Virtual reality, augmented reality, simulations, virtual communication.
Measurement	The seven basic quality tools. MSA.	Online measurement instruments, RFID, Industrial wireless networks, clouds, real-time data.
Data Analysis	Statistical analysis such as ANOVA, t-test, chi-square, etc.	Big data. Real-time data visualization, scenarios, simulations, regression and mathematical models.
Process Management and Control	Loading, sequencing, scheduling, monitoring and controlling. Jidoka. Andon. SPC.	Digital twins. Real-time detection systems. Real-time SPC. Artificial intelligence connecting demand with manufacture.
Process Improvement	5S method, SMED, Kanban, JIT, JIS.	Artificial intelligence and cognitive technologies.

Source: Author's own work

organization knowledge of their own processes. Then, research about the relationship between process approach and successful technology implementation provides evidence that support the importance of processes in organizations.

The next big aspect to develop new research relates with changes of the procedures used to manage and improve processes. Research teams have the opportunity to focus in a specific tool and investigate the changes that the execution of the tool has while using new technologies. For example, procedures such as quality audits. Digital twins, smart factories, real-time data constantly provide data and therefore, factory visit, a small part of the audit, changes its role of data caption.

The reduction of human-work in the manufacture processes is other aspect for research (Germany Trade & Invest, 2014). The manufacture activities with higher risk and routine are the best candidates for automation. Then, the investigation is about the role change of the human force in the manufacture facilities. For example, the operations manager role in the manufacture system. Decisions about loading, sequencing or scheduling become automatic as well as monitoring and control. Then, the question is about the subject of management and the respective procedures on it.

Moreover, the new main subject of research in process excellence is data. The 3C concept (Caption – Communicate – Compete) discloses several opportunities to investigate how organizations apply process approach in its own data. The processes constantly provide data but it is important to obtain the right data in the correct moment. Data Caption is about all mechanisms that organizations have to obtain the data from the processes. It is about instruments, but also the type (Analog or digital) and the amount. The phase Communicate is about taking the data from those instruments to the required clients in the appropriate format. Finally, the phase Compete refers to implementation of the data for process management or improvement. Today, organizations have many data but they fail to use it (Bares, 2016). The research is about understanding the types of data for each type of decision. Under the 3C concept for data, research teams have the opportunity to observe Mura, Mura or Muri of those processes and the organizational challenges for the improvement.

CONCLUSION

The historical review of the industrial revolutions history evidences that the concepts of process and process excellence are basic elements of the organizations and they are still valid. The review of the first three revolutions shows that these concepts endure. Then, an organization willing to obtain benefits from the fourth industrial revolution requires processes review and process excellence approach implementation.

The first three industrial revolutions determine contexts on which process excellence approaches have the opportunity to provide improvement to organizations. However, the fourth industrial revolution just began and a proper formal process excellence methodology for this new revolution is still missing. The implementation of the new technologies in the i4.0 context provides new examples, cases and evidences that eventually determine the development of new process excellence approaches.

The Quality Management System (QMS), Toyota Production System (TPS), Business Theory of Constraints (TOC), Processes Reengineering (BPR), Lean Management (LM), Six Sigma (SS) are current process excellence methodologies that provide the basic elements to implement i4.0. However, since the proposed changes from i4.0 are radical, BPR offers good perspectives to support the i4.0 implementation. Moreover, it is important to review that the combination of BPR and CI (Figure 3) gives the organization better results. Then, approaches such as Design For Six Sigma (DFSS) combines both perspectives and it becomes convenient for future implementations.

The process thinking has an important role in successful i4.0 implementations. However, the fourth industrial revolution is the next step in the evolution of process excellence thinking itself. New technologies bring to organizations the possibility to develop new procedures. This include the procedures, activities and techniques of the process excellence approach. Then, it is mandatory to review these procedures from the i4.0 perspective. For example tools such as SMED. Today, the procedure to develop a full SMED is manual based. In the future, thanks to the i4.0 context, the procedure implies the use of real-time data, simulations, digital twines and others technologies. The simple collection of documents for a quality audit to obtain a required certification utilizes today email communication. In the future, the auditor observes from their mobile device the factory performance in real time. Then, the main conclusion of this chapter is determine the necessity of process improvement to develop i4.0 but, more important, the necessity to implement i4.0 in the procedures and techniques to develop process excellence. Then, industry 4.0 provides process excellence methodologies with new aspects that enhance its activities and therefore the organizational improvement.

REFERENCES

AIAG. (2008). *Advanced Product Quality Planning and Control Plan*. Southfield, MI: Automotive Industry Action Group - AIAG.

Aksu, B., Paradkar, A., de Matas, M., Özer, Ö., Güneri, T., & York, P. (2013). A quality by design approach using artificial intelligence techniques to control the critical quality attributes of ramipril tablets manufactured by wet granulation. *Pharmaceutical Development and Technology*, *18*(1), 236–245. doi:10.3109/10837450.2012.705294 PMID:22881350

Alemi, M., & Akram, R. (2013). Measuring the leanness of manufacturing systems by using fuzzy topsis: A case study of the 'Parizan Sanat' company. *South African Journal of Industrial Engineering*, *3*, 166–174.

Bares, M. (2016). *Implications, Applications, Trends, and Topics of Industry 4.0*. Round Table session at the International Business and Management Conference, Prague, Czech Republic.

Baur, C., & Wee, D. (2015). *Manufacturing's next act*. Retrieved 04 24, 2016, from McKinsey & Company: http://www.mckinsey.com/business-functions/operations/our-insights/manufacturings-next-act

Beaudreau, B. (2005). The National Industrial Recovery Act Redux: Technology and Transitions. Lincoln, NE: iUniverse.

Brue, G. (2015). *Six Sigma for managers*. New York: McGraw-Hill Education.

Carmigniani, J., Furht, B., Anisetti, M., Ceravolo, P., Damiani, E., & Ivkovic, M. (2011). Augmented reality technologies, systems and applications. *Multimedia Tools and Applications*, *51*(1), 341–377. doi:10.100711042-010-0660-6

Comm, C. L., & Mathaisel, D. F. (2005). 09). An exploratory study of best lean sustainability practices in higher education. *Quality Assurance in Education*, *13*(3), 227–240. doi:10.1108/09684880510607963

Damelio, R. (2011). *The basics of process mapping* (2nd ed.). Boca Raton, FL: CRC Press.

Davenport, T. H., & Short, J. E. (1990). 06). The new industrial engineering: Information technology and business process redesign. *Sloan Management Review*, *31*(4), 11.

Deane, P. (1979). *The First Industrial Revolution*. Cambridge, UK: Cambridge University Press.

Deming, W. E. (1950). *Elementary Principles of the Statistical Control of Quality: A series of lectures*. JUSE.

Dixit, U. S., Hazarika, M., & Davim, J. P. (2017). *A Brief History of Mechanical Engineering*. Springer. doi:10.1007/978-3-319-42916-8

Dolejs, M. (2016). *Implications, Applications, Trends, and Topics of Industry 4.0*. Round Table session at the International Business and Management Conference, Prague, Czech Republic.

Fayol, H. (1967). *General and industrial management (Administration, industrielle et generale)* (C. Storrs, Trans.). London: Pitman.

Frenkel, K. (1990). The European community and information technology. *Communications of the ACM*, *33*(4), 404–410. doi:10.1145/77556.77557

Fukuyama, F. (1993). *The end of history and the last man*. New York: Avon.

Galbraith, J. R., & Kates, A. (2008). *Designing Your Organization: Using the STAR Model to Solve 5 Critical Design Challenges*. Hoboken, NJ: Jossey-Bass.

George, M. L., Maxey, J., Rowlands, D., & Price, M. (2005). *The Lean Six Sigma Pocket Toolbook*. New York: McGraw-Hill.

Germany Trade & Invest. (2014). *Industrie 4.0. Smart Manufacturing for the Future*. Berlin: Germany Trade & Invest.

Gesinger, S. (2016). Experiential Learning: Using Gemba Walks to Connect With Employees. *Professional Safety*, (2): 33.

Goldratt, E. M. (1984). *The Goal: A Process of Ongoing Improvement*. Great Barrington, MA: North River Press.

Goldratt, E. M. (1998). *Essays On the Theory of Constraints*. Great Barrington, MA: North River Press.

Goldratt Marketing Group. (2017). *Theory of Constraints: Goldratt Marketing*. Retrieved from Theory of Constraints: https://www.toc-goldratt.com/en/biography-of-eli-goldratt

Gonzalez Aleu, F., & Van Aken, E. M. (2016). Systematic literature review of critical success factors for continuous improvement projects. *International Journal of Lean Six Sigma*, *7*(3), 214–232. doi:10.1108/IJLSS-06-2015-0025

Greasley, A. (2009). *Operations management*. Chichester, UK: John Wiley & Sons.

Guha, S., Kettinger, W. J., & James, T. C. (1993). Business process reengineering. *Information Systems Management*, *10*(3), 13–22. doi:10.1080/10580539308906939

Haigh, T., Russell, A. L., & Dutton, W. H. (2015). Histories of the Internet: Introducing a Special Issue of Information & Culture. *Information & Culture*, *50*(2), 143–159. doi:10.7560/IC50201

Hammer, M. (1990). Reengineering work: Don't automate, obliterate. *Harvard Business Review*, *68*(4), 104.

Hammer, M., & Champy, J. (1993). *Reengineering the Corporation: A Manifesto for Business Revolution*. New York, NY: HarperCollins Publishers.

Henry Ford Heritage Association. (2017). *Henry Ford Heritage Association*. Retrieved from Henry Ford Heritage Association: http://hfha.org/

Higgins, N. J. (2007). Putting lean HR into practice. *Strategic HR Review*, *6*(4), 16–19. doi:10.1108/14754390980000981

Hines, P., Holwe, M., & Rich, N. (2004). Learning to evolve: A review of contemporary lean thinking. *International Journal of Operations & Production Management*, *24*(10), 994–1011. doi:10.1108/01443570410558049

Hsu, K.-S., Wang, C.-S., Jiang, J.-F., & Wei, H.-Y. (2015). Development of a Real-Time Detection System for Augmented Reality Driving. *Mathematical Problems in Engineering*, 1–5.

IBM Watson Health. (2017). *IBM Watson Health*. Retrieved from Cognitive Healthcare Solutions: https://www.ibm.com/watson/health/

Islam, S. R., Kwak, D., Kabir, M. H., Hossain, M., & Kwak, K.-S. (2015). The Internet of Things for Health Care: A Comprehensive Survey. *IEEE Access: Practical Innovations, Open Solutions*, *3*, 678–708. doi:10.1109/ACCESS.2015.2437951

ISO. (2015). *ISO 9001:2015 Quality Management Systems*. ISO (the International Organization for Standardization).

John, J. (2016). *Implications, Applications, Trends, and Topics of Industry 4.0*. Round Table session at the International Business and Management Conference, Prague, Czech Republic.

Kaynak, H. (2003, July). The relationship between total quality management practices and their effects on firm performance. *Journal of Operations Management*, *21*(4), 405–435. doi:10.1016/S0272-6963(03)00004-4

Kimsey, D. B. (2010). Lean Methodology in Health Care. *AORN Journal*, *92*(1), 53–60. doi:10.1016/j.aorn.2010.01.015 PMID:20619772

Knights, D., & Willmott, H. (2000). The reengineering revolution: Critical studies of corporate change. Sage Publications Ltd.

Lasi, H., Fettke, P., Kemper, H.-G., Feld, T., & Hoffmann, M. (2014). Industry 4.0. *Business & Information Systems Engineering*, *6*(4), 239–242. doi:10.100712599-014-0334-4

LaValle, S., Lesser, E., Shockley, R., Hopkins, M. S., & Kruschwitz, N. (2011). Big Data, Analytics and the Path From Insights to Value. *MIT Sloan Management Review*, *52*(2), 21–32.

Lean Enterprise Institute. (2017). *Toyota Production System in the Lean Lexicon ©*. Retrieved from Lean.org: https://www.lean.org/lexicon/toyota-production-system

Li, X., Li, D., Wan, J., Vasilakos, A. V., Lai, C.-F., & Wang, S. (2017). A review of industrial wireless networks in the context of Industry 4.0. *Wireless Networks*, *23*(1), 23–41. doi:10.100711276-015-1133-7

Liker, J. K. (2004). *The Toyota Way: 14 Management Principles from the World's Greatest Manufacturer*. New York: McGraw-Hill.

Manyika, J., Chui, M., Bisson, P., Woetzel, J., Dobbs, R., Bughin, J., & Aharon, D. (2015). The internet of things: Mapping the value beyond the hype. McKinsey & Company.

Martinez, F., Jirsak, P., & Lorenc, M. (2016). *Industry 4.0. The end Lean Management? In The 10th International Days of Statistics and Economics*. Prague: VŠE.

Martinez, F., Jirsak, P., & Lorenc, M. (2017). Implications, Applications, Trends, and Topics of Industry 4.0. In *International Business and Management Conference* (pp. 213 - 216). Prague: Oeconomica Publishing House.

Matawale, C. R., & Datta, S. (2015). Leanness metric evaluation platform in fuzzy context. *Journal of Modelling in Management*, *1*, 169–196.

Matawale, C. R., Datta, S., & Mahapatra, S. S. (2014). Leanness estimation procedural hierarchy using interval-valued fuzzy sets (IVFS). *Benchmarking: An International Journal*, *2*, 274–292.

McMillan, E. (2004). *Complexity, Organizations and Change*. London: Routledge. doi:10.4324/9780203507124

Mikulak, R. J., McDermott, R., & Beauregard, M. (2008). The Basics of FMEA (2nd ed.). Boca Ration, FL: Productivity Press.

Nadler, D. A., & Tushman, M. L. (1980, Autumn). A model for diagnosing organizational behavior. *Organizational Dynamics*, *9*(2), 35–51. doi:10.1016/0090-2616(80)90039-X

Norlyk, B. (2011). Language as a branding tool: Lean management, Lean metaphors, and the special Lean. *Language at Work - Bridging Theory into Practice*, *9*, 7.

Norman, D. (2017). Design, Business Models, and Human-Technology Teamwork. *Research Technology Management*, *60*(1), 26–29. doi:10.1080/08956308.2017.1255051

Ohno, T. (1988). *Just-In-Time for Today and Tomorrow*. Cambridge, MA: Productivity Press.

Ohno, T. (1988). *Toyota production system: Beyond large-scale production*. Cambridge: Productivity Press.

Ohno, T. (1988). *Workplace Management*. Cambridge, MA: Productivity Press.

Ota, Y. (2012). Partner Robots - From Development to Business Implementation. In Z. S. Hippe, J. L. Kulikowski, & T. Mroczek (Eds.), *Human – Computer Systems Interaction: Backgrounds and Applications 2* (pp. 31–40). Chennai, India: Springer. doi:10.1007/978-3-642-23172-8_3

Oxford Dictionaries. (2017a). *Excellence*. Retrieved 07 26, 2017, from excellence - definition of excellence in English: https://en.oxforddictionaries.com/definition/excellence

Oxford Dictionaries. (2017b). *Lean*. Retrieved from lean - definition of lean in English: https://en.oxforddictionaries.com/definition/lean

Perez, C. (2010). Technological revolutions and techno-economic paradigms. *Cambridge Journal of Economics*, *34*(1), 185–202. doi:10.1093/cje/bep051

Peters, T. J., & Waterman, J. R. (1982). *In search of excellence: lessons from America's best-run companies*. New York: Harper & Row.

Piercy, N., & Rich, N. (2009). High quality and low cost: The lean service centre. *European Journal of Marketing*, *43*(11/12), 1477–1497. doi:10.1108/03090560910989993

Rashid, M. A., Sayin, E., Oureshi, H., Shami, M.-U.-D., & Khan, N. (2011). ERP-communication framework: Aerospace smart factory & smart R&D campus. *International Journal of Computer Science and Information Security,* (7), 116-123.

Reilly, E. D. (2003). *Milestones in Computer Science and Information Technology*. London: Greenwood Press.

Ries, E. (2011). *The Lean Startup*. New York: Crown Business.

Rosing, M. V., Scheel, H. v., & Scheer, A.-W. (2015). The complete business process handbook. Volume I: body of knowledge from process modeling to bpm. Waltham, MA: Morgan Kaufmann.

Sahno, J., Shevtshenko, E., Karaulova, T., & Tahera, K. (2015). Framework for Continuous Improvement of Production Processes. *Inzinerine Ekonomika-Engineering Economics*, *26*(2), 169–180.

Schwab, K. (2016). *The Fourth Industrial Revolution*. New York: Crown Business.

Shewhart, W. A. (1931). *Economic Control of Quality of Manufactured Product*. New York: D. Van Nostrand.

Shewhart, W. A., & Deming, E. W. (1939). *Statistical method from the viewpoint of quality control.* Washington, DC: Graduate School, the Department of Agriculture.

Shingo, S. (1985). *A Revolution in Manufacturing: The SMED System*. Stamford, CT: Productivity Press.

Slack, N., Chambers, S., & Johnston, R. (2010). *Operations management* (6th ed.). Harlow: Financial Times/Prentice Hall.

Taghizadegan, S. (2013). *Mastering Lean Six Sigma: advanced black belt concepts*. New York: Momentum Press. doi:10.5643/9781606504062

Tague, N. R. (2005). *The Quality Toolbox* (2nd ed.). Milwaukee, WI: ASQ Quality Press.

Taylor, F. W. (1911). *The Principles of Scientific Management*. Harper & Row.

Temple, N. (Performer). (2016). The smart factory and the converging roles of IT, production and engineering. Smart IoT London 2016, ExCel, London, UK.

Tennant, G. (2001). *Six Sigma: SPC and TQM in Manufacturing and Services*. Aldershot, UK: Gower Publishing, Ltd.

Toyota Corporation. (2017). *Toyota Global Site | Production System*. Retrieved from Toyota Motor Corporation Global Website: http://www.toyota-global.com/company/vision_philosophy/toyota_production_system/

Toyota Motor Corporation. (2016). *Toyota Global*. Retrieved 07 13, 2016, from The origin of the Toyota Production System: http://www.toyota-global.com/company/vision_philosophy/toyota_production_system/origin_of_the_toyota_production_system.html

Tugwell, R. G. (1927). *Industry's coming of age*. New York: Columbia University Press.

Ulieru, M., & Este, R. A. (2004). The Holonic Enterprise and Theory Emergence: On emergent features of self-organization in distributed virtual agents. *Cybernetics & Human Knowing*, *11*(1).

Vinodh, S., & Balaji, S. (2011). Fuzzy logic based leanness assessment and its decision support system. *International Journal of Production Research*, *13*(13), 4027–4041. doi:10.1080/00207543.2010.492408

Vinodh, S., & Chintha, S. K. (2011). Leanness assessment using multi grade fuzzy approach. *International Journal of Production Research*, *2*(2), 431–445. doi:10.1080/00207540903471494

Walker, S. (2012). *Mine Winding and Transport*. Leicester, UK: Elsevier.

Weisbord, M. R. (1987). *Organizational Diagnosis: A workbook of theory and practice*. Addison-Wesley.

Wesseling, H. L. (2009). Globalization: A Historical Perspective. *European Review (Chichester, England)*, *17*(3-4), 455–462. doi:10.1017/S1062798709000866

Womack, J. P., & Jones, D. T. (1996). *Lean thinking: banish waste and create wealth in your corporation*. New York: Simon & Schuster.

Womack, J. P., Jones, D. T., & Roos, D. (1990). *The Machine That Changed the World*. New York: Free Press.

Womack, J. P., Jones, D. T., & Roos, D. (1990). *The Machine That Changed the World: The Story of Lean Production*. New York: Rawson Associates.

Young, T. M., Bond, B. H., & Wiedenbeck, J. (2007). Implementation of a real-time statistical process control system in hardwood sawmills. *Forest Products Journal*, *57*(9), 54.

Zhu, J., Ong, S. K., & Nee, A. (2013). An authorable context-aware augmented reality system to assist the maintenance technicians. *International Journal of Advanced Manufacturing Technology*, *66*(9), 1699–1714. doi:10.100700170-012-4451-2

KEY TERMS AND DEFINITIONS

3C Concept: It is the introduction of process approach into data.

Big Data: It is a term related with the large amount of data produced from devices and the data analytics that provide information for decision making.

BPR: Business processes reengineering is a process excellence approach that prefers radical and total changes that continuous improvement.

Cyber-Physical Systems: These are one of the revolutionary systems in manufacturing. It is about automation strongly connected with end users thru internet.

Lean Management: A process excellence approach that increases value by reducing waste in a continuous improvement philosophy.

QMS: Abbreviation stands for quality management system. It is a process excellence approach with certification at ISO 9001:2015.

Six Sigma: This process excellence methodology focuses in reduce the variability of processes.

TOC: The acronym refers to the process excellence approach theory of constraints developed by Eliyahu Goldratt.

TPS: Toyota production system is a process excellence approach from Toyota Corporation.

Compilation of References

Aas, B., & Wallace, S. W. (2012). Management of logistics planning. In J. Wang (Ed.), *Information technologies, methods, and techniques of supply chain management* (pp. 255–271). Hershey, PA: IGI Global. doi:10.4018/978-1-4666-0918-1.ch015

Abdulsomad, K. (1999). Promoting industrial and technological development under contrasting industrial policies: The automotive industry in Malaysia and Thailand. In K. S. Jomo, G. Felker, & R. Rasiah (Eds.), *Industrial Technology Development in Malaysia: Industry and Firm Studies* (pp. 274–300). London: Routledge.

Acar, O., & Acar, A. B. (2015). Modern risk management techniques in banking sector. In *Banking, finance, and accounting: Concepts, methodologies, tools, and applications* (pp. 886–906). Hershey, PA: IGI Global. doi:10.4018/978-1-4666-6268-1.ch048

Acatech-Platform Industrie 4.0. (2014). *Industrie 4.0- Whitepaper Fue Themen.* Available at http://www.acatech.de/fileadmin/user_upload/Baumstruktur_nach_Website/Acatech/root/de/Aktuelles__Presse/Presseinfos__News/ab_2014/Whitepaper_Industrie_4.0.pdf

Adalet McGowan, M., & Andrews, D. (2015). *Labour Market Mismatch and Labour Productivity: Evidence from PIAAC Data.* OECD Economics Department Working Papers, No. 1209, OECD Publishing. 10.1787/5js1pzx1r2kb-en

Adam, T. R., Fernando, C. S., & Golubeva, E. (2015). Managerial overconfidence and corporate risk management. *Journal of Banking & Finance, 60*, 195–208. doi:10.1016/j.jbankfin.2015.07.013

Adolphs, P. (2015). RAMI 4.0: An architectural Model for Industrie 4.0. In *Object Management Group meeting* (pp. 1–31). Berlin, Germany: OMG.

Agarwal, R., & Virine, L. (2017). Integration of project risk management (PRM) into enterprise risk management (ERM). In Y. Raydugin (Ed.), *Handbook of research on leveraging risk and uncertainties for effective project management* (pp. 294–317). Hershey, PA: IGI Global. doi:10.4018/978-1-5225-1790-0.ch014

Agha, H. E. (2012). Risk management and business processes reengineering, success drivers for ERP projects: A case study. In R. Valverde & M. Rao Talla (Eds.), *Information systems reengineering for modern business systems: ERP, supply chain and e-commerce management solutions* (pp. 146–184). Hershey, PA: IGI Global. doi:10.4018/978-1-4666-0155-0.ch008

Aghina, W. (2015, December). *The keys to organizational agility*. Retrieved August 21, 2017, from http://www.mckinsey.com/business-functions/organization/our-insights/the-keys-to-organizational-agility

Aghina, W., De Smet, A., & Weerda, K. (2015, December). *Agility: It rhymes with stability*. Retrieved August 5, 2017, from http://www.mckinsey.com/business-functions/organization/our-insights/agility-it-rhymes-with-stability

Ahmad, H. A. (2016). *Malaysia's Performance in 2016 GE Global Innovation Barometer.* Topline Report, Malaysian Productivity Corporation. Retrieved Aug 1, 2017, from http://www.mpc.gov.my/wp-content/uploads/2016/04/Topline-2016-GE-GIB-as-at-280116.docx

Ahmed, P., Lim, K. K., & Loh, A. (2002). *Learning Through Knowledge Management.* Oxford, UK: Butterworth-Heinemann.

AIAG. (2008). *Advanced Product Quality Planning and Control Plan.* Southfield, MI: Automotive Industry Action Group - AIAG.

Akanmu, A., & Anumba, C. J. (2015). Cyber-physical systems integration of building information models and the physical construction. *Engineering, Construction, and Architectural Management, 22*(5), 516–535. doi:10.1108/ECAM-07-2014-0097

Aksu, B., Paradkar, A., de Matas, M., Özer, Ö., Güneri, T., & York, P. (2013). A quality by design approach using artificial intelligence techniques to control the critical quality attributes of ramipril tablets manufactured by wet granulation. *Pharmaceutical Development and Technology, 18*(1), 236–245. doi:10.3109/10837450.2012.705294 PMID:22881350

Alemi, M., & Akram, R. (2013). Measuring the leanness of manufacturing systems by using fuzzy topsis: A case study of the 'Parizan Sanat' company. *South African Journal of Industrial Engineering, 3*, 166–174.

Al-Fuqaha, A., Guizani, M., Mohammadi, M., Aledhari, M., & Ayyash, M. (2015). Internet of things: A survey on enabling technologies, protocols, and applications. *IEEE Communications Surveys and Tutorials, 17*(4), 2347–2376. doi:10.1109/COMST.2015.2444095

Algahtany, M., Alhammadi, Y., & Kashiwagi, D. (2016). Introducing a new risk management model to the Saudi Arabian construction industry. *Procedia Engineering, 145*, 940–947. doi:10.1016/j.proeng.2016.04.122

Allaire, Y., & Firsirotu, M. E. (1984). Theories of organizational culture. *Organization Studies, 5*(3), 193–226. doi:10.1177/017084068400500301

Almodóvar, P., & Rugman, A. M. (2015). Testing the revisited Uppsala model: Does insidership improve international performance? *International Marketing Review, 32*(6), 686–712. doi:10.1108/IMR-04-2014-0142

Almustafa, M. M., & Alkhaldi, D. (2014). Business intelligence and agile methodology for risk management in knowledge-based organizations. In *Software design and development: Concepts, methodologies, tools, and applications* (pp. 1710–1735). Hershey, PA: IGI Global. doi:10.4018/978-1-4666-4301-7.ch082

Alvesson, M., & Sandberg, J. (2011). Generating research questions through problematization. *Academy of Management Review, 36*(2), 247–271.

Amesse, F., & Cohendet, P. (2001). Technology transfer revisited from the perspective of the knowledge-based economy. *Research Policy, 30*(9), 1459–1478. doi:10.1016/S0048-7333(01)00162-7

Anantatmula, V., & Fan, Y. (2013). Risk management instruments, strategies and their impact on project success. *International Journal of Risk and Contingency Management, 2*(2), 27–41. doi:10.4018/ijrcm.2013040102

Anderl, R., Picard, A., Wang, Y., Fleischer, J., Dosch, S., Klee, B., & Bauer, J. (2015). *Leitfaden Industrie 4.0-Orientierungshilfe zur Einführung in den Mittelstand [Guideline Industry 4.0-Guidance for the introduction into middle sized enterprises].* Frankfurt, Germany: VDMA Verlag.

Andersen, O. (1993). On the internationalization process of firms: A critical analysis. *Journal of International Business Studies, 24*(2), 209–231. doi:10.1057/palgrave.jibs.8490230

Andersson, P., & Mattsson, L. G. (2015). Service innovations enabled by the internet of things. *IMP Journal*, *9*(1), 85–106. doi:10.1108/IMP-01-2015-0002

Argote, L., & Ingram, P. (2000). Knowledge transfer: A basis for competitive advantage in firms. *Organizational Behavior and Human Decision Processes*, *82*(1), 150–169. doi:10.1006/obhd.2000.2893

Arnold, C., Kiel, D., & Voigt, K.-I. (2016, June). How industry 4.0 changes business models in different manufacturing industries. *ISPIM Innovation Conference*, 1–20.

Arnold, V., Benford, T., Canada, J., & Sutton, S. G. (2015). Leveraging integrated information systems to enhance strategic flexibility and performance: The enabling role of enterprise risk management. *International Journal of Accounting Information Systems*, *19*, 1–16. doi:10.1016/j.accinf.2015.10.001

Aronowitz, S. (2015, June). *Getting organizational redesign right*. Retrieved August 17, 2017, from http://www.mckinsey.com/business-functions/organization/our-insights/getting-organizational-redesign-right

Arthurs, J. D., & Busenitz, L. W. (2006). Dynamic capabilities and venture performance: The effects of venture capitalists. *Journal of Business Venturing*, *21*(2), 195–215. doi:10.1016/j.jbusvent.2005.04.004

Ashton, K. (2009). That 'internet of things' thing. *RFiD Journal*, *22*, 97–114.

ASM. (2015). *Akademi Sains Malaysia Science Outlook 2015: Action towards Vision.* Retrieved June 7, 2017, from http://mastic.mosti.gov.my/documents/10156/2d66a776-277e-4816-bce1-53a89afda5ed

ASM. (2017). *Malaysia 2050.* Policy Outline. Retrieved July 25, 2017, from http://www.akademisains.gov.my/download/Malaysia%202050%20Smart%20Communities%20Presentation%20MATRADE%2026th%20January%202017.pdf

Attaran, M. (2017). The internet of things: Limitless opportunities for business and society. *Journal of Strategic Innovation and Sustainability*, *12*(1), 10–29.

Atzori, L., Iera, A., & Morabito, G. (2010). The internet of things: A survey. *Computer Networks*, *54*(15), 2787–2805. doi:10.1016/j.comnet.2010.05.010

Autio, E., Sapienza, H. J., & Almeida, J. G. (2000). Effects of age at entry, knowledge intensity, and imitability on international growth. *Academy of Management Journal*, *43*(5), 909–924. doi:10.2307/1556419

Aziz, N. A. A., Manab, N. A., & Othman, S. N. (2016). Critical success factors of sustainability risk management (SRM) practices in Malaysian environmentally sensitive industries. *Procedia: Social and Behavioral Sciences*, *219*, 4–11. doi:10.1016/j.sbspro.2016.04.025

Babaev, V., Sukhonos, M., Starostina, A., & Beletsky, I. (2016). Improving the processes of cost management in the construction and energy projects. *Eastern European Journal of Enterprise Technologies, 4*(3-82), 10-17.

Baber, H. (2016). Risk mitigation practices in banking: A study of HDFC bank. *International Journal of Risk and Contingency Management*, *5*(3), 18–32. doi:10.4018/IJRCM.2016070102

Bagheri, B., Yang, S., Kao, H. A., & Lee, J. (2015). Cyber-physical systems architecture for self-aware machines in industry 4.0 environment. *IFAC-PapersOnLine*, *28*(3), 1622–1627. doi:10.1016/j.ifacol.2015.06.318

Bali, S., & Uslu, Y. D. (2017). Enterprise risk management in non-profit organization. In V. Potocan, M. Üngan, & Z. Nedelko (Eds.), *Handbook of research on managerial solutions in non-profit organizations* (pp. 75–93). Hershey, PA: IGI Global. doi:10.4018/978-1-5225-0731-4.ch004

Bälter, M., & Dennermyr, E. (2016). *Shared language, shared knowledge? Investigating barriers and facilitators to knowledge transfer in a common language context: The case of European multinational corporations.* Master Degree Project, Graduate School, University of Gothenburg. Available at http://hdl.handle.net/2077/48362

Bangemann, T., Riedl, M., Thron, M., & Diedrich, C. (2016). Integration of Classical Components into Industrial Cyber-Physical Systems. *Proceedings of the IEEE, 104*(5), 947–959. doi:10.1109/JPROC.2015.2510981

Bares, M. (2016). *Implications, Applications, Trends, and Topics of Industry 4.0.* Round Table session at the International Business and Management Conference, Prague, Czech Republic.

Barney, J. (1991). Firm resources and sustained competitive advantage. *Journal of Management, 17*(1), 99–120. doi:10.1177/014920639101700108

Barros, A., & Oberle, D. (2012). *Handbook of Service Description.* New York, NY: Springer. doi:10.1007/978-1-4614-1864-1

Bartl, M. (2008). *Open Innovation!* White Paper. Munich: HYVE. Retrieved July 8, 2017, from http://www.hyve-server.de/hyveweb/cms/upload/f_1599_WhitePaper_OpenInnovation.pdf

Bartolacci, M. R., LeBlanc, L. J., Kayikci, Y., & Grossman, T. A. (2012). Optimization modeling for logistics: Options and implementations. *Journal of Business Logistics, 33*(2), 118–127. doi:10.1111/j.0000-0000.2012.01044.x

Bar-Yam, Y. (1997). *Dynamics of complex systems.* Reading, MA: Addison-Wesley.

Bask, A., Lipponen, M., & Tinnilä, M. (2012). E-commerce logistics: A literature research review and topics for future research. *International Journal of E-Services and Mobile Applications, 4*(3), 1–22. doi:10.4018/jesma.2012070101

Bauer, W., Schlund, S., Marrenbach, D., & Ganschar, O. (2014). *Industrie 4.0 –Volkswirtschaftliches Potenzial für Deutschland [Industry 4.0-Economic potential for Germany].* Berlin, Germany: BITKOM.

Baur, C., & Wee, D. (2015). *Manufacturing's next act.* Retrieved 04 24, 2016, from McKinsey & Company: http://www.mckinsey.com/business-functions/operations/our-insights/manufacturings-next-act

Baur, C., & Wee, D. (2015, June). Manufacturing's next act. *McKinsey Quarterly.*

Baydoun, M. (2016). Risk management decisions and organizational structure in the case of a development management firm: Millennium development international. In *Project management: Concepts, methodologies, tools, and applications* (pp. 1220–1237). Hershey, PA: IGI Global. doi:10.4018/978-1-5225-0196-1.ch060

Bazigos, De Smet, & Gagnon. (2015, December). *Why agility pays.* Retrieved August 19, 2017, from http://www.mckinsey.com/business-functions/organization/our-insights/why-agility-pays#0

Beach, R., Muhlemann, A., P., Price, D, H., R., Paterson, A, & Sharp, J., A. (2000). A review of manufacturing flexibility. *European Journal of Operational Research, 122*(2000), 41-57.

Beaudoin, J., Lefebvre, G. L., Normand, M., Gouri, V., & Skerlj, A. (2016). *Prendre Part à la Revolution Manufacturière?* CEFRIO.

Beaudreau, B. (2005). The National Industrial Recovery Act Redux: Technology and Transitions. Lincoln, NE: iUniverse.

Becker, T., & Wagner, D. (2015). Identification of Key Machines in Complex Production Networks. *Procedia CIRP, 41*(2016), 69 – 74.

Becker, J., Knackstedt, R., & Pöppelbuß, J. (2009). Developing Maturity Models for IT Management - A Procedure Model and its Application. *Business & Information Systems Engineering, 1*(3), 213–222. doi:10.100712599-009-0044-5

Beede, D., Powers, R., & Ingram, C. (2017). The employment impact of autonomous vehicles. Washington, DC: Office of the Chief Economist, U.S. Department of Commerce Economics and Statistics Administration.

Bekkers, R., & Freitas, I. M. B. (2008). Analyzing knowledge transfer channels between universities and industry: To what degree do sectors also matter? *Research Policy*, *37*(10), 1837–1853. doi:10.1016/j.respol.2008.07.007

Belussi, F., & Sedita, S. (2010). Managing the fragmented value chain of global business: Exploitative and explorative offshoring toward emerging market economies. In *The Past, Present and Future of International Business & Management, Advances in International Management* (Vol. 23, pp. 399–429). Cheltenham, UK: Emerald Group Publishing Limited. doi:10.1108/S1571-5027(2010)00000230023

Bergendahl, G., & Lindblom, T. (2007). Risk management in banking: A review of principles and strategies. In H. Rao, M. Gupta, & S. Upadhyaya (Eds.), *Managing information assurance in financial services* (pp. 26–44). Hershey, PA: IGI Global. doi:10.4018/978-1-59904-171-1.ch002

Berger, T., & Frey, C. (2016). *Structural Transformation in the OECD: Digitalization, Deindustrialization and the Future of Work*. OECD Social, Employment, and Migration Working Papers, No. 193. OECD Publishing. 10.1787/5jlr068802f7-en

Berkhout, F., Hertin, J., & Jordan, A. (2001). *Socio-economic futures in climate change impact assessment: Using scenarios as 'learning machines'*. Working Paper No. 3, July 4 2001. University of Sussex: Tyndall Centre.

Bhandari, K. (2017). *Internationalization and Organizational Ambidexterity for Sustainable Performance: Moderating Effects of Firm-specific Advantages and Competitive Strategies*. Acta Wasaensia 379, Vaasan yliopisto, University of Vaasa.

Bhasin, S., & Burcher, P. (2006). Lean viewed as a philosophy. *Journal of Manufacturing Technology Management*, *17*(1), 56–72. doi:10.1108/17410380610639506

Binns, A., Harreld, J. B., III, & Tushman, M. L. (2014, December). The art of strategic renewal. *MIT Sloan Management Review*.

Binz, C., Gosens, J., Hansen, T., & Hansen, U. E. (2017). Toward Technology-Sensitive Catching-Up Policies: Insights from Renewable Energy in China. *World Development*, *96*, 418–437. doi:10.1016/j.worlddev.2017.03.027

Bird, A., & Fang, T. (2009). Editorial: Cross cultural management in the age of globalization. *International Journal of Cross Cultural Management*, *9*(2), 139–143. doi:10.1177/1470595809335713

Birkinshaw, J. (2002). The art of Swedish management. *Business Strategy Review*, *13*(2), 11–19. doi:10.1111/1467-8616.00205

Blank, S. (2013). *The four steps to the epiphany: successful strategies for products that win*. BookBaby.

Bloomberg. (2016). *Asia's Worst Currency Slump Takes Malaysian Rate Cut Off Table*. Retrieved April 25, 2017, from https://www.bloomberg.com/news/articles/2016-11-22/asia-s-worst-currency-slump-puts-malaysia-central-bank-on-guard

Bock, G. W., & Kim, Y. G. (2002). Breaking the myth of rewards: An explanatory study of attitudes about knowledge sharing. *Information Resources Management Journal*, *15*(2), 14–21. doi:10.4018/irmj.2002040102

Bodnaruk, A., Manconi, A., & Massa, M. (2016). Cross-border alliances and risk management. *Journal of International Economics*, *102*, 22–49. doi:10.1016/j.jinteco.2016.05.002

Boghean, F. (2015). Risk management in the decision-making of Romanian entities. *Procedia Economics and Finance*, *32*, 1066–1074. doi:10.1016/S2212-5671(15)01569-5

Bolumole, Y. A., Closs, D. J., & Rodammer, F. A. (2015). The economic development role of regional logistics hubs: A cross-country study of interorganizational governance models. *Journal of Business Logistics*, *36*(2), 182–198. doi:10.1111/jbl.12088

Bourlakis, C. A., & Bourlakis, M. A. (2003). Logistics, information technology, and retail internationalisation: The formation of international strategic retail networks. In L. Joia (Ed.), *IT-based management: Challenges and solutions* (pp. 257–276). Hershey, PA: IGI Global. doi:10.4018/978-1-59140-033-2.ch015

Brandon, D. M. (2006). Risk planning and management. In D. Brandon (Ed.), *Project management for modern information systems* (pp. 157–182). Hershey, PA: IGI Global. doi:10.4018/978-1-59140-693-8.ch008

Brenner, W., & Wenger, R. (2007). *Elektronische Beschaffung: Stand und Entwicklungstendenzen*. Berlin: Springer. doi:10.1007/978-3-540-34018-8

Brettel, M., Fischer, F. G., Bendig, D., Weber, A. R., & Wolff, B. (2016). Enablers for self-optimizing production systems in the context of Industrie 4.0. *Procedia CIRP*, *41*, 93–98. doi:10.1016/j.procir.2015.12.065

Brettel, M., Friederichsen, N., Keller, M., & Rosenberg, M. (2014). How virtualization, decentralization and network building change the manufacturing landscape: An industry 4.0 perspective, Int. Mech. *J. Aerosp. Ind. Mechatron. Manuf. Eng*, *8*(1).

Brettel, M., Friederichsen, N., Keller, M., & Rosenberg, M. (2014). How Virtualization, Decentralization and Network Building Change the Manufacturing Landscape: An Industry 4.0 Perspective. *International Journal of Mechanical, Aerospace, Industrial and Mechatronics Engineering*, *8*(1), 37–44.

Brettel, M., Friederichsen, N., Keller, M., & Rosenberg, M. (2014). How Virtualization, Decentralization and Network Building Change the Manufacturing Landscape: An Industry 4.0 Perspective. *International Journal of Mechanical, Aerospace, Industrial. Mechatronic and Manufacturing Engineering*, *8*(1), 37–44.

Brettel, M., Klein, M., & Friederichsen, N. (2016). The relevance of manufacturing flexibility in the context of Industrie 4.0. *Procedia CIRP*, *41*, 105–110. doi:10.1016/j.procir.2015.12.047

Brownsword, M., & Setchi, R. (2012). A formalised approach to the management of risk: A conceptual framework and ontology. In W. Lee (Ed.), *Systems approaches to knowledge management, transfer, and resource development* (pp. 263–285). Hershey, PA: IGI Global. doi:10.4018/978-1-4666-1782-7.ch018

Broy, M. (2010). *Cyber – Physical Systems: Innovation durch softwareintensive eingebettete Systeme*. Berlin: Springer Verlag. doi:10.1007/978-3-642-14901-6

Brue, G. (2015). *Six Sigma for managers*. New York: McGraw-Hill Education.

Brunet-Thornton, R., & Bureš, V. (2012). Cross-Cultural Management: Establishing a Czech Benchmark. E+M Economics and Management, 3(12), 46-62.

Brunet-Thornton, R., & Bureš, V. (2010). Meeting Czech Knowledge Management Challenges Head-On: KM-Be.At-It. In M. Al-Shammari (Ed.), *Knowledge Management in Emerging Economies: Social, Organizational and Cultural Implementation* (pp. 20–46). Hershey, PA: IGI Global.

Brynjolfsson, E. (2014). *The second machine age: Work, progress, and prosperity in a time of brilliant technologies* (1st ed.). New York: W. W. Norton and Company.

Brynjolfsson, E., & McAfee, A. (2014). *The Second Machine Age – Work, Progress, and Prosperity in a Time of Brilliant Technologies*. New York, NY: W. W. Norton & Co., Inc.

Brynjolfsson, E., & McAfee, A. (2016). *The Second Machine Age: Work, Progress, and Prosperity in a Time of Brilliant Technologies*. New York: W. W. Norton & Company.

Bughin, J. (2017, July). *Advanced social technologies and the future of collaboration*. Retrieved from http://www.mckinsey.com/business-functions/digital-mckinsey/our-insights/advanced-social-technologies-and-the-future-of-collaboration

Bughin, J., Chui, M., & Manyika, J. (2015). An executive's guide to the Internet of Things. *The McKinsey Quarterly*.

Bureš, V. (2003). Cultural Barriers in Knowledge Sharing. E+M Economics and Management, 6, 57-62.

Bureš, V. (2006). Knowledge Management and its Implementation. *WEBIST 2006: Proceedings of the Second International Conference on Web Information Systems and Technologies*, 115-118.

Bureš, V. (2006a). Knowledge Management and its Implementation. In *Proceedings of the 2nd International Conference on Web Information Systems and Technologies WEBIST 2006* (pp. 115-118). Setubal, Portugal: INSTICC.

Bureš, V. (2009). Conceptual Perspective of Knowledge Management (in Czech). E+M Economics and Management, 12(2).

Bureš, V. (2006b). Systems Thinking as a Basis for Ambient Intelligence. In *Proceedings of 11th conference on Information Technologies in Computer Science - ITiCSE06* (pp. 318). Bologna, Italy: ACM.

Bureš, V., & Čech, P. (2008). Knowledge Management: The Central European Experience. *Effective Executive*, *11*(6), 47–53.

Bureš, V., & Tučník, P. (2014). Complex Agent-based Models: Application of a constructivism in the Economic Research. *E+M. Ekonomie a Management*, *17*(3), 152–168. doi:10.15240/tul/001/2014-3-012

Bureš, V., Tučník, P., Mikulecký, P., Mls, K., & Blecha, P. (2016). Application of ambient intelligence in educational institutions: Visions and architectures. *International Journal of Ambient Computing and Intelligence*, *7*(1), 94–120. doi:10.4018/IJACI.2016010105

Burmeister, C., Luettgens, D., & Piller, F. T. (2016). *Business Model Innovation for Industrie 4.0: Why the 'Industrial Internet' Mandates a New Perspective on Innovation*. RWTH-TIM Working Paper.

Cahill, D. L., Goldsby, T. J., Knemeyer, A. M., & Wallenburg, C. M. (2010). Customer loyalty in logistics outsourcing relationships: An examination of the moderating effects of conflict frequency. *Journal of Business Logistics*, *31*(2), 253–277. doi:10.1002/j.2158-1592.2010.tb00151.x

Cäker, M., Andersson, T., & Wickelgren, M. (2011). Formal incentive systems in organizations with a Swedish management style: Conflict or interaction? In *Conference: The Actor-Reality Perspective*. Gothenburg University Publications (GUP). Retrieved from http://bit.ly/1xjBUi7

Caloghirou, Y., Kastelli, I., & Tsakanika, A. (2004). Internal capabilities and external knowledge sources: Complements or substitutes for innovative performance. *Technovation*, *24*(1), 29–39. doi:10.1016/S0166-4972(02)00051-2

Can, O. (2016). *Five million jobs by 2020: the real challenge of the fourth industrial revolution*. World Economic Forum. Retrieved September 1, 2017, from https://www.weforum.org/press/2016/01/five-million-jobs-by-2020-the-real-challenge-of-the-fourth-industrial-revolution/

Capra, F. (2015). The systems view of life a unifying conception of mind, matter, and life. *Cosmos and History: The Journal of Natural and Social Philosophy*, *11*(2), 242–249.

Capra, F., & Pier Luigi, L. (2014). *The systems view of life: A unifying vision*. Cambridge, UK: Cambridge University Press. doi:10.1017/CBO9780511895555

Carlile, P. R., & Rebentisch, E. S. (2003). Into the black box: The knowledge transformation cycle. *Management Science*, *49*(9), 1180–1195. doi:10.1287/mnsc.49.9.1180.16564

Carmeli, A., Schaubroeck, J., & Tishler, A. (2011). How CEO empowering leadership shapes top management team processes: Implications for firm performance. *The Leadership Quarterly*, *22*(2), 399–411. doi:10.1016/j.leaqua.2011.02.013

Carmigniani, J., Furht, B., Anisetti, M., Ceravolo, P., Damiani, E., & Ivkovic, M. (2011). Augmented reality technologies, systems and applications. *Multimedia Tools and Applications*, *51*(1), 341–377. doi:10.100711042-010-0660-6

Carneiro, J., Rocha, A., & da Silva, J. F. (2008). Challenging the Uppsala internationalization model: A contingent approach to the internationalization of services. *BAR - Brazilian Administration Review*, *5*(2), 85–103. doi:10.1590/S1807-76922008000200002

Carrus, P. P., & Pinna, R. (2011). Information technology and supply chain management coordination: The role of third party logistics providers. *International Journal of E-Services and Mobile Applications*, *3*(4), 21–36. doi:10.4018/jesma.2011100102

Carvalho, H., Duarte, S., & Machado, C. (2011). Lean, agile, resilient and green: Divergencies and synergies. *International. Journal of LEAN Six Sigma*, *2*(2), 151–179. doi:10.1108/20401461111135037

Čech, P. (2005). *The Potential of Knowledge in Organizations* (Dissertation). Hradec Králové: University of Hradec Králové.

Cecil, K. (2004). Walking a maze of views to the center: Teaching point of view. *English Journal*, *93*(5), 54–59. doi:10.2307/4128936

Challe, E., Lopez, J. I., & Mengus, E. (2016). *Southern Europe's Institutional Decline*. HEC Paris Research Paper No. ECO/SCD-2016-1148.

Chang, S., Kogut, B., & Yang, J. S. (2016). Global diversification discount and its discontents: A bit of self-selection makes a world of difference. *Strategic Management Journal*, *37*(11), 2254–2274. doi:10.1002mj.2574

Chapman, P., & ... . (2002). Identifying and Managing Supply Chain Vulnerability. *Logistics & Transport Focus*, *4*(4), 59–70.

Chapman, R. J. (2017). Complexity theory and system dynamics for project risk management. In Y. Raydugin (Ed.), *Handbook of research on leveraging risk and uncertainties for effective project management* (pp. 152–176). Hershey, PA: IGI Global. doi:10.4018/978-1-5225-1790-0.ch008

Chatzipoulidis, A., Michalopoulos, D., & Mavridis, I. (2016). Managing enterprise IT risks through automated security metrics. In P. Papajorgji, F. Pinet, A. Guimarães, & J. Papathanasiou (Eds.), *Automated enterprise systems for maximizing business performance* (pp. 215–243). Hershey, PA: IGI Global. doi:10.4018/978-1-4666-8841-4.ch012

Chen, J. (1995). On the Formation and Function of National Innovation System from YOFC. *Science Research of Management*, *3*.

Chen, C. J. (2004). The effects of knowledge attribute, alliance characteristics, and absorptive capacity on knowledge transfer performance. *R & D Management*, *34*(3), 311–321. doi:10.1111/j.1467-9310.2004.00341.x

Chen, D. H. C., & Dahlman, C. J. (2005). *The Knowledge Economy, the KAM Methodology and World Bank Operations*. Washington, DC: World Bank. Available http://www.worldbank.org/

Chen, F., Deng, P., Wan, J., Zhang, D., Vasilakos, A. V., & Rong, X. (2015). Data mining for the internet of things: Literature review and challenges. *International Journal of Distributed Sensor Networks*, *2015*, 12.

Cheng, J. H., & Chen, M. C. (2016). Influence of institutional and moral orientations on relational risk management in supply chains. *Journal of Purchasing and Supply Management*, *22*(2), 110–119. doi:10.1016/j.pursup.2016.01.002

Chen, H., Tian, Y., Ellinger, A. E., & Daugherty, P. J. (2010). Managing logistics outsourcing relationships: An empirical investigation in China. *Journal of Business Logistics*, *31*(2), 279–299. doi:10.1002/j.2158-1592.2010.tb00152.x

Chesbrough, H. (2003). *Open Innovation: The New Imperative for Creating and Profiting from Technology*. Boston: Harvard Business School Press.

Chesbrough, H. (2007). Business model innovation: It's not just about technology anymore. *Strategy and Leadership*, *35*(6), 12–17. doi:10.1108/10878570710833714

Childs, M. L., & Jin, B. (2014). Is Uppsala Model valid to fashion retailers? An analysis from internationalization patterns of fast fashion retailers. *Journal of Fashion Marketing and Management*, *18*(1), 36–51. doi:10.1108/JFMM-10-2012-0061

China Academy of Information and Communications Technology. (2016). *China Industry Development Report 2016*. Beijing: Posts & Telecom Press.

China State Statistics Bureau. (2017). *China's Statistical Yearbook (2007–2016)*. Beijing: China Statistical Press. (in Chinese)

Chiu, M., Ganesan, V., & Patel, M. (2017, July). Taking the pulse of enterprise IoT. *McKinsey & Company Internet of Things*. Retrieved September 1, 2017, from http://www.mckinsey.com/global-themes/internet-of-things/our-insights/taking-the-pulse-of-enterprise-iot

Choi, T. M., Chiu, C. H., & Chan, H. K. (2016). Risk management of logistics systems. *Transportation Research Part E, Logistics and Transportation Review*, *90*, 1–6. doi:10.1016/j.tre.2016.03.007

Christopher, M., & Holweg, M. (2011). Supply Chain 2.0: Managing supply chains in the era of turbulence. *International Journal of Physical Distribution & Logistics Management*, *41*(1), 63–82. doi:10.1108/09600031111101439

Christopher, M., & Towill, D. R. (2000). Supply chain migration from lean and functional to agile and customised. *Supply Chain Management*, *5*(4), 206–213. doi:10.1108/13598540010347334

Chu, Z., & Wang, Q. (2012). Drivers of relationship quality in logistics outsourcing in China. *The Journal of Supply Chain Management*, *48*(3), 78–96. doi:10.1111/j.1745-493X.2011.03259.x

Cieśla, M. (2016). Sustainable logistics strategies of transnational corporations. In T. Kramberger, V. Potočan, & V. Ipaveç (Eds.), *Sustainable logistics and strategic transportation planning* (pp. 347–367). Hershey, PA: IGI Global. doi:10.4018/978-1-5225-0001-8.ch016

CIMData. (2016). *Siemens PLM Software's Simcenter: Predictive Engineering Enables Systems-Driven Product Development*. Retrieved on March 15th, 2017, from http://www.cimdata.com/en/component/docman/cat_view/43-complimentary-reports/45-commentaries?start=30

Cisco. (2017). *Cisco 2017 Annual Cyber Security Report. WD info*. Cisco.

CNBC. (2014). *Philips: How the internet of things could affect health care*. Retrieved March 16, 2017, from http://www.cnbc.com/2014/01/23/how-the-internet-of-things-could-affect-healthcare.html

Cohen, W. M., & Levinthal, D. A. (1990). Absorptive capacity: A new perspective on learning and innovation. *Administrative Science Quarterly*, *35*(1), 128–152. doi:10.2307/2393553

Comm, C. L., & Mathaisel, D. F. (2005). 09). An exploratory study of best lean sustainability practices in higher education. *Quality Assurance in Education*, *13*(3), 227–240. doi:10.1108/09684880510607963

Cooper, T. (2016). *Medical devices cybersecurity: From best practices to standard.* Retrieved Jan. 5, 2017, from http://ceitcollaboration.org/docs/Cyber-Security-Part-II.pdf

Cordeiro, C. M. (2016a). An integrated perspective of a 'World Without Verona Walls': the Götheborg IV model. In Gränsöverskridande: Vänbok till Claes G. Alvstam. Centrum för Europaforskning vid Göteborgs Universitet (CERGU), skrift nr. 30. University of Gothenburg, Kompendiet, Göteborg, Sweden.

Cordeiro, C. M. (2016b). The Gotheborg IV (G4) Model and the Function of Language in the Globalization Process of the Firm: The Case of Swedish MNEs. In M. Khan (Ed.), *Multinational Enterprise Management Strategies in Developing Countries* (pp. 215–236). Hershey, PA: Business Science. doi:10.4018/978-1-5225-0276-0.ch011

Cordeiro-Nilsson, C. M. (2009). *Swedish management in Singapore: A discourse analysis study* (Doctoral dissertation). Gothenburg University Publications (GUP), University of Gothenburg. Available at https://gup.ub.gu.se/publication/93669

Cordeiro-Nilsson, C. M. (2010). A discourse analysis study of assimilation and integration of management style: The case of Swedish managers in Singapore. *The New English Teacher*, *4*(1), 13–53.

Cozmiuc, D., & Petrisor, I. (n.d.a). Industrie 4.0 at Siemens – steps made next. *Journal of Cases on Information Technology*, *20*(1).

Cozmiuc, D., & Petrisor, I. (n.d.b). Industrie 4.0 at Siemens – steps made today. *Journal of Cases on Information Technology*, *20*(2).

CREMA. (2015). *Providing Cloud-based Rapid Elastic Manufacturing based on the XaaS and Cloud model.* Retrieved on May 25th, 2016, from www.crema/project.eu

Crystal, D. (1990). *Linguistics* (2nd ed.). Harmondsworth, UK: Penguin.

Crystal, D. (1997). *The Cambridge encyclopedia of language* (2nd ed.). Cambridge University Press.

Cummings, J. L., & Teng, B. S. (2003). Transferring R&D knowledge: The key factors affecting knowledge transfer success. *Journal of Engineering and Technology Management*, *20*(1-2), 39–68. doi:10.1016/S0923-4748(03)00004-3

Dagiasis, A. P. (2013). Logistics modeling and forecasting with regression. In D. Folinas (Ed.), *Outsourcing management for supply chain operations and logistics service* (pp. 223–237). Hershey, PA: IGI Global. doi:10.4018/978-1-4666-2008-7.ch013

Damelio, R. (2011). *The basics of process mapping* (2nd ed.). Boca Raton, FL: CRC Press.

Darkow, I. L., Weidmann, M., & Lorentz, H. (2015). Adaptation of foreign logistics service providers' resources and capabilities to a new institutional environment. *The Journal of Supply Chain Management*, *51*(1), 27–51. doi:10.1111/jscm.12068

Datta, S. P. A. (2015). Dynamic socio-economic disequilibrium catalyzed by the Internet of Things. *Journal of Innovation Management*, *3*(3), 4–9.

Daugherty, P., Banerjee, P., Negm, W., & Alter, A. E. (2015). *Driving Unconventional Growth through the Industrial Internet of Things, s.l.* Accenture.

Davenport, T. H., & Short, J. E. (1990). 06). The new industrial engineering: Information technology and business process redesign. *Sloan Management Review*, *31*(4), 11.

Davenport, T. H., & Smith, D. E. (2000). Managing Knowledge in Professional Service Firms. In *The Knowledge Management Yearbook 2000-2001*. Oxford, UK: Butterworth-Heinemann.

Davis, D. F., & Friske, W. (2013). The role of public–private partnerships in facilitating cross-border logistics: A case study at the U.S./Canadian border. *Journal of Business Logistics*, *34*(4), 347–359. doi:10.1111/jbl.12032

De Bruin, T., Freeze, R., Kaulkarni, U., & Rosemann, M. (2005). Understanding the Main Phases of Developing a Maturity Assessment Model. *Australasian Conference on Information Systems (ACIS)*, 8–19.

de Figueiredo, J. R. J. P. Jr. (2010). A tribute to Oliver Williamson: Institutions, politics, and non-market strategy. *California Management Review*, *52*(2), 123–131. doi:10.1525/cmr.2010.52.2.123

De Man, J. C., & Strandhagen, J. O. (2017). An Industry 4.0 research agenda for sustainable business models. *Procedia CIRP*, *0*, 721–726. doi:10.1016/j.procir.2017.03.315

Deane, P. (1979). *The First Industrial Revolution*. Cambridge, UK: Cambridge University Press.

Decker, J. (2016). Business 4.0 and Generation Y/Z: Challenges and Opportunities for Human -Resources Management. In *TAKE 2016 – Theory and Applications in the Knowledge Economy* (pp. 770–785). Aveiro, Portugal: Eduardo Tomé.

Deepen, J. M., Goldsby, T. J., Knemeyer, A. M., & Wallenburg, C. M. (2008). Beyond expectations: An examination of logistics outsourcing goal achievement and goal exceedance. *Journal of Business Logistics*, *29*(2), 75–105. doi:10.1002/j.2158-1592.2008.tb00088.x

Dehghani, J., & Strandberg, M. (2015). *Well said, well done! Language as a source of power in multinational teams* (Master thesis project). Graduate School, University of Gothenburg. Available at http://hdl.handle.net/2077/39894

Deloitte. (2015). *Industry 4.0. Challenges and solutions for the digital transformation and use of exponential technologies*. Deloitte.

Deming, W. E. (1950). *Elementary Principles of the Statistical Control of Quality: A series of lectures*. JUSE.

Denis, D. J., Denis, D. K., & Yost, K. (2002). Global diversification, industrial diversification, and firm value. *The Journal of Finance*, *57*(5), 1951–1979. doi:10.1111/0022-1082.00485

Desender, K. (2011). On the determinants of enterprise risk management implementation. In N. Shi & G. Silvius (Eds.), *Enterprise IT governance, business value and performance measurement* (pp. 87–100). Hershey, PA: IGI Global. doi:10.4018/978-1-60566-346-3.ch006

Diao, X. (2017). YOFC Promote the transformation and upgrading of fiber optic cable industry. *Communications World*, *10*.

Dicken, P. (2007). *Global Shift: Mapping the Changing Contours of the World Economy*. London: Sage Publications.

Dionne, G. (2013). Risk management: History, definition, and critique. *Risk Management & Insurance Review*, *16*(2), 147–166. doi:10.1111/rmir.12016

Distefano, S., Banerjee, N., & Puliafito, A. (2016). Smart Objects, Infrastructures, and Services in the Internet of Things. International Journal of Distributed Sensor Networks.

Dittrich, P. (2016). *Reskilling for the Fourth Industrial Revolution*. Formulating a European Strategy. Policy Paper 175. Available: http://www.institutdelors.eu/media/digitalskill-jdib-nov2016.pdf?pdf=ok

Dixit, U. S., Hazarika, M., & Davim, J. P. (2017). *A Brief History of Mechanical Engineering*. Springer. doi:10.1007/978-3-319-42916-8

Doehmann, I., & Sp, G. (2016). *Industry 4.0: legal systems, the social contract and health care*. Retrieved Jan. 5, 2017, from http://www.scl.org/sitc.aspx?i=ed47630

Dolejs, M. (2016). *Implications, Applications, Trends, and Topics of Industry 4.0.* Round Table session at the International Business and Management Conference, Prague, Czech Republic.

Domingo, M. C. (2012). An overview of the Internet of Things for people with disabilities. *Journal of Network and Computer Applications, 35*(2), 584–596. doi:10.1016/j.jnca.2011.10.015

DOSM. (2017). *Salaries & Wages Survey Report, Malaysia, 2016.* Department of Statistics Malaysia (DOSM). Retrieved May 27, 2017, from https://www.dosm.gov.my/v1/index.php?r=column/pdfPrev&id=U3JoKzFiekE5WFFKK0VMRWQ0a2FDQT09

Drucker, P. F. (1993). *The post capitalist society.* Oxford, UK: Butterworth-Heinemann.

Dubey, S. (2015). *How India is poised for Industry 4.0.* Retrieved June 16, 2017, from http://rvantage.net/india-poised-industry-4-0/

Duguay, C. R., Landry, S., & Pasin, F. (1997). From mass production to flexible/agile production. *International Journal of Operations & Production Management, 17*(12), 1183–1195. doi:10.1108/01443579710182936

Dujin, A., Geissler, C., & Horstkötter, D. (2014). *Industry 4.0: The new industrial revolution.* Munich: Roland Berger Strategy Consultants.

Dujin, A., Geissler, C., & Horstkötter, D. (2014). *INDUSTRY 4.0: The new industrial revolution.* Munich: Roland Berger Strategy Consultants.

Duysters, G., Jacob, J., Lemmens, C., & Yu, J. T. (2009). Internationalization and technological catching up of emerging multinationals: A comparative case study of China's Haier group. *Industrial and Corporate Change, 18*(2), 325–349. doi:10.1093/icc/dtp006

Dworschak, B., Helmut, B., & Achtenhagen, C. (2013). Future skills needed for the Internet of Things in industrial production as part of the early identification initiative of the German Federal Ministry of Education and Research. *Frequenz (Bern).*

Dworschak, B., & Zaiser, H. (2014). Competences for cyber-physical systems in manufacturing-First findings and scenarios. *Procedia CIRP, 25*(C), 345–350. doi:10.1016/j.procir.2014.10.048

Dwoskin, E., & Adam, K. (2017, May 14). More than 150 countries affected by massive cyberattack, Europol says. *The Washington Post.* Retrieved from https://www.washingtonpost.com/business/economy/more-than-150-countries-affected-by-massive-cyberattack-europol-says/2017/05/14/5091465e-3899-11e7-9e48-c4f199710b69_story.html?utm_term=.7cd4bbf6aa42

Einsiedler, I. (2013). Embedded Systeme für Industrie 4.0. *Production Management, 18*, 26–28.

Eisenhardt, K. M. (1989). Building theories from case study research. *Academy of Management. The Academy of Management Review, 14*(4), 3–36.

Eisenhardt, K. M., & Piezunka, H. (2011). Complexity Theory and Corporate Strategy. The Sage Handbook of Complexity and Management. In B. McKelvey (Ed.), *The SAGE Handbook of Complexity and Management.* Sage Publications. doi:10.4135/9781446201084.n30

El Said, G. R. (2015). Understanding Knowledge Management System antecedents of performance impact: Extending the Task-technology Fit Model with intention to share knowledge construct. *Future Business Journal, 1*(1–2), 75–87. doi:10.1016/j.fbj.2015.11.003

Eleni-Maria, P. (2013). Logistics service providers: Collaboration with IFFs, 3PL, or 4PL providers? In D. Folinas (Ed.), *Outsourcing management for supply chain operations and logistics service* (pp. 52–77). Hershey, PA: IGI Global. doi:10.4018/978-1-4666-2008-7.ch004

Engelman, R. (2015). *The Second Industrial Revolution, 1870-1914.* Retrieved July 21, 2017, from http://ushistoryscene.com/article/second-industrial-revolution/

Englander, E. J. (1988). Technology and Oliver Williamson's transaction cost economics. *Journal of Economic Behavior & Organization, 10*(3), 339–353. doi:10.1016/0167-2681(88)90054-6

Erol, S., Schumacher, A., & Sihn, W. (2016). Strategic guidance towards Industry 4.0 – a three-stage process model. In *International Conference on Competitive Manufacturing* (pp. 495-500). Stellenbosh, South Africa: University of Stellenbosh.

Erol, S., Schumacher, A., & Sihn, W. (2016). Strategic Guidance towards Industry 4.0 - a Three-stage Process Model. *International Conference on Competitive Manufacturing, 9*, 495–501.

Espinel, V. (2016). *The digital economy: What is it and how will it transform our lives?* Retrieved June 4, 2017, from https://www.weforum.org/agenda/2016/11/the-digital-economy-what-is-it-and-how-will-it-transform-our-lives/

Essig, M., & Arnold, U. (2001). Electronic Procurement in Supply Chain Management: An Information Economics-Based Analysis of Electronic Markets. *The Journal of Supply Chain Management, 37*(4), 43–49. doi:10.1111/j.1745-493X.2001.tb00112.x

European Commission. (2017a). *Czech Republic: "Průmysl 4.0".* Available: https://ec.europa.eu/growth/tools-databases/dem/monitor/sites/default/files/DTM_Prumysl%2040_CZ%20v1.pdf

European Commission. (2017b). *Digital Transformation Scoreboard 2017: Evidence of positive outcomes and current opportunities for EU businesses.* Available: http://s3platform.jrc.ec.europa.eu/-/digital-transformation-scoreboard-2017-evidence-of-positive-outcomes-and-current-opportunities-for-eu-businesses?inheritRedirect=true

European Parliament. (2015). *Industry 4.0 Digitalisation for productivity and growth.* Retrieved on May 25th, 2016, from http://www.europarl.europa.eu/RegData/etudes/BRIE/2015/568337/EPRS_BRI(2015)568337_EN.pdf

European Union Agency for Network and Information Security (ENISA). (2016). *Review of cyber hygiene practices.* Retrieved August 17, 2017, from https://www.enisa.europa.eu/publications/cyber-hygiene

Evangelista, P. (2011). The role of information technology in supporting supply chain coordination of logistics services providers. In I. Mahdavi, S. Mohebbi, & N. Cho (Eds.), *Electronic supply network coordination in intelligent and dynamic environments: Modeling and implementation* (pp. 113–144). Hershey, PA: IGI Global. doi:10.4018/978-1-60566-808-6.ch005

Evangelista, P. (2013). Adding value to logistics services using ICT: A case study analysis of small logistics companies in Italy. In *Supply chain management: Concepts, methodologies, tools, and applications* (pp. 924–948). Hershey, PA: IGI Global. doi:10.4018/978-1-4666-2625-6.ch054

Fang, T. (2003). A critique of Hofstede's fifth national culture dimension. *International Journal of Cross Cultural Management, 3*(3), 347–368. doi:10.1177/1470595803003003006

Fang, T. (2005-2006). From 'Onion' to 'Ocean': Paradox and change in national cultures. *International Studies of Management & Organization, 35*(4), 71–90

Fang, T. (2012). Yin Yang: A new perspective on culture. *Management and Organization Review, 8*(1), 25–50. doi:10.1111/j.1740-8784.2011.00221.x

Fan, H., Li, G., Sun, H., & Cheng, T. C. E. (2017). An information processing perspective on supply chain risk management: Antecedents, mechanism, and consequences. *International Journal of Production Economics, 185*, 63–75. doi:10.1016/j.ijpe.2016.11.015

Fan, P. (2006). Catching up through developing innovation capability: Evidence from China's telecom-equipment industry. *Technovation, 26*(3), 359–368. doi:10.1016/j.technovation.2004.10.004

Fan, Y. J., Yin, Y. H., Da Xu, L., Zeng, Y., & Wu, F. (2014). IoT based smart rehabilitation system. *IEEE Transactions on Industrial Informatics, 10*(2), 1568–1577. doi:10.1109/TII.2014.2302583

Farooq, A., & Hussain, Z. (2011). Balanced scorecard perspective on change and performance: A study of selected Indian companies. *Procedia: Social and Behavioral Sciences, 24*, 754–768. doi:10.1016/j.sbspro.2011.09.043

Fayol, H. (1967). *General and industrial management (Administration, industrielle et generale)* (C. Storrs, Trans.). London: Pitman.

Fenz, S. (2011). E-business and information security risk management: Challenges and potential solutions. In E. Kajan (Ed.), *Electronic business interoperability: Concepts, opportunities and challenges* (pp. 596–614). Hershey, PA: IGI Global. doi:10.4018/978-1-60960-485-1.ch024

Firestone, J. (1999). *The Artificial Knowledge Manager Standard: A "Strawman"*. Working Paper No. One, KM ANSI/ISO Standards Committee Meeting, Executive Information Systems, Inc. Available: http://www.dkms.com/papers/akmsstrawbak.pdf

Flanagan, D. J., & O'Shaughnessy, K. C. (2005). The effect of layoffs on firm reputation. *Journal of Management, 31*(3), 445–463. doi:10.1177/0149206304272186

Flowerdew, J. (2017). Corpus-based approaches to language description for specialized academic writing. *Language Teaching, 50*(1), 90–106. doi:10.1017/S0261444814000378

Food and Drug Administration (FDA) Guidance. (2014). *Content of premarket submissions for management of cybersecurity in medical devices.* Retrieved from https://www.fda.gov/downloads/MedicalDevices/DeviceRegulationandGuidance/GuidanceDocuments/UCM356190.pdf

Food and Drug Administration (FDA) Guidance. (2016). *Postmarket management of cybersecurity in medical devices.* Retrieved from https://www.fda.gov/downloads/MedicalDevices/DeviceRegulationandGuidance/GuidanceDocuments/UCM482022.pdf

Food and Drug Administration (FDA). (2015). *What does it mean for FDA to "classify" a medical device?* Retrieved from March 20, 2017. https://www.fda.gov/AboutFDA/Transparency/Basics/ucm194438.htm

Ford, S. (2016). *Additive manufacturing and sustainability: an exploratory study of the advantages and challenges.* Academic Press.

Ford, H., & Crowther, S. (1922). *My Life and Work.* Garden City, NY: Doubleday, Page & Co.

Forsgren, M., & Hagström, P. (2007). Ignorant and impatient internationalization? The Uppsala Model and internationalization patterns for internet-related firms. *Critical Perspectives on International Business, 3*(4), 291–305. doi:10.1108/17422040710832559

Fraser, J. R. S., & Simkins, B. J. (2016). The challenges of and solutions for implementing enterprise risk management. *Business Horizons, 59*(6), 689–698. doi:10.1016/j.bushor.2016.06.007

Freeman, E. R. (1984). *Strategic management: A stakeholder approach.* Boston: Cambridge University Press.

Frenkel, K. (1990). The European community and information technology. *Communications of the ACM*, *33*(4), 404–410. doi:10.1145/77556.77557

Frey, C. B., & Osborne, M. A. (2013). *The future of employment: how susceptible are jobs to computerisation?* Working Paper. Oxford Martin School. Retrieved July 30, 2017, from http://www.futuretech.ox.ac.uk/sites/futuretech.ox.ac.uk/files/The_Future_of_Employment_OMS_Working_Paper_0.pdf

Friedman, M. (2009). *Capitalism and freedom*. University of Chicago Press.

Fu, K. (2014, April 29). *Medical devices cyber security: the first 164 years* [Video file]. Retrieved Jan. 5, 2017, from https://www.youtube.com/watch?v=QKgdvmomopw

Fuerst, S. (2010). The development of international business theory: implications for international business teaching and research in Colombia. *Cuadernos de Administración*, 33-51.

Fugate, B. S., Flint, D. J., & Mentzer, J. T. (2008). The role of logistics in market orientation. *Journal of Business Logistics*, *29*(2), 1–26. doi:10.1002/j.2158-1592.2008.tb00085.x

Fugate, B. S., Mentzer, J. T., & Stank, T. P. (2010). Logistics performance: Efficiency, effectiveness, and differentiation. *Journal of Business Logistics*, *31*(1), 43–62. doi:10.1002/j.2158-1592.2010.tb00127.x

Fukuyama, F. (1993). *The end of history and the last man*. New York: Avon.

Fuller, R. B. (1957). A Comprehensive Anticipatory Design Science. *Royal Architectural Institute of Canada*, *34*.

Fuller, R. B. (1938). *Nine Chains to the Moon*. New York: Anchor Books.

Gabrielsson, M., Seppälä, T., & Gabrielsson, P. (2016). Realizing a hybrid competitive strategy and achieving superior financial performance while internationalizing in the high-technology market. *Industrial Marketing Management*, *54*, 141–153. doi:10.1016/j.indmarman.2015.07.001

Galbraith, J. R., & Kates, A. (2008). *Designing Your Organization: Using the STAR Model to Solve 5 Critical Design Challenges*. Hoboken, NJ: Jossey-Bass.

Ganapathy-Wallace, S. (2017). *Making Industry 4.0 a reality for Malaysia*. Retrieved Aug 31, 2017, from https://www.digitalnewsasia.com/digital-economy/making-industry-40-reality-malaysia

Ganzarain, J., & Errasti, N. (2016). Three stage maturity model in SME's toward industry 4.0. *Journal of Industrial Engineering and Management*, *9*(5), 1119–1128. doi:10.3926/jiem.2073

Gao, C. (2016, November 14). Intelligent manufacturing & internationalization, YOFC in the next five years to the next big move. *Communications*.

Gao, C. (2017). YOFC Qianjiang Science and Technology Park officially put into operation, Long flight integration advantages of resources, Aiming at the international market. *Communications Weekly*, *6*.

Gao, X. D. (2014). A latecomer's strategy to promote a technology standard: The case of Datang and TD-SCDMA. *Research Policy*, *43*(3), 597–607. doi:10.1016/j.respol.2013.09.003

Garcia, D., Riedl, M., Niedermayr, F., Waid, S., & Matt, D. T. (2015, September). *Analysis and simulation of handling algorithm for intelligent movement of a woodchip gripper*. Paper presented at 10th Conference on Sustainable Development of Energy, Water and Environment Systems, Dubrovnik, Croatia.

Gardner, S. J., & Wolfe, P. S. (2015). Teaching students with developmental disabilities daily living skills using point-of-view modeling plus video prompting with error correction. *Focus on Autism and Other Developmental Disabilities*, *30*(4), 195–207. doi:10.1177/1088357614547810

Gates, D. K. (2017, May 11). *Industry 4.0: It's all about the people*. Retrieved August 28., 2017, from https://home.kpmg.com/xx/en/home/insights/2017/05/industry-4-0-its-all-about-the-people.html

Gates, D., & Bremicker, M. (2017, May). *Beyond the hype: Separating ambition from reality in i4.0*. Retrieved from https://home.kpmg.com/xx/en/home/insights/2017/05/beyond-the-hype-separating-ambition-from-reality.html

Gatewood, E. J., Shaver, K. G., & Gartner, W. B. (1995). A longitudinal study of cognitive factors influencing start-up behaviors and success at venture creation. *Journal of Business Venturing*, *10*(5), 371–391. doi:10.1016/0883-9026(95)00035-7

Gausemeier, J. (2015, February). *Szenario-basierte Entwicklung von Zukunftsoptionen für Industrie 4.0* [Scenario-based development of future options for industry 4.0]. Paper presented at Industry 4.0-Forum Science and Research, Hasso Plattner Institute, University of Potsdam, Germany.

Gavetti, G. M., Henderson, R., & Giorgi, S. (2003). Kodak (A) Case. Harvard Business School.

Gazis, V. (2017). A Survey of Standards for Machine-to-Machine and the Internet of Things. *IEEE Communications Surveys and Tutorials*, *19*(1).

Geertz, C. (1973). *The interpretation of culture*. New York: Basic Books.

Geissbauer, R., Vedso, J. V., & Schrauf, S. (2016a). *Industry 4.0: Building the Digital Enterprise Transportation and logistics key findings*. PWC - 2016 Global Industry Survey.

Geissbauer, R., Vedso, J. V., & Schrauf, S. (2016b). *The Industry 4.0: Digital Operations Self Assessment*. Academic Press.

Gelfand, M. J., Chiu, C., & Hong, Y. (2014). *Advances in culture and psychology* (Vol. 2). Oxford, UK: Oxford University Press.

Gencer, Y. G., & Akkucuk, U. (2016). Reverse logistics: Automobile recalls and other conditions. In U. Akkucuk (Ed.), *Handbook of research on waste management techniques for sustainability* (pp. 125–154). Hershey, PA: IGI Global. doi:10.4018/978-1-4666-9723-2.ch007

General Electric. (2017). *The industrial internet*. Retrieved from March 16, 2017. https://www.ge.com/digital/industrial-internet

George, M. L., Maxey, J., Rowlands, D., & Price, M. (2005). *The Lean Six Sigma Pocket Toolbook*. New York: McGraw-Hill.

Gerlitz, L. (2015). Design for product and service innovation in Industry 4.0 and emerging smart society. *Journal of Security and Sustainability Issues*, *5*(2), 181–198. doi:10.9770/jssi.2015.5.2(5)

Germany Trade & Invest. (2014). *Industrie 4.0. Smart Manufacturing for the Future*. Berlin: Germany Trade & Invest.

Gesinger, S. (2016). Experiential Learning: Using Gemba Walks to Connect With Employees. *Professional Safety*, (2): 33.

Ghoshal, S., & Bartlett, C. A. (1990). The multinational corporation as an interorganizational network. *Academy of Management Review*, *15*(4), 603.

Gilbert, M., & Cordey-Hayes, M. (1996). Understanding the process of knowledge transfer to achieve successful technological innovation. *Technovation*, *16*(6), 301–312. doi:10.1016/0166-4972(96)00012-0

Glas, A. H., & Kleemann, F. C. (2016). The impact of industry 4.0 on procurement and supply management: A conceptual and qualitative analysis. *International Journal of Business and Management Invention*, *5*(6), 55–66.

Goatly, A. (2000). *Critical reading and writing: An introductory coursebook*. London: Routledge.

Goldratt Marketing Group. (2017). *Theory of Constraints: Goldratt Marketing*. Retrieved from Theory of Constraints: https://www.toc-goldratt.com/en/biography-of-eli-goldratt

Goldratt, E. M. (1984). *The Goal: A Process of Ongoing Improvement*. Great Barrington, MA: North River Press.

Goldratt, E. M. (1998). *Essays On the Theory of Constraints*. Great Barrington, MA: North River Press.

Gong, Y. (2013). *Global operations strategy: Fundamentals and practice*. Berlin: Springer. doi:10.1007/978-3-642-36708-3

Gonzalez Aleu, F., & Van Aken, E. M. (2016). Systematic literature review of critical success factors for continuous improvement projects. *International Journal of Lean Six Sigma*, *7*(3), 214–232. doi:10.1108/IJLSS-06-2015-0025

Gonzalez, A. (2016). *Amazon's robot army grows by 50 percent*. Retrieved Aug 25, 2017, from http://www.seattletimes.com/business/amazon/amazons-robot-army-grows/?utm_source=twitter&utm_medium=social&utm_campaign=article_left_1.1

Gordon, R. (2012). *Is US economic growth over? Faltering innovation confronts the six headwinds*. CEPR Policy Insights, n. 63. Retrieved September 5, 2017, from http://cepr.org/sites/default/files/policy_insights/PolicyInsight63.pdf

Grabovy, P. G., & Orlov, A. K. (2016). The overall risk assessment and management: Implementation of foreign investment construction megaprojects by Russian development companies. *Procedia Engineering*, *153*, 195–202. doi:10.1016/j.proeng.2016.08.102

Granovetter, M. (1983). The strength of weak ties: A network theory revisited. *Sociological Theory*, *1*, 201–233. doi:10.2307/202051

Graves, C. W. (1970). Levels of existence: An open system theory of values. *Journal of Humanistic Psychology*, *10*(2), 131–155. doi:10.1177/002216787001000205

Grawe, S. J., Daugherty, P. J., & Ralston, P. M. (2015). Enhancing dyadic performance through boundary spanners and innovation: An assessment of service provider–customer relationships. *Journal of Business Logistics*, *36*(1), 88–101. doi:10.1111/jbl.12077

Greasley, A. (2009). *Operations management*. Chichester, UK: John Wiley & Sons.

Grigorenco, A., Papadopoulos, P., & Rotsios, K. (2013). Does the outsourcing of logistics services keep its promise of increased efficiency?: The case of Colgate-Palmolive, Greece. In D. Folinas (Ed.), *Outsourcing management for supply chain operations and logistics service* (pp. 162–184). Hershey, PA: IGI Global. doi:10.4018/978-1-4666-2008-7.ch010

Grimes, S. (2016). *Best practices for medical device cybersecurity management*. Retrieved from Jan. 5 2017, http://ceitcollaboration.org/docs/Cyber-Security-Part-II.pdf

Grimpe, C., & Hussinger, K. (2008). Formal and Informal Technology Transfer from Academia to Industry: Complementarity Effects and Innovation Performance. *ZEW Discussion Papers*, No. 08-080.

Grøgaard, B. (2012). Alignment of strategy and structure in international firms: An empirical examination. *International Business Review*, *21*(3), 397–407. doi:10.1016/j.ibusrev.2011.05.001

Gronau, N. (2015). The influence of Cyber-Physical Systems on the creation of production systems [in German]. *Industrial Management (Des Plaines)*, *3*, 16–20.

Gronau, N., Thim, C., Ullrich, A., Vladova, G., & Weber, E. (2016). *A Proposal to Model Knowledge in Knowledge-Intensive Business Processes*. BMSD.

Grover, R., & Froese, T. M. (2016). Knowledge management in construction using a SocioBIM platform: A case study of AYO smart home project. *Procedia Engineering*, *145*, 1283–1290. doi:10.1016/j.proeng.2016.04.165

Grover, V., & Malhotra, M. K. (2003). Transaction cost framework in operations and supply chain management research: Theory and measurement. *Journal of Operations Management*, *21*(4), 457–473. doi:10.1016/S0272-6963(03)00040-8

Guardian. (2016). *Fourth industrial revolution set to benefit richest, UBS report says.* Retrieved Sept 1, 2017, from https://www.theguardian.com/business/2016/jan/19/fourth-industrial-revolution-set-to-benefit-richest-ubs-report-says

Gubbi, J., Buyya, B., Marusic, S., & Palaniswami, M. (2013). Internet of Things (IoT): A vision, architectural elements, and future directions. *Future Generation Computer Systems*, *29*(7), 1645–1660. doi:10.1016/j.future.2013.01.010

Guha, S., Kettinger, W. J., & James, T. C. (1993). Business process reengineering. *Information Systems Management*, *10*(3), 13–22. doi:10.1080/10580539308906939

Gulev, R. (2005, December). Economic Culture Impacts on Knowledge Flows and Knowledge Sharing within Selected EU Countries. *Journal of Knowledge Management Practice*, *6*.

Gupta, O. K., Ali, S. S., & Dubey, R. (2011). Third party logistics: Key success factors and growth strategies. *International Journal of Strategic Decision Sciences*, *2*(4), 29–60. doi:10.4018/jsds.2011100103

Gupta, S., Meng, F., Goh, M., & de Souza, R. (2012). Understanding supply chain risk management: An in-depth analysis. In M. Garg & S. Gupta (Eds.), *Cases on supply chain and distribution management: Issues and principles* (pp. 349–372). Hershey, PA: IGI Global. doi:10.4018/978-1-4666-0065-2.ch016

Haigh, T., Russell, A. L., & Dutton, W. H. (2015). Histories of the Internet: Introducing a Special Issue of Information & Culture. *Information & Culture*, *50*(2), 143–159. doi:10.7560/IC50201

Hájková, V., & Hájek, P. (2011). Typology of regional innovation systems in Europe - A neural network approach. *International Journal of Mathematical Models and Methods in Applied Sciences*, *3*(5), 463–471.

Halliday, M. A. K. (1994). *An introduction to functional grammar* (2nd ed.). London: Edward Arnold.

Halliday, M. A. K., & Matthiessen, C. (2014). *Halliday's introduction to functional grammar* (4th ed.). Abingdon, UK: Routledge.

Hallikas, J., & Lintukangas, K. (2016). Purchasing and supply: An investigation of risk management performance. *International Journal of Production Economics*, *171*, 487–494. doi:10.1016/j.ijpe.2015.09.013

Hameed, B., Durr, F., & Rothermel, K. (2011). *RFID based Complex Event Processing in a Smart Real-Time Factory, Expert discussion: Distributed Systems in Smart Spaces.* Retrieved February 19, 2017, from https://www.tk.informatik.tu-darmstadt.de/fileadmin/user_upload/Group_TK/filesDownload/hameed.pdf

Hammer, M. (1990). Reengineering work: Don't automate, obliterate. *Harvard Business Review*, *68*(4), 104.

Hammer, M., & Champy, J. (1993). *Reengineering the Corporation: A Manifesto for Business Revolution.* New York, NY: HarperCollins Publishers.

Hao, H., Qiao, Q., Liu, Z., & Zhao, F. (2017). Impact of recycling on energy consumption and greenhouse gas emissions from electric vehicle production: The China 2025 case. *Resources, Conservation and Recycling*, *122*, 114–125. doi:10.1016/j.resconrec.2017.02.005

Hart, O., & Zingales, L. (2017). *Companies Should Maximize Shareholder Welfare Not Market Value.* Academic Press.

Hashweh, M. Z. (2005). Teacher pedagogical construction: A reconfiguration of pedagogical content knowledge. *Teachers and Teaching, 11*(3), 273–292. doi:10.1080/13450600500105502

Hasuike, T. (2010). Risk-management models based on the portfolio theory using historical data under uncertainty. In L. Wang & T. Hong (Eds.), *Intelligent soft computation and evolving data mining: Integrating advanced technologies* (pp. 123–146). Hershey, PA: IGI Global. doi:10.4018/978-1-61520-757-2.ch007

Hathaway, J. (2015). Developing that voice: Locating academic writing tuition in the mainstream of higher education. *Teaching in Higher Education, 20*(5), 506–517. doi:10.1080/13562517.2015.1026891

Havenga, J. (2010). Logistics costs in South Africa: The case for macroeconomic measurement. *The South African Journal of Economics, 78*(4), 460–476. doi:10.1111/j.1813-6982.2010.01252.x

Hawes, M. (2016). *The Digitalisation of the UK Automotive Industry*. KPMG report. Retrieved Aug 18, 2017, from https://www.smmt.co.uk/wp-content/uploads/sites/2/smmt_the-digitalisation-of-the-uk-auto-industry_kpmg-apr-2017.pdf

Healey, J., Pollard, N., & Woods, B. (2015). *The healthcare internet of things: rewards and risks*. Washington, DC: The Atlantic Council of the United States. Retrieved from http://www.atlanticcouncil.org/images/publications/ACUS_Intel_MedicalDevices.pdf

Hehenberger, P., Vogel-Heuser, B., Bradley, D., Eynard, B., Tomiyama, T., & Achiche, S. (2016). Design, modelling, simulation and integration of cyber physical systems: Methods and applications. *Computers in Industry, 82*, 273–289. doi:10.1016/j.compind.2016.05.006

Heier, H., & Borgman, H. P. (2002). *Knowledge Management Systems Spanning Cultures: The Case of Deutsche Bank's HRBASE*. Symposium conducted at the meeting of ECIS 2002, Gdansk, Poland.

Helu, M., Morris, K., Jung, K., Lyons, K., & Leong, S. (2015). Identifying performance assurance challenges for smart manufacturing. *Manufacturing Letters, 6*, 1–4. doi:10.1016/j.mfglet.2015.11.001 PMID:26783512

Hendrikse, G. W. J., & Veerman, C. P. (2001). Marketing cooperatives and financial structure: A transaction costs economics analysis. *Agricultural Economics, 26*(3), 205–216. doi:10.1111/j.1574-0862.2001.tb00064.x

Henke, N., & Bughin, J. (2016, December). *The age of analytics: Competing in a data-driven world*. Retrieved August 29, 2017, from http://www.mckinsey.com/business-functions/mckinsey-analytics/our-insights/the-age-of-analytics-competing-in-a-data-driven-world

Henry Ford Heritage Association. (2017). *Henry Ford Heritage Association*. Retrieved from Henry Ford Heritage Association: http://hfha.org/

Hermann, M., Pentek, T., & Otto, B. (2015). *Design Principles for Industrie 4.0 Scenarios: A Literature Review*. TU Dortmund, Working Paper No. 01 / 2015. Retrieved March 11, 2017, from http://www.snom.mb.tu-dortmund.de/cms/de/forschung/Arbeitsberichte/Design-Principles-for-Industrie-4_0-Scenarios.pdf

Hermann, M., Pentek, T., & Otto, B. (2015). *Design Principles for Industrie 4.0 Scenarios: A Literature Review*. Working Paper No. 01/2015, Technical University of Dortmund.

Hermann, M., Pentek, T., & Otto, B. (2016). *Design Principles for Industrie 4.0 Scenarios*. Retrieved on January 10th, 2017, from http://ieeexplore.ieee.org/document/7427673/?arnumber=7427673&newsearch=true&queryText=industrie%204.0%20design%20principles

Hermann, M., Pentek, T., & Otto, B. (2016). Design principles for industrie 4.0 scenarios. *Proceedings of the Annual Hawaii International Conference on System Sciences*, 3928–3937. 10.1109/HICSS.2016.488

Herrod, C. (2008). Global IT risk management strategies. In F. Tan (Ed.), *Global information technologies: Concepts, methodologies, tools, and applications* (pp. 285–298). Hershey, PA: IGI Global. doi:10.4018/978-1-59904-939-7.ch024

Herterich, M. M., Uebernickel, F., & Brenner, W. (2015). The impact of cyber-physical systems on industrial services in manufacturing. *Procedia CIRP*, *30*, 323–328. doi:10.1016/j.procir.2015.02.110

Herter, J., & Ovtcharova, J. (2016). A model based visualization framework for cross discipline collaboration in Industry 4.0 scenarios. *Procedia CIRP*, *57*, 398–403.

Hess, M. F., & Cottrell, J. H. Jr. (2016). Fraud risk management: A small business perspective. *Business Horizons*, *59*(1), 13–18. doi:10.1016/j.bushor.2015.09.005

Hevner, A. R., March, S. T., Park, J., & Ram, S. (2004). Design Science in Information Systems Research. *Management Information Systems Quarterly*, *28*(1), 75–105. doi:10.2307/25148625

Heylighen, F. (2002). *Complexity and Information Overload in Society: Why increasing efficiency leads to decreasing control*. Brussels: Free University of Brussels.

Higgins, K. (2015). *Hospital medical devices used as weapons in cyberattacks*. Retrieved March 16, 2017, from http://www.darkreading.com/vulnerabilities---threats/hospital-medical-devices-used-as-weapons-in-cyberattacks/d/d-id/1320751

Higgins, N. J. (2007). Putting lean HR into practice. *Strategic HR Review*, *6*(4), 16–19. doi:10.1108/14754390980000981

Hines, P., Holwe, M., & Rich, N. (2004). Learning to evolve: A review of contemporary lean thinking. *International Journal of Operations & Production Management*, *24*(10), 994–1011. doi:10.1108/01443570410558049

Hirsch, C., & Ezingeard, J. (2009). Aligning IT teams' risk management to business requirements. In M. Gupta & R. Sharman (Eds.), *Social and human elements of information security: Emerging trends and countermeasures* (pp. 301–315). Hershey, PA: IGI Global. doi:10.4018/978-1-60566-036-3.ch017

Hirschinger, M., Spickermann, A., Hartmann, E., von der Gracht, H., & Darkow, I. L. (2015). The future of logistics in emerging markets: Fuzzy clustering scenarios grounded in institutional and factor-market rivalry theory. *The Journal of Supply Chain Management*, *51*(4), 73–93. doi:10.1111/jscm.12074

Hirsch-Kreinsen, H. (2016). Digitalisierung industrieller Arbeit: Entwicklungspfade und Perspektiven. *Journal for Labour Market Research*, *49*(1), 1–14. doi:10.100712651-016-0200-6

Hoffmann, T., & Prause, G. (2015). How to keep open-source based innovation approaches sustainable: A view from the intellectual property perspective. *Entrepreneurship and Sustainability Issues*, *2*(3), 133–141. doi:10.9770/jesi.2014.2.3(2)

Hofmann, E., & Rüsch, M. (2017). Industry 4.0 and the current status as well as future prospects on logistics. *Computers in Industry*, *89*, 23–34. doi:10.1016/j.compind.2017.04.002

Hofstede, G. (1980). *Culture's consequences: International differences in work-related values*. Los Angeles, CA: Sage.

Hofstede, G. (1984). National cultures and corporate cultures. In L. A. Samovar & R. E. Porter (Eds.), *Communication between cultures*. Belmont, CA: Wadsworth.

Hofstede, G. (2001). *Culture's Consequences* (2nd ed.). London: Sage Publications.

Hofstede, G. (2001). *Culture's consequences: Comparing values, behaviours, institutions and organizations across nations* (2nd ed.). Thousand Oaks, CA: Sage.

Holden, N. J. (2002). *Cross-cultural management: A knowledge management perspective*. Harlow, UK: Financial Times/Prentice Hall.

Holsapple, C. W., & Joshi, K. D. (2001). Organizational Knowledge Resources. *Decision Support Systems, 31*(1), 39–54. doi:10.1016/S0167-9236(00)00118-4

Homer-Dixon, T., Walker, B., Biggs, R., Crépin, A. S., Folke, C., Lambin, E. F., ... Troell, M. (2015). Synchronous failure: The emerging causal architecture of global crisis. *Ecology and Society, 20*(3), 6. doi:10.5751/ES-07681-200306

Hou, L. (2016). Construction of Yangtze River Economic Belt and Optimization of Industrial Structure. [in Chinese]. *Journal of Nanjing University of Finance and Economics, 1*, 39–40.

House, R., Javidan, M., Hanges, P., & Dorfman, P. (2002). Understanding cultures and implicit leadership theories across the globe: An introduction to project GLOBE. *Journal of World Business, 37*(1), 3–10. doi:10.1016/S1090-9516(01)00069-4

Hsu, K.-S., Wang, C.-S., Jiang, J.-F., & Wei, H.-Y. (2015). Development of a Real-Time Detection System for Augmented Reality Driving. *Mathematical Problems in Engineering*, 1–5.

Hu, L. (2005). Independent innovation, leading the future. *China Science & Technology Industry Pars, 9*.

Hu, A., & Sun, J. (2014). Migration of Manufacturing Industries in China: Whether, How, and Where. [in Chinese]. *China Economic Quarterly, 13*(4), 1533–1554.

Huang, H. (2011). Zhuang Dan, general manager of YOFC: China's fiber optic cable industry is facing two major opportunities. *Communications World, 42*, 107.

Huang, Y. (2016). YOFC president Zhuang Dan: China is becoming the leading force in the global fiber optic cable market. *The People's Posts and Telecommunications, 11*, 10.

Huang, Y., & Yin, K. (2014). Research on the evaluation and selection of third-party logistics providers in B2C e-commerce mode. *Journal of Electronic Commerce in Organizations, 12*(2), 74–88. doi:10.4018/jeco.2014040106

Hummel, E., Slowinski, G., Matthews, S., & Gilomnt, E. (2010). Business Models for collaborative Research. *Research Technology Management, 53*(6), 51–54.

Hu, P. (2002). *China Optical Fiber and Cable Enterprises Development Strategies Research*. Wuhan University of Technology.

IBM Watson Health. (2017). *IBM Watson Health*. Retrieved from Cognitive Healthcare Solutions: https://www.ibm.com/watson/health/

International Society for Pharmacoeconomics and Outcomes Research (ISPOR). (2016). *Assessing the value of medical devices—Choosing the best path forward: Where do we go from here* [PowerPoint slides]. Retrieved from https://www.ispor.org/sigs/Assessing_Value_of_Medical_Devices_2016DC-IssueP.pdf

Islam, S. R., Kwak, D., Kabir, M. H., Hossain, M., & Kwak, K.-S. (2015). The Internet of Things for Health Care: A Comprehensive Survey. *IEEE Access: Practical Innovations, Open Solutions, 3*, 678–708. doi:10.1109/ACCESS.2015.2437951

Ismail, A., & Kastner, W. (2016). Co-Operative Peer-to-Peer Systems for Industrial Middleware. *IEEE World Conference on Factory Communication Systems (WFCS)*. 10.1109/WFCS.2016.7496497

ISO. (2015). *ISO 9001:2015 Quality Management Systems*. ISO (the International Organization for Standardization).

Ivanov, D., Sokolov, B., & Ivanova, M. (2016). Schedule Coordination in Cyber-Physical Supply Networks. *IFAC-ChaptersOnLine, 49*(12), 839–844.

Jacobson, M., & Wilensky, U. (2006). Complex systems in education: Scientific and educational importance and implications for the learning sciences. *Journal of the Learning Sciences, 15*(1), 11–34. doi:10.120715327809jls1501_4

Jarman, M. F., & Dreher, L. G. (2017). Missed opportunities from misalignment of project and operational requirements. In Y. Raydugin (Ed.), *Handbook of research on leveraging risk and uncertainties for effective project management* (pp. 363–383). Hershey, PA: IGI Global. doi:10.4018/978-1-5225-1790-0.ch017

Jeste, D. V., Ardelt, M., Blazer, D., Kraemer, H. C., Vaillant, G., & Meeks, T. W. (2010). Expert consensus on characteristics of wisdom: A Delphi method study. *The Gerontologist*, *50*(5), 668–680. doi:10.1093/geront/gnq022 PMID:20233730

Jhawar, A., & Garg, S. (2016). System dynamics modelling to study the effects of investment in information technology on logistics performance: A case study from India. *International Journal of System Dynamics Applications*, *5*(2), 19–40. doi:10.4018/IJSDA.2016040102

Jing, Q., Vasilakos, A. V., Wan, J., Lu, J., & Qiu, D. (2014). Security of the internet of things: Perspectives and challenges. *Wireless Networks*, *20*(8), 2481–2501. doi:10.100711276-014-0761-7

Jodlbauer, H., Schagerl, M., & Brunner, M. (2016). Reifegradmodell Industrie 4.0. *Industrie 4.0 Management*, *5*(32), 49–52.

Johanson, J., & Vahlne, J. (1977). The internationalization process of the firm: A model of knowledge development and increasing foreign market commitments. *Journal of International Business Studies*, *8*(1), 23.

Johanson, J., & Vahlne, J. (2009). The Uppsala internationalization process model revisited: From liability of foreignness to liability of outsidership. *Journal of International Business Studies*, *40*(9), 1411–1431. doi:10.1057/jibs.2009.24

John, J. (2016). *Implications, Applications, Trends, and Topics of Industry 4.0.* Round Table session at the International Business and Management Conference, Prague, Czech Republic.

Johnson, H. T. (2006). Lean Accounting: To become Lean, Shed Accountings. *Cost and Management*, *20*(1), 6–17.

Jönsson, S. (1995). *Goda utsikter: Svenskt management.* Göteborg: Bokförlaget BAS.

Judy, S. (2016). Construction owners face extended workers gap, productivity impacts. *Engineering News-Records*, *275*(8).

Jung, K., Morris, K. C., Lyons, K. W., Leong, S., & Cho, H. (2015). Mapping strategic goals and operational performance metrics for smart manufacturing systems. *Procedia Computer Science*, *44*(C), 184–193. doi:10.1016/j.procs.2015.03.051

Kagermann, H. (2013). *Recommendations for implementing the strategic initiative Industrie 4.0: Final report of the Industrie 4.0 Working Group.* Retrieved on January 13th, 2017, from http://www.acatech.de/fileadmin/user_upload/Baumstruktur_nach_Website/Acatech/root/de/Material_fuer_Sonderseiten/Industrie_4.0/Final_report__Industrie_4.0_accessible.pdf

Kagermann, H. (2014). Chancen von Industrie 4.0 nutzen. Bauernhansl.

Kagermann, H., Wahlster, W., & Helbig, J. (2013). *Deutschlands Zukunft als Produktionsstandort sichern. Umsetzungsempfehlungen für das Zukunftsprojekt Industrie, 4.0* [Germany's future as a production site. Implementation recommendations for the industrial sector, 4.0]. Retrieved February 20, 2017,https://www.bmbf.de/files/Umsetzungsempfehlungen_Industrie4_0.pdf

Kagermann, H., Wahlster, W., & Helbig, J. (2013). *Recommendations for implementing the strategic initiative INDUSTRY 4.0, White Paper.* National Academy of Science and Engineering.

Kagermann, H., Lukas, W. D., & Wahlster, W. (2011). Industrie 4.0: Mit dem Internet der Dinge auf dem Weg zur 4. industriellen Revolution [Industry 4.0: With the Internet of Things on the Road to the 4th Industrial Revolution]. *VDI-Nachrichten*, *13*, 2–2.

Kagermann, H., Wahlster, W., & Helbig, J. (2013). *Recommendations for implementing the strategic initiative INDUSTRY 4.0.* Berlin, Frankfurt: National Academy of Science and Engineering.

Kagermann, H., Wahlster, W., & Helbig, J. (2013). *Securing the future of German manufacturing industry: Recommendations for implementing the strategic initiative INDUSTRIE 4.0. Final report of the Industrie 4.0 Working Group. National Academy of Science and Engineering (ACATECH).* Federal Ministry of Education and Research.

Källström, A., & Solli, R. (1997). *Med takt och taktik: Om den ekonomiska krisen, våra kommuner och det kommunala ledarskapet.* Göteborg: Bokförlaget BAS.

Kalorama Information. (2017, January 3). Research firm announces top ten medical device trends to watch. *PR Newswire.* Retrieved Jan. 15, 2017, from http://www.prnewswire.com/news-releases/research-firm-announces-top-ten-medical-device-trends-to-watch-2017-300384787.html

Kang, H. S., Lee, J. Y., Choi, S., Kim, H., Park, J. H., Son, J. Y., ... Noh, S. D. (2016). Smart manufacturing: Past research, present findings, and future directions. *International Journal of Precision Engineering and Manufacturing - Green Technology, 3*(1), 111–128.

Kaplan, R. S., & Norton, D. P. (2014, July 31). *How to Implement a New Strategy Without Disrupting Your Organization.* Retrieved September 26, 2017, from https://hbr.org/2006/03/how-to-implement-a-new-strategy-without-disrupting-your-organization

Kaplan, R. S., & Norton, D. P. (1996). *Balanced Scorecard: Translating Strategy into Action, Harvard.* Harvard Business School Press.

Karagiannis, V., Chatzimisios, P., Vazquez-Gallego, F., & Alonso-Zarate, J. (2015). A Survey on Application Layer Protocols for the Internet of Things. *Transaction on IoT and Cloud Computing, 3*(1), 11–17.

Kara, M. E., & Fırat, S. Ü. (2016). Sustainability, risk, and business intelligence in supply chains. In M. Erdoğdu, T. Arun, & I. Ahmad (Eds.), *Handbook of research on green economic development initiatives and strategies* (pp. 501–538). Hershey, PA: IGI Global. doi:10.4018/978-1-5225-0440-5.ch022

Kasemsap, K. (2015a). The role of total quality management practices on quality performance. In A. Moumtzoglou, A. Kastania, & S. Archondakis (Eds.), *Laboratory management information systems: Current requirements and future perspectives* (pp. 1–31). Hershey, PA: IGI Global. doi:10.4018/978-1-4666-6320-6.ch001

Kasemsap, K. (2015b). Total quality management practices in multinational corporations. In E. Tetteh & B. Uzochukwu (Eds.), *Lean Six Sigma approaches in manufacturing, services, and production* (pp. 1–26). Hershey, PA: IGI Global. doi:10.4018/978-1-4666-7320-5.ch001

Kasemsap, K. (2016a). Advocating electronic business and electronic commerce in the global marketplace. In S. Dixit & A. Sinha (Eds.), *E-retailing challenges and opportunities in the global marketplace* (pp. 1–24). Hershey, PA: IGI Global. doi:10.4018/978-1-4666-9921-2.ch001

Kasemsap, K. (2016b). Implementing electronic commerce in global marketing. In I. Lee (Ed.), *Encyclopedia of e-commerce development, implementation, and management* (pp. 591–602). Hershey, PA: IGI Global. doi:10.4018/978-1-4666-9787-4.ch043

Kasemsap, K. (2016c). The role of strategic outsourcing in global business. In G. Alor-Hernández, C. Sánchez-Ramírez, & J. García-Alcaraz (Eds.), *Handbook of research on managerial strategies for achieving optimal performance in industrial processes* (pp. 325–357). Hershey, PA: IGI Global. doi:10.4018/978-1-5225-0130-5.ch016

Kasemsap, K. (2017a). The roles of logistics service providers and supply chain integration in global supply chain. In L. Saglietto & C. Cezanne (Eds.), *Global intermediation and logistics service providers* (pp. 265–285). Hershey, PA: IGI Global. doi:10.4018/978-1-5225-2133-4.ch014

Kasemsap, K. (2017b). Production planning: Advanced issues and implications. In U. Akkucuk (Ed.), *Ethics and sustainability in global supply chain management* (pp. 50–72). Hershey, PA: IGI Global. doi:10.4018/978-1-5225-2036-8.ch003

Kasemsap, K. (2018). The importance of electronic commerce in modern business. In M. Khosrow-Pour (Ed.), *Encyclopedia of information science and technology* (4th ed.; pp. 2791–2801). Hershey, PA: IGI Global. doi:10.4018/978-1-5225-2255-3.ch243

Katz, D., & Kahn, R. L. (1978). *The social psychology of organizations* (2nd ed.). New York: Wiley.

Kauppi, K., Longoni, A., Caniato, F., & Kuula, M. (2016). Managing country disruption risks and improving operational performance: Risk management along integrated supply chains. *International Journal of Production Economics, 182*, 484–495. doi:10.1016/j.ijpe.2016.10.006

Kavanagh, S., & Cole, J. (2013). *LEAN Achieving Critical Mass. Government Finance Review, 29*(3), 12–20.

Kaynak, H. (2003, July). The relationship between total quality management practices and their effects on firm performance. *Journal of Operations Management, 21*(4), 405–435. doi:10.1016/S0272-6963(03)00004-4

Keesing, R. M. (1974). Theories of culture. *Annual Review of Anthropology, 3*(1), 73–97. doi:10.1146/annurev.an.03.100174.000445

Khameneh, A. H., Taheri, A., & Ershadi, M. (2016). Offering a framework for evaluating the performance of project risk management system. *Procedia: Social and Behavioral Sciences, 226*, 82–90. doi:10.1016/j.sbspro.2016.06.165

Khan, A., & Turowski, K. (2016). A Perspective on Industry 4.0: From Challenges to Opportunities in Production Systems. *Proceedings of the International Conference on Internet of Things and Big Data*, 441–448. 10.5220/0005929704410448

Khan, K. S., Kunz, R., Kleijnen, J., & Antes, G. (2003). Five steps to conducting a systematic review. *Journal of the Royal Society of Medicine, 96*(3), 118–121. doi:10.1177/014107680309600304 PMID:12612111

Kim, G., & Huh, M. G. (2015). Exploration and organizational longevity: The moderating role of strategy and environment. *Asia Pacific Journal of Management, 32*(2), 389–414. doi:10.100710490-014-9399-3

Kimsey, D. B. (2010). Lean Methodology in Health Care. *AORN Journal, 92*(1), 53–60. doi:10.1016/j.aorn.2010.01.015 PMID:20619772

Knights, D., & Willmott, H. (2000). The reengineering revolution: Critical studies of corporate change. Sage Publications Ltd.

Kobara, K. (2016). Cyber physical security for Industrial Control Systems and IoT. *IEICE Transactions on Information and Systems, E99D*(4), 787–795.

Kobes, S. D. (2014). Security implications of implantable medical devices. *Graduate These and Dissertations*. 13683. Retrieved from http://lib.dr.iastate.edu/etd/13683

Koch, V., & Kuge, S. (2014). *Opportunities and challenges of the industrial internet.* Strategy PwC.

Koenig, M., & Meissner, J. (2015). Risk management policies for dynamic capacity control. *Computers & Operations Research, 59*, 104–118. doi:10.1016/j.cor.2014.12.004

Koether, R. (2006). *Taschenbuch der Logistik* (2nd ed.). Leipzig: Hanser.

Kogut, B., & Singh, H. (1988). The effect of national culture on the choice of entry mode. *Journal of International Business Studies, 19*(3), 411–432. doi:10.1057/palgrave.jibs.8490394

Kohlberg, D., & Zühlke, D. (2015). Lean Automation enabled by Industry 4.0 Technologies. *IFAC – PapersOnLine, 48*(3), 1870-1875.

Kohlegger, M., Maier, R., & Thalmann, S. (2009). Understanding maturity models results of a structured content analysis. *Proceedings of IKNOW '09 and ISEMANTICS '09*, 51–61.

Kopetz, H. (2011). Internet of things. In Real-time systems. Springer.

Kovanda, L. (2017). *Disgrace named Industry 4.0* (in Czech language). Retrieved September 5, 2017, from http://finmag.penize.cz/ekonomika/326099-blamaz-jmenem-prumysl-4-0

Krizhevsky, A., Sutskever, I., & Hinton, G. E. (2012). Imagenet classification with deep convolutional neural networks. *Advances in Neural Information Processing Systems*, 1097–1105.

Kroeber, A.L. & Kluckhohn, C. (1952). Culture: A critical review of concepts and definitions. *Harvard University Peabody Museum of American Archeology and Ethnology Papers 47.*

Krumholz, H. M., & Waldstreicher, J. (2016). The Yale Open data Access Project: How Johnson & Johnson is leading the way on clinical data transparency. *The New England Journal of Medicine*, *375*, 403–405. doi:10.1056/NEJMp1607342 PMID:27518657

Kuchler, H. (2017, Aug. 2). Medical device makers wake up to cyber security threat. *Financial Times*. Retrieved from https://www.ft.com/content/00989b9c-7634-11e7-90c0-90a9d1bc9691

Kumari, M., & Kulkarni, M. S. (2016). A complexity based look-ahead mechanism for shop floor decision making. *Procedia CIRP*, *41*, 63–68. doi:10.1016/j.procir.2015.12.032

Lai, F., Li, D., Wang, Q., & Zhao, X. (2008). The information technology capability of third-party logistics providers: A resource-based view and empirical evidence from China. *The Journal of Supply Chain Management*, *44*(3), 22–38. doi:10.1111/j.1745-493X.2008.00064.x

Lam, M. L. L. (2012a). A best practice of corporate social responsibility: Going beyond words on a page and a check. Advances in Sociology Research, 13, 157-164.

Lam, M. (2017). Empathetic Leadership as an Alternative Paradigm for Responsible Supply Chain Management. In N. Meunjohn & A. McMurray (Eds.), *The Palgrave Handbook of Leadership in Transforming Asia* (pp. 295–314). Palgrave Macmillan. doi:10.1057/978-1-137-57940-9_16

Lam, M. L. L. (2000). *Working with Chinese expatriates in business negotiations: Portraits, issues, and applications.* Westport, CT: Quorum Books.

Lam, M. L. L. (2009a). Beyond credibility of doing business in China: Strategies for improving corporate citizenship of foreign multinational Enterprises in China. *Journal of Business Ethics*, *87*(S1), 137–146. doi:10.100710551-008-9803-3

Lam, M. L. L. (2009b). Sustainable development and corporate social responsibility of multinational enterprises in China. In J. R. McIntyre, S. Ivanaj, & V. Ivanaj (Eds.), *Multinational Enterprises and the Challenge of Sustainable Development* (pp. 230–244). Cheltenham, UK: Edward Elgar. doi:10.4337/9781849802215.00023

Lam, M. L. L. (2010a). Beyond legal compliance: Toward better corporate citizenship of foreign multinational enterprises in China. *Journal of Biblical Integration in Business*, *13*, 100–109.

Lam, M. L. L. (2010b). Managing corporate social responsibility as an innovation in China. In L. Al-Hakim & J. Chen (Eds.), *Innovation in business and enterprise: Technologies and frameworks* (pp. 224–238). Hershey, PA: IGI Global. doi:10.4018/978-1-61520-643-8.ch015

Lam, M. L. L. (2010c). Political implications of the corporate social responsibility movement in China. *The Journal of International Business Research and Practice*, *4*, 125–134.

Lam, M. L. L. (2011a). Becoming corporate social responsible foreign multinational enterprises in China. *The Journal of International Business Research and Practice*, *5*, 47–61.

Lam, M. L. L. (2011b). Challenges of sustainable environmental programs of foreign multinational enterprises in China. *Management Research Review*, *34*(11), 1153–1168. doi:10.1108/01409171111178729

Lam, M. L. L. (2011c). Successful strategies for sustainability in China and the global market economy. *International Journal of Sustainable Development*, *3*(1), 73–90.

Lam, M. L. L. (2012b). An alternative paradigm for managing sustainability in the global supply chain. *International Journal of Social Ecology and Sustainable Development*, *3*(4), 1–12. doi:10.4018/jsesd.2012100101

Lam, M. L. L. (2012c). Corporate social responsibility movement in China: What can foreign corporations' corporate social responsibility programs in China do to universal values? In K. Wang (Ed.), *Dialogue among Cultures: Peace, Justice and Harmony* (pp. 221–234). Beijing, China: Foreign Language Press.

Lam, M. L. L. (2014). Empathy as a Major Contributing Factor to Sustainability in the Global Supply Chain. In M. Khosrow-Pour (Ed.), *Inventive approaches for technology integration and information resources management* (pp. 53–67). Hershey, PA: IGI Global Publications. doi:10.4018/978-1-4666-6256-8.ch002

Landes, D. S. (1969). *The Unbound Prometheus*. Cambridge, UK: University of Cambridge Press.

Langhoff, T. (1997). The influence of culture differences on internationalization processes of firms: an introduction to a semiotic and intercultural perspective. In I. Bjorkman & M. Forsgren (Eds.), *The Nature of the International Firm*. Copenhagen: Handelshojskolens Forlag.

Lasi, H., Fettke, P., Kemper, H. G., Feld, T., & Hoffmann, M. (2014). Industrie 4.0. *Business & Information Systems Engineering*, *6*(4), 239–242. doi:10.100712599-014-0334-4

Lau, K. H., & Huang, H. (2014). Adoption and utilization of ICT in the Chinese third-party logistics industry. In J. Wang (Ed.), *Management science, logistics, and operations research* (pp. 221–242). Hershey, PA: IGI Global. doi:10.4018/978-1-4666-4506-6.ch013

Lau, K. H., & Ma, W. L. (2010). A supplementary framework for evaluation of integrated logistics service provider. In K. St.Amant (Ed.), *IT outsourcing: Concepts, methodologies, tools, and applications* (pp. 763–781). Hershey, PA: IGI Global. doi:10.4018/978-1-60566-770-6.ch045

LaValle, S., Lesser, E., Shockley, R., Hopkins, M. S., & Kruschwitz, N. (2011). Big Data, Analytics and the Path From Insights to Value. *MIT Sloan Management Review*, *52*(2), 21–32.

Lean Enterprise Institute. (2017). *Toyota Production System in the Lean Lexicon ©*. Retrieved from Lean.org: https://www.lean.org/lexicon/toyota-production-system

Lebergott, S. (1966). Output, Employment, and Productivity in the United States after 1800. NBER.

Lee, E. A. (2008). Cyber Physical Systems: Design Challenges. *2008 11th IEEE International Symposium on Object Oriented Real – Time Distributed Computing (ISORC)*, 363-369.

Lee, E. A. (2012). *Cyber-physical systems*. Retrieved on April 10th, 2017, from http://cyberphysicalsystems.org/

Lee, O. & Jai, J. E. (2016). Sequence Clustering-based Automated Rule Generation for Adaptive Complex Event Processing. *Future Generation Computer Systems, 66*(2017), 100–109.

Lee, E. A. (2010). CPS Foundations. *Proc. of the 47th Design Automation Conference (DAC)*, 737-742.

Lee, E. A. (2015). The past, present and future of cyber-physical systems: A focus on models. *Sensors (Basel)*, *15*(3), 4837–4869. doi:10.3390150304837 PMID:25730486

Lee, E. A., & Seshia, S. A. (2017). *Introduction to Embedded Systems — A Cyber-Physical Systems Approach*. MIT Press.

Lee, J., Bagheri, B., & Kao, H. (2015). A Cyber-Physical Systems architecture for Industry 4.0 based manufacturing. *Manufacturing Letters*, *3*, 18–23. doi:10.1016/j.mfglet.2014.12.001

Lee, J., Kao, H. A., & Yang, S. (2013). Service innovation and smart analytics for Industry 4.0 and big data environment. *Procedia CIRP*, *16*, 3–8. doi:10.1016/j.procir.2014.02.001

Leuschner, R., Carter, C. R., Goldsby, T. J., & Rogers, Z. S. (2014). Third-party logistics: A meta-analytic review and investigation of its impact on performance. *The Journal of Supply Chain Management*, *50*(1), 21–43. doi:10.1111/jscm.12046

Levinthal, D. A., & March, J. G. (1993). The myopia of learning. *Strategic Management Journal*, *14*(S2), 95–112. doi:10.1002mj.4250141009

Lewin, K., Lippitt, R., & White, R. K. (1939). Patterns of aggressive behavior in experiementally created "social climates". *The Journal of Social Psychology*, *10*(2), 271–299. doi:10.1080/00224545.1939.9713366

Leyh, C., Schäffer, T., Bley, K., & Forstenhäusler, S. (2016). SIMMI 4.0 – A Maturity Model for Classifying the Enterprise-wide IT and Software Landscape Focusing on Industry 4.0. *Proceedings of the Federated Conference On Computer Science and Information Systems*, *8*, 1297–1302. 10.15439/2016F478

Li, M. (2013, August 2). YOFC: Layout Global Competition. *Hubei Daily*, p. 2.

Liao, K., Bayazit, O., & Wang, F. (2014). Building a natural disaster risk index for supply chain operations. *International Journal of Information Systems and Supply Chain Management*, *7*(4), 20–30. doi:10.4018/ijisscm.2014100102

Liao, Y., Deschamps, F., Loures, E. D. F. R., & Ramos, L. F. P. (2017). Past, present, and future of Industry 4.0-a systematic literature review and research agenda proposal. *International Journal of Production Research*, *55*(12), 3609–3629. doi:10.1080/00207543.2017.1308576

Lichtblau, K., Stich, V., Bertenrath, R., Blum, M., Bleider, M., Millak, A., … Schröter, M. (2015). *Industrie 4.0 – Readiness*. Frankfurt, Germany: Impuls-Stiftung für den Maschinenbau, den Anlagenbau und die Informationstechnik.

Lichtblau, K., Volker Stich, Bertenrath, R., Blum, M., Bleider, M., Millack, A., … Schröter, M. (2015). Industrie 4.O readiness. *IMPULS - Foundation for Mechanical Engineering, Plant Engineering and Information Technology*.

Liffler, M., & Tschiesner, A. (2013). *The Internet of Things and the future of manufacturing*. McKinsey & Company. Retrieved Nov 30, 2016, from http://www.mckinsey.com/business-functions/digital-mckinsey/our-insights/the-internet-of-things-and-the-future-of-manufacturing

Li, G., Fan, H., Lee, P. K. C., & Cheng, T. C. E. (2015). Joint supply chain risk management: An agency and collaboration perspective. *International Journal of Production Economics*, *164*, 83–94. doi:10.1016/j.ijpe.2015.02.021

Liker, J. K. (2004). *The Toyota way: 14 management principles from the world's greatest manufacturer*. New York: McGraw-Hill.

Liker, J. K. (2004). *The Toyota Way: 14 Management Principles from the World's Greatest Manufacturer*. New York: McGraw-Hill.

Li, L. (2016). *China's Manufacturing Industry Development Report 2015*. Beijing: Peking University Press.

Li, L. (2017). (in press). China's manufacturing locus in 2025: With a comparison of "Made-in-China 2025" and "Industry 4.0". *Technological Forecasting and Social Change.*

Li, L., Yang, H., & Liu, J. (2014). Evaluation Study on Comprehensive Developing Ability of Regional Manufacturing Industry in China: Based on the Empirical Analysis of Manufacturing Industry in East,Middle and West China [in Chinese]. *China Soft Science*, *2*, 121–129. doi:10.3724/SP.J.1001.2013.04346

Lim, A. (2017). *Holistic growth for automotive industry in 2017– MAI*. Retrieved Aug 3, 2017, from https://paultan.org/2017/01/21/holistic-growth-for-automotive-industry-in-2017-mai/

Lindell, M., & Arvonen, J. (1996). The Nordic management style in a European context. *International Studies of Management & Organization*, *26*(3), 73–91. doi:10.1080/00208825.1996.11656689

Lintukangas, K., Kähkönen, A. K., & Ritala, P. (2016). Supply risks as drivers of green supply management adoption. *Journal of Cleaner Production*, *112*, 1901–1909. doi:10.1016/j.jclepro.2014.10.089

Liu, S. X. (2016). Innovation design: Made in China 2025. *Design Management Review*, *27*(1), 52–58.

Liu, W. T., & Duff, R. W. (1972). The strength in weak ties. *Public Opinion Quarterly*, *36*(3), 361–366. doi:10.1086/268018

Li, X., Li, D., Wan, J., Vasilakos, A. V., Lai, C.-F., & Wang, S. (2017). A review of industrial wireless networks in the context of Industry 4.0. *Wireless Networks*, *23*(1), 23–41. doi:10.100711276-015-1133-7

Loffler, M., & Tschiesner, A. (2013, June). The internet of things and the future of manufacturing. *McKinsey & Company Digital McKinsey*. Retrieved September 1, 2017, from http://www.mckinsey.com/business-functions/digital-mckinsey/our-insights/the-internet-of-things-and-the-future-of-manufacturing

López de Armentia, J., Casado-Mansilla, D., & López de Ipina, D. (2012). Fighting against vampire appliances through eco-aware things. *Innovative Mobile and Internet Services in Ubiquitous Computing (IMIS), 2012 Sixth International Conference*, 868-873. 10.1109/IMIS.2012.112

López de Ipiña, D., Lorido, T., & López, U. (2011). Indoor navigation and product recognition for blind people assisted shopping. *International Workshop on Ambient Assisted Living*, 33-40. 10.1007/978-3-642-21303-8_5

Lorenz, M., Rüßmann, M., Strack, R., Lueth, K. L., & Bolle, M. (2015). Man and Machine in Industry 4.0. *The Boston Consulting Group*, *18*.

Lucke, D., Constantinescu, C., & Westkämper, E. (2008). Smart factory - a step towards the next generation of manufacturing. In M. Mitsuishi, K. Ueda, & F. Kimura (Eds.), *Manufacturing Systems and Technologies for the New Frontier* (pp. 115–118). London, UK: Springer. doi:10.1007/978-1-84800-267-8_23

Luo, Y. D. (2007). From foreign investors to strategic insiders: Shifting parameters, prescriptions and paradigms for MNCs in China. *Journal of World Business*, *42*(1), 14–34. doi:10.1016/j.jwb.2006.08.009

Lu, Y. (2017). Industry 4.0: A survey on technologies, applications and open research issues. *Journal of Industrial Information Integration*, *6*, 1–10. doi:10.1016/j.jii.2017.04.005

Lu, Y., Liu, Z., & Ma, L. (2016). Competing through logistics management: Studies on e-retailing in China. In S. Dixit & A. Sinha (Eds.), *E-retailing challenges and opportunities in the global marketplace* (pp. 256–275). Hershey, PA: IGI Global. doi:10.4018/978-1-4666-9921-2.ch014

MAA. (2017). Malaysia Vehicle Sales Report for 2016. Malaysian Automotive Association (MAA) Publication.

Maavak, M. (2018). *Managing Emerging Risks through a Net-Centric Foresight Method* (Unpublished doctoral dissertation). Universiti Teknologi Malaysia, Kuala Lumpur, Malaysia.

MAI. (2017). *The Automotive Industry*. Malaysian Automotive Institute. Retrieved July 25 2017 from http://www.mai.org.my/index.php?option=com_content&view=article&id=32&Itemid=111&lang=en

Malaysian Wireless. (2016). *Average Internet Speed in Malaysia now 6.8Mbps, still slower than Thailand, Australia – Akamai*. Retrieved Aug 15, 2017, from https://www.malaysianwireless.com/2016/10/akamai-soti-malaysia-internet-speed/

Manotas-Duque, D. F., Osorio-Gómez, J. C., & Rivera, L. (2016). Operational risk management in third party logistics (3PL). In G. Alor-Hernández, C. Sánchez-Ramírez, & J. García-Alcaraz (Eds.), *Handbook of research on managerial strategies for achieving optimal performance in industrial processes* (pp. 218–239). Hershey, PA: IGI Global. doi:10.4018/978-1-5225-0130-5.ch011

Manyika, J., & Chui, M. (2017, January). *A future that works: Automation, employment, and productivity*. Retrieved from http://www.mckinsey.com/global-themes/digital-disruption/harnessing-automation-for-a-future-that-works

Manyika, J., Chui, M., Bisson, P., Woetzel, J., Dobbs, R., Bughin, J., & Aharon, D. (2015). The internet of things: Mapping the value beyond the hype. McKinsey & Company.

Manyika, J., Chui, M., Bughin, J., Dobbs, R., Bisson, P., & Marrs, A. (2013). *Disruptive technologies: Advances that will transform life, business, and the global economy*. McKinsey Global Institute San Francisco.

March, J. G. (1991). Exploration and exploitation in organizational learning. *Organization Science*, *2*(1), 71–87. doi:10.1287/orsc.2.1.71

Marr, B. (2016). What Everyone Must Know About Industry 4.0. *Forbes Magazine*. Accessed on 31.07.2017 from https://www.forbes.com/sites/bernardmarr/2016/06/20/what-everyone-must-know-about-industry-4-0/#5ed8a614795f

Martinez, F., Jirsak, P., & Lorenc, M. (2016). *Industry 4.0. The end Lean Management? In The 10th International Days of Statistics and Economics*. Prague: VŠE.

Martinez, F., Jirsak, P., & Lorenc, M. (2016). *Industry 4.0. The end Lean Management?* Prague: VSE.

Martinez, F., Jirsak, P., & Lorenc, M. (2017). Implications, Applications, Trends, and Topics of Industry 4.0. In *International Business and Management Conference* (pp. 213 - 216). Prague: Oeconomica Publishing House.

Martin, X., & Salomon, R. (2003). Knowledge transfer capacity and its implications for the theory of the multinational corporation. *Journal of International Business Studies*, *34*(4), 356–373. doi:10.1057/palgrave.jibs.8400037

Masters, K. (2017). *The Impact of Industry 4.0 on the Automotive Industry*. Flexis AG. Retrieved on Aug 14, 2017, from https://blog.flexis.com/the-impact-of-industry-4.0-on-the-automotive-industry

Matawale, C. R., & Datta, S. (2015). Leanness metric evaluation platform in fuzzy context. *Journal of Modelling in Management*, *1*, 169–196.

Matawale, C. R., Datta, S., & Mahapatra, S. S. (2014). Leanness estimation procedural hierarchy using interval-valued fuzzy sets (IVFS). *Benchmarking: An International Journal*, *2*, 274–292.

Matt, D. T. (2008). Template based Production System Design. *Journal of Manufacturing Technology Management*, *19*(7), 783–797. doi:10.1108/17410380810898741

Matt, D. T. (2009). Design of Lean Manufacturing Support Systems in Make-to-order Production. *Key Engineering Materials*, *410-411*, 151–158. doi:10.4028/www.scientific.net/KEM.410-411.151

Matt, D. T. (2013). Design of a scalable assembly system for product variety. *Assembly Automation*, *33*(2), 117–126. doi:10.1108/01445151311306627

Matt, D. T., & Rauch, E. (2017). Designing assembly lines for mass customization production systems. In V. Modrák & D. Mourtzis (Eds.), *Mass Customized Manufacturing: Theoretical Concepts and Practical Findings* (pp. 15–35). Boca Raton, FL: CRC Press Francis & Taylor.

Matt, D. T., Rauch, E., & Fraccaroli, D. (2016). Smart Factory für den Mittelstand: Gestaltung eines ganzheitlichen Produktionssystems nach der Industrie 4.0 Vision in kleinen und mittelständischen Unternehmen (KMU) [Smart Factory for small and medium-sized enterprises: design of a holistic production system according to industry 4.0 vision in small and medium-sized enterprises (SMEs)]. *ZWF*, *111*(1-2), 52–55. doi:10.3139/104.111471

Mayer, R. E. (2009). *Multimedia learning*. Cambridge University Press. doi:10.1017/CBO9780511811678

Mayo, E. (1933). *The human problems of an industrial civilization*. New York: Macmillan.

Mazzei, M. J., & Noble, D. (2017). Big data dreams: A framework for corporate strategy. *Business Horizons*, *60*(3), 405–414. doi:10.1016/j.bushor.2017.01.010

McGinnis, M. A., Kohn, J. W., & Spillan, J. E. (2010). A longitudinal study of logistics strategy: 1990–2008. *Journal of Business Logistics*, *31*(1), 217–235. doi:10.1002/j.2158-1592.2010.tb00136.x

McMillan, E. (2004). *Complexity, Organizations and Change*. London: Routledge. doi:10.4324/9780203507124

McSweeney, B. (2002). Hofstede's model of national cultural differences and their consequences: A triumph of faith – a failure of analysis. *Human Relations*, *55*(1), 89–118. doi:10.1177/0018726702551004

McSweeney, B. (2009). Dynamic diversity: Variety and variation within countries. *Organization Studies*, *30*(9), 933–957. doi:10.1177/0170840609338983

Medtronic. (2015). *Integrated Performance Report: Governance and engagement*. Retrieved Jan. 25, 2017, from http://www.medtronic.com/content/dam/Medtronic/US/Citizenship/mdt_2015_integrated_report.pdf

Messina, D., Santos, C., Soares, A. L., & Barros, A. C. (2017). Risk and visibility in supply chains: An information management perspective. In G. Jamil, A. Soares, & C. Pessoa (Eds.), *Handbook of research on information management for effective logistics and supply chains* (pp. 34–57). Hershey, PA: IGI Global. doi:10.4018/978-1-5225-0973-8.ch003

Meyer, K. E., & Peng, M. W. (2016). Theoretical foundations of emerging economy business research. *Journal of International Business Studies*, *47*(1), 3–22. doi:10.1057/jibs.2015.34

Michael Clark, J. N., Quast, L., Jang, S., Wohkittel, J., Center, B., Edwards, K., & Bovornusvakool, W. (2016). GLOBE Study culture clusters: Can they be found in Importance ratings of managerial competencies? *European Journal of Training and Development*, *40*(7), 534–553. doi:10.1108/EJTD-03-2016-0016

Michael, R., Markus, R., Philipp, G., Manuela, W., Jan, J., Pascal, E., & Harnisch, M. (2015). Industry 4.0: The Future of Productivity and Growth in Manufacturing Industries. *The Boston Consulting Group*. Available online: http://industry.gov.au/

MIDA. (2006). *IMP3: Third Industrial Master Plan 2006-2020. Malaysia – Towards Global Competitivenes*. MITI.

Mikulak, R. J., McDermott, R., & Beauregard, M. (2008). The Basics of FMEA (2nd ed.). Boca Ration, FL: Productivity Press.

Mikulecký, P., Ponce, D., & Hynek, J. (1997) Knowledge-Based Projects in Industrial Applications. *Proceedings of 4th International Seminar on Mathematical Simulation in the Glass Melting, Horní Bečva*, 191- 201.

Miley, J. (2017). *New Report Says Robots Will Take Over Construction Industry by 2020*. Retrieved September 5, 2107, from https://interestingengineering.com/new-report-says-robots-will-take-over-construction-industry-by-2020

Miragliotta, G., Macchi, M., & Terzi, S. (2016a). Smart manufacturing: tecnologie e quadro applicativo. *Osservatorio Industria 4.0/Smart Manufacturing*.

Miragliotta, G., Macchi, M., & Terzi, S. (2016b). Smart Manufacturing in Italia: Stato dell'Arte e Stima di Mercato. *Osservatorio Industria 4.0/Smart Manufacturing*.

Misra, S. C., Kumar, V., & Kumar, U. (2009). Project-based software risk management approaches. In M. Khosrow-Pour (Ed.), *Encyclopedia of information science and technology* (2nd ed.; pp. 3142–3146). Hershey, PA: IGI Global. doi:10.4018/978-1-60566-026-4.ch501

MITI. (2009). *Review of National Automotive Policy*. Kuala Lumpur: MITI.

Mohammed, H. K., & Knapkova, A. (2016). The impact of total risk management on company's performance. *Procedia: Social and Behavioral Sciences*, *220*, 271–277. doi:10.1016/j.sbspro.2016.05.499

Moher, D., Liberati, A., Tetzlaff, J., & Altman, D. G. (2009). Preferred Reporting Items for Systematic Reviews and Meta-Analyses: The PRISMA Statement. *PLoS Medicine*, *6*(7), e1000097. doi:10.1371/journal.pmed.1000097 PMID:19621072

Moher, D., Shamseer, L., Clarke, M., Ghersi, D., Liberati, A., Petticrew, M., ... Stewart, L. A. (2015). Preferred Reporting Items for Systematic Review and Meta-Analysis Protocols (PRISMA-P) 2015 statement. *Systematic Reviews*, *4*(1), 1. doi:10.1186/2046-4053-4-1 PMID:25554246

Mojtahedi, M., & Oo, B. L. (2017). Critical attributes for proactive engagement of stakeholders in disaster risk management. *International Journal of Disaster Risk Reduction*, *21*, 35–43. doi:10.1016/j.ijdrr.2016.10.017

Monostori, L. (2016). Cyber-physical systems in manufacturing. *CIRP Annals - Manufacturing Technology*, *65*(2016), 621–641.

Monostori, L. (2014). Cyber-physical production systems: Roots, expectations and R&D challenges. *Procedia CIRP*, *17*, 9–13. doi:10.1016/j.procir.2014.03.115

Moon, K. K., Mo, P. L., & Chan, R. L. (2014). Enterprise risk management: Insights from a textile-apparel supply chain. *International Journal of Risk and Contingency Management*, *3*(2), 18–30. doi:10.4018/ijrcm.2014040102

Moore, J., Loughran, A., McCusker, E., Solvang, W. D., Szicbig, G., Yu, H., . . . Kaartinen, H. (2016, June). *Developing a Toolbox of supports for small and medium sized manufacturing companies*. Paper presented at 2016 International Symposium on Small-scale Intelligent Manufacturing Systems (SIMS), Narvik, Norway. 10.1109/SIMS.2016.7802907

Moreno-Vozmediano, R., Montero, R. S., & Llorente, I. M. (2013). Key challenges in cloud computing: Enabling the future internet of services. *IEEE Internet Computing*, *17*(4), 18–25. doi:10.1109/MIC.2012.69

Morgan. (2016). *Cybercrime damages expected to cost the world $6 trillion by 2021*. Retrieved Aug 1, 2017, from http://www.csoonline.com/article/3110467/security/cybercrime-damages-expected-to-cost-the-world-6-trillion-by-2021.html#

Morgan, N. A., Vorhies, D. W., & Schlegelmilch, B. B. (2006). Resource-performance relationships in industrial export ventures: The role of resource inimitability and substitutability. *Industrial Marketing Management*, *35*(5), 621–633. doi:10.1016/j.indmarman.2005.05.018

Mosterman, P. J., & Zander, J. (2016). Industry 4.0 as a Cyber-Physical System study. *Software & Systems Modeling*, *15*(1), 17–29. doi:10.100710270-015-0493-x

Mrugalska, B., & Wyrwicka, M. K. (2017). Towards Lean Production in Industry 4.0. *Procedia Engineering, 182*, 466–473. doi:10.1016/j.proeng.2017.03.135

Mrugalska, B., & Wyrwicka, M. K. 2017. Towards lean production in Industry 4.0. *Procedia Engineering, 182*, 466–473.

Mueller, G. C., & Barker Iii, V. L. (1997). Upper echelons and board characteristics of turnaround and nonturnaround declining firms. *Journal of Business Research, 39*(2), 119–134. doi:10.1016/S0148-2963(96)00147-6

Müllner, J. (2016). From uncertainty to risk: A risk management framework for market entry. *Journal of World Business, 51*(5), 800–814. doi:10.1016/j.jwb.2016.07.011

Mu, Z., Wenli, L., Jing, L., Xiang, Y., Congying, R., & Chengjuan, W. (2012). Research on innovation mechanism and model of logistics enterprise: A Chinese perspective. In Z. Luo (Ed.), *Innovations in logistics and supply chain management technologies for dynamic economies* (pp. 227–252). Hershey, PA: IGI Global. doi:10.4018/978-1-4666-0267-0.ch014

Nadler, D. A., & Tushman, M. L. (1980, Autumn). A model for diagnosing organizational behavior. *Organizational Dynamics, 9*(2), 35–51. doi:10.1016/0090-2616(80)90039-X

National Institute of Standards and Technology (NIST). (2016). *Framework for improving critical infrastructure cybersecurity*. Retrieved from https://www.nist.gov/sites/default/files/documents/cyberframework/Cybersecurity-Framework-for-FCSM-Jan-2016.pdf

Nehru, V. (2012). *Modern Industrial Policy: Lessons from Malaysia's Auto Industry*. Carnegie Endowment for International Peace report. Retrieved March 21, 2017, from http://carnegieendowment.org/2012/03/22/modern-industrial-policy-lessons-from-malaysia-s-auto-industry-pub-47625

Neugebauer, R., Hippmann, S., Leis, M., & Landherr, M. (2016). Industrie 4.0- From the perspective of applied research. *49th CIRP Conference on Manufacturing Systems, Procedia CIRP 57*, 2-7. 10.1016/j.procir.2016.11.002

Niedermayr, F., Waid, S., Garcia, D., Riedl, M., & Matt, D. T. (2015, September). *Design of a scalable and robust woodchip handling control system*. Paper presented at 10th Conference on Sustainable Development of Energy, Water and Environment Systems, Dubrovnik, Croatia.

Nielsen. (2014). *Rising Middle Class will Drive Global Automotive Demand in the Coming Two Years*. Retrieved July 17, 2017, from http://www.nielsen.com/my/en/insights/reports/2014/rising-middle-class-will-drive-global-auto-demand-in-the-coming-two-years.html

Nikbakhsh, E. (2012). Supply chain risk management. In R. Farahani, S. Rezapour, & L. Kardar (Eds.), *Supply chain sustainability and raw material management: Concepts and processes* (pp. 176–204). Hershey, PA: IGI Global. doi:10.4018/978-1-61350-504-5.ch010

Nikolaos, V., Dimitris, A., Charisios, A., Dimitrios, T., & Nicolas, M. (2014). Selection of the 3rd/4th party logistics provider: A multi-criteria approach. In *Cross-cultural interaction: Concepts, methodologies, tools, and applications* (pp. 197–213). Hershey, PA: IGI Global. doi:10.4018/978-1-4666-4979-8.ch013

Niu, G. (2004). The Interview with Xu Xizhou, the General Manager of YOFC. Interviews With Famous Enterprises, 7.

Nolin, J., & Olson, N. (2016). The internet of things and convenience. *Internet Research, 26*(2), 360–376. doi:10.1108/IntR-03-2014-0082

Nonaka, I. A., & Takeuchi, H. A. (1995). *The knowledge-creating company: how japanese companies create the dynamics of innovation*. Oxford, UK: Oxford University Press.

Nonaka, I., & Takeuchi, H. (1995). *The Knowledge Creating Company*. New York: Oxford University Press.

Norlyk, B. (2011). Language as a branding tool: Lean management, Lean metaphors, and the special Lean. *Language at Work - Bridging Theory into Practice*, *9*, 7.

Norman, D. (2017). Design, Business Models, and Human-Technology Teamwork. *Research Technology Management*, *60*(1), 26–29. doi:10.1080/08956308.2017.1255051

NST. (2017). *Proton would have recorded RM1 billion loss this year if not for Geely deal: Najib.* Retrieved July 30, 2017, from https://www.nst.com.my/news/nation/2017/06/245114/proton-would-have-recorded-rm1-billion-loss-year-if-not-geely-deal-najib

O'Leary, D. E. (2013). 'Big Data', The 'Internet Of Things' and The 'Internet Of Signs.' *Intelligent Systems in Accounting, Finance & Management*, *20*(1), 53–65. doi:10.1002/isaf.1336

Ocasio, W. (1997). Towards an attention-based view of the firm. *Strategic Management Journal*, *18*(S1), 187–206. doi:

Ochuko, R. E., Cullen, A., & Neagu, D. (2012). E-banking operational risk management using soft computing tools. In K. Mohammed Rezaul (Ed.), *Strategic and pragmatic e-business: Implications for future business practices* (pp. 176–202). Hershey, PA: IGI Global. doi:10.4018/978-1-4666-1619-6.ch008

OECD. (2016). *Skills for a Digital World.* Policy Brief on The Future of Work. OECD Publishing. Retrieved from http://www.oecd.org/els/emp/Skills-for-a-Digital-World.pdf

Oesterreich, T. D., & Teuteberg, F. (2016). Understanding the implications of digitization and automation in the context of Industry 4.0: A triangulation approach and elements of a research agenda for the construction industry. *Computers in Industry*, *83*, 121–139. doi:10.1016/j.compind.2016.09.006

Ogewell, V. (2017, April 27). Is industry 4.0 realistic? Face to face with Siemens CEO Tony Hemmelgarn—TV report. *Engineering.Com Websites*. Retrieved from June 15, 2017 http://www.engineering.com/PLMERP/ArticleID/14814/Is-Industry-40-Realistic-Face-to-Face-with-Siemens-CEO-Tony-Hemmelgarn-TV-Report.aspx

Ohno, T. (1988). *Just-In-Time for Today and Tomorrow*. Cambridge, MA: Productivity Press.

Ohno, T. (1988). *Toyota production system: Beyond large-scale production*. Cambridge: Productivity Press.

Ohno, T. (1988). *Workplace Management*. Cambridge, MA: Productivity Press.

Olechowski, A., Oehmen, J., Seering, W., & Ben-Daya, M. (2016). The professionalization of risk management: What role can the ISO 31000 risk management principles play? *International Journal of Project Management*, *34*(8), 1568–1578. doi:10.1016/j.ijproman.2016.08.002

Osland, J. S., Bird, A., Delano, J. & Jacob, M. (2000). Beyond sophisticated stereotyping: cultural sensemaking in context [and executive commentaries]. *The Academy of Management Executive (1993-2005)*, *14*(1), 65-79.

Osterwalder, A., Pigneur, Y., & Tucci, C. (2005). Clarifying Business Models: Origins, Present, and Future of the Concept. *Communications of the Association for Information Systems*, *16*, 1–25.

Ota, Y. (2012). Partner Robots - From Development to Business Implementation. In Z. S. Hippe, J. L. Kulikowski, & T. Mroczek (Eds.), *Human – Computer Systems Interaction: Backgrounds and Applications 2* (pp. 31–40). Chennai, India: Springer. doi:10.1007/978-3-642-23172-8_3

Oviatt, B., & McDougall, P. (1994). Toward a theory of international new ventures. *Journal of International Business Studies*, *25*(1), 45–64. doi:10.1057/palgrave.jibs.8490193

Oxford Dictionaries. (2017a). *Excellence*. Retrieved 07 26, 2017, from excellence - definition of excellence in English: https://en.oxforddictionaries.com/definition/excellence

Oxford Dictionaries. (2017b). *Lean*. Retrieved from lean - definition of lean in English: https://en.oxforddictionaries.com/definition/lean

Panetto, H., & Molina, A. (2008). Enterprise integration and interoperability in manufacturing systems: Trends and issues. *Computers in Industry*, *59*(7), 641–646. doi:10.1016/j.compind.2007.12.010

Park, S. (2016). Development of Innovative Strategies for the Korean Manufacturing Industry by Use of the Connected Smart Factory (CSF). *Procedia Computer Science, 91*, 744–750.

Park, Y. B., & Kim, H. S. (2016). Simulation-based evolutionary algorithm approach for deriving the operational planning of global supply chains from the systematic risk management. *Computers in Industry*, *83*, 68–77. doi:10.1016/j.compind.2016.09.003

Parry, V. K., & Lind, M. L. (2016). Alignment of business strategy and information technology considering information technology governance, project portfolio control, and risk management. *International Journal of Information Technology Project Management*, *7*(4), 21–37. doi:10.4018/IJITPM.2016100102

Peng, K., & Nisbett, R. E. (1999). Culture, dialectics, and reasoning about contradiction. *The American Psychologist*, *54*(9), 741–754. doi:10.1037/0003-066X.54.9.741

Peng, K., & Nisbett, R. E. (2000). Dialectical responses to questions about dialectical thinking. *The American Psychologist*, *55*(9), 1067–1068. doi:10.1037/0003-066X.55.9.1067 PMID:11036717

Penrose, E. T. (1959). *The theory of the growth of the firm*. New York: Sharpe.

Perez, C. (2010). Technological revolutions and techno-economic paradigms. *Cambridge Journal of Economics*, *34*(1), 185–202. doi:10.1093/cje/bep051

Peters, T. J., & Waterman, J. R. (1982). *In search of excellence: lessons from America's best-run companies*. New York: Harper & Row.

Piercy, N., & Rich, N. (2009). High quality and low cost: The lean service centre. *European Journal of Marketing*, *43*(11/12), 1477–1497. doi:10.1108/03090560910989993

Pisano, G. (2015). *A normative theory of dynamic capabilities: connecting strategy, know-how, and competition*. Harvard Business School Working Paper, No. 16-036.

Plattform Industrie 4.0. (2014). *Plattform Industrie 4.0, 2014: Industrie 4.0. Whitechapter FuEThemen*. Retrieved on January 13th, 2017, from http://www.plattformi40. de/sites/default/files/Whitechapter_Forschung%20Stand%203.%20April%202014_0.pdf

Plattform Industrie 4.0. (2017). *Shaping the Digital Transformation Within Companies –Examples and Recommendations for Action Regarding Basic and Further Training*. Retrieved on January 13th, 2017, from https://www.plattform-i40.de/I40/Redaktion/EN/Downloads/Publikation/digital-transformation-training.pdf?__blob=publicationFile&v=3

Ponemon Institute. (2017, Mau 27). Medical device security: An industry under attack and unprepared to defend. *Ponemon Institute Research Report*. Retrieved August 11, 2017, from https://www.synopsys.com/content/dam/synopsys/sig-assets/reports/medical-device-security-ponemon-synopsys.pdf

Porter, M. E. (1980a). *Strategy toward buyers and suppliers*. Academic Press.

Porter, M. E. (1980c). *Industry Evolution*. Academic Press.

Porter, M. E., & Advantage, C. (1985). *Creating and Sustaining Superior Performance*. Academic Press.

Porter, M. E. (1979). How competitive forces shape strategy. *Harvard Business Review*, *57*(2), 137–145. PMID:18271320

Porter, M. E. (1980b). Industry structure and competitive strategy: Keys to profitability. *Financial Analysts Journal*, *36*(4), 30–41. doi:10.2469/faj.v36.n4.30

Porter, M. E. (1985). *Competitive advantage*. New York: Free Press.

Porter, M. E., & Heppelmann, J. E. (2015). How smart, connected products are transforming companies. *Harvard Business Review*, *93*(10), 96–114.

Posada, J., Toro, C., Barandiaran, I., Oyarzun, D., Stricker, D., Amicis, R., & de. (2015). Visual Computing as a Key Enabling Technology for Industrie 4.0 and Industrial Internet. *IEEE Computer Graphics and Applications*, *35*(2), 26–40. doi:10.1109/MCG.2015.45 PMID:25807506

Potti, R., & Saurav, S. (2016). Logistics for global automobile manufacturing industry. In A. Dwivedi (Ed.), *Innovative solutions for implementing global supply chains in emerging markets* (pp. 129–140). Hershey, PA: IGI Global. doi:10.4018/978-1-4666-9795-9.ch008

Prause, G. (2015). Sustainable business models and structures for Industry 4.0. *Journal of Security and Sustainability Issues*, *5*(2), 159–169. doi:10.9770/jssi.2015.5.2(3)

Prikladnicki, R., Evaristo, R., Audy, J. L., & Hideki Yamaguti, M. (2010). Risk management in distributed IT projects: Integrating strategic, tactical, and operational levels. In K. St.Amant (Ed.), *IT outsourcing: Concepts, methodologies, tools, and applications* (pp. 1723–1738). Hershey, PA: IGI Global. doi:10.4018/978-1-60566-770-6.ch109

Pujari, D., Wright, G., & Peattie, K. (2003). Green and competitive: Influences on environmental new product development performance. *Journal of Business Research*, *56*(8), 657–671. doi:10.1016/S0148-2963(01)00310-1

PwC. (2015). *PwC, 2015 Global Digital IQ Survey*. Retrieved July 10, 2017 from https://www.pwc.com/gx/en/advisory-services/digital-iq-survey-2015/campaign-site/digital-iq-survey-2015.pdf

PwC. (2016). *Industry 4.0: Building the digital enterprise*. Retrieved July 11, 2017 from https://www.pwc.com/gx/en/industries/industries-4.0/landing-page/industry-4.0-building-your-digital-enterprise-april-2016.pdf

Pyle & San Jose. (2015, June). *An executive's guide to machine learning*. Retrieved September 20, 2017, from http://www.mckinsey.com/industries/high-tech/our-insights/an-executives-guide-to-machine-learning

Qian, F., Zhong, W., & Du, W. (2017). Fundamental Theories and Key Technologies for Smart and Optimal Manufacturing in the Process Industry. *Engineering*, *3*(2), 154–160. doi:10.1016/J.ENG.2017.02.011

Qin, J., Liu, Y., & Grosvenor, R. (2016). A categorical framework of manufacturing for Industry 4.0 and beyond. *Procedia CIRP*, *52*, 173–178. doi:10.1016/j.procir.2016.08.005

Quann. (2017). *Malaysian companies are unprepared for cyber attacks*. Retrieved May 25, 2017 from https://www.quannsecurity.com/downloads/resource/MYIDC.pdf

Radziwona, A., Bilberg, A., Bogers, M., & Madsen, E. S. (2014). The Smart Factory: Exploring Adaptive and Flexible Manufacturing Solutions. *Procedia Engineering*, *69*, 1184–1190. doi:10.1016/j.proeng.2014.03.108

Rakhmatullin, R. (2014). *Triple/Quadruple Helix in the context of Smart Specialisation*. Retrieved July 19, 2017 from https://www.surrey.ac.uk/sbs/sar/centres/bcned/BCNED%20Files/1%20Ruslan_Rakhmatullin.pdf

Ramsauer, C. (2013). Industry 4.0 – Die Produktion der Zukunft. *WINGbusiness*, *3/2013*, 6–12.

Rao, H. (1994). The social construction of reputation: Certification contests, legitimation, and the survival of organizations in the American automobile industry: 1895-1912. *Strategic Management Journal*, *15*(Winter), 29–44. doi:10.1002mj.4250150904

Rashid, M. A., Sayin, E., Oureshi, H., Shami, M.-U.-D., & Khan, N. (2011). ERP-communication framework: Aerospace smart factory & smart R&D campus. *International Journal of Computer Science and Information Security*, (7), 116-123.

Rauch, E., Seidenstricker, S., Dallasega, P., & Hämmerl, R. (2016). Collaborative Cloud Manufacturing: Design of Business Model Innovations Enabled by Cyberphysical Systems in Distributed Manufacturing Systems. Journal of Engineering.

Raye, J. (2012). Fractal organization theory. In *Proceedings of the 56th Annual Meeting of the ISSS*. International Society for the Systems Sciences.

Reilly, E. D. (2003). *Milestones in Computer Science and Information Technology*. London: Greenwood Press.

Reinhard, G., Jesper, V., & Stefan, S. (2016). Industry 4.0: Building the digital enterprise. *2016 Global Industry 4.0 Survey*.

Renault, B. Y., Agumba, J. N., & Balogun, O. A. (2016). Drivers for and obstacles to enterprise risk management in construction firms: A literature review. *Procedia Engineering*, *164*, 402–408. doi:10.1016/j.proeng.2016.11.637

Rennung, F., Luminosu, C. T., & Draghici, A. (2016). Service Provision in the Framework of Industry 4.0. *Procedia: Social and Behavioral Sciences*, *221*, 372–377. doi:10.1016/j.sbspro.2016.05.127

Richardson, F., & Walker, C. (1948). *Human relations in an expanding company*. New Haven, CT: Yale University Press.

Riedl, M., Garcia, D., Rauch, E., & Matt, D. T. (2016). Industrie 4.0: Wissenstransfer von der Forschung in die Praxis [Industry 4.0: Transfer of knowledge from research to practice]. In C. M. Schlick (Ed.), *Megatrend Digitalisierung – Potenziale der Arbeits- und Betriebsorganisation?* (pp. 111–129). Berlin, Germany: Gito.

Ries, E. (2011). *The Lean Startup*. New York: Crown Business.

Ries, E. (2011). *The lean startup: How today's entrepreneurs use continuous innovation to create radically successful businesses*. Crown Books.

Rifkin, J. (2011). *The Third Industrial Revolution: How Lateral Power Is Transforming Energy, the Economy, and the World*. New York: Palgrave Macmillan.

Ritchie, B., & Brindley, C. (2009). Risk management in the digital economy. In M. Khosrow-Pour (Ed.), *Encyclopedia of information science and technology* (2nd ed.; pp. 3298–3305). Hershey, PA: IGI Global. doi:10.4018/978-1-60566-026-4.ch525

Roblek, V., Meško, M., & Krapež, A. (2016). A complex view of Industry 4.0. *SAGE Open*, *6*(2), 2158244016653987. doi:10.1177/2158244016653987

Rockwell Automation. (2014). The Connected Enterprise Maturity Model. *Rockwell Automation*, *12*. Available online: http://www.rockwellautomation.com/

Rodan, S. (2005). Exploration and exploitation revisited: Extending March's model of mutual learning. *Scandinavian Journal of Management*, *21*(4), 407–428. doi:10.1016/j.scaman.2005.09.008

Rodriguez, E., & Edwards, J. S. (2015). Knowledge management in support of enterprise risk management. In *Transportation systems and engineering: Concepts, methodologies, tools, and applications* (pp. 108–127). Hershey, PA: IGI Global. doi:10.4018/978-1-4666-8473-7.ch005

Roethlisberger, F. J., & Dickson, W. J. (1939). *Management and the worker: An account of a research program conducted by a western electric company, Hawthorne Works, Chicago*. Cambridge, MA: Harvard University Press.

Rojas, R., Rauch, E., Vidoni, R., & Matt, D. T. (2017, June). *Enabling Connectivity of Cyber-Physical Production Systems: A Conceptual Framework*. Paper presented at 27th International Conference on Flexible Automation and Intelligent Manufacturing, Modena, Italy. 10.1016/j.promfg.2017.07.184

Romie, C. (2017). Small business cybersecurity: federal resources and coordination. *National Institute of Standards and Technology*. Retrieved August 17, 2017, from https://www.nist.gov/speech-testimony/small-business-cybersecurity-federal-resources-and-coordination

Rosenmann, A. (2017). Mapping lay perceptions of contemporary global culture and its ideological and political correlates. *Political Psychology*, *38*(2), 351–369. doi:10.1111/pops.12316

Rosing, M. V., Scheel, H. v., & Scheer, A.-W. (2015). The complete business process handbook. Volume I: body of knowledge from process modeling to bpm. Waltham, MA: Morgan Kaufmann.

Rostek, K. B. (2016). Risk management: Role and importance in business organization. In D. Jakóbczak (Ed.), *Analyzing risk through probabilistic modeling in operations research* (pp. 149–178). Hershey, PA: IGI Global. doi:10.4018/978-1-4666-9458-3.ch007

Rubera, G., Chandrasekaran, D., & Ordanini, A. (2016). Open innovation, product portfolio innovativeness and firm performance: The dual role of new product development capabilities. *Journal of the Academy of Marketing Science*, *44*(2), 166–184. doi:10.100711747-014-0423-4

Ruiz-Ortega, M. J., & García-Villaverde, P. M. (2008). Capabilities and competitive tactics influences on performance: Implications of the moment of entry. *Journal of Business Research*, *61*(4), 332–345. doi:10.1016/j.jbusres.2007.07.029

Rusman, M., Lorenz, M., Gerbert, P., Waldner, M., Justus, J., Engel, P., & Harnish, M. (2015). *Industry 4.0. The Future of Productivity Growth in Manufacturing Industry*. Retrieved from http://www.zvw.de/media.media.72e472fb-1698-4a15-8858-344351c8902f.original.pdf

Saatcıoglu, O. Y., Denktas-Sakar, G., & Karatas-Cetın, C. (2014). Logistics innovation: A service-dominant logic-based conceptual framework. In B. Christiansen, S. Yıldız, & E. Yıldız (Eds.), *Handbook of research on effective marketing in contemporary globalism* (pp. 1–26). Hershey, PA: IGI Global. doi:10.4018/978-1-4666-6220-9.ch001

Sachsenmeier, P. (2016). Industry 5.0 – The relevance and implications of bionics and synthetic biology. *Engineering*, *2*(2), 225–229. doi:10.1016/J.ENG.2016.02.015

Sackmann, S. A., & Phillips, M. E. (2004). One's many cultures: A multiple cultures perspective. In N. A. Boyacigilller, R. A. Goodman, & M. E. Phillips (Eds.), *Crossing Cultures: Insights from Master Teachers* (pp. 38–47). New York: Routledge.

Sadeghi, A., Wachsmann, C., & Waidner, M. (2015). Security and privacy challenges in industrial internet of things. *Proceedings of the 52nd Annual Design Automation Conference (DAC '15)*. 10.1145/2744769.2747942

Sahno, J., Shevtshenko, E., Karaulova, T., & Tahera, K. (2015). Framework for Continuous Improvement of Production Processes. *Inzinerine Ekonomika-Engineering Economics*, *26*(2), 169–180.

Salk, J. E., & Brannen, M. Y. (2000). National culture, networks, and individual influence in a multinational management team. *Academy of Management Journal*, *43*(2), 191–202. doi:10.2307/1556376

Sandberg, J., & Alvesson, M. (2011). Ways of constructing research questions: Gap-spotting or problematization? *Organization*, *18*(1), 23–44. doi:10.1177/1350508410372151

Sandel, M. J. (2012). *What money can't buy: The moral limits of markets.* New York: Farrar, Straus, and Giroux.

Sanders, A., Elangeswaran, C., & Wulfsberg, J. (2016). Industry 4.0 implies lean manufacturing: Research activities in industry 4.0 function as enablers for lean manufacturing. *Journal of Industrial Engineering and Management.*, *9*(3), 811–833. doi:10.3926/jiem.1940

Santucci, G. (2009). *From internet of data to internet of things.* Paper for the International Conference on Future Trends of the Internet.

Sato, H., Kanai, A., Tanimoto, S., & Kobayashi, T. (2016). Establishing Trust in the Emerging Era of IoT. *2016 IEEE Symposium on Service-Oriented System Engineering (SOSE)*, 398-406. 10.1109/SOSE.2016.50

Sauvage, T., & Haouari, M. (2012). Risk management: A new way to improve logistics outsourcing. In P. Evangelista, A. McKinnon, E. Sweeney, & E. Esposito (Eds.), *Supply chain innovation for competing in highly dynamic markets: Challenges and solutions* (pp. 315–331). Hershey, PA: IGI Global. doi:10.4018/978-1-60960-585-8.ch020

Schaefer, D. (2017). *Industry 4.0 – A holistic perspective.* University of Bath.

Schein, E. H. (1990). Organizational culture. *The American Psychologist*, *45*(2), 109–119. doi:10.1037/0003-066X.45.2.109

Schmidt, R., Möhring, M., Haering, R. C., Reichstein, C., Neumaier, P., & Jozinovic, P. (2015). Industry 4.0 - Potentials for creating smart products: Empirical research results. In W. Abramowicz (Ed.), Business Information Systems. Springer International Publishing.

Schmidt, R., Möhring, M., Härting, R. C., Reichstein, C., Neumaier, P., & Jozinović, P. (2015). Industry 4.0 - Potentials for Creating Smart Products: Empirical Research Results. *Lecture Notes in Business Information Processing*, *208*, 16–27. doi:10.1007/978-3-319-19027-3_2

Schoenthaler, F., Augenstein, D., & Karle, T. (2015). Design and governance of collaborative business processes in Industry 4.0, In *Proceedings of the Workshop on Crossorganizational and Cross-company BPM (XOC-BPM)* (pp. 1-8). Lisbon, Portugal: IEEE.

Schram, H., Prockl, G., & Kolar, P. (2017). About Claims and Realities of Digitization in Current Maritime Transportation Chains. In *Annual conference of the International Association of Maritime Economists (IAME) 2017*. Graduate School of Management, Kyoto University.

Schröder, C. (2016). *The Challenges of Industry 4.0 for Small and Medium-sized Enterprises.* Retrieved January 13, 2017, from http://library.fes.de/pdf-files/wiso/12683.pdf

Schuh, G., Potente, T., Varandani, R., Hausberg, C., & Fränken, B. (2014). Collaboration Moves Productivity To The Next Level. *Procedia CIRP*, *17*, 3–8. doi:10.1016/j.procir.2014.02.037

Schulze, A., Brojerdi, G., & von Krogh, G. (2014). Those Who Know, Do. Those Who Understand, Teach. Disseminative Capability and knowledge Transfer in the Automotive Industry. *Journal of Product Innovation Management*, *31*(1), 79–97. doi:10.1111/jpim.12081

Schumacher, A., Erol, S., & Sihn, W. (2016). A Maturity Model for Assessing Industry 4.0 Readiness and Maturity of Manufacturing Enterprises. *Procedia CIRP*, *52*, 161–166. doi:10.1016/j.procir.2016.07.040

Schwab, K. (2015). The Fourth Industrial Revolution: What It Means and How to Respond. *Foreign Affairs Magazine.* Retrieved Nov 1, 2017, from https://www.weforum.org/agenda/2016/01/the-fourth-industrial-revolution-what-it-means-and-how-to-respond/

Schwab, K. (2016). *The Fourth Industrial Revolution.* New York: Crown Business.

Schwartz, S. (2016, May 26). *Medical devices and cybersecurity* [Video file]. Retrieved Jan. 15, 2016, from https://www.youtube.com/watch?v=d9RUHXWWiO8

Schweichhart, K. (2016). *Reference Architectural Model Industrie 4.0*. RAMI 4.0.

Shackleford, D. (2015). Combatting Cyber Risks in the Supply Chain. *A SANS Whitepaper*. Available online: https://www.sans.org/reading-room

Shafiq, S. I., Sanin, C., Szczerbicki, E., & Toro, C. (2017). Towards an experience based collective computational intelligence for manufacturing. *Future Generation Computer Systems*, 66.

Shalan, M. A. (2010). Managing IT risks in virtual enterprise networks: A proposed governance framework. In S. Ponis (Ed.), *Managing risk in virtual enterprise networks: Implementing supply chain principles* (pp. 115–136). Hershey, PA: IGI Global. doi:10.4018/978-1-61520-607-0.ch006

Shamim, S., Cang, S., Yu, H., & Li, Y. (2016). Management approaches for Industry 4.0: A human resource management perspective. In *2016 IEEE Congress on Evolutionary Computation* (pp. 5309-5316). Vancouver, Canada: IEEE. 10.1109/CEC.2016.7748365

Shamseer, L., Moher, D., Clarke, M., Ghersi, D., Liberati, A., Petticrew, M., ... The PRISMA-P Group. (2015). Preferred Reporting Items for Systematic Review and Meta-Analysis Protocols (PRISMA-P) 2015: Elaboration and explanation. *BMJ 2015*, *349*, g7647.

Shenkar, O. (2001). Cultural distance revisited: Towards a more rigorous conceptualization and measurement of cultural differences. *Journal of International Business Studies*, *32*(3), 519–535. doi:10.1057/palgrave.jibs.8490982

Shenkar, O. (2012a). 2011 Decade Award Winning Article. Cultural distance revisited: Towards amore rigorous conceptualization and measurement of cultural differences. *Journal of International Business Studies*, *43*, 1–11. doi:10.1057/jibs.2011.40

Shenkar, O. (2012b). Retrospective. Beyond cultural distance revisited: Switching to a friction lens in the study of cultural differences. *Journal of International Business Studies*, *43*, 12–17. doi:10.1057/jibs.2011.42

Shewchuk, J. P., & Moodie, C. L. (1998). Definition and Classification of Manufacturing Flexibility Types and Measures. *International Journal of Flexible Manufacturing Systems*, *10*(4), 325–349. doi:10.1023/A:1008062220281

Shewhart, W. A. (1931). *Economic Control of Quality of Manufactured Product*. New York: D. Van Nostrand.

Shewhart, W. A., & Deming, E. W. (1939). *Statistical method from the viewpoint of quality control*. Washington, DC: Graduate School, the Department of Agriculture.

Shingo, S. (1985). *A Revolution in Manufacturing: The SMED System*. Stamford, CT: Productivity Press.

Shin, M., Mun, J., & Jung, M. (2009). Self-evolution framework of manufacturing systems based on fractal organization. *Computers & Industrial Engineering*, *56*(3), 1029–1039. doi:10.1016/j.cie.2008.09.014

Siemens. (2013a). *Future of manufacturing, View on enabling technologies*. Retrieved on April 10th, 2017, from http://www.bicc-net.de/workspace/uploads/subfeatures/downloads/bicctalk_cps-ictlabs_2013_hahn-524ad62786aaf.pdf

Siemens. (2013b). *Shaping the Future of Production with Siemens: On the way to Industry 4.0*. Retrieved on April 10th, 2017, from http://www.siemens.com/press/pool/de/events/2013/industry/2013-04-hannovermesse/presentation-russwurm-e.pdf

Siemens. (2013c). *Siemens annual report*. Retrieved on April 10th, 2017, from https://www.siemens.com/annual/13/en/download/pdf/Siemens_AR2013.pdf

Siemens. (2013d). *Siemens – Industries 4.0 et smart mechatronics objects*. Retrieved on April 10th, 2017, from http://www.emm-mechatronics.eu/sts/www-emm-mechatronics-eu/img/ht/files/emm2014/ppt/siemens-caisson.pdf

Siemens. (2014a). *Digitalization of manufacturing*. Retrieved on April 10th, 2017, from https://www.siemens.com/content/dam/internet/siemens-com/customer-magazine/old-mam-assets/print-archiv/2/industry-journal/industry-journal-1-2014-en.pdf

Siemens. (2014b). *Future of Manufacturing*. Retrieved on April 10th, 2017, from https://opcfoundation.org/wp-content/uploads/2014/09/3_140805_OPC_Foundation_Redmond_v7a_incl_Siemens_Slides_20140731.pdf

Siemens. (2014c). *Industry 4.0, What is it, and what does it mean for us?* Retrieved on April 10th, 2017, from https://www.iica.org.au/upload/education/Siemens_Industry4_0_IICA.pdf

Siemens. (2014d). *Maximizing PLM Value in an Innovation Economy*. Retrieved on April 10th, 2017, from http://media.plm.automation.siemens.com/se_se/plm-connection/Hemmelgarn-Nordic-PLM.pdf

Siemens. (2015a). *Combining the Virtual and Physical Worlds*. Retrieved on April 10th, 2017, from http://www.siemens.com/press/pool/de/events/2015/corporate/2015-11-innovation/presentation-digitalization-automation-e.pdf

Siemens. (2015b). *Cyber-Physical Systems - contradicting requirements as drivers for innovation*. Retrieved on April 10th, 2017, from http://www.slideshare.net/heisss/cyberphysical-systems-49324556

Siemens. (2015c). *The digital twin*. Retrieved on April 10th, 2017, from https://www.siemens.com/content/dam/internet/siemens-com/customer-magazine/old-mam-assets/print-archiv/advance/adv152-en-screen.pdf

Siemens. (2015d). *Industrie 4.0 – Digitalization strategy*. Retrieved on April 10th, 2017, from https://community.plm.automation.siemens.com/siemensplm/attachments/siemensplm/tecnomatix-forum@tkb/163/1/29_Dr_Ulrich_Rossgoderer_Siemens_Industry_4_0_Siemens_Plant_Simulation_Usermeeting_2015_approved.pdf

Siemens. (2015e). *Innovation for the Future*. Retrieved on April 10th, 2017, from https://www.siemens.com/press/pool/de/events/2015/corporate/2015-09-analyst-conference/presentation-grindstaff-e.pdf

Siemens. (2015f). *Siemens Digitalization Strategy & Sinalytics Platform*. Retrieved on April 10th, 2017, from https://www.siemens.com/digitalisierung/public/pdf/Sinalytics-and-Digital-Services-Presentation.pdf

Siemens. (2015g). *Web of systems for a digital world*. Retrieved on April 10th, 2017, from http://www.siemens.com/press/pool/de/events/2015/corporate/2015-12-internet-of-things/presentation-iot-russwurm_web-of-systems-e.pdf

Siemens. (2015h). *Web of Systems – From research to real world*. Retrieved on April 10th, 2017, from http://www.siemens.com/press/pool/de/events/2015/corporate/2015-12-internet-of-things/presentation-iot-stephan-from-research-to-real-world-e.pdf

Siemens. (2016, Feb. 21). *Spirit of innovation: The fourth industry revolution* [Video file]. Retrieved March 16, 2017, from https://www.youtube.com/watch?v=0Sj6miQif6s

Siemens. (2016a). *Agile Global Manufacturing Networks are Critical for Your Industry 4.0 Strategy*. Retrieved on April 10th, 2017, from http://camstar.industrysoftware.automation.siemens.com/en/the-essential-role-of-mes-in-industry-4-0/blog/agile-adaptive-manufacturing-networks-making-industry-4-0-real/

Siemens. (2016b). *Defects: A Vanishing Species?* Retrieved on April 10th, 2017, from http://camstar.industrysoftware.automation.siemens.com/en/the-essential-role-of-mes-in-industry-4-0/industry-4-0-ready/

Siemens. (2016c). *Keys to success in the age of smart innovation.* Retrieved on April 10th, 2017, from https://www.plm.automation.siemens.com/en_us/about_us/facts_philosophy/smart-innovation-portfolio/#lightview%26url=/en_us/Images/Siemens-PLM-Smart-Innovation-Infographic-Part-3_tcm1023-237750.pdf%26title=Infographic: Keys to Success in the Age of Smart Innovation%26description=The same forces changing what you innovate are changing how you innovate.%26docType=pdf

Siemens. (2016d). *Industrie 4.0 from both a user's and a vendor's perspective.* Retrieved on April 10th, 2017, from http://www.sysint-conference.org/uploads/media/SysInt2016_Keynote_Volkwein.pdf

Siemens. (2016e). *Innovation for the Future.* Retrieved on April 10th, 2017, from http://web.stanford.edu/class/archive/ee/ee392b/ee392b.1166/lecture/may17/Siemens.pdf

Siemens. (2016f). *Sinalytics enables Digitalization: Industrial Data Analytics.* Retrieved on April 10th, 2017, from https://indico.cern.ch/event/524996/contributions/2193648/attachments/1287431/1915652/SiemensSinalytics-Roshchin.pdf

Siemens. (2016g). *Semantics-related Challenges in Data Analytics Applications @ Siemens.* Retrieved on April 10th, 2017, from http://dbonto.cs.ox.ac.uk/workshop16/Stephan_Siemens.pdf

Siemens. (2016h). *Siemens Digitalization Strategy & Sinalytics Platform.* Retrieved on April 10th, 2017, from https://m.siemens.com/en/about/core-topics/digitalization/media/pdf/Sinalytics-and-Digital-Services-Presentation.pdf

Siemens. (2016i). *The new age of smart innovation.* Retrieved on April 10th, 2017, from https://www.plm.automation.siemens.com/en_us/about_us/facts_philosophy/smart-innovation-portfolio/#lightview%26url=/en_us/Images/Siemens-PLM-Smart-Innovation-Infographic-Part-1_tcm1023-236310.pdf%26title=Infographic: The New Age of Smart Innovations%26description=Smart Innovation Portfolio Infographic Series, Part 1%26docType=pdf

Siemens. (2017). *Siemens Vision 2020 – Focus on profitable growth.* Retrieved on April 10th, 2017, from https://www.siemens.com/investor/pool/en/investor_relations/financial_publications/speeches_and_presentations/170110_presentation_commerzbank_conference.pdf

Siems, T. (2015). *Industry 4.0 in the Automotive Industry – Hype and Hurdle in One!* Retrieved July 24, 2017, from https://www.detecon.com/sites/default/files/DMR_Automotive_Hype_Siems_E_12_2015.pdf

Sihn, W. (1997). Paradigm Shift in the Corporation: The Fractal Company. *IFAC Proceedings, 30*(19), 131-136.

Simpson, P. (1993). *Language, ideology and point of view.* London: Routledge. doi:10.4324/9780203312612

Siu, K. W. M., & Contreras, G. J. (Eds.). (2016). *Design Education for Fostering Creativity and Innovation in China.* IGI Global.

Skinner, J., & Gormley, G. J. (2016). Point of view filming and the elicitation interview. *Perspectives on Medical Education, 5*(4), 235–239. doi:10.100740037-016-0278-0 PMID:27438056

Slack, N., Chambers, S., & Johnston, R. (2010). *Operations management* (6th ed.). Harlow: Financial Times/Prentice Hall.

Smet, A. D. (2014, July). *The secrets of successful organizational redesigns: McKinsey Global Survey results.* Retrieved August 22, 2017, from http://www.mckinsey.com/business-functions/organization/our-insights/the-secrets-of-successful-organizational-redesigns-mckinsey-global-survey-results

Smith, C. D., & Mentzer, J. T. (2010). User influence on the relationship between forecast accuracy, application and logistics performance. *Journal of Business Logistics, 31*(1), 159–177. doi:10.1002/j.2158-1592.2010.tb00133.x

Smith, K. M. (2014). Risk management in aviation: The challenge of discrimination. *International Journal of Aviation Systems, Operations and Training, 1*(1), 35–43. doi:10.4018/ijasot.2014010104

Smith, V., Devane, D., Begley, C. M., & Clarke, M. (2010). Methodology in conducting a systematic review of systematic reviews of healthcare interventions. *BMC Medical Research Methodology*, *11*(1), 15. doi:10.1186/1471-2288-11-15 PMID:21291558

Sniderman, B., Mahto, M., & Cotteleer, M. (2016). *Industry 4.0 and manufacturing ecosystems: Exploring the world of connected enterprises*. Deloitte University Press.

Sogeti. (2017). *The fourth industrial revolution: Things to tighten the link between IT and OT.* VINT research report 3. Retrieved March 16, 2017, from https://www.sogeti.com/explore/reports/vint-research-3-things---the-fourth-industrial-revolution/

Sommer, L. (2015). Industrial Revolution – Industry 4.0: Are German Manufacturing SMEs the first Victims of this Revolution? *Journal of Industrial Engineering and Management.*, *8*(5), 1512–1532. doi:10.3926/jiem.1470

Sosna, M., Trevinyo-Rodríguez, R. N., & Velamuri, S. R. (2010). Business model innovation through trial-and-error learning: The Naturhouse Case. *Business Models*, *43*(2–3), 383–407.

Spanos, Y. E., Zaralis, G., & Lioukas, S. (2004). Strategy and industry effects on profitability: Evidence from Greece. *Strategic Management Journal*, *25*(2), 139–165. doi:10.1002mj.369

Spath, D., Ganschar, O., Gerlach, S., Hämmerle, M., Krause, T., & Schlund, S. (2013). *Studie: Produktionsarbeit Der Zukunft – Industrie 4.0*. Retrieved June 8, 2015, from http://www.iao.fraunhofer.de/images/iao-news/produktionsarbeit-der-zukunft.pdf

Spiess, P., Karnouskos, S., Guinard, D., Savio, D., Baecker, O., & De Souza, L. M. S. (2009). SOA-based integration of the internet of things in enterprise services. *Web Services, 2009. ICWS 2009. IEEE International Conference on*, 968-975.

SPIS. (2007). *Manifest of Knowledge Society*. Prague: Association for Information Society. Available: http://www.spis.cz

Staudinger, U. M. (2008). A psychology of wisdom: History and recent developments. *Research in Human Development*, *5*(2), 107–120. doi:10.1080/15427600802034835

Steenkamp, J., & Geyskens, E. (2012). Transaction cost economics and the roles of national culture: A test of hypotheses based on Inglehart and Hofstede. *Journal of the Academy of Marketing Science*, *40*(2), 252–270. doi:10.100711747-011-0266-1

Steers, R. M., Sánchez-Runde, C., & Nardon, L. (2013). *Management across cultures: Developing global competencies* (2nd ed.). Cambridge, UK: Cambridge University Press.

Steward, J. H. (1955). *Theory of culture change: The methodology of multilinear evolution*. Urbana, IL: University of Illinois Press.

Stock, T., & Seliger, G. (2016). Opportunities of sustainable manufacturing in Industry 4.0. *Procedia CIRP*, *40*, 536–541. doi:10.1016/j.procir.2016.01.129

Strange, R., Strange, R., Zucchella, A., & Zucchella, A. (2017). Industry 4.0, global value chains and international business. *Multinational Business Review*, *25*(3), 174–184. doi:10.1108/MBR-05-2017-0028

Strategy+business. (2016). *Thought Leaders. Siemens CEO Joe Kaeser on the Next Industrial Revolution.* Retrieved on January 13th, 2017, from http://www.strategy-business.com/chapter/Siemens-CEO-Joe-Kaeser-on-the-Next-Industrial-Revolution?gko=efd41

Suh, N. P. (1990). *The principles of design*. New York: Oxford university press.

Susarla, A., Barua, A., & Whinston, A. B. (2009). A transaction cost perspective of the "software as a service" business model. *Journal of Management Information Systems*, *26*(2), 205–240. doi:10.2753/MIS0742-1222260209

Systemy-Logistiky, C. Z. (2016). *Trh industrialnich nemovitosti: shrnuti 2016 a vyhled 2017*. Retrieved Jully 14, 2017, from http://www.systemylogistiky.cz/2017/01/13/trh-industrialnich-nemovitosti-v-cr-shrnuti-2016-a-vyhled-2017/

Szulanski, G. (1996). Exploring internal stickiness: Impediments to the transfer of best practices within the firm. *Strategic Management Journal*, *17*(S2), 27–43. doi:10.1002mj.4250171105

Szulanski, G. (2000). The process of knowledge transfer: A diachronic analysis of stickiness. *Organizational Behavior and Human Decision Processes*, *82*(1), 9–27. doi:10.1006/obhd.2000.2884

Szulanski, G., & Jensen, R. J. (2004). Overcoming stickiness: An empirical investigation of the role of the template in the replication of organizational routines. *Managerial and Decision Economics*, *25*(6–7), 347–363. doi:10.1002/mde.1195

Taghizadegan, S. (2013). *Mastering Lean Six Sigma: advanced black belt concepts*. New York: Momentum Press. doi:10.5643/9781606504062

Tague, N. R. (2005). *The Quality Toolbox* (2nd ed.). Milwaukee, WI: ASQ Quality Press.

Tallman, S. B. (1991). Strategic management models and resource-based strategies among MNEs in a host market. *Strategic Management Journal*, (12), 14–69.

Tapu, R., Mocanu, B., Bursuc, A., & Zaharia, T. (2013). A smartphone-based obstacle detection and classification system for assisting visually impaired people. *Proceedings of the IEEE International Conference on Computer Vision Workshops*, 444-451. 10.1109/ICCVW.2013.65

Taylor, F. W. (1911). *The Principles of Scientific Management*. Harper & Row.

Teece, D. J. (2007). Explicating dynamic capabilities: The nature and microfoundations of (sustainable) enterprise performance. *Strategic Management Journal*, *28*(13), 1319–1350. doi:10.1002mj.640

Teece, D. J. (2010). Business Models, Business Strategy and Innovation. *Long Range Planning*, *43*(2-3), 172–194. doi:10.1016/j.lrp.2009.07.003

Teece, D. J. (2014). A dynamic capabilities-based entrepreneurial theory of the multinational enterprise. *Journal of International Business Studies*, *45*(1), 8–37. doi:10.1057/jibs.2013.54

Teece, D. J., Pisano, G., & Shuen, A. (1997). Dynamic capabilities and strategic management. *Strategic Management Journal*, *18*(7), 509–533. doi:

Teller, J., Kock, A., & Gemünden, H. G. (2014). Risk management in project portfolios is more than managing project risks: A contingency perspective on risk management. *Project Management Journal*, *45*(4), 67–80. doi:10.1002/pmj.21431

Temple, N. (Performer). (2016). The smart factory and the converging roles of IT, production and engineering. Smart IoT London 2016, ExCel, London, UK.

ten Hompel & Vogel-Heuser (Eds.). (2014). Industrie 4.0 in Produktion, Automatisierung und Logistik. *Anwendung, Technologien und Migration*, 603–614.

Tennant, G. (2001). *Six Sigma: SPC and TQM in Manufacturing and Services*. Aldershot, UK: Gower Publishing, Ltd.

Thames, L., & Schaefer, D. (2016). Software-defined cloud manufacturing for Industry 4.0. *Procedia CIRP*, *52*, 12–17. doi:10.1016/j.procir.2016.07.041

Thamhain, H. (2013). Managing risks in complex projects. *Project Management Journal*, *44*(2), 20–35. doi:10.1002/pmj.21325

The Atlas of Economic Complexity, Centre for International Development at Harvard University. (n.d.). Retrieved from http://www.atlas.cid.harvard.edu

The Economist. (2017, March 2). Wonder drug: A digital revolution in health care is speeding up. *The Economist*. Retrieved from https://www.economist.com/news/business/21717990-telemedicine-predictive-diagnostics-wearable-sensors-and-host-new-apps-will-transform-how

Theisens, H., Hooge, E., & Waslander, S. (2016). Steering dynamics in complex education systems. An agenda for empirical research. *European Journal of Education*, *51*(4), 463–477. doi:10.1111/ejed.12187

Thekdi, S., & Aven, T. (2016). An enhanced data-analytic framework for integrating risk management and performance management. *Reliability Engineering & System Safety*, *156*, 277–287. doi:10.1016/j.ress.2016.07.010

Thoben, K. D., Wiesner, S. A., & Wuest, T. (2017). "Industrie 4.0" and smart manufacturing – a review of research issues and application examples. *International Journal of Automotive Technology*, *11*(1), 4–16. doi:10.20965/ijat.2017.p0004

Thoben, K.-D., Busse, M., Denkena, B., & Gausemeier, J. (2014). Editorial: System-integrated Intelligence - New Challenges for Product and Production Engineering in the Context of Industry 4.0. *Procedia Technology*, *15*, 1–4. doi:10.1016/j.protcy.2014.09.028

Thompson, M. K. (2013). A Classification of Procedural Errors in the Definition of Functional Requirements in Axiomatic Design Theory. In *Proceedings of the 7th International Conference on Axiomatic Design* (pp. 107-112). Worcester, MA: Worcester Polytechnic Institute.

Thuemmler, C., & Bai, C. (2017). Health 4.0: Application of industry 4.0 design principles in future asthma management. In C. Thuemmler & C. Bai (Eds.), *Health 4.0: How Virtualization and Big Data are Revolutionizing Healthcare* (pp. 23–37). Cham: Springer. doi:10.1007/978-3-319-47617-9_2

Tian, Q. (2012). BPR Help to Improve Enterprises High Speed Developing, Mission and Responsibility - Promoting Quality Upgrade by Quality Method. *Proceedings of the 5th China Forum on Quality and Academic Innovation.*

Tipton, F. B. (2009). Modeling national identities and cultural change: The western European, Japanese and United States experiences compared. *International Journal of Cross Cultural Management*, *9*(2), 145–168. doi:10.1177/1470595809335722

Todd, J. (2006). Introduction. *Nationalism & Ethnic Politics*, *12*(3), 315–321. doi:10.1080/13537110600882320

Tokman, M., Richey, R. G., Deitz, G. D., & Adams, F. G. (2012). The retailer's perspective on the link between logistical resources and perceived customer loyalty to manufacturer brands. *Journal of Business Logistics*, *33*(3), 181–195. doi:10.1111/j.2158-1592.2012.01051.x

Torabi, S. A., Giahi, R., & Sahebjamnia, N. (2016). An enhanced risk assessment framework for business continuity management systems. *Safety Science*, *89*, 201–218. doi:10.1016/j.ssci.2016.06.015

Törngren, M., Bensalem, S., Cengarle, M. V., Chen, D.-J., McDermid, J., Passerone, R., … Runkler, T. (2014). *CPS State of the Art, EC FP7 Project 611430 CyPhERS*. Tech. Rep. Deliverable D5.1.

Toro, C., Barandiaran, I., & Posada, J. (2015). A perspective on Knowledge Based and Intelligent systems implementation in Industrie 4.0. *Procedia Computer Science*, *60*, 362–370. doi:10.1016/j.procs.2015.08.143

Toth, T., & Sebestyen, Z. (2016). Project risk management process for professionals: A value-based approach. In C. Bodea, A. Purnus, M. Huemann, & M. Hajdu (Eds.), *Managing project risks for competitive advantage in changing business environments* (pp. 128–149). Hershey, PA: IGI Global. doi:10.4018/978-1-5225-0335-4.ch007

Tourk, K., & Marsh, P. (2016). The new industrial revolution and industrial upgrading in China: Achievements and challenges. *Economic and Political Studies*, *4*(2), 187–209. doi:10.1080/20954816.2016.1180769

Toyota Corporation. (2017). *Toyota Global Site | Production System*. Retrieved from Toyota Motor Corporation Global Website: http://www.toyota-global.com/company/vision_philosophy/toyota_production_system/

Toyota Motor Corporation. (2016). *Toyota Global*. Retrieved 07 13, 2016, from The origin of the Toyota Production System: http://www.toyota-global.com/company/vision_philosophy/toyota_production_system/origin_of_the_toyota_production_system.html

Trade Department. (2016). Medical technology industry United States. *SelectUSA.gov Websites*. Retrieved Jan. 15, 2017, from https://www.selectusa.gov/medical-technology-industry-united-states)

Trappey, A. J. C., Trappey, C. V., Hareesh Govindarajan, U., Chuang, A. C., & Sun, J. J. (2017). A review of essential standards and patent landscapes for the Internet of Things: A key enabler for Industry 4.0. *Advanced Engineering Informatics*, *33*, 208–229. doi:10.1016/j.aei.2016.11.007

Travkina, I. (2015). Export and GDP Growth in Lithuania: Short-run or Middle-run Causality? *Entrepreneurship and Sustainability Issues*, *3*(1), 74–84.

Trefke, J., Rohjans, S., Uslar, M., Lehnhof, S., Nordstrom, L., & Saleem, A. (2013). *Smart Grid Architecture Model use case management in a large European Smart Grid project. In 4th IEEE/PES Innovative Smart Grid Technologies Europe* (pp. 1–5). Lyngby, Denmark: IEEE.

Triandis, H. C. (1988). Collectivism vs. individualism: A reconceptualization of a basic concept in cross-cultural social psychology. In G. K. Verma & C. Bagry (Eds.), *Cross-cultural studies of personality, attitudes and cognition*. London: Macmillan. doi:10.1007/978-1-349-08120-2_3

Triandis, H. C. (1990). Cross-cultural studies of individualism and collectivism. In J. Berman (Ed.), *Nebraska symposium on motivation, 1989* (pp. 41–133). Lincoln, NE: University of Nebraska Press.

Triandis, H. C. (1993). Collectivism and individualism as cultural syndromes. *Cross-Cultural Research*, *27*(3-4), 155–180. doi:10.1177/106939719302700301

Triandis, H. C. (1995a). *Individualism and collectivism*. Boulder, CO: Westview.

Triandis, H. C. (1995b). Motivation and achievement in collectivist and individualist cultures. In M. L. Maehr & P. R. Pintrich (Eds.), *Advances in motivation and achievement: Culture, motivation and achievement, 9* (pp. 1–30). Greenwich, CT: JAI Press.

Triandis, H. C., Brislin, R., & Hui, C. H. (1988). Cross-cultural training across individualism- collectivism divide. *International Journal of Intercultural Relations*, *12*(3), 269–289. doi:10.1016/0147-1767(88)90019-3

Trompenaars, F., & Hampden-Turner, C. (1998). *Riding the waves of culture: Understanding Cultural Diversity in Global Business* (2nd ed.). New York: McGraw-Hill.

Tsai, C., Lai, C., Chiang, M., & Yang, L. T. (2014). Data Mining for Internet of Things: A Survey. *IEEE Communications Surveys and Tutorials*, *16*(1), 77–97. doi:10.1109/SURV.2013.103013.00206

Tsang, E. W. K. (2014). Generalizing from research findings: The merits of case studies. *International Journal of Management Reviews*, *16*(4), 369–383. doi:10.1111/ijmr.12024

Tsiakis, T., Kargidis, T., & Chatzipoulidis, A. (2015). IT security governance in e-banking. In *Banking, finance, and accounting: Concepts, methodologies, tools, and applications* (pp. 247–281). Hershey, PA: IGI Global. doi:10.4018/978-1-4666-6268-1.ch014

Tučník, P., & Bureš, V. (2013). Inclusion of Complexity: Modelling Enterprise Business Environment by Means of Agent based Simulation. *International Review on Modelling and Simulations*, *6*(5), 1709–1717.

Tugwell, R. G. (1927). *Industry's coming of age*. New York: Columbia University Press.

Ukil, A., Bandyoapdhyay, S., Puri, C., & Pal, A. (2016). IoT Healthcare Analytics: The Importance of Anomaly Detection. *2016 IEEE 30th International Conference on Advanced Information Networking and Applications (AINA)*, 994-997.

Ulieru, M., & Este, R. A. (2004). The Holonic Enterprise and Theory Emergence: On emergent features of self-organization in distributed virtual agents. *Cybernetics & Human Knowing*, *11*(1).

Uotila, J., Maula, M., Keil, T., & Zahra, S. A. (2009). Exploration, exploitation, and financial performance: Analysis of S&P 500 corporations. *Strategic Management Journal*, *30*(2), 221–231. doi:10.1002mj.738

Vahlne, J.-E., Ivarsson, I., & Johanson, J. (2011). The tortuous road to globalization of Volvo's heavy truck business - extending the scope of the Uppsala model. *International Business Review*, *20*(1), 1–14. doi:10.1016/j.ibusrev.2010.05.003

Vahlne, J., & Ivarsson, I. (2014). The globalization of Swedish MNEs: Empirical evidence and theoretical explanations. *Journal of International Business Studies*, *45*(3), 227–247. doi:10.1057/jibs.2013.60

Vaill, P. B. (2007). Organizational epistemology: Interpersonal relations in organizations and the emergence of wisdom. In E. Kessler & J. Bailey (Eds.), *The handbook of managerial and organizational wisdom* (pp. 327–355). Thousand Oaks, CA: Sage. doi:10.4135/9781412982726.n15

Van Dijk, T. A. (2006). Ideology and discourse analysis. *Journal of Political Ideologies*, *11*(2), 115–140. doi:10.1080/13569310600687908

VDMA. (2014). *Maschinen- und Anlagenbau* [Mechanical engineering and plant engineering]. Retrieved March 10, 2017, from http://www.berufsstart.de/unternehmen/branchen/maschinen-anlagenbau/verband.php

Venaik, S., & Brewer, P. (2013). Critical issues in the Hofstede and GLOBE national culture models. *International Marketing Review*, *30*(5), 469–482. doi:10.1108/IMR-03-2013-0058

Veza, I., Mladineo, M., & Gjeldum, N. (2014). Managing Innovative Production Network of Smart Factories. *IFAC-ChaptersOnLine, 48*(3), 555–560.

Vinodh, S., & Balaji, S. (2011). Fuzzy logic based leanness assessment and its decision support system. *International Journal of Production Research*, *13*(13), 4027–4041. doi:10.1080/00207543.2010.492408

Vinodh, S., & Chintha, S. K. (2011). Leanness assessment using multi grade fuzzy approach. *International Journal of Production Research*, 2(2), 431–445. doi:10.1080/00207540903471494

Vonderembse, M. A., Uppal, M., Huang, S. H., & Dismukes, J. P. (2006). Designing supply chains: Towards theory development. *International Journal of Production Economics*, *100*(2), 223–238. doi:10.1016/j.ijpe.2004.11.014

Voros, J. (2003). A Generic Foresight Process Framework. *Foresight*, *5*(3), 10–21. doi:10.1108/14636680310698379

Vuori, T. O., & Huy, Q. N. (2016). Distributed attention and shared emotions in the innovation process: How Nokia lost the smartphone battle. *Administrative Science Quarterly*, *61*(1), 9–51. doi:10.1177/0001839215606951

Wade, M., & Hulland, J. (2004). The resource-based view and information systems research: Review, extension, and suggestions for future research. *Management Information Systems Quarterly*, *28*(1), 107–142. doi:10.2307/25148626

Wad, P., & Govindaraju, V. G. R. C. (2011). Automotive industry in Malaysia: An assessment of its development. *International Journal of Automotive Technology and Management*, *11*(2), 152. doi:10.1504/IJATM.2011.039542

Wagner, T., Herrmann, C., & Thiede, S. (2017). Industry 4.0 Impacts on Lean Production Systems. *Procedia CIRP*, *63*, 125–131. doi:10.1016/j.procir.2017.02.041

Walker, S. (2012). *Mine Winding and Transport*. Leicester, UK: Elsevier.

Wang, S., Wan, J., Li, D., & Zhang, C. (2016). Implementing Smart Factory of Industrie 4.0: An Outlook. *International Journal of Distributed Sensor Networks*.

Wang, H. (2005). *Research on BPR Based on Business Process Modeling - A Case Study of YOFC's Inventory Management Business Process Reengineering*. Xi'an University of Technology.

Wang, S., Wan, J., Li, D., & Zhang, C. (2016). Implementing Smart Factory of Industrie 4.0: An Outlook. *International Journal of Distributed Sensor Networks*.

Wang, S., Wan, J., Zhang, D., Li, D., & Zhang, C. (2016). Towards smart factory for Industry 4.0: A self-organized multi-agent system with big data based feedback and coordination. *Computer Networks*, *101*, 158–168. doi:10.1016/j.comnet.2015.12.017

Wan, J., Tang, S., Shu, Z., Li, D., Wang, S., Imran, M., & Vasilakos, A. V. (2016). Software-defined industrial internet of things in the context of industry 4.0. *IEEE Sensors Journal*, *16*(20), 7373–7380.

Warnecke, H. (1996). *The Fractal Company: A Revolution in Corporate Culture*. New York: Springer-Verlag.

Warner, W. L., & Low, J. (1947). *The social system of the modern factory: The strike, a social analysis*. New Haven, CT: Yale University Press.

Webster, J., & Watson, R. T. (2002). Analyzing the past to prepare for the future: Writing a literature review. *Management Information Systems Quarterly*, *26*(2), xiii–xxiii.

Wee, D., Kelly, R., Cattel, J., & Breunig, M. (2015). *Industry 4.0—how to navigate digitization of the manufacturing sector*. McKinsey & Company.

WEF. (2014). *The Global Competitiveness Report 2014–2015*. Retrieved July 23, 2017, from http://www3.weforum.org/docs/WEF_GlobalCompetitivenessReport_2014-15.pdf

WEF. (2016a). *Global Information Technology Report 2016*. Retrieved July 30, 2017, from http://www3.weforum.org/docs/GITR2016/WEF_GITR_Full_Report.pdf

WEF. (2016b). *The future of jobs: Employment, skills, and workforce strategy for the fourth Industrial Revolution*. Retrieved Aug 2, 2017, from http://www3.weforum.org/docs/WEF_Future_of_Jobs.pdf

WEF. (2016c). *The 10 countries best prepared for the new digital economy*. Retrieved Nov 1, 2017, from https://www.weforum.org/agenda/2016/07/countries-best-prepared-for-the-new-digital-economy/

WEF. (2017). *Global Risk Report 2017*. Retrieved Jan 20, 2017, from http://www3.weforum.org/docs/GRR17_Report_web.pdf

Wehn, U., & Montalvo, C. (2016). Knowledge transfer dynamics and innovation: Behaviour, interactions and aggregated outcomes. *Journal of Cleaner Production*.

Weinberger, M., Bilgeri, D., & Fleisch, E. (2016). IoT business models in an industrial context. *Automatisierungstechnik*, *64*(9), 699–706. doi:10.1515/auto-2016-0054

Weisbord, M. R. (1987). *Organizational Diagnosis: A workbook of theory and practice*. Addison-Wesley.

Wellington, K. B. (2014). Cyberattacks on medical devices and hospital networks: legal gap and regulatory solutions. *Santa Clara High Technology Law Journal*, *30*(2), 139-198. Retrieved from http://digitalcommons.law.scu.edu/chtlj/vol30/iss2/1

Wendler, R. (2012). The maturity of maturity model research: A systematic mapping study. *Information and Software Technology*, *54*(12), 1317–1339. doi:10.1016/j.infsof.2012.07.007

Wesseling, H. L. (2009). Globalization: A Historical Perspective. *European Review (Chichester, England)*, *17*(3-4), 455–462. doi:10.1017/S1062798709000866

Weyer, S., Schmitt, M., Ohmer, M., & Gorecky, D. (2015). Towards industry 4.0 - Standardization as the crucial challenge for highly modular, multi-vendor production systems. *IFAC-PapersOnLine*, *28*(3), 579–584. doi:10.1016/j.ifacol.2015.06.143

Whelan, R. (2016). Fully autonomous robots: The warehouse workers of the near future. *The Wall Street Journal*. Retrieved from https://www.wsj.com/articles/fully-autonomous-robots-the-warehouse-workers-of-the-near-future-1474383024

Wiengarten, F., Humphreys, P., Gimenez, C., & McIvor, R. (2016). Risk, risk management practices, and the success of supply chain integration. *International Journal of Production Economics*, *171*, 361–370. doi:10.1016/j.ijpe.2015.03.020

Wilber, K. (1980). *The atman project: A transpersonal view of human development*. Wheaton, IL: Theosophical Publishing House.

Wilber, K. (2000). *Sex, ecology, spirituality: The spirit of evolution* (2nd ed.). Boston: Shambhala.

Wittenberg, C. (2016). Human-CPS Interaction – requirements and human-machine interaction methods for the Industry 4.0. *IFAC-PapersOnLine*, *49*(19), 420-425.

Womack, J. P., & Jones, D. T. (1996). *Lean thinking: banish waste and create wealth in your corporation*. New York: Simon & Schuster.

Womack, J. P., Jones, D. T., & Roos, D. (1990). *The Machine That Changed the World*. New York: Free Press.

Womack, J. P., Jones, D. T., & Roos, D. (1990). *The Machine That Changed the World: The Story of Lean Production*. New York: Rawson Associates.

Woodside Capital Partners. (2017). The industrial internet of things: Making factories "smart" for the *next* industrial revolution. *Silicon Valley London*. Retrieved June 15, 2017, from http://www.woodsidecap.com/wp-content/uploads/2017/04/WCP-IIoT-Report-Spring-2017-1.pdf

World Health Organization (WHO). (2010). *Barriers to innovation in the field of medical devices*. Retrieved Jan. 10, 2017, from http://apps.who.int/iris/bitstream/10665/70457/1/WHO_HSS_EHT_DIM_10.6_eng.pdf

World Health Organization (WHO). (n.d.). *Medical Devices*. Retrieved Jan. 23, 2017, from http://www.who.int/medical_devices/definitions/en/

Wübbeke, J., Meissner, M., Zenglein, M. J., Ives, J., & Conrad, B. (2016). Made in China 2025: The making of a high-tech superpower and consequences for industrial countries. *Mercator Institute for China Studies, 17.*

Wu, D., Liu, S., Zhang, L., Terpenny, J., Gao, R. X., Kurfess, T., & Guzzo, J. A. (2017). A fog computing-based framework for process monitoring and prognosis in cyber-manufacturing. *Journal of Manufacturing Systems, 43*, 25–34. doi:10.1016/j.jmsy.2017.02.011

Wu, M., Lu, T., & Ling, F. (2010). Research on architecture of Internet of Things. In *3rd International Conference on Advanced Computer Theory and Engineering (ICACTE)*, Washington, DC: IEEE.

Xia, F., Yang, L. T., Wang, L., & Vinel, A. (2012). Internet of things. *International Journal of Communication Systems, 25*(9), 1101–1102. doi:10.1002/dac.2417

Xia, J. (2017). A Review to the Development of Foreign Capital Manufacturing Industry in China: Looking forward to Made in China, 2025. *American Journal of Industrial and Business Management, 07*(05), 604–613. doi:10.4236/ajibm.2017.75045

Xiaomin, X., & Yi, L. (2017). Customer satisfaction of the third-party logistics enterprise based on AHP: A case study. *International Journal of Information Systems and Supply Chain Management, 10*(1), 68–81. doi:10.4018/IJISSCM.2017010105

Xiao, X., Liu, Y., & Zhang, Z. (2012). The analysis of the logistics mode decision to e-commerce. *Journal of Electronic Commerce in Organizations, 10*(4), 57–70. doi:10.4018/jeco.2012100105

Xu, S. (2014). YOFC's senior product manager Zhou Qinmin: Focus on next generation fiber. *Communications Weekly, 17.*

Xu, X. (2003). Enhance its strength to participate in international competition. *Communications World, 21*, 6.

Xu, X., Sheng, Q. Z., Zhang, L. J., Fan, Y., & Dustdar, S. (2015). From big data to big service. *Computer, 48*(7), 80–83. doi:10.1109/MC.2015.182 PMID:27110033

Yahya, B. (2017, March). *Malaysia's experience to increase broadband penetration.* Paper presented at the meeting of the Standing Committee for Economic and Commercial Cooperation of the Organization of the Islamic Cooperation (COMCEC), Ankara, Turkey.

Yang, Z., &Luo, H. (2001). On the Development of Chinese Enterprises from the Growth of YOFC. *Science & Technology Progress and Policy, 5.*

Yang, H., Li, L., & Liu, J. (2015). Impact of Home Market Scale on Technological Innovation and Its Regional Differences [in Chinese]. *Forum on Science and Technology in China, 1*, 27–32.

Yang, Z., Yue, Y., Yang, Y., Peng, Y., Wang, X., & Liu, W. (2011). Study and application on the architecture and key technologies for IoT. *International Conference on Multimedia Technology (ICMT)*, 747-751.

Yoon, J. S., Shin, S. J., & Suh, S. H. (2012). A conceptual framework for the ubiquitous factory. *International Journal of Production Research, 50*(8), 2174–2189. doi:10.1080/00207543.2011.562563

Young, T. M., Bond, B. H., & Wiedenbeck, J. (2007). Implementation of a real-time statistical process control system in hardwood sawmills. *Forest Products Journal, 57*(9), 54.

Yu, W. (2002). Current Situation and Development of China 's Fiber Optic Cable Industry. *Information System Engineering, 5.*

Zander, L. (2004). Editorial: Dialogue on identifying culture. *International Journal of Cross Cultural Management, 4*(3), 275–290. doi:10.1177/1470595804047812

Zezulka, F., Veselý, I., & Braun, V. (2017). Introduction to Industry 4.0 and fundamental models (in Czech language). *SystemOnLine, 1-2.*

Zezulka, F., Marcon, P., Vesely, I., & Sajdl, O. (2016). Industry 4.0 – An Introduction in the Phenomenon. *IFAC PapersOnline*, *49*(25), 8–12. doi:10.1016/j.ifacol.2016.12.002

Zhang, P., & Chen, H. (2006). VMI model implementation research of YOFC. *Journal of Wuhan Institute of Technology*, *3*.

Zhang, G. (2005). *EIQ Analysis of Fiber Warehouse Operation of YOFC*. Huazhong University of Science and Technology.

Zhang, X., Peek, W. A., Pikas, B., & Lee, T. (2016). The Transformation and Upgrading of the Chinese Manufacturing Industry: Based on" German Industry 4.0. *The Journal of Applied Business and Economics*, *18*(5), 97.

Zhao, Y., & Cao, H. (2015). Risk management on joint product development with power asymmetry between supplier and manufacturer. *International Journal of Project Management*, *33*(8), 1812–1826. doi:10.1016/j.ijproman.2015.08.008

Zhou, H., Benton, W. C. Jr, Schilling, D. A., & Milligan, G. W. (2011). Supply Chain Integration and the SCOR Model. *Journal of Business Logistics*, *32*(4), 332–344. doi:10.1111/j.0000-0000.2011.01029.x

Zhou, K. (2015). Industry 4.0: Towards Future Industrial Opportunities and Challenges. *12th International Conference on Fuzzy Systems and Knowledge Discovery (FSKD)*, 2147–2152. 10.1109/FSKD.2015.7382284

Zhu, J., Ong, S. K., & Nee, A. (2013). An authorable context-aware augmented reality system to assist the maintenance technicians. *International Journal of Advanced Manufacturing Technology*, *66*(9), 1699–1714. doi:10.100700170-012-4451-2

Zhu, Q., Sarkis, J., & Lai, K. (2008). Confirmation of a measurement model for green supply chain management practices implementation. *International Journal of Production Economics*, *111*(2), 261–273. doi:10.1016/j.ijpe.2006.11.029

Zou, Y. (2016). *The efficient working capital- Working capital management experience of YOFC*. YOFC.

Zuehlke, D. (2010). Smart Factory - towards a factory-of-things. *Annual Reviews in Control*, *34*(1), 129–138. doi:10.1016/j.arcontrol.2010.02.008

Zukunftsprojekt Industrie 4.0. (2017). *Digitale Wirtschaft und Gesellschaft*. Retrieved on January 13th, 2017, from https://www.bmbf.de/de/zukunftsprojekt-industrie-4-0-848.html

Zwikael, O., & Ahn, M. (2011). The effectiveness of risk management: An analysis of project risk planning across industries and countries. *Risk Analysis*, *31*(1), 25–37. doi:10.1111/j.1539-6924.2010.01470.x PMID:20723146

Zyngier, S. (2008). Risk management: Strengthening knowledge management. *International Journal of Knowledge Management*, *4*(3), 19–32. doi:10.4018/jkm.2008070102

About the Contributors

Richard Brunet-Thornton, FRSA, MIM, MBA, Ph.D. Dr. Brunet-Thornton holds two full-time positions in both Montréal (Canada) and Prague (Czech Republic). As an assistant professor at VŠE, his expertise encompasses Cross-Cultural Management and Communications, Knowledge Management, Project Management, and Academic Writing. His area of speciality is the Czech Republic. In addition, he is a native speaker of both French and English. He has published numerous articles in various scholarly journals and textbooks as well as holding various editorial positions in numerous journals. On the application side, he is responsible for an international business practice with the fifth largest global IS/IT consultancy. In this field, his expertise is in telephony. During his many years of business tenure, Dr. Brunet-Thornton has worked on every continent within the telecommunications domain.

Felipe Martinez career covers process excellence, specifically two main areas: Lean Management and Organisational Design. His offer as a consultant includes both topics and other process excellence issues related such as Industries 4.0. The research in Lean Management explores the creation of a leanness measurement system and it investigates the application of Lean SixSigma methodologies in non-traditional institutions and fields such as Lean Health Care, Lean Higher Education and Lean HR. He teaches Lean Management in Prague and Porto and Operations Management in Prague. The research in Organisational Design focuses on the Procedures to set up the organisational structure. His PhD presents more than 10 years of work in this topic. He teaches the course of Organisational Design in Prague and Riga. He also teaches Harvard Case Studies Colombia CS and Dutch Flower Cluster CS in the framework of the Microeconomics of Competiveness network. Additionally, He teaches general management in Prague and Bogota. He is Industrial Engineer (Pontificia Universidad Javeriana, Bogotá) and PhD in management (University of Economics, Prague). He has work experience in Colombia, India and the Czech Republic.

***

Anirudh Agrawal is a PhD Fellow at Copenhagen Business School and Former Assistant professor at Jindal Global University, Visiting Assistant professor at Bennett University India His research focus is Entrepreneurship, Venture Capital, SME Strategy, Social Entrepreneurship, Bottom of the Pyramid and Impact Investing. He is a community member at TechQuartier where he collects data on building entrepreneurship ecosystem.

Aini Suzana Ariffin is a senior lecturer at the Perdana School of Science, Technology and Innovation Policy, Universiti Teknologi Malaysia (UTM) She specialises in Science, Technology and Innovation Policy, Innovation Management & Governance, Technological Commercialisation and Valuation, Innovative Entrepreneurship, Human Capital & Strategic Human Resource, Talent Management, Transformation & Change Management and Standards Development.

Fabiano Armellini holds B.Eng., MSc. and DSc. degrees in Mechanical Engineering from Escola Politécnica da Universidade de São Paulo (Brazil), with exchange studies at Michigan State University (USA). He is an assistant professor in the Department of Mathematics and Industrial Engineering at Polytechnique Montréal (Canada) and member of the Centre Interuniversitaire de Recherche sur la Science et la Technologie (CIRST). Dr. Armellini is co-founder of two successful Brazilian consulting companies focused on engineering design, product development and innovation management. He has several years of professional experience in performing and managing innovative product development, as well as in the design and implementation of innovation processes as a consultant. His experience embraces several different industry sectors, such as aerospace, automotive, telecommunications, industrial automation, food, mining and chemical sectors. In research, Dr. Armellini's interests lie on innovation management, with special interest on open innovation, industry 4.0, technological entrepreneurship and new product development.

Catherine Beaudry, Rhodes Scholar, has a Ph.D. in economics from the University of Oxford where she also obtained an M.Phil. in economics. From her first degree in electrical engineering specialised in satellite technology, she has kept a strong interest on technology, science and innovation. She is a professor at the Mathematics and Industrial Engineering Department of École Polytechnique de Montréal where she also holds a Tier I Canada Research Chair on the Creation, development and commercialisation of innovation. The Canada research chair (CRC) that she holds at Polytechnique is centered around the university-industry interface and on the role that government and policy may have on fostering a flourishing and productive science, technology and innovation relationship at all phases of the innovation process.

Krishna Bhandari, a PhD from the University of Vaasa, Finland combines academic and practitioner's perspectives in his research in strategy, innovation and sustainable performance. Earlier Dr. Bhandari worked for Nokia and born globals from Finland.

Alessandro Brun holds a Master Degree with distinction in Production and Management Engineering and a PhD on the same subject. He is professor at MIP-Politecnico di Milano where he teaches the Quality Management and Luxury Management courses and is currently the deputy director of the MBA program. Dr. Brun presently works as Director of Master in Global Luxury Goods and Services Management. His main research streams are related to Supply Chain Management, Operational Improvements in manufacturing and service industries and Total Quality Management.

Vladimír Bureš was born in Jaroměř, Czech Republic on 4th August, 1977. He earned his bachelor degree in Financial Management (1999), master degree in Information Management (2001), PhD. in Information and Knowledge Management (2005) at the University of Hradec Králové, Czech Republic, and MBA in Global Management (2015) at the City University of Seattle (WA, USA). He has already published five books (as author or a member of the authoring team) and tens of scientific papers published at several journals or in conference proceedings. He has attended both international and national research projects (e.g. 6th or 7th European Framework Program projects). In his research he focuses on systems engineering, systems dynamics, knowledge management, and application of ICT in areas such as education or business administration. Associate Professor Bureš is a member of program committees and editorial boards of several scientific conferences and journals respectively.

Cheryl Marie Cordeiro has a doctoral degree in general linguistics from the University of Gothenburg. She is Research Fellow at the Centre for International Business Studies (CIBS), School of Business, Economics and Law at the University of Gothenburg. She is currently a Flexit scholar of the Bank of Sweden Tercentenary Foundation, Riksbankens Jubileumsfond (RJ). In this program, she is attached for a two year period with ABB Corporate Research, with the User Experience & Industrial Design group in Västerås, Sweden. She has a Master of Science in Information Studies from the Nanyang Technological University (NTU) of Singapore, and a Master of Arts in the English Language from the National University of Singapore (NUS). She is former Miss Universe Singapore 1999. Her CV can be found on her webpage at www.cherylmariecordeiro.com.

Cozmiuc Diana is a Business Controller at Siemens, Continental and Academic Researcher in Value Based Management.

Thomas Funke has been fascinated by entrepreneurship since he set up a course at university in 2008 that allowed students to start their own businesses. He is especially motivated by seeing how starting a business can release new forces in young people that lead to a completely strengthened self-efficacy. Thomas Funke is particularly fascinated by training and educating young entrepreneurs. Furthermore, he loves measuring and decoding the different entrepreneurship ecosystems. He just recently published a book on entrepreneurship ecosystems with FAZ Buchverlag with the title: "Beyond Silicon Valley: Examples of Successful Entrepreneurship Ecosystems". He also serves as academic contributor for the renown Global Startup Ecosystem Report by Silicon Valley based company Compass, which just recently published the top 20 startup ecosystems ranking.

Egemen Hopali EDUCATION: 2016- Marmara University Engineering Management Ph.D. 2013-2016 Marmara University Industrial Engineering M.S. 2015- Universitad Politecnico de Catalunya-ETSEIB Barcelona (Erasmus). 2009-2013 Işık University Industrial Engineering. WORK INFO: 2016- Üsküdar University- Industrial Engineering Research Assistant. 2012-Pegasus/Simulator. 2011-Onur Air/Strategic Planning & Business Development. PUBLICATIONS: 7th International Scientific and Expert Conference TEAM 2015(Belgrade): "Evaluating Competitive Position of An Airline Company". (Sennaroglu B., Hopali E.). PROJECTS: "Havayolu Endüstrisinde Rekabet Gücü Analizi". Marmara University Scientific Research Projects Committee (BAPKO). Project Number: FEN-C-YLP-130515-0185. Total Budget: 15000 TL, Researcher, 13.05.2015-13.05.2016.

Ma Huimin is the Associate Professor in the Department of Information Management, School of Management, Huazhong University of Science & Technology. Additionally he is also the Vice director of the Electronic Business Center of HUST in 2004. His major research field is the application of information technology in corporation, especially the application of Electronic Business.

Petr Jirsak works at the University of Economics in Prague at the department of Logistics and at the Centre for Digital Transformation. He specializes in supply chain management strategies and operation as well as automation and digitalization in 3PL and in Automotive industry.

Kijpokin Kasemsap received his BEng degree in Mechanical Engineering from King Mongkut's University of Technology, Thonburi, his MBA degree from Ramkhamhaeng University, and his DBA degree in Human Resource Management from Suan Sunandha Rajabhat University. Dr. Kasemsap is a Special Lecturer in the Faculty of Management Sciences, Suan Sunandha Rajabhat University, based in Bangkok, Thailand. Dr. Kasemsap is a Member of the International Economics Development and Research Center (IEDRC), the International Foundation for Research and Development (IFRD), and the International Innovative Scientific and Research Organization (IISRO). Dr. Kasemsap also serves on the International Advisory Committee (IAC) for the International Association of Academicians and Researchers (INAAR). Dr. Kasemsap is the sole author of over 250 peer-reviewed international publications and book chapters on business, education, and information technology. Dr. Kasemsap is included in the TOP 100 Professionals–2016 and in the 10th edition of 2000 Outstanding Intellectuals of the 21st Century by the International Biographical Centre, Cambridge, England.

Martin G. Kaspar is Head of Business Development at a German Mittelstands-company within the automotive industry; he is a regular speaker / panellist at FDI and internationalization conferences and PhD candidate at Durham University.

Maria Lai-ling Lam is now a senior consultant. She had been a Professor of Marketing at Point Loma Nazarene University, San Diego, California and Malone University, Canton, Ohio in the United States for fourteen years. She holds a Ph.D. in marketing and organization behavior from George Washington University, a M.A. degree in Religion Studies focusing on Christianity and Chinese religions, a M.B.A. degree in Marketing and International Business, and a B.B.A degree in Marketing from the Chinese University of Hong Kong. She has published one book and more than 80 peer-reviewed journal articles, book chapters and proceedings published in refereed academic and professional outlets. Her research interests are corporate social responsibility, cross-cultural negotiation, and business education.

Radek Liska obtained Masters degree at Faculty of Business administration at University of Economics, Prague. Specializes in an area of IT process simplification and digitalization of related processes. Ph.D. researcher of an impact of virtual teams collaboration within international organization structures. Up to date experience with international IT projects from a role of Technical project manager.

Mathew Maavak is a doctoral candidate who is currently developing a virtual Risk Foresight model for his thesis at the Perdana School of Science, Technology and Innovation Policy, Universiti Teknologi Malaysia (UTM). Mr Maavak is a prolific Op-Ed contributor to the international media. He is also regularly sought for his expert opinion on various geostrategic issues.

Dominik Matt holds the Chair for Production Systems and Technologies and heads the research department "Industrial Engineering and Automation (IEA)" at the Faculty of Science and Technology at the Free University of Bozen-Bolzano. Moreover, Prof. Matt is the Director of the Research Center

Fraunhofer Italia in Bolzano. He has authored more than 150 scientific and technical papers in journals and conference proceedings and is member of numerous national and international scientific organizations and committees (e.g.: AITeM - Associazione Italiana di Tecnologia Meccanica I WGAB - Academic Society for Work and Industrial Organization I EVI - European Virtual Institute on Innovation in Industrial Supply Chains and Logistic Networks).

Ioan Petrisor is a University Professor PhD at the West University of Timisoara, Romania, the Faculty of Economics and Business Administration; Research competencies: strategic management organization; strategic intelligence; author or co-author in 13 books, over 100 articles published in international journal databases.

Erwin Rauch received his B.Sc. in Logistics and Production Engineering from the Free University in Bolzano (Italy). He also holds a M.Sc. in Mechanical Engineering from the Technical University Munich (TUM) and a M.Sc. in Business Administration from the TUM Business School. He obtained his Ph.D. degree in Mechanical Engineering from the University of Stuttgart. Currently he is an Assistant Professor for Manufacturing Technology and Systems at the Free University of Bolzano. His current research is on Axiomatic Design in Manufacturing, Flexible and Reconfigurable Manufacturing Systems, Industry 4.0 and Distributed Manufacturing. In addition he is the Head of the mini-factory laboratory for smart manufacturing at the Free University of Bolzano.

Michael Riedl obtained his Ph.D. degree at the Technical University of Munich in mechanical engineering with a specialization in systematic product development, automotive engineering and simulation technologies. Subsequently he worked at AUDI AG in the department for technical development with a focus on concept development. At Fraunhofer Italia, he is deputy director and team leader of the research group "Automation and Mechatronics Engineering". His current research is on automation technologies as well as the development of mechatronic and cyber physical systems and their application in smart buildings, precision agriculture and the factory of the future.

Sebastian Schaefer has a passion for entrepreneurship and innovation. With many years of practical experiences in different positions in and outside of academia he has gained valuable insights and has developed a unique perspective of how to design and foster dynamic ecosystems. Together with his team and his partners, Sebastian aims at promoting the startup scene Frankfurt Rhine-Main as one of the leading Startup- and Fintech Hubs in Europe.

Luca Scremin holds B.Sc and M.Sc degrees in Management Engineering from Politecnico di Milano. His researches focus on the Industry 4.0 topic, with particular emphasis on its implementation in manufacturing companies. Over the course of his studies, he completed an internship in the semiconductors sector, a research internship at École Polytechnique de Montréal, and he is currently the Responsible of the Quality Management System of an Italian manufacturing company (RGV srl).

Laurence Solar-Pelletier holds a Ph.D. (2013) and an MSc. (2007) in administration from HEC Montreal. She also completed her undergrad studies in industrial engineering at Polytechnique Montreal (2003). Since 2005, she has been working as a consultant and research assistant for various organizations, including universities, colleges and enterprises. Her research interests include innovation, strategic management, technological ecosystems and adult training. She currently works at Polytechnique Montreal as a coordinator of a Tier 1 Canada's Research Chair on Creativity, Development and Commercialization of innovation, and of the Research group on Globalization and Management of Technology.

Özalp Vayvay is the Engineering Management department head at Graduate Institute of Pure and Applied Sciences. He is also serving as a rector consultant. He gives several courses in industrial engineering and business departments The main research areas are Supply Chain Management, Technology/Innovation Management, Operations Management, Risk Management, Quality and Process Management, Industry 4.0 There are many articles published in these areas There are many Master and Ph.D. students working in these subjects.

Ke Wang is an undergraduate of the School of Management, Huazhong University of Science and Technology.

Kei-Wing Wong has been in the Dean list for four years. She has worked as an intern in a medical device company during 2013 to 2017 summers. She is now the mentor to a group of undergraduates. She is pursuing her graduate education in the area of sustainability, climate change, and architecture.

Han Wu is a PhD student at Rennes School of Business, France.

Xiang Wu is a postdoctoral researcher at School of Management, Huazhong University of Science & Technology.

Lu Xu is a PhD student of Rennes School of Business (France).

Jinlong Zhang is a professor of Information System & Management Science at School of Management, Huazhong University of Science & Technology.

Index

E

F

G

H

I

J

K

L

T

U

V

W

Y

CPSIA information can be obtained
at www.ICGtesting.com
Printed in the USA
BVOW09*1339290318
511782BV00012B/167/P

9 781522 534686